Case Conceptualization and Treatment Planning

Third Edition

I would like to dedicate this book to Devora Berman, Irene Berman-Vaporis, Rachel Berman-Vaporis, Irene Birnbaum, Esther Clenott, Catherine Dugan, and Alisa Zucker. These strong women have always served as an inspiration to me whenever the going got tough.

Case Conceptualization and Treatment Planning

Integrating Theory With Clinical Practice

Third Edition

Pearl S. Berman
Indiana University of Pennsylvania

Los Angeles | London | New Delhi
Singapore | Washington DC | Boston

Los Angeles | London | New Delhi
Singapore | Washington DC | Boston

FOR INFORMATION:

SAGE Publications, Inc.
2455 Teller Road
Thousand Oaks, California 91320
E-mail: order@sagepub.com

SAGE Publications Ltd.
1 Oliver's Yard
55 City Road
London EC1Y 1SP
United Kingdom

SAGE Publications India Pvt. Ltd.
B 1/I 1 Mohan Cooperative Industrial Area
Mathura Road, New Delhi 110 044
India

SAGE Publications Asia-Pacific Pte. Ltd.
3 Church Street
#10-04 Samsung Hub
Singapore 049483

Copyright © 2015 by SAGE Publications, Inc.

Printed in the United States of America.

A catalog record of this book is available from the Library of Congress.

ISBN 978-1-4833-4371-6

This book is printed on acid-free paper.

Acquisitions Editor: Kassie Graves
Editorial Assistant: Carrie Montoya
Production Editor: Bennie Clark Allen
Copy Editor: Rachel Keith
Typesetter: C&M Digitals (P) Ltd.
Proofreader: Laura Webb
Cover Designer: Anupama Krishnan
Marketing Manager: Shari Countryman

14 15 16 17 18 10 9 8 7 6 5 4 3 2 1

Contents

3   Behavioral Case Conceptualizations and Treatment Plans   107

4   Cognitive Case Conceptualizations and Treatment Plans   135

5   Cognitive-Behavioral Conceptualizations and Treatment Plans   163

6   Feminist Case Conceptualizations and Treatment Plans   197

7   Emotion-Focused Case Conceptualizations and Treatment Plans   237

8   Dynamic Case Conceptualizations and Treatment Plans   277

12 Transtheoretical Case Conceptualizations and Treatment Plans   429

13 Discussion and Extension of the Model   467

Preface

This book is designed to help clinicians develop effective case conceptualization and treatment-planning skills. *Clinicians* is a general term used to refer to individuals who have obtained, or are in the process of obtaining, professional training in psychology, counseling, education, or social work departments at universities, medical centers, or training institutes.

The goal of case conceptualization is to provide a clear, theoretical explanation for *what the client is like* as well as theoretical hypotheses for *why the client is like this*. Based on this conceptualization, the clinician develops a treatment plan that will help the client change. The treatment plan also provides a mechanism for assessing client progress in the change process. When progress is not being made, the conceptualization is a resource for assessing barriers to progress. Case conceptualization and treatment-planning skills have always been important in providing quality care to clients. These skills are even more vital in today's managed-care market, as they can be used to document the need a client has for treatment and to support recommendations for brief, intermediate, or long-term services.

The model this text presents addresses skill building in four areas of clinical practice: integrating psychological theory, integrating domains of human complexity, self-reflection on issues relevant to human complexity, and organizing and writing effectively using your own personal style. Exercises will be provided to aid this skill building.

The psychological theories highlighted in the text include behavioral, cognitive, cognitive-behavioral, feminist, emotion-focused, family systems, dynamic, cultural, constructivist, and transtheoretical. The domains of human complexity introduced include age, gender, race and ethnicity, sexual orientation, socioeconomic status, and violence. The intent of practicing case conceptualization and treatment-planning skills using diverse theoretical orientations and incorporating many domains of human complexity is to encourage clinicians to think about clients in an in-depth and flexible manner.

This is not a *know it all* book. There are many psychological theories and many domains of human complexity that might be relevant to a particular client beyond those presented in this text. In addition, readers will not become experts in any of the systems of psychotherapy or domains of human complexity that are introduced. The clinician who seeks to master the full richness of any of these knowledge bases will need further reading and extensive study. This is a *know how to* book. This book teaches a process that can be used in integrating any theory, any domain of complexity, or any new knowledge base into clinical work. It is implicit in this approach that clinicians need to keep up-to-date on new developments within the treatment literature and integrate this new knowledge into their work in order to maintain ethical and effective treatment. This text will also help clinicians sharpen their professional writing skills.

OVERVIEW OF CHAPTERS

Chapter 1 will provide a discussion of the case conceptualization and treatment-planning process used within the text. In addition, it includes a discussion of personal writing styles. Six styles of case conceptualizations and treatment plans are modeled within the text to help clinicians identify their own style. These styles have been labeled assumption-based, theme-based, historically based, symptom-based, interpersonally based, and diagnosis-based. In addition, three formats for presenting treatment goals are modeled. These formats have been labeled the basic format, the problem format, and the SOAP format.

The text instructions for case conceptualizations and treatment plans use a variety of key words to explain important concepts. The intent is for readers to use the key word that is most congruent with the way they think about and understand information. This variety of key words is maintained in the exercise instructions contained in Chapters 3 through 12. You can locate specific client examples and exercises quickly by theoretical perspective using the table of contents. To locate case conceptualization and treatment plan examples quickly by domain, conceptualization style, or treatment goal style, use Table 1.1.

Chapter 2 will provide clinicians with an introduction to the following domains of human complexity: age, gender, race and ethnicity, sexual orientation, socioeconomic status, and violence. This quick reference information, as well as the additional resources that are recommended, can be used by clinicians in the integration exercises that follow in Chapters 3 through 12. To locate domains of complexity quickly as they relate to presenting problems, referral sources, and treatment settings, see Table 2.1. To locate additional work that will help you compare different theories and different domains of complexity for particular clients, see Table 2.2.

Chapters 3 through 12 follow a parallel format. First, the case conceptualization and treatment-planning process is modeled from a specific theoretical viewpoint integrating one domain of human complexity. This is done first using an assumption-based style and then using a second style. Second, clinicians are given the opportunity to develop a theoretically driven case conceptualization and treatment plan that integrates a domain of human complexity and to reflect on how to make themselves an effective therapeutic match for their clients. Exercises are provided to aid clinicians in this process. Finally, an exercise is provided to help clinicians critically think about theory, complexity, ethics, and personal growth using the specifics from a particular client case. Recommended resources for further skill building are provided, including book references, Internet websites, and video materials.

The client interviews used within Chapters 3 through 12 have been simulated by the author of this text. Any similarities between the simulated clients and real individuals are coincidental. These interviews all take place after an earlier, brief appointment in which the limits of confidentiality, fees, and other treatment issues have been discussed. The clients, unlike many of those in real life, will always provide the clinician with enough information to formulate a conceptualization based on the first interview. Why the interview format? It is through interviews that clinicians gather information about clients in real-world settings. Although the text author shifts her perspective in different theoretical chapters, her own personal style and sense of herself in the world is likely to pervade all the interviews in the text. Do your best to put yourself into the role of the clinician even though your own style and sense of yourself may differ significantly from hers.

Chapter 3 provides practice integrating behavioral theory into clinical practice. Interview 1 is with an assaultive White man who is filled with rage. Two sample behavioral case conceptualizations and treatment plans are presented, one using an assumption-based focused style and one using a historically based style; both integrate the domain of violence. Interview 2 is with a White teen male who hates himself and is phobic about mirrors. Exercises follow to help clinicians integrate the domain of age into a behavioral case conceptualization and treatment plan.

Chapter 4 provides practice integrating cognitive theory into clinical practice. Interview 1 is with a White widow struggling to grieve but inhibited in this process by her rigid gender beliefs. Two sample cognitive case conceptualizations and treatment plans are provided, one using the assumption-based style and one using a diagnosis-based writing style; both integrate the domain of gender. Interview 2 is with a White teen male struggling with his sexual identity. Exercises follow to help the clinician integrate the domain of sexual orientation into a cognitive case conceptualization and treatment plan.

Chapter 5 provides practice integrating cognitive-behavioral theory into clinical practice. Interview 1 is with a White woman who has been abused by her adult daughter and is struggling with feelings of depression. Two sample cognitive-behavioral case conceptualizations and treatment plans are provided, one using an assumption-based style and one using a theme-based writing style; both integrate the domain of socioeconomic status. Interview 2 is with a White teen female who is struggling with her desire to be independent and is misusing alcohol. Exercises follow to help clinicians integrate the domain of age into a cognitive-behavioral case conceptualization and treatment plan.

Chapter 6 provides practice integrating feminist theory into clinical practice. Interview 1 is with a White man struggling to understand why his wife left him and their marriage right as they were on the brink of becoming even wealthier than before. Two sample feminist case conceptualizations and treatment plans are provided, one using an assumption-based style and the second using a historically based style; both integrate the domain of race and ethnicity. Interview 2 is with a White mother of two who has recently remarried. Exercises follow to help clinicians integrate the domain of socioeconomic status into a feminist case conceptualization and treatment plan.

Chapter 7 provides practice integrating emotion-focused theory into clinical practice. Interview 1 is with a White woman struggling to integrate her sexual identity into her relationships. Two sample emotion-focused case conceptualizations and treatment plans are provided, one using an assumption-based style and the other an interpersonally based style; both integrate the domain of sexual orientation. Interview 2 is with an abused White teen female struggling with fears of intimacy. Exercises follow to help clinicians integrate the domain of violence into an emotion-focused case conceptualization and treatment plan.

Chapter 8 provides practice integrating dynamic theory into clinical practice. Interview 1 is with a Mexican American adolescent male facing a drug conviction as he struggles to be a man. Two sample dynamic case conceptualizations and treatment plans are provided, one using an assumption-based style and the other a symptom-based style; both integrate the domain of race and ethnicity. Interview 2 is with a White man complaining of emotional detachment. Exercises follow to help clinicians integrate the domain of gender into a dynamic case conceptualization and treatment plan.

Chapter 9 provides practice integrating family systems theory into clinical practice. Interview 1 is with a White mother and daughter. The daughter is immature and caught in her parents' divorce war. Two sample family systems case conceptualizations and treatment plans are provided, one using an assumption-based writing style and one using a symptom-based style; both integrate the domain of age. Interview 2 is with a bereaved African American couple. Exercises follow to help clinicians integrate the domain of race and ethnicity into a family systems case conceptualization and treatment plan.

Chapter 10 provides practice integrating cultural theory into clinical practice. Interview 1 is with an African American female who is the CEO of a company and experiencing chronic loneliness. Two sample cultural case conceptualizations and treatment plans are provided, one using an assumption-based style and one using a diagnosis-based style; both integrate the domain of age. Interview 2 is with a retired White male who is being psychologically and physically abused by his adult daughter. Exercises follow to help clinicians integrate the domain of violence into a cultural case conceptualization and treatment plan.

Chapter 11 provides practice integrating constructivist theory into clinical practice. Interview 1 is with an African American college student who believes he was wrongly accused of violent behavior. Two sample constructivist case conceptualizations and treatment plans are provided, one using an assumption-based style and the other a symptom-based style; both integrate the domain of socioeconomic status. Interview 2 is with a Mexican American mother accused of child abuse. Exercises follow to help clinicians integrate the domain of violence into a constructivist case conceptualization and treatment plan.

Chapter 12 provides practice integrating transtheoretical theory into clinical practice. Interview 1 is with a White man who has abused his son. Two sample transtheoretical case conceptualizations and treatment plans are provided, one using an assumption-based style and one a theme-based style; both integrate the domain of violence. Interview 2 is with a Sioux woman who complains of malaise. Exercises follow to help the clinician integrate the domain of race and ethnicity into a transtheoretical case conceptualization and treatment plan.

Chapter 13 provides a discussion and extension of the model for developing case conceptualizations and treatment plans, using as an example a Sioux woman who is a poly-victim, having experienced emotional abuse, physical abuse, and sexual abuse throughout her childhood and adolescence. The following issues are discussed: increasing clinical effectiveness through individualizing treatment, integrating psychotherapy research findings into clinical practice, changing case conceptualizations and treatment plans over time as part of deliberate practice, and red-flag guidelines for developing case conceptualizations and treatment plans.

The final section of the text is a complete reference list of all scholarly work that has been cited in the theoretical discussions within each chapter.

Acknowledgments

I would like to thank the psychology doctoral students of Indiana University of Pennsylvania for inspiring me to write this book and for completing many questionnaires to help me improve the exercise instructions and the case examples. I would also like to thank specific students who provided me with in-depth feedback on certain aspects of the book: Camille Interligi, Shannon Kovalchick, Kate McGann, and Marissa Perrone.

Developing Case Conceptualizations and Treatment Plans

This book was designed to help you develop effective case conceptualization and treatment-planning skills. In this chapter, a structure for developing these tools is introduced that includes four steps: (a) selecting the theoretical perspective that is most appropriate to the client; (b) utilizing a premise, supporting material, and a conclusion as key features of a case conceptualization; (c) utilizing a treatment plan overview, long-term goals, and short-term goals as key features in developing a treatment plan; and (d) developing an effective personal writing style that is comfortable for you and may be motivating to your client.

The text provides exercises for helping you through these steps while paying close attention to the extratherapeutic factors that the client brings into treatment, including his or her strengths and resources. The exercises also stress writing treatment goals in a manner that helps the client see them as relevant and credible, creates a sense of hope and expectancy, and builds trust between you and the client. These factors are critical to developing a positive therapeutic alliance and in achieving a positive treatment outcome (Hubble, Duncan, & Miller, 1999).

Developing conceptualizations is time-consuming, so why not just go directly to the treatment plan? When there is no careful conceptualization, there may be treatment chaos. For example, assume that Veona, a White female in her mid-30s, comes in to consult with you because her teenage son has just been arrested and she doesn't know what to do. She expresses a lot of fears for his safety in jail. Since she presents with this crisis, you go into crisis management mode and provide her with emotional support and advice about how to get legal representation. You intend to do a careful intake at the next session. Week 2 arrives, however, and before you can try to do this, she presents with a new crisis: Her relationship with her significant other seems to be breaking up, and she's desperate for help in saving it. You try to initiate a conversation about her son, but she quickly diverts back to this relationship crisis. You go into crisis management mode and give her emotional support to calm her down and try to initiate a constructive conversation about her relationship issues. You're determined to conduct your intake at the next session. However, when that day arrives, Veona comes in drunk. You make several attempts to find out what happened with her teenage son and her significant other but quickly give up and send her home. Your plan is to be very firm when she comes in for her fourth session; thus, before she has a chance to tell you anything, you indicate the need to conduct a thorough intake. Veona interrupts you and indicates she is about to become homeless if she can't find the money to pay her rent by tomorrow. She has used her rent money to pay the attorney you recommended she get to represent her son. Frustrated, you go into crisis intervention mode and try to connect her with community resources so she won't become homeless.

Treatment is in a state of chaos because you don't know whether Veona's son is out of jail or not, you don't know if Veona is still with her significant other, and you don't know if she has a long-standing problem with alcohol or if her drunkenness was just a reaction to extreme stress. You may also be exhausted from all these crises.

Rewind and assume that, while you acknowledge the seriousness of the client's son's difficulties when she brings them up, you still carry out an intake during the first session. Based on this intake, you come up with a behavioral conceptualization to capture what you consider to be her basic issues. The following is the premise of, or theory-driven introduction to, this conceptualization:

> Veona is a 35-year-old Caucasian woman who was raised by parents who modeled aggressive expressions of anger and aggressive or neglectful problem-solving. Veona's parents either ignored how she was behaving or what was happening to her or overreacted to her mistakes and developmental struggles and used abusive punishment. Veona survived this history by developing a people-pleasing style where she carefully observed the people around her and tried to meet their needs so that they would accept her and not hurt her. Her passive approach to her own needs led to an early pregnancy outside of marriage. As she raised her son alone, she sought to be a "better parent" than her own parents were to her. She strove to attend to all of her son's needs and deny him nothing. As she had no role models for effective parenting, her wish to be a loving parent led her to overindulge the desires of her son. Her desire to avoid abusive parenting practices has led her to avoid setting limits on her son's behavior. Veona's strengths lie in her sincere desire to be a good parent, her ability to observe and predict the moods of others, and her average level of intelligence that allows her to understand the consequences of her son's present behavior. At this time, Veona is very aware that she and her son are having serious difficulties, but she is not aware of how her permissive and people-pleasing style is related to these difficulties.

After completing the full conceptualization process, you decide that Veona would profit from a treatment plan that will teach her communication and problem-solving skills. Your long-term goals are as follows:

> LONG-TERM GOAL 1: Veona will learn how to recognize and express her feelings assertively.

LONG-TERM GOAL 2: Veona will learn to express concerns in a relationship without blaming others.

LONG-TERM GOAL 3: Veona will learn how to negotiate solutions that respect the needs of self and others.

LONG-TERM GOAL 4: Veona will learn how to recognize her goals for a relationship.

LONG-TERM GOAL 5: Veona will learn how to break down goals into small steps that can be accomplished.

When Veona comes in for Session 2, if she wants to talk about her son's legal problems, you will (a) work on Veona's ability to communicate clearly to the police and her teen and (b) help Veona set goals around the arrest situation. If she wants to discuss imminent relationship failure, you will (a) work on Veona's ability to communicate clearly to her significant other and (b) help Veona set goals around the relationship. In both situations, you are not ignoring the crisis Veona wants to discuss. However, you are helping her build the skills she needs no matter what "issue" she wants to talk about. As she progresses through the treatment plan, her new skills may help her avert a life full of emergencies. Thus, while the process of developing a case conceptualization and treatment plan is time-consuming at first, over time it will increase the likelihood that you will provide effective and time-efficient treatment. The four-step case conceptualization and treatment-planning process will now be discussed in detail using the case of Pat.

SELECTING A THEORETICAL PERSPECTIVE

Pat is a 25-year-old European American male who was released four and a half months ago from prison after serving three years of a five-year prison sentence for assault. He was sentenced to jail after beating a man unconscious in a drunken brawl following a football game; Pat denies any memory of the reason for the fight, but he is sure the other man started it. This was Pat's only stint in prison, but he had been arrested on a regular basis before this for getting into fights in bars. For these incidents, he received first fines, then probation, and finally time in prison. His current probation officer has insisted he attend treatment to decrease his aggressive behavior and alcohol abuse in an attempt to break his cycle of getting into trouble at bars.

Pat was an average student in high school and went on to get an associate's degree in computer repair. Before going to prison, Pat spent a year working as a computer technician in a small company. He is proud of holding down this job so long and admits to enjoying work with computers. He indicates he would return to computer repair if he could ever get a break. After prison, he quickly found out that no one wanted a computer technician with a history of violent behavior. Determined to work, Pat finally gained employment as the custodian of a large department store. Pat has treated his boss very respectfully, both because he had to work very hard to find any job and because this man was the only one who would give him a try despite his criminal record. Although he is a self-described loner,

Pat has been carefully observing his boss and the other store employees trying to understand what makes them "tick"—this is a game he has played with himself since high school. Pat does not intend to lose this job, unless it is to move upward. His probation officer meets with him weekly and has made it very clear that he plans to monitor Pat's progress in treatment. There have been no aggressive episodes within the work environment to date, nor does he have any history of fighting at work.

Pat has never been married and presently has no children. He is currently involved in an intimate relationship with Alice, a 19-year-old European American female; this relationship is in its second month. Pat has had a number of intimate relationships, none of which has lasted beyond six months. He meets these women in his neighborhood and, after a brief dating period, invites them to move in. He says that he always finds the relationships satisfying but that the women always disappear one day when he is at work. He reports that they move out of the neighborhood and he never sees them again. Pat denies understanding why women run out on him. Pat does admit that he has been in quite a few fights with men. Pat has never been married and has no children. During his time in jail, Pat realized he was tired of problems with the police and tired of changing women; he wants Alice to "stay put."

When asked about his childhood, Pat says that he was raised by two people who never stopped drinking or fighting. He denies having any memories of home that didn't involve his parents being violent, or passed out somewhere in the house. Pat has been responsible for himself for as long as he can remember. Neither of his parents seemed to take responsibility for making sure he had meals. He learned early on how to grab food and then run off to a corner of the house to eat. Otherwise, one or the other of his parents was bound to find him, give him a few swift kicks, and then grab his food. No one in Pat's neighborhood or at school seemed to notice that he was mostly skin and bones and always covered in bruises. However, there were people in the neighborhood who would pay him to walk their pets or clean out their garages. Pat quickly learned the value of work, as the money he earned bought him food to eat at the local store.

At school, Pat intentionally kept a low profile, doing the minimum necessary to stay out of trouble. He was socially isolated until high school, when he was old enough to begin work after school at a gas station. When the station closed down late at night, he and the other attendants would go drinking in the woods after long hours of pumping gas. Once they started drinking, they would keep drinking until all the alcohol was gone. Currently, Pat binges on the weekends, but he never drinks on a work day.

There are many theoretical approaches or systems of treatment currently available for understanding Pat. Research on a variety of talk therapies has found them to be effective (Editors of Consumer Reports, 2004; Lambert, Garfield, & Bergin, 2004). So, how will you choose an approach to use with Pat? You could choose an orientation based on your personal preferences. When a client isn't appropriate for your approach, you can refer this individual to another clinician; this is a completely ethical choice. However, the outcome literature suggests that you will maximize treatment effectiveness if you use Pat's characteristics and presenting concerns to guide your choice (Hubble et al., 1999). The type of approach that "fits" the theoretical orientation to the client is referred to as *integrationism* or *systematic eclecticism* (Lambert et al., 2004).

While it is legitimate to conceptualize Pat's concerns from many different theoretical perspectives, the theory chosen will have important repercussions for treatment, including how hard it will be for Pat to understand/perceive his problems, how unconscious or how deep in the unconscious the precipitants of his problems will be conceived to be, and how long treatment will take to resolve these problems (Prochaska & Norcross, 1999, 2009). For example, a behavioral approach to Pat's case would involve analyzing his symptoms and immediate life circumstances. The focus of a treatment session might be on the immediate antecedents and consequences of a recent violent episode. The precipitants of a particular episode of violence, and the immediate consequences of it, would be located in his immediate past and therefore relatively easy for Pat to recall and contemplate.

In contrast, a dynamic approach to Pat's case would focus on unconscious psychological conflicts as the root cause of his violence. Pat would need to become aware of events in his distant past that resulted in his experiencing, for example, unmet needs for security and nurturance. Perhaps, to avoid the anxiety generated by these unmet needs, Pat had to develop an aggressive lifestyle, whereby through acts of violence he provided himself with a facade of security and safety. As an adult, he has perfected a violent interpersonal style that provides him with "protection" from a hostile world. Only under the influence of alcohol might Pat's anxiety be low enough for him to try to relate to women and address his need for nurturance. From this dynamic perspective, Pat will need to develop significant insight into his unconscious conflicts before he can address his current issues with violence.

Thus, Prochaska and Norcross (1999, 2009) assume that Pat would need more treatment sessions to change constructively using dynamic treatment than he would using behavioral treatment.

DEVELOPING YOUR THEORETICAL UNDERSTANDING

The first step in developing a case conceptualization of Pat is to choose the theoretical viewpoint that will guide an understanding of him at the time that he enters treatment. This theoretical viewpoint will determine the types of questions you ask him and thus the type of information that is included in your case conceptualization and treatment plan.

A case conceptualization of Pat will provide a theoretical perspective for understanding who he is and why he behaves as he does. In general, conceptualizations contain case history information that is theoretically based and includes a formulation of the client's difficulties as well as his or her strengths. Professionals prepare many other types of reports on clients that may include this type of information, such as case histories, intakes, and assessment reports. There is no consensus across clinical settings on what constitutes each type of report. In general, case histories provide the greatest detail about the client's past history, intakes focus more on the client's present functioning, assessment reports focus on the interpretation of psychological testing, and case conceptualizations stress a theoretical understanding of the client to use in guiding treatment decisions. Comprehensive client files may include several types of reports, and what a clinician includes in the case record will be a combination of legal or funding requirements and what is most useful clinically (American Psychiatric Association, 2002, Section 2; American Psychological Association [APA], 2007c, Guideline 2).

A treatment plan for Pat will be a theory-driven action plan for helping him change constructively. It may focus on the goals to be attained, such as "Pat will learn new methods of anger control," or on what needs to change, such as "Pat will stop assaulting others when angry." Research links positive outcomes with treatment plans that are designed around a client's unique characteristics and that take advantage of the client's personal strengths and resources (Hubble et al., 1999). Treatment progress within the first three sessions is also related to positive outcomes for 80% of clients (Haas, Hill, Lambert, & Morrell, 2002). Thus, a treatment plan that aids the clinician in conducting effective and time-efficient treatment sessions may improve client outcomes.

There are no standard criteria for evaluating treatment plans beyond their conformity to legal and ethical mandates and adherence to a format acceptable to licensing agencies and insurance companies (American Psychiatric Association, 2002; APA, 2007c). However, the research literature indicates that treatment goals stated in small and specific terms that Pat can understand and in such a way that he can see them as valuable to attain are most likely to influence him (Hubble et al., 1999). In addition, goals written in a manner that fits Pat's expectations, wishes, and values may be more motivating (Egan, 2007). This text recommends an overall strategy for writing goals of this type that also, whenever possible, take advantage of Pat's strengths and resources. The effectiveness of treatment can be documented through the step-by-step attainment of these specific goals. In addition, seeing progress documented in this way may help maintain Pat's hope; this is an important common factor in effective treatment (Hubble et al., 1999).

KEY FEATURES IN DEVELOPING A CASE CONCEPTUALIZATION

In writing conceptualizations, two key organizational features are recommended. The first feature is the premise. The premise is a succinct analysis of the client's core strengths and weaknesses, tied to the assumptions of a selected theoretical perspective. It can be organized in many ways but should always set up an organizational structure for the entire conceptualization and be theoretically sound. If *premise* is not a meaningful term to you, think of this feature as serving to provide an overview of the client, or as *preliminary* or *explanatory* statements, or as a summary of the key features of the client, or as a *proposition* on which arguments are based, or as *hypotheses*, or as a *thesis statement*, or as a *theory-driven introduction*. This series of alternative key words is provided so that you can select the words that have the clearest meaning for you.

A premise at the beginning of a case conceptualization gives the reader a concise understanding of the main issues to be covered in the conceptualization, and the topic sentence of the premise serves the same function for this introductory paragraph by setting up what is going to be discussed. The premise topic sentence could include an overview of the client demographics and reason for referral—for example, "Pat is a 25-year-old, European American male who was referred for treatment of his violent behavior by his probation officer." However, there are many other possibilities. For example, the topic sentence might read, "Pat enters treatment with two major goals: to keep Alice in his life and to keep himself out of jail" or "Pat doesn't agree that he has problems with aggressive behavior, but he does agree that his current life consists of a controlling probation officer, an unstable relationship with Alice, and a boring job." After the topic sentence, the premise will go on to consider both Pat's strengths and his weaknesses, as understood through the lens of the theory that has been selected to guide treatment, and it will end with a sentence that draws a general conclusion about Pat's prognosis or ties the paragraph together in some way before transitioning to the next one.

The second organizational feature, which follows the premise, is the theoretically based *supporting material*. It can also be understood as a *detailed case analysis* that provides evidence to back up the statements made in the premise. This supportive material includes an in-depth analysis of the client's strengths (strong points, positive features, successes, coping strategies, skills, factors facilitating change) and weaknesses (concerns, issues, problems, symptoms, skill deficits, treatment barriers) considered from within the same theoretical perspective that guided the premise. Information from the client's past history, the client's present history, behavioral observations in the treatment session, and other sources may be included in the overall case conceptualization as appropriate to building an effective analysis of the client.

The support paragraphs should be written following a coherent organizational structure set up by the premise. At the end of these support paragraphs, the conceptualization should draw conclusions about the client's overall level of functioning at this time, contain broad treatment goals, include any windows of opportunity for achieving these goals, and note any barriers to goal attainment that exist at this time.

KEY FEATURES IN DEVELOPING A TREATMENT PLAN

Three organizational features are suggested for developing an effective treatment plan. The first feature is the treatment plan overview. This is a brief paragraph that provides a brief explanation for how the treatment plan will be implemented. It can be written in client-friendly language that could help increase clients' ownership of their treatment plan and responsibility for their own outcome in treatment. The overview can also be used to help a referral source understand the intent of your treatment plan and your respect for his or her role in it as appropriate.

The second feature is the development of long-term (major, large, ambitious, comprehensive, broad) goals that stem from the main concepts developed in the premise of the case conceptualization. These are goals that the client ideally will have achieved by the time treatment is terminated. The information contained in the premise, and the topic sentences of the support paragraphs, should provide the information needed to develop your long-term goals, as they should reflect the most important or basic needs, issues, or goals of the client at this time.

The third organizational feature is the development of short-term (small, brief, encapsulated, specific, measurable) goals that the client and clinician will expect to see accomplished within a brief time frame. These goals will assist in charting treatment progress, instill hope for change, and help the clinician plan treatment sessions. Early positive change is part of the trajectory toward successful treatment (Hubble et al., 1999, Chapter 14). Therefore, a plan that helps highlight for the client even small steps taken toward change is more likely to lead the client toward a positive outcome.

Every long-term goal should have a series of short-term goals that will be used to move the client toward its accomplishment. Expect to need more short-term goals to support ambitious, versus moderately difficult, long-term goals. If treatment has stalled, it may be that the short-term goals were too large or difficult and need to be broken down further. It also may be that the goals were inappropriate and need to be redesigned.

Ideas for the development of short-term goals may come from the supportive details contained in the case conceptualization. While a client's difficulties have a clear connection to treatment goals, so do strengths. For example, if Pat has strategies that help him keep his aggression under control at work, then treatment goals for expanding his use of these strategies at home and in the neighborhood would capitalize on these strengths. Additional ideas for goals will come from the theoretical model that is chosen to guide treatment. For example, in behavioral therapy, the clinician takes on the role of an educator. Therefore, treatment goals may center on the skills, or information base, that the clinician will help the client master. Taken together, the long- and short-term goals provide an action plan for helping the client change effectively.

The text exercises will guide you to develop goals that are (a) stated in specific terms that the client can understand, (b) congruent with what the client wants to achieve, and (c) viewed as attainable by the client, as such goals are the most motivating (Egan, 2007; Hubble et al., 1999). In some cases, all the long-term goals may be worked on simultaneously. In other cases, goal achievement will follow a specific order as each goal builds on what came before. The strategy for implementing the plan should be included in the treatment plan overview and clearly explained to the client, since a collaborative, working relationship has been found to be critical in achieving positive treatment outcomes (Hubble et al., 1999; Lambert et al., 2004).

DEVELOPING YOUR PERSONAL WRITING STYLE

Professional writing requires a clear and specific organizational plan. Within this plan, there are many different styles for organizing an effective case conceptualization and treatment plan. Based on your prior training or style of viewing the world, it may seem at first as if professional writing requires you to abandon the style that comes most easily to you. This viewpoint often develops because the examples provided during training may follow one specific style (or use one type of organizational strategy). This text seeks to demonstrate the power and legitimacy of different writing styles by modeling the effective use of six different styles of conceptualizations and treatment plans; the intent is to encourage you to identify, and practice developing, your own professional writing style.

Each theoretical chapter in this book contains two complete case conceptualizations and treatment plans. The first always uses the assumptions of the theory to guide its organization. The second follows another style that might be particularly potent in connecting with the client (see Table 1.1). Research shows that instilling hope is an important factor in positive treatment outcomes (Wampold, 2010). Thus, when clinicians adapt their writing style to reflect the personal perspectives of their clients, it can increase their clients' sense of hope and ownership of their treatment. At the end of this chapter, abbreviated examples of six different styles for adapting your clinical work are provided. These examples include premises, treatment plan overviews, and partially completed treatment plans. All of these examples are based on a behavioral analysis of the case of Pat in order to highlight differences based on writing style versus theory. The labels used to describe each style have been created by the author and include assumption-based, symptom-based, interpersonally based, historically based, theme-based, and diagnosis-based.

Table 1.1 Location of Case Conceptualization and Treatment Plan Examples by Domain, Chapter, Style, and Format

Domain	Chapter	Style	Format
Violence	3	Assumption, Historical	Basic, Problem
Gender	4	Assumption, Diagnosis	Basic, SOAP
Socioeconomic Status	5	Assumption, Thematic	Basic, Problem
Race & Ethnicity	6	Assumption, Historical	Basic, Problem
Sexual Orientation	7	Assumption, Interpersonal	Problem, Basic
Race & Ethnicity	8	Assumption, Interpersonal	Basic, Basic
Age	9	Assumption, Symptom	Problem, Basic
Age	10	Assumption, Diagnosis	Problem, SOAP
Socioeconomic Status	11	Assumption, Symptom	Problem, Problem
Violence	12	Assumption, Thematic	Problem, Problem

The assumption-based style organizes information about Pat in terms of the major assumptions of the psychological theory chosen for understanding his dynamics. The topic sentences of the premise, support paragraphs, and long-term goals are all constructed around the assumptions of the theory. There is a complete conceptualization and treatment plan using this style in each chapter.

The symptom-based style organizes information about Pat in terms of the major symptoms he presents with in treatment. Therefore, the topic sentence of the premise will highlight all the symptoms that will be dealt with in the conceptualization, and each long-term goal in the treatment plan will focus on each of these symptoms in turn. To read full conceptualizations and treatment plans using this style, read the cases of Alice in Chapter 9 or that of Zechariah in Chapter 11.

The interpersonally based style organizes information about Pat in terms of his relationships with significant others. The topic sentence of the premise lists the significant relationships that will be discussed in the conceptualization. Each of these relationships will have a long-term goal associated with it. Each support paragraph will discuss one of these relationships. If appropriate, another support paragraph may focus on the client's relationship with himself or herself. This can be useful in dealing with personal identity, self-esteem, one's personal view of the world, or other self-focused issues as appropriate to the theoretical orientation chosen for the conceptualization. To read full conceptualizations and treatment plans using this style, see the cases of Ellen in Chapter 7 and Sergio in Chapter 8.

The historically based style organizes information about Pat based on his personal history using selected time periods from past to present or vice versa. The time periods selected are individualized to the client's needs and current situation. Examples could be early childhood, elementary school, high school, college/vocational school, and adulthood. Or, for a therapeutic issue that occurred during disrupted adult development, examples could be early college years, tour of duty in war zone, return to civilian life, and divorce. If the client is a young child, it might be relevant to organize information based on such issues as physical development, cognitive development, and psychosocial development. For complete examples of the historically based style, see the cases of Jeff in Chapter 3 and John in Chapter 6.

The theme-based style organizes information about Pat around an important theme or metaphor that epitomizes Pat's behavior or view of the world. In this style, the theme is introduced within the topic sentence of the premise. Each long-term goal utilizes the theme under the assumption that it was selected because it captures something meaningful to the client in a "nutshell." The topic sentence of each support paragraph in the conceptualization introduces an important aspect or realm of the client's life within the context of the theme. For a complete example, see the case of Ann in Chapter 5 and Jake in Chapter 12.

The diagnosis-based style organizes information about Pat around the framework of the formal diagnostic system created by the American Psychiatric Association (2013) in the fifth edition of its *Diagnostic and Statistical Manual of Mental Disorders* (DSM-5). The diagnosis style is very similar to the symptom style, as the DSM-5 is organized primarily around symptoms. A diagnosis-based style is most often required within medical settings. The premise for this style should include the major data, but not supportive details, indicating a diagnosis of one or more mental disorders, a situation or interaction between people that provides a focus of clinical attention, or the lack of such a disorder or need for treatment. The topic sentence of the premise highlights the major symptoms of the client. Each long-term goal of the treatment plan might likewise highlight one symptom. Or, if there is only one primary symptom, each long-term goal might address the client's level of functioning within one of the client's primary roles, such as worker, husband, and father. Each support paragraph will focus on one symptom or, when there is only one symptom, may discuss the client's current level of functioning within one of his or her primary roles. Full examples of the diagnosis-based style, the cases of Marie and Amber, can be found in Chapters 4 and 10, respectively.

The six styles discussed in this chapter are not intended to be all-inclusive. Other strategies could be used to effectively organize your clinical work. Professional writing allows for a great deal of flexibility in style; however, there must be a clear organizational plan that will easily communicate to other professionals your current understanding of your client and your client's treatment plan. This may be needed to support clinical supervision of your work, case reviews by accreditation boards, court-ordered evaluations, or emergency coverage of your cases by another clinician (APA, 2007c, Guideline 5).

Do your conceptualization and treatment plans have to follow a parallel structure? No. An assumption-based case conceptualization does not have to be followed by treatment goals expressed in terms of the theory's assumptions. However, this can be an effective strategy in that the reader, whether it is your supervisor or a judge, can easily follow your professional reasoning. Similarly, if Pat blames his problems on the alcoholic parents who neglected him, he might be most motivated to work on treatment plan goals that are developmentally expressed. If his treatment plan meets his expectations that his problems today are not "his fault" but due to his alcoholic parents not giving him what he needed, he may be more motivated to work on them.

There is no standardized format for presenting the goals of a treatment plan. Different clinicians and different clinical settings have preferred formats. Three formats will be modeled in the examples at the end of this chapter. These have been labeled the *basic format* (Treatment Plans 1–3), the *problem format* (Treatment Plans 4–5), and the *SOAP format* (Treatment Plan 6).

The basic format has goals stated in terms of what the client needs to achieve, learn, or develop. This may be a motivating format for the client, as it is stated in terms of the goals the client wants to achieve. It is also useful when the client has a very negative reaction to any indication that he or she has any "problems" or "issues." The problem format has goals stated in terms of what maladaptive behavior or issues need to be reduced. This may be most motivating for clients who are very frustrated by their own behavior and ready for change. Similarly, it may be a good format for parents who are very frustrated by the maladaptive behavior of one of their children or for a probation officer who is determined to prevent recidivism in a parolee. The final format is an adaptation of the "SOAP" note that is commonly used in medical settings. This note was first developed by Lawrence L. Weed, MD. He developed it to go along with his "Problem-Oriented Medical Record (POMR)."

Dr. Weed wanted the medical record to clearly draw attention to the client's presenting problem, the current status of this problem, and the immediate plan for dealing with the problem and then conclude with why this plan was chosen. The clinician was to write a new SOAP note each day (a short-term plan) rather than coming up with goals for a more long-term plan. The letter *S* refers to the subjective data provided by the client. The letter *O* refers to the clinician's objective data developed through testing or informal assessment of the client. The letter *A* refers to the clinician's assessment of the client based on the *S* and *O* data. The letter *P* refers to the clinician's immediate plan vis-à-vis the client. For the purposes of this book, the *S*, *O*, and *A* parts of the note will be used following the procedures described by Bacigalupe (2008) and Keenan (2008) in their web documents for training students in the use of Dr. Weed's SOAP note. The *P* section of the SOAP note will be extended to include the long- and short-term goals described in this volume.

The three formats modeled in this text are intended to encourage you, if you have the freedom to choose, to select the format you believe will be most likely to engage the client in constructive change.

EXAMPLES OF PREMISES AND TREATMENT PLAN STYLES

All the following examples provide insights concerning the case of Pat described earlier in this chapter. Assume that the clinician has carried out a comprehensive intake with him as well as conferred with his probation officer. As you read each example, assume that the clinician will be monitoring Pat's potential for harm toward others, whether or not this is made explicit in the treatment goals. All the examples are based on behavioral theory so that differences in writing style can be highlighted.

Behavioral theory is chosen because it has a number of strengths for considering Pat's unique characteristics at this time. It is action oriented, and he prefers a quick pace. He was recently in prison, so a highly structured approach should not seem unusual or burdensome to him. In fact, it should provide significantly less structure than he has been used to in the last three years. In addition, his jail term was reduced due to his learning how to be a "good inmate," and this past learning might be effectively incorporated into the treatment plan. Finally, achievement of behavioral goals is relatively quick, and this fast response may be needed to prevent Pat from being sent back to jail.

Premise 1: Assumption-Based Style

Pat's childhood learning experiences taught him that dysfunctional behavior, such as verbal and physical aggression, is rewarded and emotional vulnerability is punished. Pat learned a lot from observing his parents; he is a master of verbal and physical assault and has also learned to associate physical dominance with sexual arousal and fear with emotional vulnerability. He also saw how to take alcohol in gulps rather than sips and to consider the needs of children irrelevant. His parents provided no positive consequences for Pat and gave no demonstration of emotional regulation or nonviolent problem-solving; the only strategy he had for dealing with his parents that led to positive consequences was to eat fast and learn how to hide effectively. Despite this violent upbringing, Pat did learn to inhibit any aggressive impulses he might have in his dealings with neighborhood adults. These neighbors were a good source of income if he was reliable and worked hard. Pat also learned that if he kept a low profile at school, he would be safe. While Pat has trouble inhibiting his aggression, particularly when drinking, he did graduate from high school and did gain an associate's degree. He has also learned that he wants to have a stable relationship with a woman rather than a revolving door of sexual partners. Pat's consistent interest in observing others, and his ability to inhibit his aggression within some environments, are all signs that he may be able to stop, think, and learn from prosocial role models at work, within the probation arena, and in the therapy environment.

Treatment Plan 1: Assumption-Based Style

Treatment Plan Overview. Pat is most motivated to maintain a romantic relationship and to stay out of jail; thus, his treatment goals will focus on these issues. Pat's probation officer meets with him weekly to ensure that Pat has not engaged in any violent behavior. Pat has found these meetings aversive, as the focus has been exclusively on reviewing Pat's past acts of violence. The officer will be asked to reinforce Pat's attempts to exert positive control in relationships within the past week as well as reviewing probation expectations. Long-Term Goals 1 and 2 will be addressed simultaneously. (This treatment plan follows the *basic format*.)

LONG-TERM GOAL 1: Pat will learn to recognize the positive and negative consequences that follow behavior and determine which behaviors he would like to use to strengthen his relationship with Alice.

Short-Term Goals

1. Pat's behaviors in therapy, such as arriving on time, coming regularly, being polite, and not making threats during discussions, will be noted as relationship-building behavior whenever they occur.

2. Pat will consider whether the clinician's responses to him (smiles, a relaxed posture, leaning forward, etc.) serve to build a relaxed or a stressful relationship.

3. Pat will gain practice tuning in to his own immediate behavior within the treatment session, identify the obvious and subtle cues he is using in his interactions with the clinician, and ask the clinician whether they are being experienced as building a relaxing or a stressful relationship.

4. Pat will discuss with the clinician what Alice does when he comes home that he wants to continue and consider telling Alice that he likes these behaviors and wants them to continue.

5. Pat will discuss with the clinician the pros and cons of providing Alice with positive consequences for doing what he likes, and ignoring any of Alice's behavior that he doesn't like, for building a positive relationship with Alice.

6. Pat will learn about the power of deep breathing, progressive muscle relaxation, and self-hypnosis as consequences he can give to himself to control behaviors that could damage his relationship with Alice or lead to jail time.

7. Pat will select a method of controlling his own negative behaviors and practice it in session with the clinician in role plays of situations he finds provoking.

8. Pat will use his preferred method of relaxing immediately before walking into his home after work.

9. Other goals will be developed as needed for mastering Long-Term Goal 1.

LONG-TERM GOAL 2: Pat will use his observational skills to determine how his boss, his coworkers, and the store customers provide positive and negative consequences to each other that don't involve verbal or physical aggression.

LONG-TERM GOAL 3: Pat will learn how to tune in to his body and recognize when he is having reflexive positive or negative responses to the behavior of others and decide whether he wants to continue to learn or unlearn this behavior.

Premise 2: Symptom-Based Style

Pat's most serious problems are that he engages in violent fights with men, drinks excessively, and can't maintain adaptive relationships with women. Pat learned to fight from modeling his parents' violent behavior and being physically abused by them for being visible within their home. His parents also taught him that the purpose of alcohol was to get drunk. These learning experiences around alcohol were further reinforced by his peers at the gas station, who also drank to excess. Thus, Pat didn't learn how to develop nonviolent conflict resolution strategies. Pat did learn how to work hard, persevere, and inhibit his anger in the school and work environment. He also developed strong observational skills due to his curiosity about why people do what they do. These strengths may support Pat in learning new behaviors within the therapy experience.

Treatment Plan 2: Symptom-Based Style

Treatment Plan Overview. Pat's probation officer is monitoring his aggressive behavior and level of drinking. If Pat loses control of his aggressive behavior, his parole will be violated, and he will be sent back to jail. Pat will develop behavioral strategies that ensure he maintains control of his aggressive impulses. He will learn to recognize when he needs to stop drinking so he can think clearly and avoid a situation that could land him back in jail. While Pat does not agree with the probation officer that he has a problem with aggression and excessive alcohol use, he does agree with the clinician that he does not want to go back to jail and that he does not want to lose his relationship with Alice. Long-Term Goals 1, 2, and 3 will be worked on simultaneously to decrease the likelihood that Pat will come into conflict with the law. (This treatment plan follows the *basic format.*)

LONG-TERM GOAL 1: Decrease Pat's violent behavior to keep him out of jail.

Short-Term Goals

1. Pat will discuss the antecedents to the fight that resulted in his prison sentence.

2. Pat will discuss the immediate and long-term consequences (positive, negative) of the fight that resulted in his prison sentence.

3. Pat will consider what consequences he would prefer to have following his fights with other men.

4. Pat will become aware of what happens immediately before he becomes verbally or physically aggressive (thoughts, feelings, behavior) so he can be in control of himself at all times.

   a. During the session, after warning him this is about to happen, the clinician will intentionally bring up incidents involving treatment sessions and probationary appointments that have made Pat angry in the past to help him develop personal awareness of when his anger is rising.

b. The clinician will follow the same procedure as in (a) but first ask Pat about a recent provocation at work.

c. The clinician will follow the same procedure as in (a) but first ask Pat to describe a recent provocation by Alice or a neighbor.

5. Pat will become aware of what happens immediately after he has been verbally or physically aggressive (thoughts, feelings, behavior) and decide if these are positive or negative consequences.

a. Pat will reenact with the clinician a recent act of his aggression within the treatment session to heighten his awareness of his thoughts, feelings, and behavior and whether or not he was in control of himself.

b. Pat will reenact with the clinician a recent act of his aggression at work to heighten his awareness of his thoughts, feelings, and behavior and whether or not he was in control of himself.

c. Pat will reenact with the clinician a recent act of his aggression at home to heighten his awareness of his thoughts, feelings, and behavior and whether or not he was in control of himself.

6. Pat will consider taking a personal time-out (taking several deep breaths, looking away, walking away, etc.) when he becomes aware that he might be verbally or physically aggressive.

a. Pat will develop the ability to calm himself down using strategies such as deep breathing, progressive muscle relaxation, and self-hypnosis.

b. Pat will select the method of relaxation he prefers based on its making him feel most in control of himself.

c. Pat will try using this method when he is in a session but recalling a recent confrontation at home or at work so that he can feel in control of himself.

d. Pat will be aware of when he becomes angry with the clinician within a session and practice taking control of his anger in the moment.

e. Pat will try to use one of these methods when he becomes angry with Alice at home so he is in control of what he does.

f. Other goals will be developed as appropriate to ensure Pat is in control of his actions when he feels that others are provoking him.

7. Pat will learn, within sessions, problem-solving strategies that do not involve aggressive behavior that he can use during provoking situations if he wants to.

a. Pat will try to identify what he wanted to achieve in his most recent interpersonal conflict and whether he achieved it.

b. Pat will learn to recognize verbally assertive, aggressive, and passive responses within conflict situations that are role-played within the session with the clinician.

    c. Pat will consider which type of response gives him what he wants without leading to a consequence that could send him to jail.

    d. Within role-plays with the clinician, Pat will practice assertive verbal responses for getting what he wants, as these are least likely to get him in trouble with the law.

    e. Pat will practice using assertive responses within his next conflict with the probation officer. (The probation officer will be notified, in advance, that Pat will be practicing assertiveness within the probationary appointment so that he provides appropriate consequences for this effort.)

    f. If Pat has developed enough behavioral control, he will practice how to use assertiveness in conflicts with Alice via reenactments within the treatment setting.

8. Other goals will be developed once Pat is able to practice new behaviors with Alice, both within sessions and later at home, without harming his relationship with her or coming into conflict with the law.

9. Other goals involving men at work will be developed once it is safe for Pat to practice his new behaviors within the employment setting without being in danger of losing his employment or coming into conflict with the law.

LONG-TERM GOAL 2: Decrease the level of Pat's drinking to the point where he feels in control at all times in order to decrease the danger of his being sent back to jail.

LONG-TERM GOAL 3: Increase Pat's relationship-building skills so that it will be more likely that he can maintain his relationship with Alice or another woman.

Premise 3: Interpersonally Based Style

    Whether in relation to his parents, peers, or intimate partners, Pat has not learned how to develop relationships that are free from physical violence unless he keeps both physically and emotionally at a distance. His parents modeled a violent, drunken relationship with each other. To avoid physical abuse, he had to hide from them. The closest thing Pat has ever had to friends has been the peers he has gone drinking with. From them he learned that you never drink unless you continue until you black out. During bar experiences, he learned to always fight to win. He continued to fight, despite receiving steadily increasing sanctions from the police; the feelings of dominance he gained during the fight were more powerful reinforcement than the punishments he was getting from the police— until he was sent to jail. Despite the lack of intimacy his past relationships have brought, Pat is determined to have a long-term intimate relationship with a woman. In addition, with coworkers, he has shown no verbal or physical aggression; he views work as critical to his survival and is motivated to maintain this employment. Pat is very intelligent and can learn quickly when he is motivated to do so. He has shown a long-standing interest in learning through observing others. Maximizing these skills in treatment may help improve Pat's guarded prognosis for overcoming his destructive learning history. Focusing on what Pat cares about most, having a solid relationship with Alice and staying out of jail, may be most motivating to him at this time.

Treatment Plan 3: Interpersonally Based Style

Treatment Plan Overview. Pat's greatest motivations at this time are to keep his relationship with Alice and stay out of jail. Thus, his goals will be designed to take advantage of these motivations by focusing on the building of relationship skills. Treatment will start with his reading a book on relationship-building skills and discussing the different skills with the clinician to discover how and why they might build rather than damage relationships. Once this has been achieved, he will analyze the major relationships he has experienced in his life and determine when using new skills with other people could help him stay out of conflict with the law, get a better job, and maintain a relationship with Alice. Long-Term Goal 1 will be achieved first, and then he will work on Long-Term Goals 2, 3, and 4 simultaneously. (This treatment plan follows the *basic format.*)

LONG-TERM GOAL 1: Pat will read a book that explains the concepts of relationship building, relationship damaging, and neutral behaviors and consider whether he wants to be more conscious of when he uses these types of skills in his own relationships.

Short-Term Goals

1. Pat will discuss what he has read in the book during treatment sessions and discuss in what ways he agrees or disagrees with how behaviors are categorized as relationship building, relationship damaging, or neutral.

2. Pat will observe relationships in the TV shows that he watches and keep a record of the relationship-building, relationship-damaging, and neutral behaviors that he observes and discuss this record during treatment sessions.

3. Pat will observe his boss and keep a record of the relationship-building, relationship-damaging, and neutral behaviors that he observes and discuss this record during treatment sessions.

4. Pat will observe and keep a record of the relationship-building, relationship-damaging, and neutral behaviors that he observes on his way to work and discuss this record during treatment sessions.

5. Pat will watch a movie with the clinician that covers relationship skills and discuss the advantages and disadvantages of his using them within his own relationships.

6. Other goals will be set as needed to clarify the differences between types of relationship behaviors.

LONG-TERM GOAL 2: Pat will analyze his relationship with his parents for examples of relationship building, relationship damaging, and neutral relationship behavior and consider the consequences these behaviors had for him and for their marital relationship.

LONG-TERM GOAL 3: Pat will analyze his relationships with his peers for examples of relationship building, relationship damaging, and neutral relationship behavior and consider whether he wants to make any changes in his current or future relationships.

LONG-TERM GOAL 4: Pat will analyze his relationship with Alice for examples of relationship building, relationship damaging, and neutral relationship behavior and consider whether he wants to make any changes in his relationship with her.

Premise 4: Historically Based Style

As Pat developed from childhood through adolescence, he learned that his personal world was either violent or neglectful and that only he could ensure his own survival. While adults in his neighborhood and school reinforced the idea that his abused body was normal, these other environments did teach him that hard work could lead to money and enough to eat. Adult Pat has been very motivated to have a relationship with an adult woman. However, while he knows that he doesn't want a relationship like the one his parents had with each other, he doesn't know what makes relationships succeed or fail. While motivated to be "different," he lacks the skills he needs to develop a stable adaptive relationship; however, he is persistent, and despite a number of failures, he continues to try again. His strengths lie in his ability to learn through observation, his ability to inhibit his physical aggression in certain situations, and his curiosity about why people do what they do. This curiosity may provide Pat with motivation to try new behaviors in pursuit of his goals of keeping Alice engaged in a relationship and keeping out of jail.

Treatment Plan 4: Historically Based Style

Treatment Plan Overview. Due to the neglectful and violent behaviors of his parents, Pat raised himself and did not get help learning how to get what he wanted from life without the use of aggression. Pat has little motivation at this time to explore his own aggressive behavior, as he does not agree that it is a problem. He is overtly angry with his parents and feels they "screwed him up." Furthermore, Pat wants to have a better relationship with Alice than his father had with his mother. Thus, he will consider learning the relationship-building skills his parents neglected to teach him. Long-Term Goal 1 will be achieved before progressing to further goals. (This treatment plan follows the *problem format.*)

PROBLEM: Pat did not learn how to solve relationship problems without violence when he was growing up.

LONG-TERM GOAL 1: Pat will examine what he learned from his parents about conflict resolution when he was a young child and teen.

Short-Term Goals

1. Pat will describe what he observed about his parents' behavior toward other adults, such as neighbors and extended family members, and consider whether they had relationships he would call friendships.

    a. Pat will articulate how well his parents' violent style of relating supported their getting their human needs for companionship, respect, and trust met from adult friends.

    b. Pat will reflect on whether he learned any viable friendship skills by observing his parents.

    c. Pat will reflect on how his parents' behavior influenced his choice to be a loner.

2. Pat will discuss his parents' behavior toward each other as spouses and speculate on the consequences of that behavior for each of them in getting their needs for intimacy, respect, and security met.

    a. Pat will reflect on what he learned about how men and women relate to each other by observing his parents.

    b. Pat will consider the impact his violent upbringing had on his ability to relate to women in a way that would sustain a positive relationship.

3. Pat will discuss his parents' aggressive and neglectful behavior toward him as a child and the consequences of this in regard to his receiving the care and support every child needs.

4. Pat will discuss the impact his violent upbringing had on his ability to consider other people trustworthy.

5. Pat will discuss the impact his violent upbringing had on his ability to succeed at schoolwork.

6. Other goals will be developed as appropriate to helping Pat see the impact of his past violent and neglectful learning history on his current life.

LONG-TERM GOAL 2: Pat will examine what he learned from his teachers' and neighbors' failure to respond to his physical signs of being abused and neglected when he was a child and a teen.

LONG-TERM GOAL 3: Pat will examine what he learned from his neighbors' giving him money for working for them but not responding to his physical signs of being abused and neglected when he was a child and a teen.

Premise 5: Theme-Based Style

"Can I make her stay put?" This may be a question Pat never asked himself until his recent alliance with Alice. Faced with a history of relationship failure and in danger of losing yet another relationship, Pat may finally be open to thinking about his life and what has taught him to be who he is today. From a behavioral perspective, many of his difficulties stem from faulty learning experiences in which the use of aggression and an overindulgence in alcohol were modeled and reinforced as much as direct caregiving and nurturing were ignored. In his family, the young Pat was left to learn that only in not staying put, but rather in hiding, was he safe. These experiences led him to consider it safer to keep others at a distance, and thus he didn't develop social skills through ongoing peer interactions. As a result, he did not learn the skills that might invite people to stay put and relate to him rather than melting away when he isn't looking. Pat's strengths can be seen in his ability to reflect on, and try to learn from, watching others and his recognition that it was his violent behavior that landed him in jail. This recognition may be an opening for Pat to learn new strategies that could help him motivate Alice to "stay put." In the past, he has struggled against heavy odds to survive. This persistence has the potential to serve him well. He can use his intelligence and ability to learn from observing others to develop the power to maintain relationships.

Treatment Plan 5: Theme-Based Style

Treatment Plan Overview. Pat has started and then lost many relationships with women in the past. He is currently very interested in Alice "staying put" and not disappearing while he is at work, as prior partners have. The only stable relationship he observed was the one between his two alcoholic parents. When they weren't drinking, he only saw them engaging in violent exchanges. Thus, he doesn't have relationship-maintaining skills. He may be motivated by treatment focused on his being able to maintain a stable relationship with Alice. Long-Term Goal 1 is to be completed before beginning Long-Term Goal 2. (This treatment plan follows the *problem format*.)

PROBLEM: Pat did not learn how to help a woman want to "stay put" in a relationship with him.

LONG-TERM GOAL 1: Pat will examine stable interpersonal relationships and determine which skills he may want to learn in order to encourage Alice to stay put.

Short-Term Goals

1. Pat will observe current interpersonal relationships in his neighborhood, work environment, and so on and explore the question "Who has stable relationships and why?"

2. Pat will consider which verbal and physical behaviors provide evidence that these relationships are stable.

3. Pat will observe the consequences (neutral, negative, positive) during new social interactions that he witnesses between people who have stable relationships and determine which skills result in neutral, negative, or positive consequences.

4. Pat will make a list of skills he would like to learn to use in his own relationships.

5. Pat will watch a movie that he enjoys and observe whether the men and women are using the behaviors that lead to stable or unstable relationships.

6. Pat will watch a movie selected by the clinician and observe whether the men and women are using behaviors that lead to stable or unstable relationships.

7. Pat will discuss which verbal behaviors he would like to try using in developing a positive relationship with his probation officer.

8. Other goals will be set as appropriate to identify skills Pat considers to be of value to him.

LONG-TERM GOAL 2: Pat will practice relationship-maintaining strategies with Alice, within the context of treatment sessions, to make it more likely that she will stay put and continue relating to him.

Premise 6: Diagnosis-Based Style

Pat has a lifelong history of being either abused or neglected by individuals who were responsible for his welfare. His parents never showed emotional regulation in their interactions with each other or him. His neighbors and teachers did not reach out to help raise him. He developed survival techniques that included ducking and hiding to keep safe and observing others to try to understand what made them "tick." While he has come to view the world as a basically hostile place in which sane people have learned to be on their guard, he does recognize that some people, like his current boss, are not dangerous and deserve respect. He has also learned that hard work and responsibility can get him physical security (i.e., a warm place to live and enough food to eat). Pat works hard and has the ability to learn new skills, such as computer skills, if given the opportunity. In addition, he shows evidence of regretting the time he spent in prison and the loss of some of his past interpersonal relationships. However, he lacks awareness of how episodes in which he lost control of his anger led to his difficulties with the law and his relationship failures. This profile of episodic losses of control of anger leading to serious consequences can be considered compatible with a primary DSM-5 diagnosis of 312.34 Intermittent Explosive Disorder (American Psychiatric Association, 2013). Further assessment is needed to determine if a diagnosis of an Alcohol-Related Disorder is appropriate. Both of Pat's parents may have been alcoholics, and there are indications that excessive alcohol use occurred prior to Pat's most violent outbursts. While showing serious episodes of loss of control of his anger, Pat also has a long-standing history of seeking constructive employment and learning new job skills. He had pride in his earlier work as a computer technician and currently shows a sense of loyalty to his current employer despite feeling underemployed. These bode well for his ability to profit from new learning experiences that will teach him how to regulate his emotions and sustain intimate relationships.

Treatment Plan 6: Diagnosis-Based Style

Treatment Plan Overview. Pat is motivated to stay out of jail and continue his relationship with Alice. He does not currently believe that learning emotional regulation skills and ending or reducing his alcohol use is necessary to achieve these goals. The current situation will first be described from his point of view. Then, information that the clinician has garnered from other sources will be summarized. Finally, a plan based on an integration of this information will be offered to help Pat stay out of jail and strengthen his relationship with Alice. (This treatment plan follows the *adapted SOAP format.*)

Subjective Data

Personal history: Pat is a 25-year-old, European American male who was the only child of two alcoholic parents. He describes being treated by his parents with indifference and hostility. He states that he was often beaten for reasons he did not understand. He witnessed many acts of violence between his parents. He got into trouble in school for aggressive behavior and received poor grades beginning in elementary school. He began coming into conflict with the law as a teenager. This was also the time when he began to drink. He considers himself a loner who never had friends. He says friends are for "losers."

Relationship history: Pat has been involved in many short-term relationships with women. He met these women in bars or in his neighborhood and, after a few weeks of dating, invited them to move in with him; then, just as suddenly, they secretly moved back out. He has observed other people having longer-term relationships than he has had, and he expresses the desire to maintain a long-term relationship with Alice.

Legal history: Pat was recently released from prison. He was convicted of assault with intent to harm and given a prison sentence of two to five years. Pat was released after three years for good behavior. He is currently on parole. He has weekly appointments with his parole officer and is participating in treatment as a requirement of his parole. The officer wants him to decrease his alcohol use and develop nonaggressive strategies for dealing with conflict.

Work history: Pat began seeking employment as a child and has been gainfully employed since he graduated from high school. The only disruption of this was his time in prison. Immediately on release from prison, he set out to get a job and is now a custodian at a store.

Objective Data

Standardized intellectual testing using the Wechsler Adult Intelligence Scale, Fourth Edition (WAIS-IV), revealed that Pat has an above-average level of intelligence. Pat denied any memory loss, cognitive disorientation, or history of head injury, so no neuropsychological testing was considered necessary at this time. Personality testing utilizing the Minnesota Multiphasic Personality Inventory–2 (MMPI-2) revealed no signs of cognitive confusion, personal turmoil or distress, or physical symptoms. Rather, his profile suggested a history of severe family and interpersonal discord. His relationships with others can be characterized by suspiciousness, jealousy, and hostility. His scores on items reflective of alcohol abuse are ambiguous, and thus further assessment in this area is called for. His profile suggests a pattern of behavior consistent with episodic losses of control and risk-taking tendencies as well as severe family disruption. As a result, Pat is not likely to view the clinician as trustworthy. The clinician must take responsibility for demonstrating trustworthiness. His working diagnosis at this time is 312.34 Intermittent Explosive Disorder. His current functioning at this time reflects at least an average level of intelligence, stable employment, and motivation to develop a stable relationship with Alice. He has minimal social support in the form of weekly parole meetings; there is no evidence at this time regarding whether Alice does or does not seek to remain in a relationship with Pat.

Assessment

At this time, Pat shows no signs of significant emotional turmoil or distress related to his past violent behavior or alcohol abuse except for a clear desire to not return to jail and not lose his relationship with Alice. Pat's behavior is consistent with a diagnosis of 312.34 Intermittent Explosive Disorder. His adult behavior is also consistent with a view of Pat as an adult survivor of an abusive and neglectful upbringing. Based on his self-report, he was not given needed physical or emotional support as a child to develop emotional regulation skills or constructive relationship skills. Both Pat's high level of intelligence and his ability to observe and analyze others might be utilized in supporting his learning of these needed skills. However, safety issues must be monitored carefully, as Pat is angry about the referral for treatment. While there were no signs of any loss of control of anger within the treatment session, he has a history of explosive, violent outbursts. Thus, Pat's potential for being a danger to others, including the clinician, will need to be monitored on an ongoing basis.

Plan

Treatment plan overview: Pat has a significant potential to be a danger to others, and thus his level of anger will need to be monitored on an ongoing basis. All the fights that the clinician is aware of involved men. It is unknown at this time if he has ever physically abused Alice. Involving the probation officer in assessing Alice's safety as well as monitoring Pat's level of anger will be an asset to treatment. Pat is most motivated to maintain a relationship with Alice, to maintain constructive employment, and to stay out of jail. His relationship with Alice will be worked on first, as he is unambiguously motivated to do something different than he has in his past relationships with women. Pat has strong observational skills. Utilizing these within the treatment plan will aid success.

LONG-TERM GOAL 1: Pat would like to maintain his relationship with Alice.

Short-Term Goals

1. Pat will read a book on relationship building and discuss with the clinician any skills within it that he thinks might be useful in his relationship with Alice.

2. Pat will observe men and women in his neighborhood and at work and discuss with the clinician any relationship skills he sees that he thinks might be useful in his relationship with Alice.

3. Pat will observe TV broadcasts, videos, and movies and discuss with the clinician any relationship skills he sees that he thinks might be useful to him in building a stronger relationship with Alice.

4. Pat will practice relationship skills he has found useful within role plays with the clinician as a way of strengthening these skills prior to trying them with Alice.

5. Pat will read a book about the destructive impact violence has on relationships and discuss with the clinician any skills within it that he observed in his parents' relationship and consider whether violence played a role in any of his prior relationships with women.

6. Pat will observe TV broadcasts, videos, and movies that involve realistic relationship violence and discuss with the clinician the impact he observed that this violence had on the couple's relationship.

7. Pat will read a book about emotional regulation skills and consider whether there are one or more skills within the book that might be of value in his attempts to achieve his personal goals with Alice.

8. In role plays with the clinician, Pat will practice using emotional regulation skills that he considers useful for maintaining his relationship with Alice.

9. Pat will practice skills he has found useful within conjoint treatment sessions with Alice.

10. Other goals will be set as needed to accomplish Long-Term Goal 1.

LONG-TERM GOAL 2: Pat would like to maintain constructive employment.

LONG-TERM GOAL 3: Pat would like to remain out of jail.

CONCLUSIONS

The types of case conceptualizations and treatment plans recommended within this chapter require a great deal of critical thinking prior to actually implementing treatment. Although this is initially time-consuming, this critical thinking will serve you well in planning effective and time-efficient treatment sessions overall.

Developing new skills can create temporary chaos for the learner. As you practice these new case conceptualization and treatment-planning skills, you may enter a temporary period in which your writing seems awkward, rigid, or simplistic and in which you feel confused and uncomfortable. This period of "bad" or "stressful" writing will dissipate with practice, and you will have developed a scholarly approach to writing that reflects your personal style.

RECOMMENDED RESOURCES

American Psychiatric Association. (2013). *Diagnostic and statistical manual of mental disorders* (5th ed.). Washington, DC: American Psychiatric Publishing.

American Psychological Association. (2007). Record keeping guidelines. *American Psychologist, 62*(9), 993–1004.

Dunn, D. S. (2004). *A short guide to writing about psychology.* New York, NY: Pearson Education.

Pan, M. L. (2008). *Preparing literature reviews: Qualitative and quantitative approaches.* Glendale, CA: Pyrczak.

The Complexity
of Human Experience

Malika is referred to you for treatment of acute anxiety attacks. Is her age, sexual orientation, gender, or racial background relevant to her treatment? What about her medical history, her religious upbringing, her socioeconomic status, her educational achievements, her history of physical or sexual abuse, or other aspects of her background? All these domains may reveal insights to help you evaluate Malika. Which should you choose in conceptualizing her case?

The greater the differences between you and Malika, the greater the difficulty you will have in making this decision. There is no absolute standard of mental health, as all norms are influenced by the history and politics of when they were developed. As a result, professional organizations such as the American Psychological Association (APA; 2002a) and the Association for Multicultural Counseling and Development (Sue, Arredondo, & McDavis, 1992) call on clinicians to develop multicultural competencies and keep informed of new research on the complexity of human experience. Special populations such as older adults, individuals with disabilities, women, and, sexual minorities have also come to be considered areas of cultural difference that require specific competencies (APA, 2006, 2007a, 2007b, 2013, 2014).

You are the clinician. Thus, it is your task to determine whether Malika's anxiety is a "healthy reaction" to a problematic environment, a "different but healthy reaction," or a pathological level of anxiety. It would be overwhelming, and overly time-consuming, to evaluate everything that makes up Malika's complex and unique identity when trying to decide if she needs treatment for anxiety. Hays (2008) recommends that you begin by asking Malika to describe herself. Supporting self-definition is important, because research suggests that it can be damaging to invalidate Malika's self-attributions or describe her identities for her (Pedrotti, Edwards, & Lopez, 2008). Some aspects of her identity may be very salient to her worldview and influence her on a continuous basis. Other aspects may be more or less salient depending on time and place as she takes on different roles or life challenges (Delphin & Rowe, 2008).

There will also be an interaction between your personal identity and Malika's; this interaction can support or inhibit the development of an effective working relationship. Thus, Hays (2008) recommends that you start each new treatment relationship by evaluating potential differences between you and your client on nine critical domains of identity: (a) age and generational influences, (b) developmental disabilities and disabilities acquired later in life, (c) religion and spiritual orientation, (d) ethnic and racial identity, (e) socioeconomic status, (f) sexual orientation, (g) indigenous heritage, (h) national origin, and (i) gender. Within each of these domains, you may find that you differ from Malika in terms of privilege, power, and experiences with oppression. Clarifying the power differentials between you and Malika will be your first step in avoiding microaggressions, that is, the unintentional taking on of an oppressor role with her, or the infusion of a negative bias into your conceptualization and treatment plan (Hays, 2008; Sue & Sue, 2013). These aggressions or invalidations may appear small to you, the person with the greatest power within the treatment relationship, but they can cause substantial psychological harm to Malika, the less powerful individual, because she is the one seeking help (Sue & Sue, 2013). We all have ingrained, automatic behavioral responses to other people that we have developed over our life span. Some of this may involve unintentionally taking on an oppressor role in relation to someone else. Changing this ingrained behavior can be difficult. It requires a great deal of self-awareness to recognize when your ingrained biases may be acting automatically to influence you. For example, in a friendly moment, I, a European American, might ask a new male neighbor, "How long have you been in the United States?" The frown I receive in return tells me that I've made a mistake. I committed a microaggression by assuming this individual was a foreign national or a recent immigrant when, in fact, he is the third generation of his family born in the United States. His family have been citizens longer than mine. It isn't enough to apologize. If you were Asian American, you might never have committed this microaggression toward this particular man. But what if this new neighbor is of Latino descent? Then you, too, might have made the same microaggression that I did. Or, on the other hand, your own experiences with microaggressions might have sensitized you to being more careful in this situation.

We all have the potential to engage in these destructive practices. As a result, we must all take responsibility for developing greater self-awareness of our stereotypes of people who are different from ourselves. It is our responsibility to educate ourselves further and learn to slow down our immediate reactions to someone who looks different from us. Returning to Malika, you, as the more powerful person in the therapeutic relationship, must take personal responsibility for adapting your approach to Malika so that a positive treatment alliance can be developed. While we will learn directly from Malika, it is not her responsibility to educate us about her background. Expecting this of her is a microaggression when she's come to you to talk about her acute anxiety attacks, not her cultural heritage.

The following sections represent introductions to the domains of age, ethnic and racial background, gender, sexual orientation, socioeconomic status, and violence history. Only an overview of information relevant to each domain is included. There are also "red-flag" guidelines to help you integrate critical information from each domain into your case conceptualizations and treatment plans. The last section under each domain helps you reflect on your level of understanding of the cultural domain. These self-awareness questions are based on the multicultural competencies described by Sue and colleagues (1992). You can use the information from each of these domains to deepen your analyses of clients as you complete the integration exercises found at the end of Chapters 3 through 12.

These exercises mark the beginning stage of learning how to incorporate human complexity into your work. If you are ready for a more in-depth understanding, there are recommended resources at the end of this chapter.

THE DOMAIN OF AGE

Darla, age 16, has been suspended from school for drinking on school grounds (Chapter 5). Kevin, age 14, is struggling with self-hate and a phobia of mirrors (Chapter 3). Alice, age 9, is caught in the middle of her parents' conflicts before and after their divorce (Chapter 8). Each minor has been mandated into treatment by adults. How relevant are Darla's, Kevin's, and Alice's ages to you as their clinician? How will what constitutes adaptive behavior be different for a 9-year-old and a 14-year-old? What is considered normal for a child or youth is influenced by the child's level of intelligence, his or her caretakers' attitudes, and current social norms. In addition, the age of a child is highly related to what types of behaviors would be considered typical or normal for the age group versus what would be considered untypical or abnormal.

As a clinician, you will need to be grounded in normal development to conduct valid assessment and treatment decisions for minors. This section will provide you with a brief introduction to development to use in the case conceptualizations and treatment plans that follow in this textbook. First, census data relevant to minors will be provided. Then, brief summaries of the developmental periods of early childhood, late childhood, and adolescence in terms of physical, cognitive, and psychosocial development will be used as an introduction to how children of different ages differ from each other and from adults. These overviews apply only to individuals of at least average intelligence who are in good health and receiving adequate care. Issues of cognitive or physical disabilities, gender, culture, and the influence of different types of traumas on development are beyond the scope and intent of this section. While information about children is presented in terms of discrete developmental periods, it is important to underscore that growth is a continuous process that doesn't just start and stop at particular ages. In addition, the social context in which children live is critical to their development (H. Werner, 1957). Werner posits that a child's development occurs through the social interactions they have. As they are exposed to new thoughts, feelings, actions, and bodily sensations, they come to integrate new information into what they already understand. As they see how this new information or these new experiences are similar to or different from prior knowledge, they create new, more individualized knowledge for themselves (Raeff, 2014). Thus, your decisions about children always need to take into account their social interconnections with others.

Census Data

In 2012, 74 million children were living in the United States. While they are not often thought of as a minority group, children have significantly less power than adults. They have no choice as to what type of family they are born into, where they live, where they go to school, and many other basic aspects of daily living. At this time, 64% of children are living with married parents, 24% are living with only their mother, and 12% are living with unmarried parents, with only their father, or without parents (Vespa, Lewis, & Kreider, 2013). It is unlikely that any of these children had a lot to say about whether their parents got married or not or whether their parents live together or not. Economically, children living with married parents are in the most affluent circumstances; 70 % of them are living at 200 % of the poverty level or more. However, 1 in 2 children living with only their mother, with unmarried parents, or without parents is living below the poverty level. Not all children are equally vulnerable to growing up in poverty. Fifty-two percent of African American children live in poverty with only one parent, followed by 28 % of Hispanic children of any race and 20 % of White children (Vespa et al., 2013). The relative powerlessness of children is often overlooked. Development is influenced by context, and children do not have the power to control the contexts in which they live, including their homes, their neighborhoods, their schools, and their countries (Raeff, 2014; H. Werner, 1957). Consider this lack of power as you read through the cases in the text and consider in what ways this helplessness should be considered as you set out to support the healthy development of minors.

Early Childhood (Approximately Ages 4–7)

A 4-year-old looks very young and incompetent compared to a 7-year-old, while at the same time appearing highly sophisticated and coordinated in comparison to a toddler. This is because early childhood is a time of very rapid physical development. Young children can walk, run, jump, and climb with ever-increasing speed and coordination. As they age, gross motor skills, such as running and climbing, are mastered more easily than fine motor skills, such as holding a knife and fork or writing with a pencil. Tasks are valued for kinesthetic pleasure rather than for goal directedness (Brems, 2008). Thus, children might play with mud endlessly without any intention of building something specific. Intrinsic motivation to master new physical skills is the norm. However, how adults respond to the child's behavior is critical to the child's brain development and will set the stage for later skill development (National Scientific Council on the Developing Child, 2007).

While they enjoy unstructured play, young children can effectively focus their attention on challenging tasks when they are provided with appropriate, guided structure (Vygotsky; 1978, 1986–1987). Intense frustration may result when young children are pressured by others to master tasks they are not neurologically ready for. Physical maturity that allows for greater speed and agility builds faster than cognitive skills that help children stop and think. This results in a high rate of injuries in this group (National Center for Health Statistics, 2002). The injury rate is highest for children under the age of 15 (12 %) and individuals 75 and older (15 %), with falls being the leading cause of harm (Bergen, Chen, Warner, & Fingerhut, 2008).

Cognitively, young children are curious and active learners. They are in Piaget's stage of preoperational thought where they can begin to think about something (manipulate symbols) before acting on it (Piaget, 1952). They enjoy make-believe and use symbolic play to gratify their needs and increase their understanding of the world. Preoperational thinking is egocentric, and these children have an exaggerated view of their impact on the world. They often see themselves as responsible for what has happened. This can be true of positive as well as negative events (Piaget, 1952). For example, a child may think, "Dad beat my mom because I left my clothes on the floor today."

Despite this type of egocentrism, young children do have a theory of mind that allows them to recognize that other people have thoughts and feelings that are different from their own. Children learn from copying their parents long before verbal instruction is possible (Meltzoff, 2005). Thus, a child can realize that another child is hurt when hit with a ball and that one teacher will be angry when a rule is broken while another will not. Young children always look to immediate events to understand cause and effect. Their theory of mind develops first through imitation, and then through firsthand experience, and then to the view that others that "act like me" have "internal states like me" (Meltzoff, 2005, p. 56). Their views of rules are very concrete and inflexible. They master new learning best through guided participation, repetition, and scaffolding (Vygotsky, 1978, 1986–1987). Their cognitive abilities grow the most smoothly when the challenge of the new tasks is kept within reasonable limits. In this situation, the child is intrinsically motivated to move toward mastery (Vygotsky, 1978, 1986–1987).

In terms of language development, these children can communicate with adultlike verbal and nonverbal speech. They use complex sentences and can use speech as a tool for developing more complex thinking skills (Vygotsky, 1978). They need concrete and simple explanations that are tied to the here and now to learn new concepts (Brems, 2008). Despite having improved verbal skills, these young children still prefer learning through modeling rather than learning through verbal directions (Brems, 2008). Advances in their language development allow parents, siblings, and others to guide their learning experiences. The development of private speech also plays a role in aiding self-control and guiding the child during the learning process. This learning occurs over the course of a long series of developmental steps (Vygotsky, 1978, p. 57).

The earliest forms of social development have been studied in terms of the attachment patterns of infants as secure or insecure (Bowlby, 1973). Sroufe (2005) has found that infants who are securely attached are more likely to develop the ability to regulate emotions and to become the toddlers, preschoolers, and older children who have a positive network of social relationships. They may also view themselves as worthy and valued (Masten & Narayan, 2012). This is posited because social skills build on each other, and as an individual grows from one age to the next, his or her repertoire of behaviors that can lead to successful relationships increases (Feeney, 2008). Children need help learning to label their internal sensations with emotional labels, to understand how to reduce the level of felt emotion, and to understand the emotions of others. Adults can effectively coach children to master these skills (Denham, Basset, & Wyatt, 2007, p. 622).

Infants first show attachment using proximity-seeking behavior, then they use the attachment figure as a safe haven in times of stress, and finally they see the attachment figure as a secure base from which to explore the world (Bowlby, 1973). When adults consistently respond to the needs of infants with warmth, as well as expecting the child to show age-appropriate maturity, the infant develops a positive model for his or her self as well as for others. This serves as the foundation for forming healthy intimate relationships with adults (Baumrind, 1967).

On the other hand, if caretakers provide inconsistent or insufficient responsiveness in childhood, children can develop a negative working model of themselves and a fear that all intimate relationships will result in abandonment (Mallinckrodt & Wei, 2005). Children in these circumstances may not learn how to regulate their emotions—particularly anger, frustration, and fear. This may lead to explosions of fear or rage and violent behavior (Ryder, 2014). When parents do not correct children when they are disruptive, these children may be set up for rejection by other adults and children as they become ever more involved in society outside their immediate caretaker's realm.

Children ages 4 through 7 are in Erikson's psychosocial stage of "initiative versus guilt." Children have a strong desire to fit in with their families and be valued as a member of the family. They model their caregivers and take in the socialized rules of their community and culture (Erikson, 1963). These children can identify how they feel and can communicate this to others when helped to do so. Typically, they can be aware of one emotion at a time, although they can understand a variety of emotions and have begun to learn emotional regulation skills. The ability to inhibit, moderate, and direct emotions—that is, to regulate them—allows a child to learn to talk about being angry rather than just kicking the dog (Halberstadt & Eaton, 2003; National Scientific Council on the Developing Child, 2004). Children without these skills may develop either internalizing problems from over-controlling their emotions or externalizing problems from under-controlling their emotions (Bates & Pettit, 2007).

Emotional and behavioral self-regulation will influence how well children interact with adults and peers. Children need to learn how to cope with their negative emotions, inhibit their impulses to act out in a negative way when angry or upset, and see that they have many choices in how to respond (D. Schwartz & Proctor, 2000). While emotional regulation is a skill that will continue to develop as the child ages, increasing self-regulatory strategies can improve social functioning. Effective strategies may include saying soothing things to oneself, shifting one's attention away from the distressing situation, attempting to cognitively understand the unpleasant event and reframing it to be less emotionally evocative, and acting in ways that reduce exposure to stressful situations (D. Schwartz, Toblin, Abou-ezzeddine, Shelley, & Stevens, 2005). This type of social competence is an important protective factor, supporting resiliency in development in the face of stressful circumstances.

Biological research suggests that children have inborn temperaments that can reflect being behaviorally inhibited, behaviorally uninhibited, or neither (Kagan, 1997; C. E. Schwartz et al., 2010). In addition, social withdrawal has been found to be a heterogeneous category that is influenced by situational context, motivational tendencies, and developmental consequences (Coplan, Prakash, O'Neil, & Armer, 2004). In socializing with other children, young children can begin displaying a give-and-take style in which cooperation and sharing are important. While peer influences are beginning, approval and attention, particularly from caregivers, are still primary. Parents and other valued role models in the environment can help children develop empathy or antipathy for others; mirror neurons in children's brains facilitate this emotional development, and in many ways, children's emotional skills become wired into the brain (Meltzoff, 2005; National Scientific Council on the Developing Child, 2004).

What happens during early childhood provides the foundations for weak or strong social skills in adulthood (National Scientific Council on the Developing Child, 2007). Self-esteem develops from learning new skills and developing a sense of competency and relationships with adults that encourage skill development (Erikson, 1963; National

Scientific Council on the Developing Child, 2007). Children begin to form a self-concept based on what they can and can't do. Their sense of pride in taking on a new task helps them concentrate and persist. They are usually optimistic that they can accomplish a new project. However, they feel guilt over their mistakes (Erikson, 1963). Connections between their mistakes or misdeeds and a punishment must be immediate and clear; otherwise the child will not learn from them (Skinner, 1938). Laible and Thompson (2007, p. 184) indicated that warmth in parenting can help increase positive mood states in children. There is a cascading effect of having a trustworthy relationship with a parent whereby you come to expect that other relationships will involve trustworthy others and, as a result, are more cooperative with others, which facilitates warmer relationships. When caretakers are neglectful, the architecture of the brain can be negatively impacted such that children develop less ability to regulate their emotions and control their behavior (Laible & Thompson, 2007; National Scientific Council on the Developing Child, 2005).

Middle Childhood (Approximately Ages 7–12)

Children in the elementary school years master one new physical challenge after another. While gross motor skills continue to be mastered more quickly than fine motor skills, the overall process of physical development reflects a relatively smooth increase in coordination and competence. The ability to follow the rules of competitive games increases, and variability in success in individual and team sports provides a new arena for winners and losers. Myelination continues in the brain along with increases in interconnections between areas of the brain. This, along with the assistance of supportive adults, helps school-age children show a reduction in temper tantrums, impulsiveness, inattention, and insistence on rigid routines in comparison to younger children. When schools foster warm relationships between teachers, staff, and children, the supports are in place for the development of positive self-esteem, persistence, and the ability to work cooperatively with peers and resolve conflicts (National Scientific Council on the Developing Child, 2007).

Children of elementary school age are in Piaget's concrete operational stage of thought (Piaget, 1952). They can understand logical reasoning when it is presented to them using concrete events or tools that they can experience or directly see. This makes them much more logical and more able to use strategies for learning. In following rules and directions, these children are able to process more than one or two steps at a time, and they are able to plan ahead if the task has concrete and specific goals. Present-oriented explanations are still more effective than abstract, general discussions in helping these children understand complex life events such as divorce and death. They have begun to anticipate the consequences of their behavior (Brems, 2008). Language skills are well developed; these children have wide vocabularies and an expanded understanding of grammatical rules. They have learned to talk differently to parents than to friends (code switching). Most children master learning to read in this period, and reading skills become increasingly important for educational success—school success being a protective factor supporting resilience reactions to stress (Masten, 2014).

Psychosocially, Erikson puts these children in the stage of "industry versus inferiority." These youths busily set about learning new skills, which can give them a sense of competence and a positive sense of self. This seeking of competence is an inborn tendency; however, it is impacted by the reactions of the environment (National Scientific Council on the Developing Child, 2007). These children's increased skill at social cognition makes them more aware of their social status vis-à-vis their peers. This ability to compare their skills to those of others may lead them to feel inferior, resulting in a negative self-concept (Erikson, 1963). In addition, emotional rejection or physical abuse by caretakers causes hypervigilance to cues of danger and a tendency to misperceive neutral social cues as negative, leading to more aggressive behavior (National Scientific Council on the Developing Child, 2005). Being socially isolated can be a risk factor for the development of psychopathology. However, research indicates that there are at least three forms of social isolation that have different implications for children. Conflicted shyness (Asendorpf, 1990, 1993) represents a child with social competencies who has an approach–avoidance conflict. These shy children need encouragement and support to become more comfortable in group and new situations but are not at risk for peer isolation. The shy child may have good social skills but feel conflicted about approaching other children. Another child who has less social contact than the outgoing child may spend less time with peers because he or she is industriously involved in activities that are very rewarding to the child and socially appropriate. Industrious children can become at risk as development proceeds if their unique interests keep them so preoccupied that they fall behind in age-appropriate social skills. Finally, the child at significant risk is the one who is actively rejected by peers; however, positive parental relationships can mitigate this risk (Asendorpf, 1993; Wright, Masten, & Narayan, 2013).

While parents are still important, these children actively seek out others of their own age for advice and self-validation, and they model themselves after popular peers (Luthar & Latendresse, 2005). Children can be popular because they have positive social skills, such as kindness, cooperativeness, and trustworthiness, or because they are athletic, highly attractive, dominating, and arrogant. Sixth-graders in both suburbia and the inner city tend to respect peers who openly flaunt authority and do not passively follow rules (Luthar & Latendresse, 2005).

Research with suburban families has shown that physical attractiveness is a more important criterion for girls than for boys; physical attractiveness was also a less important factor in popularity in the inner city than in suburbia (Luthar & Latendresse, 2005). Children who are unpopular can be neglected but socially accepted, or they can be rejected due to either their withdrawn behavior or their aggressive behavior. Being actively rejected is a risk factor for the development of emotional problems, while shyness per se is not (Asendorpf, 1993).

Most boys and girls are at their most aggressive during kindergarten and become increasingly less aggressive as they age. The children who were overly aggressive in kindergarten may now be the bullies in elementary school. Some gender differences have been found, with boys being more likely to use physically aggressive behavior as their primary mode of bullying and female bullies showing a heavier reliance on relational aggression. However, both boys and girls can be physically aggressive and use relational aggression (Watson, Andreas, Fischer, & Smith, 2005). In examining groups of girls and boys across six sites, Broidy and associates (2003) found that there was a larger percentage of girls than boys who were rarely physically aggressive and more boys than girls who were consistently aggressive. While anxious and withdrawn children may now be the ones who are victimized at school, effective parents can serve as buffers to help their children negotiate problems with peers (Wright et al., 2013). Stress, when it is short term and paired with responsive parenting, can serve to spur psychological growth by giving the child more control over his or her impulses and a sense of mastery over difficult tasks. When stress is constant and children have to find ways of coping on their own, it is toxic. This type of stress can lead to either a constant state of vigilance and response to the smallest perceptions of threat, or the numbing of the body's response to threat so that the child doesn't stay out of harm's way. In either case, toxic stress interferes with brain chemistry, disrupting emotional regulation, memory, and learning (National Scientific Council on the Developing Child, 2007).

Children are active agents of their own socialization, as they may accept or reject information coming in from the environment and there is a reciprocal impact of children with their primary caretakers that continues to promote or discourage healthy development (Grusec & Goodnow, 1994; National Scientific Council on the Developing Child, 2007). What has begun in early and middle childhood will set the groundwork for what will come next. The children who are relating well with peers and developing effective social skills through interactions with nurturing caretakers now have a firm foundation for building further interpersonal skills (National Scientific Council on the Developing Child, 2007). These youths have a greater ability to modulate their emotions and express their emotions in words rather than acting them out. They can understand two emotions at the same time as long as they are either both positive and both negative. Children become more able to recognize the causes and effects behind their feelings and actions and become more self-directed. Schools demand more and more of this self-direction with each passing year. Students who have difficulties with this, for example, due to learning disabilities or attention deficit disorder, or who come from disadvantaged homes, may fall behind in their schoolwork (National Scientific Council on the Developing Child, 2007).

Adolescence (Approximately Ages 12–19)

As children progress through puberty, dramatic physical changes occur. Some teens seem to "change overnight." For others, the process is more gradual. Onset anytime between the ages of 8 and 15 is considered normal, but puberty typically starts between the ages of 10 and 13. In general, females start the process earlier than males (Hofmann & Greydanus, 1997). Self-image and identity may be influenced by early versus late development, as teens prefer to mature at the same time as everyone else. Being off "the norm" can lead to additional stress. Early-maturing girls have been found to have increased risk of internalizing and externalizing problems (Ge, Conger, & Elder, 2001). Late-maturing boys may be at greater risk for bullying at school, and they show higher rates of internalizing problems (Graber, Lewinsohn, Seeley, & Brooks-Gunn, 1997). Adolescents' responses to puberty are moderated by whether they have been prepared for the changes they are undergoing and whether their home and neighborhood environments are supportive or destructive. For example, early-maturing girls may not be prepared to handle the advances that older boys and even adult males may make toward them. Adults can show positive support by not making comments about adolescents' physical development and teaching them how to identify and respond effectively to unwanted sexual attention (APA, 2002b).

While the timing of puberty is genetic and influenced by nutrition and physical health, there are still powerful environmental influences. While an earlier-maturing boy could be the football star at high school due to his large size and fast reflexes, he could also join a gang in the inner city as an enforcer of destructive norms. While hormonal fluctuations can cause more moodiness in teens, overall adolescent testiness is more a result of the higher demands placed on them by society due to their more mature appearance.

Adults may make the mistake of judging maturity by height rather than brain maturation; adults need to understand that they should respond to the social and emotional development of the adolescent, not his or her physical appearance (APA, 2002). Whatever the timing of puberty, both male and female teens take their appearance seriously and spend more time trying to look "right" so that their peers will approve of them (APA, 2002).

Studies show that sleep deprivation is a significant problem facing teens. Biologically, teens need about two more hours of sleep than adults. Lack of sleep is responsible for teen drowsiness, fatigue, and greater impulsivity; this leads to greater disciplinary problems and decreased learning at school (Carpenter, 2001). Studies also indicate that today's adolescents are using more birth control then in previous generations and have decreased their use of cigarettes (World Health Organization [WHO], 2014).

Piaget (1952) considered all adolescents to be in the stage of formal operational reasoning and able to think logically in the same manner as adults. However, brain research reveals a more complex pattern. In tasks involving cognitive capacity, the ability to reason with facts and basic information, significant differences have been found between early and late adolescents, but no significant differences have been found between teens over 16 and adults (Steinberg, Cauffman, Woolard, Graham, & Banich, 2009). However, different types of cognitive reasoning are out of sync with each other during adolescence. Adults use both their prefrontal cortex and their limbic system to make complex decisions. However, the limbic system is developing faster than the prefrontal cortex during the teen years. This makes adolescents more vulnerable to overly emotional reasoning in a number of situations.

First, adolescents may use sophisticated reasoning within academic subjects in which they excel while at the same time making highly impulsive decisions in contexts in which they have less experience. Second, adolescents have been found to rely much more heavily on their emotional reasoning system when highly aroused due to anxiety, fear, anger, or sexual feelings. Thus, while teens can think logically in terms of hypothetical situations involving drugs and sexual behavior, when they are actually in these situations and experiencing emotional and physical excitement, their feelings are likely to preempt logic. Finally, adolescents are more vulnerable to peer pressure and conformity than adults. Deciding to use alcohol or drugs "because everyone is doing it" is the type of reasoning that puts teenagers at risk of violent death and unprotected sex (APA, 2004; Steinberg, 2007; Steinberg & Scott, 2003).

In summary, while adolescents show cognitive capacities similar to those of adults in terms of general intellectual functioning, they show significant differences from adults in many types of reasoning tasks that involve peers, high states of arousal, and impulse control (APA, 2004). The neurobiological evidence clearly reveals differences between adolescents and adults in a number of brain areas. These involve the ability to regulate emotions, impulse control, evaluation of risk and reward, and long-term planning (Steinberg, 2008; Steinberg et al., 2008; Steinberg, Graham, et al., 2009; Steinberg & Monahan, 2007). The neurobiological evidence is considered so compelling that the APA (2004) wrote a legal brief indicating that adolescents are less blameworthy for their anti-social behavior, even when it resulted in the murder of someone else, due to brain imma-turity. In addition, not all adolescents are alike. Significant differences in psychosocial maturity have been found between 16- to 17-year-olds and those 22 and older. Similar significant differences were found between those who were 18 to 21 and those who were 26 or older (Steinberg, Cauffman, et al., 2009). The brain adapts to new learned experi-ences. Thus, while the reward-seeking centers of the brain develop before the areas involved in emotional regulation and decision-making, adolescent exploration and risk-taking can lead to improved decision-making (WHO, 2014).

Adolescents who are less mature, and thus make more snap decisions, have been found to engage in more risky, illegal, or dangerous activities (APA, 2002). Who are these youth? On the Youth Surveillance Survey from the CDC (Kann et al., 2014), 10.8% of male youth and 7.8% of female youth had smoked before the age of 13 (p. 13). Within a 30-day period, 25.3% of male youth and 21.1% of female youth had drunk five or more drinks in a row (p. 19). Of the 64.3% of youth who had driven a car within the last 30 days, 12% of males and 7.8% of females had driven after drinking (p.6). Forty-one percent of youth who had driven in the last month had texted or e-mailed while driving (p. 6). In the same time period, 28% of males and 7.9% of females had carried a weapon (p.7), and 7.4% of males and 13% of females had been involved in dating violence (p. 10). Within the last year, 24.7% of male youth and 19.2% of female youth had been involved in a physical fight (p. 8). Almost half (46.8%) of the youth had had sexual intercourse, and 5.6% had had intercourse before the age of 13. As a final example, in the year before the survey, 24.5% of males and 19.7% of females had been sold, offered, or given illegal drugs on school property (p. 24). According to Moffitt (1993), substance use, for example, is a much stronger risk factor at age 9 than it is at age 14, as most antisocial behavior that begins in adolescence ends in early adulthood.

Fear of losing an intimate relationship, no matter how poor the relationship is, may lead girls from highly neglectful and violent homes to respond with both verbal and physical assaults to anyone who criticizes their highly deficient parent. Such parents have not been effective emotional coaches who support their child in learning how to understand and regulate their emotions (Denham et al., 2007). Thus, a teen girl who has been abused and neglected and has no emotional regulation skills could violently lash out on an impulse. Ironically, the teens whom society views as most dangerous and as "violent predators" may sit in prison recognizing that they committed a crime but not viewing themselves as vio-lent. How can they be so "naive"? The context in which they have grown up contained so much family and neighborhood violence that they see their behavior as typical anger (Ryder, 2014). For most youth—all but about 7% of chronically offending boys—aggressive behavior is on a steadily declining trajectory from childhood through adolescence. A much larger group (19% in Broidy et al.'s 2003 study) exhibit little physical aggression in child-hood, and this remains consistent through the teen years (Broidy et al., 2003).

Psychosocially, teens are in Erikson's stage of "identity versus role confusion." As such, they focus a great deal on their own identity and may feel a great deal of anxiety if they are unsure about what they want to do with their lives. They can experiment with sexual, family, political, religious, and career identities, trying different things on for size and trying to find where they fit in the world (Erikson, 1963). While they may struggle for a sense of separateness and independence from their caregivers, they still may use, as role models, older individuals from their families or their social environment and media personalities. Most teens experience only moderate caregiver–adolescent conflicts and maintain positive relationships with their caregivers. Adolescents with serious conflicts with their caregivers have been found to come from families with chronic conflict (APA, 2002b).

At this time in life, peer acceptance transcends adult approval. Teens initiate and maintain effective peer group relationships without adult support. For most teens, earlier same-gender preferences now change to an interest in developing intimate relationships with a partner of the other sex. Teens struggle as they try to understand what it means to be an adult man or woman while at the same time attempting to integrate their new sexual identity into their sense of self (Brems, 2008). In a study of the complete cohort, minus health absences, of 9th- through 12th-graders in an affluent school system (1,185 students), approximately 2.5% of them exhibited higher-than-average levels of substance use, higher levels of externalizing behaviors, earlier engagement in sexual activity, and lower grade point averages than other teens in their school (Jensen Racz, MacMahon, & Luthar, 2011); no gender differences were found. While a subset of students engaged in a cluster of negative behaviors, there was also a cluster of students who showed the reverse pattern. These prosocial students engaged in less of all these negative activities and had higher grade point averages. Sexual minority teens may face significant challenges in developing a positive self-identity in families and/or communities that provide support only for heterosexual development (Beckstead & Israel, 2007).

Overall, the teen years are less happy than earlier school years, although it is not the time of tremendous turmoil that past myths suggested. Each year teens become aware that the standards are getting more difficult, and they face increased life stress. As a result, they have the capacity to understand the full complexity of emotional reactions and to recognize that the same situation may evoke very different feelings for different people. Based on their past experiences, they can understand and empathize with the feelings of others (Brems, 2008); however, this is more likely if they have parents or an environment that supports the learning of empathy. Teens who have dinner with at least one parent most nights show fewer emotional and behavioral difficulties than teens who do not. Overall, approximately 50% of all mental health problems begin by age 14 (WHO, 2014).

While valuing peer relationships, teens do want adults to remain a part of their lives (APA, 2002b). Physical and emotional isolation are risk factors among both wealthy and inner city teens for anxiety, depression, substance abuse, and poor scholastic achievement (Luthar & Latendresse, 2005). Teens who have developed antipathy rather than empathy may already have begun victimizing others. The aggressive kindergarteners, who became the bullies in elementary school, may now be involved in both violent and nonviolent delinquency in the teen years (Broidy et al., 2003; Watson et al., 2005). Emotional regulation skills continue to be key in successful social development, with teens benefiting from help in being consciously aware of how they feel and what choices they have for dealing with feelings so that they do not seek to numb their emotions using destructive behaviors such as alcohol and drug use, withdrawal from social relationships, and dysfunctional eating. Due to gender role socialization, girls may need more help than boys in learning how to assert themselves and deal with anger, while boys may need more help in learning how to put competition aside and be cooperative. Teens who have strong ethnic identities may develop higher self-esteem than those who do not (APA, 2002b).

Schools can provide an at-risk environment for teens by bringing them into contact with antisocial peers or adults. On the other hand, educational success, and programs that can be offered in schools to promote well-being, are consistently found to be protective factors that promote resiliency in development (WHO, 2014). While educational achievement is stressed more and more by society, school performance declines for many individuals during adolescence. They are more likely than younger children to describe school as boring and teachers as hostile, and intrinsic motivation for school success sags. This decrease in positive attachment to the school may occur because teachers see a student for only one period, because classmates change each period, or because rules and structure become more rigid at a time when adolescents desire more autonomy. Tasks that adolescents need to master as they enter adulthood, such as how to hold down employment, how to sustain an enriching romantic relationship, and how to care for children effectively, can all be seen to follow from the basic social skills that start with a secure attachment in infancy and deepen with age (McCormick, Kuo, & Masten, 2011). In fact, in a longitudinal study of infancy through age 28, quality of infant and child attachment continued to be predictive of each subsequent stage of social attachment, leading to improved romantic relationships and overall life adjustment at age 28 (Englund, Kuo, Puig, & Collins, 2011). Insecurity about the ability to form attachments and avoidance of attachments are negatively associated with perceived support from a social network and positively associated with psychological distress (Mallinckrodt & Wei, 2005).

The life of an adolescent is embedded within a complex web of peers, family, teachers, neighborhoods, work environments, and so forth, and complex interactions among these influences contribute to both positive and negative trajectories for youth as they make the transition from adolescence to early adulthood (Masten, 2014). While adolescence is the time when individuals may first actively strive to understand their own uniqueness, it is not the only time in life where this type of exploration occurs (APA, 2002b). Most individuals emerge into adulthood attached to their families, successful at school and in community endeavors, and not having serious emotional or behavioral problems (APA, 2002b).

Resilience Versus Risk

If an adolescent dies, it is most likely to be the result of an accident, with homicide being the second leading cause of death and suicide the third (Centers for Disease Control and Prevention, 2014). In a nationwide survey of youth in high schools, 16% of students reported seriously considering suicide and 8% reported trying to take their own life during the past year. While girls attempt suicide more often, boys are more likely to die. The risk factors noted by the Centers for Disease Control and Prevention (CDC) include at least one previous attempt at committing suicide; a family history of attempted suicide; depression, bipolar disorder, or another severe mental illness; alcohol or drug use; a recent stressful life event or loss; easy access to a lethal mechanism for committing suicide; exposure to suicide as a potential solution through the suicidal behavior of others; and previous incarceration (CDC, 2014). According to the CDC (2013a), children who are between the ages of 3 and 17 are most likely to have the following three problems: attention deficit disorder (6.8%), behavioral or conduct problems (3.5%), and anxiety (3.0%). Adolescents between the ages of 12 and 17 years are most likely to use illicit drugs (4.7%), use alcohol (4.2%), and be dependent on cigarettes (2.8%).

A variety of criteria have been used to judge resilience during development (Masten, 2014). For example, the National Survey of Children's Health 2007 (U.S. Department of Health and Human Services, Health Resources and Services Administration, Maternal and Child Health Bureau, 2009) estimated that 2.8% of children ages 6 to 17 had severe behavior problems. If freedom from severe difficulties is the criterion, than the vast majority of children are resilient. On the other hand, there are an estimated 13% to 20% of children who experience some type of emotional or behavioral disorder every year. Thus, if these children are considered, many children are at risk. Wright and associates (2013, p. 17) define resilience as "positive adaptation in the face of risk or adversity; capacity of a dynamic system to withstand or recover from disturbance" and risk as "an elevated probability of a negative outcome."

In some ways, the ability to show a resilient reaction to trauma is highly related to factors outside of a child's control—neighborhood environment and family income (G. W. Evans, Li, & Whipple, 2013). Children growing up in disadvantaged neighborhoods were found to have a higher rate of these severe problems (6%) and were three times more likely to have severe behavior problems than children in the most favorable neighborhoods (2%). These risks, brought on by poor neighborhood social conditions, remained even when the parents' income was taken into account. Living below the poverty line gave children almost four times the risk of developing a severe behavioral problem as those coming from families living at 400% of the poverty threshold. Measures of disadvantage in the neighborhood included safety concerns, such as vandalism, dangerous conditions in housing and on the street, and garbage and litter in the street (Singh & Ghandour, 2012).

Masten's research outlined four global factors that have been found to determine whether a child will show a resilient or pathological reaction to stress during the course of development. The first factor is whether the child has formed positive connections with a confident and effective adult within the family or community. An effective parent, for example, monitors his or her child's behavior and environment to ensure safety and provides a warm and supportive atmosphere. A caregiver who is competent, responsive, and caring provides many protective factors that support the child's growth. These parents, when faced with adversity, respond effectively to the threat and adapt their behavior to try to protect the child (Masten & Narayan, 2012). Family characteristics that promote positive development and constitute resilience factors include warm parenting, the provision of appropriate structure and monitoring of the child's behavior, age-appropriate expectations for the child, positive relationships with siblings, a stable home environment, and parental involvement in the child's education. Support is also provided by an effective school where the curriculum and teachers reflect quality training, the teachers are enthusiastic, and after-school programs help children develop positive connections as well as provide services for children whose parents are not home.

The second factor in resilience is the child's having at least average cognitive and emotional self-regulation skills that enable him or her to succeed in school and other social environments. While intelligence is continuously variable, at this point research has found that individuals with higher levels of intelligence show more resilient reactions and individuals with less than average intelligence show less resilient reactions; this is also related to attendance at effective schools (Wright et al., 2013). The third factor is the presence of a positive view of the self. This includes such qualities as self-confidence, self-efficacy, an appropriate view of one's strengths, hopefulness, and a sense of meaning in life. The final factor is the child's motivation to be effective within the environment, which may also be enhanced by socioeconomic advantages and the postsecondary education of parents. With these factors in place, children may be protected from the negative consequences of adverse life events, such as growing up in disadvantaged circumstances. The resilient youth seeks to take advantage of healthy opportunities for success, seeks connections with prosocial mentors, is less likely to associate with deviant peers, and engages in less novelty seeking (Masten, 2001; Masten & Narayan, 2012). Resilience in the face of economic disadvantage is influenced by good communication with family members, which can serve to buffer children from the impact of negative events, and positive peer relationships that help individuals develop prosocial identities, good self-esteem, and social skills. Adolescents who have a positive social network report fewer health concerns, a greater sense of well-being, and more health-enhancing behaviors than health damaging-behaviors, such as smoking and drinking to excess. When students find their school to be supportive of their success, they report greater life satisfaction and have fewer health complaints. Finally, living in a neighborhood that builds social capital resources to turn to when needed, enhances self-esteem, and discourages negative social behaviors is related to more positive health outcomes (Currie, Zanotti, et al., 2012). Neighborhood social cohesion serves to decrease the risk of both physical and mental health problems (Rios, Aiken, & Zautra, 2012). Wright and colleagues (2013), in evaluating research on the complex interactions between variables related to risk or resiliency in development, consider that it is most appropriate to talk about a continuum of both of these concepts rather than risk or resiliency per se and to stress that level of resiliency, for example, while containing some factors internal to the child, is highly affected by interpersonal relationships and contexts.

Red-Flag Developmental Guidelines

1. Assess how age appropriate clients' physical and cognitive development have been, and in what ways this has influenced their performance and level of motivation at home, at school, and within community activities.

2. Assess how age appropriate clients' relationships with adults have been in terms of limit setting, monitoring, skill building, and emotional connection, and in what ways these relationships have supported or hindered the developmental process.

3. Assess how age appropriate the clients' relationships with peers have been in terms of companionship and social skill building, and in what ways these relationships have supported or hindered the developmental process.

4. Assess how age appropriately clients are functioning at this time, including consideration of clients' self-image and self-efficacy, what they need most to support healthy development, and what, if any, barriers to maturation or maturation-facilitating factors exist.

5. Assess the current level of situational risk in clients' lives and how much control they have in mitigating these risks.

6. Assess the current level of situational support in clients' lives and how much control they have in increasing these situational supports.

Self-Analysis Guidelines

1. What is your current knowledge of issues relevant to development?

   a. How many courses have you taken that give you background on this age group?

   b. How many workshops have you attended that give you background on this age group?

   c. What professional experiences have you had with this age group?

   d. What personal experiences have you had with this age group?

   e. What cohort effects might influence your worldview of this age group in terms of what is important in the world, how people communicate, and what is rewarded and punished in this world?

2. What is your current level of awareness of how development can influence your clinical work?

   a. How do your current age and current amount of contact with the client's age group influence your reactions to the client?

   b. What stereotypes of this age group do you know about?

   c. What experiences have you had that could support your effective work with the client? What experiences have you had that might lead to a negative bias or marginalization of the client's points of view or current situation?

3. What are your current skills in working with clients of different ages?

   a. What skills do you currently have that are of value in working with this age group?

   b. What skills do you feel it would be important to develop to work effectively with this age group?

4. What action steps could you take?

   a. What could you do to prepare yourself to be more skilled in working with this age group?

b. How might you structure the treatment environment to increase the likelihood of a positive outcome with clients in this age group?

c. What processes of treatment might you change to make them more welcoming to clients in this age group?

THE DOMAIN OF GENDER

Marie, a recent widow, gives herself no time to grieve; she feels she must focus all her attention on her children (Chapter 4). Steve, an art student, is emotionally detached from others (Chapter 8). Could their gender roles be influencing their psychological well-being? Do you need to understand the worldview of men to fully understand Steve as well as the worldview of women to fully understand Marie? Gender-informed treatment can occur only when clinicians are aware of their own gender stereotypes of Marie and Steve; their gender-influenced biases toward themselves; and the role that gender may be playing in providing strengths or difficulties within their clients' personal and social lives. Marie and Steve will profit more from their treatment with you when treatment strategies have been chosen with their self-identification of their gender roles in mind (Liu, 2005).

Census Data

On the 2010 census, individuals were presented with the categories *male* and *female* and self-identified as one or the other (U.S. Census Bureau, 2010a). Based on this, women represented 51% of the population of the United States and men represented 49%. This difference could be surprising, as there were more baby boys born than baby girls, with this sex disparity lasting up until age group 35–39; at this point, females slowly began to outnumber males. By age group 65–69, women represented 53% of the population and men 47%. By age 85, women represented 65% of the population and men 35% (U.S. Census Bureau, 2010a).

If gender were not relevant to our understanding of our male and female clients, then these census statistics would also show that women constitute a slight majority in all employment classifications and at all levels of authority within society. In later years, women would begin to dominate all employment classifications and positions of authority as they came to represent a larger and larger majority. However, this isn't the case. While the 21st century has seen the emergence of some powerful female political leaders, such as Senator Dianne Feinstein, who took office in 1992; Nancy Pelosi, who became Speaker of the House in 2007; and Hillary Clinton, who became the third woman to be secretary of state in 2009, in 2014, women still represented only 18% of the House and 20% of the Senate at the federal level. At the state level, they represented only 21% of the Senate and 25% of the House. In addition, only 12 of the 100 largest cities in the country have women as mayors (Eagleton Institute of Politics, 2014). Research on gender indicates that, within the United States, men continue to have privileges and opportunities that women do not (Liu, 2005).

How men and women perceive their roles in society has changed as family households have decreased from 81% in 1970 to 66% in 2012; 27% of households are now single people (Vespa et al., 2013). The 21st-century family has been taking longer to develop as men and women are remaining single longer, marrying later, and having fewer children (Worell & Remer, 2003). However, married couples still constitute the clear majority of households (63%), as indicated by 2012 census data (Vespa et al., 2013). Families have gotten smaller over time; 40.3% of married couples had children in 1970, whereas only 19.6% had children in 2012. As adults are older when they marry, they are older when they have children. Women are still marrying younger than men (Vespa et al., 2013), with the average age at first marriage being 26 for women and 28 for men. Men aged 18 to 24 are more likely to be living with their parents than young women are (59% vs. 51%). Cohabitation increased from 3% in 1982 to 11% in 2010 (Copen, Daniels, Vespa, & Mosher, 2012). Cohabitating couples tend to be younger than married couples, and 86% of men and 89% of women marry (Vespa et al., 2013).

Despite marrying later, 50% of first marriages are ending in divorce (Copen et al., 2012). On the other hand, 52% of women and 56% of men see their first marriages reach their 20th anniversary. Women with a bachelor's degree are more likely to have their first marriage last than women with less education (Copen et al., 2012). Once married, men and women are divorcing at high rates and then remarrying. Thus, families may consist of two parents and their children, single parents and their children, or stepfamilies (U.S. Census Bureau, 2004). Men and women have faced the need to adapt to changing family structures and increased role strain (Worell & Remer, 2003). Marriage moderates life stress for men but not for women, as women still take on most of the responsibilities for caring for the home and children (APA, Joint Task Force, 2006). Family dissolution has led to financial strain. This has been especially true for children living with mothers; children have been five times more likely to be living in poverty when living with a single mother than with married parents (U.S. Census Bureau, 2003). In terms of parenting skills, when single men are confronted with the need to actively parent, they take on similar behaviors and attitudes as women who parent (Kimmel, 2008).

Brief History

Biological differences between males and females are a constant. However, what it means to be female or male has been socially constructed and varies across cultural groups, historical periods, and political climates. It is not a static concept but rather something that can always be open to change (Liu, 2005). Worell and Remer (2003, p. 15) defined gender roles as "patterns of culturally approved behaviors that are regarded as more desirable for either females or males in a particular culture." Thus, a person's sex is based on biology, while a person's gender pertains to what he or she learned that influences the person's behavior at the social level, the interpersonal level, and the individual level (Crawford, 2006). Despite the large body of research documenting greater heterogeneity of abilities within genders than across them, gender stereotypes have still been used to define, and limit, the roles males and females take on in their personal and social identities (Worell & Remer, 2003). Masculinity and femininity have often been defined in opposition to each other (Kimmel, 2008). However, your gender identity is also influenced by your internal sense of yourself as male or female. For transgender individuals, their internal sense of gender identity is different from their externally defined sex (APA, Committee on Lesbian, Gay, Bisexual, and Transgender Concerns, 2006).

How might constructs of gender influence an individual? At the social level, gender is a construct that has influenced who has the most power to influence society. In the United States, society is based on a patriarchal model, as men are making the laws that we must obey, men own the media and thus public discourse, wealth is concentrated in male hands, the major religions in society define the deity in masculine terms, and men control the military (Crawford, 2006).

At the interpersonal level, gender has been found to influence how males and females interact with each other. People will often act in response to what they think others expect of them. If others expect males and females to behave in certain ways, individuals will tend to move toward these norms, and they will be socially rewarded for behaving according to these expectations (Crawford, 2006). For a woman to be perceived as feminine by others, she must seek to express her gender by being very concerned about the clothes she wears, the shape of her body, and the appearance of her hair and her face, and engage in many other tasks that might enhance her appearance. Thus, femininity requires that women devote a great deal of time to enhancing their appearance rather than accomplishing their goals. While there are constraints on how men must behave to be masculine, they do not take time away from accomplishing their goals (Crawford, 2006; Just the Facts Coalition, 2008).

How might gender influence interpersonal behavior? Men feel more comfortable interrupting what a woman is saying, dominating the conversation, touching women without overt permission, and blaming women for having lesser power in society while placing barriers in the way of their achieving that power (Crawford, 2006). For example, being masculine is linked to ideas of what is normal behavior in society, including being dominant within relationships, being competent, and being aggressive in pursuing goals. A woman who engages in this same behavior is often not valued, as this behavior is counter to social expectations for her gender (Crawford, 2006).

At the individual level, each individual needs to make a decision about how much to accept gender distinctions. Gender typing refers to how individuals begin to view their own traits and behaviors through the lens of masculinity or femininity, and it influences the roles they take on with other people (Crawford, 2006).

In addition to the unequal hierarchy of power, societal institutions reinforce the idea that men's accomplishments are more valuable and deserve more respect than women's; this serves to preserve the power status quo (Kimmel, 2008). While this inequality of privileges and opportunities suggests that our female clients may come in with distress as a result of gender biases in society, Mellinger and Liu (2006) have pointed out the importance of understanding male gender–based difficulties as well. When men have experienced family and social pressure to submit to strict gender roles, this can be a major factor in their psychological distress. However, these are just part of stereotypical views of masculinity, as if all cultural groups within the United States viewed masculinity in the same way. In fact, there is an intersection between gender and racial or ethnic group as well as many other types of interpersonal difference (Liu, 2005). This may lead to stress as men try to understand these changing expectations for their behavior (Liu,

2005). Gender-competent clinicians understand how socialization can lead to stress, and healthy as well as unhealthy behavior (Feder, Levant, & Dean, 2007). Physical activities, such as twisting a towel, may help males express emotions in a manner that is less directly opposed to their gendered identity (Rabinowitz & Cochran, 2002). According to Mahalik and colleagues (2003), the norms for masculinity within the United States include expecting power over women; taking on a dominant position in interpersonal relationships; placing a high emphasis on sexual experiences, including sexual titillation through reading sexual magazines such as *Playboy*; and an antigay ethic. Their roles in work are considered primary, and pursuing status, taking risks, and the pursuit of winning are valued. Self-reliance and emotional control are emphasized, along with an acceptance of the world as a violent place (Mahalik et al., 2003).

The following discussion of the impact of gender roles on males and females has been based on research derived from primarily White, Western, middle-class, Christian samples within the United States. The generalizations presented may have less or limited validity for other populations, as gender constructions vary across socially identifiable groups. However, culturally different youth, as they attempt to assimilate into dominant society, have been found to incorporate the gender stereotypes of the dominant population into their own experiences (APA, Joint Task Force, 2006; Mazure, Keita, & Blehar, 2002; Worell & Remer, 2003). The issues relevant to transgender individuals will not be discussed due to a lack of population studies that account for the range of gender identities and gender expressions currently included within the term *transgender* (APA, Committee on Lesbian, Gay, Bisexual, and Transgender Concerns, 2006).

How are men supposed to behave? There is a culture of masculinity (Liu, 2005). This culture includes what society expects from men, what men are intended to value, what typical male behavior is, and the customs to which men are expected to adhere. Traditional stereotypes have encouraged them to be self-reliant, tough, aggressive, dominant, and emotionally controlled (Addis & Mahalik, 2003). Male behavior is conforming if it meets social expectations in both private and public life. Boys' peer groups have supported teamwork and competition, and boys and men who are assertive in expressing their opinions may be viewed as leaders (Worell & Remer, 2003). However, males have also been discouraged from experiencing a full range of emotions. They have been socialized to view their emotions as something to act on rather than to experience. "What American men have been taught for centuries when they are upset and angry," according to Kimmel (2008, p. 122), is that "men don't get mad; they get even." As a result, they may have "alexithymia," or an inability to articulate their emotions (Feder et al., 2007). Men have been allowed to be angry, but males who cry or show other vulnerable emotions have been perceived as weak, emasculated, and in need of toughening up. As a result, some men have had their emotional awareness truncated. Help-seeking behavior has also been discouraged in males. As a result, they have been less likely to access either health or mental health services than women; if men feel that asking for help jeopardizes their autonomy, they avoid it (Addis & Mahalik, 2003). The male standard of health has required them to "prove" their masculinity through success at work and in sports, dominance with women, and a heterosexual and married lifestyle (Kimmel, 2008). The pursuit of power and privilege comes at a cost for young boys and adolescents, as they may experience trauma, pain, and isolation if they are not successful (Kaufman,

1994; Messner, 1997). Eleven factors have been found to be related to the masculine gender role, including an emphasis on winning, emotional control, dominance, risk-taking, violence, power over women, self-reliance, primacy of work, disdain for sexual minorities, the pursuit of status, and playboy inclinations (Mahalik et al., 2003).

Societal messages exhorting men to seek dominance and prove their masculinity may be directly responsible for their higher rates of violent behavior as teens and young adults. While acts of violence have been referred to as "teen violence," "drug violence," "school violence," and "terrorist hijacker violence," the perpetrators were in fact almost always males (Kimmel, 2008). Society pressures all males to think, feel, and behave in similar ways despite their heterogeneity. The external pressure for them to be emotionally stoic and self-reliant at all times may have resulted in role stress. Books written by women and goals achieved by women have been analyzed for their "gendered" influences. However, the parallel process has not occurred for males; this has left issues of masculinity invisible. Thus, the challenges faced by, for example, male scientists who also want to be good fathers have never been discussed (Kimmel, 2008). Men are oppressed by cultural norms that limit their individuality and jeopardize their physical and mental health by setting unrealistic standards of behavior, yet these issues have been socially ignored (Kimmel, 2008; Worell & Remer, 2003). Media images of women are linked to men's having an unrealistic, narrow vision of what type of woman to seek out as a partner (Schooler & Ward, 2006). When men show psychological disorders, they are more likely to have externalizing behavior, such as substance abuse or intermittent explosive disorder (Kessler, Chiu, Demier, & Walters, 2005). If they show a comorbid disorder, it is most likely to be depression or substance abuse (Russo & Tartaro, 2008).

How are women supposed to behave? Traditional stereotypes of women include their being submissive, passive, nurturing, emotionally attuned in relationships, and dependent on others (APA, Joint Task Force, 2006; Papp, 2008). Factors related to the feminine gender role include being friendly and supportive in relationships, being invested in romantic relationships and being committed to sexual fidelity, being modest about abilities and talents, desiring to take care of and be with children, desiring to maintain a home, being highly investing in maintaining and improving their physical appearance, and pursuing a thin body ideal (Mahalik et al., 2005). Women who act assertively are viewed as "bitchy," not as leaders (Worell & Remer, 2003), and women are more rewarded socially for interpersonal behavior that fits the gender expectations of society (Crawford, 2006). Girls' peer groups have supported the development of emotionally intimate relationships, and adult women are encouraged to tune in to their emotions and talk through problems. This may be why women report experiencing greater emotional intensity than men in terms of both positive and negative emotions (Brannon, 2002). Women are also encouraged to make relationships with others, both friends and romantic partners, central to their view of themselves (Nolen-Hoeksema, 2000).

Societal messages encourage women to believe that sexual attractiveness is the key to success in relationships with men. When problems have arisen in these relationships, women have been encouraged to internalize or deny anger (APA, Joint Task Force, 2006). Despite this emphasis on sexual attractiveness, society leaves women confused about themselves as sexual people. Language traps women with derogatory sexual labels such as *bitch*, *frigid*, and *ho*. This leaves them insecure as to how to behave as a sexual person (Worell & Remer, 2003). Societal standards continue to stress virginity as the standard for unmarried women. Thus, when a single woman has been the victim of sexual assault or abuse, she is less likely to seek out help for fear of being blamed for the assault (Russo & Tartaro, 2008). In addition, women and girls are deluged with unrealistic media images and societal norms of attractiveness. These images require women to espouse a cult of thinness in order to feel feminine. Women are encouraged to focus a great deal of time on grooming and grooming products. Inability to meet unrealistic media images may lead many women to have low self-esteem and increased vulnerability to depression, anxiety, and eating disorders in comparison to men (APA, Joint Task Force, 2006; Mazure et al., 2002). A female who expresses anger rather than depression may feel guilty about it or receive the disapproval of others.

When women show psychological disorders, they are most likely to show internalizing symptoms such as depression and anxiety. When they show disorders "atypical" for their gender, such as alcoholism, these problems are less likely to be addressed (Russo & Tartaro, 2008). In addition, the sexualization of girls has been associated with eating disorders, low self-esteem, depression, and an internalized view of oneself as a sexual object (Zurbriggen et al., 2007). Finally, interpersonal violence is a significant force in gender relations, with more than 20% of women reporting having been physically assaulted by a partner and 12% having experienced a sexual assault (APA, 2005b). Women continue to outlive men, but older women have been found to be at greater risk for depression and substance abuse (APA, 2004).

The traditional mother role is to take responsibility for raising the children and caring for the home. Women's reproductive capacities and ability to nurse have been taken to indicate that women are born to be mothers. Good mothering is treated as a natural ability rather than as consisting of difficult skills that need to be learned (Goodrich, 2008). Although mothers can be idealized for being loving and caring and for sacrificing their own needs for their children, they are also blamed for any types of psychopathology found in their children (Papp, 2008). Women have been criticized for mothering too much or too little, as well as for working outside the home too much or too little; this puts women in a double bind (Papp, 2008). Women who emphasize their family role over their others roles are more negatively impacted by family conflicts, partner violence, and pressure to be a caretaker of others (Russo & Tartaro, 2008). Being unable to have healthy children, while painful for both parents, may be particularly problematic for women due to the coupling of femininity with motherhood. On the other hand, the greater availability of birth control and fertility options gives women more freedom to choose whether and when they will become mothers (APA, Joint Task Force, 2006).

The traditional father role is to provide financial support for the family. Fathers typically play a comparatively minor role in the management of their home, the development of their children, the caring for other dependents, and the maintaining of social networks (Papp, 2008). While fathers today are more likely than fathers in the past to express the attitude that they should be involved in child rearing and household responsibilities, they overestimate their time doing these tasks. Social norms in the United States continue to support the idea that men's work is more demanding and significant and a man's leisure time is more necessary for him than for his wife. This leads to inequities in the home, where women have taken on more domestic responsibilities than men even while they are likely to be working outside the home (Brannon, 2002). When fathers spend more time caring for and mentoring their sons, their sons have higher self-esteem, a greater understanding of their emotions, and lower levels of aggression in comparison to boys without involved fathers (Feder et al., 2007).

Husbands and wives often accept the power imbalances and privileges within the home. These are interpreted as reflecting differences between masculinity and femininity rather than cultural expectations that men "deserve" more power and privileges than women (Goodrich, 2008; Papp, 2008). Thus, male oppression within the home can be conscious, with men refusing to share household chores or take care of children on the basis of its being "women's" work. Male oppression may also occur at the unconscious level, with a husband getting very angry if his wife makes a decision that goes against his advice (McIntosh, 2008). When men become more equal partners in caring for children, they gain a greater sense of confidence in themselves as parents (Barnett & Hyde, 2001).

What do children learn about their genders? Starting at birth, males and females are socialized differently and inculcated with the belief that males deserve more power than females; differential sex role socialization serves to maintain this power differential (Kimmel, 2008). Parents often model a relationship in which the father is dominant. Children see their mothers as being more expressive and loving and their father as being more detached, in control, and dominant (Worell & Remer, 2003). At early ages, children begin to identify some professions as being for males rather than females based on whom they see in those positions. In the school system, most teachers are female and most principals and superintendents are male; this reinforces gender stereotypes and gender-based power differentials (Worell & Remer, 2003). At school, boys receive more mentoring and encouragement. Girls are more likely to be victimized by discriminatory testing and counseling by school officials that discourages their achievement (APA, Joint Task Force, 2006). Television programming indicates that gender harassment is at least acceptable, if not funny (Montemurro, 2003). Girls begin to experience anxiety over their body's appearance because of media images of perfect bodies (Monro & Huon, 2005).

What happens to men and women at the office? Women are more likely to be underemployed than men, feeling trapped in jobs that underutilize their abilities. They also earn less than men with equal qualifications; women currently earn $0.77 to men's $1.00 (DeNavas-Walt, Proctor, & Smith, 2013). Women, due to their decreased earning power, have more limited economic resources to use during times of need (APA, Joint Task Force, 2006).

Women are not as psychologically welcome in the workplace as men. They are often faced with sexual or general harassment at work. They may not mention small slights at work to coworkers or supervisors for fear of being considered "too sensitive." Over time, these slights create hostile environments that leave women feeling less appreciated and more devalued than men (Goodrich, 2008). However, when given equal opportunities, powerful women exhibit the same work behaviors as powerful men—using language to exert power and authority—while subordinate men exhibit the same behavior as subordinate women, such as providing ego strokes to the boss and being sensitive to this person's moods (Kimmel, 2008).

Most men expect to dedicate themselves to their worker role, while most women expect that they will be trying to balance family and work roles (Brannon, 2002). In 2009, the U.S. Bureau of Labor Statistics' *Monthly Labor Review* revealed that 70 % of working women had children at home in the mid-1990s. Even when women start out in high-status jobs, they frequently face slower rates of advancement than men because of their need to take pregnancy leave. Once a woman takes this leave, a company may hold the prejudice that she was not as dedicated to their work as her male counterpart and receive slower promotion (Goodrich, 2008). In families with a child under 15, 24 % have a stay-at-home mother. While stay-at-home fathers have increased recently, they still represent only 3 % of married households with minor children. Mothers who stay home with their children are more likely to be younger, and to have younger children, than working mothers. In addition, they are more likely to be Hispanic or foreign born, and their families are more likely to live in poverty (Krieder & Elliot, 2009).

Working women have, of necessity, divided loyalties. Since they continue to be disproportionately responsible for the parenting role, they are subject to disadvantages in the workplace. For example, when a child gets sick, it is the mother who is most likely to rush out of the workplace to take the child to the doctor (Goodrich, 2008). While taking on multiple roles can lead to greater life stress, success in one role can also buffer the effects of problems within another (Barnett & Hyde, 2001). Society encourages men to evaluate their success based exclusively on their earning capacity and employment status. Thus, unemployment or underemployment may have a greater negative effect on their physical and mental health, sense of identity, and general outlook on life than it does on women, who have multiple arenas for success (Papp, 2008). The majority of married couples (66 %) are both working (Krieder & Elliot, 2009); while this leads to greater financial resources, it also decreases time to spend with family, exercise, and relax.

How might gender influence psychological health? Men and women may learn to use different coping mechanisms when faced with stress. Men frequently socialize within the context of physical activities and use these activities to distract themselves from their problems. This strategy is a healthy one when it provides an immediate feeling of relief from stress that later leads to effective problem-solving. However, it represents an unhealthy strategy if it leads to minimizing, rather than solving, the problems behind the stress (Mazure et al., 2002). Women are more likely to seek out companionship within which to discuss their problems. This represents a healthy strategy when it brings first social support and then effective problem-solving. However, it can represent an unhealthy strategy if it leads to a ruminative mindset in which they spend more time thinking about their problems than they do problem-solving (Mazure et al., 2002).

Gender may influence whether a client seeks treatment and the types of physical and emotional problems that clients present with. Men are more frequently diagnosed with substance abuse and antisocial personality disorder, and women are more frequently diagnosed with depression, anxiety, and eating disorders (Kessler et al., 2005). Women may be more vulnerable to psychological stress due to their multiple roles and decreased access to occupational and educational resources in comparison to men. Women have higher levels of poverty and victimization, which have been linked with greater vulnerability to stress-related disorders (APA, Joint Task Force, 2006; Mazure et al., 2002). However, seeking help is more difficult for men, as their roles contain expectations of self-sufficiency (Papp, 2008). This may make them less likely to seek help for any reason but particularly reluctant to seek help for emotional problems (Addis & Mahalik, 2003; Liu, 2005).

In summary, individuals are raised to believe that males have been given more power than females in society because of innate differences in their abilities; in fact, these differences are created by unequal treatment and supported by the devaluation of women's roles compared to men's (Kimmel, 2008). As adults, men are given the most culturally respected roles both at home and at work, and female contributions to society are minimized. Men are treated as the "norm" or the "neutral point" against which women are measured and found deficient. For example, female scientists are expected to act like male scientists, while the effect of men's masculinity on their work as scientists is ignored (Kimmel, 2008). Thus, in differing ways, men and women have their unique potentials limited by rigid gender role stereotypes that ignore the reality that there are more differences within sexes than between them (APA, Joint Task Force, 2006; Kimmel, 2008). Flexible expectations and standards for behavior that allow each individual to fully explore his or her own interests and abilities may increase the well-being of both men and women (Kimmel, 2008; Worell & Remer, 2003). Providing gender-informed treatment means that the clinician understands the role that gender may play in the client's life. For example, masculine-focused therapy means that the clinician understands the male gender role and worldview. The clinician will need to provide the information that will help male clients feel more comfortable with the therapy process. For example, the clinician should show a willingness to discuss the process of therapy and to focus on identifiable objectives that are relevant to the client. Male clients may also require more information from the clinician to develop an effective therapeutic alliance (Liu, 2005). For example, clinicians may strengthen the therapeutic relationship by clarifying that they are not in competition with their male clients (Liu, 2005).

Red-Flag Gender Guidelines

1. Assess the personal costs and benefits of the gender role currently guiding clients in terms of self-image, emotional life, expectations, perceptions, behavior, and access to personal resources.

2. Assess the interpersonal costs and benefits of the gender role currently guiding clients in terms of their relationships with romantic partners, family, and friends.

3. Assess the social costs and benefits of the gender role current guiding clients in terms of educational or work relationships and access to social resources.

4. How much are traditional gender roles positively or negatively influencing clients' mental and physical health, and how aware are clients of these influences?

5. Overall, how much power and choice do clients have to live life as nongendered individuals with unique needs and goals, and how strong are the counterpressures on clients to be gendered individuals?

Self-Analysis Guidelines

1. What is your current knowledge of gender issues?

   a. How many courses have you taken that give you background on issues relevant to gender?

   b. How many workshops have you attended that give you background on gender issues?

   c. What professional experiences have you had with clients that were informed by a gender analysis?

   d. What personal experiences have you had in considering the impact of gender on individuals?

   e. What cohort effects might influence your worldview of gender, the roles of men and women in society, how men and women communicate, and what is rewarded and punished for males and females?

2. What is your current level of awareness of how gender has played a role in your life?

   a. What gender role is currently guiding you in your life?

   b. How similar to or different from your gender role is the gender role of the client?

   c. What stereotypes of gender within U.S. culture might influence your views of the client?

   d. What stereotypes about the gender of your client do you know about?

   e. What experiences have you had that could support your effective work with the client? What experiences have you had that might lead to a negative bias or marginalization of the client's point of view or current situation?

3. What skills do you have, or do you have the potential to develop, in working with clients of this gender?

   a. What skills do you currently have that are of value in working with clients of this gender?

   b. What skills might it be important to develop to carry out an effective gender analysis of this client?

   c. What could you do to develop a positive working relationship with clients of this gender?

   d. What aspects of your treatment approach might be gender biased, and how will you deal with this?

4. What action steps could you take?

   a. What could you do to prepare yourself to be more skilled in working with this gender?

b. How might you structure the treatment environment to increase the likelihood of a positive outcome with clients of this gender?

c. What processes of treatment might you change to make them more welcoming to clients of this gender?

THE DOMAIN OF RACE AND ETHNICITY

John, a middle-aged European American male, the chief executive officer of an international company, returns home to find his wife has abandoned him (Chapter 6). Sergio, a Mexican American high school student, was arrested for selling marijuana at school and is struggling with racial prejudice and poverty (Chapter 8). Tanisha and Marcus, a financially successful African American couple, seek help due to unresolved grief (Chapter 9). Kayla, an internationally renowned Native American writer, complains of malaise and acculturation conflicts (Chapter 12). To what degree, and in what ways, might their racial or ethnic backgrounds influence your treatment decisions?

Census Data

There are 357,134,565 people residing within the United States based on the 2012 census (U.S. Census Bureau, 2012d). You may be one of them. Are you African American? American Indian? Hispanic or Latina/Latino American? European American? Can you be biracial? Multiracial? Who has the right to decide your race or ethnicity? Only you. Who has the right to decide for clients? Only them. An important thing to remember, as you read this section, is that you should not assume you know an individual's race or ethnicity based on his or her appearance. It is important to ask clients to self-identify (Hays, 2008; Rodriguez, 2008). On the 2012 American Community Survey (U.S. Census Bureau, 2012d), individuals were allowed to indicate all their ancestries or ethnic group affiliations. Based on this ancestry data, the six largest ethnic groups currently identified in the United States are German (46,882,727), Irish (34,149,030), English (25,262,644), American (23,567,147), Italian (17,361,780), and Polish (9,500,696). The composition of the U.S. population is constantly shifting due to changes in immigration and birth rates. It is projected that by 2043 (U.S. Census, 2012e), non-Hispanic Whites will no longer be in the majority, although they will still remain the largest single group in the United States. By 2060, minority groups will constitute 57% of the population. These minority groups will include African Americans, American Indian and Alaska Natives, Asian Americans, Native Hawaiians and Pacific Islanders, and Hispanics.

Brief History

How well a racial or an ethnic group fares economically is influenced by its standing in comparison to the dominant group. This is because the dominant cultural group infuses its values into all the institutions of society, such as the school system and the court system. Dominant group members have the unnoticed privilege of perceiving their institutions as neutral and objective when in fact they are culturally influenced and put nondominant groups at a disadvantage (Sue & Sue, 2013).

Day-to-day microaggressions, perpetrated by dominant group members and institutions, cause substantial psychological harm to groups that differ substantially from the dominant society (Solorzano, Ceja, & Yosso, 2000; Sue & Sue, 2013). These negative events occur most often for individuals whose skin is not perceived as white. The "color line" (Du Bois, 1903/1997; Ignatiev, 1995) plays a substantial role in facilitating or inhibiting the acculturation of groups into dominant society within the United States; dark-skinned immigrants are the most disadvantaged when trying to immigrate and assimilate. New immigrants quickly come to see how skin color, hair texture, and facial structure can add to or decrease an individual's status and power in U.S. society. They also learn that they can better their own status if they ally themselves with the White race and against the Black race (Rodriguez, 2008).

As "Whites" or "European Americans" still make up the largest ethnic groups within the United States, helpers from these groups must actively consider when a "culturally different" client's presenting problems might reflect assimilation conflicts or oppression rather than being caused by internal or family-based problems. While presenting problems can have their major determinants in individual or family-based problems, research has shown that individuals from groups with the least power are more aware of when their problems are a result of acts of injustice and discrimination than members of the dominant group are (Sue & Sue, 2013). Therefore, if you are from the dominant group and your clients are not, listen to them, as they may be more accurate than you in determining whether oppression has a role in their presenting concerns. In addition, the White culture considers race an important category of identity, while many other cultural groups consider their national origin to be more important. In addition, they may see continua of racial affiliation that change with context rather than clear categories that are immutable aspects of their identity and that have been developed by Whites, without regard for their collaboration (Rodriguez, 2008). Whether or not a clinician is from the dominant culture or minority cultures, Sue and Sue (2013) indicate that there may be three major barriers to clinicians' correctly understanding the needs of their clients: class-based values, as clients from nondominant groups are often lower class while clinicians are often middle or upper class; language biases that lead to misunderstandings, as these groups may speak dialects or have another language as their first language and clinicians expect high facility in the English language; and clashes in cultural values, where the clinician assumes that clients implicitly understand and agree with the White values embedded within most treatment approaches (Sue & Sue, 2013).

It is important that you collaborate with your clients in making treatment an effective and empowering experience. You can do this by making your expectations explicit, modifying them to suit your clients' needs, and accurately assessing the role of realistic life constraints on your clients' presenting concerns. The following sections will include broad-brush descriptions of the heritage of African Americans, American Indians and Alaska Natives, Latinas and Latinos, and European Americans with white skin. Why were these groups included and not others? Hard decisions had to be made, keeping in mind the main goals of the text, the limitations of the author's expertise, and practical constraints set by page limitations for the text. There is no intent to demean or devalue the important contributions of other racial and ethnic groups to the United States by their exclusion from this text. For each racial or ethnic group that is covered, some important historical events are briefly reviewed. History is not necessarily the past. It is important to be aware that for many people, historical events may continue to operate directly as family or cultural stories are retold. In addition, indirectly, survival strategies may have become embedded in the psyche of racial or ethnic groups to cope with past incidences or trauma, maltreatment, and oppression.

African Americans

Census Data

Individuals self-identifying as African American or Black represent 38.9 million individuals within the 2010 Census categories; this represents 12.6% of the population of the United States (U.S. Census Bureau, 2010a). Out of this population, 3.6 million are foreign born, and 41.8% entered the country starting in the 2000s (U.S. Census Bureau, 2010a). Individuals from Latin America constitute 60.8% of these immigrants, and individuals from Africa constitute 36.2% (U.S. Census Bureau, 2011a). This is a relatively young group, with a median age of 31.7 years in comparison to 38.3 years for non-Hispanic Whites and with 32% of this population being minors (U.S. Census Bureau, 2011b).

From an educational standpoint, 84.5% of African Americans or Blacks attain at least a high school diploma; this is in comparison to 87.5% of the general population. Fourteen percent of African American women have achieved a bachelor's degree, as have 12.2% of African American men (U.S. Census Bureau, 2011b). While African American adults value education, their children experience significant problems within the current public school system. Tutwiler (2007) summarizes how schools jeopardize school success, particularly of African American boys, by treating them in a racist and classist manner. When youngsters try to resist negative stereotypes and assert their self-worth, school personnel often misunderstand and either punish the youths or intensify an already hostile environment. Statistics indicate that African American children are two to five times more likely to be suspended from school than their White peers (Monroe, 2005), and they may disconnect their self-esteem from their academic performance during middle school and high school as a result of a racist school environment (Caughy, O'Campo, & Muntaner, 2004). In addition, some students intentionally underachieve as a form of resistance to an oppressive school system (Ogbu, 2003). While toxic conditions do exist in schools, children from families that attend church regularly are less likely to exhibit problems in school (Christian & Barbarin, 2001).

In terms of vocations, 29% of all African American workers are employed within management and professional occupations, while 26.1% are employed in service jobs. African American men make $100 for each $90 made by African American women. Both African American men and African American women earn less than their counterparts in the general population (U.S. Bureau of Labor Statistics, 2013). Economically, the median African American household income is $33,321, which is significantly less than the median income of the general population of $51,017. In all, 25.8% of this population is living below the poverty line, in comparison to 14.3% of the general population. This means that one in four Black families and more than one third (38.2%) of African American children live in poverty (U.S. Census Bureau, 2011a).

The correctional system is involved with one of every 35 individuals in the United States (Glaze & Herberman, 2013); this represents 3% of the population overall. The poor have been more likely to end up in the criminal justice system. Thus, the high rate of poverty within the Black population is in part behind why 3% of all Black males were imprisoned in 2011, in comparison to .5% for all white males (Carson & Sabol, 2012). African Americans are incarcerated at greater rates than White Americans for both violent and nonviolent crimes (Carson & Golinelli, 2013). African Americans have the highest imprisonment rate of all groups, particularly in the age group of 25–39, where between 6.6% and 7.5% of Black males are imprisoned (Carson & Sabol, 2012). In part because of the war on drugs, and in part because of the epidemic of crack cocaine among poor African Americans, many Black mothers are being sent to jail—leaving their children without a parent (Ryder, 2014). People of color such as Blacks, both male and female, are imprisoned at higher rates than Whites across all age groups (Carson & Sabol, 2012).

While these statistics are grim, much of the data collected on African Americans has been drawn from predominantly lower socioeconomic groups and thus may not be representative of the experiences of middle- and upper-class individuals (Ford, 1997; Holmes & Morin, 2006). Many specialty organizations have been developed to help these more economically advantaged people continue to experience economic success. For example, Black Entertainment Television offers a free membership in "Black America Saves," and the Consumer Federation of America offers services to aid in the accumulation of wealth. In addition, the National Urban League (nul.iamempowered.com/org), the Coalition of Black Investors, the Investment Company Institute (www.ici.org), and New York Life Insurance Company (New York Life, 2008) provide seminars to aid effective investment.

Families come in many different constellations. Most African American or Black individuals have chosen to live in family households. However, African American marriage rates are still lower than those of many other groups, and African American families are more likely to be headed by women. For example, in 2012, only 27.4% of individuals within a Black household were married, in comparison to 51.2% of non-Hispanic White individuals (Vespa et al., 2013). African American women head the household 29.4% of the time, in comparison to 10.2% of non-Hispanic White women (Vespa et al., 2013). In a 2007 survey, 42.3% of all Black women had never been married, and 70% of professional Black women had never been married (Nelson, 2008). While fewer women are marrying, they are still having children. Of Black women who had a child in the last year, 67% were unmarried, in comparison to 20% of non-Hispanic White women. Finally, when grandparents are living in the household, 50% of the time they are responsible for the care of their grandchildren (U.S. Census Bureau, 2011a).

Brief History

The category *African American* or *Black* is very heterogeneous. Therefore, the following information is based on the African Americans who are descendants of the slaves who were forced to immigrate to the United States and endured 200 years of slavery. These slaves were stolen predominantly from sub-Saharan, middle African coastal communities where polygamy was a common part of clan life (Comer & Hill, 1985; Du Bois, 1903/1997). The traditions of these communities emphasized family and kinship ties as being more important to self-identification than an individualized self.

The leaders of the clan, the chief and the priest, were separated from their people during the enslavement process. Furthermore, plantation-based slavery actively worked to subvert the formation of committed relationships (Du Bois, 1903/1997). Masters would pressure their slaves to form bonds; in order to give birth to more slaves, couples might be forcibly separated, and one might be sold into slavery on another plantation, where he or she might be pressured to find a new partner. Two hundred years of this cruel practice caused deterioration of the traditional family practices of the African people.

Some of the major political events that shaped African American life following slavery and the Civil War included the development of the Freedmen's Bureau in 1866 and a series of amendments to the U.S. Constitution. The Thirteenth Amendment abolished slavery, the Fourteenth Amendment defined the rights of citizenship, and the Fifteenth Amendment gave African Americans the right to vote. Despite these legislative advances, oppression and racism continued. Overly harsh and discriminatory practices within the school systems, legal systems, housing authorities, land authorities, and so forth eventually led to the civil rights legislation that was passed in 1964 and 1965. According to Du Bois (1903/1997), the "color-line" kept African Americans from integrating into the dominant culture of society. They struggled with the integration of two identities, that of being "American" and that of being "African American" (Du Bois, 1903/1997).

Affirmative action programs, beginning in the 1970s, were designed to make reparation to African Americans for their years of oppression. The goal was to increase the numbers of qualified African Americans in higher education and employment. Clear economic gains were made by people who benefited from these affirmative action programs. However, a backlash began in the 1980s. The Fourteenth Amendment's equal protection clause, as well as Title VII of the Civil Rights Act of 1964, began to be used to make the argument that affirmative action was "reverse discrimination." Polls suggest that White males believe they are harmed by affirmative action programs. Research data suggest that discrimination against White males is rare (5% or less), while a much larger percentage of people of color and women are harmed without affirmative action (Pincus, 2001/2002).

Overall, African American families have been more likely to emphasize interconnection and interdependence among members and take on a more holistic perspective on life, in comparison to the dominant culture's emphasis on individual achievement and a more linear view of events (Hall & Greene, 2008). To deal effectively with the hostile and oppressive historical and political realities in the United States, African American families have developed four major strengths (LaRue & Majidi-Ahi, 1998). The first is to use their religious beliefs and their affiliations with the church as a starting point for their social and civic activity. The majority of African Americans are Protestants who attend Baptist churches, Methodist churches, and Churches of God; many of these churches are part of the fundamentalist movement. However, Black Muslims and the more liberal Protestant churches have been gaining in membership in recent years (LaRue & Majidi-Ahi, 1998). Spiritual beliefs serve as protective factors in the lives of African Americans. The church serves as a haven from the prejudice and discrimination faced by African Americans in the White community. The church is a place where important social connections can be made that provide comfort, economic support, and opportunities for leadership and self-expression (Boyd-Franklin & Lockwood, 2009). Many important African American leaders have come out of religious careers—for example, the Reverend Martin Luther King Jr., the Reverend

Jesse Jackson, and the Reverend Al Sharpton. When parents attend church regularly, their children show fewer behavioral problems in schools (Christian & Barbarin, 2001). Clubs that are supported by the church promote resilience for students exposed to microaggressions in college (Watkins, Labarrie, & Appio, 2010). Church leaders often know their families well and can serve as important resources to clinicians in understanding how best to help a family in trouble (Sue & Sue, 2013).

African American families have close ties to their extended families and friends, so their definition of who is in the family may differ from White cultural expectations (LaRue & Majidi-Ahi, 1998; Sue & Sue, 2013). African American families care for extended family members in trouble. For example, adolescents in need of a change in environment or in highly conflicted relationships with their immediate family members may be sent to live with other relatives (LaRue & Majidi-Ahi, 1998). The sharing of money, resources, and emotional support is critical to the survival of many poor families within the African American community. However, this also means that money can be spread too thinly across family members (Greene, 1997). Strong kinship bonds extend to friends. Thus, family structures may include extended family or nontraditional living arrangements. Older children, friends, or grandparents may take on important caretaking roles (Sue & Sue, 2013).

African American adults are willing to take on flexible roles within families based on the specific needs of the family, rather than abiding by the European American custom of dividing tasks by gender (LaRue & Majidi-Ahi, 1998). Family tasks are divided up based on what would be most functional within each person's work or school schedule (LaRue & Majidi-Ahi, 1998). Thus, African American men are often involved in child-rearing responsibilities (Sue & Sue, 2013). Economic realities fuel this more androgynous lifestyle, as African American women have always needed to work, and this work has often been within low-pay and low-prestige settings. Thus, these families are often dual-income families by necessity, not choice (Greene, 1997). In addition, a racist society offers more employment opportunities to African American women than African American men. While some women experience guilt over this, the community as a whole recognizes that many employers actively discriminate against African American men (Greene, 1997). African American women may become frustrated and overwhelmed if they take on the stereotypical role of the strong woman in the family—the one who always keeps the family going; this role leads to a neglect of their own needs as individuals. In addition, African American men are harmed by stereotypes labeling them as irresponsible, incompetent, and violent (Hall & Greene, 2008).

African American parents actively support the development of assertiveness and self-esteem in their children (Sue & Sue, 2013). African American parents are also more likely to use physical discipline than their European American counterparts. While physical punishment correlates with negative outcomes in European American populations, this is not true in African American populations (Pinderhughes, Dodge, Bates, Pettit, & Zelli, 2000). This may be because physical punishment is correlated with negative attitudes toward children in European American families, while it is correlated with parental warmth in African American families. African American families who directly teach their children how to deal with racism and oppression have children with lower levels of anxiety when confronted with injustice than those who do not (Neal-Barnett & Crowther,

2000). Children struggling with poor self-esteem are helped by programs that teach them about African American culture (Belgrave, Chase-Vaughn, Gray, Addison, & Cherry, 2000). The African American community continues to have a realistic lack of trust in dominant culture institutions based on past and continuing acts of direct and indirect oppression (Sue & Sue, 2013). For example, 61% of African American families felt that quicker and more effective help would have been given to the victims of Hurricane Katrina in New Orleans if more of these victims had been European Americans (Washington, 2005). Research by the Pew Research Center (Krogstad, 2014) finds that African Americans continue to feel race is an important factor in how people are judged. In addition, more subtle forms of oppression continue, with children's toys most often featuring White faces, powerful characters in television shows being predominantly White, and powerful people such as police officers and politicians being predominantly White (McIntosh, 2008). Despite African Americans being victimized at higher rates than the general population, they are less likely to report crimes due to concerns about how the police will intervene (C. E. Schwartz et al., 2010). Their lack of trust is supported by the February 26, 2012, shooting of 17-year-old Trayvon Martin and the November 23, 2012, shooting of 17-year-old Jordan Davis; they were both shot by White men, were without any weapons, and had not committed any crimes. Trayvon was on his way home from a convenience store in Sanford, Florida, when he was first followed and then shot by George Zimmerman, a neighborhood watch volunteer. Jordan Davis was shot by Michael Dunn in a Jacksonville, Florida, parking lot because he was playing loud music in his car. In both cases, the White men were the ones to approach the African American adolescent males, yet used in their self-defense that they felt threatened by the young men after intentionally confronting them.

African American power in society continues to increase in the 21st century. More than 50 years have passed since the Civil Rights Act of 1964 was signed into law, and many powerful African Americans have taken political office. These include Secretary of State Colin Powell, who took office in 2001; Secretary of State Condoleezza Rice, who took office in 2005; and President Barack Obama, who took office in 2009 and was reelected in 2012. These leaders make visible the contributions of African Americans to the prosperity of the United States. However, African Americans are more cautious of these advances than Whites. In 2013, when asked if African Americans are better off today than they were five years ago, 35% of Whites agreed while only 26% of African Americans agreed (Krogstad, 2014). In a poll conducted after Trayvon Martin was killed, 79% of African Americans but only 44% of White Americans felt a lot needed to be done before there would be racial equality in the United States (Krogstad, 2014). African Americans coming into treatment may experience a disconnection between what is offered and what they are seeking. This disconnection may result because (a) the client comes from the lower class while the clinician is from the middle class; (b) the client uses a Black dialect and emphasizes nonverbal behavior rather than standard English; (c) the client has a people orientation, including an emphasis on extended family, versus an individualistic one that relies on a nuclear family structure; (d) the client emphasizes immediate, short-range, and concrete goals rather than long-range goals with a focus on personal exploration; or (e) the client has a social viewpoint in which oppression, versus a belief in a just world, plays a pivotal role (Sue & Sue, 2013, Chapter 14).

American Indians and Alaska Natives

Census Data

American Indians and Alaska Natives represent the indigenous population of North America. Included in this population is anyone who originated in North, South, or Central America and maintains tribal affiliation or community attachment. As of 2011, 5.1 million people self-identified within this population, representing 1.6% of the total population of the United States. There are 324 federally recognized Indian reservations, 617 recognized Indian areas, and 566 tribes (U.S. Census Bureau, 2012a). Only recognized tribal members are covered by the Indian Health Service (IHS). This organization is part of the U.S. Department of Health and Human Services. Most individuals served by the IHS live on reservations or in rural communities.

The median family income for American Indians and Alaska Natives is $35,192, which is substantially below the general population income of $51,017 (DeNavas-Walt et al., 2013; U.S. Census Bureau, 2012a). Twenty-seven percent of all American Indians are living below the poverty line, and they have an infant mortality rate that is 1.6 times that of the White population (U.S. Department of Health and Human Services, Office of Minority Health, 2006, 2009; U.S. Census Bureau, 2011a). Along with this high poverty rate comes a high crime rate.

Department of Justice statistics reveal that Native people between the ages of 25 and 34 are 2.5 times more likely to be victimized by violent crime than the general population. Males 12 and older have a one-in-10 chance of being victimized by violent crime, and historically the perpetrator has often been a White individual under the influence of alcohol. The rate for female victimization is lower; however, Native females are twice as likely to be victimized as females in the general population. Native women who have been assaulted or raped are most likely to be attacked by someone outside the family, while non-Native women are most often attacked by an intimate partner (U.S. Department of Justice, 2002). Thus, American Indians and Alaska Natives may have a realistic fear for their safety around White people. In addition, clinicians often underestimate the rate of poly-victimization among Native people. This may lead an individual to give up hope of ending victimization and view continued life as something to be endured (Vieth & Johnson, 2013). In comparison to all other ethnic and racial groups, American Indians have the highest rates of arrest for alcohol violations (U.S. Department of Justice, 2002).

American Indians are less likely to graduate from high school than other cultural groups, although they start out very successfully in the early school years. Seventy-nine percent of Indian students receive at least a high school diploma, in comparison to 85.9% of students in the general population (U.S. Census Bureau, 2012a). A hostile school environment or a sense of social stigmatization seems to increase in the early teen years as Indians come to see that they are marginalized and treated unfairly (Sue & Sue, 2013). The U.S. government frequently sends underqualified teachers, and even teachers with criminal records, to staff schools on Indian reservations (French, 1997). While intentional oppression does exist in the schools, teachers trained in dominant society values can also unintentionally create an uncomfortable environment. For example, being singled out at school to receive an award will make an American Indian child uncomfortable unless the child sees that the whole group will benefit from this achievement. The nonverbal communication patterns of these youths may also be incongruent with dominant cultural expectations. For example, to show respect, direct eye contact with an elder is to be avoided. Teachers in schools that value competition between students could view this behavior as disrespectful and see these children as passive or uninvolved (French, 1997). In addition, Indians tend not to ask direct questions, so teachers may not know when they need help (Sue & Sue, 2013). Despite these difficulties, 13.3% of Native people go on to achieve a bachelor's degree, and some go further to attain advanced professional degrees (U.S. Census Bureau, 2012a).

Sixty-five percent of American Indians and Alaska Natives are living in family households. Twenty percent of Native families are female-headed households without a husband present, compared to 13.1% of families in the general population (DeNavas-Walt et al., 2013; U.S. Census Bureau, 2010b). More marriages are intact among families residing on tribal lands than among those living within the dominant culture.

Brief History

Catastrophic historical and political events enveloped Native people when European American immigration began. Europeans spread infectious diseases such as measles, diphtheria, cholera, smallpox, and tuberculosis for which Indians had no immunity. These diseases depopulated the land. Indigenous cultures were extensively damaged by this massive population loss, which allowed Europeans to literally take North America away from them. European immigrants moved into the homes and onto the property the Indians abandoned due to death or fleeing infection (Mann, 2005).

Once the U.S. government was formed, it used military force to continue the process of stealing Indian land away from those who had survived the pandemics. Policies of the government included acts of genocide by U.S. troops, forcible relocation of survivors away from their traditional lands, and the repeated forcing of Native populations into political treaties that were to their disservice. These treaties were later violated by the U.S. government; examples of this are the Fort Laramie treaties of 1851 and 1868.

In addition to this physical decimation, a malignant social agenda was carried out on the surviving American Indians in an attempt to wipe out their cultures. Children were forcibly abducted and raised in boarding schools as Christians with European values. At these schools, children were punished if they spoke in their native language or tried to participate in any spiritual rituals or cultural practices. American Indian children and youth were systematically abused by non-Indians—notably those employed by the federal government to be their teachers. As a result, politicians, lawyers, teachers, and social agencies of the dominant society are not perceived as trustworthy, and many Indians have a justifiable distrust and hatred of the institutions supported by the U.S. government (French, 1997). The long-standing pattern of sociocultural and historical trauma perpetrated by European Americans led to the high rates of poverty, alcoholism, drug abuse, and violence among Native peoples that still exist today (Duran, 2006). Cultural oppression by militarily imposed genocide and cultural eradication efforts led to soul wounds in Native peoples, including their losing a sense of themselves as a strong people and internalizing the negative stereotypes fostered by the Europeans (Duran, 2006).

The grouping "American Indians and Alaska Natives" represents highly diverse peoples. The largest numbers of these people report their tribal affiliation as being Cherokee or Navajo (20%), Canadian or Latin American (4.4%), Sioux (4.4%), Chippewa (4.3%), Choctaw

(3.5%), Pueblo (2.4%), Apache (2.3%), Lumbee (2.1%), or Iroquois (1.8%). All together, the other tribal groupings identified by people affiliating with one tribe represent 24% of the population. In addition, 2.1% indicated more than one tribal affiliation, and 20.7% reported no tribal affiliation (U.S. Census Bureau, 2012a). More specific cultural information will be provided using the Lakota Sioux as a reference group.

The Sioux Nation is itself highly diverse, containing three major subdivisions: the Lakota, which has seven bands; the Dakota or Santee, with four bands; and the Nakota or Yankton, with three bands (Snow Owl, 2004). The people who originally made up the Sioux were mound builders who lived in the woods (French, 1997). They survived using hunting, gathering, and horticulture. Historic migrations led to the development of the three basic groups. These groups met episodically but were not united as a coordinated Sioux Nation until White persecution began. Lewis and Clarke attempted to develop a relationship between the United States government, as led by President Thomas Jefferson, and the Lakota people. However, this effort failed due to a combination of cultural misunderstanding and language misinterpretation (Jefferson National Expansion Memorial, 2013).

To many citizens of the United States, the Plains Sioux fulfilled the characteristics of the stereotypical Indian. They were nomadic, lived in teepees, and hunted buffalo. They were a warrior-oriented society whose warriors wore feather headdresses as they raided other tribes. They have a complex belief system that has at its center the "Great Mystery," or *Wakan Tanka*, which also has the name "Chief God, Great Spirit, Creator, and Executive" (French, 1997, p. 114). This Great Mystery has a complex and sometimes contradictory nature and is an amalgamation of 16 superior and subordinate Sioux gods and godlike beings. The numbers four and seven are very important to the Sioux and are tied to nature (such as the four directions), to animals (crawling, flying, two-legged, four-legged), and to the Sioux virtues (bravery, fortitude, generosity, and wisdom). Every summer, the "Seven Council Fires" powwow occurred, at which the most important ceremony—the Sun Dance—took place. This ceremony focuses on the warrior's fulfillment of important vows. The Sioux view all power as coming from Wakan Tanka. Thus, the warrior turns to this supernatural power to draw strength. The warrior also seeks visions to aid in this process of gaining strength from the creator. There are six other sacred ceremonies in addition to the Sun Dance, including Purification, Vision Seeking, Ball Throwing, Making a Buffalo Woman, Making as Brothers, and Owning a Ghost. Integral to Sioux spirituality is the use of the sacred pipe, which represents the universe. Smoking this pipe is part of making the connection with Wakan Tanka (French, 1997).

Sioux chiefs are not rulers who tell their people what to do; it is an honorary title. They are men who have fought well during wars and whose actions and opinions are respected by the tribe (French, 1997). Important decisions result from the unanimous vote of a Council of Chiefs (Snow Owl, 2004). Some important chiefs in history were Sitting Bull, Big Foot, and Crazy Horse. The Lakota are not originally from the Black Hills, but they migrated toward the West due to the encroachment of White settlements in the East. They came to see the Black Hills as sacred and the center of their spiritual culture (Jefferson National Expansion Memorial, 2013).

The Sioux moral code is grounded in the beliefs that good is stronger than evil and that good is a result of harmony within the group. Mind, body, and spirit are considered interconnected and inseparable (French, 1997). A lack of harmony between them may cause physical or psychological difficulties (Sue & Sue, 2013). The tribe is very important to the Indian and is an extension of himself or herself. The value of each person is contained in his or her usefulness to the tribe. The tribal land or reservation is also critical to the identity of an American Indian. When an individual leaves ancestral land to pursue economic prosperity, the individual's sense of identity may be damaged (Sue & Sue, 2013). Indians tend to live in the present rather than planning for the future. Their manner of being contains both a psychological and spiritual world (Duran, 2006). Thus, Indians might keep a job only long enough to pay basic expenses so that they can dedicate themselves to spiritual rituals; unfortunately, this may serve to perpetuate poverty (Sue & Sue, 2013).

Historically, the Lakota used 12 virtues to help them live in the world (Marshall, 2001). Stories were the traditional teaching tools, and children were taught about Sioux virtues in this way. Males and females were expected to be virtuous, and their status in the tribe came from how well they demonstrated these virtues (Marshall, 2001). While men and women took on defined sex roles, with men being warriors and women being bearers of children, both sexes were to show the virtue of bravery (*woohitike*) and its related virtue, fortitude (*cantewasake*). Bravery required self-sacrifice (*icicupi*). For a warrior, this could be shown through acts of bravery, such as counting coup (a nonviolent act of bravery where an enemy is touched briefly with a hand or a stick and then the warrior runs away), dog soldiering (being an elite warrior who would fight to the death in defense of the tribe), and participating in the Sun Dance (a public demonstration of bravery and self-discipline). *Fortitude* describes how men and women would demonstrate bravery (French, 1997). While stories demonstrating bravery and fortitude were encouraged as teaching devices, at the same time, humility (*unsiiciyapi*) was highly prized; warriors recognized that it was the deed, not the telling of it, that was important (Marshall, 2001). The Sioux considered humility to validate the virtues of generosity, bravery, respect, and wisdom. "The burden of humility is light because a truly humble person divests him or herself of the need for recognition. The burden of arrogance, on the other hand, grows heavier day by day" (Marshall, 2001, p. 19).

Success that comes with little effort was not worth telling stories about. Perseverance (*wowacintanka*) despite repeated challenges to success was worthy of remembering. While love (*catognake*) and enduring attachment were valued, in public, both males and females were socialized to show self-discipline and emotional self-control in positive experiences as well as when confronting fear and pain. Physical intimacies were private behaviors, and it was taboo to engage in public displays of affection. Respect (*wawoohola*) referred to holding someone in high regard—treating the person with consideration and behaving toward the person as he or she deserved (Marshall, 2001); if a Lakota gave in to the temptation to behave disrespectfully, his or her spirit might never heal. Thus, while a woman might truly love a man, if he was not the choice of her father, she would marry the man her father chose. She would behave impeccably in building a home, having children, and caring for her husband, but he would know her heart belonged to someone else. Stories, such as this one about a virtuous woman, would be told as a lesson to the next generation so that they would learn to live in balance within the personal and spiritual worlds of the Lakota people (Marshall, 2001).

Generosity (*canteyuke*), or sharing of food and possessions, was another key virtue (Marshall, 2001). It illustrated the profound differences between the Sioux ethic and that of the early White immigrants. The European immigrants gained respect from each other by making money and owning individual property. Among the Sioux, respect came from participating in the "giveaway" (French, 1997, p. 118). Individuals who could give away their possessions to be distributed among the tribe, particularly to the neediest in the tribe, were those who earned prestige and respect. Those who gave away the most achieved the highest status. These generous individuals were showing compassion (*waunsilapi*), demonstrating that they understood the needs of others, sympathized with their situation, and cared about their welfare over the accumulation of possessions (Duran, 2006).

The way of honor (*wayuonihan*) was the path of integrity, honesty, and having a steadfast character (Marshall, 2001). The Lakota could show honor as much by what they did as by what they did not do. Honor underlay many other virtues, such as generosity and telling the truthful (*wowicake*), so that others knew you would stand by your word and be trustworthy. A combination of age and life accomplishments was used to determine status within the tribe. Wisdom (*woksape*) came from accumulating knowledge. Elders in the tribe were valued for their opinions based on life experience and were often used to help bring conflicts to an acceptable conclusion (French, 1997). The Sioux strongly endorsed the concept of harmony and had traditions that were designed to keep conflicts down. They did not interfere in other people's business. They were taught to observe and consider carefully rather than act impulsively. Dreams and visions were taken seriously as conveying supernatural power (Jefferson National Expansion Memorial, 2013).

The family group, while changing over time, was all important. A family was compared to others in terms of how many horses they owned, the success they had in hunting, whether the men participated in important societies, and how many religious ceremonies they sponsored (Jefferson National Expansion Memorial, 2013). Children were prized and treated indulgently. Even after misbehaving, they were not physically punished, as tribal harmony included the happiness of children. The most severe punishment given to children was for angry parents to dump a bucket of cold water over the child (History Learning Site, 2008). Young people were encouraged to be sensitive to the feelings of others and not seek competition, as this would lead to discord (French, 1997). The Lakota believed that adults, as well as children, should listen more than talk. Thus, listening to stories about the 12 virtues was an important teaching tool for everyone. The stories contained lessons in how to live in ways that were consonant with being virtuous and led to honorable outcomes (Marshall, 2001). Historical circumstances were incorporated into stories and became a part of the oral tradition of the Sioux people.

Tragically, the dominant culture of the United States continues to take actions that suppress traditional Sioux ways. As a direct result of generations of this cultural oppression, many American Indian tribes have lost contact with their traditional ways. A pan-Indian movement has developed as one response to try to rectify this. Sioux ceremonies and spiritual songs are being incorporated into the traditional healing ceremonies of other Indian groups; indeed, Sioux leaders are training healers from many different tribes (French, 1997). At the present time, American Indians have selected lifestyles that are most appropriate to their own personal needs, ranging from living totally within their Native culture to being completely assimilated within the dominant culture of the United States. Duran (2006) considers that many Native people might benefit from help in achieving a balance between their cultural and personal identities. For this to happen, the psychological abuse and microaggressions embedded within the dominant culture need to come to an end. For example, history books within the United States continue to teach that Christopher Columbus discovered America when in fact there had been Native people living throughout America prior to his "discovery." By celebrating Columbus Day, we are suggesting that until European Americans arrived, there was nothing of value in North and South America. Some American Indians want to abolish Columbus Day for this reason. Pacific Northwest tribes hold an annual protest against Columbus Day (Pan Tribal Secession Against the Empire, 2012). In addition, sports teams across the United States have used names, symbols, and imagery that are not respectful of American Indian culture. The National Collegiate Athletic Association (NCAA) required universities to retire any offensive words or symbols on their uniforms and other clothing starting on November 1, 2005, at championship events if they wanted to stay in the league (ESPN.com News Services, 2005). At that time, the NCAA listed 18 schools as having mascots that were considered offensive or unacceptable; however, not all Native American tribes were offended by the use of their names or symbols. The Seminal Tribe of Florida showed support for Florida State by passing a resolution approving the university's use of their name and symbols. This controversy underscores how important it is for Native Americans to participate in all dialogues involving aspects of their culture rather than having dominant culture representatives make decisions for them (Billie, 2013). Changes in the policies of sports teams represent some acknowledgment of the dominant culture's oppression of Native Americans; however, much more serious violations of their human rights have continued and have had tragic results.

Oppressive practices by the United States government, racial and ethnic prejudice, and Indians' high rates of poverty are all factors behind the much higher rates of unemployment, substance abuse, suicide, posttraumatic stress disorder, and victimization in Native Americans than in the dominant culture of the United States. A past history of victimization by White neighbors and the government has led Native Americans to distrust non-Indian individuals when seeking help (French, 1997; Sue & Sue, 2013; U.S. Department of Justice, 2002). When they do seek help from non-Indian clinicians, problems that may arise include the following: Clients may speak tribal dialects and use nonverbal communication patterns that are very different from those used in English and within the White culture; tribal customs may emphasize cooperation over competition; tribal goal setting may focus on present needs and immediate, short-range goals rather than the future and long-term goals; and tribal family structure may rely on active participation from extended family rather than the nuclear family (Sue & Sue, 2013). Other complications include how far from helpers many Native people may live, their lack of highly trained helpers, and the disruptions that have occurred within their traditional styles of learning (i.e., through stories) and their spirituality.

Many culturally specific treatments have been developed to empower Indians in the recovery process, such as bibliotherapy for traumatized children and youth, Cherokee cultural therapy, the traditional healing practices of the Sioux, and the Navajo Beauty Way perspective. Each of these treatments seeks to revitalize cultural connection and pride and promote religious freedom (French, 1997). Duran (2006) believes that the Sioux need liberation discourse to heal the soul wounds created as a result of the rape of the people and the land by colonialism in the United States. Unlike the past colonial view of one truth as defined by White society, liberation psychology takes the narrative perspective that there is more than one way to see the truth and more than one way to live in the world. Western psychology doesn't talk in terms of the spirit world or the soul. However, it is critical to discuss the spirit world and the soul in helping the Lakota to heal.

Duran talks of a number of treatment strategies that have been developed out of traditional practices of the Lakota people. It is valuable to incorporate these traditional practices into clinical work, because the American Indian culture does not fit well with the expectations of treatment orientations that stem from White, middle-class culture and because the problems that the Lakota are experiencing right now are a direct result of cultural and historical trauma that has not been processed in a way that empowers the Lakota people to be freed of the internal hatred brought on by colonialism. Part of what is necessary for healing is for Whites to acknowledge the atrocities committed against Native peoples, including the Sand Creek Massacre, the Wounded Knee Massacre, the Long Walk of the Navajo, the Trail of Tears, the Long Walk of the Maidu People, and the burning of hundreds of Original People at Jamestown. By acknowledging these atrocities, part of the soul wound of the Lakota may be healed, because the people who died will have been honored for their sacrifice (Duran, 2006).

National statistics indicate that rates of child abuse and neglect are higher for American Indian children than for the general population (U.S. Department of Health and Human Services, Office of Minority Health, 2006). Duran (2006) considers these statistics a result of the soul wounds of Native people. Many of these wounds are a result of intentional acts of the dominant culture to force acculturation of Native people and of the domino effect in which Native people have become ignorant of the important traditions that helped them structure their lives in adaptive ways. Helpers must listen to Native people, share information freely, and support traditional practices, such as their oral tradition of telling stories (Vieth & Johnson, 2013). Duran (2006) recommends a liberation discourse in treatment that starts with an acknowledgment of the holocaust that was carried out against Native people. He believes that, like the schools provided by the United States government, social service agencies are replete with "clinical racism." These clinicians do not honor or respect Native people and don't provide the same standard of care, such as just keeping appropriate case notes, as they would for Whites (p. 36). Duran believes Native people would best be served by hybrid services that honor both the Western worldview and the Native worldview. Strengths of the Native people need to be recognized, such as their respect for their extended family and their elders and their desire to protect the land and animals (Sue & Sue, 2013).

Traditional approaches to healing may also be incorporated that attempt to restore harmony among the spirit, mind, and body, such as sweat lodges, fasting to remove body impurities, and the use of herbal remedies (Indians.org, 2014). Native American healing practices focus on healing the person as a whole rather than on curing a specific disease. Storytelling and the use of tribal proverbs can also be used as learning tools. Examples of proverbs include "You can't wake a person who's pretending to be asleep" (Navajo), "Don't be afraid to cry; it will free your mind of sorrowful thoughts" (Hopi), "There is nothing as eloquent as a rattlesnake tail" (Cheyenne), "Our first teacher is our own heart" (Cheyenne), "Do not judge your neighbor until you walk two moons in his moccasins" (Cheyenne), and "When a man moves away from nature, his heart becomes hard" (Lakota).

Recent leaders known for fighting for justice for the Indian people come from groups such as the American Indian Movement, the National Congress of American Indians, and the National Indian Youth Council. The Lower Brule Sioux tribal reservation works with nine tribal governments in South Dakota, including the Cheyenne River Sioux tribe, the Crow Creek Sioux tribe, the Flandreau Santee Sioux tribe, the Lower Brule Sioux tribe, the Oglala Sioux tribe, the Rosebud Sioux tribe, the Sisseton Wahpeton Oyate, the Standing Rock Sioux tribe, and the Yankton Sioux tribe (South Dakota Department of Tribal Relations, 2011). Within the Lower Brule reservation, each tribe operates as a separate government. Each tribe has its own unique land, with its own language, religion, and culture that may vary from those of the other tribes (South Dakota Department of Tribal Relations, 2011). For example, the Rosebud Sioux seek to preserve the traditions of the Sicangu Lakota Oyate. The Rosebud Sioux tribe consists of 20 communities, including Antelope, Black Pipe, Bull Creek, Butte Creek, Corn Creek, Grass Mountain, He Dog, Horse Creek, Ideal, Milk's Camp, Okreek, Parmelee, Ring Thunder, Rosebud, St. Francis, Soldier Creek, Spring Creek, Swift Bear, Two Strike, and Upper Cut Meat (Official Site of the Rosebud Sioux Tribe, 2013).

Hispanic or Latina and Latino Americans

Census Data

According to the 2010 census, there are roughly 50.4 million Hispanics living in the United States (Ennis, Ríos-Vargas, & Albert, 2011; U.S. Census Bureau, 2012b). "Hispanic" is a category created by the census that defines people by their country of origin rather than by their racial group. It consists of people from Mexico, Puerto Rico, Cuba, El Salvador, Nicaragua, and other Central and South American countries as well as Spain (U.S. Census Bureau, 2012b). While 53% of them identify themselves as White (U.S. Census Bureau, 2012b), they often have an ethnic and racial heritage that could include full Aztec Indian or other Indian heritage, along with biracial or multiracial heritage involving Indian, African, Spanish, and White ancestors (Comas-Diaz, 2008). Hispanics consider racial mixtures and multiple identifications typical. There is great variability in skin color among these groups, which may lead people who are not Latina or Latino to misidentify them as White when they don't view themselves as White, to misidentify them as Black when they don't view themselves as Black, and so forth. They may be highly offended when others select a racial identification for them rather than asking them to self-identify. Latinas and Latinos identify themselves more by national origin than through racial categorization. In fact, their self-identification of race is more fluid. They tend to see race more as a social construction influenced by context than as a biological reality. For example, some contexts may lead to a national origin self-designation, some to a Latina/Latino designation, some to an Afro-Latina/o designation, some to a Black Cuban designation, and so forth (Rodriguez, 2008). One third of the foreign-born population of the United States comes from Mexico, and 55% are of Latin America origin. Mexican Americans are the largest subgroup within the Hispanic population, representing 31.8 million people. Puerto Ricans are the next largest group, followed in order by Central Americans, South Americans, and Cubans (U.S. Census Bureau, 2010e). Immigration from Latin America has been steadily increasing. The majority of Hispanics live within three states. California has 27.8% of the Hispanic population, Texas has 18.7%, and Florida has 8.4%.

The median household income for Hispanics is $39,005 in comparison to $51,017 for the general population (DeNavas-Walt et al., 2013). While male Hispanics earn less than the general population of men, they earn more than Hispanic women. Seventy percent of Hispanic males and 58.2% of Hispanic females are in the workforce (U.S. Census Bureau, 2011b). Both Hispanic males and females are most likely to be employed in management, professional, and related occupations. A total of 23.2% of Hispanics are living below the poverty line, compared to 14.3% of the general population. One in three Hispanic children lives in poverty, and their poverty rate is 15.3 percentage points higher than that of White children (Anderson, 2011; Macartney, Bishaw, & Fontenot, 2013).

Higher poverty rates are accompanied by higher crime rates. The Hispanic population has an incarceration rate of 9% in comparison to the 5% rate for the general population (Carson & Sabol, 2012). People of color such as Hispanics, both male and female, are imprisoned at higher rates than Whites across all age groups (Carson & Sabol, 2012).

The educational attainment of Hispanics has been lower than that of the general population. Only 64.3% of Hispanic individuals over the age of 25 have a high school diploma, which is substantially below the general population figure of 87.5%. However, 14.1% of Hispanics have earned a bachelor's degree. Educational background varies considerably among Hispanic groups, with South Americans showing the highest educational attainment and Mexican and Central Americans showing the lowest. Only 29.7% of individuals who were born in Mexico have at least a high school education (U.S. Census Bureau, 2011a).

There are gaps in educational achievement that begin prior to school. Research has found that only 23% of Hispanic 4-year-olds are ready to start school, compared to 37% of White 4-year-olds (Aud, Fox, & KewalRamani, 2010). Latina and Latino parents have also been found to be less likely than White parents to be involved in their children's school activities due to language barriers, feelings of being unwelcome at school (Nzinga-Johnson, Baker, & Aupperlee, 2009), cultural misunderstandings, and employment that prevents their involvement (Carreon, Drake, & Barton, 2005). Despite this, there has been an increase in college enrollment for Hispanics; in fact, 49% of 18- to 24-year-old high school graduates have gone on to college in comparison to 47% of White graduates (Krogstad & Fry, 2014).

Passel and Cohn (2009) have estimated that there are 11.9 million unauthorized immigrants in the United States, 7 million of whom are from Mexico. The United States has been prosecuting "unlawful entry" into the country. Unlawful entry is a charge used when an individual has attempted to enter the United States illegally more than once. Prosecutions for this offense more than doubled between 1992 and 2012. While 48% of the growth in sentencing in federal court was for unlawful entry, only 22% of the growth was for drug offenses. Nearly all individuals sentenced for unlawful entry receive time in prison (Light, Lopez, & Gonzalez-Barrera, 2014). While in this country illegally, undocumented people bring significant benefits to the economy, having contributed $1.9 billion dollars in tax income and billions more in consumer spending. This money contributes to all the services provided to U.S. citizens in terms of education, health care, and social services (Capps & Fix, 2005). Undocumented workers do not receive the same services as legal immigrants. For example, while illegal immigrants pay into Social Security, they will never have any access to Social Security benefits (Chung, Bemak, & Kudo-Grabosky, 2011). Even if they are aware that they need social services, illegal immigrants may not seek mental health services due to language barriers, a lack of interpreters, and cultural differences (Bemak & Chung, 2008).

The majority of undocumented workers are believed to be poor and uneducated, with those coming from Mexico being even poorer and less educated than those from other countries. Estimates suggest that while 25% of unauthorized immigrants have not completed high school, 64% of illegal Mexican immigrants have not. However, 4% of undocumented Mexican immigrants do hold a college degree. More than other illegals, undocumented Mexican adults are more likely to be parents with children, with their children having been born in the United States (Passel & Cohn, 2009).

Immigration policy has a personal impact on Latinas and Latinos. When asked about the current year, 24% of them indicated knowing someone who had been either detained or deported (Lopez, Gonzalez-Barrera, & Motel, 2011). Thus, many Latina and Latino citizens experience anxiety about the possibility that a family member or friend who is not a citizen will be deported (Lopez et al., 2011).

Immigration policy has shifted during the Obama administration. There has been a huge decrease (70%) in apprehensions at the border, and instead, deportations have increased (Passel & Cohn, 2009). Fifty-nine percent of Latinas and Latinos disapprove of this (Lopez et al., 2011). Forty-two percent of Latina and Latino citizens, in comparison to 24% of the general population, approve of providing a pathway to citizenship for illegal immigrants. Roughly the same percentage of Latinas and Latinos (46%) in comparison to the general population (43%) say that border enforcement and a pathway to citizenship should have equal weight in immigration policy. Border security and enforcement is endorsed by 10% of Latinas and Latinos and 29% of the general public as being of top priority (Lopez et al., 2011).

There have been many different attempts to deal with undocumented populations, for example, the DREAM (Development, Relief, and Education for Alien Minors) Act introduced in the Senate in 2001 by Dick Durbin and Orrin Hatch. The DREAM Act encountered a great deal of opposition from the beginning. It would have provided permanent resident status to undocumented students who graduated from a United States high school, lived here for at least five years, and were documented to be of good character. In addition, it would have allowed Latina and Latino youth who were born into their undocumented circumstances to receive public education. While proposed in 2001, this act has still not passed at the federal level. However, as of November 2013, 15 states had enacted their own version of this act to help undocumented youth. The vast majority (91%) of Latinas and Latinos support the DREAM Act (Lopez et al., 2011).

Concerns about illegal immigration have led to acts of prejudice and discrimination against Latina and Latino citizens. After Hurricane Katrina, they were required to provide proof of residency to get hurricane relief services (Terhune & Perez, 2005). In 2010, Arizona passed a bill (Arizona S.B. 1070) titled "Support Our Law Enforcement and Safe Neighborhoods Act" to decrease its problems with illegal immigration. The bill included three provisions that were later deemed unconstitutional by the *United States v. Windsor* Supreme Court decision (2013), including penalties for working without a permit, penalties for not registering appropriately as an alien, and the granting of authority to police to arrest, without a warrant, any individual perceived to be an illegal alien. However, the fourth provision, which allowed police officers to request identification of anyone they stopped because of some other offense or potential offense, was not struck down.

Due to tremendous diversity within the Hispanic population, the more in-depth analysis that follows is focused on Mexican Americans, which is the largest Latina/o population in the United States (Ennis et al., 2011).

Brief History

Mexicans originally became citizens of the United States through acts of conquest and purchase. The largest changeover in citizenry occurred at the conclusion of the Mexican–American War in 1849, when Mexico lost 45% of its national territory to the United States. In this Southwest Territory, citizenship was granted to all Mexican and Spanish people. Later, an ambivalent and destructive cycle began, wherein Mexicans were encouraged to immigrate to the United States when their labor was needed and then were expected to return to Mexico when it was not. For example, during the depression years of the 1930s, 300,000 Mexicans and Mexican Americans were repatriated or deported. During World War II, the Bracero agreement encouraged Mexicans to work for short periods within the United States. When the war ended, politicians enacted legislation to again restrict immigration of Mexican workers into the United States (Bernal & Enchautegui-de-Jesus, 1994).

At this time, major problems with Mexico stem from the activities of their drug syndicates. Mexico is the second largest producer of opium in the world. Drug syndicates send ecstasy, heroin, marijuana, and methamphetamines across the border to the United States (Central Intelligence Agency, 2013).

Despite the ambivalent and sometimes actively hostile attitude of the U.S. government, many Mexicans continued to immigrate to the United States in search of economic opportunities. Mexico has approximately 118.8 million people, 51% of whom live below the poverty line (Central Intelligence Agency, 2013). A lack of economic opportunities has encouraged many people to immigrate to the United States (Santana & Santana, 2001). The legal status of an individual as "documented" or "undocumented" has a huge influence on his or her ability to attain any rights within the employment, educational, medical, and social structures in the United States. Fear of disclosure may prevent undocumented workers from seeking the services they need (Atkinson, Morten, & Sue, 1979). However, they remain in the United States because of shortages of paid work in Mexico. In their turn, many agricultural communities in the United States are dependent on Mexican workers (Santana & Santana, 2001) For example, it is estimated that 25% of farmworkers, 19% of groundskeepers, and 17% of construction workers are unauthorized immigrants (Passel & Cohn, 2009).

There is considerable heterogeneity across Mexican American families due to family dynamics and patterns of acculturation to the dominant culture of the United States; however, common Latino values include the importance of family membership and pride in the family. The term *familismo* refers to the importance placed on family needs over the individual family member. Family includes an extended network of relatives, some of whom are tied by customs of obligation and feeling rather than blood; family unity and honor are emphasized (Atkinson et al., 1979). For example, even families three or more generations removed from Mexico may maintain extended kinship ties back home. Mexican families may also rely on *compadres* (godparents) for financial, emotional, and social support (Ramirez, 1998).

Coming from a collectivist culture, Mexican Americans draw their personal identities from the sociopolitical and historical context in which they have developed as well as their ancestral histories (Comas-Diaz, 2008). Family histories may include multigenerational dislocations and disruptions, including traumas that have not been processed. Deep family ties and cross-generational influences may have resulted in the continued transmission of racial and gender oppression from past injustices. Elders pass down family history through stories so that past trauma continues to have an impact on younger family members (Comas-Diaz, 2008).

Mexican families have a 25% poverty rate (Macartney et al., 2013). There are approximately 7 million children in the United States who speak Spanish as their primary language at home. As schools are primarily providing instruction in English, these children may be at a disadvantage in keeping up with the curriculum (Sanchez, Bledsoe, Sumabat, & Ye, 2004), and their parents may lack the facility with English to help them (Aud et al., 2010).

Latinas and Latinos have a strong sense of hierarchy and deference for authority and may consider it impolite to disagree with an authority figure. This may inhibit them from asserting their rights (Ramirez, 1998; Santana & Santana, 2001). Traditionally, men have assumed the role of provider and final decision maker. They are to have *machismo* by being strong, being loyal, and doing everything possible to ensure the happiness of family members. In fact, even if suffering from severe pain, the man is expected to stoically bear it while continuing to support his family. A man is expected to take pride in his role as husband, father, and son and put the well-being of his family first (Santana & Santana, 2001). The concept of *machismo* has sometimes taken on sexist and authoritarian elements. Men may be considered the superiors of women and exert unjust power over them. Rather than being protective, they may be restrictive of their girlfriends or wives due to jealousy.

The tradition in which the eldest male in the household holds the most dominant role in the family may be changing because of economic realities that push women to work outside the home to provide financial support for the family. Immigrant women using their sewing, cleaning, and cooking skills may find it easier to gain employment than immigrant men using their agricultural skills (Santana & Santana, 2001). This has led to a shift toward more egalitarian households (Ramirez, 1998). For some families, these shifting roles cause stress and turmoil (Santana & Santana, 2001).

Traditional women take on the role of homemaker and caretaker of children. They are to show *marianismo*. The word stems from a belief in the Virgin Mary as the ultimate example of motherhood. *Marianismo* includes being warm and supportive to family members, literally as a sacred duty. Women are to work to bring pleasure to others while not seeking pleasure for themselves, even to the level of martyrdom. They are also to show devotion to the home. The family home is expected to be the center of the family, and women are to put family loyalty first. Mothers, while appearing very submissive, actually have a great deal of power within the home, as their skills at caring for others are considered even more important than skills at providing financial support. Mother love is considered stronger than romantic love. The role of parents is considered primary over the role of being a spouse. While motherhood and a mother's authority to run the household are highly respected, paradoxically, the father is given the most authority in making final family decisions (Santana & Santana, 2001).

Mexican Americans are generally very accepting of the individual needs and qualities of their children. They are less likely to push their children through developmental stages. Young children are indulged and dealt with affectionately by both parents. The father takes on a very playful role while children are young and is a disciplinarian when they are older. The mother continues to take on a very loving role with her children throughout their development and serves as an intermediary when needed to reduce conflicts between her children and her husband. Having proper *respeto* for authority is emphasized within the home. Children are to listen to and obey parents, and younger children are to obey and model the behavior of older siblings. As children enter the later elementary school years, they are expected to take on more and more family responsibilities (Ramirez, 1998). Self-worth is defined in terms of children's inner qualities of uniqueness, goodness, and integrity that give them self-respect and dignity and earn for them the respect of others.

Family members are expected to be dependent on rather than independent of each other. Young people are to work hard to improve themselves beyond what was achieved by their parents' generation. Rebellion against parental authority is unacceptable within traditional families. Teenage girls are traditionally afforded less freedom than boys and are channeled into homemaker activities, while boys are encouraged to socialize with their male peers. Adolescents who push for freedom, due to greater levels of acculturation, may cause crises within the home and may struggle trying to bridge the identities they develop within each culture (Santana & Santana, 2001). Young adults are expected to live with their parents until marriage, and when parents become frail it is assumed that they will move in with one of their adult children (Santana & Santana, 2001). Girls are to be chaste before marriage and not to show interest in their sexuality. In fact, women who do so may be considered "bad" women (Santana & Santana, 2001).

Families who are just beginning to acculturate to the dominant culture within the United States may be forced to use their children as interpreters at times. This may disrupt the traditional family hierarchy of authority and cause stress. In addition, it may result in the clinician's gaining inaccurate information (Sue & Sue, 2013).

Mexican Americans emphasize friendliness and warmth in their interactions with others. They value *personalismo*, or an individualized and personal manner of interacting with others, rather than the more professional or distant method of interacting often favored in dominant culture institutions. When Mexican Americans interact with individuals who behave in a distant and impersonal manner, they feel disrespected and uncomfortable.

The church is integral to family life, and priests are highly respected and officiate in important religious rituals as well as weddings and the *quinceañera* where 15-year-old girls cross into adult roles (Santana & Santana, 2001). The majority of Mexican Americans are Catholics (70%); however, Mexicans have begun to enter Protestant faiths such as the Church of Jesus Christ of Latter-Day Saints and the Presbyterian Church (Delgado, 2006). Evangelical churches have seen an increase in Mexican American membership over the last 10 years (Delgado, 2006). While beliefs are diverse, the *Virgen de Guadalupe* is an important spiritual mother for many Mexican women. She is considered a Black Virgin Mary (Comas-Diaz, 2008; Santana & Santana, 2001). Guadalupe stems from the Catholic Church but has also been used within more indigenous belief systems. She is believed to provide nurturance, warmth, and acceptance to the oppressed. She has been used as a symbol of hope in political struggles within both Mexico and the United States (Comas-Diaz, 2008).

Overall, the Mexican American population is younger, less educated, and poorer than the general population of the United States. This population continues to grow due to its high birth rate, despite the relatively stable rate of immigration (Passel, Cohn, & Gonzalez-Barrera, 2012). Intergenerational history plays an important role in how family members interact with each other and with society (Comas-Diaz, 2008). Family context is so important to identity that immediate and extended families try to live close to each other (Santana & Santana, 2001).

Current treatment practices may come into conflict with Latino expectations and competencies, including (a) an emphasis on Spanish rather than English within the home, which may reduce facility with communicating in English; (b) a family rather than an individualistic orientation; (c) a style of being silent and compliant with an authority figure; (d) an expectation that communication will be unidirectional from the clinician within a highly structured approach; and (e) an expectation that treatment will be action oriented and focused on short-range goals that are concrete and specific (Sue & Sue, 2013).

White Americans/European Americans

Census Data

The classification "White American" was created by the U.S. Census Bureau at its inception. "White" is a heterogeneous group that includes individuals of European American descent who are perceived to have white skin, as well as individuals who are perceived to have white skin whose ancestors were not from Europe. Currently, "White" Americans represent the dominant group within the United States. They represent 78% of the population when White Hispanic people are included as "White" and 64% of the population when Hispanics are not included (DeNavas-Walt et al., 2013). The median household income of non-Hispanic Whites is $57,009. This is significantly higher than the median income of the population at large, which is $51,017. The percentage of this population living below the poverty level is 11.6% in comparison to 14.3% for the general population (U.S. Census Bureau, 2011b). Only 17% of non-Hispanic White children live in poverty (U.S. Census Bureau, 2011a; DeNavas-Walt et al., 2013); this represents the lowest poverty rate of any racial or ethnic group within the United States. As economic welfare is related to crime rates, White individuals have only a 2% chance of spending time in prison; this is a significantly lower rate than the 9% rate for the general population (U.S. Department of Justice, 2006).

From an educational perspective, 92.4% of the White population has graduated from high school, and 34% have attained a bachelor's degree or more (U.S. Census Bureau, 2011b). Vocationally, the greatest percentage of White workers are in the management, professional, and related occupations category (42.7%), followed by sales and office occupations (24.2%) and service occupations (14.5%). Only 10.1% of White workers have classified themselves as working within production, transportation, and material-moving occupations; 8.2% consider themselves to be in construction, extraction, and maintenance occupations; and 0.5% have classified themselves as working in farming, fishing, and forestry occupations (U.S. Census Bureau, 2011b).

Brief History

The first politically powerful or "privileged" population within the United States comprised White Protestants. Only Protestant males had the right to vote. They were also the heads of the household in their families. They used the values from their belief system to create the institutions and rules of society. More recently emigrated and less financially successful groups needed to adhere to these already created institutions. Early in the nation's history, many Caucasian populations were actively discriminated against and were not considered White. A case in point was the treatment of early Irish American immigrants. They were treated with the same type of discrimination and oppression as African Americans and were part of a highly exploited working class in the 19th century. They were referred to as "white Negros" (Ignatiev, 1995, p. 34). Before the Civil War, the Irish played an active role in the abolitionist movement. Southern slaveholders came to realize that to maintain their power, they needed support among the Northern working class. They funneled money into political battles to give the Irish citizenry the right to vote in exchange for their support against the abolitionists. Over time, the Irish came to see their white skin as their ticket out of marginalization, and they took it (Ignatiev, 1995).

During the World War II era, other formerly marginalized groups from so-called "inferior" races or European ethnic groups became accepted as White once they earned enough money to enter the middle class and gain some political clout. Despite quotas that tried to keep them out, they were able to pursue higher education for their children. These more educated offspring learned skills that were needed in the workforce (Brodkin, 2001). This type of entry into Whiteness was further accelerated after World War II. The new industrial complex had a need for skilled labor, and this employment boom spread economic prosperity among white-skinned groups.

Similarly, as a result of the 1944 Servicemen's Readjustment Act and loans from the Federal Housing Administration, White male service members gained loans that allowed them to buy homes for the first time; this further set the stage for economic prosperity. It was their white skin and their male gender that gave them these privileges (McIntosh, 2008). These same benefits were systematically denied to women and minority veterans who had similar military service and economic stability. Brodkin (2001) considered the "GI Bill" the largest affirmative action movement in U.S. history; it provided privileges that allowed white-skinned Catholic and Jewish men to enter the middle class. Being a member of the White race conferred privileges beyond access to better housing. It carried with it the cachet of social respectability where you were assumed to be a good employee, a good citizen, and a safe neighbor (McIntosh, 2008; Sue & Sue, 2013).

However, "true" Whiteness came at the expense of separating from allegiance to country of origin. If a family continued to, for example, speak Italian in the home, then it was considered White but of "such and such descent" and thus an inferior type of White (Frankenberg, 2008, p. 83). A racial and cultural hierarchy developed where skin color, hair texture, facial features, and language were used as criteria for where one fit in the hierarchy. A carryover from colonialism, the view that non-White cultures were less sophisticated, less civilized, or deviant pervaded this hierarchy. White was made equivalent to being "average" or "typical" and a quality of the true American. White was what everybody who was "normal" was, and true Whites spoke only English (Frankenberg, 2008).

The "Protestant ethic," a term coined by Weber (1904–1905/1958), is thought to epitomize what has come to be called White culture. This ethic incorporated aspects of aesthetic Protestantism, which values hard work, self-reliance, self-denial, emotional control, and guilt as a mechanism of control (Albee, 1977). These values were intermixed with the qualities needed by the newly developing capitalist system, as conceived by wealthy Protestant businessmen. They wanted loyal workers who would find more satisfaction in their job success than in their relationships with family and friends. Workers who would sacrifice their time with their families to support company growth were rewarded with financial success (Weber, 1904–1905/1958). A more individualistic orientation was fostered in which success was measured by accumulating wealth and social status rather than fulfilling societal obligations (Albee, 1977). Capitalism and industrialization were powerful forces, transforming the values of White groups so that they considered the production and consumption of goods their primary goals (Frankenberg, 2008).

This new cultural ethic redefined the concept of breadwinner for men. Now, they were to be the major financial support of their families, rather than an active participant in day-to-day family life. Family members were to support the breadwinner in his single-minded pursuit of advancement in the workplace. Having children was delayed so that the breadwinner could become more educated and upwardly mobile. Smaller families were encouraged so that each individual child could be given the education and financial support needed to climb the ladder (Albee, 1977). Breadwinners were expected to have self-discipline so that they would pursue long-term goals, not hedonistic short-term ones. They needed a sense of agency within the context of independent thinking, rather than within the context of interdependence with others (Weber, 1904–1905/1958). These pressures brought on by capitalism actively worked to homogenize Whites, driving them to have the same values and to speak English (Frankenberg, 2008). Legal and educational institutions were developed to fit in with the specific schedules and lifestyles that were congruent with the new capitalism. Social reform moments and developments within the school system served to further socialize white-skinned immigrants to take on these values and behaviors (Frankenberg, 2008; Ignatiev, 1995). Partitioning time into segments that were useful for business became the norm. "Wasting time" became a serious offense. This new ethic selectively disadvantaged employees from cultures that had a different sense of time and that encouraged active involvement in family life (Weber, 1904–1905/1958). All cultural groups were measured in terms of how similar they were to the "norms" set by the White culture; the more different they were, the more they were excluded and considered inferior or deviant (Frankenberg, 2008).

A social myth of the United States as a meritocracy was created; success was assumed to come to all who had merit and who worked hard. People were assumed to be the masters of their own destiny. A malignant corollary was that individuals who were financially successful were morally superior to individuals who had less money and possessions. Thus, the idea of "agency" came to be intermixed with the idea that only the morally weak or lazy would be poor or disadvantaged (Quinn & Crocker, 1999). In addition, the active exclusion of non-White groups from employment opportunities, and how this served as a serious barrier to success, was ignored (Zweig, 2008). Parenting practices were changed to support the ideals of White cultural success. Parents trained their sons to focus on long-range goals, be sensitive to signs of success, and actively pursue it. Parents might promote the view that short-term failure was acceptable, as long as the son learned important lessons that would support success in the long run (Ng, Pomerantz, & Lam, 2007). This fostered the view that healthy males were independent and competitive. To build a self-confident and independent son, White parents have been found to provide positive feedback for successes while downplaying situations involving failure. As some segments of society have become more androgynous, these parenting practices have also been applied to girls. Middle-class, White parents may use reasoning strategies, within their disciplinary practices, to encourage their children to take the initiative and behave independently. A side effect of this may be that adolescents have less respect for authority figures during decision-making (S. V. Dixon, Graber, & Brooks-Gunn, 2008). Overall, White adolescents have been found to consider autonomy from their parents a high priority (Fuligni, 1998).

White people are a heterogeneous group composed of people from different ethnicities and religions. What they have in common is the privilege that comes with being White in the United States. As a result, white-skinned immigrants automatically have an advantage when they are trying to integrate into the society of the United States. They have the implicit privilege of considering their racial category as nonexistent or "unmarked," their values and behaviors as natural or the norm in society, and their cultural values as the reference point for all other cultures (Frankenberg, 2008, p. 81; L. Smith, Constantine, Graham, & Diz, 2008). White parents assume they can keep their children out of situations where they will be mistreated, and White children turn on the television and see members of their race portrayed as the "good guys" (McIntosh, 2008).

D. W. Sue and D. Sue (2013) call these advantages "unearned privileges" because they haven't come as the result of any positive action on the part of the individual. Members of the White culture have more social and political power than other races and ethnic groups, and they maintain this greater power through carrying out explicit and implicit policies that maintain a society of racial inequality (Frankenberg, 2008). Whites can continue to believe they live in a meritocracy and be blind to their unearned power (McIntosh, 2008). Whites may find it difficult to recognize that they are racists, as the oppressive nature of society toward people of color is built into the structures of society. One possible solution would be to make whiteness visible, such as by challenging racist comments and overpowering attempts to silence the voices of people of color, and by recognizing internal negative reactions that may be a result of internalized racism (Case, 2012).

The people in power in the United States are primarily White. As a result of prejudice, discrimination, and marginalization, most non-White populations in the United States express strong negative feelings against Whites (Sue & Sue, 2013). However, many Whites do not have access to power and have worked in sweatshops and experienced financial oppression (Frankenberg, 2008). However, the fact that they have White skin has given them the ability to assimilate, while other groups have been actively excluded from assimilation. It has allowed these individuals to live in any neighborhood where they can afford the cost, to vote without facing impediments on Election Day, to take it as a given that the school system and judicial system will be responsive to their needs, and to have the right to fight against injustice (Frankenberg, 2008; Sue & Sue, 2013). Many White individuals perceive themselves as "color-blind" and think that they judge people only by their own unique qualities; while they may acknowledge the existence of racism, they vastly underestimate its prevalence and impact. These types of beliefs support the racism of today, which consists of microaggressions carrying a highly negative impact on people of color (L. Smith et al., 2008; Sue & Sue, 2013). Whites are unaware of the privileges their skin gives them. For example, in missing a college class, a White student may feel comfortable asking the professor, who is probably White, for extra help. In addition, this student may feel comfortable asking to copy the notes of anyone else in class; most of his or her classmates are likely to be White. In contrast, an African American student may not feel comfortable approaching a White professor, having experienced many directly racist acts, as well as many microaggressions, in school in the past. In addition, this student may only feel comfortable asking another African American student for notes, and there may not be another African American student to ask. This might lead the student to fall behind in class while the White student is able to catch up (McIntosh, 2008).

The current domination of White culture within the United States, and the domination of the United States in world affairs, serves as implicit justification of the superiority of White culture and the justice of its imposition of its values on other cultural groups (Frankenberg, 2008). Economics is inextricably linked to race. The middle and upper class formed the attitudes and behaviors now assumed to be from White culture. Lack of money brings with it crowded housing, little privacy, and jobs that involve intense, physical labor. These factors keep non-White cultural groups from living in the ways that Whites consider "traditional," "normal," and "healthy" (Frankenberg, 2008).

Two general forms of White privilege exist within society. One is the privilege to be treated with respect and to have fair access to education, housing, and so forth. This type of privilege should be extended to all racial and ethnic groups. The second type of privilege is the malignant kind; it confers the power to dominate others. This type of privilege needs to be eradicated (McIntosh, 2008).

The values of White middle-class culture have been infused into the treatment strategies used by clinicians, and thus most White clients will feel more comfortable than non-White clients in the treatment setting. These embedded values include (a) an individualistic orientation, (b) an emphasis on verbal expressiveness and thus a reliance on a facility with English, (c) an emphasis on active participation of the client in communicating needs and solving problems, (d) an emphasis on emotional expressiveness as key to health, and (e) a future orientation with an emphasis on long-term goals (Sue & Sue, 2013).

Red-Flag Racial and Ethnic Guidelines

1. Assess the role of clients' self-identified racial and ethnic group(s) in their lives in terms of the strengths, resources, and power it (they) may be bringing to them within personal, family, social, vocational, and political spheres.

2. Consider what entrenched dominant cultural worldviews, institutions, policies, and practices may be leading to discrimination, prejudice, and racism and setting up barriers to clients' healthy development at this time.

3. Consider what current events may be leading to increased discrimination, prejudice, and racism and thus setting up barriers to clients' healthy development at this time.

4. Consider what historical events have influenced clients' identified racial and ethnic group(s) and assess whether any of their current problem(s) could be a result of direct or indirect oppression or trauma, their responses to this oppression, assimilation stress, discrimination, prejudice and racism, or a mismatch in values with the dominant society and its institutions.

5. Assess how well clients are functioning overall in terms of their values, beliefs, and behaviors, both through the worldview of their racial and ethnic heritage and through the worldview of the dominant cultural group; discuss whether any of their behavior within the dominant society might represent a healthy adaptation to injustice that would be supported by their racial and ethnic community.

6. Consider whether successful treatment will involve more internal awareness or actions on the part of the client or if it will involve more actions to change policies, procedures, and values of an environment that is oppressing the clients; consider if there are any culturally specific resources, treatment strategies, or helpers clients would value at this time that might be effectively used within your treatment plan.

Self-Analysis Guidelines

1. What is your current knowledge of your client's racial or ethnic group(s)?

   a. How many courses have you taken that give you background on the client's racial or ethnic group(s)?

   b. How many workshops have you attended that give you background on the client's racial or ethnic group(s)?

   c. What professional experiences have you had with the client's racial or ethnic group(s)?

   d. What personal experience have you had with the client's racial or ethnic group(s)?

   e. What is the worldview of the client's racial or ethnic group(s).

2. What is your current level of awareness of issues relevant to the client's racial or ethnic group(s)?

   a. What stereotypes have you heard about the client's cultural and racial groups?

   b. What are some ways in which the dominant culture's biases may have operated in your life?

   c. What role have your racial and ethnic groups played in your life?

   d. In comparing your racial and cultural affiliations to those of the client, what differences could lead to communication problems, value conflicts, difficulties in understanding the client's lifestyle or experiences, or an invalidation of the client's strengths?

3. What are your current skills in working with clients of this (these) racial or ethnic group(s)?

    a. What skills do you currently have that are of value in working with this client's cultural and racial identifications?

    b. What skills do you feel it would be important to develop to work effectively with the client's cultural and racial identifications?

4. What action steps can you take?

    a. What might you change in how you interact within the rapport-building phase to develop a more effective working alliance with a client of this (these) racial or ethnic group(s)?

    b. How might you structure the treatment environment to increase the likelihood of a positive outcome with clients from this (these) racial or ethnic group(s)?

    c. What aspects of the theoretical orientation you are planning to use with this client might contain implicit cultural or racial biases? What will you change to promote effective treatment?

    d. What might you change in the treatment-planning phase to increase the likelihood of a positive outcome with clients from this (these) racial or ethnic group(s)?

THE DOMAIN OF SEXUAL ORIENTATION

Sixteen-year-old Eric is struggling to come to terms with his sexual identity amid family chaos (Chapter 4). Ellen is lonely and trying to improve her relationships with her family now that she has come out as a lesbian (Chapter 7). While sexual orientation is often discussed as an individual characteristic, the American Psychological Association (2008) considers this definition inadequate, as sexual orientation is embedded within an individual's interactions with others. These interactions are intended to meet the individual's need for intimacy, love, and attachment. Thus, Eric's and Ellen's sexual orientations should be taken into account as you try to help them strengthen their interpersonal relationships. If someone's sexual orientation is expressed within interpersonal interactions, how might it influence the therapeutic relationship?

A common misconception is that same-sex couples are different than heterosexual couples. Discrimination and prejudice aside, these couples form families for the same reasons (APA, 2008). In 2011, 1% of households in the United States, or 605,000 households, reported themselves to be same-sex couples. Of these, 28% reported themselves as same-sex spouses (Lofquist, 2011). There were greater discrepancies in age between same-sex partners than between heterosexual partners. In addition, there was a gender difference, with more males having a partner 10 years older than himself (25%) than females having a partner 10 years older than herself (18%); this difference from heterosexual couples may be due to a more restricted partner pool for gay and lesbian individuals (Lofquist, 2011).

Attitudes around sexual exclusivity for sexual minority couples have been found to differ from those for heterosexual couples. The American Couples Study found that only 36% of gay males valued monogamy in comparison to 75% of heterosexual males. In addition, while 71% of lesbians valued monogamy, 84% of heterosexual women did. In both cases, females valued monogamy more than males (Peplau & Fingerhut, 2007).

The United States Supreme Court struck down the Defense of Marriage Act (DOMA) on June 26, 2013 (*United States v. Windsor*). It was considered unconstitutional as it violated the Fifth Amendment, which indicates that citizens should have equal liberty. Still, in 2014, there remains significant political controversy over whether same-sex couples should be allowed to marry, and it's still considered acceptable by some politicians to make homophobic comments. For example, in 2011, Representative Franks (R-Arizona) indicated, "Marriage equality is a threat to the nation's survival in the long run" and in 2013, Representative Michele Bachmann (R-Minnesota) stated that Christians must engage in "spiritual warfare" to combat same-sex marriage (Hagan, 2013). Homophobia aside, as of this writing, same-sex couples have the freedom to marry in 27 states and Washington, D.C. In addition, nearly 44% of the population of the United States lives in states where same-sex couples have the freedom to marry. Finally, 48% of the population lives in states that offer some form of protection to same-sex couples (Freedom to Marry, 2013).

Sexual orientation was defined by the American Psychological Association (2008) as

an enduring pattern of emotional, romantic, or sexual attractions to men, women, or both sexes. Sexual orientation also refers to a person's sense of identity based on those attractions, related behaviors, and membership in a community of others who share those attractions.

While it is common to think about sexual orientation as a categorical variable, in fact it appears to range along a continuum, where at one end an individual is attracted exclusively to individuals of the same sex and at the other end an individual is attracted exclusively to individuals of the other sex (APA, 2008). Sexual orientation is different from a person's biological sex, which is defined genetically, and an individual's gender attitudes and behaviors, which are defined culturally.

Eric's and Ellen's gender identity includes both their psychological sense of being male or female as well as how closely they are adhering to what society defines as feminine or masculine behavior (APA, 2008). Sexual orientation is also different from the sexual activities a person engages in. For example, some individuals engage in sexual behavior with an other-sex partner or a same-sex partner purely for the sake of convenience (Savin-Williams, 2001). Eric and Ellen express their sexual orientation—unlike their biological sex—in relation to others. Whatever the specific behaviors (hand-holding, kissing, barebacking), the intent is to get needs met for love, attachment, or intimacy. Sexual orientation does define the social group from which one is most likely to find a fulfilling romantic relationship but does not define emotional stability (APA, 2008).

Sexual minorities can self-identify in a variety of ways, including as gay or lesbian, bisexual, questioning, queer, or pansexual (Zea & Nakamura, 2014). Self-identification of sexual orientation is important for self-respect and emotional well-being. Thus, treatment for sexual orientation concerns should involve helping an individual cope with social prejudices against sexual minorities and come to his or her own self-definition of sexual orientation. There is no evidence that "reparative" or "conversion" therapy is safe, and it reinforces negative stereotypes of sexual minorities that can be harmful (APA, 2008).

Recent statements about the psychological health of sexual minority youth, and ethical guidelines of the American Psychological Association (2005a, 2012), the American Psychiatric Association (American Psychiatric Association, Commission on Psychotherapy for Psychiatrists, 2000), and the Association for Lesbian, Gay, Bisexual, and Transgender Issues in Counseling (2012), stress the importance of recognizing sexual minorities as following a different but normal developmental pathway. These guidelines also stress that providers must learn how to respond to these clients in affirming and constructive ways. In a policy statement on lesbian and gay issues, the American Psychological Association's Committee on Lesbian and Gay Concerns (1991, p. 1) stated that "homosexuality per se implies no impairment in judgment, stability, reliability or general social and vocational capabilities" and went on to indicate that practitioners have an obligation to educate the public about this. Public attitudes toward homosexuality are not static and have rapidly been changing (T. Smith, 2011). In the General Social Survey taken in 2010 by the National Opinion Research Center (NORC) at the University of Chicago, a sharp divide in public opinion was revealed when 44% of their population sample indicated that "sexual relations between two adults of the same sex" were always wrong while 41% indicated that such relations were "not wrong at all." This may be a result of cohort effects, as younger individuals were much more likely to indicate acceptance of homosexuality than older individuals (Smith, 2011).

Sexual minority individuals may come to treatment more often than their heterosexual peers. Prejudice and discrimination can have a negative social and personal impact (APA, 2008). While some sexual minority individuals cope in an adaptive way to the negative stereotypes and social stigma associated with nonheteronormative behavior, this type of stress can bring sexual minority group members into treatment more often than heterosexuals (Cochran, 2001). Discrimination may include easily definable actions such as being denied a job or bank loan. It may also include subtler negative actions that leave the individual feeling disrespectfully treated. At the present time, federal laws do not protect sexual minorities from discrimination in housing or in the workplace (Human Rights Campaign, 2000). Due to the greater likelihood of facing daily discrimination and prejudice in their neighborhoods and of being bullied and harassed at school or in the workplace, some sexual minority individuals will engage in high-risk activities, including unprotected sex and drug and alcohol use (APA, 2008). Sexual minority individuals have also been found to have a higher risk for depression, suicidal ideation, and suicide attempts than heterosexuals (APA, 2008; Herek & Garnets, 2007).

Therefore, the ability to "come out" may at times rest on whether it is economically viable to do so. While there are realistic risks to the coming-out process, there are also clear benefits. Individuals have cited gaining a sense of personal freedom to be who they are as an individual. This freedom also allows them to develop deeper relationships with others that are based on self-affirming behavior rather than social facades (Riggle, Whitman, Olson, Rostosky, & Strong, 2008). In a two-year longitudinal research project by Bauermeister and colleagues (2010), women reported that being involved in a same-sex relationship decreased their internal homophobia, and men reported that being in a same-sex relationship increased their self-esteem. Unlike in previous studies, being involved in a heterosexual relationship had neither a positive nor a negative impact on well-being, while being involved in a same-sex relationship was associated with feeling happy. Social climates that don't tolerate harassment, bullying, and discrimination do much to support the healthy development of sexual minority youths (APA, 2008).

Recognition that one is a member of a sexual minority group often emerges during middle childhood and adolescence. While some people recognize their sexual orientation early on, some sexual minority individuals may engage in a variety of sexual activities before being clear about their self-identification (APA, 2008). Biologically timed changes in physical development bring with them a budding interest in sexuality for most youth. Sexual activity is not necessary for an individual to recognize their sexual orientation. However, sexual minority youth can struggle to come to a sense of their sexual orientation when they are living within a "heterosexist" or "homonegative" context (Beckstead & Israel, 2007, p. 222). This is because cultural messages about sexuality, as expressed by parents, religious leaders, the media, and other influential socialization agents, can be exclusively heterosexual and homonegative—that is, suggesting that homosexual development is inherently less healthy than heterosexual development (Savin-Williams, 2001). Surveys of sexual minority youth have indicated that they self- identify in a variety of ways: 61% as gay or lesbian, 32% as bisexual, 3% as questioning, and 4.5% as "other" (Kosciw, Greytak, Diaz, & Bartkiewicz; 2010).

Public opinion has become increasingly against discrimination and increasingly for tolerance (T. Smith, 2011). Despite this, there is still a great deal of antigay prejudice in society. Research finds verbal harassment and abuse to be universal experiences for sexual minorities, and there are still high rates of severe acts of harassment and violence against sexual minorities. In fact, gay and lesbian individuals may discriminate against bisexuals or transsexuals (APA, 2008).

It is common for youth to experience their sexual orientation as something they have little or no choice about. Scientific study of sexual orientation generally considers it to be a complex interaction of nature and nurture (APA, 2008). When heterosexual youth are confused about their identity, they can try out new roles and behaviors they see modeled by other overtly heterosexual individuals. They will receive at least some parental acceptance of this exploratory behavior. These same types of exploratory opportunities may not exist for homosexuals and bisexuals. If they do find potential partners, they usually do not receive validation from family, peers, or the media in regard to exploring their feelings. Instead, they often face prejudice and disapproval from adult peers, violence at home, and hate crimes in their communities (Schneider, Brown, & Glassgold, 2002). Fears about AIDS also have intensified prejudice and discrimination against sexual minorities despite evidence that it is not a "gay" disease (APA, 2008). While individuals are increasingly disapproving of overt discrimination, it is still common for sexual minorities to experience a great deal of hostility from others (APA, 2008).

School can be a dangerous place for lesbian, gay, bisexual, and transgender (LGBT) youth. Victimization at school contributes to lower academic achievement and lower self-esteem. Institutional supports, such as the presence of adults in school who are supportive of LGBT students, is related to lower absenteeism. Inclusive school policies that increase sexual minority youth connection and engagement, such as curricula that include education about sexual minority issues, clubs such as gay–straight alliances, and comprehensive anti-bullying and anti-harassment policies, have been found to positively influence self-esteem, increase school achievement, and decrease absenteeism (Kosciw, Palmer, Kull, Greytak, 2014).

Some heterosexual parents, while not overtly rejecting their minority teens, may still not be fully accepting. Parents assume their children will be heterosexual and may be unprepared for the truth. They may invalidate their teens' growing sexual awareness by saying their children are too young to decide and by encouraging them not to rush into making any decisions (Schneider et al., 2002). Sexual minority teens have sometimes given in to psychological pressure to ignore their sexual feelings so that they will fit within religious and cultural norms (Haldeman, 2000). Savin-Williams (2001) reported that overall, 25% to 84% of sexual minority youth did not come out to their families out of fear of losing either financial or emotional support.

The coming-out process for teens may be a complex one due to discrimination and prejudice against sexual minorities (APA, 2008). The first step might involve an increasing personal awareness and an ability to label one's sexual identity; the next step might be making the first disclosure to someone else and then proceeding to tell "important" others. However, many people don't go through such a linear process, and there may be many different trajectories to development rather than one stage model (Savin-Williams, 2001). There also may be a multiplicity of reasons a youth decides not to come out fully or to stay fully closeted until he or she is ready to be independent from the family (Hershberger & D'Augelli, 2000). Some sexual minority teens have felt that their family relationships would be jeopardized if they came out, while others find that this leads to improved relationships. Youth don't have control of the neighborhoods they live in or the schools they attend. Sexual minority youth who come out to others may be bullied and harassed at school (APA, 2008). Acculturation into the LGBT community takes place later in life, as these youth are usually born to heterosexual parents. They may seek to join a LGBT community in adolescence or adulthood. Each individual needs to determine how integrated he or she wants to be in this community, which is separate from the mainstream (Zea & Nakamura, 2014).

In addition, individuals have complex identities. Aspects of an individual's identity do not exist in a vacuum. One common point of intersection is that of an individual's racial or ethnic identification with his or her sexual orientation. Another example is the intersection of someone's sexual orientation with his or her gender (Zea & Nakamura, 2014). This might result in few opportunities for individuals to explore their identity without risking being outed by peers from their other social groups (Hershberger & D'Augelli, 2000). A sexual minority individual can choose to pass as heterosexual within communities in which he or she has concerns about coming out. This can result in dating in bars and clubs outside his or her neighborhood. Bars and clubs have been designed for adults and may have a highly sexualized atmosphere. Thus, sexual minority youth may need strategies for navigating through these shoals and selecting safe and appropriate partners for dating (Hershberger & D'Augelli, 2000).

Even in adulthood, society pressures sexual minorities to change to a heterosexual identity (Beckstead & Israel, 2007). Human beings have unique personalities and backgrounds and want to participate in a broad spectrum of social groups (Bartoli & Gillem, 2008). However, sexual minorities frequently feel forced to choose between their sexual identity and another aspect of their identity, such as their religious or ethnic beliefs (Beckstead & Israel, 2007). It has been found that more individuals self-identify as lesbian, gay, or bisexual than report engaging in same-sex behavior (Gates, 2010). This may well be due to external and internal homophobia (Zea & Nakamura, 2014). As a result, a period of questioning one's own sexuality may occur, which could last for years as individuals try to make peace between diverse aspects of themselves. These ambivalent struggles with "who am I" are a common part of the coming-out process and are likely to lead eventually to a healthy and sexually integrated identity. However, some ambivalent individuals have participated in conversion therapies; 66% of them do this to fit in with their religious beliefs. Conversion therapy has negative consequences for most individuals, including an increased level of homophobia and self-loathing because of an inability to change, hatred for parents whose parenting mistakes are blamed for a nonheterosexual orientation, feelings of depression and loneliness, the loss of support from sexual minority communities, misinformation about the causes of sexual minority desires, and fear of being or becoming a child abuser (APA, 2014; Shidlo & Schroeder, 2002). While therapy that helps individuals clarify their sexual identity can be helpful, the American Academy of Pediatrics, the American Counseling Association, the American Psychiatric Association, the American Psychological Association, the American School Counselor Association, and the National Association of Social Workers all clearly state that any treatment that treats homosexuality as a sickness, a mental disorder, a sign of emotional problems, or a sin is harmful to the individual's well-being (APA, 2014).

Sexual minority members often become parents. Sometimes this occurs because the individual was living a heterosexual lifestyle. However, some cohorts, such as lesbians in the 1980s, began using reproductive technologies to become parents within same-sex unions. In addition, sexual minority members became foster parents and adoptive parents around this same time due to the needs of the child welfare system (Cooper & Cates, 2006). Research has found that they are just as likely as heterosexual parents to provide appropriate parenting. No significant differences have been found between the developmental patterns and psychological adjustment of children raised by lesbians and those of children raised by heterosexuals (Cooper & Cates, 2006). In addition, young children have been found to be highly accepting of their sexual minority parents. This dynamic might change during puberty. Teens may go through a period where they are embarrassed by their parents' same-sex attractions and partners.

Sexual minority parents may have realistic fears of losing custody of their children during divorce proceedings (American Civil Liberties Union, 1999). If their same-sex families break up, the legal precedents are still scant and unstable. Individual judges have significant power in interpreting the custody statute of "best interest of the child," and there have been significant levels of discrimination documented in states such as Alabama, Mississippi, North Carolina, and Virginia (Cooper & Cates, 2006; DeAngelis, 2002).

While sexual minorities face significant stress from prejudice and discrimination, there are protective factors that support resiliency in the face of this stress, including satisfactory relationships with family, a positive gay identity, and a sense of belonging to a group

(Zea & Nakamura, 2014). Clinicians are ethically mandated to advocate for the full human rights of sexual minorities, as what these individuals may need for increased mental health is increased civil rights. The media have also been a driving force in support of these human rights. While motivated by profit rather than ethics, the media have provided a growing stream of sexual minority role models within movies and television. Stars such as Ellen DeGeneres have been able to maintain their popularity after coming out to the public. There have also been growing numbers of political leaders who were open about their sexual minority status prior to their election to office. For example, Senator Tammy Baldwin from Wisconsin identifies herself as a lesbian, Representative Jared Polis from Colorado identifies himself as gay, and Representative Kyrsten Sinema from Arizona identifies herself as bisexual.

The Internet provides a private forum where individuals can gain a wealth of information on sexuality. Agencies such as PFLAG (Parents, Families and Friends of Lesbians and Gays) and GLSEN (the Gay, Lesbian, Straight Education Network) support the healthy development of sexual minorities, and COLAGE (Children of Lesbians and Gays Everywhere) provides education and support for children of sexual minority parents. Thus, while negative stereotyping, discrimination, and hate crimes are still forces to contend with, many positive forces also exist that provide a background of normality to individuals as they explore their sexual identities.

Red-Flag Sexual Orientation Guidelines

1. Assess where clients are in the process of identifying their sexual orientation in terms of their desires, fantasies, attitudes, emotions, and behavior related to sexuality and whether their sexual identification is stable, ambivalent, questioning, or shifting.

2. Assess the past and present environments that are influencing clients' comfort with their sexual identification, including strengths and barriers within their work or school environment, family relationships, and social relationships and their level of access to information and resources.

3. Assess the (potential) benefits of clients' coming out. If they have not yet come out, assess which aspects of their world might benefit the most from their coming out at this time, considering their personal identity, family relationships, peer relationships, and educational or vocational relationships.

4. Assess the (potential) costs of clients' coming out. If they have not yet come out, assess which aspects of their world might carry the most risk in the coming-out process, considering their personal identity, family relationships, peer relationships, and educational or vocational relationships.

5. Assess whether clients need to find a common ground between their sexual identity and other aspects of their identity, such as religious affiliation or racial or ethnic heritage, and consider how to connect them with resources and decrease barriers to this process.

Self-Analysis Guidelines

1. What is your current knowledge of issues relevant to sexual orientation?

   a. How many courses have you taken that give you background on sexual orientation?

   b. How many workshops have you attended that give you background on sexual orientation?

   c. What professional experiences have you had with clients about issues relevant to sexual orientation?

   d. What personal experiences have you had with individuals who are sexual minorities?

   e. What cohort effects might influence the worldview of sexual minorities? What is important to them at this point in history? How does society reward or punish people based on their sexuality?

2. What is your current level of awareness of issues relevant to sexual orientation?

   a. What positive and negative stereotypes did you learn about heterosexuality and sexual minority identities as you were growing up?

   b. How was societal homophobia present as you were growing up?

   c. How is societal homophobia present in your current family, social, cultural, and political groups?

   d. How might societal homophobia and the assumption that everyone is heterosexual lead you to unintentionally marginalize or invalidate your client's experiences or point of view?

3. What are your current skills in working with clients of different sexual orientations?

   a. What skills do you currently have that are of value in working with issues of sexuality or sexual orientation?

   b. What skills do you feel it would be important to develop to work effectively with issues of sexuality or sexual orientation?

4. What action steps can you take?

   a. What can you do to enhance your ability to form a strong therapeutic alliance with clients of this sexual orientation?

   b. What aspects of the treatment approach that you plan to use with this client have possibly been developed from a heterosexual point of view? What can you do about it?

   c. How might you structure the treatment environment to increase the likelihood of a positive outcome with clients having this sexual orientation?

THE DOMAIN OF SOCIOECONOMIC STATUS

Ann, a 70-year-old European American woman, is being financially exploited by her adult daughter, who considers herself a member of the financial elite despite being unemployed (Chapter 5). Sharon, a 34-year-old European American woman, raised as a member of the working poor, is struggling to parent her children as a new member of the upper class (Chapter 6). Zechariah, a 19-year-old African American male, the first member of his family to enter college, is accused of being a danger to others (Chapter 11). What role, if any, might their income level and social status play in their current dilemmas? Socioeconomic status (SES) is an index that attempts to represent someone's income as well as access to resources in health care, housing, and education.

Census Data

SES can enhance or limit opportunities within a person's public and private life. December 2007 to June 2009 was a period of severe recession in the United States (Kochhar, Fry, & Taylor; 2011). Analysis of 2009 census data indicated an increase in wealth disparities between Whites, Blacks, and Hispanics. The net worth of White households was 18 times that of Hispanic households and 20 times that of Black households. One reason for this increase in wealth disparity was the sharp decline in household values, which had a disproportionately greater impact on minority households than on White households. Minority households were twice as likely to have their homes go into foreclosure as White households (Kochhar et al., 2011). Overall median household wealth showed decreases across all groups from 2005 to 2009; however, while this was a 16% drop for Whites, it was a 53% drop for Blacks, a 54% drop for Asians, and a 66% drop for Hispanics.

For most individuals, one's home is one's greatest asset. Thus, the housing crisis brought on by inappropriate loans and inappropriate banking caused a devastating reduction in many people's household wealth (Kochhar et al., 2011). Some Whites and Asians may have had the impact of the decline in their home values partially offset by an increase in the wealth they had invested in interest-earning assets, such as stocks and mutual funds. Such assets are owned by 45% of Whites and Asians but only 25% to 30% of Hispanics.

During 2007–2008 of the recession, there was a collapse of stock market values and a loss of 7.5 million jobs. The impact of the recession was quite different for low- and middle-income families in comparison to wealthy families. As the lower-SES groups were showing a sharp drop in economic well-being during 2005–2009, the wealth held by the top 10% of every racial and ethnic showed an increase. This increased the wealth disparity between the top 10% and the bottom 90% of financial worth (Kochhar et al., 2011).

The income of full-time workers went down 2% from 2010 to 2011. In the United States in 2012, the median household income within the general population was $51,017 (DeNavas-Walt et al., 2013). This is far behind the $677,900 of the wealthiest households (U.S. Census Bureau, 2006). Statistics indicate a clear chasm growing between the most and least financially successful populations within the United States. Shapiro, Greenstein, and Primus (2001) analyzed data from the Center on Budget and Policy Priorities and concluded that after-tax income for the poor has dropped by $100 in recent years, from $10,900 to

$10,800. Within the same time interval, the wealthiest households saw their income increase by 36% from $263,700 to $677,900. The middle fifth of households had their income rise by 10%. Thus, the gap between the poor and the middle class has broadened, and the middle class has been left far behind by the rich. This increased income disparity resulted from tax legislation promoted by President George W. Bush during his two presidencies. The United States is now the fourth most unequal nation among the 34 wealthiest countries in the world (Shapiro, Greenstein, & Primus, 2001).

Who are the poor in the United States? They represent 15% of the total population, or 46.2 million people (DeNavas-Walt et al., 2013). Currently, 14.3% of the U.S. population lives below the poverty line (Macartney et al., 2013). Longitudinal studies of poverty reveal a complex picture (Anderson, 2011). Over a 36-month period, 29% of the population spent at least two months in poverty; however, only 3% remained in poverty throughout the whole period. Most people are able to leave poverty within two months. Statistics on poverty vary by racial and ethnic group and gender of the adult in charge of the household. In 2012, the highest median income of $68,636 belonged to Asian households (DeNavas-Walt et al., 2013). However, White, married families have the lowest poverty rates. The real median income for a non-Hispanic White household was $57,009 (DeNavas-Walt et al., 2013). When children are living with both parents, statistics indicate they are most economically well off (U.S. Census Bureau, 2004). Seventy percent of children whose parents are still married lived in households that were at least 200% above the poverty level (Vespa et al., 2013). These married families are still the most common family arrangement (Vespa et al., 2013). However, between 1970 and 2012, the proportion of households headed by one individual increased from 17% to 27% (Vespa et al., 2013). Married-couple households numbered 56 million, while 5 million male householders and 15 million female householders lacked a spouse (Vespa et al., 2013). At all ages, there are more females living below the poverty line than males (Macartney & Mykyta, 2012).

Children living without both parents were less well off. The poverty rate for White children living only with their mothers was 28.1%, in comparison to 14.1% for those who lived only with their fathers. In 2012, it was more likely for Black and Hispanic children to live with one parent than for non-Hispanic White or Asian children to do so (Vespa et al., 2013). The ethnic or racial group with the highest poverty rate was American Indians and Alaska Natives, at 23.9% below the poverty line (Macartney et al., 2013). The populations with the lowest percentages of people living below the poverty level were Whites (11.6%), Asians (11.7%), Hispanics (23.2), members of "some other race" (24.6%), and African Americans (25.8%) (Macartney et al., 2013).

More females (16%) than males (14%) are living below the poverty level, and 22% of the poor are children (DeNavas-Walt et al., 2013). One million of these children are part of homeless families (Macartney et al., 2013). Seventy percent of poor families contain a parent who is working; a killing combination of low wages, high living costs, and high medical and other critical resource costs keeps these families living below the poverty line (Children's Defense Fund [CDF], 2008). In the United States in 2011, most poor children were White. However, proportionally, only 19% of White children were living below the poverty line compared to 37% of Black children and 34% of Hispanic children (DeNavas-Walt et al., 2013). Living below the poverty line is most likely in households where the mother is the head of the household. Fifty-seven percent of children under 6 who are living with a female householder are being raised in poverty. In addition, 5.8 million children under the age of 6 are living below the poverty level. In 2012, the real median income for households maintained by women with no spouse was $34,002 (DeNavas-Walt et al., 2013).

The United States spends more of its gross domestic product on health care than any other country, yet it ranks only 37th out of 191 countries in quality of health care, according to the 2002 World Health Report (WHO, 2002). This low ranking is caused by the large percentage of the population that is uninsured as well as the significant discrepancy that exists between the quality of health care given to the poor and that given to the rich (WHO, 2000). When a family member becomes seriously ill, it represents a crisis for poor families. Illness leads them into greater indebtedness as they try to pay for services they can't afford. Lack of access to quality care may result in family members dying or being left with disabilities that would have been preventable (WHO, 2000). In 2012, 15.4% of the U.S. population did not possess health insurance (DeNavas-Walt et al., 2013).

Within the United States, 6.6 million children have no health insurance, and this problem is much more severe for children of color than for White children (DeNavas-Walt et al., 2013). Social disadvantage has shown a relationship to increased health risk. The less affluent a child's living circumstances, the lower his or her access to health care, healthy foods such as fresh fruits and vegetables, and healthy outlets for exercise that are fee based. They are also exposed to greater health risks brought on by increased exposure to psychosocial stress (Currie, Zanotti, et al., 2012).

Brief History

The three major class distinctions in the United States could be made on the basis of how much power, independence in decision making, and quality of life a group has (Zweig, 2008). As a group, the capitalists (2% of the labor force) have the power to dominate the workplace and the political arena. Even among this top group, there is considerable diversity of power. Individuals who are in charge of the largest corporations (less than 0.2%) control not only their own money but the wealth of the nation. These predominantly White men, along with the top political leaders of the federal government, could be said to constitute a "ruling class" within the United States (Zweig, 2008, p. 132). Neighborhoods that provide the bulk of financial support for political campaigns are predominantly White, older, and conservative and come from more concentrated metropolitan areas than the individuals who live in low-donor neighborhoods (Bramlett, Gimpel, & Lee, 2011). In terms of political opinions, they are more supportive of open trade and immigration, same-sex marriage, and abortion rights, and more opposed to school prayer. On other issues, Bramlett and associates did not find them to be significantly different than average or low-donor areas.

Middle-class individuals have significantly less power than the capitalists, but they have traditionally held stable jobs, owned homes and cars, and taken paid vacations. This class contains professionals (lawyers, doctors, professors, etc.) and small-business owners, as well as supervisors in industry; this group represents 36% of the population. They may have some political clout through lobbying from their professional associations. The border between this group and the capitalists may be unclear, as some high-level corporate attorneys and accountants, for example, may make salaries commensurate with those of some capitalists. Middle-class individuals have considerable authority over what they do, but they are not final decision makers, and it is the power to control decisions that sets the capitalists apart from the middle class (Zweig, 2008).

Working-class individuals may, through overtime, make as much money as middle-class workers; however, they don't have the power to control their work tasks or work calendar and do not receive the same respect for their work as middle-class workers do. Their jobs are regimented, they have limited autonomy in how they conduct their work and in the pace of their work, and they don't have authority to make decisions. This class (62% of the labor force) has little power except as represented by the unions they may belong to, which do lobby for their membership (Zweig, 2008).

Economic welfare is highly dependent on educational achievement. As schools are funded by property taxes, there are serious disparities in quality between the schools available to wealthy children, those available to middle-class children, and those available to poor children. If a neighborhood school begins to deteriorate, middle- and upper-income households may be able to move out of these neighborhoods and into areas with better schools. This leaves an even smaller income base to support the schools, and so a further decline in quality occurs. The children left behind go to schools that are run down, poorly equipped, crowded, and often dangerous (Books, 2007). Head Start, which helps children learn to be successful in school, only receives enough funding to enroll one half to two thirds of income-eligible children (CDF, 2008).

In the 25-and-older group, 80.4% are high school graduates, and 24.4% went on to achieve either a bachelor's degree or a higher professional degree. Over one third of married men and women have a bachelor's degree (Vespa et al., 2013). Almost 25% of children live in a home with someone with at least a bachelor's degree (U.S. Census Bureau, 2004).

Schools are more effective when parents are actively involved, but poor, working parents have no time to do this. National surveys show that 60% of parents living above the poverty line are involved in school activities on a regular basis. In contrast, only 36% of poor parents are similarly involved (U.S. Department of Health and Human Services, 1999). This further increases poor children's lack of identification with their school, which has also been found to lower educational success (G. W. Evans, 2004). Current statistics reveal that two thirds of fourth graders educated in public schools can't read or do math at grade level. This deficiency is higher in minority children than White children (CDF, 2008). Due to having jobs with low wages, poor parents must work long hours to pay the bills. This leaves them little time to spend with their children. Thus, while 40% to 58% of families above the poverty line read to their preschool children, only 38% of low-income families do. Poor parents are also more likely to allow their children to watch television more and read less (U.S. Department of Health and Human Services, Federal Interagency Forum on Child and Family Statistics, 2008). A new type of educational risk factor that limits the educational attainment of poor children is their lack of access to the Internet. Ninety-four percent of poor children have no access to the Internet; this lack of access occurs for only 57% of more affluent youth (G. W. Evans, 2004).

Poor families are also more likely to live in dangerous neighborhoods where children are exposed to personal risk and trauma, including street violence and involvement in traffic accidents. In addition, they may live in neighborhoods that are closer to toxic waste dumps and other environmental hazards, placing young children at risk for lead and carbon monoxide exposure. Thus, 35% of poor toddlers are exposed to six or more environmental risk factors during development, while this occurs for only 5% of middle-income toddlers (G. W. Evans, 2004).

The longer a family remains in poverty, the more family life deteriorates, with husbands and wives fighting more, parents behaving less responsively to their children, and parents engaging in harsher disciplinary practices (G. W. Evans, 2004). The rates of depression are also higher among the poor, and depressed parents provide poorer-quality care to their children (Mazure et al., 2002). Poor children are also more likely to be separated from their families through foster care and other out-of-home placements than better-off children (G. W. Evans, 2004).

While statistics may lead to the perception that the "average" poor person is from a minority group, in fact, the average adult poor head of household is White, female, and young (U.S. Census Bureau, 2012a). Historical and political contexts can influence society's openness to helping less advantaged people within one's country and the world (Delphin & Rowe, 2008). When the general population is faced with what they consider to be clear and convincing evidence of financial need, they give freely to help others. For example, money poured in to help the victims of the 2001 attack on the World Trade Center. The RAND Corporation (L. Dixon & Stern, 2004) estimated that charitable donations reached $2.7 billion. What concerned citizens were not aware of was how a concerted series of political policies treated the poor as invisible and expendable. The disaster following Hurricane Katrina is a dramatic example. That a disaster was coming had been well predicted. However, 40 years of low-budget governmental policies left the levees in disarray. The Federal Emergency Management Agency (FEMA) had been cut by the Bush presidency and its monetary resources transferred to the war on terror. The poor, encompassing 27% of households, had no way to evacuate and nowhere to go when the hurricane struck, as the only evacuation plan was for individuals to drive themselves out (Ignatieff, 2005). This left the poor to drown. After the initial disaster, political conservatives, in a Republican-dominated Congress, blocked a plan to allow hurricane victims to gain health care using Medicaid (Krugman, 2005). The poor of New Orleans were further exploited by reconstructive efforts. The Davis–Bacon Act, which ensures a decent wage on all federal contracts, was suspended, and political cronies of President Bush and Vice President Cheney got preferential access to contracts to rebuild (Lipton & Nixon, 2005); they exploited the poor further by giving work to those who would accept the smallest wages.

How can such exploitation continue? Often there is no day-to-day evidence of the needs of the poor because middle-class, lower-class, and upper-class families have come to live in different neighborhoods, attend different schools, and are insulated from each other's day-to-day experiences. This leads to ignorance of each other's challenges and strengths and often leads to cognitive distancing where the suffering of the poor is underestimated (Lott, 2002). Middle- and upper-class families can give their children access to the Internet, higher-quality schools, and safer home and neighborhood conditions. Wealthier adults attain higher levels of education and gain greater occupational success. They have the ability to pay for services such as housekeeping, child care, and more comprehensive medical care. Thus, in times of trouble, wealthier individuals have many more resources that they can turn to for help than poor individuals do (Mellander, Florida, & Rentfrow, 2011).

While risks to adaptive emotional and behavioral health have been found among poor teens, similar difficulties with depression, anxiety, and substance abuse have been found among a similarly sized cohort of teens from wealthy families (Luthar & Latendresse, 2005). Common factors that led to these problems in both sets of teens included emotional and physical isolation from parents. These troubled teens represented 1 out of 10 teens within a cohort of all sixth-graders within a suburban school who were followed through the 11th grade. Teens who ate a family meal on most nights did not show these same difficulties. One difference between the poor and wealthy teens in trouble was that the wealthy teens scored high on achievement pressure. Perfectionistic, affluent teens who were not meeting their own or their parents' standards were at higher risk for beginning substance abuse in the early teen years that lasted through age 18. Lack of emotional closeness with affluent parents may be a by-product of the very hectic schedules of both the teens and the parents (Luthar & Latendresse, 2005). While wealthy parents can more easily access mental health services for their troubled teens, there is some evidence that privacy concerns, and the belief that as part of an elite group they should be able to handle everything on their own, might impede their seeking help (Feather & Sherman, 2002).

Individuals' level of income, along with the social context in which it is earned, influences their class identification. Research across 15 industrialized countries suggested that in times of prosperity, individuals in countries with low economic inequality had a greater sense of well-being and trust in the societal structure and the other individuals in it, regardless of their class identification. In addition, there was a tendency for individuals to all identify as middle class. However, in times of prosperity, where there is large economic inequality causing significant disparities in health care, education, and social mobility, there is more class polarization and in-group/out-group conflicts (Curtis, 2013).

Resilience in the face of economic disadvantage is influenced by good communication with family members and positive peer relationships. These supportive relationships help individuals develop prosocial identities, good self-esteem, and social skills. Finally, neighborhood social cohesion serves to decrease risk of both physical and mental health problems (Rios et al., 2012). While gaining an education can be a route out of poverty, they are many barriers to attending college beyond gaining the background and money to arrive in a seat; cultural mismatches between the faculty, institution, and the poor attendee may lead to misunderstandings that make academic success unlikely (Markus & Conner, 2013). Lee and Dean (2004) stress that the middle-class myth, which holds that anyone who consistently works hard and does quality work can become economically advantaged, ignores the role that oppression, lack of opportunity, and lack of resources plays in social mobility. They emphasize that recent immigrants, the unemployed, and the disadvantaged are helped more when these external constraints are an overt part of the therapeutic dialogue, rather than when clients are intentionally or unintentionally acculturated into the middle-class myth. To support motivation to achieve economic success, examples of successful immigrants can be pointed out. However, it is important to clarify when giving these examples that these "success stories" gained significant resources from their families and communities. People can rise out of poverty through hard work and persistence as long as they receive substantial assistance from others (Lee & Dean, 2004).

Red-Flag Socioeconomic Guidelines

1. Assess clients' economic and social class and consider how this has influenced their access to resources within the family, such as time to give and get attention from other family members and resources for daily living, safe housing, privacy, and recreation.

2. Assess clients' economic and social class and consider how this has influenced their access to resources within the community, such as medical care, educational choices, social choices, vocational choices, legal resources, and sociopolitical power.

3. Considering 1 and 2 above, assess the impact of clients' economic and social class on their self-esteem and personal welfare; family welfare; ability to make independent decisions at home, at school, and/or within a work setting; and ability to influence their own life circumstances versus having their lives subjected to the control of others within the work, social, or political sphere.

4. Consider the impact of the environment (in terms of social and economic barriers or windows of opportunity) in actively supporting or discouraging clients' economic success in the past, at the current time, and in the foreseeable future.

5. Considering 1 through 3 above, consider whether SES is serving more to constrain clients' lives or to support them; how SES might be the cause of or be related to their strengths or weaknesses at this time, their overall level of stress, or their overall level of well-being; and how SES might inhibit or facilitate any lifestyle changes for them at this time.

Self-Analysis Guidelines

1. What is your current knowledge of issues relevant to SES?

   a. How many courses have you taken that give you background on SES and its impact on clients' physical and emotional health?

   b. How many workshops have you taken that give you background on SES and its impact on clients' physical and emotional health?

   c. What professional experiences have you had with individuals of differing SES?

   d. What personal experiences have you had with individuals of differing SES?

   e. What cohort effects might influence the worldview of individuals who are lower class, middle class, and upper class at this time?

2. What is your current level of awareness of SES?

   a. What stereotypes have you heard about lower-class, middle-class, and upper-class people?

   b. What role might the socioeconomic class of your family of origin play in your life now in terms of how you vote, where you live, what you own, and how you handle your finances?

    c. What experiences have you had that could support your effective work with this client? What experiences might lead to a negative bias or marginalization of the client's point of view or current situation?

  3. What are your current skills in working with clients of this SES?

    a. What skills do you currently have in carrying out a class analysis and helping clients access needed financial or related resources?

    b. What skills do you currently have that would help you evaluate the impact of social class on this client's physical and emotional health?

    c. What could you do to increase your ability to evaluate the impact of social class on this client's physical and emotional health?

  4. What action steps can you take?

    a. What can you do to prepare yourself to be more skilled in working with clients of this SES?

    b. How might you structure the treatment environment to increase the likelihood of a positive outcome with clients of this SES?

    c. In considering the therapeutic orientation you plan to use with this client, what classist values implicitly embedded within this treatment orientation could lead to bias or marginalization of the client's experiences and point of view?

    d. What can you do to strengthen the process of building rapport with the current client?

    e. What can you change about the treatment-planning process to make it more effective for clients from this socioeconomic status?

THE DOMAIN OF VIOLENCE

Jeff, a 22-year-old European American male, is mandated into treatment after assaulting a woman in a parking lot (Chapter 3). Ann, a 70-year-old European American female, is depressed and being abused by her adult daughter (Chapter 5). Nicole, an 18-year-old European American female, is being abused by her father and brothers and witnesses their violence against her mother (Chapter 7). Dan, a 75-year-old European American male, is being physically abused by the adult daughter he used to have under his thumb (Chapter 10). Josephina, a 17-year-old Mexican American female, a victim of date rape and domestic violence, has begun abusing her infant son (Chapter 11). Finally, Jake, a 25-year-old European American male, terrorizes his son while trying to be a good father (Chapter 12). What impact will their violent histories have on their ability to develop a treatment relationship with you? What impact will their violent histories have on your treatment plan?

In 2002, the World Health Organization (WHO) identified interpersonal violence as a worldwide public health crisis (WHO, 2002). A wealth of studies have demonstrated that exposure to interpersonal violence in one context increases the likelihood of exposure in another. In addition, any incidence of victimization increases the likelihood of experiencing serious mental and physical health consequences (Felitti, 2002; Hamby & Grych, 2013). As the number of adverse childhood events, such as those involving emotional abuse, child maltreatment, and bullying in the schools, increases, the likelihood of suffering severe illness as an adult and the likelihood of early death increase (Brown et al., 2009). Interpersonal violence occurs in every community, and its prevention across the life span would increase community health and wellness by decreasing every physical health and mental health problem (Brown et al., 2009). In 1998, 1.5 million women and 800,000 men in the United States reported physical or sexual abuse by a partner, while 3 million children witnessed it (CDC, 1998). Assaultive parents may force a child to participate in abuse or subject the child to the same type of abuse (Fantuzzo & Mohr, 1999). Millions of child maltreatment cases are reported each year (Finkelhor, Turner, Ormrod, & Hamby, 2005). Elder abuse has also come to be of greater concern; as hotlines have expanded, reporting continues to increase (CDC, 2002). While acts of violence are complexly determined, many could be prevented through accurate behavioral threat assessment and effective response (APA, 2013). Individuals' exposure to violence across their life spans should be assessed; most victims of violence will have been exposed to multiple forms of victimization, which may play different roles across situations and across time (Finkelhor, Turner, Ormrod, & Hamby, 2009; Hamby & Grych, 2013). Thus, effective treatment plans needs to take each type of exposure violence into account. For each exposure to violence, clinicians should assess whether the individual was directly involved or indirectly involved as a witness, the frequency of his or her exposure, the severity of the incident, and the individual's role in the exposure (witness, victim, perpetrator, victim-perpetrator; Hamby & Grych, 2013, p. 10).

Exposure to violence can begin prenatally if a pregnant woman is assaulted (CDC, 2006). An estimated 3.3 million reports of child maltreatment were investigated in 2006. Within established cases of maltreatment, neglect was most common (64.1%), followed by physical abuse (16%), sexual abuse (8.8%), and emotional maltreatment (6.6%). The vast majority of perpetrators were parents (79.4%) or a biological relative of the victim (U.S. Department of Health and Human Services, Administration for Children and Families, 2006). Parents from maltreating households use harsh physical discipline when children make mistakes or misbehave (Consortium for Longitudinal Studies of Child Abuse and Neglect, 2006). The impact of maltreatment is a higher risk of lower cognitive and academic functioning as well as an increased risk of internalizing and externalizing behavior (Bates & Pettit, 2007). Adverse childhood events have also been found to have long-term mental health outcomes as well as long-term health outcomes, including behavioral problems that involve aggression, anxiety, and/or depression (Brown et al., 2009). This may be due to the developmental impact of both abuse and neglect on the brain of the developing child (National Scientific Council on the Developing Child, 2005). Development is an ongoing process. It occurs when circumstances and individuals provide the child with learning experiences in which he or she can trust the information as valid and both assimilate and integrate the violent or neglectful information into his or her view of the world, interpersonal relationships, and self-understandings (Raeff, 2014). Going beyond this, Ryder (2014) has proposed a model for bridging early childhood experiences at the hands of neglectful or abusive caretakers and later willingness to be involved in violent relationships or engage in violent behavior. Her model proposes that the seeds of violence begin with the traumatogenic effects of broken infant and early childhood relationships. Ryder studied adolescent girls who had been convicted of violent crimes. She found that these girls had grown up within a violent neighborhood and family contexts. Many of the adults in their communities and households were addicted to drugs. These girls never had the opportunity to form the secure attachment to responsive adults that is needed for children to develop emotional regulation and self-control of impulses. Throughout development, these girls continued to have disrupted attachments, a lack of stable housing, and a lack of stable guidance. Thus, they never received help to improve their ability to form healthy attachments to others, and they arrived within the social institutions of school, the child welfare system, and the courts unprepared and unable to conform their behavior to social norms. Their attempts to cope with their repeated victimizations by avoiding thoughts and feelings related to the events provided in-the-moment relief from pain; however, their suppressed emotions would erratically erupt into violent behavior and they would victimize someone else. Thus, the victim of violence would be transformed by repeated trauma, and lack of responsive parenting, into the violent perpetrator (Ryder, 2014).

The abuse and neglect of children may occur in the absence of domestic violence. However, there is a 30% to 60% co-occurrence with domestic violence. Men are three times more likely than women to assault both their partners and their children (U.S. Department of Health and Human Services, Administration for Children and Families, 2006). If mothers try to protect their children from maltreatment, the father may respond by assaulting her or intensifying his attack on the children, thereby teaching her that it is better not to interfere (Bancroft & Silverman, 2004/2005). Women who do not intervene are sometimes prosecuted by authorities for failing to protect their children (Kantor & Little, 2003).

When partners engage in violence, an estimated 3 million children witness it (Fantuzzo & Mohr, 1999). Children may see or hear the violent acts of the adults in their lives or witness the sequelae later. These acts may involve physical as well as sexual assaults (Kantor & Little, 2003; Wolak & Finkelhor, 1998). In addition to the negative psychological impact of secondhand violence, the assaultive parent may force the child to participate in the assaults, require the child to spy on the victimized parent, or indoctrinate the child with the message that the victim was responsible for the assault (Kantor & Little, 2003). In addition, 1,500 children die from child abuse and neglect every year, with 80% of these deaths occurring in children who are less than 4 years of age. There are 750,000 children and youth treated in hospitals each year as a result of an assault (CDC, 2013b).

Boys and girls exposed to prolonged domestic violence may take on the beliefs that men are superior to women, that the use of violence against women is justifiable, and that violence is an appropriate problem-solving tool (Bancroft & Silverman, 2002). Male batterers may use destructive parenting practices. They may choose favorites among their children and ridicule their children for showing an attachment to their mother (Bancroft & Silverman, 2004/2005). They may unintentionally undermine the mother's authority in parenting children by modeling contempt for her abilities. They may also deliberately overrule her decisions. For example, if she forbids an activity, the batterer may help the child engage in it. He may also reward his children for defying their mother. Overall, boys may be socialized to become victimizers while girls may be indoctrinated to tolerate abuse (Jaffe & Geffner, 1998). This may be because children try to incorporate what they are learning from a violent society into what they have already learned about their gender roles. Gendered behaviors include men's assertion of dominance and control and women's attempts to be nurturant and meet the needs of others (Worell & Remer, 2003).

When they go to school, maltreated children are at increased risk of being bullied by other children. While poly-victimization may continue to occur, these children over time may become the aggressors themselves. Patterns of poly-victimization and poly-perpetration have been found to be more likely than mono-victimization or mono-perpetration (Hamby & Grych, 2013). Maltreated children with uninhibited temperaments are likely to act aggressively. They develop maladaptive cognitive schemas for processing social information and attribute hostile intentions to others, who are often engaging in neutral behavior. These children respond impulsively and get angry quickly. They have learned a repertoire of aggressive retaliatory behavior at home, they view aggression as morally acceptable, and their parents are tolerant of their aggressive behavior toward peers (Dodge, Pettit, Bates, & Valente, 1995; Watson et al., 2005).

In contrast, children who are behaviorally inhibited may be more likely to respond with internalizing symptoms to victimization at school. However, they can become aggressive over time in certain circumstances or within certain family contexts (Watson et al., 2005). Holt, Finkelhor, and Kantor (2007) investigated victimization using a social ecological framework. They investigated how victimization and victimizing behavior across many different settings did and did not relate to each other. They found that anyone who was involved in bullying within the schools reported greater internalizing behavior than anyone who was not involved in bullying in any role. However, the causes of the internalizing behavior differed. Bullies developed this behavior due to being victimized themselves within conventional forms of crime. Individuals who were victimized by bullies developed internalizing behavior directly. In addition, bullies and bully-victims had higher rates of exposure to indirect forms of victimization, such as witnessing domestic violence. Victims and bully-victims showed similarities in being victimized, both at school and in their sibling or other peer relationships. Bully-victims reported higher rates of victimization by conventional crime than either bullies or victims. Most striking, 32.1% of bully-victims reported sexual victimization in the last year in comparison to 3.1% of those who had no role in school bullying, and the children with the highest rates of internalizing symptoms were those with the highest rates of child maltreatment and victimization by conventional crime.

Longitudinal studies show that children who are physically aggressive at age 5 often continue to be aggressive throughout the elementary years and even into adolescence (Broidy et al., 2003; Watson et al., 2005). Teens who have been abused as children are more likely to be arrested for both violent and nonviolent offenses; they are also more likely to engage in violence in their dating relationships and more likely to have externalizing behavior problems. They are also at greater risk of dropping out of high school, getting fired from employment, and teen parenthood (Lansford et al., 2007).

The likelihood of youth violence increases as several risk factors increase. These risks include the presence of substance abuse in the home, easy access to weapons, the child's moving back and forth between different family households, exposure to violence in the community, participation in deviant peer groups, and living in poverty (Garbarino, 1999; Hanson et al., 2006; Surgeon General, 2001; Watson et al., 2005). Gender is also a major risk factor for committing acts of violence, especially during the teen and early adult years

(Kimmel, 2008). Starting in kindergarten, boys show more aggression than girls at all levels of aggressiveness (Watson et al., 2005), and young men are 10 times more likely to commit murder than young women (Garbarino, 1999).

White and Smith (2004) found that males who have been sexually assaulted in childhood, then physically abused in childhood or made to witness domestic violence in childhood, are twice as likely to commit a sexual assault as teens. Of maltreatment experiences, parental physical abuse showed the highest relationship to sexual assault in the teen years, followed by witnessing domestic violence and then childhood sexual abuse. White and Smith also found that perpetration of sexual assault in college was only related to childhood victimization through the pathway of teen sexual assault. Those men who had been victimized in childhood, but had not been engaged in sexual assault in adolescence, did not victimize women in college. In following male college students across four years of college, White and Smith found that most were not perpetrators of sexual assault. However for the subset that was engaged in sexually coercive behavior, including rape, the number of assaults increased with each of the four years of college.

Promoting a community environment in which beliefs, attitudes, and messages include the importance of treating romantic partners, peers, family members, and strangers with respect and counter messages that condone sexual violence, stalking, and physical violence is critical in ending victimization of both males and females. The media often reinforce societal and community norms that portray victimizing and perpetrating behavior as normal and find stereotypes of a masculinity that objectifies and degrades women acceptable (Black et al., 2011).

In addition to examining the risk factors for continued violence, research has sought to understand the factors related to children's being exposed to violence in the home or school, yet not becoming violent themselves. One important factor is a caregiver who provides social and emotional support to the child. In addition, practical guidance in how to cope with the violence is critical (Consortium for Longitudinal Studies of Child Abuse and Neglect, 2006). Other protective factors include a positive attachment to adults who do not tolerate violent or deviant behavior and parental commitment to children's school success (Surgeon General, 2001). Wright and associates (2013) indicated that the strongest family factors in protecting children from the negative impact of trauma include positive and responsive caretaking from a family member or surrogate family member and a stable and safe home environment. Child characteristics that have protective features include the ability to regulate emotions and view oneself as worthy and valued, average or above-average intelligence, adaptive problem-solving abilities, and a positive outlook on life. Community characteristics that have been found to be protective in dealing with trauma include a safe neighborhood, low levels of community violence, affordable housing, access to recreational centers, effective schools, and employment opportunities. Finally, there are cultural or societal characteristics that serve as protective factors, such as laws that protect the welfare of children at home, at school, and in the labor force; that support health care; and that do not tolerate physical violence (Wright et al., 2013).

Preventing all interpersonal violence starts with healthy and respectful family relationships developing between the parent and child (Wright et al., 2013). A healthy parent–child relationship includes a child being the recipient of positive and effective parenting from both the mother and the father. This creates a family environment that is emotionally supportive and includes open communication. Children require many complex skills from their parents, and their needs change as they develop. Parents need to learn new behaviors and develop new skills and resources as their children age and place differing demands on them. Parents are also children's role models for how adults should behave in intimate relationships. Thus, a respectful intimate relationship, free of aggression or violence, provides children with a compelling example of what they should be developing in their own future relationships. Adolescents can use this example of a good relationship to guide them as they go on to develop relationships with peers and dating partners. Children and teens will come into conflict with others and need to hold the belief that violence is not acceptable in relationships as well as have strategies for nonviolent communication and problem-solving. Parents are critical in helping their children and teenagers learn how to negotiate conflict, reduce stress, and manage negative emotions in a safe manner (Black et al., 2011).

Violence between adults occurs within a context of individuals, stimuli, and physical settings, not as isolated events (U.S. Department of Justice, Office of Violent Crimes, 2010). It may include physical assaults, sexual assaults, threats of physical or sexual assault, or emotional abuse (CDC, 2006). Assaults between partners can range from temporary injuries due to slaps and scratches to fatal injury as a result of repeated punching, kicking, use of weapons, and so forth. Nonlethal injury can result in acute medical conditions or chronic consequences. While legal statutes label all partner abuse "battery," men's attacks often show a higher level of lethality than those initiated by women (Samuelson & Campbell, 2005; Stuart, 2005). Violence may begin with one partner, but this often serves to elicit violence from the other, either for self-defense or for revenge (Archer, 2002; Graham-Kevan & Archer, 2005).

While it is more common for women to be sexually assaulted, men are also sexually assaulted. The National Intimate Partner and Sexual Violence Survey found that 1 in 5 women and 1 in 71 men in the United States have been raped at some point in their lives. These rapes are usually perpetrated by an intimate partner, second most often by an acquaintance, and least frequently a stranger. Most female victims experienced their first completed rape prior to the age of 25, and 42% experienced their first completed rape before they were 18. More than 25% of male victims experienced a completed rape when they were 10 years of age or younger. Most males and females indicate that men were the perpetrators of their assaults (Black et al., 2011).

Emotional abuse includes acts such as name-calling, deliberate public embarrassment of the victim, isolation of the victim from family and friends, taking control of finances, and so forth (CDC, 2006). Partner abuse is often a family secret. Many reasons for this have been posited, including victims' belief that the victimization is their own fault, that victimization is a universal family experience, or that it would be dangerous to oneself or one's family to reveal its existence (Stuart, 2005). Victims of partner violence are heterogeneous and come from all socioeconomic levels, ethnic and racial groups, educational backgrounds, and sexual orientations (CDC, 2006). A commonality among victims is that they view the violent experience as a betrayal of their prior relationship with the perpetrator; even those who are not physically injured experience significant emotional disturbance, often losing self-confidence and feeling worthless. Victims may also show fearfulness and become vigilant for signs of danger from the partner (Stuart, 2005).

Violence between couples fits roughly into two broad categories. The first, common or situational couple violence, occurs in a broad range of couples, including gay and straight, married and cohabitating (Frieze, 2005). For these couples, violence is mutual and occurs in reaction to negative experiences within the day-to-day life of the family. These individuals consider violence an acceptable reaction to stress (M. P. Johnson & Leone, 2005). The other type of couple violence, "intimate terrorism," occurs less frequently and involves the most extreme behavior. The perpetrator uses violence and fear to maintain absolute control over the partner, who experiences severe emotional reactions to the victimization (M. P. Johnson, 1995; Koss, Bailey, Yuan, Herrera, & Lichter, 2003). The perpetrator also uses intense psychological abuse as another mechanism of control (Dye & Davis, 2003).

There are no simple explanations for the occurrence of intimate partner violence beyond the fact that a previous history of adverse childhood events makes it more likely (Felitti, 2002). A complex model that examines predisposing factors, potentiating factors, and eliciting factors may have the most potential for use in preventing and treating violence (Stuart, 2005). Predisposing factors include biological and cultural variables that together explain the individual's mental capacity and worldview. Potentiating factors include internal and situational variables that together encompass the individual's potential for volatility and the couple's relationship dynamics. Eliciting factors include internal and situational events that lower self-restraint and increase vulnerability in the immediacy of the situation.

Not all violent individuals are equally amenable to treatment, and research has tried to determine which perpetrators are most amenable to treatment. Stuart (2005) has developed a typology that offers some guidance to practitioners. His research classifies individuals as predatory abusers, affectively motivated abusers, or instrumental abusers. The abusers who are least motivated to change, and most dangerous to their victims, are the predatory abusers. They engage in frequent and recurrent violence that is instigated for their own idiosyncratic purposes unrelated to their partner's behavior. Prior to the assault, they may be calm, and they find the violent episode arousing. They severely injure their victims both physically and emotionally, yet after the incident show a lack of empathy or regret for what they have done to the victim.

The instrumental abuser engages in violence in order to gain something from the partner, and incidences of violence are rare. These individuals are calm before the assault and mildly aroused upon gaining whatever it is they wanted from the partner. They have limited motivation to change because their desire for personal gain is more important to them than their concern for the victim. The injuries inflicted are incidental to the perpetrator's trying to get what he or she wants from the victim.

The perpetrator most amenable to change is the affectively motivated assailant. This individual has actually been provoked by the victim or at least interprets the behavior of the victim as provoking. Violent behavior occurs only occasionally. The perpetrator is highly aroused before the assault and calms down afterward. The violent acts occur impulsively, may involve relatively less severe actions, and may result in only mild consequences to the victim in comparison to the acts of other abusers. The acts may have the greatest impact on the victim's self-esteem, and the perpetrator may show empathy for the victim's injuries and regret for having caused them.

Violent relationships that fall within the domain of common couple violence or that stem from an affectively motivated abuser may be most open to change (Frieze, 2005;

Stuart, 2005). Motivation for change may come from dynamics such as regret over harming the partner, the wish to be a good parent, the desire to protect children from harm, or a future orientation (CDC, 2006). Violence, however, may continue throughout 50 years of an intimate relationship or marriage (U.S. Department of Justice, Office of Violent Crimes, 2010). Women over 50 are more likely than men over 50 to be victims of physical and sexual violence. Homicide-suicides are most likely to occur with the husband first killing his wife and then killing himself (U.S. Department of Justice, Office of Violent Crimes, 2010). However, men are also victimized in this way, and some data indicate that there may be relatively more male victims of exploitation or neglect (Pritchard, 2002). The most common perpetrators of violence against senior citizens are members of their family. The victims trust them and have ongoing relationships with them (U.S. Department of Justice, Office of Violent Crimes, 2010). However, elder abuse can occur within new relationships after there's been some type of significant family disruption.

Late-onset interpersonal violence can also occur in a long-standing relationship where some type of significant change, such as a medical or mental health condition, has led to an increase in aggressive behavior or where a power and control dynamic has deepened into violence (U.S. Department of Justice, Office of Violent Crimes, 2010). Abusive individuals find ways to justify their use of actual violence or threats of violence to get what they want from their victim. It has been estimated that 2 million seniors are abused every year, and there are many forms of such abuse, including physical abuse, sexual abuse, emotional abuse, neglect, confinement, and financial abuse (Dong et al., 2011). The National Elder Maltreatment Study (Acierno et al., 2010) found that the most common form of mistreatment of elders is financial abuse (5.2%), followed by neglect (5.1%), emotional abuse (4.6%), physical abuse (1.6%) and sexual abuse (.6%). Evidence suggests that certain seniors are more vulnerable to abuse than others; not having many social contacts and having had previous exposure to trauma were most related to vulnerability (Acierno et al., 2010). The most vulnerable seniors also indicated low levels of psychological and social well-being. A question that remains is whether high depression, a marginal social network, and little engagement are the results of elder abuse or increase the risk of being abused (Dong et al., 2011).

In conclusion, whether the violence involves a child, an adult, or a senior, research indicates that poly-victimization is common, and thus clinicians should not be misled by the report of one form of violence into not assessing for the potential presence of other forms. In addition, across forms of violence, clients' roles as victims or victimizers may shift; thus, different forms of violence may require different interventions (Hamby & Grych, 2013). Barriers to treatment success can include the fact that violence may be viewed as commonplace by both victim and perpetrator. Growing up surrounded by a context of violence, clients may view clear communication and nonviolent problem-solving goals as unrealistic. These clients may have a hostile or suspicious bias that influences their interpretation of the clinician's behavior and the behavior of others. Clinicians need to carefully assess the level of danger within the home, school, neighborhood, and treatment session itself for the immediate, short, and long term (Samuelson & Campbell, 2005). The victim's experiences need validation, but at the same time the clinician must clarify that the abusive behavior is illegal and causing the victim both physical and psychological damage; damage to child witnesses should also be underscored, and this may enhance motivation for change in some parents. Reducing risk factors for violence and increasing protective factors should be the first priority in treatment, and a safety plan should be in place before clients are expected to make other changes in their lives. While past violence is still the best predictor of future violence, for most perpetrators, there is a decrease of both physical and emotional violence across a 10-year period (Timmons Fritz & O'Leary, 2007).

Red-Flag Violence Guidelines

1. Assess the risk factors for engaging in violence and the protective factors discouraging violence that are currently in place for clients, considering the following:

    a. The adverse childhood events clients have been exposed to in the past, which might include living with a drug addict; having divorced parents; severe family disruption, such as repeated moves or homelessness; having a parent who was depressed or mentally ill; having someone in the household who committed suicide or attempted to commit suicide; having someone in the household who committed a serious crime or went to prison; being the victim of physical, sexual, or emotional abuse or neglect; or witnessing violence.

    b. The adverse events clients have been exposed to as adults, which may include living with a drug addict; severe family disruption; living with someone who was depressed or mentally ill; having someone in the household who committed suicide or attempted to commit suicide; having someone in the household who committed a serious crime or went to prison; being the victim of physical, sexual, or emotional abuse; witnessing violence; or living in fear of violence.

    c. The *internal* factors within clients, such as their ability to control their impulses and set limits on their own behavior, regulate their emotions, engage in reflective problem-solving, and understand the emotions and behaviors of others.

    d. The *long-term* social network and environment that were in place during clients' childhood and whether they supported or constrained violence, such as whether there were traumatic, ambivalent, or nonexistent emotional bonds or positive emotional bonds; whether or not there was family violence; the level of family toleration for violence as a problem-solving strategy; whether school and neighborhood experiences were generally positive or negative; and religious background.

    e. The *current* environmental supports or constraints on violence from family relationships, peer relationships, educational attainment, vocation, current neighborhood, and current religious beliefs.

    f. Any *immediate* eliciting or triggering factors that might serve to justify and/ or make a violent or prosocial response more likely, such as the presence of a weapon, alcohol or drug use, a high level of frustration or anger, and encouragement of violence from others.

2. Assess clients' exposure to violence across their life span on a variety of aspects:

   a. Types of exposure (direct, indirect)

   b. Frequency of exposure

   c. Severity of incidents

   d. The client's role in the exposure (witness, victim, perpetrator, victim-perpetrator)

   e. The current impact of the exposure in terms of emotional, cognitive, physical, and social functioning

3. Assess clients' worldview, whether violence plays a generalized or circumscribed role in it, and whether they are currently generating or promoting violence or generating or promoting prosocial behavior.

4. Assess clients' level of danger and that of others within their environment at this time. Assess whether, and how, their safety could be enhanced, both in the immediate and in the longer term, including careful consideration of the *characteristics* of the perpetrator of the violence in their life. On a scale of 1 to 10, how dangerous is the client's environment at this time? How much control of this danger does the client have?

5. Assess clients' safety and that of others within their personal, social, and cultural worlds.

6. Assess the overall psychological and physical impact of violence on clients and others, determine whether there are more forces supporting violence or supporting nonviolence, and consider clients' prognosis in regard to their ability to live a life free of violence in their current circumstances.

Self-Analysis Guidelines

1. What is your current knowledge of the impact of violence or neglect on individuals and their families?

   a. How many courses have you taken that give you background on the impact of neglect, violence, and trauma on the physical and emotional welfare of clients?

   b. How many workshops have you attended that give you background on the impact of neglect, violence, and trauma on the physical and emotional welfare of clients?

   c. What professional experiences have you had that give you background on the impact of neglect, violence, and trauma on the physical and emotional welfare of clients?

   d. What personal experiences have you had that give you background on the impact of neglect, violence, and trauma on the physical and emotional welfare of clients?

    e. What cohort effects might influence the worldview of individuals with a background of neglect, violence, and trauma as to what is important in the world, how people communicate, and what is rewarded and punished in this world?

2. What is your current level of awareness of issues relevant to clients who come from violent or neglectful backgrounds?

    a. What stereotypes of neglectful and violent lifestyles do you know about? How might they influence your view of the client at this time?

    b. How might your past experiences with or exposure to violence influence your view of the client at this time?

    c. What stereotypes of good romantic relationships and good parent–child relationships do you know about? How might these influence your view of the client at this time?

    d. How might your past exposure to violence and neglect influence your reactions to this particular client?

    e. What experiences have you had that could support your effective work with this client? What experiences have you had that might lead to a negative bias or marginalization of clients' point of view or current situation?

3. What are your current skills in working with clients from violent or neglectful backgrounds?

    a. What skills do you currently have that are of value in working with individuals who have a background of neglect, violence, and/or trauma?

    b. What skills do you feel it would be important to develop to work effectively with individuals who have a violent or neglectful background?

    c. What can you do to increase the likelihood of a positive outcome with this client who has a violent or neglectful background?

4. What action steps can you take?

    a. What can you do to prepare yourself to be more skilled in working with clients who come from violent or neglectful backgrounds?

    b. In considering your chosen treatment approach, what potential biases do you see in terms of neglect of or inappropriate interventions for individuals who were victims or perpetrators of violence?

    c. How might you structure the treatment environment to increase the likelihood of a positive outcome with this client who comes from a violent or neglectful background?

    d. What processes of treatment might you change to make them more welcoming to this client from a violent or neglectful background?

CONCLUSIONS

A theoretical perspective—behaviorism, for instance—may be helpful in acquiring an understanding of *who clients are* and *why they do what they do.* Will it be worthwhile to further investigate the client's individuality by considering the impact of gender, sexual orientation, violence history, or other domains of complexity? The exercises in Chapters 3 through 12 are first steps in answering these questions and in providing a framework for practicing your skills at integrating human complexity into your clinical work. As your comfort with complexity increases, expand your readings on the domains introduced within this text as well as studying the many important domains that have not been covered, such as religion and developmental disabilities.

Table 2.1 provides a quick guide to locating the domains of human complexity highlighted in client interviews by chapter, presenting problem, referral source, and treatment setting. Table 2.2 provides a quick reference to how theories and areas of complexity are compared within Exercise 6 in Chapters 3 through 12.

Table 2.1 Location of Domains Highlighted in Client Interviews

Domain	Chapter	Presenting Problem	Referral Source	Treatment Setting
Age				
Kevin	3	Self-hate, phobia	School	School
Alice, Katherine	9	Immaturity, divorce, war	School	Outpatient
Amber	10	Chronic loneliness	Self	Outpatient
Gender				
Marie	4	Bereavement, parenting	Self	Outpatient
Darla	5	Alcohol abuse, neglect	School	Outpatient
Steve	8	Emotional intimacy	Self	School
Race and Ethnicity				
John	6	Marital crisis	Self	Outpatient
Sergio	8	Drug conviction, racism	Court	Outpatient
Tanisha, Marcus	9	Bereavement	Self	Outpatient
Kayla	12	Malaise, emotional intimacy	Self	Outpatient

(Continued)

Table 2.1   (Continued)

Domain	Chapter	Presenting Problem	Referral Source	Treatment Setting
Sexual Orientation				
Eric	4	Sexual confusion, neglect	School	School
Ellen	7	Divorce, sexual intimacy	Self	Outpatient
Socioeconomic				
Ann	5	Depression, elder abuse	Friend	Outpatient
Sharon	6	Marital, parenting	Internist	Outpatient
Zechariah	11	Racism, adjustment	School	School
Violence				
Jeff	3	Assault, rage	Court	Outpatient
Nicole	7	Physical abuse, intimacy fears	Self	Outpatient
Dan	10	Physical and emotional abuse	Aging Services	Outpatient
Josephina	11	Child abuse, violence	Court	Outpatient
Jake	12	Child abuse, parenting	Court	Outpatient

Table 2.2   Comparisons of Theories and Areas of Human Complexity Within Exercise 6

Chapter	Theory	Client	Theory Comparison	Complexity Comparison
3	Behavioral	Kevin	Cognitive-behavioral	Age, Violence
4	Cognitive	Eric	Cognitive-behavioral	Sexuality, Violence
5	Cognitive-behavioral	Darla	Family systems	Age, Violence
6	Feminist	Sharon	Cognitive	SES, Gender
7	Emotion-focused	Nicole	Feminist	Violence, Age
8	Dynamic	Steve	Emotion-focused	Gender, SES
9	Family	Tanisha and Marcus	Feminist	Race, Gender
10	Cultural	Dan	Dynamic	Violence, Race
11	Constructivist	Josephina	Family systems	Violence, Race
12	Transtheoretical	Kayla	Constructivist	Race, Sexuality

RECOMMENDED RESOURCES

The Domain of Age

American Psychological Association Help Center. http://www.apa.org/helpcenter/

Brems, C. (2008). *A comprehensive guide to child psychotherapy and counseling* (3rd ed.). Long Grove, IL: Waveland Press.

Harvard University, Center on the Developing Child, National Scientific Council on the Developing Child. http://developingchild.harvard.edu/activities/council/

Zero to Three: National Center for Infants, Toddlers, and Families. www.zerotothree.org

The Domain of Gender

Association for Women in Psychology. http://awpsf2015.com/

Crawford, M. (2006). *Transformations: Women, gender and psychology* (2nd ed.). New York: NY: McGraw-Hill.

Feminist Psychology Institute. https://feminism.org

Kimmel, M. S. (2008). The gendered society. In K. E. Rosenblum & T. C. Travis (Eds.), *The meaning of difference: American constructions of race, sex and gender, social class, sexual orientation, and disability* (5th ed., pp. 81–87). Boston, MA: McGraw-Hill.

Landrine, N. F., & Russo, N. F. (2010). *Handbook of diversity in feminist psychology*. New York, NY: Springer.

U.S. Department of Labor, Women's Bureau. http://www.dol.gov/wb/

The Domain of Race and Ethnicity

Hays, P. (2008). *Addressing cultural complexities in practice: Assessment, diagnosis, and therapy* (2nd ed.). Washington, DC: American Psychological Association.

National Alliance for Hispanic Health (NAHH). http://www.hispanichealth.org/

National Black Child Development Institute (NBCDI). http://www.nbcdi.org/

National Indian Child Welfare Association (NICWA). http://www.nicwa.org/

The Domain of Sexual Orientation

Association for Lesbian, Gay, Bisexual, & Transgender Issues in Counseling. www.algbtic.org

Biescheke, K. J., Perez, R. M., & DeBord, K. (2007). *Handbook of counseling and psychotherapy with lesbian, gay, bisexual, and transgender clients* (2nd ed.). Washington, DC: American Psychological Association.

Children of Lesbians and Gays Everywhere. http://www.colage.org

Gay, Lesbian and Straight Education Network. www.glsen.org

Parents, Families and Friends of Lesbians and Gays. http://www.PFLAG.org

The Domain of Socioeconomic Status

Books, S. (2007). *Invisible children in the society and its schools* (3rd ed., pp. 1–22). Mahwah, NJ: Lawrence Erlbaum.

Centers for Disease Control and Prevention. http://www.cdc.gov

Children's Defense Fund. http://www.childrensdefense.org/

Institute for Research on Poverty. http://www.irp.wisc.edu/

The Domain of Violence

Child Welfare Information Gateway. http://www.childwelfare.gov/

Hamby, S., & Grych, J. (2013). *The web of violence: Exploring connections among different forms of interpersonal violence and abuse*. New York, NY: Springer.

National Council on Child Abuse and Family Violence. http://www.nccafv.org/

Stop It Now! http://www.stopitnow.org

Zorza, J. (2006). *Violence against women: Vol. III. Victims and abusers*. Kingston, NJ: Civic Research Institute.

Behavioral Case Conceptualizations and Treatment Plans

INTRODUCTION TO BEHAVIORAL THEORY

You have just received a phone referral from the probation department. Jeff is a 22-year-old White male. He dropped out of high school at the age of 16. He has been working since that time as a cook at a fast-food restaurant. He has recently begun pursuing his GED. He has been married to Karen, who is 21 years old, for two years. They have a son, John (3 years old), and Karen is 4 months pregnant. Jeff was convicted of assaulting a 50-year-old woman and was sentenced to 100 hours of community service and the same number of hours of treatment focusing on anger management. Assume that during a brief intake, Jeff showed no signs of cognitive confusion or suicidal ideation. However, he became very angry in response to mental status questions about harm to others. However, he signed release forms to the court and his probation officer. He did this to prove that he had a laid-back personality.

You are a behaviorist and assume that all behavior is learned. How did Jeff learn to be violent? Your model assumes that this occurred according to the principles of classical conditioning, operant conditioning, and/or social learning (Bandura, 1986; Pavlov, 1927; Skinner, 1938). How would treatment proceed? The focus would be on a behavioral analysis of Jeff's overt adaptive and maladaptive behaviors and the specific circumstances in which they occur (Ingram, 2012). Within sessions, Jeff will actively participate in learning experiences to modify or extinguish maladaptive behavior patterns as well as teach or increase the frequency of adaptive behavior. If Jeff's overt behavior changes, it is assumed that related cognitive and affective changes will follow. However, there are times when conditioned emotional responses, or mediating cognitions, might be the focus of change (Ingram, 2012).

If Jeff has learned violent responses through classical conditioning, it was unintentional learning (Pavlov, 1927). Classical conditioning involves reflexive, elicited behavior that occurs outside the person's conscious control. For example, as Jeff was growing up, an initially neutral stimulus (a door slamming) was present at the same time as an unconditioned stimulus (Jeff receiving a physical blow from his father). Over time, Jeff developed an unlearned, reflexive response (respondent) to this unconditioned stimulus—a fear reaction (increase in blood pressure, heart rate, body temperature). Through repeated association between the neutral stimulus (a door slamming) and the unconditioned stimulus (receiving a physical blow from his father), Jeff learned to show the respondent (fear reaction) when the neutral stimulus occurred even though it was no longer paired with the unconditioned stimulus.

A door slamming has now become a conditioned (learned) stimulus for Jeff. The fear response to this conditioned stimulus is now considered a conditioned (learned) response. Unlearning of a classically conditioned response requires a break in association between the conditioned stimulus (door slamming) and the unconditioned stimulus (physical blow). Throughout the course of his childhood, Jeff may have learned to generalize his fear response to any sudden loud noise when his father was present. However, if he learned to discriminate loud noises where his father was present from loud noises where his father was absent, Jeff's fear response may play a functional role in his life. However, if Jeff has generalized his fear reaction to loud noises in any circumstances, his fear may be immobilizing him or leading him to take dysfunctional actions.

If Jeff has learned violent responses through operant conditioning, then he learned by intentionally doing something (operating on his environment) and experiencing the consequences (Skinner, 1938). If there is a positive consequence, the behavior increases in frequency. If there is a negative consequence, the behavior decreases in frequency. Positive consequences can consist of receiving positive reinforcement (getting something you want) or receiving negative reinforcement (having something you don't want removed). For example, if Jeff yelled at his wife that he was hungry and she rushed to get him food, then her giving him food served as positive reinforcement, thereby increasing his yelling. Similarly, if he hated being asked questions, her being quiet the moment he raised his voice could increase his yelling through negative reinforcement. What serves as reinforcement is specific to the individual.

Jeff's behavior can also be modified by either positive or negative punishment. If a young Jeff yelled at his father and his father punched him, the punch would serve as positive punishment to discourage his yelling. If Jeff's father wouldn't let him watch TV because he yelled at him, this would be using negative punishment to discourage yelling. Positive punishment involves getting something you don't want, while negative punishment involves something you want being taken away. Across environments, Jeff could learn to discriminate when yelling would result in punishment and when it would lead to reinforcement.

One incident of a reinforcement or punishment does not usually cause a lasting impact on an individual. It is Jeff's overall history of reinforcements and punishments that produced his current behavioral repertoire. Jeff may need to be taught new behaviors that will be functional in his life. In this case, he should be given reinforcement for taking small steps toward development of this new competency. If he needs skills in an area where he is unlikely to spontaneously take a "step in the right direction," prompts or shaping should be used. Prompts are antecedent events (cues, instructions, gestures) that can initiate a behavior so that it is then possible to reinforce it. Shaping refers to reinforcing successive approximations of the desired response. Unlearning (operant extinction) occurs when a previously reinforced behavior ceases to produce positive consequences.

Jeff may have learned violent behavior and its consequences through observing a model or models (Bandura, 1986). Whether this learned behavior is later performed depends on the consequences that are associated with it. Jeff will be more likely to learn from a model that he perceives as similar to himself or a model he considers high in prestige, status, or expertise. Jeff's father, who had total power within the family, may have served as a powerful role model for teaching violent behavior. Jeff may have received vicarious reinforcement for his own dominating behaviors from seeing his mother acquiesce to his father's verbally and physically controlling behavior. The extinction of an observationally learned response can occur through direct or observed (vicarious) punishing consequences.

While behaviors are the primary focus of attention, it is possible for cognitions or emotions to be "learned behaviors." For example, through classical conditioning, Jeff could have been taught to associate anger and feelings of hostility with women. Therefore, in any interaction involving women, he may have a conditioned emotional response that leads him toward maladaptive behavior. Similarly, he may have learned the belief, from his father, that any attempt to ask a question is, in fact, an attempt to dominate him. Therefore, whenever anyone asks him a question today, he may have automatic thoughts such as "This person is trying to control me. I must show who's boss, or I'll be this person's slave." These types of thoughts might fuel Jeff's aggressive behavior in situations that most people would find neutral or benign (Ingram, 2012).

THE ROLE OF THE CLINICIAN

How will you help Jeff? You will be a teacher, trainer, and contingency manager who actively guides treatment. First, you will assess Jeff's behavior and define his current problems in behavioral terms, including the dimensions of frequency, intensity, duration, form or quality, and appropriateness to context. Jeff's behavioral strengths also will be noted in a similar manner. This information may be collected through self-report inventories, interviews with Jeff and significant others, behavioral observations, and other methods. Concomitant with this process, you will analyze the conditions maintaining Jeff's problems in terms of the antecedents (the triggers—where, when, whom) and consequences (reinforcements, punishments) and the environmental supports or barriers to the change process. After making these determinations, you will plan sessions to provide Jeff with the learning experiences that he needs in order to change. Jeff may need to initiate, increase in frequency, or modify certain behaviors. Similarly, he may need to terminate, decrease, or alter others. You will take an active and directive role in structuring the learning environment to support these changes.

An active search for adaptive behavior will also be part of this behavioral analysis, as modifying potentially adaptive behavior, increasing already present adaptive behavior, and teaching new skills are integral to achieving treatment success. While Jeff's problems with violent behavior should not be underestimated, there may be many areas in which true behavioral strengths can be found. For example, Jeff has shown the ability to discriminate situations in which it is and isn't safe to yell at others; this demonstrates that even when angry, he has some self-control. Jeff is motivated and has a finely tuned ability to observe others. He may learn most effectively if given the opportunity to use these skills. For example, he might more quickly recognize antecedents and consequences to aggressive behavior if he is given a homework assignment that deals with observing his "buddies" after work rather than one where he is directed to reflect on his own behavior. As a final example, behavioral treatment is very action oriented, rather than insight focused. Jeff may find concretely described homework assignments that involve him in "doing something" more congruent with his personal style than activities that involve pure self-reflection.

You might introduce many types of learning experiences, including relaxation training, anger management training, and social skills training, in trying to help Jeff. Historically, behavior therapy did not focus on cognitions or emotions (Skinner, 1938). However, many current behaviorists believe that "cognitions" and "emotions" may be conditioned and thus serve as appropriate targets for intervention (Ingram, 2012).

How will Jeff's progress be measured and monitored? Goals will be set that are specific, clear, functional, and attainable, and they may involve modifying or decreasing maladaptive behaviors as well as modifying, enhancing, or learning adaptive behaviors. Interventions targeted at providing environments that will support constructive change may be initiated. Jeff's wife will be involved in changing the consequences she gives Jeff for his behavior at home if it is safe for her to do so. An effective teaching environment will not occur within the treatment sessions if Jeff and you do not develop a trusting, and mutually respectful, working relationship in which you design individualized learning experiences and Jeff actively participates in them.

CASE APPLICATION: INTEGRATING THE DOMAIN OF VIOLENCE

Jeff's case will now be examined in detail. There are many domains of complexity that might provide insights into his behavior. The domain of violence has been selected for consideration within a behavioral case conceptualization and treatment plan. When asked if he had any preferences about who was assigned as his clinician, Jeff said he would take anyone who was available, as he wished to get treatment over with as soon as possible; as an afterthought, he said he preferred a clinician who was "not an idiot."

Interview With Jeff (J) From a Behavioral Perspective

C: I understand that you are coming here as a condition of your probation. Why are you on probation?

J: (tensely) Because this woman stole my parking space and I wouldn't put up with it.

C: How did she steal your parking space?

J: (angrily) I was running late for work because my wife Karen was having a hysterical fit. When I got to work, the whole lot was full. I circled and circled until a space opened up. I put on my turn signal to back up for the space when this woman pulled into it. Well, I got out and banged on her car window and told her to move. She ignored me. I pretended to walk away. She got out of the car, and I was on her in a second. I told her to get back in the car and move out of my space. She tried to push past me. So, I gave her a shake.

C: How badly was she hurt?

J: (emphatically) She wasn't hurt. Someone in the parking lot ran into the restaurant and called the police. The police jerked me around and sent her to the hospital. She didn't need a Band-Aid!

C: What did the police do?

J: (angrily) They took me to court. The judge asked me why I lost control. I told him I had just had a bad fight with my wife and was running late for work. Then I told the judge my wife was pregnant and I would lose my job if I went to jail; Karen was sitting there crying. I got probation.

C: Karen being there helped to get you probation?

J: (angrily) The whole stupid mess was her fault to begin with. She made me late to work. My boss was furious about the fight. It frightened off some customers. He said one more false step and I'm out!

C: Is this job important to you?

J: (rigidly) I will qualify for a management training program at the restaurant when I have finished the GED. Then I can earn enough money for the kids Karen keeps producing.

C: You are working hard to support your family. Can you stay in control at work and keep your job?

J: (glaring at *C*, tensely) I won't hit my boss, if that's what you mean.

C: When your boss pressures you, you can control your anger. Why didn't you control your anger with the woman in the parking lot?

J: (firmly) Women don't step on me. If she had backed down when I threatened her, I would have backed off but just felt tense. *Her* behavior pushed me to the boiling point. I felt relaxed once I looked down at her and heard her wimpering. I didn't stay calm long because the police began jerking me around.

C: Did you explode again?

J: (dismissively) No, I had to control it.

C: You could control your anger with the police.

J: (irritably) I didn't want to go to jail—but I felt jumpy.

C: What does it mean to feel jumpy?

J: (tensely) At first, I just have trouble concentrating. After a while, if I still can't let the tension out I begin to feel hot. If I get too hot I go onto autopilot—I fight until I win.

C: Is that what happened with that woman?

J: (angrily) I had been jumpy in the car, it got worse as I circled, and then when she tried to push by—that was it.

C: What helped to get rid of the tension after you went to court?

J: (matter-of-factly) I went to work, and I overcooked the food. The burning smell always gives me some satisfaction.

C: What about at home—how do you release tension?

J: (intently) When I get home, Karen better have everything the way I want it.

C: If it's not?

J: (hostilely) Then, I'm all over her.

C: What do you do?

J: (matter-of-factly) It depends how mad she has made me. Maybe I just shove her around a little. Maybe I have to get more physical.

C: Has Karen ever needed medical attention after a fight?

J: (slowly and emphatically) Noooo. I don't hit her that hard.

C: Could you give me a recent example?

J: (tensely) The day I got into the fight, she wanted to know when I would be home so she could take the car to the store. I shoved her away from me, just hard enough to make the point that she had better not try to control me.

C: On a scale from one to ten, how hard a shove was it?

J: (irritably) Don't fret over Karen; she can handle it. She whines a lot when she is pregnant, but she got a dozen whacks from her parents for every one I give her!

C: How many times a day do you hit or kick her?

J: (highly frustrated) *Karen is OK.* The push I gave didn't stop her mouth at all. She grabbed my arm as I was opening the door. I kicked her, hard. She let go of me and I was able to get out the door, but it left me all worked up.

C: Why didn't kicking Karen leave you feeling relaxed?

J: (intently) I didn't get much relief because I hadn't made her completely back down and show me I'm in charge. If she begs . . . big time, I end up feeling good.

C: What do you do when you are in a good mood?

J: (matter-of-factly) I'm ready for sex. (pause) I may insist on it.

C: You feel sexually aroused after a physical fight with your wife?

J: (calmly) Only after a big blowout, because then all my frustration gets released. That fight right before I went to work didn't do it for me; I was still tense and edgy as I left.

C: What happens after you have sex?

J: (smugly) I feel really relaxed.

C: Do you have any other way to handle being angry besides physically fighting?

J: (smugly) I'm pretty good with my mouth too. Often, a few threats will go a long way.

C: Can anything stop you from fighting once you are mad?

J: (tensely) If the person backs down, I still feel edgy, but I can let it go. If I haven't got hot yet, I can walk away if it's a work situation. I must control myself. I hate it.

C: Having to control yourself?

J: (angrily) I hate feeling edgy and having to wait to get rid of it.

C: If you get hot?

J: (emphatically) As I said, I'm on autopilot. But, I'm in control most of the time. In fact, I'm always razzed by everyone for being an underachiever and taking things too easily.

C: Who is "everyone"?

J: (dismissively) My mom and dad. They only did three things: complain that I was lazy and wouldn't ever get anywhere, beat on me, and ignore me.

C: What would happen when you were growing up?

J: (reflectively) If my dad was home and he noticed me, he would find a reason to hit me for being lazy. If he wasn't hitting or kicking me it was because he was too busy to notice me. Now my mom would wait for me to screw up, like getting an F from school or being truant. Then she would pounce. My only break was when my parents were too busy fighting each other to notice me.

C: Did you ever need medical attention after a beating?

J: (dismissively) My arm was broken a few times.

C: Did any medical personnel or other adults recognize you were being abused?

J: (calmly) No one cared. Even when I showed up at school with loads of bruises no one seemed to see them. The teachers thought I was lazy. By about 14, I had learned to disappear if my dad was around. I'd learned to keep my mom in her place.

C: How did you learn that?

J: (intently) From listening to my dad and watching TV day and night.

C: What did you watch?

J: (intently) I always liked to watch action shows about police, spies, war. That's still what I watch.

C: What do you like about the action shows?

J: (intently) The quick action, the rage. I have gotten some good tips from these shows, how to use intimidation as well as my fists. My parents think I'm an idiot. But, I can learn fast when I want to.

C: What are you interested in learning right now?

J: (emphatically) As long as no one tries to push me, I will get the GED.

C: If I don't push you, are you willing to learn to express your anger and feel relaxed with ways that don't risk jail time? (*J* looks hesitant) I know a lot of ways to help people relax.

J: (challengingly) You think you can teach me more than I already know about sex?

C: I am talking about nonsexual and nonviolent ways to relax.

J: (sarcastically) We're going to drink together?

C: No. (pause) Does drinking help you relax?

J: (matter-of-factly) No, but I like the taste.

C: How much alcohol and drugs do you consume a day?

J: (irritably) I don't take drugs. I drink a couple of beers after work with the guys.

C: At home?

J: (intently) Maybe, if I'm watching football.

C: Do you ever get drunk? (*J* shakes his head no) Does drinking make you more or less edgy?

J: (angrily) If I'm edgy, I'm edgy whether I'm drinking or not.

C: There is no connection between when you lose control and when you drink?

J: (frustratedly) I've told you. I'm an easygoing guy most of the time.

C: What do you do for fun?

J: (reflectively) Watching TV is OK. I also like to swap stories with the guys at work about situations we've handled.

C: Do you ever get into physical fights with these guys?

J: (intently) No, I don't fight that much. The guys—maybe we push and shove a little at a bar after work just to get some material for a story session at work the next day.

C: Have you ever physically fought with your son?

J: No.

C: Is he scared of you?

J: No.

C: Is there anything that he does that makes you angry?

J: (emphatically) *No.* He is only three. Karen takes care of him.

C: What does he do when you and Karen are fighting?

J: (reflectively) He always runs into his room. Sometimes he seems to know, before the first blow, that a fight is going to start, and he goes off to watch TV.

C: Smart kid—he knows what triggers a fight. You are slumped pretty low in that chair. Are you feeling edgy or tense now?

J: (angrily) I'm in control. This is how I usually am.

C: Are you angry now?

J: (dismissively) No. (pause) Why would you ask?

C: Well, you were pushed into coming, and I have asked you a lot of questions. You have told me it makes you mad when people push you.

J: (frustratedly) It was this or jail; the choice was clear.

C: We need to talk very specifically about what things are making you feel tense and lose control. We need to develop nonaggressive ways to help you feel relaxed. Is it going to be safe for me to help you with this?

J: (challengingly) Safe?

C: If I make you feel tense and edgy, will you be able to tell me, or will you move in to shake me up?

J: (emphatically) I don't want to end up in jail.

C: You think you can control it here. (long pause during which *J* shakes his head yes) If I make you edgy, will you go home and shake Karen?

J: (irritably) I don't know. I don't plan to shake Karen up. If it happens, it's her fault.

C: Do you recognize when the tension is building?

J: (dismissively) Sometimes I do.

C: If you feel that in here, will you tell me?

J: (angrily) My probation officer says if I beat anyone up while I am on probation, I go straight to jail.

C: I'll come up with a plan to show you next week. If you want to follow it, you will gain control over your edgy, tense feelings. I will make sure to include skills that can help you stay out of jail and be an effective manager. I need to remind you that if I think Karen, or anyone else, is in danger, I'll have to call them and the police.

J: (intently) I'm not going to hit Karen or anyone else. I don't want to go to jail.

Behavioral Case Conceptualization of Jeff: Assumption-Based Style

Jeff's learning history is replete with observed acts of verbal and physical aggression, reinforcement of aggressive acts, and the association of domination over others with sexual satisfaction and relaxation. He watched countless violent interchanges between his parents, admired violent characters on television, and learned how to use his mouth and his fists to intimidate others. Just as his parents were successful in getting him to do what they wanted when he was little, the bigger he grew the more Jeff had his acts of verbal and physical aggression rewarded by getting what he wanted from his mother and from targeted others. While teachers at school did not abuse him, they showed a lack of interest or concern with his frequent injuries. This served to further reinforce Jeff's hostile view of the world, including his perception that violent individuals have power and control and nonviolent individuals are passive and useless in helping him. Jeff has a strong tendency to go on automatic pilot when he is angry and is only able to stop fighting once he has thoroughly dominated his opponent; if the opponent is female, feelings of domination seem to be associated with sexual satisfaction and relaxation. Jeff can control his urge to be violent if he is at work or confronted with police. As an adult, Jeff is hypervigilant to the behavior of others and quick to interpret the behavior of others—whether actually negative or neutral—as threatening. However, he has also learned to take seriously his responsibility to stay gainfully employed and to financially support his wife and child. These are assets that bode well for Jeff's potential to learn new behaviors if they provide consequences that meet his current goals, such as attaining a GED.

Jeff began building his repertoire of verbal and physical aggression through observing his parents. He remembers feeling safe from his parents' violence only when they were too busy assaulting each other to notice him. He learned that the precursors to his father's violent assaults could be anything. However, his mother's acts of aggression would originate in something Jeff had arguably done wrong. Trying to stay out of their way as much as possible, Jeff became an avid television watcher. While his first acts of verbal or physical aggression may have been mirror images of parental behaviors, Jeff is proud of how much he learned from watching violent role models on television. Pulling apart these observational influences may be impossible. However, whether from observing his father dominate his mother or from watching men dominate women on television, Jeff may have begun to vicariously experience emotional satisfaction and pleasure from the domination of women by men. As he entered puberty, this indirect learning may have become direct as he became more and more successful at dominating his mother. However, he never speaks of trying to dominate his father. Thus, whether from this relationship or from television, Jeff may have learned that to lose control with an authority figure can lead to self-harm. While it is unclear at this time who they might be, Jeff's dedication to his work suggests that he had role models for being responsible and earning a living. Thus, if angry at work, Jeff may engage in passive-aggressive behavior, such as burning food, but he will not overtly lose control of his behavior with his boss or fellow employees.

Jeff's violent skills were further reinforced through operant conditioning. His father found verbally and physically abusing Jeff to be rewarding and lost no opportunity to harm him. Jeff's mother had learned to value an education, and she would only verbally or physically abuse Jeff if she felt he was not working hard enough in school. When Jeff did not work as hard on his schoolwork as she wanted, she punished him by beating him verbally or physically. As he grew older, he began to be truant. This initially resulted in his mother's assaulting him, but as he grew larger, she became more and more Jeff's victim than the reverse. As a growing child, Jeff would have come more and more in contact with other youth within the neighborhood and school environments. While it is unclear, his upbringing makes it likely that Jeff was very aggressive within these environments and that the bigger he became, the more he was successful in victimizing those who were smaller or less intellectual agile than him. The joy that Jeff expresses about learning to dominant his mother clearly continues as he discusses his relationship with his wife Karen and the incident with the woman in the parking lot. He has learned that many respond with sympathy to pregnant women. Knowing this, he had Karen attend his court hearing and cry. As he expected, Jeff was put on probation rather than sent to jail. Jeff appears to find working for money rewarding. He goes to work regularly even when in a bad mood and is very aware that any obvious loss of control at work will get him fired. In addition, while he has nothing good to say about school, he has indicated a willingness to study for the GED if it will result in his earning more money and no one punishes him through nagging.

Jeff's violent behaviors are tied to physiological sensations of heat and tension that appear to have been classically conditioned in his youth. Jeff doesn't remember exactly when it started. He just knows that now, once the autopilot of rage gets turned on, he fights till he drops his victim. He has selected women to be his prime victims. This may be because of an association he has built up between sexual satisfaction and calmness with the domination of a woman. Clear subservience to his will must occur for Jeff to feel satisfied and relaxed. On the critical day when he came under the eye of the police, Jeff arrived at the parking lot at work, late and angry. He was angry because Karen had tried to gain his attention when he had chosen to ignore her. Because there was only time for Jeff to give her a few quick kicks, Karen hadn't been thoroughly dominated, so he drove to work still angry. Similarly, scaring the woman in the parking lot was not enough; if she wasn't going to move her car, he had to beat her up. With his male boss, the male police officers, and the male judge, he has been able to interfere with his tension cycle enough to stop himself from entering the rage phase. This may be partly because he continued to have mixed success in his aggressive encounters with his father and other men. He has also learned that many people behave in softer ways around a crying, pregnant woman. He utilized this effectively with Karen to move himself toward parole rather than prison. Jeff has also somehow managed to learn something that supports his role as a nonabusive father. None of the predictable behavior of infants or young children, such as impulsiveness, crying, and neediness, appears to have elicited any anger or frustration from Jeff. As a father, he has been able to perceive how helpless a young child is and approves of how Karen takes care of their son.

Currently, Jeff denies experiencing any feelings of anger, tension, of frustration. He claims to be a relaxed, laid-back guy. He may feel that he must maintain this persona with the clinician in order to avoid the punishing consequence of ending up in jail. However, unless treatment has a significant impact on his learning history, Jeff is likely to harm a woman again, probably Karen. Jeff himself was a poly-victim as a child and has become a poly-perpetrator of violence against women as a man. His current perpetration of violence has left women with physical injuries that have required hospitalization. His desire to avoid jail and enter a management training program appears genuine. Thus, this may be a time in Jeff's learning history when he is open to new strategies for living and interacting with others without violence.

Behavioral Treatment Plan: Assumption-Based Style

Treatment Plan Overview. Jeff's present goals are to stay out of jail by attending anger management training and to attain a GED so that he can become promoted at work. These goals may provide enough incentive to engage Jeff in treatment at this time. The clinician and probation officer will need to collaborate and evaluate Jeff for dangerousness on a session-by-session basis. Karen and other women are at most risk should he lose control. Progress on Long Term Goal 1 should be the initial focus of treatment, as this will make it less likely that he will be a risk to the clinician, probation officer, Karen, and women in general. (This treatment plan follows the *basic format.*)

LONG TERM GOAL 1: Jeff will learn emotional regulation skills in order to take control of his living situation and stay out of jail.

Short-Term Goals

1. Jeff will be given introductions to a number of relaxation and anger control strategies so that he can select the ones he wants to learn to increase his control over whether he is sent to jail.

2. Jeff will learn to identify, within sessions, the physical signs that he is becoming angry or tense and practice the skills he has selected.

3. Jeff will practice using his preferred relaxation strategies to prevent himself from getting "hot" during role plays of conflict situations with his probation officer and men at work.

4. Jeff will use avoidance to remove himself from out-of-session situations, as soon as he begins to feel angry or tense, to keep himself out of jail.

5. Jeff will learn to identify his anger and frustration before he feels hot and practice using relaxation exercises if he is experiencing any negative emotions.

6. Jeff will evaluate the most recent time he became angry or frustrated and identify the antecedents of this event; if talking about the event makes him angry, he will use his relaxation exercises.

7. Jeff will make a list of behaviors from others from least to most provoking and talk about each one in detail, using his relaxation exercises if his anger begins to rise from talking about these behaviors.

8. Jeff will begin to use strategies he has learned in session to prevent himself from getting hot out of session.

9. Other goals will be developed as appropriate to ensure he can stop and cool off if he is getting too hot.

LONG TERM GOAL 2: Jeff will use his observational skills to determine the successful and unsuccessful strategies that his GED classmates, people at the probation office, and his coworkers use to stay on the positive side of the teacher/probation officer/boss in order to take control of his living situation and stay out of jail.

Short-Term Goals

1. Jeff will observe how the teacher of the GED class behaves when a student is late, asks a question, or does something else that might cause the teacher frustration, and will discuss what the antecedents and consequences of this frustrating behavior were.

2. Jeff will make a list of the teacher's behaviors toward himself and the other students and determine if any of these behaviors "may be" skills he wants to learn.

3. Jeff will go early to probation appointments so that he can observe what happens between staff members when a person on the phone or in the office behaves in a way that might cause the probation officer frustration and discuss in session whether any of the behaviors he sees "may be" skills he wants to learn.

4. Jeff will make a list of the probation officer's behaviors toward himself and others and determine if any of these "may be" skills he wants to learn.

5. Jeff will observe his boss when a staff member is late, makes a mistake, or does something else that might cause frustration for the boss and discuss what the antecedents and consequences of this frustrating behavior were.

6. Jeff will make a list of the boss's behaviors toward him and others and determine if any of these "may be" skills he wants to learn.

7. Jeff will watch his wife interacting with his son and consider whether she is talking or behaving in a way that "may be" useful to him at work, in school, or when dealing with the courts.

8. Jeff will decide which of the "maybe" skills he wants to learn.

LONG TERM GOAL 3: Jeff's will identify consequences that follow his use of "maybe" or nonviolent problem-solving skills at work, during probation appointments, in his home life, and at work and decide if they are consequences that help him gain control of whether or not he goes to jail or gets his GED.

Short-Term Goals

1. Jeff will gain control of his probation requirements by developing a daily log of frustrating events that occurred at work and how he responded to each in order to not behave with violence.

2. Jeff will take control of the beginning of each weekly probation appointment by handing the probation officer the logs of his attempts during the week to maintain control during frustrating circumstances.

3. Jeff will take control of the end of each weekly probation appointment by asking his probation officer if he is currently meeting the expectations of the probation department.

4. Jeff will take control of the beginning of each treatment appointment by reviewing both his log and the probation officer's reaction to it within the session and discussing whether keeping the logs is helping or not in his having more control over staying out of jail.

5. Jeff will take control over his feelings of anger by considering any places in his neighborhood, or any situations, such as being late, that provide triggers to his aggressive behavior, and develop a schedule that could give him the personal control to avoid these triggers.

6. Jeff will plan, in sessions, how to maximize his learning within the GED program in order to keep his arousal level low and impress his teachers and employer with his learning potential.

7. Other goals will be developed as appropriate.

Behavioral Case Conceptualization of Jeff: Historically Based Style

As a developing person, Jeff had needs for physical, cognitive, and psychosocial mentoring that were met with verbal intimidation and physical aggression by his parents and with neglect from other adults such as teachers and medical personnel. No one actively taught him prosocial or nurturant life skills. Jeff became an active self-learner, concentrating on mastering violent responses that he could use to get his survival needs met. He did not recognize the need to learn prosocial competencies or perceive the value of them. As an adult, Jeff is quick to perceive and respond aggressively to any sign of attention from others. Neutral, positive, or negative behaviors by others are experienced as negative or threatening consequences, and his most common response is aggression. Jeff's current behavioral assets are his ability to learn quickly when motivated and his present motivation to stay out of jail and support his family through gainful employment.

As a young child, Jeff learned that adults were aggressive. His parents had many violent interchanges with each other, thereby serving as role models for the use of aggression in intimate relationships, the use of aggression in communicating about problems, and the use of aggression to solve problems. This emphasis on aggression "to teach people how to behave" or "as punishment for misdeeds" was further entrenched by its use as the sole active parenting strategy used to influence Jeff's behavior. Both parents were supportive of each other's physical abuse of Jeff. When not providing violent consequences, Jeff's parents may have ignored his behavior. Jeff had the ability to learn nonviolent skills, but he wasn't provided with an environment that supported this type of skill development.

As Jeff entered the school years, he perceived teachers as providing only negative consequences to his behavior, such as calling him lazy and ignoring obvious signs of abuse. These learning experiences further reinforced Jeff's negative identifications with his parents. Jeff turned to TV for company and for learning how to negotiate through a hostile world. The shows that he selected to watch confirmed his prior learning that the world was a hostile place and that self-esteem and security were gained through mastery of verbal and physical aggression. He developed a positive identification with the characters in the action shows who earned respect through their use of physical violence and lack of toleration for bending to the authority of others. He was highly attentive to these role models and began to actively learn through observing them.

As a teenager, Jeff had developed the physical strength and had mastered enough violent techniques to use verbal and physical intimidation with his mother. He began using the skills he had learned by observing his father and his TV role models. His mother provided reinforcement for this behavior by acquiescing to his demands and not beating him anymore. Jeff used physical avoidance to protect himself from his father. Thus, Jeff learned how to keep himself safe at home. The quality and extent of his peer interactions as he was developing are unclear. His teachers continued ignoring obvious signs he was a victim of abuse, such as a broken arm, and he didn't receive any consequences from them that he found reinforcing. As a result, he did not consider them role models. He did not actively try to learn nonviolent ways of relating to others from observing them, and he did not learn to find academic success rewarding; he dropped out of high school.

As an adult, Jeff continues to have his violent view of the world reinforced by the environmental experiences he selects. He socializes exclusively with other violent men. These peer activities focus on demonstrating who is most expert at the use of verbal and physical aggression. Women (his wife, his mother) have reinforced his verbal and physical aggression by acquiescing to his demands. Jeff's knowledge of Karen's abuse by her parents, as well as his memories of his mother's abuse by his father, further underscores to him the acceptability and usefulness of violence against women. A further positive reinforcer for Jeff's violence is the feeling of relaxation he gains after physically dominating a woman. Classical learning also may play a role in the autonomic symptoms he describes as being immediately antecedent to his losses of control. Jeff was repeatedly a victim and witness of violence within his home. It is possible that many neutral stimuli within his home environment became conditioned stimuli as they were unintentionally paired with physical assaults. Jeff may enter these loss-of-control states only with women. He has learned to control the level of his anger in situations in which he might lose a fight (with his dad, other men) or in which his income or personal freedom is at stake (with his boss, the probation officer). While his life is full of rage, he maintains gainful employment and is committed to supporting his wife, son, and future children. He also plans to improve his employment opportunities through completing a GED and attending management training; thus, he has a willingness to learn new skills when the consequences for doing so are clear and motivating to him.

At the present time, Jeff's violent behavior is determined in complex ways and supports his poly-victimization of women as an adult male. He has had his violent responses consistently reinforced by Karen's doing his bidding. He is exposed daily to violent role models that serve to further reinforce his violent worldview. He may also respond violently when exposed to certain classically conditioned stimuli. Yet, there is more to Jeff than his propensity for violence. As a child, he developed a facility for learning through observation despite receiving little if any help from others in doing so. As an adult, he is showing a willingness to work hard and learn new skills in order to better support his family. At this point in his learning history, Jeff has come into conflict with the legal system. Prior to being sentenced to probation, Jeff did not receive any consequences for his violent behavior that he found negative. Thus, he had no motivation to change. The knowledge that he could go to jail if he commits another violent offense has provided him with an incentive to increase his self-control. This probationary period is a window of opportunity for engaging Jeff in learning experiences that could increase his range of nonviolent responses to anger, frustration, and tension as well as increase or modify his prosocial skills or teach him new ones.

Behavioral Treatment Plan: Historically Based Style

Treatment Plan Overview. Jeff's present goals are to stay out of jail by attending anger management training and to attain a GED so that he can become promoted at work. These goals may provide enough incentive to engage Jeff in treatment at this time. The clinician and probation officer will need to collaborate and evaluate Jeff for dangerousness on a session-by-session basis. Karen and other women are at most risk should he lose control. Long-Term Goals 1 and 2 will be worked on simultaneously, followed later by first Goal 3 and then 4. (This treatment plan follows the *problem format.*)

PROBLEM: Jeff raised himself and did not get help learning how to get what he needed or wanted from life without the use of aggression. The clinician and probation officer will need to take on the educational role (not taken by his parents) of inhibiting his aggression and encouraging the development of adaptive competencies. For each goal, either the probation officer or the clinician will underscore the consequence of negative behavior (going to jail) and the consequences of positive behavior (success as a manager, staying out of jail, developing intimacy).

LONG-TERM GOAL 1: Jeff will receive the learning experiences not provided by his parents and teachers on how to use environmental controls to inhibit his aggressive behavior so that he will stay out of jail.

Short-Term Goals

1. Jeff will attend weekly probation appointments and receive positive social consequences for arriving on time, being polite, and not making threats.

2. Jeff will attend weekly treatment appointments and receive positive social support for arriving on time, being polite, and not making threats.

3. Jeff will avoid bars and socializing outside of work with violent individuals to decrease triggers for aggressive behavior that could lead to jail time.

4. Jeff will seek out opportunities within GED study sessions and management training sessions to observe how others manage to keep their arousal level low in social situations, and he will consider the value of copying this behavior himself.

5. Other goals will be developed as appropriate.

LONG-TERM GOAL 2: Jeff will receive the learning experiences not provided by his parents and teachers on how to use anger control and stress reduction strategies to control his edgy feelings.

Short-Term Goals

1. Jeff will be given introductions to a number of relaxation and anger control strategies so that he can select the ones he wants to learn.

2. Jeff will learn to identify, within sessions, the physical signs that he is becoming angry or tense.

3. Jeff will practice using his preferred relaxation strategies to prevent himself from getting hot during role plays of conflict situations.

4. Jeff will use avoidance to remove himself from out-of-session situations, as soon as he begins to feel angry or tense, to keep himself out of jail.

5. Jeff will begin to use strategies he has learned in session to prevent himself from getting hot out of session.

6. Other goals will be developed as appropriate.

LONG-TERM GOAL 3: Adult Jeff will learn new nonaggressive communication and problem-solving strategies he was not taught in childhood so that he can gain positive reinforcement from his boss, his probation officer, his clinician, and so forth for showing self-control in conflictual situations and be prepared to be a manager.

Short-Term Goals

1. Jeff will be introduced to alternative strategies for effective listening, assertive communication, and problem-solving so that he can select the ones he would like to learn.

2. Jeff will practice effective listening strategies, first within treatment sessions, then within probation sessions, then at work, and finally at home.

3. Once he has mastered listening skills, Jeff will practice (in session) assertive responses to conflict situations involving others; if he gets angry, he will stop the role play and help himself relax.

4. Jeff will practice assertive responses to conflict out of session; if he gets angry, he will remove himself from the situation and help himself relax.

5. Other goals will be developed as appropriate.

LONG-TERM GOAL 4: Jeff will learn strategies for developing emotional intimacy that he was not taught in childhood.

Short-Term Goals

1. Jeff and the clinician will discuss what emotionally intimate behavior refers to and the concrete rewards that can follow this type of behavior.

2. Jeff will observe others and develop a list of the positive, neutral, and negative consequences that he has seen following emotionally intimate behavior.

   a. Jeff will observe nurturing behavior between Karen and his son John and then discuss his observations with the clinician.

   b. Jeff will observe nurturing behavior between coworkers or customers and then discuss his observations with the clinician.

3. Jeff will practice play skills with the clinician to use in later sessions with Karen and John that will use nurturant behavior such as encouragement and praise when John is behaving well, leaving Karen in charge if John misbehaves.

4. Jeff will discuss with the clinician the types of behavior John engages in at home that he finds frustrating and will practice with the clinician how he might remove himself from the situation and take time to reduce any of his feelings of anger and frustration while leaving Karen in charge of John.

5. Jeff will practice play skills with Karen and John during treatment sessions, using only nurturant behavior with John and removing himself from the situation and calming himself down if he experiences anger and frustration.

6. Jeff will use effective listening and assertive communication to discuss with Karen, during sessions, the consequences they are receiving from playing together with John and whether they are ready to try this at home.

7. Jeff will keep a log of his experiences of trying to calm himself down when frustrated, using nurturant behaviour, and using nonaggressive problem-solving strategies and discuss this log in session.

8. Jeff will use effective listening and nurturant behavior in talking to John in session about whether he feels scared at home, and Jeff will remove himself, and leave Karen in charge, if he begins to feel angry about anything John says or does.

9. Jeff will use effective listening and problem-solving skills to talk with Karen about what they could do at home to be the best possible parents for John and keep the home a safe place for everyone.

10. Other goals will be developed as appropriate.

PRACTICE CASE FOR STUDENT CONCEPTUALIZATION: INTEGRATING THE DOMAIN OF AGE

It is time to do a behavioral analysis of Kevin. There are many domains of complexity that might provide insights into his behavior. You are asked to integrate the domain of age into your behavioral case conceptualization and treatment plan.

Information Received From Brief Intake

Kevin is a 14-year-old White male going to high school in a rural area. He has a long history of high scholastic achievement and plans to attend college after finishing high school. He is living with his biological parents and two older sisters. His father is a self-employed farmer. At the age of 7, Kevin was diagnosed with an inoperable brain tumor. Extended chemotherapy arrested the tumor growth but resulted in temporary loss of his hair. Because of this tumor, Kevin had extended school absences in the first and second grades. Kevin's high school counselor referred him for treatment; Kevin had told the counselor that he couldn't look in mirrors and hated himself. His parents disapproved of his coming for this appointment but did not prevent it.

During a brief mental status exam, there were no indications of suicidal or homicidal ideation or severe psychopathology. Kevin was asked to sign release forms for consultations with school personnel and his family. Kevin was willing to sign these forms only for the school system. When asked if he had any preference for whom he saw in treatment, Kevin indicated he would take the first appointment available.

Interview With Kevin (K) From a Behavioral Perspective

C: Kevin, I understand that you consider yourself to be phobic of mirrors. Can you tell me exactly what you mean by this?

K: (openly) I can't look in mirrors. If I try, I break out into a sweat and begin to feel dizzy.

C: Can you remember a time when you could look in mirrors?

K: (reflectively) Before I had chemotherapy and my hair fell out, I looked in mirrors all the time. After my hair fell out, I looked like a freak—it was scary. I can still remember the day I came home from the hospital and the way my older sisters ran when they saw how I looked.

C: You were frightened by losing your hair or by their reaction to it?

K: (intently) Both. After they ran away, I rushed into the bathroom and stared at myself for a while. Until that moment, I was so glad to get out of the hospital that I hadn't thought about my looks. I came to realize I was a freak.

C: A freak?

K: (angrily) That's what all of the kids at school called me after I returned to school.

C: All of the kids, even your friends?

K: (angrily) I had no friends from the time I left the hospital. No one wanted to associate with a freak. (long pause) I was alone.

C: Did anyone associate with you?

K: (thoughtfully) Some of the teachers. They were repulsed by me, but they were nice and always gave me additional assignments.

C: How, specifically, did they react toward you?

K: (sadly) They looked other kids in the face but not me.

C: What did the doctors tell you?

K: (intently) They saved my life. (long pause) What more could I expect?

C: Has there ever been a time, since your operation, that you could look into mirrors?

K: (anxiously) No, every time I try, I break into a sweat, and my heart feels like it will burst open. It's a real phobia.

C: What have your parents done to help you?

K: (matter-of-factly) I'm on my own. They took me to the hospital when I was sick but never visited. (long pause; scornfully) Surprise, I didn't die. They had to bring me home.

C: Didn't they want you home?

K: (calmly) Sure, it was spring planting time. They needed my help.

C: Did they ever try to help you with your phobia?

K: (anxiously) My father tried to make me get over it in the third grade by forcing me to look in a mirror; I passed out.

C: What happened exactly?

K: (anxiety rising) I was getting ready to catch the school bus. My father said that I had forgotten to comb my hair. I disagreed. We argued about it for a while, and then he dragged me into the bathroom to look in the mirror. When I came to, my mother handed me a comb and told me to hurry or I would miss the bus.

C: What brought you in to see me now?

K: (sweating profusely) Other boys in my class have started to grow beards. How will I shave if I can't look into a mirror? If I don't shave, I'll look even more like a freak. (desperately) Can you help me?

C: Yes, phobias can be cured. Together we will work out a plan to overcome yours.

K: (intently) Other people may be able to stop being afraid, but can a freak like me?

C: You sweat and feel like your heart will burst when you go near a mirror, but you are not a freak. I know that you have the brains and skills to combat your problems just by the way you have come forward today.

K: (hopefully) What do you mean?

C: Most people are afraid when they come here and don't want to talk. Most people can describe having trouble breathing or feeling faint but don't know the term *phobia*. That's a professional description of your problem. You already have an insight and expertise into your problem that few adults have. You also show an open-mindedness to seeking out help.

K: (excitedly) What's next?

C: I need to ask a few more questions. Is there anything that makes the phobia worse?

K: (reflectively) After the kids or someone in my family has taunted me, I can't even go near a room that has a mirror in it without feeling panicky.

C: Does someone have to taunt you about your appearance to bring on this reaction, or can someone taunt you about something else, like calling you an idiot?

K: (painfully) No one sees me as anything but a freak, except for some of my teachers. They've always encouraged me and thought I could make it to college.

C: How is your physical health now?

K: (dismissively) I haven't needed any medical exams for years. My mom still tries popping pills or vitamins into my mouth.

C: Your mom seems worried about your health, but it's not necessary?

K: (irritably) I'm fine; the doctors don't even follow up with me anymore. My mother doesn't get what the real problem is—I'm an outcast. My father only cares about problems that relate to our farm.

C: Is there anything besides mirrors that triggers your fear?

K: (thoughtfully) Anything that is really shiny so that it reflects an image. At school there's a corridor where one side is all windows. The hallway is lit in a strange way. I have to look down at the floor or I can see my reflection in the windows.

C: What happens if you see your reflection?

K: (anxiously) I have to run out of there as fast as I can or else I'll be sick.

C: How often have you had to do this?

K: (intently) Maybe once a month, I get distracted by something, and I forget to keep my eyes on the floor.

C: Have any of your teachers or peers noticed?

K: (calmly) No teacher has ever said anything to me. The kids know better by now. I learned early on that the only way to stop their mouths was to kick ass. At first, it was my ass that got kicked, but now, I know how to handle things. They may think I'm a freak, but they keep their distance if they know what's good for them.

C: What happens before you kick ass?

K: (reflectively) It could be anything from a direct statement, to someone shoving me in the hall, to giving me a nasty look. I don't always beat kids up; sometimes I just give them my *look*, and if they back off, I leave them alone. When I was little, I always had to fight. Since I reached six feet tall, my look has gone a long way.

C: What happens after you kick ass?

K: (proudly) No one bugs me for a long time. Sometimes the teachers tell me to cool off. I think my school counselor, the one who sent me here, thinks that I need more self-control. He doesn't know what it's like to be a freak.

C: What have you tried to do to help yourself with this problem?

K: (nervously) Once in a while I try to get myself to look in mirrors. I usually try the mirror in the basement bathroom at home because no one else in the family likes to go down there. I start walking down the basement stairs telling myself to be cool—I can handle the mirror. As I get to the bottom of the stairs, my heart starts to pound. Usually, I cannot get into the bathroom. I have also tried rushing down the stairs trying not to think. Once, I actually got the door open before I panicked.

C: What helped make this time work better?

K: (reflectively) I was going down to the basement to get something for my mom, so I hadn't planned in advance to try to look into a mirror.

C: Have you tried anything else?

K: (tense) Don't you think I tried enough?

C: I think you are a very strong person. I'm impressed with the efforts you have made. I just want to make sure I understand everything you have tried.

K: (apologetically) I'm sorry I lost my cool. I know you are here to help.

C: It's been a tough hour for you. I am going to spend the time between now and our next session working out our battle plan. I'll share my ideas with you next week, and you can make any suggestions you think might make it work better.

K: (anxiously) Can anything be done?

C: If it wasn't hard, you'd have handled it by yourself years ago—you've got guts. But it's hard. You did the right thing to come for help. I would like you to keep a record this week of each time your anxiety about mirrors begins to build. Try to describe how anxious you are each time, on a scale of one to ten. Then, indicate what happened right before the anxiety started. Try to do something to help yourself chill out. Then, write down what you did, and, on a scale of one to (Kevin interrupts)

K: ten, write down how successful I was.

C: Absolutely right! I know you can do it.

Exercises for Developing a Case Conceptualization of Kevin

Exercise 1 *(four-page maximum)*

GOAL: To verify that you have a clear understanding of behavioral theory.

STYLE: An integrative essay comprising Parts A through C.

NEED HELP?   Review this chapter (pages 107–110).

A. Develop a concise overview of all the assumptions of behavioral theory (the theory's hypotheses about key dimensions in understanding how clients change; think broadly, abstractly) as an introduction to the rest of this exercise.

B. Develop a thorough description of how each of these assumptions is used to understand a client's progression through the change process in paragraphs that provide specific examples to fully explain each assumption.

C. Conclude your essay by describing the role of the clinician in helping the client change (consultant, doctor, educator, helper), the major approach taken to treatment, and common treatment techniques. Provide enough specific examples to clarify what is distinctive about this approach.

Exercise 2 *(four-page maximum)*

GOAL: To aid application of behavioral theory to Kevin.

STYLE: A separate sentence outline for each section, A through C.

NEED HELP?   Review this chapter (pages 107–110).

A. Create a list of Kevin's behavioral deficits/excesses and behavioral assets/skills, and for each provide:

1. An operational definition; frequency, duration, and intensity of the behavior; what, if anything, decreases its frequency or intensity; what, if anything, increases its frequency or intensity; and the antecedents and consequences of the behavior.

2. A discussion of the type(s) of learning that might be involved: operant, classical, and/or social learning.

3. A discussion of the environmental factors that exist that would support change in the problematic behavior and/or would enhance more adaptive behaviors as replacements, as well as those that might provide barriers to change.

    C. Discuss the strategies Kevin has used to adapt to his environment in the past, his preferred manner of learning, and his present attitude toward new learning.

    D. Discuss how adaptively Kevin is functioning within his environment at this time.

Exercise 3 (four-page maximum)

GOAL: To develop an understanding of the potential role of development in Kevin's life.

STYLE: A separate sentence outline for each section, A through H.

NEED HELP?   Review Chapter 2 (pages 27–41).

    A. Assess how age appropriate Kevin's physical development and cognitive development have been and how, and in what ways, they have influenced his performance and level of motivation at home, in school, or within community activities, both at age 8 and at age 14.

    B. Assess how age appropriate Kevin's relationships to adults have been in terms of their providing limit setting, monitoring, skill building, and emotional connection and in what ways these relationships have supported or hindered the developmental process, both at age 8 and at age 14.

    C. Assess how age appropriate Kevin's relationships to peers have been in providing casual social skill building and friendship and in what ways these relationships have supported or hindered the developmental process at ages 8 and 14.

    D. Assess how age appropriately Kevin is functioning overall at this time; include consideration of his self-image and self-efficacy, what he needs most to support his healthy development as a teen, and what, if any, barriers to maturation or maturation-facilitating factors exist at this time.

    E. Assess your current knowledge of issues relevant to Kevin's age group.

       1. How many courses have you taken that give you background on adolescence?

       2. How many workshops have you attended that give you background on adolescence?

       3. What professional experiences have you had with adolescents?

       4. What personal experiences have you had with adolescents?

       5. What cohort effects might influence your worldview of adolescents in terms of what is important in the world, how they communicate, and what is rewarded and punished in this world?

    F. Assess your current level of awareness of how Kevin's age may influence your clinical work.

1. How might your current age and current amount of contact with adolescents influence your reactions to Kevin?

2. What stereotypes about adolescents do you know about?

3. What experiences have you had that could support your effective work with Kevin? What experiences have you had that might lead to a negative bias or marginalization of Kevin's point of view or current situation?

G. Assess your current skills in working with adolescents.

1. What skills do you currently have that are of value in working with adolescents?

2. What skills do you feel it would be important to develop to work effectively with this age group?

H. What action steps can you take?

1. What can you do to prepare yourself to be more skilled in working with adolescents?

2. How might you structure the treatment environment to increase the likelihood of a positive outcome with adolescents?

3. What processes of treatment might you change to make them more welcoming to adolescents?

Exercise 4 (five-page maximum)

GOAL: To help you integrate your knowledge of behavioral theory and development into an in-depth conceptualization of Kevin (who he is and why he does what he does).

STYLE: An integrated essay consisting of a premise, supportive details, and conclusions following a carefully planned organizational style.

NEED HELP?   Review Chapter 2 (pages 27–41) and Chapter 1 (pages 1–7).

STEP 1: Consider what style you could use for organizing your behavioral understanding of Kevin that (a) would support you in providing a comprehensive and clear understanding of his learning history and how this influences him at this time and (b) would support language that he'd find persuasive as a teenager.

STEP 2: Develop a concise premise (overview, preliminary or explanatory statements, summary of key features, proposition, hypotheses, thesis statement, theory-driven introduction) that explains Kevin's strengths and weaknesses as a teenager who has a mirror phobia and has often been in charge of his own learning. If you have trouble with Step 2, remember that it should be an integration of the key ideas of Exercises 2 and 3 and that it should (a) provide a basis for Kevin's long-term goals, (b) be grounded in behavioral theory and include a developmental context for understanding his past and current behavior, and (c) highlight the strengths he might bring to behavioral treatment.

STEP 3: Develop your supporting material or detailed case analysis of strengths and weaknesses from a behavioral perspective, incorporating within each paragraph a deep understanding of Kevin as a socially rejected teen. If you have trouble with Step 3, consider the information you'll need to (a) support the development of short-term goals, (b) be grounded in behavioral treatment that is sensitive to development, and (c) integrate an understanding of Kevin's strengths in the learning process whenever possible.

STEP 4: Develop your conclusions and broad treatment recommendations, including (a) Kevin's overall level of functioning, (b) anything facilitating or serving as a barrier to his learning new skills at this time, and (c) his most basic needs as a learner at this time, being careful to consider what you said in Parts F and H of Exercise 3 (be concise and general).

Exercise 5 (three-page maximum)

GOAL: To develop an individualized, theory-driven action plan for Kevin that considers his strengths and is age appropriate.

STYLE : A sentence outline consisting of long- and short-term goals.

NEED HELP? Review Chapter 1 (pages 7–24).

STEP 1: Develop your treatment plan overview, being careful to consider what you said in Part F and H of Exercise 3 to prevent any negative bias in your treatment plan and insure that you adapt your approach to Kevin's unique needs as an individual.

STEP 2: Develop long-term (major, large, ambitious, comprehensive, broad) goals that Kevin will *ideally* reach by the termination of treatment in order to learn adaptive and/or unlearn maladaptive skills to support his development as a teen and overcome his mirror phobia. If you have trouble with this step, reread your premise and support topic sentences and transform them into goals that might involve classical conditioning, operant conditioning, and/or observational learning (use the *style* you selected for Exercise 4).

STEP 3: Develop short-term (small, brief, encapsulated, specific, measurable) goals that Kevin and you can expect to see accomplished within a few weeks and that will help you chart his progress in learning, instill hope for change, and plan time-effective treatment sessions. If you have trouble with this step, reread your support paragraphs, looking for ideas to transform into goals that (a) might help him learn adaptive or unlearn maladaptive skills using particular modes of learning that are sensitive to his being a teen, (b) might enhance factors facilitating or decrease factors inhibiting his ability to learn new skills at this time, (c) utilize his strengths in the learning process whenever possible, and (d) are individualized to his issues as a teen from a neglectful home rather than generic.

Exercise 6

GOAL: To critique behavioral treatment in the case of Kevin.

STYLE: Answer each question in essay format or discuss in a group format.

A. What are the strengths and weaknesses of this model for helping Kevin (a teenager with a mirror phobia, self-hatred, and problems with aggression)?

B. What beliefs might Kevin have learned from his family based on the interview, and how might an expansion of your conceptualization, to include self-talk, attributions, expectations, and perceptions, strengthen your treatment plan?

C. Based on information from the domain of violence, how dangerous do you think Kevin is at this time? In what ways should his propensity toward violent problem-solving influence your treatment planning, both in the short run and over time?

D. Assume that you were a clinician working at the hospital when 8-year-old Kevin came in to receive treatment for his brain tumor. His doctors referred Kevin to you for support in dealing with his medical condition. What ethical issues would have arisen for you once you learned that Kevin's family never visited or called him? How specifically would you handle the situation?

E. Kevin was quick to take offense at things the clinician said during the interview and has a history of aggressive behavior to things he considers provocative. Reread the interview, taking note of your reactions to this behavior. Then discuss these reactions along with your ideas for how to handle them effectively, within a behavioral framework, to support the development of an effective treatment alliance.

RECOMMENDED RESOURCES

Books

Antony, M. M., & Roemer, L. (2011). *Behavior therapy.* Washington, DC: American Psychological Association.

Ingram, B. L. (2012). *Clinical case formulations: Matching the integrative treatment plan to the client* (Chapter 11, pp. 225–255). Hoboken, NJ: John Wiley & Sons.

Martin, G., & Pear, J. (2010). *Behavior modification: What it is and how to do it* (9th ed.). Upper Saddle River, NJ: Prentice Hall.

Michael, J. L. (2004). *Concepts and principles of behavior analysis* (Rev. ed.). Kalamazoo, MI: Society for the Advancement of Behavior Analysis.

Videos

American Psychological Association (Producer), & Persons, J. B. (Trainer). (n.d.). *Cognitive behavior therapy* (Motion Picture #4310774). (Available from the American Psychological Association, 750 First Street, NE, Washington, DC 20002–4242)

Chapman, A. L. (Featured). (2014). Dialectical behavioral therapy [Video series episode]. In *APA psychotherapy video series II: Specific treatments for specific populations*. Washington, DC: American Psychological Association.

Gondim, P. (2006, October 22). Behaviour therapy [Video file]. Retrieved from https://www.youtube.com/watch?v=MCyfMFXR-n0

Smethells, J. (2012, December 5). Snake phobia behavioral therapy [Video file]. Retrieved from https://www.youtube.com/watch?v=zKTpecooiec

Websites

Association for Behavioral Analysis International. http://www.abainternational.org/

The Linehan Institute: Behavioral Tech. http://behavioraltech.org

Cognitive Case Conceptualizations and Treatment Plans

INTRODUCTION TO COGNITIVE THEORY

You received a phone call last week from Marie, a 30-year-old, White widow with two daughters, Amy (age 8) and Nancy (age 5). Marie's husband, Allen, along with two business associates, was killed when their chartered plane crashed during a severe thunderstorm one month ago. Allen had been hurrying home to come to the engagement party of Marie's younger sister and had taken the chartered plane because his original flight, on a national airline, was delayed because of the weather. This sudden death ended what Marie described as a happy and satisfying 10-year marriage. She and the girls continue to live in the family home, which is located in a suburb of a large city. Marie is self-referred. She is very concerned about her ability to parent her two daughters in the aftermath of Allen's death. She participated in a mental status interview and psychometric testing last week. The results indicate that Marie is depressed but having no suicidal ideation. There were also no signs of homicidal ideation, cognitive confusion, or impulsivity.

You take the cognitive approach to treatment developed by Aaron Beck (1991; Beck Institute for Cognitive Therapy and Research, 2008; J. S. Beck 2011). This approach focuses on the role of maladaptive cognitions in psychological distress. From this perspective, it is not the death of her husband and its aftermath that will be the focus of Marie's treatment but rather her cognitive representation of these events. Problems are considered to be a result of self-defeating belief systems (cognitive structures) that increase the power of distorted images and thoughts Marie may have as a result of her husband's death. The goals of treatment will be to assess and modify Marie's cognitive distortions by reappraising her automatic thoughts; teaching her the role of distorted negative thinking in her current difficulties; and recording, challenging, and modifying her thinking (A. T. Beck, 1991; J. S. Beck, 2011; Sudak, 2006).

How has Marie developed her belief systems (cognitive schemata)? Cognitive theory posits that as individuals develop from infancy through old age, they develop and maintain beliefs about themselves and the world. These beliefs develop around important themes or social issues such as success and failure, acceptance and rejection, and respect and disdain (A. T. Beck, 1991). Some of these are core beliefs and have overarching influences on an individual. Others are more specific, intermediate beliefs that consist of working rules and assumptions for more specific situations and events. All these beliefs become part of the individual's cognitive representations of the world and are reflected in a stream of self-talk or automatic thoughts. This self-talk is the individual's internal communication system. Some individuals are more aware of this internal communication than others are. Through learning, the individual's self-talk comes to include evaluations of the self, others, and the environment as well as recollections of the past and expectations about the future (A. T. Beck, 1991; J. S. Beck, 2011).

What impact will this internal communication system have on Marie? Her stream of self-talk will monitor, initiate, and inhibit her behavior. In areas where she shows adaptive behavior (high self-esteem and self-efficacy), this is assumed to result from adaptive beliefs with their concomitant positive stream of self-talk. Conversely, maladaptive behavior (low self-esteem, self-criticism) is assumed to result from maladaptive beliefs with their concomitant negative stream of self-talk. Marie has learned both her adaptive and her maladaptive beliefs.

How does this learning occur? Caretakers and others may explicitly teach these beliefs to children, or children may learn them implicitly through modeling. For example, a child may see a parent drop a glass on the floor. The parent might say, "Oh no, I dropped a glass! Oh well, I can clean it up; it's just a mistake, no big deal." The child might learn from this that everyone makes mistakes and mistakes can be fixed. On the other hand, the parent might say, "Oh no, this is a disaster! I can never do anything right; now the evening is ruined." The child might learn from this that mistakes are awful and cannot be fixed.

From long-term exposure to a positive view of the world, children may develop positively biased cognitive schemata (core and intermediate beliefs) and self-talk in which they interpret their own behavior and that of others with positive expectations, attributions, and evaluations. These individuals have a positive bias to their inferences about the future and their recollections of the past. Mistakes and unpleasant experiences do not in and of themselves lead to the blockage of positive information (A. T. Beck, 1991; J. S. Beck, 2011; Sudak, 2006).

In contrast, from long-term exposure to a negative view of the world, children may develop negatively biased cognitive schemata and self-talk, leading to a negative lens for viewing their own and others' behavior. A negative cognitive bias makes people more vulnerable to negative thinking and may prevent them from noticing or being influenced by positive events. Anything that fits the negative worldview is taken in easily. Individuals with a negative bias often interpret anything ambiguous as negative. Aaron Beck (1991) postulates the existence of elevated, depressed, anxious, and angry cognitive biases. Cognitive biases can be restricted to specific realms of experience, or they may be comprehensive (A. T. Beck, 1991; J. S. Beck, 2011; Sudak, 2006).

THE ROLE OF THE CLINICIAN

How will you help Marie? You will be an educator and a hypothesis generator who takes an active role in directing treatment and helping Marie assess and modify her self-defeating belief systems. First, Marie will be educated about the model so that she understands how her thoughts lead to her feelings and behavior (A. T. Beck, 1991; Sudak, 2006). Second, you will help Marie become aware of her self-talk and take on the view that her thoughts are hypotheses that can be tested. This assessment or examination of cognitions involves a partnership between you and Marie. Together you will collect data about, and test the usefulness and validity of, her belief systems using a Socratic dialogue (A. T. Beck, 1991; Ingram, 2012). Overall, this process involves your asking Marie questions, pushing her to test out her conclusions, increasing her ability to recognize distortions of thinking, and increasing the imagination and flexibility that she brings to her thinking about her life. Marie will learn to recognize her common errors in thinking in terms of specific here-and-now events in the treatment room and/or in her daily life; this step-by-step refutation of maladaptive thoughts will serve as a means to challenge Marie's underlying maladaptive beliefs (A. T. Beck, 1991; J. S. Beck, 2011; Ingram, 2012; Sudak, 2006).

Specifically, you two will investigate (a) the attributions she makes about herself and others; (b) her expectations about the future; (c) her perceptions of what happens, including any negative biases she may have; and (d) her perceptions of past events and any biases in her interpretation of these events. Errors in thinking may involve all-or-nothing thinking (dichotomous thinking), arbitrary inference (jumping to conclusions), emotional reasoning (using feelings, not facts, to draw conclusions), fortune telling (believing that the future can be predicted), magnification and minimization (misrepresenting the realistic impact of something), mind reading (believing that you can know what another person is thinking), personalization (assuming something must have something to do with you personally), overgeneralization (overly broad inference), selective abstraction (deleting or ignoring information), and exaggeration or distortion (A. T. Beck & Weishaar, 2000; Ingram, 2012).

Marie will investigate her thoughts both within the session and through homework assignments such as keeping a thought log that can make her more aware of how her thinking is connected to her feelings of depression and anxiety. After learning to identify her cognitive errors, Marie will be helped to see the connections between these maladaptive cognitions and her current life stress. She will be helped to understand how constant self-criticism and negative predictions, recollections, and interpretations have all fed on one another to create self-blame, low self-esteem, and low self-efficacy. Then, through in- and out-of-session activities, Marie will be encouraged to notice, catch, monitor, interrupt, and challenge her negative thoughts and then give herself reinforcement for more adaptive coping responses. She will be helped to identify high-risk situations and consider ways to prepare for, handle, and deal with any failures.

Marie will also be encouraged to engage in activities that promote feelings of competence and pleasure and to make positive self-attributions concerning these activities, such as "I can influence the world" and "I don't have to be a passive victim of life events." These attributions of control are assumed to have the potential to increase Marie's self-efficacy and to enable her to alter the negative attributions she imposes on herself, others, and the environment. As more positive cognitions become part of Marie's automatic stream of consciousness, her mood and overt behavior will be positively influenced (A. T. Beck, 1991; J. S. Beck, 2011; Sudak, 2006).

CASE APPLICATION: INTEGRATING THE DOMAIN OF GENDER

Marie's case will now be examined in detail. There are many domains of complexity that might be relevant to her case. The domain of gender has been chosen for examination within a cognitive case conceptualization and treatment plan.

Interview With Marie (M) From a Cognitive Perspective

C: I understand your husband died recently and you have concerns about your children. What are you concerned about specifically?

M: (calmly) My husband and I have always prided ourselves on our parenting. It was very important to both of us that our girls be raised correctly. (pause) Now that I am alone, I feel I am betraying my husband's trust.

C: How do you think you are betraying your husband?

M: (calmly) He was my best friend and perfect husband. We had the same ideas about how to live and raise children; everything was going the way we planned. (with agitation) Now, my eight-year-old, Amy, is having one temper tantrum after another at home, is constantly picking fights with her sister Nancy, and is being rude to her teachers.

C: Your daughter is misbehaving at home and at school. How is this your fault and a betrayal?

M: (regretfully) Amy had a perfect record at school before Allen died. She never missed a day and had the report card of an angel. Now . . . I fight with her every morning just to get her dressed, and she is *rude* to her teacher.

C: You find rudeness unacceptable.

M: (emphatically) Girls do not behave that way. Allen and I never tolerated back talk. He would be so upset by Amy's behavior.

C: What specifically have you tried to do about it?

M: (earnestly) I have always set an example of self-control. I am never rude to anyone, including the children, no matter how badly they have misbehaved.

C: Is it wrong to show anger? (*M* nods) Do you think that humans, particularly children, can always control their anger?

M: (sadly) I know that they need to be taught self-control, but the way Amy has been slipping, I just don't know what I am doing wrong that she is . . . (*M* sobs softly)

C: What thoughts are overwhelming you?

M: (sounding sad and tired) How can I bear it? I am letting Allen down.

C: Would he expect you to set such a high standard for Amy?

M: (back in control) That's the only kind of standard we have in our family. Allen was the best husband and father. He could control the girls' high spirits with just a look or a raise in his voice.

C: Allen did more than set a good example. He also intervened with his eyes and his voice.

M: (emphatically) Yes. He could always control them, so I never needed to.

C: He could set limits on them, but now the limits are gone. (long pause) Should Allen be here?

M: (intently) It's not his fault that he's gone. He was coming to my sister's engagement party; he knew he needed to be there. (long pause; sadly) The weather prevented him from coming.

C: Coming back was the *right* thing?

M: (confidently) Yes. Allen would never have intentionally missed the party. It would have been so disrespectful to my family.

C: Can people control the weather?

M: (irritably) We knew the storm wasn't Allen's fault. (pause) But, if you plan well enough, things like this don't happen.

C: You believe bad things don't happen if you plan well.

M: (irritably) The engagement party date was set before Allen's business meeting. He had been consulted about the date out of respect for his work. He felt he had to rush off to this meeting. He knew it was his responsibility to get back. My parents were talking about this, even at the funeral.

C: Did someone tell him that he had to get back for the party?

M: (confusedly) No, it wasn't necessary.

C: The standard was automatic.

M: (confident again) Yes, it was. When the kids act disrespectfully, I can hear Allen's voice in my head saying, "This is not acceptable." There is this little voice—evaluating what is going on and telling me what I should do.

C: What kind of voice?

M: (anxiously) It's just me. Like my conscience. I always hear myself citing the standards . . . keeping me from giving up.

C: What happens if you make a mistake?

M: (sad again) I feel so awful. (pause) I just can't forgive myself.

C: Have you ever felt so bad you thought of harming yourself?

M: (in control again) No. The girls need me. I will not let them down. It's just hard because I keep making mistakes.

C: Does everyone make mistakes?

M: (determinedly) I can't let myself. The girls have only me now; I couldn't forgive myself if I didn't make things right.

C: Can you forgive the girls for their mistakes?

M: (emphatically) Of course. They are just kids. They need to be taught how to behave correctly. (pause) But . . . they have only me now.

C: The standards tell you to be perfect. Does your family expect this perfection too?

M: (stridently) Oh yes. I know my parents are disappointed by the girls' behavior.

C: How do you know?

M: (intently) They have never said anything, but . . . I saw it in their faces for the first time as they watched the girls fight with each other at Allen's funeral. In the past few weeks, they have stopped coming to the house. (pause; *M* shakes her head) My father says they will be back when I have things under control.

C: You interpret their withdrawal as disapproval of you or the girls?

M: (long pause, desperately) I must be making terrible mistakes as a mother. The girls haven't been well mannered or respectful since Allen died. My parents set a good example for me. My mother is a real lady. She taught me how to keep my temper under control and how to attend to the needs of others. (pause) I am trying to teach the girls . . . (long pause)

C: Your parents hold high standards for you and the girls. You want to reach them. But, are they too high?

M: (emphatically) Standards weren't too high when Allen was alive. We knew we could reach them. He's dead now. I can't let Allen's death ruin my girls' futures.

C: Could their whole futures depend on their behavior now?

M: (uncertainly) I don't know . . . Behavior can become ingrained. Allen was so proud of my femininity, my manners, my poise. No good men will want to marry my girls if they are rough and undisciplined.

C: You are thinking all the time about your children's welfare. Do you have time to think of anything else?

M: (long pause; calmly) I'm lucky in a way . . . Allen had a lot of life insurance, so I can continue at home with the girls. I don't have to abandon the type of home Allen and I wanted for them. He was always so wonderful.

C: Financially, Allen is still caring for you and the girls; he always cared for you. Now that he's died, are you getting help from anyone else?

M: (calmly) Two of the men from Allen's office have been very kind. They take turns coming over to mow the grass, and they help with home repairs.

C: Were these Allen's jobs?

M: (anxiously) Yes. But . . . (sobbing for a minute; controlled) I may have to tell them to stop coming over because (pause) some of my neighbors are talking.

C: What thoughts are behind your tears?

M: (sadly) They are spreading rumors about me and Allen's friends. (pause) I am lost without Allen. (determinedly) How can people think I would be interested in someone else? (intently) And these men are married!

C: You and Allen's friends know the rumors are untrue. What are you thinking about these rumors that is bothering you so much?

M: (sadly) Clearly, my neighbors have so little respect for me that . . . (sobbing)

C: It's very painful to feel you aren't respected. (*M* nods) What contacts are you having with your neighbors now?

M: (dismissively) None, really. I don't really know any of them. Our family has moved a lot to help Allen be successful in his work. I never put down roots in any neighborhood. My life was the family.

C: Your neighbors are strangers to you. How could they know anything about you?

M: (pause, uncertainly) I don't know. I should get along with them, and I want them to know I am a respectable woman. I don't want them thinking ill of me. (long pause) I guess I need to tell Allen's friends to stop coming.

C: Do you have any other choices? (long pause) You want help, and Allen's friends are willing to help.

M: (uncertainly) If the neighbors are talking about me, I must be doing something wrong!

C: Must you? (long pause) Could you approach them and let them see who you are?

M: (tearful but no longer crying) Maybe, I could . . . Allen wouldn't want me to cut the grass and things. Those are men's jobs. (pause, controlled) I'm sorry I have acted poorly. You must have no respect for me.

C: You worry about this because your family so highly values self-control. (*M* nods) Is there anything you feel is under control for you and the girls?

M: (calmly) Well, I took books out from the library about explaining death to children. I know I have helped the girls understand Allen's death better. Right after the accident, the girls had terrible nightmares. Now, these have stopped.

C: In the midst of your own pain, you are still physically caring for your children. You are aware that they are having problems, *and* you are trying to help them with these problems. (long pause) Does this mean you are a good mother?

M: (regretfully) No. When you get to know me better, you will see how inadequate I have been since Allen's death. I will be a good mother again when everything is going well for my girls.

C: Your standards are very high. Could anyone reach them?

M: (painfully) You don't think I have to try? (long pause) I feel crazy and out of control without Allen.

C: People in grief feel overwhelmed. It's what happens when a loved one dies.

M: (anxiously) I don't have time to deal with myself. (emphatically) I must take care of these girls!

C: Allen was so important to you. Is grieving realistic?

M: (intently) He would want me to focus exclusively on the girls.

C: You have put yourself under intense pressure. Could you be a good woman and a good mother but not be perfect?

M: (anxiously) If I let go of my standards, I won't know myself. I thought about not wearing makeup yesterday . . . who would care? But, I had to. (desperately) Already, the girls want things from me that I can't give. Allen always used to carry them around the house and play chase games. They miss this fun so much.

C: If the kids need playfulness, can you be playful?

M: (anxiously) I can't take their dad's place. I guess they need me to find them another dad . . . I can't face this now. I am suffocating! (desperately) Will it ever be better?

C: Yes, but it will take some time because Allen was so important. The two of us will explore the standards of behavior for a family in grief.

M: (anxiously) I shouldn't be asking for help. I should be able to control this situation myself.

C: Those are the type of thoughts we will need to explore together.

Cognitive Case Conceptualization of Marie: Assumption-Based Style

Marie has a perfectionist belief system around the roles of women in society, including that good women can always maintain self-control, that a good wife will always defer to her husband's wishes, and that a good mother will have perfect children. While her husband was alive, she was able to maintain functional moods, relationships, and behavior while maintaining this perfectionist set of beliefs. However, the sudden death of her husband has made this impossible. She cannot remain a perfect lady while grieving and can't keep her children performing as perfect little ladies as they grieve for their father. In addition, Marie has a nonending stream of negative self-talk about her worth as a woman and her daughters' worth as women of the future. This self-talk encourages her to engage in black/white thinking, overgeneralization, and magnification of small failings as she examines her own missteps and her children's misbehavior. Marie has no prior history of depression and her children were functioning well at home and at school prior to the accident. She has shown herself well able to care for their physical needs, and even while grieving, she helped them understand the meaning of death and has communicated regularly with the school system. This indicates that Marie still maintains many adaptive beliefs, with their accompanying emotional and behavioral competencies, that can be used to demonstrate the "exceptions" to her current litany of incompetence. With support for grieving, Marie should be able to learn constructive self-talk that can guide her and her children into a new worldview of family life with a deceased husband and father.

Marie's thinking is dominated by the gendered belief that a good woman always looks and acts like a perfect lady. She gives herself no quarter for having lost her husband in a tragic plane accident. To Marie and her husband Allen, women should always look and behave as perfect ladies. As such, there were no excuses for not being correctly dressed, including keeping one's makeup looking fresh at all times. In addition, women were always polite and never lost control of their emotions, no matter how angry. Marie and Allen shared these beliefs, and it was possible to for Marie to maintain this role of perfect lady until Allen died. However, now Marie must try to take care of the home and the children on her own. Her stream of perfectionistic self-talk does not allow her to care for them and forget about her makeup; perfect ladies have perfect appearances. Fortunately, perfect women are allowed to need men to do chores around the yard. Thus, when several of Allen's friends stepped in to help, Marie initially gratefully accepted. Now, however, she is guilt-stricken because rumors have circulated that she must be having affairs with these men. She says punishing things to herself, believing that if people are gossiping about her, she must deserve it—she must be a bad woman.

Marie believes that it was her responsibility to be a perfect wife to Allen and that he was her best friend and a perfect father. This has led to self-talk that she will always be alone, will never have another friend, can never make up for the loss her children will experience growing up without a father, and is betraying her husband's trust. Marie is facing her husband's death without a single friend in the community because she felt it was her job to move whenever it would support Allen's employment. She had been involved in so many previous moves that upon moving to this community she made no effort to make friends. This may in part be the reason that neighbors are gossiping about her rather than coming over to help her. She is engaging in black/white thinking, such as that either she must tell the men not to come over and flounder under more work, or she can continue to have them come and perpetuate her reputation of being a promiscuous woman. The idea that she could talk to her neighbors about what is going on does not occur to her despite the fact that she is a woman with good social skills. She also holds inflexible gender roles that guide her behavior. Allen was the playful one with the girls, and rather than taking on this role herself, Marie believes that the children will now have to go without having this playful influence in their lives. Allen also held himself to inflexible rules of behavior. If he planned correctly, as a man should, he would not have missed the engagement party. Thus, he traveled home during bad weather and was killed when the plane he was on crashed. Even now, when Marie is asked if this was a mistake, she says that Allen knew what was expected of him. It was his "job" to get there.

Marie believes that a good mother is a perfect mother. In the past, she was satisfied with her performance as a parent. She may have engaged in self-talk whereby she told herself that mothers plan their children's lives, mothers make sure their children do well in school, mothers cook their children meals, and so forth. It wasn't clear if she had fun as a mother, as she says things suggesting that only Allen got to be the parent who was playful with the girls. Marie considers herself far from perfect now. She has self-talk where she berates herself with comments such as "If I had any competency as a parent, my girls would never show anger or engage in aggressive behavior." The only conclusion Marie draws from her "errors" and "mistakes" as a parent is that she must be a bad mother. As Marie talks of her life with Allen, it seems clear that they both held perfectionist plans for their perfect little ladies. This tyranny of perfection has become impossible for Marie to maintain on her own. She can't give herself respite from perfection even while she is still grieving and her children are still grieving.

Marie believes that good children are perfect children. Marie can accept the idea that her children might temporarily, maybe for a few weeks, have difficulties in the direct aftermath of their father's death. Marie mentions some self-talk to the effect that it was acceptable for her children to have nightmares immediately after the death of their father. However, continuing to have nightmares and misbehaving at school after a full month should not be happening. This tyranny of the "should" is accompanied by Marie's magnification of the severity of the children's aggressive symptoms as they grieve the death of their father. It is to be expected that the children's performance, both emotionally and academically at school, would decline in the aftermath of their father's death. However, rather than engaging in soothing self-talk about giving herself and her children longer to adjust to this loss, Marie is engaging in minimization of all actions that are positive and magnification of everything that is negative. She has gone from the extreme of expecting them to be perfect little ladies, even when faced with the loss of their father, to the other extreme of feeling they are now hopelessly flawed and that Allen would be ashamed of her and them. Marie wonders if anything can be done to rescue her children from their flawed futures.

In the past, while Marie's perfectionistic and demanding beliefs created stress in her life, she was able to see the future with a positive lens. She would remain married to her best friend and husband Allen. They would raise happy, healthy, achieving, perfect little ladies. She was able to recognize when her family members were happy and achieving well and she was able to show them how much they were loved. Thus, she must have had constructive self-talk that underlay all this adaptive behavior. While she has experienced a negative cognitive shift following the death of her husband, she has no history of prior incapacitation. If she challenges her negative expectations about herself and her children, evaluates whether her attributions about their behavior are accurate, and reevaluates herself and others through a neutral lens, she should be able to reestablish her prior level of adaptive thinking.

Cognitive Treatment Plan: Assumption-Based Style

Treatment Plan Overview. Marie's grief over her husband's death has led to dysfunctional behavior due to perfectionistic belief systems supported by rigid gender-role stereotypes. Marie will be helped to engage in hypothesis testing in regard to each of these perfectionistic belief systems and replace any maladaptive thinking with adaptive thinking. Long-Term Goals 1 through 3 can be addressed simultaneously or in any order. (This treatment plan follows the *basic format.*)

LONG-TERM GOAL 1: Marie will examine her belief that women must always be perfect ladies to be good women.

Short-Term Goals

1. Marie will internalize her attention so that she becomes aware of her stream of self-talk around her expectations about the daily appearance of a perfect woman.

2. Marie will explore the thoughts, feelings, and actions relative to this standard that she has experienced or carried out since the death of her husband.

3. Marie will consider whether there are any times when it might be understandable or appropriate to not have a perfect appearance and articulate her reasons for this.

4. Marie will take a walk in her neighborhood, notice the appearance of other women, consider whether any of them do not look perfect, and become aware of her self-talk related to this.

5. Marie will engage in hypothesis testing in regard to why each woman might not have looked perfect and consider whether there could be any valid reasons that a good woman might not look perfect.

6. Marie will take on Allen's role and describe her reputation as a woman prior to his death, including all the thoughts, feelings, and actions that might have been related to this.

7. Marie will take on Allen's role and describe her reputation as a woman since his death, including how she has handled accepting help from his friends.

8. Marie will ask each of Allen's friends if they found any of her behavior inappropriate prior to Allen's death and if they have noticed any inappropriate behavior from her since his death.

9. Marie will think back to an event in which Allen was not a perfect husband and discuss whether it is possible to perceive him as a good husband even if he made mistakes.

10. Marie will formulate more adaptive self-talk around the thoughts, moods, and behaviors of a good woman who has experienced the recent death of her spouse.

LONG-TERM GOAL 2: Marie will explore her belief that women must always be perfect mothers to be effective mothers.

Short-Term Goals

1. Marie will internalize her attention so that she becomes aware of her stream of self-talk around her expectations for the behavior of a perfect mother.

2. Marie will explore the thoughts, feelings, and actions relative to this standard that she has experienced since the death of her husband.

3. Marie will think back to an incident where Allen made a mistake as a parent and consider whether or not this mistake indicated that he was not a good parent.

4. Marie will think back to an incident where she performed in a way that she considered "right" for a parent but the children did not respond in the expected way.

5. Marie will think back to an incident where she did not perform to a perfect standard and yet her children responded in an adaptive way.

6. Marie will watch other parents at the park and note when they make mistakes and when they perform in a way she considers "right" and consider whether it is possible to perceive someone to be a good parent when he or she does not always do everything right.

7. Marie will formulate more adaptive self-talk around parenting that includes the idea that making mistakes is human and does not lead to permanent damage to children.

LONG-TERM GOAL 3: Marie will explore her belief that little girls must always be perfect little ladies to be good children.

Short-Term Goals

1. Marie will internalize her attention so that she becomes aware of her stream of self-talk around her expectations for the behavior of her daughters.

2. Marie will explore the thoughts, feelings, and actions relative to this standard that she has experienced or carried out since the death of her husband.

3. Marie will watch other children at the park and come up with at least three reasons why a child who is misbehaving might be misbehaving for reasons other than not being a good child.

4. Marie will consider a recent event in which one of her daughters did not behave as a perfect little lady and consider whether there is any meaning that she could derive from this misbehavior other than that the girl is not a good child.

5. Marie will come up with at least three reasons why a child who is sick might not be able to be well behaved.

6. Marie will come up with at least three reasons why a child who has lost a father might misbehave at school but still, overall, be a well-behaved child.

7. Marie will take on Allen's role within the family and try to imagine his expectations for a daughter who was trying to accept his death.

8. Marie will take on the school principal's role and try to image her expectations for the behavior of a child at school in the aftermath of a parent's death.

9. Marie will develop adaptive self-talk around her children's behavior that allows them to be imperfect as they grieve for their father and as they go through stresses and growth in the future.

Cognitive Case Conceptualization of Marie: Diagnosis-Based Style

Whether within her role as a widow, as a mother, as a daughter, or as a friend, Marie is feeling depressed and anxious and is suffering from feelings of low self-esteem and personal efficacy. Marie has experienced a negative cognitive shift in which she has trouble perceiving anything positive about herself, her children, or her immediate social environment. This negative shift, and its accompanying symptoms, began after her husband was killed suddenly in a plane accident one month ago. Marie has no prior history of depression; however, she does have a history of core perfectionist and rigid belief systems, along with strong intermediary beliefs about the proper roles of men and women that are serving to complicate her ability to grieve effectively for her husband. Although she shows significant symptomatology at this time, her bereavement is recent, and her continued positive attention to her children's developmental, academic, and social needs reflects an individual with significant intellectual and functional competencies. Her total constellation of behaviors is most accurately reflected in a DSM-5 diagnosis of V62.82 Uncomplicated Bereavement (American Psychiatric Association, 2013). Marie exhibits signs of obsessional and perfectionist thinking. Her past high level of functioning, however, suggests that these reflect her personal style based on core beliefs rather than a personality disorder. Because of her high level of distress, her strong motivation for treatment, and her prior history of adaptive functioning, her treatment prognosis is considered good to excellent.

How does Marie view herself as a widow? She believes that she and her husband had a strong and satisfying relationship that lasted for 10 years. Sharing core and intermediary beliefs on gender role stereotypes and ideal family functioning, they were each other's strong support system. Due to their frequent moves in support of Allen's career, they maintained an isolated family unit. As a result, Marie has lost her husband and only intimate friend. Her ability to grieve has been inhibited by her rigidly held gender role beliefs. These intermediary beliefs contain assumptions such as "women cannot be angry," "women cannot lose control," and "women must always help others." These gender role stereotypes are superimposed on perfectionist core belief systems that dictate to Marie that "only the highest standards are acceptable," "if you plan properly, things do not go wrong," and "you are either perfect or inadequate." These maladaptive belief systems are reflected in a stream of self-talk that criticizes Marie for experiencing her very normal reactions of grief and exhorts her to perfection even in the immediate aftermath of loss. At a time when she really needs the support of others, her negative lens leads her to view all the "others" in her environment as disapproving. Even in the face of positive support from the clinician, she reinterprets this support as misguided: "When you get to know me better, you will see how inadequate I have been since Allen's death." Using overgeneralizations and distortions, she looks back at her husband as a perfect spouse and evaluates herself now as betraying his trust through her inadequacies; she did have positive thoughts about herself as a woman and wife before her bereavement.

How does Marie view herself as a parent? Based on her belief systems, Marie strives to be a perfect mother and despite her loss has continued to provide well for most of her children's needs. She attends well to their physical needs, she communicates regularly with their teachers, and she has helped them understand the reality of their father's death. Her perfectionist and gender-typed beliefs, however, are inhibiting her from recognizing her abilities as a mother and maintaining a sense of competency in her role. Furthermore, these beliefs lead to negative assumptions about her children's recent acting-out behaviors; she views their misbehavior as unacceptable rather than as understandable stress reactions to the death of their father. Marie exaggerates the seriousness of their difficulties, even to the point of making catastrophic predictions about their futures. She sees their only hope for life success as tied to their ability to always be little ladies, even in the direct aftermath of their father's death. She views her role in their lives strictly in terms of setting standards, being a perfect role model, and taking care of their physical needs. The role of a father is that of financial supporter and perfect playmate. Marie sees remarriage as her only option to provide for her children's need for this perfect playmate. In addition to her own critical voice, Marie hears the voice of Allen and sees the looks of her parents as a critical chorus disapproving of her every parenting move. Despite feeling overwhelmed by their current behavioral outbursts, she does perceive her daughters to have achieved well academically and socially prior to Allen's death.

How does Marie view herself as a daughter? She and Allen remained actively involved with her family after their marriage. She recognizes that she took her core beliefs, and her beliefs about how to be a perfect woman, from her mother, who she describes as "a real lady." Her parents continue to reinforce her belief systems involving perfectionism and rigid gender role stereotypes. Even after Allen's death, her parents do not consider his rushing home during a storm to have been inappropriate. They say things such as "He knew it was his responsibility to be back on time; he was doing what he was supposed to do." Perhaps there was some softly voiced criticism of Allen at the funeral from extended family members, such as "If he had planned better, this wouldn't have happened." Marie may be sharing this criticism implicitly when she says, "The engagement party date was set before Allen's business meeting . . . He had been consulted about the date . . . He felt he had to rush off . . . He knew it was his responsibility to get back." Marie does not believe that women should be angry, but deep down, she may be angry at Allen for going to the business meeting. She may also feel guilty that he got killed flying home for a party in her sister's honor. Allen and Marie both knew that her family would accept no excuses for his absence from the party. Marie's extended family is not providing Marie with any emotional support for her own grief reactions or for her parenting dilemmas. Her parents plan to stay withdrawn from Marie and the children until Marie has "gained control" of the situation. Marie does not complain about this withdrawal. She interprets it as their justified reaction to her "failings" as a woman and a mother.

How does Marie view herself as a female friend and neighbor? Her past roles were as perfect wife and mother. She had no other role for herself and no friends of her own because she always put Allen and the children first. She has tried to maintain her past perfectionist standards by dressing and acting like a perfect lady at all times despite her state of bereavement. She has not directly solicited help from her neighbors because of her beliefs that "everything will turn out right if you plan enough" and "it's shameful to be out of control of your children." This may have led her neighbors to assume that she does not need help or in fact is not really grief-stricken. It may also be part of the reason why her neighbors gossip about the role Allen's friends currently play in her life. Their gossip unintentionally serves to reinforce Marie's assumption that she is betraying Allen's trust and that her parenting "mistakes" mean she is defective and unacceptable. Marie has the social skills to develop positive relationships with her neighbors, as well as to develop personal friendships, if she develops the belief that it is acceptable for her to have these relationships.

In many ways, Marie's family is functioning well in the aftermath of Allen's death. Everyone is getting enough to eat, everyone is living in the family home, the children are attending their neighborhood school, and after only one month, they have progressed through the denial stage of grief. Unfortunately, maladaptive belief systems are inhibiting Marie from proceeding further in the grief process, leaving her feeling depressed, anxious, and incompetent. These beliefs are also preventing her from recognizing that her children's acting-out behaviors are legitimate grief reactions and that a relaxation of her "high standards" is appropriate at this time. The behavior of Marie's parents, in reinforcing her perfectionistic core beliefs, may serve to impede Marie's ability to function more flexibly at this time. However, Marie's stress level has become so intense that she has violated one of her own standards and is actively seeking help from a clinician. She is also questioning whether all her assumptions about what it means to be a perfect lady, such as wearing a lot of makeup each day, are really necessary at this time of loss. This may represent a window of opportunity in which she can be helped to reevaluate the efficacy of her current belief systems in guiding her behavior and that of her children.

Cognitive Treatment Plan: Diagnosis-Based Style

Treatment Plan Overview. Marie is verbal, intelligent, in distress, and motivated for change; thus, she is a good candidate for treatment, and her prognosis for improvement is good to excellent. (This treatment plan follows the *adapted SOAP format*. A more complete treatment plan overview and a detailed treatment plan can be found below under the "Plan" subsection.)

Subjective Data

Marie comes in expressing concerns about her children. She views their behavior to have seriously deteriorated following the recent death of their father from a plane accident. She finds herself to be inadequate and a failure as a woman and a mother. She is guilt-ridden because she believes that she is failing her own and her husband's standards as a parent. She considers her own functioning to be irrelevant at this time; only her children are important.

Objective Data

Standardized intellectual testing using the Wechsler Adult Intelligence Scale IV (WAIS-IV) revealed that Marie has an average level of intelligence. Personality testing utilizing the Minnesota Multiphasic Personality Inventory-2 (MMPI-2) revealed signs of rigid, perfectionist thinking; traditional sex role stereotypes; mild cognitive confusion; significant personal turmoil; and distress. Her profile is most consistent with a DSM-5 diagnosis of V62.82 Uncomplicated Bereavement.

Assessment

Marie is depressed, anxious, and suffering from feelings of low self-esteem and low personal efficacy. Due to a negative cognitive shift brought on by her recent bereavement, she has trouble perceiving anything positive about herself, her children, or her immediate social environment. Marie is a highly functioning and competent woman and parent whose grieving process has become complicated by her core beliefs involving perfectionism and her intermediary beliefs involving rigid gender roles. Although she is showing significant symptomatology at this time, her continued positive attention to her children's developmental, academic, and social needs reflects an individual with significant intellectual and functional competencies.

Her DSM-5 working diagnosis is V62.82, Uncomplicated Bereavement. Her current functioning represents at least an average level of intelligence, good social skills, good parenting skills, and financial stability. Her level of social support is currently inadequate.

Plan

Treatment plan overview: Marie's adaptive and maladaptive belief systems will be explored within her roles as a widow, a mother, an adult daughter, a friend, and a neighbor. All her perfectionistic belief systems involve rigid gender roles, and thus her long-term goals can be worked on simultaneously.

LONG-TERM GOAL 1: Marie will become aware of her belief systems about herself as a newly widowed woman and consider how these are helping her or creating stress for her.

Short-Term Goals

1. Marie will become aware of her self-talk around the idea that a good woman is never angry and how it is or is not helping her cope realistically with the sudden death of her husband.

2. Marie will become aware of her self-talk around the idea that a good woman never loses control and how it is or is not helping her cope realistically with the sudden death of her husband.

3. Marie will become aware of her self-talk around the idea of whether a good woman must always focus on helping others and how it is or is not helping her cope realistically with the sudden death of her husband.

4. Marie will engage in hypothesis testing in regard to whether these thoughts are realistic through reading books on bereavement, talking with the clinician, and initiating discussions with other people who are grieving.

5. Based on her greater knowledge of bereavement issues, Marie will replace any perfectionist and unrealistic thoughts with more adaptive ones in her discussions about herself with others and within her own head when she considers her own "performance" as a recent widow.

6. Other goals will be developed as appropriate.

LONG-TERM GOAL 2: Marie will become aware of her belief systems around her view of herself as a mother and consider how these are helping her or creating stress for her.

Short-Term Goals

1. Marie will become aware of her self-talk around the behavior of her daughters and consider whether it represents a realistic appraisal of the behavior of recently bereaved children.

2. Marie will become aware of her self-talk around her disciplinary strategies with her daughters and consider whether they represent realistic interventions for young girls in grief.

3. Marie will engage in hypothesis testing around her self-talk through reading about grief and young children, talking with the clinician, and observing other parents with their young children.

4. Marie will replace any perfectionistic or unrealistic self-talk with constructive self-talk based on her new level of understanding of child development and grief.

5. Other goals will be developed as appropriate.

LONG-TERM GOAL 3: Marie will become aware of her belief systems around her view of herself as an adult daughter and consider how these are helping her or creating stress for her.

Short-Term Goals

1. Marie will become aware of her self-talk that she learned as a daughter and that her parents continue to emphasize (e.g., "If you plan, things always turn out right"; "It is an adult's responsibility to do things right").

2. Marie will become aware of her self-talk about the responsibilities of a husband that she learned as a daughter and that her parents continue to emphasize (e.g., "It was his responsibility to get back for a family party").

3. Marie will engage in hypothesis testing regarding whether or not this self-talk is adaptive based on reading about the differences between rational and unrealistic thinking and the differential impact these types of thinking have on moods such as anger, depression, and anxiety; discussing these issues with the clinician; and keeping a thought diary to monitor her own emotions in relation to her thinking in these absolutist terms.

4. Marie will replace any negative self-talk with more adaptive self-talk that will support more positive emotions and adaptive, flexible behavior, free of perfectionism, in her interactions with her parents.

5. Other goals will be developed as appropriate.

LONG-TERM GOAL 4: Marie will become aware of her belief systems around her view of herself as a female friend and neighbor and consider how these are helping her or creating stress for her.

Short-Term Goals

1. Marie will become aware of her self-talk around her role as a female friend and neighbor and how it requires her to always look perfectly groomed, always be in emotional control, and always be in complete control as a parent.

2. Marie will engage in hypothesis testing around her idea that she cannot show the world that she is grieving and in distress and cannot ask for help for anything; otherwise, she isn't a lady and deserving of respect. She will do this through reading about the importance of social support, discussing the issues with the clinician, and watching other adults interacting with their peers.

3. Marie will replace any maladaptive talk with adaptive talk that will enable her to request help when needed with her home, her children, and her feelings of loneliness following the death of her husband and best friend.

4. Marie will consider what adaptive talk would help her in discussing with her neighbors the current false rumors that have begun circulating about her since her husband's death.

5. Other goals will be developed as appropriate.

PRACTICE CASE FOR STUDENT CONCEPTUALIZATION: INTEGRATING THE DOMAIN OF SEXUAL ORIENTATION

It is time to do a cognitive analysis of Eric. There are many domains of complexity that might provide insights into his behavior. Within this analysis, you are asked to try to integrate the domain of sexual orientation into your case conceptualization.

Information Received From Phone Intake

Eric is a 16-year-old White male living in a poor and deteriorating section of a large midwestern city. He is presently a junior in high school. He is an average student with no record of school adjustment problems. His parents were divorced seven years ago, but they remain in a conflictual relationship. Over the past seven years, Eric has switched households five times. In addition to living with his parents, he has sometimes gone to live with his maternal aunt and uncle. These moves have also involved his switching back and forth between three school systems. Eric was referred by his history teacher, Mr. Jenkins, to a clinician who provides treatment at the high school. Mr. Jenkins considers Eric to be depressed, and he is also worried about whether Eric's home environment is safe.

During a brief mental status exam, there were moderate signs of distress but no indications of suicidal or homicidal ideation or severe psychopathology. Eric showed some anxiety during the discussion of the limits of confidentiality. However, he said he would agree to treatment in order to please Mr. Jenkins.

Interview With Eric (E) From a Cognitive Perspective

C: Mr. Jenkins told me a little about you. Could you tell me what's on your mind?

E: (angrily) Well, I feel like a bouncing ball all the time. Sometimes my mom seems to want me, sometimes my dad, and sometimes neither does and I end up at my aunt and uncle's house. My dad always has to control everything. He always tries to jerk me around. (pause) I've never been sure if there was anything about me he liked. It was pathetic how much I tried to please him when I was little. (pause) But I've given up on that now. When I am at his house, I just keep out of his way. (reflectively) My dad and mom seem to hate each other. My mom has let her new drinking buddy move into our home. One thing I'm sure about is that he hates me.

C: What makes you think that?

E: (reflectively) If I even say hello to Mom, he screams his lungs out. She has to give him one hundred percent of her time. (shaking his head, intently) *He* is the intruder, not *me*.

C: When your mom pays attention to you, he gets angry?

E: (caustically) That's an understatement. If I say hello to Mom when I come in from school, she'll ignore me if he's home. Even the sound of my voice alone often starts him screaming.

C: How exactly does your mom react to this?

E: (furiously) She tells me to shut up. She says if I drive him away, we'll starve.

C: What do you think will happen when she threatens you with this?

E: (resignedly) She'll kick me out for a while, and it's back to my aunt and uncle again.

C: What will happen there?

E: (desolately) They let me stay. They feed me. (pause) Once when I needed a new coat, they bought it for me. They never really talk to me . . . but they don't talk to each other either. At school, it's the same deal. I have no one.

C: What stops you from making friends at school?

E: (sadly) I have changed schools so many times I've never had a chance to make any real friends. (long pause) I feel alone, different. I don't fit in anywhere.

C: You can't think of any times when you thought you fit in.

E: (anxiously) I have to figure out who I am besides the fact that my parents can't waste their time on me. (explosively) This can't go on!

C: Are you pressuring yourself for insight? (pause) You feel alone in this struggle. Have you noticed any other teens struggling with this?

E: (tensely) No one has gone through what I have.

C: You say this to yourself, and it increases your distress.

E: (pause; reflectively) Maybe. Other people seem to have close friends. I want that, but whenever I start to make a friend, I think, what if it is just more pain?

C: Your family relationships are painful. Does this mean all relationships must be that way?

E: (intently) Well, my folks can't do anything but hurt each other. Their new relationships don't seem so great either. (with resignation) Good relationships seem impossible.

C: If I tell you good relationships are possible, what goes through your mind?

E: (confidently) I'll get hurt, I'll be rejected, and I won't be able to take any more pain.

C: If someone rejects you, you think everyone will?

E: (matter-of-factly) Everyone rejects me. Only Mr. Jenkins cares.

C: I understand you spend a lot of time with him.

E: (explosively) *What's wrong with that!*

C: You sound angry. What are you thinking?

E: (long pause; intently) Yesterday, some guys harassed me in the locker room. They called me a loser, a queer with a crush on Mr. Jenkins. (long pause) One of them had been mouthing off in class to Mr. Jenkins, so I sort of shoved him in the hall after class. Then he got a bunch of his friends to shove me around by the lockers.

C: Are you OK?

E: (surprised) Yeah. They just wanted to make me feel small. Once they felt they had done it real well, they left me alone.

C: They shoved you out of revenge. But why did they call you a queer?

E: (explosively) *I have never thought about it!* (long pause, calmly) I don't know. (dejectedly) Maybe I am.

C: You have slumped down in the chair. What's on your mind?

E: (sarcastically) Well, it's not like it's a good thing to be queer.

C: What do you think is good or bad about being gay?

E: (shaking his head, tensely) I can't talk about this with you or anyone else.

C: It might be hard for you to talk about. (pause) Our sexuality is an important part of who we are. (long pause) I don't know if you're gay or not. (long pause) Could it be OK if you are?

E: (firmly) I'm only willing to talk about this if I am gay. (pause) How will I know?

C: When you think about Mr. Jenkins right now, what specific thoughts and feelings do you have?

E: (quietly) I think I would rather be with him than anyone else. If he says hello to me, I feel great. If he is sick, I feel low. I think about him all the time, what he would think of everything I do. Does this mean I'm gay?

C: Mr. Jenkins is important to you. Is there a difference between feeling very emotionally close and the desire for something more?

E: (uncertainly) What do you mean?

C: Well, when teens go through puberty, most of them begin to have special thoughts, wishes, or fantasies about a particular person or type of person that are different from how they think about most people.

E: (dejectedly) I think I'm a loser like those guys said.

C: Are you a loser or something else? (pause) Are you shaving yet? (*E* shakes his head no) Could you have a lot more growing to do? (long pause) Is it possible that it isn't time yet for you to have these feelings?

E: (sarcastically) The guys who beat me up made a big deal about my size.

C: Is it a big deal to you? (long pause)

E: (frankly) I didn't really care till I got into that fight. I could have used some extra inches then. (long pause) What does this all mean about Mr. Jenkins and me?

C: I don't know if you have special feelings about Mr. Jenkins or not. You don't seem to know either. If I give you some stuff to read and you give yourself time to grow up, might it all become clear to you in time? (*E* shakes his head no) Questioning is a normal part of learning who you are.

E: (furiously) I can't take my whole life to figure this thing out. (long pause; calmly) I've wondered a lot if I should tell Mr. Jenkins about this. This is the one important thing I haven't shared. He knows something is up.

C: What are you imagining he will do if you tell him?

E: (desperately) I hear him screaming abuse in my mind, just like the guys in the locker room; then I see myself disintegrating, alone, no one caring about me.

C: Those consequences are catastrophic. Could anything else be possible?

E: (dejectedly) I can't imagine anything else.

C: I don't know what he would do. He could freak out, or he might understand and talk to you about it. What risks are involved in telling or not telling?

E: (sadly) Sometimes I think to myself that he won't want me, but he will pity me instead and still let me hang around him.

C: What else might happen?

E: (intently) Nothing. He's very into right and wrong. I know that from our talks about my parents. He will be my teacher and nothing else. I guess I must be a real jerk to consider anything else.

C: You say very harsh things to yourself. Do you think any other students may have had personal thoughts about their teachers?

E: (hopefully) Yeah, I guess. (long pause; agitatedly) My dad would just hate me if I was gay.

C: What makes you expect this?

E: (anxiously) He never has had much interest in me. I've heard him say a lot of ugly stuff about fags . . . if he thought I was one, it might just push him into hate.

C: Have you met any gay or lesbian individuals?

E: (uncertainly) I think I did once. I was walking down the street with my dad, when some guy brushed up against him. I thought it was an accident, but Dad said the guy was a faggot and beat the crap out of him. (long pause)

C: What was that guy like, the one your dad called a faggot?

E: (confused) He looked like anyone else, but my dad says he can always tell. (pause) He hasn't seemed concerned about me yet. If he did, he might beat the crap out of me like he did that guy on the street.

C: Some dads do that. But, some parents and friends learn to understand. Could anyone in your family try to understand? (long pause) Would they all be extreme and beat you up or kick you out?

E: (intently) My parents do everything to the extreme. They married young. They drank a lot, fought a lot. My dad finally walked out after so much fighting and jealousy. (pause) I don't have that crap with Mr. Jenkins; with him it's calm. On my own it's a nightmare. (long pause, yelling) *I have to know now! I can't stand this!*

C: Are things bad enough that you are thinking about hurting yourself or running away?

E: (Taking a deep breath, calmly) No. I'm OK.

C: Are you safe at home?

E: (calmly) Home is an angry place, but no one hits me or anything.

C: What about school?

E: (calmly) No one but those guys have ever threatened me. The principal overheard them the other day and threatened them with something. They avoid me now.

C: OK. If you come back next week, we need to focus on your thoughts about yourself and others and how this self-talk might be influencing you. I'd like you to keep a record of your thoughts about yourself and being gay.

E: (anxiously) If I do the assignment, will it tell me if I'm gay?

C: It's normal to need time to question and explore. You may need to allow yourself to be like everyone else and take time to work it out.

Exercises for Developing a Case Conceptualization of Eric

Exercise 1 (four-page maximum)

GOAL: To verify that you have a clear understanding of cognitive theory.

STYLE: An integrative essay comprising Parts A through C.

NEED HELP?   Review this chapter (pages 135–138).

A. Develop a concise overview of all the assumptions of cognitive theory (the theory's hypotheses about key dimensions in understanding how clients change; think broadly, abstractly) as an introduction to the rest of this exercise.

B. Develop a thorough description of how each of these assumptions is used to understand a client's progression through the change process in paragraphs that provide specific examples to fully explain each assumption.

C. Conclude your essay by describing the role of the clinician in helping the client change (consultant, doctor, educator, helper), the major approach taken to treatment, and common treatment techniques. Provide enough specific examples to clarify what is distinctive about this approach.

Exercise 2 (four-page maximum)

GOAL: To aid application of cognitive theory to Eric.

STYLE: A separate sentence outline for each section, A through D.

NEED HELP?   Review this chapter (pages 135–138).

A. Create a list of Eric's weaknesses (concerns, issues, problems, symptoms, skill deficits, treatment barriers) and indicate which of them Eric wants help with.

B. Create a list of Eric's strengths (strong points, positive features, successes, skills, factors facilitating change) and indicate which of them Eric is aware of having.

C. Discuss what Eric thinks is related to these weaknesses and strengths, considering his (a) belief systems, (b) self-talk, (c) attributions about himself and others, (d) perceptions of current and past events and any biases in these perceptions, and (e) expectations for the future. If you have not already done so, consider how his thinking influences his affect, behavior, and motivations within his strengths and weaknesses.

D. Discuss Eric's overall worldview, what forces in the environment are reinforcing or contradicting this worldview, and, overall, how adaptive his thinking is at this time.

Exercise 3 (four-page maximum)

GOAL: To develop an understanding of the potential role of sexual orientation in Eric's life.

STYLE: A separate sentence outline for each section, A through I.

NEED HELP?   Review Chapter 2 (pages 77–84).

A. Assess where Eric is in the process of identifying his sexual orientation in terms of desires, fantasies, attitudes, emotions, and behavior related to sexuality and whether his sexual identification is stable, ambivalent, questioning, or shifting.

B. Assess the past and present environments that are influencing Eric's comfort with his sexual identification, including strengths or barriers within himself, his school environment, his family and social relationships and his level of access to information and resources.

C. Assess the benefits there might be if Eric came out at this time, and which aspects of his world might benefit the most from his coming out, considering his personal identity, family relationships, peer relationships, and educational relationships.

D. Assess the costs there might be if Eric came out at this time, and which aspects of his world might carry the most risk in the coming-out process, considering his personal identity, family relationships, peer relationships, and educational relationships.

E. Assess whether Eric needs to find a common ground between his sexual identity and other aspects of his identity, such as religious affiliation or racial or ethnic heritage, and consider how to connect him with resources and decrease barriers to this process.

F. Assess your current knowledge of issues relevant to sexual orientation.

1. How many courses have you taken that give you background on sexual orientation?

2. How many workshops have you taken that give you background on sexual orientation?

3. What professional experiences have you with clients about issues relevant to sexual orientation?

4. What personal experiences have you had with individuals who are sexual minorities?

5. What cohort effects might influence the worldview of sexual minorities? What is important to them at this point in history? How does society reward or punish people based on their sexuality?

G. What is your current level of awareness of issues relevant to sexual orientation?

1. Discuss the positive and negative stereotypes you learned about heterosexuality and sexual minority identities as you were growing up.

2. Discuss how societal homophobia was present as you were growing up.

3. Discuss how societal homophobia is present in your current family, social, cultural, and political groups.

4. Discuss how societal homophobia and the assumption that everyone is heterosexual could lead you to unintentionally marginalize or invalidate Eric's experiences or point of view.

H. Assess your current skills in working with clients of different sexual orientations.

1. What skills do you currently have that are of value in working with issues of sexuality or sexual orientation?

2. What skills do you feel it would be important to develop to work effectively with issues of sexuality or sexual orientation?

I. Consider the action steps you can take.

1. What can you do to enhance your ability to form a strong therapeutic alliance with gay or questioning clients?

2. Discuss the aspects of the treatment approach you plan to use with Eric that might have been developed from a heterosexual point of view and what you can do about it.

3. How might you structure the treatment environment to increase the likelihood of a positive outcome with gay or questioning clients?

Exercise 4 (six-page maximum)

GOAL: To help you integrate your knowledge of cognitive theory and issues relevant to sexual orientation into an in-depth conceptualization of Eric (who he is and why he does what he does).

STYLE: An integrated essay consisting of a premise, supportive details, and conclusions following a carefully planned organizational style.

NEED HELP?   Review Chapter 1 (pages 1–7) and Chapter 2 (pages 77–83).

STEP 1: Consider what style you should use to organize your cognitive understanding of Eric. This style should (a) support you in providing a comprehensive and clear understanding of his beliefs, self-talk, attributions, perceptions, and expectations and (b) support language that he might find persuasive in his current state of desperation.

STEP 2: Develop a concise premise (overview, preliminary or explanatory statements, proposition, thesis statement, theory-driven introduction, hypotheses, summary, concluding causal statements) that explains Eric's overall level of functioning as an individual who is struggling to understand his sexuality amid family chaos. If you have trouble with Step 2, remember that it should be an integration of the key ideas of Exercises 2 and 3 and that it should (a) provide a basis for Eric's long-term goals, (b) be grounded in cognitive theory and be sensitive to sexual orientation issues, and (c) highlight the strengths Eric brings to cognitive treatment whenever possible.

STEP 3: Develop your supporting material (a detailed case analysis of strengths and weaknesses, supplying data to support an introductory premise) from a cognitive perspective that incorporates an in-depth understanding of Eric, a homophobic teen. If you have trouble with Step 3, consider the information you'll need to include in order to (a) support the development of short-term goals, (b) be grounded in cognitive theory and sensitive to sexual orientation issues, and (c) integrate an understanding of Eric's strengths in analyzing his beliefs and self-talk.

STEP 4: Develop your conclusions and broad treatment recommendations, including (a) Eric's overall level of functioning, (b) anything facilitating or serving as a barrier to his developing more constructive beliefs at this time, and (c) his basic needs as he evaluates his thinking, being careful to consider what you said in Parts G and I of Exercise 3 (be concise and general).

Exercise 5 (three-page maximum)

GOAL: To develop a theory-driven action plan for Eric that considers his strengths and is sensitive to his sexual orientation issues.

STYLE: A sentence outline consisting of long- and short-term goals.

NEED HELP?   Review Chapter 1 (pages 7–24).

STEP 1: Develop your treatment plan overview, being careful to consider what you said in Parts G and I of Exercise 3 to try to prevent any negative bias from coloring your treatment plan and to insure that you adapt your treatment approach to Eric's unique needs as an individual.

STEP 2: Develop long-term (major, large, ambitious, comprehensive, broad) goals that Eric will *ideally* reach by the termination of treatment and that will lead to an adaptive worldview and a healthy integration of his sexuality into his identity. If you have trouble with Step 2, reread your premise and support topic sentences for ideas, paying careful attention to how they could be transformed into goals that are realistic in terms of Eric's needs and situation (use the *style* of Exercise 4).

STEP 3: Develop short-term (small, brief, encapsulated, specific, measurable, subsidiary) goals that Eric and you can expect to see accomplished within a few weeks and that will help you to chart Eric's progress in learning to analyze, challenge, and replace his maladaptive thoughts, particularly around sexuality; instill hope for change; and plan time-effective treatment sessions. If you have trouble with Step 3, reread your support paragraphs, looking for ideas to transform into goals that (a) might help Eric engage in hypothesis testing about his specific beliefs or replace maladaptive thoughts with adaptive ones, (b) might enhance factors facilitating or decrease factors inhibiting his ability to explore his sexuality at this time, (c) might utilize his strengths in analyzing his life whenever possible, and (d) are individualized to him as a neglected teen rather than generic.

Exercise 6

GOAL: To critique cognitive treatment in the case of Eric.

STYLE: Answer Questions A through E in essay format or discuss them in a group format.

A. What are the strengths and weaknesses of this model for helping Eric (a teen with sexual orientation issues)?

B. Consider how taking a cognitive-behavioral perspective, in which you would help Eric integrate an understanding of the role of his thoughts with an understanding of his learning history, would change the treatment plan. What modes of learning does Eric seem to use most? What role models have influenced his thoughts and behaviors? Which approach do you consider most valuable to Eric at this time, and why?

C. Assume that Eric's comments about his mother's boyfriend and his father are understatements and that there are realistic threats to his safety at this time. Considering what you know from the domain of violence, what issues must you assess, and what specifically will you do, to encourage the change process without jeopardizing Eric's safety?

D. Considering Eric's family situation and the research on sexual orientation, discuss Eric's current risk for suicide. Are there particular issues you need to assess in more depth to develop an accurate assessment of this? What could happen if his family becomes aware that his treatment with you focuses on issues related to his sexuality? Might this increase or decrease his risk of suicide?

E. What did you learn about your own attitudes toward sexuality and helping teenagers with their sexuality as you were working through the case of Eric?

RECOMMENDED RESOURCES

Books

Beck, J. S. (2011). *Cognitive behavior therapy: Basics and beyond* (2nd ed.). New York, NY: Guilford Press.

Dobson, K. S. (2012). *Cognitive therapy.* Washington, DC: American Psychological Association.

Greenberg, L. S., McWilliams, N., & Wenzel, A. (2013). *Exploring three approaches to psychotherapy.* Washington, DC: American Psychological Association.

Ingram, B. L. (2012). *Clinical case formulations: Matching the integrative treatment plan to the client* (Chapter 10, pp. 197–223). Hoboken, NJ: John Wiley.

Videos

American Psychological Association (Producer), & Beck, J. S. (Trainer). (n.d.). *Cognitive therapy* (Motion Picture #4310736). (Available from the American Psychological Association, 750 First Street, NE, Washington, DC 20002–4242)

Owen, P. (2013, September 15). Depression: A cognitive therapy approach [Video file]. Retrieved from https://www.youtube.com/watch?v=G1ALHcCRpkE

Websites

American Institute for Cognitive Therapy. http://www.cognitivetherapynyc.com

Beck Institute for Cognitive Behavior Therapy. http://www.beckinstitute.org

Cognitive-Behavioral Case Conceptualizations and Treatment Plans

INTRODUCTION TO COGNITIVE-BEHAVIORAL THEORY

Ann, 70 years old, is brought in by her best friend, Karen, who waits outside your office. Ann has been living with Karen, a next-door neighbor, for the past week. Ann had needed to leave her home to get time away from her daughter Laurie (age 43). Laurie had shaken her back and forth repeatedly and then shoved her down hard on the living room couch; this happened after Ann refused to give Laurie a credit card to use at the store. Ann felt frightened by what happened and ran out her back door to Karen's house. Karen took Ann to the doctor and has been caring for Ann since the incident. Ann is recovering well from the effects of a mild concussion she developed as a result of the abuse.

Ann's husband Jason died a year ago of a heart attack while cutting the grass around their suburban home. Laurie was served divorce papers by her husband soon after Jason's death. Ostensibly to take care of Ann, Laurie moved back home; this has led to a lot of conflicts between Laurie and her mother. Ann has one other child, Brian (age 47), who lives about two hours away. Ann has told you on the phone that while she was frightened of Laurie during the incident, now she just wishes that Laurie would move out. Ann feels the real problem is a deep depression she has been suffering for the past year since the death of her husband.

On psychometric testing and a mental status screen, Ann shows no signs of residual cognitive confusion as a result of her concussion. She shows no signs of homicidal ideation or impulsivity. While there are no signs of suicidal ideation, she does admit to symptoms of significant depression.

Although there were significant concerns about elder abuse during the brief intake, Ann refused to contact an elder advocate and indicated she would deny the altercations with Laurie if she was contacted by elder protective services. You made the mandated report, and Ann did indeed deny the incident to elder protective services. However, Karen drove Ann to her treatment appointment with you, and Ann didn't significantly resist coming in.

In traditional cognitive-behavioral treatment, your first step would be to teach Ann how thoughts, feelings, and behaviors are related to each other. Ann's depression is not a result of Jason's death or Laurie's assault, but rather her interpretation of these events. You might also introduce her to the concept that antecedents and consequences have powerful influences on both her and Laurie's behavior. However, unlike the traditional cognitive-behavioral approach, you will not go on to teach Ann how to change her maladaptive thoughts into more adaptive ones. You do not necessarily believe that Ann needs to change these to relieve her depression. Instead, she may need to change her relationship to her thoughts and behaviors as they exist within the internal world of her mind. Your approach to treatment is based on mindfulness-based cognitive therapy (MBCT), developed by Segal, Williams, and Teasdale (2013). MBCT combines cognitive treatment and psychoeducation so that Ann will become aware of her mental model for how she interacts in the world. MBCT also adds meditative practices so that Ann can become fully present in the moment—in a nonjudgmental, patient, and kind manner.

Using MBCT, Ann will learn that she has a mental model for how to interact in the world that includes her beliefs about herself, others, and the situations she is in. Her problems with depression are the result of her living on automatic pilot, allowing ingrained patterns to control her behavior, and thus reducing her ability to challenge the validity of her current beliefs and thoughts. She will be helped to come out of her depression, and to reduce the likelihood that she will relapse, by increasing her awareness of her own mental life so that she becomes aware of the choices that she has. She will learn how to be fully present in the moment rather than operating on automatic pilot.

Rather than getting stuck ruminating on her inability to stop being depressed, Ann will become aware that her rumination is holding her back from overcoming her depression. Rather than thinking about her past failure to overcome depression, or her fear that she won't overcome it in the future, Ann will be helped to fully experience her depression in the present moment. Ann needs to be consciously aware of her experiences as they are happening so that she can make careful judgments about when she should and should not be tolerating certain aspects of them. There will always be distressing events in life that can interfere with living a satisfying life. Ann has many choices for how to respond to these distressing events. For example, she could choose to act on her thoughts and impulses; she could choose to accept that she has them but then choose not to act on them; or she could challenge their validity for her current life and change them. Mindfulness will teach Ann to welcome all aspects of her experiences with the world, attend to them, and make decisions about whether to tolerate these experiences or distract herself from them. MBCT assumes that the attempts Ann makes to fight off negative thoughts, emotions, sensations, and impulses can cause more distress than simply experiencing them does.

Segal and associates (2013) view the mind as having a variety of modes of operation. One of them is *doing mode* (getting something done). In this mode, Ann might have had a goal she wanted to achieve, such as raising her daughter Laurie to be a responsible adult. She took actions she thought would help Laurie develop the skills she needed to become a responsible adult. As Ann noticed discrepancies between how Laurie behaved and how Ann wished she would behave, Ann tried to engage in a variety of activities to decrease or erase this discrepancy. This problem-solving strategy, while not inherently flawed for some types of goal attainment, may be inappropriate when the context of the goal has so many aspects outside the individual's control. By acting (doing) as if she could in fact be in control, Ann was setting herself up for repeated episodes of depression. Segal and associates refer to this dysfunctional doing as the "driven-doing mode" (p. 68) that involves obsessional, ruminative thinking errors.

Rather than allowing "driven-doing" to make her miserable, Ann could put herself in "being mode" (Segal et al., 2013, p. 72). In this mode, Ann would be fully aware, accepting herself and allowing herself to get back in touch with the bodily sensations that tell her that she is truly in her life rather than just talking about her life. Ann would be experiencing what was happening, while at the same time not necessarily changing what was happening. Since Ann won't be attempting to achieve a goal while she is in being mode, she can experience the full richness of her experiences in the present moment without being concerned about plans for the past or future. Thoughts, feelings, and impulses are all aspects of moment-to-moment experiences that Ann will be fully aware of. In being mode, unlike in doing mode, actions are not taken. Ann will just experience what *is*—which may, or may not, lead to a more multidimensional experience. When Ann learns to recognize that she is in driven-doing mode, she can shift herself back into being mode. This content-to-process shift will help Ann protect herself from relapsing into depression in the future.

THE ROLE OF THE CLINICIAN

In MBCT, your role is that of an instructor who will help Ann learn how to become profoundly attuned to the here and now of her internal experience so that she can free herself from entrenched maladaptive thinking. There are many types of exercises you could use to help Ann to be more aware of her experiences. Whatever you choose to do, you will be a role model of warmth, caring, and kindness. It is critical that your therapeutic environment and your behavior be welcoming. You must create a space where Ann can fearlessly explore the world of her mind. As you provide instructions, you will directly tell her to be gentle and kind to herself. As you talk to her, you will be gentle and kind to her.

Eventually, Ann may be able to show this same sense of kindness and caring toward her own experiences, even her negative ones. It is counterproductive for Ann to be harsh toward herself when the old autopilot begins. She needs you to teach her how to gently disengage herself from autopilot and reenter her focus on the here and now. Just as you will be warm and gentle as you guide her to be mindful, once Ann has mastered mindfulness skills, she will practice them with warmth, compassion, and interest. She will no longer hate or fear her experiences; she will truly understand them. While the name *MBCT* could give Ann the impression that learning to pay careful attention to her in-the-moment experiences is paramount, this can be harmful if Ann has not also learned to be kind and self-compassionate as she does so (Segal et al., 2013, p.137).

Ann may experience heightened negative emotions when she begins to process her internal experiences. You will need to encourage her to have a gentle curiosity about her difficulties that can help her explore them further, without making judgments or putting herself under pressure to achieve a goal. In all, there are eight skills to be learned (Segal et al., 2013, pp. 91–92). These include concentration, awareness/mindfulness, being in the moment, decentering, acceptance, letting go, being, and bringing awareness to a manifestation of the problem.

You will be helping Ann *concentrate* when you help her learn to maintain sustained, focused attention. You will help her be more *aware or mindful* when you help her attune to the patterns that have been unhelpful to her. She will be *in the moment* when you do not provide her with helpful instructions unless the instruction is needed right at that moment. If Ann is able to let thoughts, feelings, impulses, and bodily sensations just seem to pass through her body rather than personally identifying with them, you have helped her *decenter*. If she is able to *accept* an experience and have a kindly awareness of even a negative emotion or sensation, that will help her reduce the power of prior maladaptive habits to cause her distress. In *letting go*, Ann will be helped to not initiate, or at least to step out of, unhelpful cycles of thoughts, feelings, sensations, or impulses. In *being*, she will be supported in not achieving or setting a goal but just experiencing. Finally, Ann's body is the key space in which she can learn how to relate in a different way to her experience. When you help her *become aware of a manifestation of the problem*, you are helping her learn a key strategy for staying attuned with healthy processes rather than getting into driven-doing efforts to escape from discomfort.

Once you have completed an interview with Ann and determined that she is appropriate for MBCT, Segal and associates (2013) recommend an eight-session group treatment program. This group treatment will involve intensive work within a two-hour weekly meeting as well as one hour of daily practice of mindfulness exercises at home. It is not easy to get off autopilot; to do so, Ann will need to learn to recognize the signs of driven-doing mode, practice being mode, and learn how to switch from driven-doing to being mode when needed. This will require Ann to tolerate negative emotions, sensations, and thoughts at times as she explores difficult and uncomfortable emotions. As a result of treatment, Ann will have a full range of options for how to respond to her internal world while staying attuned to her external needs as well.

There are many mindfulness exercises that can be used within treatment sessions. After every exercise, you will need to ask Ann for feedback about the experience. It is through discussions of experiences, not lectures from you, that most of the learning will take place. The aim of treatment is to get Ann out of her mental ruts and allow her to respond to situations from a position of choice rather than from a position of automatic pilot. Each exercise will help Ann become more mindful and take on a warmer and more compassionate stance toward herself.

Examples of how Ann will learn to bring a deep awareness to her experience are the raisin exercise and the body scan exercise. In the *raisin exercise*, Ann will literally be given a raisin in her hand to fully attend to. She will be coached to explore all facets of the raisin using each of her sensory systems, including tactile, olfactory, visual, and gustatory. Ann will learn how to note the differences between being mindfully aware and being on automatic pilot. She will be gaining practice in how paying attention to detail can reveal increased information; how careful attention to something can transform it; and how having her mind wander as she tries to pay attention is normal. After this experience, she will be engaged in a discussion of what the exercise was like for her. This exercise was designed to increase her awareness in the moment and increase her curiosity about her sensory experiences.

An exercise that will help Ann practice deliberately engaging and then disengaging her attention is the *body scan exercise*. The intent of this exercise is to help Ann get back in touch with her bodily sensations. She will start the exercise by lying down on the floor and closing her eyes. She will then slowly move her attention around to different parts of her body to become aware of how it feels where her body connects with the floor. She will become aware of her breathing in the sensations in her body. For each outbreath, she will allow herself to feel as if she's sinking deeper into the floor. She will be reminded that she may or may not feel any different as she does this exercise. She may or may not feel more relaxed. She will be advised that this practice exercise only requires that she try to focus her attention on each part of her body in turn; there is no success or failure connected to any part of this exercise. The exercise starts with Ann's being directed to note her sensations around her stomach. Ann may be told that as she breathes in, her awareness of the sensations in her stomach may increase; if they don't, it's not a problem. When it's time for Ann to move her awareness to another body part, Ann may be instructed that as she breathes out, she may experience her breath as moving out of her stomach and into a new area of her body; however, if this doesn't happen for her, it is not a problem. If Ann's attention wanders away, she will be told that it is normal for the mind to wander and that when she notes that it is happening, she should just bring her attention back to the part of the body that she was scanning. After Ann has been directed gently to scan her entire body, she will spend a few moments just breathing in and out allowing her breath to flow freely. After a few minutes of breathing, Ann will be engaged in a discussion of what the body scan exercise was like for her. Within this discussion, Ann will be asked if she is curious about what happened. If she criticizes her performance, she will be encouraged to take a gentle stance rather than a blaming stance toward herself. You will encourage her to consider letting go of "judging" her performance because the point of the exercise was just to experience it—period.

To educate Ann about the role that interpretation plays in her feelings, she can be engaged in the *thoughts and feelings exercise*. In this exercise, she will settle into a comfortable position, close her eyes, and then imagine a scenario as you describe it aloud. In the scenario, Ann is walking down the street, sees somebody that she knows, and smiles and waves at the person. However, this person walks by without any sign of recognition. Ann will process what is going through her mind as she imagines this scenario. How does her body feel? What actions does she feel like doing? You can then discuss with Ann how her interpretation of the person's behavior, rather than the behavior itself, is what led to her feelings about it (worried, angry, depressed, or untouched by the event). The response of the observed person was in many ways neutral. However, since Ann is depressed, she is likely to interpret the person's behavior as rejection. A ruminative pattern will have put her on automatic pilot. For example, she might look down and start to cry, her stomach might tighten up, and she might feel alone. Two important points will be made to Ann. One point is that the exercise occurred solely in her mind, and that therefore it was her thoughts, not the event, that led her to feel isolated. The hypothetical acquaintance who walked by without waving might have done so for many reasons that had nothing to do with Ann herself. For example, the acquaintance may have just had drops placed in her eyes by the ophthalmologist and not been able to see Ann. Or, perhaps Ann waved at someone who looked like her acquaintance but was not. These are just two of the many different interpretations that meet the facts of the scenario. The person passed her, without waving, in the imagined scenario, but Ann's thinking that the person was rejecting her was just an idea she had in her mind, not a fact. The second point is that MBCT may help Ann prevent another relapse into depression if she can learn that this automatic pattern of response is a warning sign of depression. Whenever she becomes aware of this pattern, Ann needs to realize that she has to get herself out of driven-doing mode and into being mode or she will relapse into depression.

Whatever exercises you introduce to Ann, she will need to practice mindfulness outside of treatment sessions if she is to develop the skills she needs to free herself from her past negative patterns. This practice will take at least an hour a day. In addition to this formal hour of practice, she will informally practice mindfulness while doing one thing she selects from her everyday life, such as brushing her teeth, putting her clothes on, or eating breakfast.

As a clinician, you will also need to practice mindfulness every day. You cannot be an effective instructor of mindfulness if you have not rigorously practiced it. Segal and associates (2013) indicate that "how" you talk to Ann about mindfulness, coming from a deep understanding of your own experiences in being mindful, will in some ways help Ann more than the exercises per se.

CASE APPLICATION: INTEGRATING THE DOMAIN OF SOCIOECONOMIC STATUS

Ann's case will now be examined in detail. There are many domains of complexity that may be relevant to her case. The domain of SES has been chosen to examine within the cognitive-behavioral approach of mindfulness-based cognitive therapy in case conceptualization and treatment planning.

Interview With Ann (A) Using Mindfulness-Based Cognitive-Behavioral Theory

C: On the phone, you said your friend Karen was concerned that your daughter Laurie was physically abusing you. Is this why you are here today?

A: (anxiously) No. Karen is overly concerned about Laurie. She's my daughter. She has always had a hot temper and always will. I am so depressed—that is what I need help with. My husband died last year and I just can't seem to get myself past it. I try but I just can't live without him. I have plenty of money, a beautiful home, I could travel the world if I wanted to (deep sigh) but there's no point to living life without him.

C: He is gone and you want him back.

A: (deep sigh) We were together for 45 years. I met him accidentally on the train. The attraction was mutual and immediate. I had to get off the train first. It was so impossible to part that he actually just got off the train and walked me home. (long pause, crying) We married two weeks later.

C: You are crying.

A: (anxious again) I can't stop. It doesn't matter if I am alone or with someone else. Whatever we are talking about disappears and I can only cry. I don't know where to start to change this. What should I say?

C: You have so many different people in your life and so many different experiences, yet your response is always the same: You cry.

A: (crying, softly) Can you help me stop?

C: We will be working on your depression together, but first, could you give me more background so I understand more clearly what is going on?

A: (softly) Family life has always been important to me. Jason loved our kids, but he would get on the train early in the morning and not get home till seven at night, right about the time the children needed to be in bed. He was very successful at work and gave us everything we could possibly want. The house was full of beautiful things; the children participated in any activity they found interesting.

C: You had everything you needed. (pause; *A* nods) How did things go?

A: I didn't have much trouble with our son Brian. He had a solid head on his shoulders and was very logical, even as a little boy. Not Laurie; she was a whirlwind of energy, and she was always having temper tantrums. She always had to have her way. She could never accept my no. (long pause, looking down)

C: You are looking down. (pause) What are you thinking about?

A: (regretfully) I really failed Laurie. I loved that child so much. I was so happy to have a daughter, but . . . (pause, crying softly; *C* hands her the tissue box) I always told Jason when I was struggling with Laurie. He would tell me to put my foot down but always in a hesitant voice—he was a very indulgent dad. He never came home without candy in his pockets when the kids were little. They would run to him in their pajamas and put their hands in his pockets. (pause, crying softly)

C: You were remembering him loving your children and bringing them treats, yet you are crying, not smiling.

A: (small sigh) Yes, I know I should pull myself together.

C: I was just trying to describe what was happening. It makes sense to cry when you feel depressed. (long pause) I was just noticing that remembering a pleasant memory was bringing up painful thoughts and emotions, not happy ones. I was curious how you were interpreting the memory of Jason and the candy.

A: (sad) He never let the children down; he never forgot their candy. But I was responsible for raising them. Brian has a good job and is doing well with his own family, but Laurie is divorced and her life is a complete mess. It's her temper. (shaking her head) I tried so many times to get her to calm down and compromise with her husband. Her marriage was always rocky because she and her husband were constantly in a battle of wills.

C: They were on automatic pilot where they couldn't stop fighting, whether they were getting what they wanted or not.

A: (sad, slipping down in the chair) Laurie and Frank were both so stubborn. Each one was always trying to control the other. I talked to both of them, oh so many times. I needed to help them but failed, (pause) completely failed. Frank is not my child, but I am responsible for Laurie.

C: When you interpreted their behavior as stubborn, you slipped down in your chair. I was curious about what that means?

A: (crying, long pause) Everyone blames me for being such a bad mother. (pause) I blame myself more than everyone else does.

C: I have no reason to blame you for anything. You loved your child and did everything that you could to take care of her. Jason was gone most of the time. You were the one with both Laurie and Brian day and night. Brian is doing well. (pause) Do you get credit for this?

A: (anxiously wringing her hands) Even though you are speaking in a gentle voice, I can tell by what you said that you blame me too. Jason was gone, so it couldn't have been his mistakes that led to Laurie's problems. It must have been mine.

C: You are very hard on yourself. (pause) I was curious about what it meant that you had slipped down into your chair. You responded by saying, "Everyone blames me." I asked if you got any credit for Brian's success, and you said the mistakes were entirely your fault because Jason was always gone. Your thoughts and feelings are on automatic pilot right now. Even though there are many possible factors involved in the situations we have been talking about, you automatically say the cause is you and the result is that you have to take full responsibility and suffer for it. (pause, A still looking down) Does that sound right?

A: (softly, looking up with some sniffling) I guess I would agree that I'm on automatic pilot; I do spend a lot of time blaming myself and feeling sad about Laurie or Jason. I have had troubles with depression on and off as I started raising the children. Karen told me many times to just buck up. She thought I would feel better if I stood up for myself and was firm with Laurie. She said if I didn't, Laurie would have big problems in her adult life. Karen was a hundred percent right! If only I had listened to her.

C: Is Karen helping you blame yourself?

A: (softly) Oh no. Karen has been my perfect friend for more than forty years. She has always been there to help me. We married brothers, you see. She married the outgoing one—Ted. I married the shy one—Jason. They both worked together at the big department store their folks owned in downtown Los Angeles. (emphatically) We really raised our kids together while the boys worked. She was always there for me.

C: You two raised the kids together? (A nods) You say she was always there for you, but "always" is a tough standard.

A: (choking back her tears) She was always there to help; she didn't always agree. She knows her own mind and she knew my children well. She never hesitated to tell me what she thought. (sigh) That's what friends are for, to be brutally honest if that is what you need.

C: Could you describe a time you remember when you think she was being brutally honest?

A: (pause; agitated) Well, Laurie was about ten years old and screaming at the top of her lungs in the backyard. Laurie didn't want to come in and do her homework. I was trying to reason with her. Brian had already come in, and I was trying to point out to her that she should follow his good example. (pause, squeezing eyes shut) Karen came running over and said to me that Laurie could be heard all over the neighborhood. She told me I was acting like a wet dishrag and I should buck up and tell my daughter to shut up. I started to cry, which irritated her. I wanted Laurie to love me. I wanted us to be close. And whenever I tried to be firm, she only said she felt unloved.

C: You wanted to be loved by your daughter. That is very understandable. (pause) Karen was brutally frank and labeled you a wet dishrag. Your response was to cry, so while she was trying to help you, (pause) it didn't work.

A: (softly) Karen was always right. She just yelled at Laurie to shut up and get inside. She told her to stop acting like a big baby or she would get a spanking like she was one. Laurie stomped in the house and threw me a bitter look.

C: Since Laurie went into the house, this means that Karen was right and you were wrong? Could there be any other reason? (*A* shakes her head no) Could Laurie be afraid of Karen because of her loud voice and threats but not afraid of you?

A: (curious) Do you think so? That wouldn't be good; children shouldn't be afraid of their parents. But that couldn't be it. They would never be afraid of Karen; they love her. I'm the big baby. It doesn't matter if it's a little four-year-old Laurie or a big Laurie, loud voices always make me step back inside myself. (pause) Karen was right again, and I am getting what I deserve. Laurie is forty-three years old, still pushing me around and spending all my money (softly crying again). If I try to say no, she starts crying and telling me that it's always been the same: I never really loved her like I loved Brian.

C: When she said you didn't really love her, did you give her the money she wanted? (*A* nods and then stares into her lap) It sounds like there was a pattern of Laurie being able to get what she wanted from you because in a contest of wills, you would go for the soft response of reason and she wouldn't hesitate to yell. If you would ever be firm, even without yelling, she would say you didn't love her, and you would give in.

A: (brittle) You have it; I am a coward. I raised her. (pause) I have to be firm now. I can't be weak. She has been spending more money than I'm bringing in. If I don't stop her, I will have so many financial problems. I already had to let my medication run out because I couldn't afford to pay for the renewal. My property taxes are coming up, and she's emptied my savings account. (starts crying) I am responsible for this debt Laurie has run up. (crying hard) I tried to be firm and now I have a concussion. Even Jason's death is my fault.

C: You can be understanding about Laurie shaking you, even though she is an adult, because you understand her quick temper. Yet you have no sympathy for yourself. You are in financial problems from trying to help Laurie feel loved. You lost your beloved husband. You add to your pain by blaming yourself for everything—even Jason's death.

A: (crying) It was my fault. Not the heart attack itself; he was seventy-two and had been a heavy smoker. But the thing is, I ran out of dish-washing fluid and ran off to the store to buy more. Had I been at home when he had his attack, I might have been able to get him to the hospital in time to save him.

C: I can hear the pain in your voice and see it in your posture. Let's slow things down. I would like us to both take some deep breaths together, the type of long, (pause) slow (pause) breaths where we have a chance to really feel the air going in (pause) and out (pause). Don't try to say anything. As best you can, just feel your breath coming in and then going out. That's good. Take the breath in even more deeply; feel your chest expanding with air. Try to be curious about what it feels like to just let your lungs fill slowly up with air, and then the change in your body as you slowly exhale.

A: (choking back her tears) I am trying, but I just keep thinking about everything I have done wrong.

C: Whenever you start thinking about something else, just notice that your mind wandered and then bring it back to being aware of every sensation, even the smallest one, of your air coming in and then going out.

A: (long pause, breathing gradually slowing down) Am I doing it right now that I stopped crying?

C: Just continue to breathe. There is no doing it right or wrong. Just breathe and try to turn your attention fully to the sensations in your body. If your mind starts to wander, that is normal; just bring yourself gently back to your breathing. Try to be fully aware of how your body feels as you breathe. (five minutes go by)

A: (choking back tears) I just keep thinking about how inadequate I am and how I failed as a wife, failed as a mother; now I am failing as a widow!

C: Try to step back from these thoughts of criticism as if you were a neutral observer of them. You understand what the thoughts are, but you don't judge whether they are right or wrong. Your mind needs to have thoughts like your lungs need to have air; otherwise it can't work. Acknowledge your thoughts when they are there, but then return your focus to your breathing. (three minutes go by)

A: (calm) I have stopped crying, finally!

C: The goal was not for you to cry or stop crying. I just wanted to give you the experience of what we might do in treatment together. We will not be evaluating you or grading you. I will be helping you become aware of your mental model for relating to the world. This model includes the beliefs that you have that fuel your depression. I will be supporting you as you decide what relationship you want to have with these thoughts.

A: (crying again) I didn't do things right. I was judging my thoughts. (pause) Oh, dear, I am crying again!

C: You can cry here. You can have any thoughts or feelings. They are yours to have. But, are you curious at all about whether you can be aware of these thoughts of being inadequate, yet not feel inadequate?

A: (anxious) I may not be able to do it.

C: Your thoughts are part of your internal world. It feels as if you don't have the choice to think them or not. However, you do have a choice. I want you to experience, in the moment, whether you have a choice to think or not think those depressing thoughts.

A: (calm, breathing slowly; five minutes go by) This feels good.

C: Can you tell me, in as much detail as you can what you are experiencing?

A: (calm) I feel my breathing is what I am paying the most attention to. I periodically notice that my chest gets tight as I think about being responsible for my Jason being dead, but then I just return to feeling my breathing and it goes away.

C: While you are aware of some negative experiences in your body and your mind, you found that you could decide to bring your attention back to your breathing. (pause; A nods) You have thoughts, feelings, sensations, impulses to act, yet you can decide whether to have any of these leave your internal world and influence your external interactions.

A: (anxious) I can feel in control of my thoughts in here, but when I leave, I won't be able to.

C: It will take lots of practice, but you will be able to do it. It is easy to get into automatic pilot and let your thoughts control you rather than recognizing that you control your thoughts.

A: (softly) How long will it take?

C: Everyone is different. However, when you are ready, we will be going through a program of exercises together with other people who are trying to learn the same things you are. The group sessions will be once a week for eight weeks. I will be asking you to practice skills at home for an hour every day. If you can do these things, you will be ready to stop coming in when the eight weeks of group are over.

A: (getting very red) While I was breathing, I did have a moment when I felt very afraid of Laurie. (sobbing) It feels terrible; she's my daughter. I can't be afraid of her.

C: Your feelings are your feelings. She did shake you. She did push you down. You did get a concussion. This was elder abuse under the law.

A: (stronger) I knew you were going to report the incident. (looking down) I told you I would deny the incident, and I did.

C: I did understand that you didn't want me to report Laurie, but I was concerned about your safety and I still am. You talked a lot today about Laurie's quick temper. I am a mandated reporter under the law, and must report to elder protective services any suspicions I might have that you are being abused, neglected, or financially exploited.

A: (looking up) I won't press charges, whatever you do. But I did understand why you made the call, and I appreciate you and Karen both caring about me. I don't know why you do (sigh). I am so useless, but (pause, looking directly at *C*) thank you. I have thought about what happened. Laurie can yell at me if she wants, but she can't shake me. I am her mother. I worked hard to take good care of her all her life. She owes me more respect than that.

C: You look like you are sitting straighter in your chair, and your voice has more confidence in it.

A: (calm) I do wish I had a better relationship than I have with Laurie. But it isn't true that I was never there for her. I called her this morning and told her what you did. She was shocked. I think that will take care of things, her knowing she was committing abuse under the law.

C: Are you sure you are safe?

A: (stiffly) Karen may be bossy, but she loves me. She isn't going to let me go home till Laurie has moved out. What will happen next?

C: We will talk alone again next week, and we will decide when you are ready to join those group sessions I told you about. In the meantime, I'm going to give you some exercises to practice at home during the week. Take a moment, and ask me any questions you have about completing them.

A: (reads the materials; three minutes of silence) I understand them. But it might be hard to do it.

C: Just do it every day. Don't evaluate it. Just do it.

Cognitive-Behavioral Case Conceptualization of Ann: Assumption-Based Style

Ann's mental model for operating in the world is currently on autopilot, full of perfectionistic beliefs and depressive thoughts and locking her into an internal struggle with depression rather than guiding her to have an active life. Ann's mental model guides her to think everything through carefully to come up with the perfect solution. It has been effective in guiding her to care for her home and make many life decisions. However, when faced with problems that evoke deep negative emotions, Ann gets caught in automatic pilot, where she ruminates about the situation evoking the emotion rather than taking effective action. Life is complex, and there will always be both negative and positive events; it is Ann's perceptions of these events, rather than the events per se, that lead to her emotional and behavioral reactions to them. Jason's death and Laurie's physical abuse were traumatic, and her perfectionistic beliefs, not these events, have led to her unproductive rumination where she is depressed and inactive. This is not the first time that Ann has become stuck in a ruminative cycle, and she has been able to break out of this dysfunctional state in the past. Ann maintained a relationship with her husband for 45 years that she remembers with love and affection despite her episodic bouts of depressive rumination. In addition, she maintained a lifelong friendship with Karen, who is committed to Ann's current safety. Thus, if Ann can become more fully aware of her experiences and regain her ability to make choices about how to react to her thoughts and feelings, it is likely that she already has the skills and social support needed to respond to her beliefs and either tolerate them, modify them, or distract herself from them as needed. Learning to be more mindful of what's going on in the moment can help Ann learn to recognize warning signs that she is getting stuck in automatic pilot and may prevent her from further lapses into depression. Ann recently told Laurie that elder protective services had been called about Laurie's abusive behavior. By defining Laurie's behavior as elder abuse, Ann thinks Laurie will never assault her again. While it is unclear if this is true, this is a positive sign that Ann can step out of her internal world to try to protect her own physical safety.

Ann's model for operating in the world has involved always thinking about what she needs to accomplish in the future and evaluating what she has done in the past to ensure that she always does things exactly right. If things go wrong, she always considers it possible to fix them if she takes the right actions. While her model has always contained the belief that she should do things exactly right, this belief can be functional in some situations, guiding Ann to make thoughtful decisions. Unfortunately, strong negative emotions have set off a ruminative pattern where she just keeps thinking and criticizing herself and not taking effective action. When she came home from shopping to find her husband dead of a heart attack, the pain of loss sent her into a ruminative loop in which she perceived that this event could have been prevented if only she had made better decisions. When her daughter exploited her financially and physically abused her, fear sent Ann into rumination about her past failures as a parent. Since she has always longed for a supportive and intimate relationship with her daughter Laurie and didn't have it, she believes this must have been her fault because she wasn't a good enough parent. During the interview, Ann ignored all positive signs of her competency as a parent with Brian and exaggerated any signs of having parental difficulties with Laurie. Brian may have had an analytic and logical way of operating in the world similar to Ann's, making it easier for her to understand how to parent him. Laurie may have operated more based on her feelings and expressed these at such an intense level that they overwhelmed Ann. As Laurie's yelling didn't overwhelm Karen, who could match Laurie's intensity with her own, this was further evidence to Ann that if she had only planned better, she wouldn't be having problems with Laurie now. Ann needs to recognize when her mental model is helping her make carefully thought out decisions and when it is operating automatically based on faulty beliefs that do not guide her effectively.

Life is full of positive and negative events, and it is Ann's perceptions of these events that can lead to constructive or destructive thoughts and feelings. Jason's death and Laurie's abuse are negative events, but it is Ann's rumination that has prevented her from having constructive self-talk, experiencing supportive emotions, and taking effective action to cope with these events. For example, Ann needs to recognize that ruminating about the mistakes she made when Laurie was a young child is standing in the way of her dealing effectively with adult Laurie. At this time, Ann is using all-or-nothing thinking in viewing her relationships. On the one hand, she believes her marriage was perfect, her husband was a perfect parent, Karen is a perfect friend, and Brian's life is successful. On the other hand, she believes that she always let Laurie down and that Laurie's life is a complete mess. Ann's model of the world filters her experiences to give the credit for everything good to others and the blame for everything bad to herself. Ann attributes all of what was good in their marriage to Jason's efforts and none to her own. Ann believes that Jason, although he rarely interacted with the children, always knew what they needed.

Ann has filled her mental world with "shoulds." She should not have gone to the grocery store the day of Jason's heart attack. She should have listened to Karen's advice about parenting. These all-or-nothing thoughts that tell Ann that, for instance, she either helped Laurie or failed Laurie keep Ann frozen and inactive. Due to this self-criticism and her all-or-nothing thinking, Ann frequently misperceives how others are viewing her. For example, she assumed the clinician was criticizing her when she was asked why she was slumping in the chair. Ann has broken out of her depressions in the past. To do so again, she needs to carefully attend to her experiences with people as they are happening in the present. Ann needs to be mindful in the here and now and evaluate the validity of her perceptions and expectations for guiding her relationships at the present time. She can resolve her current depression if she can increase her awareness in the moment and notice where she has choices for how to feel and how to behave. She doesn't necessarily need to stop feeling sad about Jason or feeling fearful about Laurie. Ann just needs to change her relationship to these feelings. For example, when sad feelings about Jason flood her consciousness, Ann needs to decide if she wants to tolerate them, if she needs to alter them to include memories of his mistakes, or if she needs to distract herself from them. Currently, she is lost in her internal world of depression, ruminating about her past behavior and her fears for the future. This mental stuckness is why Ann can allow 43-year-old Laurie to exploit her financially and abuse her physically, yet deny this when elder protective services comes to speak to her. Instead of fully facing the current situation with Laurie, Ann is ruminating about an event that occurred when Laurie was 10 years old. Laurie's expenditures have taken away Ann's ability to acquire needed medication and may have put her home in jeopardy, as Laurie has spent all the money Ann saved to pay her real estate taxes. Rather than taking control of her checking account and credit cards, Ann is concerned that Laurie will feel unloved if she turns the money faucet off.

While these issues of physical abuse and financial exploitation are serious, Ann can recognize exceptions to her perfectionistic thinking. For example, she can recognize that

Jason provided very well for the family financially but wasn't home very much. She can say that he was a perfect father yet recognize that he may have overindulged Laurie. Ann has also been able to take one step out of frozen immobility. She called Laurie and told her that the clinician had made a mandated report labeling Laurie a perpetrator of abuse. Ann believes that by telling Laurie about this, Laurie will be less likely to lay hands on her again. Thus, while denying the clinician's report when contacted by elder protective services, Ann has shown the ability to step out of her mental world of depressive thoughts and take effective action to increase her physical safety.

Ann has undergone two very traumatic events in the last year. One was the sudden death of her husband Jason, and the second was being physically assaulted by her daughter Laurie. In response to both events, Ann retreated into a long-established pattern of withdrawing from intense, negative feelings and blaming herself for the events that evoked the feelings. While a dangerous event, Laurie's abusing her mother opened up a window of opportunity for Ann to move out of automatic pilot. It set in motion a number of changes that put Ann in the position of evaluating whether she wants to be controlled by her internal world or be in control of it.

While Ann is having recurrence of a depressive state, she has shown the ability to recognize the signs that she is on automatic pilot and not fully processing her experiences. While unsure if her efforts will be successful, Ann is trying a new way of breathing to help herself be more aware of what is happening in the present moment. In addition, she has committed to returning for another treatment session, in which she will actively practice new skills while not criticizing the quality of her skills. A barrier to success is Ann's longstanding pattern of not accepting anything but perfect behavior from herself. Ann needs to learn to be as kind and forgiving toward herself as she has always been toward her daughter Laurie. Another critical skill for Ann will be to learn to recognize the difference between when she is carefully thinking and moving toward a solution and when she is ruminating and stuck. Being stuck is a sign that Ann is on automatic pilot and unable to evaluate the value of her thoughts in guiding her in the present moment. Ann's ability to make this distinction is key to her ending her cycles of depression.

Cognitive-Behavioral Treatment Plan: Assumption-Based Style

Treatment Plan Overview. Ann wants help with her depression. Long-Term Goals 1, 2, and 3 need to be addressed sequentially, as each follows from the skill building contained within the earlier ones. (This treatment plan follows the *basic format.*)

LONG-TERM GOAL 1: Ann will become fully aware of her model for interacting in the world in which she withdraws from negative feelings, such as the pain of Jason's death and fears of what Laura might do.

Short-Term Goals

1. Ann will practice the raisin exercise in session, trying not to shift into rumination about her depression, and afterward describe in what ways being fully aware of a raisin differs from being on automatic pilot and thinking about her depression.

2. Ann will discuss the physical sensations that she had in her body as she was chewing the raisin and how this active engagement differed from how she withdrew from a negative thought or feeling that came up during the raisin exercise.

3. Ann will learn to identify and label the physical sensations in her body when she is withdrawing from a negative thought or feeling that comes up during home practice of the body scan exercise.

4. Ann will practice recognizing when she is on automatic pilot and withdrawing from negative thoughts by practicing full awareness in the present moment three times a day as she brushes her teeth after each meal.

5. Ann will keep a daily log of how attentive she can be in the moment as she brushes her teeth during the day and as she practices the body scan exercise daily.

6. In treatment sessions, Ann will discuss her experiences at home and whether (and if so, when) she noticed that she was on automatic pilot.

7. Ann will continue to practice being fully aware each time she brushes her teeth and will add being fully aware as she gets dressed in the morning.

8. Other goals will be developed as appropriate to ensure that Ann can recognize when she is fully attending to the present and when she is on automatic pilot.

LONG TERM GOAL 2: Ann will consider how her perceptions and interpretations of Jason's death and Laurie's financial exploitation and abuse have caused her feelings of depression and inadequacy and her withdrawal into her internal world.

Short-Term Goals

1. Ann will be introduced to the ABC model of antecedent, behavior, and consequences within a session, and she will discuss it with the clinician to make sure she understands it clearly.

2. As homework, Ann will nonjudgmentally evaluate her thoughts about Jason's parenting style by remembering specific events from the past and evaluating them based on the ABC model; in the next treatment session, she will discuss what she experienced from doing the homework.

3. In session, on the basis of the ABC model, Ann will nonjudgmentally consider whether the consequences Jason provided Laurie for her behavior could have had any impact on how Laurie is currently behaving as an adult.

4. Ann will discuss her memories of Jason by recalling one specific event from the past where they were getting along well and one where they were not, and she will come up with at least three possible explanations for why each event happened as it did.

5. As homework, Ann will keep a log of one memory she has about Jason each day and come up with at least three possible explanations for his behavior.

6. Ann will discuss her memories of Brian as a young son through remembering one event where she understood his behavior and one event where she did not, and she will come up with at least three possible explanations for why each event happened as it did.

7. As homework, Ann will keep a log of one memory she has about Brian each day and come up with at least three possible explanations for his behavior.

8. Ann will discuss her memories of Laurie as a young daughter through remembering one event where she understood her behavior and one event where she did not, and she will come up with at least three possible explanations for why each event happened as it did.

9. As homework, Ann will keep a log of one memory she has about Laurie each day and come up with at least three possible explanations for her behavior.

10. Ann will discuss her perceptions of how the clinician behaves in treatment sessions and come up with at least three possible explanations for the clinician's behavior.

11. Other goals will be determined as needed.

LONG TERM GOAL 3: Ann will decrease her depression by actively attending to her internal perceptions in the moment, evaluating their validity, and discovering where she can make choices about how to behave in the external world.

1. Ann will actively attend to her internal experience as she considers whether it is all her fault that Jason died.

    a. Ann will breathe deeply in and out for five minutes, carefully attending only to her breathing.

    b. Ann will consider her bodily sensations, cognitions, feelings, and action tendencies as she directs her mind to the idea that Jason is dead.

    c. Ann will breathe deeply in and out for five minutes and then discuss what choice points she currently has for either tolerating her pain at Jason's death, moderating it, or distracting herself from it.

    d. Ann will practice, as homework and during sessions, the actions that she has decided are most beneficial to her at the present time in relation to Jason's death, such as when to tolerate her pain, when to distract herself from her pain, and when to remember things he did that were not perfect.

2. Ann will actively attend to her internal experiences as she considers whether it is all her fault that Laurie financially exploited her and physically abused her.

    a. Ann will breathe deeply in and out for five minutes, carefully attending only to her breathing.

    b. Ann will consider her bodily sensations, cognitions, feelings, and action tendencies as she directs her mind to the idea that Laurie spent her money and shook her back and forth.

    c. Ann will breathe deeply in and out for five minutes and then discuss what choice points she currently has for either tolerating her feelings of guilt and loss over Laurie's behavior, moderating those feelings, or distracting herself from them.

    d. Ann will practice, within homework and during sessions, the actions that she has decided are most beneficial to her at the present time in relation to Laurie's behavior, such as when to tolerate her anger, when to distract herself from Laurie's anger, and when to set limits on how much time she spends with Laurie or whether she spends time alone with Laurie.

3. Ann will actively attend to her internal experiences as she considers whether it is all her fault that she is reexperiencing a serious depression.

    a. Ann will breathe deeply in and out for five minutes, carefully attending only to her breathing.

    b. Ann will consider her bodily sensations, cognitions, feelings, and action tendencies as she directs her mind to the idea that this is not her first episode of depression.

    c. Ann will breathe deeply in and out for five minutes and then discuss what choice points she currently has for either tolerating her anger and disappointment with herself for experiencing depression again, moderating that anger and disappointment, or distracting herself from it.

    d. Ann will practice, within homework and during sessions, the actions that she has decided are most beneficial to her at the present time in relation to her current episode of depression, such as tolerating her feelings of sadness, distracting herself from her feelings of sadness, or actively trying to influence how she is feeling.

Cognitive-Behavioral Case Conceptualization of Ann: Theme-Based Style

"It's all my fault." This is Ann's mantra as she ruminates about the death of her husband, her daughter's abusive behavior, and her current depression. Ann believes that if she had planned perfectly, her husband would not have had a heart attack. The thought that goes with this belief is that if she hadn't been shopping, she could have called 911 and emergency workers would have saved him. Ann believes that if she had provided Laurie with proper consequences as a young child, she would not have grown up to be physically abusive and emotionally exploitive. Ann believes that if she could think more effectively, she would not be depressed despite the traumas of her husband's death and her daughter's abusive behavior. Ann is frozen on autopilot, where she withdraws from negative emotions and gets locked in a ruminative cycle in which she thinks about her life but doesn't engage with it. On the other hand, Ann has more functional thoughts in her head, such as that she is an advantaged person who leads a luxurious life. She can recognize that she met many of her daughter's needs when she was growing up. She can recognize that her husband was a heavy smoker and that this may have contributed to his heart attack. In addition, she has relationship skills that allowed her to maintain a marriage for 45 years, raise two children to adulthood, and maintain a lifelong friendship with Karen. Thus, if Ann can become more fully aware of her experiences and regain her ability to make choices about how to react to her thoughts and feelings, she can regain control of her life.

"It's all my fault that Jason is dead." Ann was married to Jason for 45 years, and she describes the marriage as happy and Jason as being an excellent provider. From her perspective, he provided them with a luxurious lifestyle where each member of the family could have everything he or she wanted. While Jason smoked heavily and didn't die until he was 72, Ann can give credence to these factors only briefly before retreating to her perfectionistic belief that if she had been a good enough wife, he would still be with her. The thoughts that go through her head are that she should have known better than to go to the store and that if she had been home, she would've been able to get him to the hospital in time for his life to be saved. It is this stream of negative thinking that fuels her view that she can never get over his death or enjoy life again.

"It's all my fault that Laurie shook me." Ann describes always having wanted to develop a close relationship with her daughter. She indicates that she loves her daughter but has always had difficulty dealing with Laurie's quick temper. Despite her perception that she gave Laurie everything she needed, Laurie was easily frustrated. Ann remembers trying to help Laurie learn to calm herself and to use reason, but she cannot bring up any memories of being effective in helping Laurie calm down. Ann observed a lot of fighting between Laurie and her now ex-husband; Ann feels that neither would compromise with the other. Ann frequently tried to intervene and help them work out their problems but perceives that she always failed to do so. From Ann's perspective, people who were competent, such as Jason and Karen, never let Laurie down. Jason always had candy for Laurie and always bought her gifts that soothed her when she was angry. Karen could always gain control of Laurie by yelling at her and telling her what to do. Ann views herself as the only one who was inadequate in dealing with Laurie and thus that it is all her fault that Laurie physically shook her and pushed her down on the couch, despite the fact that Laurie's behavior meets the criteria for elder physical abuse. In addition, Laurie's spending of the money that Ann needed for her own medication and living expenses fully meets the criteria for financial exploitation, another form of elder abuse. There was one moment when Ann was able to state that she had met most of Laurie's needs as a child, that she did deserve to be treated with respect, and that Laurie should not have shaken her.

"It's all my fault that I'm depressed." Ann describes having been depressed on and off since she began raising children. She may already have had perfectionist tendencies prior to having children; however, being solely responsible for them until bedtime may have intensified her need to do everything right. While things with her older child, Brian, went according to what may have been her "plan" as a mother, Laurie's temperament was more difficult for her to handle. Repeated experiences that she perceived to reflect her own failure as a mother may have sent her down into her first depression. The fact that her husband would give Laurie gifts, rather than helping Ann teach their daughter emotional regulation, may have added to the burden Ann was under to guide her daughter in self-control. Having a perfect friend, Karen, tell her that she was handling things wrong may have further entrenched Ann's belief that she was an inadequate parent. At the same time, Ann filters out all evidence that Brian was doing well, and that on many incidences she might have been meeting Laurie's needs well. Her model of how to operate in the world is now in a ruminative loop that ends with her being paralyzed with thoughts of her inadequacies and failures: It is all her fault that she can't get herself out of the depression that began with Jason's death. The fact that some people do recover from heart attacks is all that it might have taken for Ann to blame herself. However, this self-blame may have been instigated by the trauma of coming home and being alone with a dead loved one. Ann's typical pattern of pulling away from strong, negative emotions could not have had a stronger initiating incident. With support from the treatment relationship, Ann was able to consider that Jason's age and smoking habit may have played strong roles in his death.

"Must everything be all my fault?" At this point in her life, Ann quickly responds "yes." However, with support from the treatment relationship, Ann was able to temporarily pull out of automatic pilot and be mindful while considering Laurie's behavior. The idea that Jason encouraged Laurie to be demanding by giving her constant gifts occurred to her—which made everything not her fault. However, Ann fears she will never be able to be mindful like this on her own. There are several windows of opportunity that may support Ann in breaking out of autopilot at this time. One is that Ann doesn't want to stay afraid of her beloved daughter Laurie. Second, her friend Karen is supporting her change efforts by driving her to treatment and telling Ann she is going to stay her guest until Laurie moves out of the family home. In addition, threats of being held accountable for abusive actions by elder protective services may help Laurie inhibit her aggressive and exploitive behavior, at least in the short run. Barriers to change are Ann's entrenched patterns of withdrawal from negative emotions and the secondary gain that will come to Laurie if Ann doesn't change.

Cognitive-Behavioral Treatment Plan: Theme-Based Style

Treatment Plan Overview. It is unclear at this time when and if Ann will be ready to join an eight-session mindfulness group program. This treatment plan will proceed individually until it is determined whether she should join this group. Ann frequently uses the self-blaming statement that everything is always her fault. Therefore, having a treatment plan where the goals help her evaluate her level of blame may be powerful for her. Long-Term Goals 1, 2, and 3 can be processed in any order, as they will all help her become more aware of her present experience, evaluate whether she should tolerate or change her internal thoughts, and take control of her life. (This treatment plan follows the *problem format*.)

PROBLEM: Ann considers everything her fault, and this is depressing for her to think about.

LONG-TERM GOAL 1: Ann will decide what level of responsibility she has for Jason's death—how much it is her fault.

Short-Term Goals

1. Ann will practice being fully aware of her present experience by considering what level of responsibility she had for the health that Jason had during his adult life.

2. Ann will practice being fully aware of any experiences she had where she discussed Jason's health with him.

3. Ann will practice being fully aware of any experiences she had where she regretted health choices that Jason made.

4. Ann will practice being fully aware of any experiences she had early during the day that Jason had his heart attack that suggested it was a normal day.

5. Ann will practice being fully aware of any experiences she had with Jason immediately before she went to the store that suggested it was not a normal day.

6. Ann will practice being fully aware of any experiences she had immediately after coming home and finding Jason dead.

7. Ann will think about Jason's death and the beliefs that she currently has about it, and she will evaluate the validity of these beliefs for guiding her external behavior at this time.

8. Ann will decide what choice is most appropriate for her at this time: to tolerate these beliefs, to modify them, or to take steps to avoid them.

9. Other goals will be added if needed.

LONG-TERM GOAL 2: Ann will decide what level of responsibility she has for Laurie's temper—how much it is her fault.

Short-Term Goals

1. Ann will practice being fully aware of her present experience by considering what level of responsibility she had for the first temper tantrum she can remember Laurie having.

2. Ann will practice being fully aware of at least three experiences she can remember where she discussed Laurie's temper with her when she was a child.

3. Ann will practice being fully aware of at least three experiences she can remember where she discussed Laurie's temper with her when she was an adolescent.

4. Ann will practice being fully aware of at least three experiences she can remember where she discussed Laurie's temper with her when she was an adult.

5. Ann will practice being fully aware of the experience she had with Laurie when Laurie physically abused her.

6. Ann will think about Laurie's abuse and the beliefs that she currently has about it, and she will evaluate the validity of these beliefs for guiding her external behavior at this time.

7. Ann will decide what choice is most appropriate for her at this time: to tolerate these beliefs, to modify them, or to take steps to avoid them.

8. Other goals will be added if needed.

LONG-TERM GOAL 3: Ann will decide what level of responsibility she has for her current depression—how much it is her fault.

Short-Term Goals

1. Ann will practice being fully aware of the first experience she can remember where she recognized that she was depressed. She will articulate the event, her perceptions of her control over this event, her feelings, and any help she received from others.

2. Ann will practice being fully aware of at least three experiences she can remember where she was depressed while her children were young. She will articulate the events, her perceptions of her control over these events, her feelings, and any help she received from others.

3. Ann will practice being fully aware of at least three experiences she can remember where she was not depressed when her children were young. She will articulate the events, her perceptions of her control over these events, her feelings, and any help she received from others.

4. Ann will practice being fully aware of at least three experiences she can remember where she was depressed when her children were adolescents. She will articulate the events, her perceptions of her control over these events, her feelings, and any help she received from others.

5. And will practice being fully aware of at least three experiences she can remember where she was not depressed when her children were adolescents. She will articulate the events, her perceptions of her control over these events, her feelings, and any help she received from others.

6. Ann will practice being fully aware of at least three experiences she can remember where she was depressed when Laurie and Brian were adults. She will articulate the events, her perceptions of her control over these events, her feelings, and any help she received from others.

7. Ann will practice being fully aware of at least three experiences she can remember where she was not depressed when Laurie and Brian were adults. She will articulate the events, her perceptions of her control over these events, her feelings, and any help she received from others.

8. Ann will practice being fully aware of at least three experiences within the past week where her depression had a grip on her external behavior. She will articulate the events, her perceptions of her control over these events, her feelings, and any help she received from others.

9. Ann will practice being fully aware of at least three positive experiences during the past week, no matter how small. She will articulate the events, her perceptions of her control over these events, her feelings, and any help she received from others.

10. Ann will meditate during the week, both at home and in session, about her current depression. She will log the thoughts, feelings, and impulses to act that crossed her mind during this meditation.

11. Ann will meditate in session, starting by allowing her mental model to proceed automatically and then beginning to interrupt it periodically and either tolerate what is streaming through her mind, make a decision to modify it, or decide how to distract herself from it.

12. Other goals will be added if needed.

PRACTICE CASE FOR STUDENT CONCEPTUALIZATION: INTEGRATING THE DOMAIN OF AGE

It is time to do a cognitive-behavioral analysis of Darla. There are many domains of complexity that might provide insights into her behavior. Within this analysis, you are asked to try to integrate the domain of age into your case conceptualization.

Information Received From Phone Intake

Darla is a 14-year-old White female living in a suburban section of a large midwestern city with her mother, who is a single parent; Darla doesn't remember her father, who left shortly after her sister Susan (age 12) was born. She is presently a freshman in high school. Her mother reports that she was a straight-A student with no record of school adjustment problems until junior high school. Darla's grades started nose-diving at the same time as her breasts started budding. Her mother indicates that Darla seemed to have forgotten everything she had been taught about proper decorum and family responsibilities. She was neglecting taking care of her younger sister, just as she was neglecting her grades. Fortunately, young Susan was still doing well in school despite her older sister's bad example. Things came to a head when Darla was caught, in the parking lot of the junior high, drinking with a group of students. The students were suspended for six months based on the school's policies against underage drinking on school property. Darla's mother indicates that Darla is out of control and that this alcohol incident is just one example. She believes Darla needs treatment because she is addicted to alcohol and needs more self-control.

During a brief mental status exam, Darla seems highly poised and gives no signs of any psychological distress, including no indications of suicidal or homicidal ideation or severe psychopathology.

Interview With Darla (D) From a Cognitive-Behavioral Perspective

C: I know that you have a lot of doubts about coming here, and (*D interrupts*)

D: (snarling and looking down in her lap) Doubts? That's rich. My mother is controlling this whole thing; I have zero interest in being here.

C: You sound very angry.

D: (snarling but looking up briefly) Wouldn't you be angry if someone forced you in here? It is ridiculous. I am fine—see her. (long pause)

C: I knew from our brief intake appointment that you didn't want to (*D interrupts*)

D: (furious) *Shit, shit, shit!* You just don't get it! (long pause as she hits her fists against her legs)

C: Your anger is boiling over. (long pause) Your mom said you were suspended from school, and she sounded (*D interrupts*)

D: (furious) I know what she sounded like. She sounded like she was concerned, but that is all a big act. She tells everyone she fears I have become an alcoholic like my dad is supposed to be. (taking a big breath, blowing out, and speaking softly but very intensely) It's just all bullshit. First, *she*, not *me*, is the one who's drinking every single night. (looking up briefly) Second, I don't know about my dad, but if I drink too much, it's because of her. (*D* is now looking down and swearing into her lap in a soft but vicious voice)

C: You are furious with your mom. (pause) You think she drinks too much. (pause) It seems even worse that she blames your behavior on a father who disappeared long before you started drinking. (long pause; *D* is knocking her fists down on her legs again) I have no idea what you are going through, but it feels so strong that I hope you will consider getting help with it.

D: (angry, looking stonily over the clinician's shoulder) I hate her. I wish she would just leave like dad; we would be better off without them both.

C: We? (long pause)

D: (finally looking up and smiling) I have a sister Susan. She's 12; she's a good kid. Not me, (smiling) I'm the black sheep of the family. (chuckles)

C: What's it like being the black sheep?

D: (angry again) Are you kidding me? Do you think I want to be the one who is always such a disappointment? Do you think I wanted to be kicked out of school when all my real friends are there and I'm here? (glares into *C*'s eyes)

C: What do you mean by your "real friends"?

D: (sarcastic) Duh, everyone I hang out with at school.

C: I thought you got suspended with your friends?

D: (angry) Those were just kids I drink with. I'm done with them.

C: Did you decide to be done with them, or does it have something to do with the school?

D: (angry) Of course it was my decision. I decide what I do. If I want to drink, I'll drink. If I don't, I won't. My body, my decision; I make good decisions. (long pause)

C: (long pause, looking gently at D)

D: (quiet but intense) Aren't you going to say something?

C: I was thinking that you seem angry most of the time. It's like you're in a rut and not giving yourself a chance to feel anything else.

D: (quiet but intense) Well, I have a damn right to be angry!

C: Are you curious at all about why you have gotten so angry so fast in here?

D: (furious) Why would I be curious? *I'm angry because my mother has fucked everything up!* (long pause, choking back tears; quietly) I can't be responsible for everything, make the lunches, make sure the refrigerator has food, help Susan get to school and do her homework.

C: You feel pressured to hold your family together. You feel Susan needs you to take care of things because, in different ways, both of your parents have disappeared from view.

D: (calm, tears streaming down her face) It is so hard. Why is it so hard?

C: You are just fourteen. You know a lot more than Susan, but still, it's hard to be a mother at fourteen.

D: (trying to choke the tears back) It is supposed to be her. Can you make her be a mother?

C: We could try to invite her in here, if you want her. I can't make her do anything—just like you can't. (long pause, D looking down) If you came back, it would be time for you. It would be time for you to look at your model for living in this world. You would be in control of the process; I would just help you.

D: (sarcastic, looking up) Well, I have nothing better to do with Susan gone all day. But I don't see how this will change how my mother is behaving.

C: Whatever is happening at home, in here, the focus would be on you. You are on automatic pilot now, being very angry at all the experiences that you're having. I want you to have more choices in your life.

D: (sarcastic, looking up) Well, that sounds great, but what does it really mean?

C: If you're willing, I can begin to show you what we might be doing together. (*D* nods) We'll be doing an exercise that helps you focus your attention on your internal world, what's going on within your own mind and body.

D: (angry) No one is going to be touching my body, I've had enough of this type of crap from the guys who were supposed to be my boyfriends.

C: It's your body, and no one should be touching it if you don't want them to. (pause) I didn't mean I would be touching you. I meant you would be aware of what was going on within your own body. It is yours and you have the right to be in control of it.

D: (calm) That sounds okay. (pause) I'll do it.

C: Get as comfortable as you can in the chair, and then close your eyes. (pause) First, try to become aware of how your backside and abdomen feel as you are sitting in the chair. Be aware only of the sensations of those parts of your body.

D: (tense) I'm not comfortable. I'm not going to be able to relax.

C: This isn't about relaxing or not relaxing. It's just about tuning in to the sensations in your body. It is your body to be aware of. Just take some deep breaths and notice how your body feels. It might feel the same or it might feel different.

D: (tense, angry) It doesn't feel different. (pause) I want it to feel different. What am I doing wrong? I hate this.

C: Notice how fast you become angry and how critical you become of yourself. (pause) As you are aware of the feelings of anger, can you say what thoughts are going through your mind?

D: (tense) I want to drink. All I can think about is a beer.

C: Just be aware of the thoughts going through your mind about having a beer. Don't try to stop the thoughts or change them in any way; just try to be aware of them. (Pause) Now take a deep breath in. As you do this, you may or may not feel more intense sensations of your backside sinking down into the chair.

D: (angry) I'm a black sheep; that's why I have to do bad things like run around with boys and drink a lot of beer. I have to do things, and I have to do things right away. I hate to wait for things. What's wrong with me?

C: Everything feels like a burden, (pause) even sitting in this chair. Being a black sheep is a heavy burden for a fourteen-year-old. Try and let go of the burden for now and be aware of your bodily sensations as you sit in the chair. (pause) As you breathe in and out, let the out-breath seem to travel down your legs, and be very aware of the sensations you may or may not have as you imagine the breath traveling down through your legs.

D: (frustrated) I don't know what to do. It kind of feels good to do this sitting in the chair thing, but I kind of feel like I have to do something else right away. How do I sit still?

C: You just do it. (long pause)

D: (tense) Okay, I'm breathing and sitting still. What next?

C: What we are practicing is your ability to pay close attention to something, like how your backside feels sitting in the chair, and then disengage your attention from your backside and focus your attention on your legs. We are practicing you being in control of your attention and what you do with it.

D: (angry) I want to be in control. I'm so tired of having to be the good big sister who gets great grades and always takes care of Susan. I want to take care of myself. (pause) I'm not able to do it. I keep screwing up. Boys take control of me, yet I still go out with them and drink till I'm out of control. What's up with that? My mother is such a jerk when she's drinks heavily, so why am I acting like her?

C: Why don't you open your eyes now. (*D* looks at *C*) You have a lot of questions about who you are and why you do what you do. These questions make sense to ask. There are many ways to work toward answers to these questions. My way would be to help you tune in to your world that is inside yourself, to help you become aware of the model you have developed for yourself, for operating at school, with your family, when you're out on dates.

D: (tense) How long would this take? I'm in a hurry. I have a lot of things I have to get done.

C: You are on automatic pilot again, Darla, wanting to rush to do something immediately; this is your way of dealing with stress. I can't promise you exactly how long it will take to have a better plan for taking care of yourself, but it often takes about eight sessions before you don't need to come in here anymore—if you do your homework every day.

D: (sarcastic) I don't do homework anymore.

C: This won't work unless you commit to practicing the skills we're working on. Without practice, you won't be able to stop your automatic pilot and you won't get answers to your questions. (long pause) This process will require one hour of homework every day. Responding with anger to everything that is happening is not getting you what you want with your life. Something needs to change.

D: (tense) Fine, okay, what is it I have to do? (*C* hands her a sheet of homework instructions; two-minute pause) I get it.

C: One more thing. Besides doing this exercise, I would like you to practice being fully aware of what you're doing during one simple task that you do every day. While you do it, you'll try to only think, feel, and be fully attentive to what you're doing. When might you do this?

D: I'll do it while I pick out my outfit in the morning.

Exercises for Developing a Case Conceptualization of Darla

Exercise 1 (four-page maximum)

GOAL: To verify that you have a clear understanding of cognitive-behavioral theory.

STYLE: An integrative essay comprising Parts A through C.

NEED HELP?   Review this chapter (pages 163–168).

A. Develop a concise overview of all the assumptions of the cognitive-behavioral model (the theory's hypotheses about key dimensions in understanding how clients change; think broadly, abstractly) as an introduction to the rest of this exercise.

B. Develop a thorough description of how each of these assumptions is used to understand a client's progression through the change process in paragraphs that provide specific examples to fully explain each assumption.

C. Conclude your essay by describing the role of the clinician in helping the client change (consultant, doctor, educator, helper), the major approach taken to treatment, and common treatment techniques. Provide enough specific examples to clarify what is distinctive about this approach.

Exercise 2 (four-page maximum)

GOAL: To aid application of cognitive-behavioral theory to Darla.

STYLL: A separate sentence outline for each section, A through I.

NEED HELP?   Review this chapter (pages 163–168).

A. Create a list of Darla's weaknesses (concerns, issues, problems, symptoms, skill deficits, treatment barriers) and indicate which of these Darla wants help with.

B. Create a list of Darla's strengths (strong points, positive features, successes, skills, factors facilitating change) and indicate which of these Darla is aware of having.

C. Describe Darla's mental model of how to interact in the world.

   1. How does this model fuel/represent any of her weaknesses?

      a. What is her maladaptive self-talk?

      b. What maladaptive beliefs are behind her self-talk?

      c. What behaviors stem from these beliefs?

      d. What feelings stem from these beliefs?

      e. When she is on autopilot, is the pattern of thoughts, feelings, and behavior always the same?

2. How does this model fuel/represent any of her strengths?

    a. Does she have adaptive self-talk?

    b. What adaptive beliefs are behind her self-talk?

    c. What behaviors stem from these adaptive beliefs?

    d. What feelings stem from these adaptive beliefs?

    e. Does she have strategies she has attempted to use to solve her problems that are functional for her at this time?

E. How open is Darla to evaluating her mental model at this time?

1. How difficult is it for her to be aware of her experience in the moment, on a scale of 1 to 10?

2. When her mind wanders, how difficult is it for her to bring her mind back to the here and now, on a scale of 1 to 10?

3. How difficult is it for her to see moments of choice as she evaluates her internal experience?

4. Overall, how adaptive is Darla's mental model at this time, and how aware is she of the need for change? (Give specific and concrete examples.)

Exercise 3 *(four-page maximum)*

GOAL: To develop an understanding of the potential role of age in Darla's life.

STYLE: A separate sentence outline for each section, A through J.

NEED HELP?   Review Chapter 2 (pages 27–41).

A. Assess how age appropriate Darla's physical and cognitive development have been, and how, and in what ways, this has influenced Darla's performance and her level of motivation at home, in school, and within community activities.

B. Assess how age appropriate Darla's relationships with adults have been in terms of providing age-appropriate limit setting, monitoring, skill building, and emotional connection, and in what ways these relationships have supported or hindered her developmental progress.

C. Assess how age appropriate Darla's relationships with peers have been in terms of providing age-appropriate companionship and social skill building, and how, and in what ways, these relationships have supported or hindered her developmental progress.

D. Assess how age appropriately Darla is functioning at this time; include consideration of self-image and self-efficacy, what Darla needs most to support healthy development at this time, and what, if any, barriers to maturation or factors facilitating maturation exist at this time.

E. Assess the level of situational risk in Darla's life at this time and how much control Darla has in trying to mitigate these risks.

F. Assess the level of situational support in Darla's life at this time and how much control Darla has in trying to increase these situational supports.

G. What is your current knowledge of issues relevant to development?

1. How many courses have you taken that give you background on adolescence?

2. How many workshops have you taken that give you background on adolescence?

3. What professional experiences have you had with adolescents?

4. What personal experiences have you had with adolescents?

5. What cohort effects might influence your worldview of adolescents as to what is important in their world, how people communicate, and what is rewarded and punished?

H. What is your current level of awareness of how development can influence your clinical work?

1. Discuss how your current age and current amount of contact with adolescents might influence your reactions to Darla.

2. Discuss the stereotypes of adolescents that you know about.

3. Discuss the experiences you have had that could support your effective work with Darla as well as experiences you have had that might lead to negative bias or marginalization of Darla's point of view or current situation.

I. What are your current skills in working with clients of different ages?

a. What skills do you currently have that are of value in working with adolescents?

b. What skills do you feel it would be important to develop to work effectively with Darla?

J. What action steps can you take?

1. What could you do to prepare yourself to be more skilled in working with Darla?

2. How might you structure the treatment environment to increase the likelihood of a positive outcome with Darla?

3. What processes of treatment might you change to make them more welcoming to Darla?

Exercise 4 (six-page maximum)

GOAL: To help you integrate your knowledge of cognitive-behavioral theory and issues relevant to development into an in-depth conceptualization of Darla (who she is and why she does what she does).

STYLE: An integrated essay consisting of a premise, supportive details, and conclusions following a carefully planned organizational style.

NEED HELP? Review Chapter 1 (pages 1–7) and Chapter 2 (pages 27–41).

STEP 1: Consider which style you should use for organizing your cognitive-behavioral understanding of Darla. This style should (a) support you in providing a comprehensive and clear understanding of Darla's mental model for operating in the world, (b) support you in emphasizing the importance of operating in the present moment rather than in the past or in expectation of the future, and (c) support language that Darla might find persuasive in her current state of distrust of adults.

STEP 2: Develop a concise premise (overview, preliminary or explanatory statements, proposition, thesis statement, theory-driven introduction, hypotheses, summary, concluding causal statements) that explains Darla's overall level of functioning as a teen who is struggling to understand how to develop as an adolescent within a neglectful household. If you have trouble with Step 2, remember that it should be an integration of the key ideas of Exercises 2 and 3 and that it should (a) provide a basis for Darla's long-term goals, (b) be grounded in cognitive-behavioral theory, (c) be sensitive to developmental issues, and (d) highlight the strengths Darla brings to cognitive-behavioral treatment whenever possible.

STEP 3: Develop your supporting material (a detailed case analysis of strengths and weaknesses, supplying data to support an introductory premise) from a cognitive-behavioral perspective, incorporating an in-depth understanding of Darla as an alcohol-abusing teen. If you have trouble with Step 3, consider the information you'll need to include in order to (a) support the development of short-term goals, (b) be grounded in cognitive theory and sensitive to developmental issues, and (d) integrate an understanding of Darla's strengths in analyzing what she values in her life.

STEP 4: Develop your conclusions and broad treatment recommendations, including (a) Darla's overall level of functioning; (b) anything facilitating or serving as a barrier to her developing a greater awareness of her emotions or her ability to regulate them without alcohol; and (c) her basic needs as she determines what she values and wants to have more of in her life, considering what you said in Part H and J of Exercise 3 (be concise and general).

Exercise 5 (three-page maximum)

GOAL: To develop a theory-driven action plan for Darla that considers her strengths and is sensitive to her difficulties as an adolescent from a neglectful household who uses alcohol abuse as an escape.

STYLE: A sentence outline consisting of long- and short-term goals.

NEED HELP? Review Chapter 1 (pages 7–24).

STEP 1: Develop your treatment plan overview, being careful to consider what you said in Part H and J of Exercise 3 to try to prevent any negative bias in your treatment plan and insure that you adapt your treatment approach to Darla's unique needs as an individual.

STEP 2: Develop long-term (major, large, ambitious, comprehensive, broad) goals that *ideally* Darla will reach by the termination of treatment and that will lead to an adaptive mental model of the world that takes advantage of her adaptive beliefs. If you are having trouble with Step 2, reread your premise and support sentences for ideas, paying careful attention to how they could be transformed into goals that are realistic considering Darla's needs and situation (use the *style* of Exercise 4).

STEP 3: Develop short-term (small, brief, encapsulated, specific, measurable, subsidiary) goals that Darla and you can expect to see accomplished within a few weeks so that you can chart Darla's progress in learning to be fully aware in the present moment and to recognize choice points where she can decide to tolerate negative experiences, modify negative experiences, or engage in distracting activities. If you have trouble with Step 3, reread your support paragraphs, looking for ideas to transform them into goals that (a) might help Darla carry out hypothesis testing in regard to specific beliefs to determine how adaptive they are for her at the present time, (b) might facilitate her ability to recognize choice points in her experience of negative internal events, (c) might teach her new skills for adaptively coping with negative internal events, (d) will utilize her strengths whenever possible, and (e) are individualized to her as a neglected teen rather than generic.

Exercise 6

GOAL: To critique cognitive-behavioral treatment and the case of Darla.

STYLE: Answer Questions A through E in essay format or discuss them in a group format.

A. What are the strengths and weaknesses of this model for helping Darla (a teen with an alcohol problem from a neglectful background)?

B. Consider how taking a family systems perspective, where you would help Darla integrate an understanding of her role in the family and of how her family's boundaries, subsystems, and hierarchy could be used to understand her current situation, would change the treatment plan. In what ways does Darla seem to be the symptom barrier for her family? How might a reframe indicating that Darla is actually the most responsible member of her family, rather than the black sheep, influence Darla's attitude toward treatment at this time? Which approach do you consider most valuable to Darla at this time, and why?

C. Assume that Darla's comments about her current acting out reflect understatements and that she has actually been raped and assaulted.

Considering what you know from the domain of violence, what issues must you assess, and what specifically will you do, to encourage the change process without jeopardizing her safety at this time?

D. Considering Darla's family and current school situations and the information on resiliency in development, discuss Darla's current risk for further victimizing experiences. Are there particular issues you need to assess in more depth to develop an accurate assessment of this? What could happen if her mother became aware that she had been victimized? Might this increase or decrease Darla's risk for continued alcohol abuse?

E. What did you learn about your own attitudes toward alcohol, and toward helping teenagers manage their emotions, as you were working through the case of Darla?

RECOMMENDED RESOURCES

Books

Beck, J. S. (2011). *Cognitive behavioral theory: Basics and beyond* (2nd ed.). New York, NY: Guilford Press.

Farmer, R. F., & Chapman, A. L. (2008). *Behavioral interventions in cognitive behavior therapy: Practical guidance for putting theory into action.* Washington, DC: American Psychological Association.

Hays, S. C., & Lillis, J. (2012). *Acceptance and commitment therapy* (Theories of Psychotherapy). Washington, DC: American Psychological Association.

Herbert, J. D., & Forman, E. M. (2011). *Acceptance in mindfulness in cognitive behavior therapy: Understanding and applying the new therapies.* Hoboken, NJ: John Wiley.

Ingram, B. L. (2012). *Clinical case formulations: Matching the integrative treatment plan to the client* (pp. 191–228). Hoboken, NJ: John Wiley.

Polk, K. L., & Schoendorff, B. (2014). *The ACT matrix: A new approach to building psychological flexibility across settings and populations.* Reno, NV: Context Press.

Strosahl, K. D., Robinson, P. J., & Gustavsson, T. (2012). *Brief interventions for radical change: Principles and practice of focused acceptance and commitment therapy.* Oakland, CA: New Harbinger.

Wenzel, A. (2013). *Strategic decision making in cognitive behavioral therapy.* Washington, DC: American Psychological Association.

Videos

aggiementalhealth. (2013, March 7). Cognitive behavioral tools [Video file]. Retrieved from https://www.youtube.com/watch?v=IEsYiCDoJks

Association for Behavioral Cognitive Therapies. (2007). Clinical grand rounds: Mindfulness-based cognitive therapy and the prevention of depression [Video file]. Retrieved from http://www.abct.org/docs/mov/GWilliams_1.htm

Beck Institute for Cognitive Behavior Therapy. (2014, February 19). Determining treatment length in CBT [Video file]. Retrieved from https://www.youtube.com/watch?v=ZSIO3itZS_I

DrAhmedHaroun. (2013, March 13). CBT for depression 1/6 [Video file]. Retrieved from https://www.youtube.com/watch?v=9QkbF197HGs

Global Presentations. (2008, November 16). Applying principles of evidence-based practice to three treatments of PTSD [Video file]. Retrieved from http://www.globalpres.com/mediasite/Viewer/?peid=1213ec7d20a74cb0abf7bc4cadb3186a

Websites

American Academy of Cognitive and Behavioral Psychology. http://aacbp.org/index.htm
Association for Behavioral and Cognitive Therapies. http://www.abct.org
National Association of Cognitive-Behavioral Therapists. http://www.nacbt.org

Feminist Case Conceptualizations and Treatment Plans

INTRODUCTION TO FEMINIST THEORY

John is a 56-year-old Protestant White male who wants an immediate appointment to discuss a marital problem. He is the chief executive officer (CEO) of an international corporation that has its corporate headquarters across the street from your office in a large northeastern city. Your office location was his sole reason for choosing you as his clinician.

In a mental status screen, John appeared to be functioning at a superior level intellectually. There were no signs that he was having any issues with cognitive confusion or memory difficulties. He denied any suicidal or homicidal ideation or substance abuse and showed no signs of impulse control problems. However, he was very domineering during the assessment and indicated many times that he felt all the questions he was being asked were just wasting his time.

John has been married to 53-year-old Margaret for the last 30 years. For most of that time, his family lived on an estate in Connecticut. There is extended family living in the same town for both John and Margaret, and both sides of the family contained founding members of the Protestant church in town. John came home from a business trip last week to find that Margaret had moved out of the house and left him with a note saying she wanted a divorce. He has been able to locate her only via cell phone, and she has refused to come home. Starting a few days ago, she stopped answering his calls. They have two daughters, Juliet (age 25) and Kimberly (age 22), who recently moved to California. They are starting their own company using trust fund money recently inherited when Margaret's father died.

As a proponent of empowerment feminist therapy (EFT), you recognize the power of the environment, in terms of social and political forces, to shape John's values, expectations, and behaviors within his marriage to Margaret. Your first step will be to help John deepen his understanding of his complex personal and social identities and the roles power, privilege, and oppression play in them. Through consciousness raising, John will recognize that rather than developing his own unique marriage with Margaret, he has been adapting to the status quo and following many unconscious "shoulds" within a socially designed marriage. Socializing forces have led John and Margaret to take on rigid gender roles within their marriage that deny them the right to express themselves as individuals. John's current mindset is that Margaret's behavior is pathological and stems from internal causes such as a psychotic breakdown or midlife crisis. You will help him recognize how differential power, within society and within their marriage, is what is actually behind Margaret's current behavior. She has been actively discriminated against, oppressed, and denied opportunities for expressing herself as a unique individual and setting her own unique life goals. While John will not be blamed for Margaret's distress—as he, like her, has been shaped by external pressures—he will come to recognize that to have a healthy marriage, he must work to develop an egalitarian relationship with Margaret in which her values as a woman are respected (Worell & Remer, 2003).

Who is John? While he may view himself primarily as a successful businessman, in fact, according to the first principle of EFT, he has multiple social and personal identities that are interdependent and that, taken together, serve to define him (Worell & Remer, 2003). Each of his identities may be more or less salient to him depending on the time period and the social context. You will help John become consciously aware of this complex matrix of personal and social identities that together govern his thoughts, feelings, behaviors, and values within different aspects of his life. How these identities may support his strengths, as well as how they may contribute to his current difficulties, will be considered in depth. Each carries with it a potential "seat of advantage" within the dominant society where John experiences privilege, or a potential "seat of oppression" where John might have experiences that deny him power or freedom of choice (Worell & Remer, 2003, p. 58). Power is intrinsic to all relationships. The person with more power in a relationship experiences more privilege. For example, as the CEO of a company, John has the most power. This means he has the ability to decide when a meeting should be held, what the agenda should be, and who at the meeting will be assigned what tasks to do. He could make fair or unjust decisions. Other people at the meeting are in a one-down position relative to him and, depending on what John does, may be treated with respect and fairness or may experience oppression.

A gendered social order promotes the myth that men and women are fundamentally different from each other and that individuals within each gender are highly similar to each other; thus, gender homogenization is made to seem natural and healthy, and anyone who departs from rigid gender roles is pathologized. Sexist society has determined that males have more privilege than females within the institutions of society, including the institution of marriage. Thus, women are oppressed within marriage in a parallel manner to how they are oppressed within public institutions. For example, society has given John, as a husband, more power than Margaret, as a wife. This illustrates the second principle of EFT: "The personal is political." The same oppression that exists in society also exists in personal relationships (Worell & Remer, 2003, p. 6).

In treatment, John's consciousness will be raised so that he can recognize how traditional sex role stereotypes homogenize people by gender. Men are socialized into the role of breadwinner, and women are socialized into the role of caretaker of home and children. Even within her role as caretaker of the home, Margaret still has to defer to John on important family decisions. Men are allowed to pursue their own personal goals, as long as they earn money, and they are free to use direct power in their relationships. For example, John can directly tell Margaret what to do, such as prepare a party for his business colleagues.

Margaret has been placed in a subordinate role and is expected to support John's goals. As subordinates, women may have only indirect methods of gaining power, such as through manipulating, rather than asking, men to do what they want (Worell & Remer, 2003). Women are expected to become attuned to the moods of their husbands and adapt their behavior accordingly. They pick what to fight about, and when, in an effort to keep their marriage secure (Goodrich, 2008). Thus, if Margaret is sick and doesn't want to prepare for a party, she might suggest that the weather is predicted to be better next week and mention that she knows how much John likes to grill outside at parties. She doesn't directly express her needs. She couches her needs within a framework John might find motivating. John and Margaret are likely to view their behavior as guided by personal choice. However, through consciousness raising, they could learn to recognize the influence of gender role socialization and institutionalized sexism on their functioning and consider the value of living a more androgynous lifestyle.

What is needed for a healthy marriage? According to the third principle of EFT, egalitarian relationships foster healthy thoughts, emotions, and behaviors. While John's genuine strengths will be supported and prized, all of his oppressive thoughts, feelings, and actions will be explored for their impact on others. Treatment will seek to transform the hierarchical, power-imbalanced relationship between John and Margaret into an egalitarian one in which both partners can thrive as individuals. John will have to take responsibility for his oppressive behavior within and outside the marriage; however, social pressures will work against this change from the status quo. John will need to be aware of these pressures and take responsibility for resisting them within his personal identities as well as, ideally, within his social identities. He will be encouraged to use the knowledge he gains in treatment to become an agent of positive social change in his personal, social, and work relationships.

Society has encouraged John and Margaret to take on gendered perspectives. In addition, it has socialized them to believe that male values are superior to female values. John will be encouraged to throw off this bias and treat Margaret's perspective as equal to his own. The mindset that "women's perspectives are valued in addition to men's" represents the final principle of EFT (Worell & Remer, 2003, p. 73). From a male point of view, meaning is constructed out of life through wielding power in the workplace. It is important to be a leader and take initiative in setting the agenda and solving problems. To be successful at taking on this role, men are taught to value independence and emotional detachment; it is assumed that emotional detachment is needed for logical decision-making. From a female point of view, meaning is constructed through nurturing others and building emotional attachments. Society encourages women to develop an expressive orientation toward the world where warmth, nurturance, kindness, and a concern for the welfare of others are paramount over competition in the workplace. Yet, society devalues women who are successful at taking on this role, treating their achievements as if they were commonplace (American Psychological Association, Joint Task Force, 2006; Worell & Remer, 2003).

The devaluation of women may occur overtly or subtly. In society, John's opinion might be taken over Margaret's at a parent-teacher conference. In the home, John may override Margaret's economic choices whenever she disagrees with him, citing his greater business savvy. Or, John might just grimace when Margaret makes a suggestion about finances. Even subtle slights, when they are repetitive, have been found to undermine the self-esteem and emotional well-being of women (Goodrich, 2008). To have a just society, the achievements of men and women must be given equal respect. To improve his marriage, John will need to listen to Margaret and treat her perspective as valuable; Margaret will need to do the same for John. Treatment will empower John to view himself as a human being who can freely choose what behaviors and attitudes are most relevant to him within each specific situation in which he finds himself; he will no longer be a gendered male who must fit neatly into a prescribed identity.

THE ROLE OF THE CLINICIAN

How will you help John? You will actively use a variety of techniques that challenge John to consider a fuller range of choices in how to act, think, and feel as an individual rather than as a gendered self. The first step will be to work toward an egalitarian relationship with him. While a truly egalitarian relationship is more of an ideal than a reality, as John is here for help and you are here to help him, there are two major strategies you can use to establish a collaborative relationship. The first strategy is to discuss, with John, the values embedded in EFT. It is important to demystify the treatment process so that he is an educated consumer. John should be educated about the theory and the techniques that are available to help him. After an initial session, John will be given the opportunity to provide you with feedback about the session and whether he feels that you and EFT can help him.

You will also make selective self-disclosures when you feel these will help him understand his experiences more fully. You will make responses to John that allow him to perceive your emotional reaction to what he is saying and doing. Empathy, nurturance, and mutual respect will be modeled, as will a nonblaming attitude. You will actively explore John's strengths and encourage him to value his selfhood at the same time as you will discourage any of his oppressive thoughts, feelings, and behaviors. Finally, John will be treated as the expert on his experiences.

In addition to building a collaborative relationship, you will help John identify each of his personal and social identities. Within each, you will help him identify how much, and what type, of privilege he experiences, and how much, and in what ways, he is oppressed in any of them. He will then identify which of his many identities are most salient to him at this time and how they may be influenced by sex role socialization and environmental pressures. He will be educated as to how interdependent his identities are and how together they give him a sense of who he is.

What will you do next? Feminist clinicians can choose from myriad treatment techniques to use with clients like John as long as they aren't inconsistent with the principles of EFT. Commonly used techniques include reframing and relabeling, cultural analysis, bibliotherapy, assertiveness training, consciousness raising, gender role analysis, and power analysis; the last two techniques are unique to feminist treatment.

If you use the technique of reframing, you're shifting John's definition of his problem. This will usually involve changing an intrapersonal definition of the problem to one in which interpersonal, social, or political pressures are suggested as causative. You might help John see how Margaret's problems are not caused by something internal, such as being menopausal. Rather, they are caused by her lifelong experiences of being homogenized and devalued as an individual.

In relabeling, you take something that the client has viewed with a negative lens and relabel it using a positive lens or vice versa. You might relabel John's "marital crisis" as a "life opportunity." This might get John to examine his situation from a different perspective and may open up the possibility of trying new solutions.

In a cultural analysis, you will help John see how his White culture has provided him with a context for understanding his presenting concerns. The definition his cultural group gives for understanding marital problems will be explored along with any cultural myths that may exist relevant to these problems. This will include an analysis of how the very language or labels typically used by White culture to describe his marital problems will suggest intrapersonal causality and personal blame, such as that Margaret is suffering from "the empty nest syndrome." He will be educated about the incidence rate of his problems within White culture. Through understanding the full power of the cultural context in which his difficulties are embedded, he will come to see how the pressures from his White culture have played an important role in "causing" his marital problems.

In bibliotherapy, John will be encouraged to read articles and books that are relevant to helping him understand his marital problems and the cultural context in which they are embedded. He will engage in a dialogue with you about what he is learning. This will help him become more aware of experiences he is having that are a result of privilege or oppression.

In assertiveness training, John will learn how to stand up for his own rights without trampling the rights of other people. This might be a particularly valuable treatment option for John. In the past, he has always expressed his needs and wishes through the exertion of power; this has led to the oppression of others. Consciousness raising is a significant part of assertiveness training and can be done individually or in groups. The intent is to help John become aware of how gender role socialization has encouraged men to use domination and control to get what they want without regard for the needs and wishes of others; thus, John is following the path in his marriage that men have been socialized to take.

Men and women may differ in their thoughts, feelings, and actions, but these differences are caused by socialization pressures, not biology. In gender role analysis, John will be helped to see how men and women have been socialized differently and how this is the direct cause of their differences. How gendered expectations for males may have helped or hindered his development will be discussed. This will include helping him identify both direct and indirect messages and pressures he has experienced to fulfill specific gender role tasks and to experience things in a gender-prescribed manner. He will be taught skills for breaking free of these gendered pressures so he can think, feel, and behave in ways that support his uniqueness as an individual.

Finally, in a power analysis, John will be made aware of the types of power that exist and the differential power that exists between groups. For example, society has been structured to give men more power than women, Whites more power than people of color, wealthy people more power than the poor, physically able people more power than people with disabilities, and so forth. Power can be exerted either directly or indirectly. Being male and having access to personal resources such as accumulated wealth, possessions, and high-quality health care make John highly privileged and thus give him access to a great deal of power. People who are privileged are free to use direct power strategies. Less privileged people must rely on more indirect strategies to get what they need. John will be encouraged to explore both the direct and the indirect ways he has expressed power over other people. Rather than controlling others, John will be encouraged to develop egalitarian relationships and use constructive power, which is the power to create personal or external change.

The treatment process will be considered effective when John has become empowered to recognize external causes of stress and respond effectively to them, have an increased resilience in the face of stress, thrive within his social and personal spheres, and work to end oppressive practices against others. Feminist treatment attempts to foster a more just society. Thus, the deepest form of change would occur if John worked to end sexism on a social level.

CASE APPLICATION: INTEGRATING THE DOMAIN OF RACE AND ETHNICITY

John's case will now be examined in further detail. While there are many domains of human complexity that could provide insights into his behavior, the domain of race and ethnicity has been selected to integrate within a feminist case conceptualization and treatment plan.

Interview With John (J) From a Feminist Perspective

C: From our brief phone contact, I understand that you're deeply concerned because your wife has suddenly abandoned the family home and won't talk with you.

J: (tensely) Yes. I'm probably wasting time, but I'm out of ideas for fixing things.

C: You sound angry.

J: (angrily) I'm feeling trapped. My wife has me in a vice. She won't return my calls. My daughters deny they know what's going on. I'm stuck with being here.

C: You're angry and you wish you had a better option than coming here. Choices are important. Part of what makes this work is if you are honest with me and tell me if you're dissatisfied at any time. If you still want treatment but don't want to see me, I will help you locate someone else.

J: (calmly) Fair enough. You need to understand that I must get this problem under control by the end of next week, when I'm leaving the country to complete crucial business.

C: Time keeps coming up. (pause) You really value it.

J: (surprised) Doesn't everyone?

C: No, it's really a cultural issue. You might not think of it this way, but you're part of the business culture. It's been critical to your life. This culture has a huge respect for time, and there's that saying "Time is money." On the phone, you suggested that you were under a great deal of work pressure right now.

J: (impatiently) Of course I'm under pressure. I'm the CEO. I have a huge deal to close—but this is just what my job is.

C: While I might consider it pressure, it's part of your normal day-to-day life as a CEO. On the phone, you said you're confused about why your wife left, but that you're leaving the country in two weeks. (long pause) What is your expectation of what we can do in two weeks?

J: (angrily, changing subject) Margaret left me suddenly, (emphatically) and she won't answer my calls. I need more data to figure this thing out.

C: It was sudden and shocking. (long pause) You want more information, but she won't talk to you. (pause) Has she ever done this before?

J: (frustrated, changing subject again) I've given Margaret everything. She has a beautiful home, a closet full of gorgeous clothes, memberships in exclusive clubs.

C: John, you may not realize it, but twice now, I've asked you a question and you've changed the subject. What do you think this means?

J: (emphatically) I gave you information that was more relevant.

C: You are a leader at work. You set the agenda of what is important and what isn't. (*J* nods) But this isn't your office, and we aren't engaged in a business deal. Might I know anything about what is relevant to discuss?

J: (emphatically) I need you to understand that this deal is not just a deal. It's *the* deal. Margaret and I have been working for this since we graduated from college.

C: It's been the goal of your life, and you're assuming it was Margaret's too. (pause) Did you ever discuss this with her?

J: (irritably) We didn't have a meeting about it, if that's what you're asking. This is our marriage; she knew what she was signing on for.

C: You're sounding like a CEO, not a husband. Your work is critical to who you are. But I think we need to explore John the husband more. (pause) As a man, you were under a lot of pressure to put your work first and leave the home front to Margaret. She left, so she's dissatisfied with something. Do you think she wanted the life that you two were sharing?

J: (reflectively) I met Margaret at college; she had a clear head. She was analytical, ambitious, and busy planning her own future in the business world. Of course, once we married, she got pregnant and needed to stay home. It took her time, but she came to excel at it.

C: You and Margaret both had business aspirations— that's how you met. But you also shared expectations that having children meant her ambitions needed to change. Do you think that Margaret resented in some way that you were pursuing your business ambitions and she had to give hers up?

J: (with hostility) Are you trying to tell me Margaret didn't want to put our family life first?

C: I'm just wondering if there were social pressures on Margaret that made her feel she had to give up her business ambitions. You met in college and you were both ambitious. You've continued to be able to focus on your own unique talents and abilities. Margaret, because she was a woman, was under social pressure to put family life first. You seem to suggest that Margaret might not have been happy with shifting her ambitions to the home front.

J: (emphatic) Both my mother and hers helped her adjust; we all live in the same town in Connecticut. Margaret has been a great organizer for our local church for the last thirty years. Hell, she was even school board president for ten years! She arranged the best parties in town; everyone wanted to come. Now she's just cutting herself off from everything—right when I'm at the peak of my success. (scornfully) My golf foursome thinks she's just gone menopausal. Could that be it?

C: She might've started menopause. Stop and think about what you just said from Margaret's point of view. She's taken the very serious step of moving out. Yet your golf buddies are trivializing it as if it's unimportant and irrational.

J: (insistently) Well, women do go through menopause and get too emotional. I need to help her get back on a rational track, but she won't return my phone calls.

C: You want her to think like you, use the data in the way that feels rational to you. You're thinking of feelings as illogical. But it really isn't logical for human beings to discount feelings. Feelings are very powerful and have a big influence on people. (*J* looks down and grimaces; pause) What I'm trying to help you do is look at the situation from a different perspective to see if it provides us with any useful data for understanding the current situation with Margaret.

J: (angrily) My marriage is fine!

C: If you really thought that, you wouldn't be here. (*J* looks down, looks furious) It's okay to be angry and confused. You're on uncharted ground. Let me throw out a hypothesis here for you to consider. (*J* looks up) Is it possible that Margaret left when you were out of the country, and avoids your calls, so you can't have the opportunity to make her serious decision seem stupid and unimportant?

J: (hostilely) It's ironic. She's avoiding my calls after years of complaining I didn't call enough.

C: You were aware she was unhappy with something?

J: (dismissively) I knew she was lonely sometimes, but she needed to adjust to it. I was on the fast track, and she benefited from it as much as I did.

C: Your very ambitious work record has rewarded you with status and money. This is what you wanted at least since college. You were the CEO, both at work and at home. It sounds like Margaret, like one of your subordinates, needed to adjust her expectations and goals to fit in with yours.

J: (insistently) She needed to be a wife and mother if that's what you're talking about. (pause) Maybe Margaret has that empty nest syndrome?

C: Blaming Margaret's behavior on some syndrome seems to feel good to you right now. (long pause) That is certainly a hypothesis. She may have found a homemaker role more satisfying when your daughters were children. She might be sad or anxious now that her "nest" is empty. On the other hand, the social pressures for her to be only a wife and mom, rather than that ambitious student you met, may have decreased since your daughters became adults. Another possibility is that she is reconnecting with her own individual ambitions.

J: (frustrated) What are these social pressures you keep bringing up?

C: You both grew up in a White, upper-class culture that emphasized the importance of money and status. You and Margaret attended the same Protestant church—both your families contained founding members of the church, which sets up certain expectations in the community that you will be role models. While that's flattering in some ways, it's also social pressure to behave in a prescribed way. What was expected of you fit well with what you seem to enjoy, which is being a CEO and being very ambitious and successful in the business world. When you met Margaret, she had the same ambitions. However, social expectations in Connecticut, coming strongly from both your mothers, pressured her to fit into the role of the wife of a successful man rather than a successful woman.

J: (angrily but quietly) I don't like your suggestion that I've been forcing anything on her. Sure, her original plans were to start a business, but I allowed her total control of the house and the girls.

C: Did you notice that you use the words, "I allowed her total control of the house and the girls?" You were part of the social pressure, telling Margaret that you were in charge, and she could have control over whatever you decided she could have control of. I'm just asking you if it is possible that Margaret might have wanted to have control in the business world just like you did.

J: (tense) We discussed it and agreed that it wasn't realistic. She was pregnant, end of story.

C: Was the child planned?

J: (angry) No. It just happened, but we made it work.

C: While you hadn't expected to have a child at that particular time, you were able to integrate the event into your plan. You are angry that your wife is rejecting the plan.

J: (furiously) You bet I'm angry. You can't even begin to imagine the time I've put in, the ideas I've had to generate, and the crises I've had to resolve in order to make my company as strong as it is. Margaret knew I was going to be out of the country to orchestrate a new deal, and while my back was turned, she pulled this power play on me.

C: After all your hard work, ingenuity, and success, you have come to expect that every-one, including Margaret, will treat you with deference, and you're feeling infuriated, right now, by what you feel is her disrespectful behavior.

J: (angrily) I have a right to respect!

C: Was Margaret leaving when you were gone a mark of disrespect, or was it a sign that she did in fact know how powerful you are? Maybe she only had enough power of her own to leave if you were absent.

J: (with hostility) She should have faced me with this. What she did was very cowardly. I always faced my bosses whenever I was moving on to another job.

C: Whenever we begin to talk of you and Margaret as husband and wife, your business role of CEO keeps coming up. This identity is so salient to you it pervades every aspect of your life.

J: (argumentatively) Are you telling me it's wrong to be a leader?

C: I'm trying to ask you if you should be a CEO at work and a husband at home. I'm wondering if social pressure is part of your life too. The business community may be pressuring you to put work first and take control in all your relationships. I want you to be consciously aware of all these influences. Then, you have the freedom to make your own unique choices free from social pressure.

J: (furiously) I can make any choices I want!

C: You do have a lot of privilege. You are a powerful businessman. (*J* looks calmer) As wealthy, White Protestants, you and Margaret can live in any neighborhood you choose. You have money for buying beautiful possessions and can afford quality health care and so on. One thing you don't seem to have is time. (long pause) Work is pressuring you to leave the country in two weeks. If losing Margaret is a crisis for you, does work have the right to pressure you to take only two weeks to try to resolve such a serious situation? You've always given so much to work. Shouldn't it be possible to delay this trip so that you can focus on your marriage?

J: (furiously) If I delay the trip, the deal is off.

C: The CEO part of you says take the trip. What about Margaret's husband? Do people at work ever have the choice to give a family crisis top priority?

J: (long pause, reflectively) Most of the men I know are divorced, sometimes from mar-riages two and three.

C: How would you feel if divorce papers were waiting for you after the trip?

J: (quietly) I would be angry at Margaret for forcing it on me.

C: You look more sad than angry as you say that.

J: (furiously) Don't try to push that emotional crap on me, that it's good for men to cry.

C: You certainly seem angry now. Strong men are supposed to ignore any feelings they might have of depression, anxiety, or insecurity. Only anger is considered manly, so sometimes men express anger instead. That's not logical or natural. Our very DNA is behind our expression of emotions. They are a biological imperative, and they have a potent impact on human relationships.

J: (intently) I don't want a divorce, but you can't tell me to blow off this deal.

C: I would never tell you or anyone else what to do. This process is about collaboration. You're bringing your strengths to the table; I am bringing mine. You have highly developed strategy skills. (pause) But I'm wondering if you were taught that if you related to people on an emotional level, it would impede your success as a man.

J: My father trained me well, if that's what you mean.

C: What did your father tell you being a man meant?

J: He showed me more than told me. He was very busy. I wanted to see him more than I did, so I tended to listen in on a lot of his phone conversations when he was at home. He didn't stop me as long as I didn't interrupt. I come from a long line of successful businessmen; it's instinctual, inborn.

C: It feels natural. Like you automatically knew it, but you were taught. He taught just by letting you listen in on his phone conversations. But what did it feel like, as a son, having him at home but having him thinking about work and not the family?

J: (confusedly) I don't know. What kind of question is that? Dad did what he had to do. I knew what I needed to do. My part was to get the most out of my education so I would be ready for success. I worked really hard at school to show him I could do it. He bought me a car when I was valedictorian of my high school class—his note said this was a family tradition. (pause) But I wished he had shown up at graduation. (pause) His absence really infuriated my mother.

C: How did you know?

J: (dismissively) She embarrassed the family by drinking too much at my graduation party.

C: She was in a lot of pain, and she drank too much to dampen it. What do you think she should have done?

J: (matter-of-factly) Just accept it. Dad was always going to put work first; it was necessary. He would have made it up to her with a present—usually jewelry. She needed to be happy with that.

C: He showed that he cared by buying her beautiful things. You learned to do this for Margaret. You both learned to expect that women should be satisfied with what men give them and not ask for anything else.

J: (angrily) You think I'm not being a good husband?

C: I think you are doing everything that you thought a good husband was supposed to do. But I don't think you recognize how much power and control you were exerting over Margaret. Did you ever ask her if she wanted to continue with her plans to work after graduation? (*J* shakes his head no) Did you ask if what she wanted from you was lots of money?

J: (angrily) Of course she wanted money. She came from a very wealthy family. She could never have been happy with a dinky little house in the suburbs.

C: The two of you shared a wealthy family background. As your wife, she lived a life of privilege. She could buy anything she wanted and live on an estate. What she didn't have was the power and control to set her own life goals.

J: (intently) Sacrifices are part of life. I can't remember a week when I didn't have to skip a game of golf or miss out on a party to close a deal.

C: You missed out on things that you would have preferred to do. You were trying to be an excellent provider, and you did provide everything money can buy. (pause) What's your relationship like with your daughters?

J: (intently) I've given them everything they've ever asked for. I sent them to private schools and paid for all their special clubs and activities. I did plan to be around more for them than my dad was for me, but their recitals and events always conflicted with important work.

C: Do you have any intuition about what they might say about their mother moving out?

J: (angrily) Intuition is crap. I need facts and logical reasons for Margaret disappearing. They refuse to answer my questions. I'm their father. I deserve their respect.

C: You expect to be treated with respect, and since they're not answering some of your questions, you feel disrespected. Analytic thinking has an important place in the world. But so does intuition, as it relies on what our emotions tell us. Could you think about your girls for a moment and see if you have any gut feelings about what they would say about your marriage?

J: (long pause, sad) To be honest, my gut feeling is I don't really know what they would say.

C: Your voice sounds a little sad as you say that. (pause) You are a very goal-oriented person. And, (pause) you didn't achieve your goal of getting to know your girls better than your dad knew you.

J: (long pause, reflectively) I do have some regrets; I can admit that. I'm proud of them. They're very independent. They started a new life far away, not asking for anything from me, although the money they inherited when Margaret's dad died three months ago sealed the deal.

C: You aren't as proud because they received some money from their grandfather?

J: (emphatically) It would have been a bigger achievement if they had made their own money before inheriting it from the family. That's just my point.

C: Why did they move so far away?

J: (matter-of-factly) I've got no idea. A lot of this happened last month when I was out of state. I don't have many facts to go on. Like Margaret, they just took off.

C: They took off too, but they'll talk to you, but not answer your questions. Maybe they are being disrespectful, or maybe they don't want to get in the middle between their mother and father. (pause) Why don't you take a moment to consider Margaret's feelings and why she might have left while you were away.

J: (long pause, looking down) I guess if Margaret had been home and told me she was going to walk out, (long pause) I probably would've told her to forget it because she couldn't make it without me.

C: Would you have listened to her point of view before telling her what to do?

J: (intently) Probably not. (pause) I'm feeling very stupid. I should have seen this thing coming.

C: You aren't the least bit stupid. You are an expert on everything business but not on recognizing the emotional needs of other people. You were trying to learn every-thing you needed to know about how to be a man from your father, and he showed no value for building strong intimate relationships. (pause) You are very smart and goal oriented. If you decided to become more emotionally connected to your daugh-ters, you could learn how to do it. It's hard to say if this would help the situation with Margaret, as she refuses to speak to you. She might be more willing to talk to you if she heard from your daughters that you were being a more attentive father. Would you be willing to try?

J: (sincerely) I don't know. I really want to hear your opinion of why Margaret left.

C: I haven't spoken to Margaret, so I can only raise ideas—not know. (pause; *J* is looking directly at *C*) The moment we are born and people see that we are male or female, they treat us as if biology is destiny (*J* interrupts)

J: (emphatic) It does define us.

C: Did you realize you interrupted me? You have done this several times before. This is how you use your power to control the agenda. It makes me wonder why you would ask for my opinion if my ideas hold no value for you.

J: (pause; sincerely) I do want to know your opinion.

C: Sex defines what we physically look like but not what our unique talents are going to be once our minds are fully developed. Margaret wanted to start her own business. You were drawn to her because she was like you—logical, goal oriented, ambitious! But both your mothers decided that Margaret should give up these ambitions. You agreed. And you were all making your logical decisions based on stereotypes of what men and women were supposed to do, not Margaret's own unique talents as an indi-vidual. This isn't logical. Logic says you had enough money to pay a babysitter so that

Margaret could stay in the business world whether she was a mother or not. (*J*'s head is hanging down; long pause) Margaret may have done what everybody told her she was supposed to do while her children were young. Now, maybe she's finally free to pursue what she wants to do because the girls are grown up.

J: (calmly) I need more time to think about this. I don't know if I buy into your ideas.

C: If you decide to come back, we would work on how you have developed your strengths, following the "shoulds" of manhood, and also explore how these "shoulds" may have contributed to your problems with Margaret. When you understand social pressure, you are in a greater position to freely choose how to reach out to Margaret and what to say to her. I can't promise you anything. But maybe, if you reach out to Margaret in a way that she will find respectful, she will be willing to talk to you.

J: (looking at *C*) I can't say I'll come back.

C: You've made a lot of important decisions by weighing the facts. Let me give you some things to read that will give you more facts about what we've been talking about today. (pause) If you want Margaret to recognize that you want her, not just a wife, I think you need to make your marriage a priority now, rather than scheduling it around your work. I will wait to hear from you one way or the other as to whether you want to talk with me again.

J: (quietly but emphatically) I won't give up being strong!

C: The goal would be to give you more choices and more strengths.

Feminist Case Conceptualization of John: Assumption-Based Style

John's most prominent identity is that of a CEO; however, his other identities of being White, wealthy, and male are also having a potent impact on him at this time. These identities consume most of his time. In contrast, he has allowed his identities as a husband and father to fall by the wayside. There are no egalitarian relationships in John's life. He wields the same power in his relationships with his wife and daughters that he wields at work with his employees, and he is unaware of this parallel or the injustices that derive from it. His reaction to his wife's setting the agenda for his marriage is to demean her thoughts and emotions; only his perspective as a husband is valid. From the perspective of White culture, he is fulfilling his role as a male to perfection—he is powerful, wealthy, analytical, and in control of his emotions. John's strengths include the ability to learn quickly and analyze the pros and cons of a decision. In addition, he has the financial resources to gain greater work flexibility and gain more of that commodity "time" that his White culture has taught him to consider so precious. These will serve him well if he is willing to form an egalitarian treatment relationship that allows him the freedom to explore how powerful socialization messages, rather than "inborn abilities," are playing a role in both his business successes and his personal failures.

John's identity as a CEO is his most salient identity, but how his identity as a White person eased his path to this position goes unrecognized. He considers his success a result of his internal qualities of independence, ambitiousness, and aggressiveness. White culture encouraged him to develop these qualities, but it was the environmental resources of inherited wealth and an excellent education that gave him an entry into the world of financial success. His father directly modeled absolute dedication to work and reinforced the White cultural message that a man's success is measured by the amount of money he earns. Attending graduation ceremonies or playing with your children never show up on the radar screen if you want to make it big. Currently, John's business identity thoroughly dominates his personal identities as a husband and a father. He uses business metaphors to try to understand his current family crisis. He has been treating his family members as subordinates, ignoring their wishes and values as if these were irrelevant. He isn't interested in giving up some of his authority in the family so that his wife and daughters will feel more respected. In addition, John hasn't even considered using his professional status and power to change the timing of his upcoming business deal. "Time" has become his dictatorial and oppressive boss, and he has become the loyal subordinate who automatically makes any sacrifice demanded of him. John may have difficulty recognizing that by keeping his personal and social identities so closely aligned, he may lose his family roles as husband and father. Man, as head of the family and the economic provider, is iconic for White Protestants. Thus, John may find it very difficult to recognize how oppressively he has treated Margaret and his daughters and that a different type of family life is possible. However, he has learned to work very hard and persist when trying to solve complex problems within the business world; he could learn to do this within his personal world.

John's identity as a wealthy man is entwined and interdependent with his identity as a member of the White culture. This "Whiteness" exists outside his conscious awareness, but he is very aware of his inherited wealth and considers it a natural part of himself. John started his work career already buoyed up by economic privilege. He passed this privilege on to his daughters by giving them a private school education and membership in exclusive clubs and activities—those that are dominated by Whites. He considers these privileges a result of his hard work and dedication to success, and thus believes he has the "right" to be treated deferentially. He is unaware that society has given White people and wealthy people unearned privilege that has been systematically denied to people of color and the poor. John's feeling of entitlement was passed down to him, just as his Whiteness and inherited wealth were. He, in his turn, has passed it down to his daughters. The ability they had to start their own business in their 20s is a concrete example of how inherited wealth and white skin have brought John's family a lot of power. They can select high-status employment and relocate to the community of their choice; no neighborhoods or business opportunities will be closed to them. John may be resistant to the idea of developing egalitarian relationships, as society has encouraged him to consider himself superior to many other people. He may struggle with the idea that empowering others, through treating their thoughts and feelings with respect, is an issue of social justice. John may also struggle with developing respect for a female perspective on what is important, since emotional intimacy doesn't equate with dollars and cents.

John's view of himself as a man entails taking on rigid gender role stereotypes that in many ways had their origins in his White culture. This culture emphasized independence, achievement, and emotional control over nurturance and emotional connection as well as workforce achievements over family achievements. John began learning his gender role through watching his father and mother. They had a hierarchical relationship, with his father clearly having the most power. His dad chose when and how he would relate to his family. His mother's only recourse was to dampen her disappointments with alcohol. White culture carries with it the myth of a just society. Thus, to John, if his mother was powerless, she must have deserved it. John regretted his father's frequent absences but came to believe that his father was doing what he had to do—that it was natural for a father to always put work first. His mother was to supply the "impeccable background" of a beautiful home and high-achieving children. Unlike Latino culture, where the mothering role carries a great deal of respect, within the White culture his mother's work was unpaid and therefore unimportant. John learned that autonomy (a male value) was more important than emotional connection (a female value). John learned to view his dad's behavior as strong and worth emulating and to treat his mother with condescension. Finally, John came to believe that less powerful family members, children and wives, should appreciate what they are given and adjust to their powerlessness in the family. Thus, while he recognized his mother's unhappiness, John doesn't understand that his father's devaluation of her role as a woman, wife, and mother, not a weak character, was the cause of her turning to alcohol. John is not aware that his parents' marriage, and his own with Margaret, faces challenges caused by an oppressive society that tries to enforce gendered behavior patterns. While John is currently relating to family members as a stereotypical male, husband, and father, he recognizes that he has lost something he valued by doing so. John's view of himself as a husband maintains the same rigid marital pattern that he observed between his parents; this was a common pattern among the White and wealthy community he grew up in, and it had a powerful impact on John's expectations. While he was initially attracted to a personally ambitious Margaret, he considered it natural and inevitable that she would take on the homemaker role once they were married. As a wife, Margaret was given access to any resources that money could buy—except power within her relationship with John or the freedom to choose her own life goals. To be a successful husband, John was socialized to believe he must supply a lot of money and possessions; he assumed Margaret preferred this to time with him. This led him to work very long hours and bring work home. Margaret was often psychologically, if not physically, alone. Margaret succumbed for many years to taking on the role prescribed by her gender, under pressure from John, her own mother, and his.

Now, John is both puzzled and angered by his sudden loss of power in their marital relationship. John had been unwilling to seek out help for these marital problems as they were building up over the years; this is in keeping with his White cultural beliefs in extreme independence and self-sufficiency. However, Margaret's act of desertion was too dramatic to be ignored. Why she left is unknown; however, the money Margaret inherited from her father gave her access to money that John couldn't control. She may have finally felt capable of exerting power to control her own destiny. Margaret's identity as an independent woman may have become more salient, and she may be pursuing goals relevant to her past wish to enter the business world. If she believed John would respect and value her viewpoint, she might not have left abruptly without attempting to negotiate a more satisfying and perhaps egalitarian relationship with him. While John doesn't want to give up his greater authority within the family, he doesn't want a divorce; this may serve as an opening to his developing a less oppressive relationship with Margaret.

What about John's identity as a father? John is only vaguely aware that he didn't make good on the promise he made to himself—to be around more for his daughters than his father was for him. He couldn't find the type of balance between his personal and work identities that would have allowed him to know his daughters better, and he does regret this; it is unlikely that there was anything in his White business community or White, affluent neighborhood to guide him in achieving such a balance. His daughters did learn many of the life lessons he values; they pursued higher education, and they are currently valuing business success over family life. Their choice to leave the East Coast and build their company out in California may be an indirect exertion of power. They may need physical distance between themselves and their dad to maintain a sense of control over their own lives. They may be following John's example and allowing their work identities to dominate their lives. If so, they may be identifying with the male perspective and placing more value on financial success than on developing emotionally intimate relationships. The social pressures within their White community may have led them to believe this was a choice they "had" to make. John is torn between pride in their achievements and confusion as to why they're making choices independent of his influence; he may not have experienced this type of internal struggle if these were his sons rather than his daughters. In a reciprocal fashion, rigid gender roles may be limiting the quality of the relationship between John and his daughters. John's vague dissatisfaction with his fathering may serve as an opening for him to reconsider his devaluation of the female perspective.

John might find a new role, that of a client in treatment, difficult to embrace, as in many ways this role is counter to the values that White, male, Protestant society has taught him. However, through the course of his first appointment, he did not walk out when he wasn't allowed to be in charge of the session. He didn't refuse to come back when it became clear he would have to take responsibility for his own role in his marital difficulties as well as consider the role societal pressures may have played in it. John has noticed that many of his successful White peers have had more than one marriage fail; he doesn't want to follow this pattern. In addition, he is a highly skilled learner who enjoys being challenged by complex problems. Thus, while he is currently still on the fence about changing, should he commit to treatment, it won't take long for him to recognize that a clash between the male and female perspectives is at the root of his current marital crisis. The time may be right for John to take on a new challenge: that of being a more androgynous male.

John, as a family man who is a CEO, is struggling to decide if his goals of salvaging his marriage and understanding his daughters are important enough to overcome his desire to close another business deal. This decision is causing him significant emotional distress, because his White cultural background and status, as a successful CEO, bring with them powerful environmental pressures to maintain the status quo. He has been brought up to be "a man" and regard expressing emotions and sharing power as weaknesses; yet, these are the very skills that might help him build bridges to Margaret and his daughters. However, his highly developed problem-solving skills, learned on the business front, may motivate him to want to have this same edge on the home front, thus opening up some willingness to consider learning new skills. John hasn't developed the skills needed to be attuned and responsive to the needs of others because society has not helped him develop these skills. This may be why his marital problems are currently hitting him like a ton of bricks. John is at an important choice point within his social identities; he needs to decide if developing more emotionally connected relationships with Margaret and his daughters is "worth his time."

Feminist Treatment Plan: Assumption-Based Style

Treatment Plan Overview. John's White cultural background has reinforced his oppressive use of power within all his relationships; thus, becoming aware of this will come first. Then, the identities that are most salient to him right now, those of being male, a CEO, and from a wealthy background, will be addressed simultaneously. (This plan follows the *basic format.*)

LONG-TERM GOAL 1: John will examine how his social identity as a White person was shaped by socialization forces and consider the ways it has brought him privilege and reinforced his dominating behavior when engaged in interactions with less powerful individuals such as Margaret.

Short-Term Goals

1. John will take notes on his role as a White individual with social power, both as a member of the community where he resides and on his international trips.

   a. He will read materials on "White" as a race and consider the validity of this within his note taking.

   b. He will discuss his notes within the treatment session and consider the pros and cons of being consciously aware of his Whiteness rather than having it influence his thoughts and actions on an automatic level as he deals with individuals with less social power, such as his wife, Margaret.

2. John will explore his thoughts, feelings, and actions as he relates to non-White individuals and whether these differ when he is relating to other White individuals.

   a. In treatment sessions, he will discuss his recent interactions with White and non-White people.

   b. He will explore how White culture has pressured and continues to pressure him to relate to people differently if they have less social power than he has.

3. John will discuss the justice of his unearned privilege based on his being White and how he may or may not have used this privilege to intentionally or unintentionally oppress non-White individuals as well as White individuals with less power, such as Margaret.

4. John will consider in which situations, with people of less power, he needs to maintain a role of authority to succeed in achieving a goal, and in which situations treating people in a more egalitarian manner might lead to better results.

5. John will practice in role plays different strategies for interacting with people who have less power and come to conclusions about how he could maintain his authority when appropriate, yet treat others with respect rather than oppression.

LONG-TERM GOAL 2: John will examine how his social identity as a male was shaped by rigid gender role socialization and how his gender has brought him privilege as well as limited his choices in developing a mutually satisfying relationship with Margaret.

Short-Term Goals

1. John will read literature on gender role stereotypes and then analyze his behavior, for a week, as he relates to men and women and come to tentative conclusions about the validity of gender stereotypes for his own values, attitudes, emotions, and behavior.

2. John will consider his childhood and analyze what socialization pressures from his family, his community, and the media might have shaped his current gender role and his gendered expectations about marriage and family life.

3. John will discuss, in sessions, the way his being male has given him a privileged or dominant relationship to women and in what ways taking on this role has limited his freedom of choice in relating to his wife, Margaret, and his daughters.

4. John will read articles about relationship-building skills and use his analytic skills to determine which skills might be useful as he attempts to develop an egalitarian relationship with Margaret and his daughters.

5. John will use his analytic skills to determine in which situations he might achieve his social and work goals more effectively by taking on an authoritarian role with women and in which situations relating to them in an egalitarian manner might be more effective.

LONG-TERM GOAL 3: John will examine how his social identity as a CEO was shaped by socialization forces and the ways this has brought him privilege and financial success while at the same time reducing his success as a husband and father.

Short-Term Goals

1. John will observe interactions between the president, vice presidents, and department heads of his company over the course of a week, and he will take notes on their communication styles and the direct and indirect uses of power he witnesses.

   1a. John will consider whether they achieved their work goals efficiently in directing their subordinates using direct power (in terms of how quickly their subordinates worked, whether effective teamwork was involved, and the quality of the work that was done).

1b. John will consider whether they achieved their work goals efficiently in directing their subordinates using indirect power (in terms of how quickly their subordinates worked, whether there was effective teamwork involved, and the quality of the work that was done).

1c. John will consider the pros and cons of using a more egalitarian style with subordinates and whether this has the potential to lead to better ideas, more teamwork, and efficient progress toward goals.

2. John will compare his behavior toward subordinates at work with his past behavior toward Margaret and his daughters.

   2a. John will consider whether the authoritarian stance he took toward Margaret and his daughters might have played a role in their current estrangement from him.

   2b. John will consider whether using a more egalitarian stance toward Margaret and his daughters might lead them to feel more respected by him and provide an opening for improving their relationships with him.

3. John will use role plays to practice different relationship skills and then decide which skills he would like to try in reconnecting with Margaret and which he would like to try in reconnecting with his daughters.

LONG-TERM GOAL 4: John will examine how his primary social identity as a wealthy individual was shaped by socialization forces and the ways this has brought him privilege as well as prevented him from engaging in egalitarian and mutually satisfying relationships with Margaret and his daughters.

Short-Term Goals

1. John will read articles about the history of wealth accumulation in the United States and create a new family biography based on this to discuss within treatment sessions.

2. John will create a history of his own accomplishments on a timeline and consider the role of inherited wealth in these accomplishments.

3. John will create a strengths-and-weaknesses chart and then evaluate the role that unearned privilege versus earned privilege played in each strength and weakness.

4. John will consider what values, attitudes, emotions, and behaviors support him in experiencing success within his work and family identities without oppressing others.

5. John will practice, in role plays with the clinician, strategies for reconnecting with Margaret and his daughters.

6. John will develop a list of strategies for reconnecting with his daughters in a respectful and nurturant manner.

7. John will develop a list of strategies for reconnecting with Margaret if a time came when she was willing to receive a letter, call, or visit from him.

8. John will call his daughters and, using new skills he believes might be successful, start taking steps to reconnect with his daughters.

9. John will share his struggles and successes in treatment sessions to determine when he might have success in gaining his daughters' help in making some level of contact with Margaret without jeopardizing his relationships with them.

10. Other goals will be developed as appropriate if Margaret is willing to establish some level of contact with John.

Feminist Case Conceptualization of John: Historically Based Style

John and Margaret started their relationship with intense excitement, but this excitement began spiraling down for Margaret once they married and then had children. Societal pressure, in the form of their parents, transformed fiancée Margaret from the businesswoman she wanted to be into the White, wealthy, stay-at-home mom who served as a foil to her wealthy and powerful husband John. When John and Margaret met in college, they both had complex social identities that included personal ambitions as well as attractions to each other that were based on sexual attraction, mutual interests, and a similar wealthy, well-educated background. John describes their relationship as egalitarian in that they had developed a joint agenda together in which they would both pursue careers in business and both contribute to their goals of becoming powerful and wealthy leaders. The environment holds more power to control the behavior of men and women than John and Margaret might have realized. As their relationship went from superficial to committed, societal pressure persuaded them to take on more gendered roles in relation to each other while at the same time making these pressures seem internally right rather than externally imposed. The personal may have become political the first time Margaret met members of John's family or brought John home to meet her family. Sex role stereotypes may have led John to talk about his plans for work once he graduated from college. On the other hand, Margaret might have been pushed to discuss her plans for motherhood, and any work commitments she may have discussed may have elicited direct or indirect disapproval from her parents or John's. Facing vastly different pressures, John may have been approved of by her parents on the basis of his wealthy background and his ambitious goals for his future success. While having some basis in egalitarianism, their initial relationship was becoming increasingly weighted, with more power falling into John's hands. The negativity of this might have been ameliorated if John had shown any appreciation for the difficulties facing Margaret. He describes their parents as helping Margaret. He indicates that he did not ask her if she wanted to leave the workforce. Whether intentional or not, he devalued her women's perspective. John's current strengths include that at this time of crisis in his marriage, he has recognized that he doesn't understand what Margaret and his daughters want and that he needs help. While it was extremely difficult for him, as society has deeply inculcated in him the belief that he is the wealthy powerful one who makes all the decisions, he asked the clinician's opinion about why Margaret left. While it annoyed him, he was able to recognize that Margaret's decision to leave was not the sudden result of menopause but had rather had been building for a long time. This suggests he may be capable of taking on a more flexible role as a husband if Margaret will consider working on their marriage.

John and Margaret first met when they were college students. He respected that she had a clear head and was ambitious, analytical, and carefully planning her future in the world of business. For both of them, their future business identities monopolized a lot of their time. While they must have been sexually attracted to each other, when John talks of their relationship it is within the context of developing an agenda for how they would become powerful and wealthy. John and Margaret's relationship became integrated into the values of their extended families when they decided to marry, and this led to an expansion of John's role in the workforce and the beginning of restrictions on Margaret's work, friendships, and family identities. Their plan to be married created the environment of "planning for the wedding," which further pushed John and Margaret into gendered personal identities.

While John was free to put his creative energies into work, Margaret may have been pressured to be fascinated by decisions regarding her physical appearance and endless details concerning the wedding. The personal was quite political for John and Margaret, for while other women in the family, his mother and hers, pushed her to accept the role of a wealthy man's wife, it is unclear whether he did anything to counter this pressure so that Margaret would be more free to choose her identity. Sex role stereotypes might have placed different pressures on John and Margaret. He might have heard many messages about his duty to provide very substantially for his wife and future children. She might have heard many messages about her duty to provide a proper foil for her husband and promote his success. Any signs of an egalitarian relationship were likely to be gone at this point as Margaret's social identities became more and more constrained by John's career path. However, the newness of their relationship may have kept Margaret invigorated as she thought of how they would both be a part of the financial success that John would ostensibly achieve for both of them.

John hit his stride as a financial provider as their extended families pushed Margaret out of the workforce and into motherhood. Within his life as part of the full-time workforce, John was likely to be receiving kudos for his business skills from both inside and outside the family. As he perceived himself to be achieving "their" goals, and as he spent long hours away from their home, John may have found it easier and easier to be unaware of Margaret's needs. He indicated that she would complain about being lonely and wanting more contact from him. His response was to tell her that she would get used to it. He had no sympathy or understanding of how rigid gender role stereotypes had forced Margaret out of the life path she had chosen for herself while he had been allowed to continue in his. Margaret filled her life by channeling her ambitious nature into doing things that wealthy stay-at-home moms were supposed to do. She attended all the social events and participated in all the fund-raising activities and volunteered for leadership roles in activities dominated by moms. Her intelligence led her to be quite successful at this, and her success may have misled John into feeling that she was satisfied with her life.

Margaret might have found her social identities as a mother, wife, and school board president satisfying or she might not have; it's unlikely she considered that she had other choices. John never asked her, and she may have given up on telling him. In underestimating the power of the gendered environment, John and Margaret may have become more and more emotionally distant from each other. John had been devaluing her point of view for so long that he had lost touch with the clear-thinking, ambitious, analytical woman he'd been attracted to. Margaret may have become so embedded in her socialized identity as a wife and mother that she may have attributed her unhappiness more and more to having selected the wrong young man to marry rather than recognizing she had been forced to abandon her personal ambitions. His financial success may have invalidated any of her complaints to her friends or extended family, and her social isolation within a wealthy community makes it unlikely that she would have heard diverse viewpoints.

John is now 56 years old and unexpectedly on his own without contact with either his wife of 30 years or his two 20-something daughters. He is perplexed by how Margaret could leave him as they are about to achieve their crowning glory—his achievement of an international business deal that will bring him so much money that he feels he is finally achieving the ambition he and Margaret set for themselves way back in college. He can only imagine that menopause or the empty nest syndrome is sending Margaret into some sort of out-of-control, emotional woman thing. His lack of respect for a woman's perspective has become deeply entrenched. At one time in his life, he deeply regretted how little time he'd had with his father and planned to spend more time with his daughters. However, like Margaret, both of his daughters have chosen to cut themselves off from him. While he expresses some regret over not spending the time with them that he wanted to, he doesn't understand their attitude. He can't imagine how they would feel, and he admits that he doesn't really know them at all.

It may be particularly relevant that Margaret and her daughters decided to opt out of the family when the daughters reached the age that Margaret had been when many of her social identities became constrained by extended family. Unlike Margaret, Kim and Juliet are getting the chance to move forward toward their own, self-determined goals. This is partially because these goals are in sync with White, upper-class values and require the money they have recently inherited from Margaret's father. It is unclear if their grandfather would have supported this flouting of their father's authority to control their own destinies. While John was at the peak of his power as a CEO of a major company, Margaret may have been both at the nadir of her own personal power as well as having this lack of power made crystal clear by the personal decisions her daughters were making. Her perspective at this time is unknown beyond the fact that she has, at least for a time, refused to allow John to control her life. If John wants back the analytical, ambitious, clearheaded woman he married, it might be possible for him to reengage with Margaret. At this time, this is all hypothetical, her point of view being unknown. When John sets his sights on the goal, he is able to pursue it with deep commitment. Therefore, if he decides to try to learn about the power of society's pressures on Margaret and him apart from the couple they originally were, it may be possible for him to consider taking on a more androgynous identity that will allow him to get to know his daughters and develop a respectful and giving relationship with Margaret.

Feminist Treatment Plan: Historically Based Style

Treatment Plan Overview. John and Margaret's wealthy, White cultural background has reinforced the downward trajectory of her satisfaction within their relationship. The changes in their relationship over time, and how his being male, a CEO, and from a wealthy background have affected that relationship, will be examined to help him understand why Margaret might be seeking a divorce. (This plan follows the *problem format.*)

PROBLEM: Margaret has left John and no longer wants to be married to him, while he would like to continue being married to her.

LONG-TERM GOAL 1: John will examine the relationship that he and Margaret had when they first met and how their shared identity of coming from wealthy, White families influenced their relationship over time.

Short-Term Goals

1. John will look through all the memorabilia he can find that documents his early relationship with Margaret.

   a. John will discuss in treatment sessions what courses and organizations they took part in and how this may have related to their identities as college students.

   b. John will discuss in treatment sessions the social networks they had in college and how diverse they were in terms of race, religion, socioeconomic status, and so forth so that he can understand how a lack of contact with diverse individuals allowed him to be more unaware of social pressures on him and Margaret to fulfill sex role stereotypes.

2. John will contact any old friends he and Margaret had who might be able to tell him stories about his early relationship with Margaret.

   a. John will discuss in treatment sessions what social background, roles, interests, and so forth these friends had and in what ways they were similar to or different from Margaret and him.

   b. John will discuss in treatment sessions how much these similarities or differences may have led to unconscious assumptions, on their parts, for what life together would look like.

   c. John will discuss in treatment how much he and Margaret were acting within gender role stereotypes.

3. John will research how diverse the college population was when he and Margaret were attending, in terms of both economics and racial and ethnic diversity.

   a. John will discuss in treatment how "White" the college was and if he ever had experiences that illustrated for him the role of power and oppression in relationships.

   b. John will discuss in treatment how much the White and wealthy backgrounds that he and Margaret shared influenced or did not influence their choice in colleges.

   c. John will discuss in treatment how much the White and wealthy backgrounds that he and Margaret shared influenced or did not influence their choice of major and career.

d. John will discuss in treatment how much the lack of diversity in student population may have led to his lack of awareness of the power differential that occurred between him and Margaret when he became the sole breadwinner.

4. John will consider how much Margaret shared her own personal values and personal plans with him as they began their relationship and whether he was aware of disagreeing with her about her values and personal plans.

   a. He will discuss what he remembers that she got excited about regarding her university courses and future plans, and whether he ever directly or indirectly indicated to her that he expected that she would have to change some of these plans if she intended to marry him.

   b. He will discuss what he remembers that he got excited about regarding his university courses and future plans, and whether she ever directly or indirectly indicated to him that he would need to change some of these plans if he intended to marry her.

5. John will consider in what ways he did and did not value Margaret's perspective and in what ways she did and did not value his.

6. John will consider in what ways the relationship he had with Margaret was egalitarian and in what ways he exerted more power and control.

LONG-TERM GOAL 2: John will examine the relationship that he and Margaret had when they began planning to be married and how their shared identity of coming from wealthy, White families influenced their relationship during this time.

1. John will read literature on gender role stereotypes and then analyze the behavior of his mother and father and other adults in his social circle to consider whether in fact gender role stereotypes could have played a role in the changes that occurred when John and Margaret went from dating to newlyweds.

2. John will consider his childhood and analyze what socialization pressures from his family, his community, and the media might have shaped his current gender role and gendered expectations about marriage and family life.

3. John will consider whether men in his childhood, such as gardeners, cleaning people, and car mechanics, had the same freedom to choose that he did, and how this might have influenced the gender roles they took on within their families.

4. John will talk to both his parents and Margaret's to hear stories about how Margaret behaved as she prepared for the wedding in terms of how much control of the wedding she had and how much control they had.

5. John will reflect on his own behavior as he prepared for the wedding and was married and how much control he had versus how much control other people had in making decisions about the wedding.

6. John will reflect on how egalitarian the decisions were that were made in regard to where they would get married, where they would live after they were married, and how this might have affected his relationship with Margaret.

7. John will try to remember if Margaret might have expressed to him that she was dissatisfied about how their life was progressing at this time and how much he attended to what she said.

8. John will reflect on whether Margaret ever expressed a lack of interest in moving to the country and how he might have responded to this.

9. John will reflect on whether Margaret ever indicated that she wanted to keep working and not be a stay-at-home wife and how he might have responded to this.

10. John will reflect on the power of the environment, in the form of their parents and their social group, and how much this might have influenced the decisions that were made about where they would live and whether or not he and Margaret would pursue their careers.

LONG-TERM GOAL 3: John will examine the relationship that he and Margaret had when they first began to have children and how their shared identity of coming from wealthy, White families influenced their relationship during this time.

1. John will reflect on whether he and Margaret ever discussed whether or not they wanted to have children, and if so when they wanted to start having children and what their roles would be.

2. John will reflect on whether he ever told Margaret that he wanted to be an involved father and what her reaction might have been to this.

3. John will reflect on whether Margaret ever told him that she wanted to go back to work and be a working mother and how he might have responded to this.

4. John will reflect on the power of the environment, in the form of their parents and their social network, and how this might have influenced their decisions about the roles they would take on as parents.

5. John will discuss whether the gender role stereotypes they took on as parents led to his having a privileged or dominant position in relation to Margaret.

6. John will discuss whether the gender role stereotypes they took on as parents led him to lose the opportunity to be an active parent of his daughters.

7. John will read articles about relationship-building skills and use his analytic skills to determine which skills might be useful if he decides to try to reconnect with his daughters and Margaret in an egalitarian manner.

LONG-TERM GOAL 4: John will examine the relationship that he and Margaret had as they entered this recent period of their relationship where he felt he was close to achieving their mutual life goal, and how their shared identity of coming from wealthy, White families influenced their relationship during this time.

1. John will read articles about the history of wealth accumulation in the United States and then describe in treatment how much he believes the power and control his family has in society is based on personal effort and how much is based on inherited wealth.

2. John will create a history of his own accomplishments on a timeline and consider the role of inherited wealth in these accomplishments.

3. John will create a strengths-and-weaknesses chart and then evaluate the role that unearned privilege versus earned privilege played in each strength and weakness.

4. John will consider what values, attitudes, emotions, and behaviors that he learned from being a member of a wealthy, White family led him to neglect his family roles in order to continue accumulating wealth.

5. John will consider whether it is more important to him to continue accumulating more wealth by finalizing the international business deal or to try to reconnect with his family members in this time of crisis.

6. John will compare his behavior toward subordinates at work with his past behavior toward Margaret and his daughters and consider what he could do to show respect for their perspectives.

   6a. John will talk with his subordinates about the need for someone to take a trip to close an important deal and ask for their ideas about what needs to happen before, during, and after the trip to make it a success.

   6b. John will consider whether one of these subordinates has the requisite skills to handle work issues while he attends to his family crisis.

7. John will use role plays to practice egalitarian relationship skills that might be useful to him if he decides to follow through with contacting his subordinates about closing the business deal for him.

8. John will brainstorm with the clinician various ways to show his two daughters that he recognizes he has behaved oppressively toward them and clarify that he wants to make amends and try to relate to them as a supportive father who shows respect for their point of view.

   8a. John will decide whether he will call his daughters and try to start a respectful dialogue with them about their father–daughter relationship.

   8b. John will discuss with the clinician when it might be acceptable for him to ask his daughters to contact Margaret for him and request a chance to talk about his regrets that she wants a divorce.

9. John will brainstorm with the clinician various ways to show Margaret that he recognizes he has behaved oppressively toward her and clarify that he wants to make amends and try to relate to her in an egalitarian manner that shows respect for her point of view.

10. Other goals will be developed as appropriate if Margaret is willing to have contact with John.

PRACTICE CASE FOR STUDENT CONCEPTUALIZATION: INTEGRATING THE DOMAIN OF SOCIOECONOMIC STATUS

It is time to use empowerment feminist therapy to do an analysis of Sharon. Within this analysis, you are asked to integrate the domain of socioeconomic status into your case conceptualization and treatment plan.

Information Received From Brief Intake

Sharon is a 34-year-old White female living in a small city set within a large rural county. She has currently been married for one year. This is her second marriage. Her first marriage lasted for 10 years and ended in divorce due to her husband's long-term alcohol abuse. She has two children with her first husband, Adrian, age 10, and Susie, age 8. Sharon and her children lived alone for a year before she began dating Edward, her second husband. They married after six months of dating. Edward is the regional manager of a large bank, and Sharon is the manager of one of these banks. She was referred by her internist due to losing weight steadily over the past year and exhibiting signs of anxiety and depression.

During a brief mental status exam, Sharon expressed significant anger over her physician's referral for treatment; however, out of respect for him, she agreed to come. Sharon showed no signs of homicidal or suicidal ideation or serious pathology. She repeatedly insisted she was happily married and excited by her work at the bank.

Interview With Sharon (S) From a Feminist Perspective

C: Would you like to start by talking about your work at the bank?

S: (earnestly) I love my work. I had been a stay-at-home mom. I love my kids, but it feels very exhilarating to have responsibilities that test my limits.

C: You love it because you are intellectually challenged. (pause) Can you tell me more?

S: (smiling) I started as a teller, and I was petrified my first week on the job. But I was amazed by how easily I took to the whole banking process. I began studying on my own, and the manager noticed my work and promoted me for the first time. (excitedly) It really felt thrilling to have my work acknowledged.

C: I can see the pleasure in your face when you talk about this. It feels good to me too when people recognize my efforts.

S: (smiling) It was just the start of an exciting ride. The bank helped pay for me to go to college part time. I loved the university setting and taking courses. Once I got my degree, I was promoted again, first to assistant manager and now to manager.

C: Your hard work and top skills were appreciated . . . .(S starts frowning) What's wrong?

S: (dismissively) It's not a big deal. Most people did recognize my skills, but I was just thinking about some rumors that started circulating since I was promoted last year.

C: Can you tell me about them?

S: (angrily) I have been accused of sleeping my way to the top. It's because Edward and I were married around the time of my last promotion. I met Edward at church. I only found out once we started dating that he was the regional manager. He had been promoted a few weeks before from a bank two hours away; we had never met!

C: Edward had nothing to do with your promotion. You deserved it and deserve to feel good about it. Unfortunately, there is still a lot of sexism in our country that tends to invalidate the achievements of women.

S: I think it was just spiteful people at my office. I don't believe feminist nonsense.

C: You know what happened in your office, and of course, I don't. However, government statistics show men earn more, at every job classification, than women. It's possible that understanding what's happening to women in general could enhance your understanding of what's happening to you now.

S: (irritably) I don't mean to contradict you, but Edward and I feel very strongly that we live in a country of equal opportunity. He isn't going to want me coming in here if you are going to be indoctrinating me with propaganda.

C: You can contradict me whenever you want to. I would never want to indoctrinate you into anything. I do have a treatment philosophy that influences everything I do. I believe that men and women should be treated equally and accorded the same respect for their efforts.

S: (sincerely) Well, I agree with that. I just don't want to be told what to think.

C: I can understand that. Since you enjoyed your time at the university so much, I wonder if you'd like to take out some of the books that I have on this subject. You could read the federal statistics and come to your own conclusions.

S: (sincerely) I think I would enjoy that. But what if I don't agree with you?

C: You can tell me what you don't agree with, and we can discuss it. If you find that my treatment philosophy is wrong for you, I have a list of the other clinicians in our community that you can use to find someone you would feel comfortable with.

S: (intently) You say I can disagree. I need to know you mean it. I want you to tell me what you're thinking since I said your beliefs were feminist nonsense.

C: I don't agree that it's nonsense, but we don't have to agree on everything. I am very impressed with how you have educated yourself, learned banking, and raised two children at the same time. You don't need me or anyone else to tell you what to think.

S: (matter-of-factly) Good. For a start, my life is just great right now. Work is going great; the rumors are just irritating; there is no point in talking about them further.

C: What does seem worth discussing?

S: (looking anxious) I'm worried about my kids. They are having a hard time adjusting to my new marriage. Even when I was married to their father, it was really just them and me—their dad took a hands-off approach to child rearing. Edward is very different. He has rules, and Adrian and Susie are having trouble adjusting.

C: Did Edward discuss these rules with you?

S: (intently) No. He started to be an active father from day one. I really appreciate his efforts; however, he is older than I am and lived a long time without children. He doesn't realize that I know a lot more than he does about children. He expects too much.

C: Have you discussed this with him?

S: (earnestly) Not exactly, because even at home, we tend to talk about banking business. I periodically raise the issue of the children, but it seems we get quickly back to business. He really appreciates having a partner who shares his work interests.

C: Even as a couple at home, it is your work identities that are most important.

S: (confusedly) I don't understand what you mean.

C: Everyone has many identities that define who they are. For example, you are a bank manager, a newlywed, a mother. Each of these identities is interdependent with the others. It sounds like even when you are in your wife role, your banking skills come into play. Each identity carries with it a certain level of power or oppression in relationships with other people. At work, you are the manager. All the other people at the bank are your subordinates. So, you have more power than they do to decide how the bank should be conducted.

S: (defensively) Well, I worked hard to be in a position of authority.

C: You did work hard, and you deserved your position. I'm trying to point out that your position brings with it power and control to make things happen at the bank. On the other hand, Edward, as the regional manager, has still more power than you.

S: (sincerely) Yes, of course that's true.

C: If you talk about work, even when you're at home, he is still in a position of greater power. Does Edward ever feel more like your boss than your husband? (S looks confused) You said that whenever you bring up the children, he changes the topic back to work. Bosses set the topic with subordinates.

S: (reflectively) Thinking about it, yes, he does control the topic of conversation most of the time at home. He also decides what we do at home, but it's because he is introducing us to new things.

C: What does he decide for you?

S: (defensively) Nothing big—just things that will help me fit in with his friends. He wanted me to take up tennis because we belong to a country club. He's been champion of the men's singles tournament for a long time.

C: Edward really enjoys competition.

S: (emphatically) He does, and he was a little disappointed to find out that we didn't play tennis and golf—we are all in lessons now. Edward grew up in a wealthy home. He still doesn't really understand what it was like for me when I was growing up. I worked at any dead-end job I could get. In my first marriage, we lived paycheck to paycheck. Expensive sports were not an option.

C: Edward grew up with wealth. He takes for granted many of the privileges that are new to you, like playing sports that require expensive equipment. I'm wondering if he also had the privilege of a faster career path than you.

S: (calmly) That's an understatement. His father was in banking too. Edward had to start on his own, but he had the benefit of his dad's advice. This job has been a big step up for me and my family; I'm so thankful. I took the first steps myself, but Edward is a huge help. (excitedly) He feels we will be an unstoppable team!

C: You've really experienced a change in personal power.

S: (pause; uncertainly) Yes, it's all been great except Adrian really isn't enjoying golf lessons, but Edward says he needs the golf to be successful in business.

C: Edward is trying to help Adrian with a future goal, being successful in business. But Adrian is still young. Should he have a choice about what he does in his free time?

S: (defensively) Edward is really dedicated to Adrian. He wants to make a success out of him. I really appreciate that. After all, Adrian isn't really his son.

C: Does your family spend time just relaxing?

S: (softly) Edward feels that it is just wasting time to do what Adrian calls "hanging out." (pause) I realize Edward can be domineering, but that's only one side of him. He's been very generous to us. The day we got home from our wedding, he surprised the kids by changing two rooms in his house to be their bedrooms. He made a study corner with a personal computer in both their rooms. We were all stunned.

C: I've noticed that you use "we" rather than just giving me your own reaction.

S: (intently) I meant the children and me. Edward picked our wedding day for the delivery so everything would be a big surprise when we got back to the house.

C: He is very generous with possessions. (pause) But would you like to be consulted about these decisions rather than being surprised by them?

S: (intently) He's not intentionally leaving me out. He is a very action-oriented person and makes quick decisions. He's not the type to consult with other people.

C: Does this ever make you feel that your opinions aren't valued?

S: (anxiously) He values my opinion, but his experience is wider.

C: In our society, the husband and father often has the most power in making decisions.

S: (irritably) I don't think I'm letting him do it because he's the man. I really admire his intellect and his decision-making abilities. I think he just underestimates my experiences as a mother.

C: How serious a problem do you think this is?

S: (defensively) I don't think it's serious. Adrian and Susie are getting so much out of having him as a father. But Susie has been crying a lot, and I don't like that. It also makes Edward edgy; he feels she should have more self-control. I keep trying to remind the kids of all Edward has given us. They do love the clothes and the house. We lived in a very small apartment before. The children had to share a room; we didn't have money for extras like going to the movies.

C: You gained a lot of resources since your marriage. Why was Susie crying?

S: (angrily) She's getting bullied in ballet class because they say her clothes are stupid. Everybody else has been together in classes since kindergarten, and she's the newcomer. I've told her things will get better with time and her clothes are beautiful.

C: Women and girls are under a lot of social pressure to look certain ways. It can squelch their individuality.

S: (emphatically) I agree. That's what's happening to Susie. I wish I had more time to help her. One regret I have about my life changing is that my time is so limited with the kids. When I was a stay-at-home mom, I could put them first and give them a lot of my time. But they didn't have nice clothes and toys. Now it's the reverse; I'm always in a rush, but I can get them pretty much anything money can buy.

C: As a mom, you wish you could give more time to your children. At this point, there's constant tension between your identity as a wife and that of a mother.

S: (sadly) It does feel like that. I feel pulled between them. Edward doesn't understand. I just want to be with my kids. Whenever I've planned a weekend just to be quietly at home with them, I find that Edward has signed them up for something. My role is just to drive them somewhere and drop them off.

C: I can see the pain in your face. Does Edward know how you feel?

S: (sadly) He tends to minimize my concerns—without a plan, he feels time is wasted. My mother thinks I'm nuts to ever disagree with Edward.

C: She doesn't validate your concerns. (pause) You have a right to have them. You love your kids, and it makes sense that you want time with them.

S: (irritably) Mom actually told me I'm crazy to worry. She just reminds me how bad things used to be and how Edward really has been the savior of the family. He's helped her refinance her home so that she's a lot more comfortable financially now.

C: When it comes to money, Edward really comes through for everyone. When you are struggling to stay out of debt, more money does really seem to be the savior of the situation. However, has the money you have now made the children happier?

S: (sadly) The kids are happy right after they have been given something. But they don't seem to like the new private school they're enrolled in. Those other kids are brats, and I really don't want my children to be like them. (anxiously) I'm worried about the kids, but Edward thinks they just need time to adjust.

C: Change is hard. People often need time to adjust, but you don't want to be adjusting to something that isn't healthy for you.

S: (long pause) Adrian is having the most trouble with Edward. He works hard in school, but sometimes he just wants to lie around and not do anything. I wish Edward could understand this. Last week, Edward really lost it when Adrian's baseball bat accidentally broke a vase in the living room.

C: What do you mean, "lost it"?

S: (sadly) Edward hit him on the butt a few times. I definitely wouldn't call it abuse, but I don't hit my kids. Adrian yelled into Edward's face that he was a child abuser, and then Edward grounded him for a month; this is too long. Adrian was disrespectful, but kids lose their cool sometimes. (anxiously) I wish Edward could understand this.

C: Has Edward ever left bruises or other marks on one of the kids after he disciplined them?

S: (intently) No; he does spank both of them, but he's never left any marks. Edward's sharpest weapon is his tongue. He says demeaning things if he's displeased with them. He is trying to motivate them to try harder. He believes that his father helped him by setting hard standards and making him live up to them. He believes Adrian is really intelligent but too emotional. I guess I have encouraged my kids to talk to me about their feelings. Edward thinks Adrian's a wimp and needs to toughen up.

C: Do you want this?

S: (calmly) I think Adrian's fine, but it wouldn't hurt him to try to learn from Edward.

C: Edward is very powerful both at work and in the home. What about you? It doesn't seem as if your role as the mother is being given as much respect as you deserve.

S: (nervously) He's given me so much.

C: He's given you material possessions and training opportunities at work. Have you given him anything?

S: (intently) Yes. I've been a good wife to him, supported his interests, cared for him. But (long pause) I don't know really what I could want that I don't have.

C: It's up to you to define a good marriage for yourself. But I believe that both partners' opinions should have equal say and equal respect. Edward has the right to be treated with respect for his knowledge of banking, but your knowledge of parenting also deserves respect.

S: (uncertainly) I'm new to feeling like I deserve respect.

C: Edward has been a good partner in many respects. But, like many powerful men, he isn't stopping to consider if you have valuable knowledge he doesn't—about how to raise children. How are you handling the stress of Edward not understanding the kids?

S: (anxiously) I guess I need to tell you that I've lost a lot of weight recently. I just don't feel like eating. I know that's crazy. (sadly) Edward likes it. (emphatically) He says I'm going to be the most beautiful woman at the country club.

C: What did your doctor say about your weight?

S: (uncertainly) He says I'm too thin. But I'm not hungry, and I'm getting a lot of compliments.

C: There is a lot of social pressure on women to be thin. It comes from TV, movies, and advertisements. It sells a lot of diet products, but it's not healthy for women.

S: (sadly) I'm really not trying to diet. But Susie has begun to copy me and eat less. I don't want that for her!

C: There are a lot of positives from building this new family of yours. I know it made you angry when your doctor said it, but I have to be honest with you, and say that you do seem anxious and depressed. I think it may be coming from the terrible pressure you are under to be a good wife and a good mother in this new family.

S: (anxiously) I don't want to lose Edward.

C: If you choose to come back, we need to think about the ways you can balance your identities as a wife and mother without losing your appetite.

S: (long pause; calmly) I guess I do need to come back.

Exercises for Developing a Case Conceptualization of Sharon

Exercise 1 (four-page maximum)

GOAL: To verify that you have a clear understanding of EFT.

STYLE: An integrative essay comprising Parts A through C.

NEED HELP?   Review this chapter (pages 197–202).

A. Develop a concise overview of all the assumptions of EFT (the theory's hypotheses about key dimensions in understanding how clients change; think broadly, abstractly) as an introduction to the rest of this exercise.

B. Develop a thorough description of how each of these assumptions is used to understand a client's progression through the change process in paragraphs that provide specific examples to fully explain each assumption.

C. Conclude your essay by describing the role of the clinician in helping the client change (consultant, doctor, educator, helper), the major approach taken to treatment, and common treatment techniques. Provide enough specific examples to clarify what is distinctive about this approach.

Exercise 2 (four-page maximum)

GOAL: To aid application of feminist theory to Sharon.

STYLE: A separate sentence outline for each section, A through D.

NEED HELP?   Review this chapter (pages 197–202).

A. For each of Sharon's identities as a mother, wife, daughter, and bank manager, discuss, where appropriate:

1. The role, if any, of past gender role stereotypes in the development of this identity.

2. The role, if any, of current pressures from family and/or society in maintaining gender stereotypes within this identity.

3. How much privilege or oppression Sharon experiences within each identity.

4. How much or how little of a woman's perspective is valued within this identity.

5. How egalitarian Sharon's relationships are with others when she functions in this identity.

6. What, if any, significant changes have occurred in this identity since Sharon's first marriage.

7. What Sharon's current weaknesses (concerns, issues, problems, symptoms, skill deficits, treatment barriers) are at this time within this identity.

8. What Sharon's current strengths (strong points, positive features, successes, skills, factors facilitating change) are at this time within this identity.

B. Discuss how interdependent Sharon's identities are with each other at this time, which identity or identities are most salient to her, how empowered Sharon currently is, and how androgynous her current lifestyle is.

C. In what ways are Sharon's current environmental and social contexts facilitating or inhibiting her growth as an individual at this time? How aware is she of how societal expectations that she be a gendered female are influencing her life? What role do these social pressures play in her weight loss, anxiety, and depression?

D. How well is Sharon functioning overall? How might her strengths be utilized to support her greater empowerment and her development of egalitarian relationships with other adults? What, specifically, might EFT have to offer her at this time?

Exercise 3 (four-page maximum)

GOAL: To develop an understanding of the potential role of socioeconomic status (SES) in Sharon's life.

STYLE: A separate sentence outline for each section, A through I.

NEED HELP? Review Chapter 2 (pages 85–92).

A. Assess Sharon's economic and social class and consider how this has influenced her access to resources within the family, such as time to spend with family members as well as resources for daily living, safe housing, privacy, and recreation.

B. Assess Sharon's economic and social class and consider how this has influenced her access to resources within the community, such as medical care, educational choices, social choices, vocational choices, legal resources, and sociopolitical power.

C. Considering A and B above, assess the impact of Sharon's economic and social class on her self-esteem and personal welfare; family welfare; ability to make independent decisions at home, at school, and/or within a work setting; and ability to influence her own life circumstances as opposed to having her life be under the control of others within the work, social, or political sphere.

D. Consider the impact of the environment in actively supporting or discouraging Sharon's economic success in the past, currently, and in the foreseeable future (social and economic barriers or windows of opportunity).

E. Considering A through D above, consider whether SES is serving more to constrain Sharon's life or to support it, how SES might be the cause of or be related to her strengths or weaknesses at this time, her overall level of stress, her overall level of well-being, and how SES might inhibit or facilitate any lifestyle changes for Sharon at this time.

F. What is your current knowledge of issues relevant to SES?

1. How many courses have you taken that give you background on SES and its impact on clients' physical and emotional health?

2. How many workshops have you taken that give you background on SES and its impact on clients' physical and emotional health?

3. What professional experiences have you had in working with individuals of differing SES?

4. What personal experiences have you had with individuals of differing SES?

5. What cohort effects might influence the worldview of individuals who are lower class, middle class, and upper class at this time?

G. What is your current level of awareness of SES?

1. Discuss the stereotypes you have heard about lower-class, middle-class, and upper-class people.

2. Discuss the role that the socioeconomic class of your family of origin might play in your life now in terms of how you vote, where you live, what you own, and how you handle your finances.

3. Discuss the experiences you have had that could support your effective work with Sharon as well as experiences you have had that might lead to negative bias or marginalization of Sharon's point of view or current situation.

H. What are your current skills in working with clients of this SES?

1. What skills do you currently have in carrying out a class analysis and helping clients access needed financial or related resources?

2. What skills do you currently have that would help you evaluate the impact of social class on Sharon's physical and emotional health?

3. What could you do to increase your ability to evaluate the impact of social class on Sharon's physical and emotional health?

I. What action steps can you take?

1. What can you do to prepare yourself to be more skilled in working with clients of this SES?

2. How might you structure the treatment environment to increase the likelihood of a positive outcome with clients from this SES?

3. Describe the therapeutic orientation you plan to use with this client and discuss the classist values implicitly embedded within this treatment orientation that could lead to bias or marginalization of Sharon's experiences or point of view.

4. What can you do to strengthen the process of building rapport with Sharon?

5. What can you change about the treatment-planning process to make it more effective for clients from this SES?

Exercise 4 (six-page maximum)

GOAL: To help you integrate your knowledge of EFT and the role of SES into an in-depth conceptualization of Sharon (who she is and why she does what she does).

STYLE: An integrated essay consisting of a premise, supportive details, and conclusions following a carefully planned organizational style.

NEED HELP? Review Chapter 1 (pages 1–7) and Chapter 2 (pages 85–92).

STEP 1: Consider what style you should use for organizing your feminist understanding of Sharon. This style should (a) support you in providing a comprehensive and clear understanding of her identities and her power in the world and (b) support language she might find persuasive in spite of her ambivalence toward EFT.

STEP 2: Develop a concise premise (overview, preliminary or explanatory statements, proposition, thesis statement, theory-driven introduction, hypotheses, summary, concluding causal statements) that explains Sharon's strengths and weaknesses as a newly upper-class woman who is concerned about how her children and their new stepfather are relating to each other. If you have trouble with Step 2, remember that it should be an integration of the key ideas of Exercises 2 and 3 and that it should (a) provide a basis for Sharon's long-term goals, (b) be grounded in feminist theory and be sensitive to issues of social class, and (c) highlight the strengths that Sharon brings to feminist treatment.

STEP 3: Develop your supporting material (a detailed case analysis of strengths and weaknesses, supplying data to support an introductory premise) from a feminist perspective, incorporating within each paragraph an in-depth understanding of Sharon as a woman whose struggle to find a balance between her personal and work identities has resulted in anxiety, depression, and weight loss. If you have trouble with Step 3, consider the information you'll need to include in order to (a) support the development of short-term goals; (b) be grounded in the principles of EFT, especially as they relate to SES; and (c) integrate an understanding of Sharon's strengths into your evaluation of the role of social forces in her life.

STEP 4: Develop your feminist conclusions and broad treatment recommendations, including (a) Sharon's overall level of functioning, (b) anything facilitating or serving as a barrier to her empowerment at this time, and (c) her basic needs as she tries to develop egalitarian relationships that allow her to develop her own unique abilities (be concise and general).

Exercise 5 (four-page maximum)

GOAL: To develop an individualized, theory-driven action plan for Sharon that considers her strengths and is sensitive to issues of SES.

STYLE: A sentence outline consisting of long- and short-term goals.

NEED HELP? Review Chapter 1 (pages 7–24).

STEP 1: Develop your treatment plan overview, being careful to consider what you said in Parts G and I of Exercise 3 to try to prevent any negative bias in your treatment plan and to ensure that you adapt your treatment approach to Sharon's unique needs as an individual.

STEP 2: Develop long-term (major, large, ambitious, comprehensive, broad) goals that Sharon will *ideally* reach by the termination of treatment and that will lead to her empowerment. If you have trouble with Step 2, reread your premise and support topic sentences and transform them into goals that will meet her needs as a mother, wife, and bank manager (use the *style* of Exercise 4).

STEP 3: Develop short-term (small, brief, encapsulated, specific, measurable) goals that Sharon and you can expect to see accomplished within a few weeks and that will help you chart Sharon's progress toward understanding the impact of social forces in her life, instill hope for change, and plan time-effective treatment sessions. If you have trouble with Step 3, reread your support paragraphs looking for ideas to transform into goals that (a) might facilitate change that is relevant to the principles of EFT and issues of SES, (b) might enhance anything facilitating or decrease anything serving as a barrier to her empowerment at this time, (c) utilize her strengths whenever possible in understanding the role of societal pressures in her life, and (d) are individualized to her needs as a newly married mother of two rather than generic.

Exercise 6

GOAL: To critique empowerment feminist therapy in the case of Sharon.

STYLE: Answer Questions A through E in essay format or discuss them in a group format.

A. What are the strengths and weaknesses of this model for helping Sharon (a newly married mother of two who went from the lower to the upper class)?

B. Discuss the power of using cognitive-behavioral theory with this case, looking for any signs in the interview of thinking errors such as absolutist standards, right/wrong thinking, and maladaptive emotions, behaviors, and so forth. Then, compare and contrast the power of using a cognitive-behavioral versus a feminist approach to this case. Conclude with a discussion of which theory you consider most powerful for helping Sharon at this time, and explain why.

C. Apply the domain of gender to Sharon and Edward. Then discuss whether you think gender or SES is having the greatest impact on Sharon's spousal relationship at this time. Also, discuss how the dynamics in her spousal relationship might change if Edward was the owner of a small landscaping business and she was still manager of the bank.

D. What ethical issues might arise in working with Sharon, considering her overt rejection of the idea that gender role stereotypes are relevant to her and her marriage? A principle of EFT is that Sharon has the right to find her own unique identity. What specifically will you do if, after a few weeks, she tells you that her choice is to allow Edward to remain in control of family decisions and that she wants your help in discussing this with her children?

E. What did you learn about your own gender role assumptions as you tried to implement this model for Sharon? How did you react to Sharon's comments involving her relationship to Edward and his relationship to her children? How might this support or inhibit your ability to develop a positive working relationship with her?

RECOMMENDED RESOURCES

Books

Brown, L. S. (2010). *Feminist therapy*. Washington, DC: American Psychological Association.

Enns, C. Z., & Byars-Winston, A. M. (2010). Multicultural feminist therapy. In H. Landrine & N. F. Russo (Eds.), *Handbook of diversity in feminist psychology* (pp. 367–388). New York, NY: Springer.

Worell, J., & Remer, P. (2003). *Feminist perspectives in therapy: Empowering diverse women*. New York, NY: John Wiley & Sons.

Videos

American Psychological Association (Producer), & Brown, L. S. (Trainer). (n.d.). *Feminist therapy* (Systems of Psychotherapy Video Series, Motion Picture #4310828). (Available from the American Psychological Association, 750 First Street, NE, Washington, DC 20002–4242)

Amber May (Producer). (2012, August 1). Feminist therapy [Video file]. Retrieved from https://www.youtube.com/watch?v=YuFmc3y72Nw

Websites

Feminist Psychology Institute. https://feminism.org

Psychology's Feminist Voices. http://www.feministvoices.com

Emotion-Focused Case Conceptualizations and Treatment Plans

INTRODUCTION TO EMOTION-FOCUSED TREATMENT

Ellen calls and leaves a message on your answering machine. She is a 32-year-old White female who has recently divorced Frank, her husband of 10 years. She is currently living in the city with her two sons, ages 8 and 10. Ellen divorced Frank, after a chronically unhappy marriage, when she recognized that she was a lesbian. She says that Frank has not yet accepted the divorce or her sexual orientation. Ellen wants help in resolving her relationship with Frank and in developing a constructive relationship with another lesbian adult. Her parting words are "Don't call me back if you think my lesbianism is the problem. I want it clear from the start that it's part of the solution to my problems."

A brief mental status screen during an intake indicated that Ellen showed no signs of homicidal or suicidal ideation, cognitive confusion, or impulsivity. However, she did indicate a history of being abused and neglected as a child as well as a long-standing history of alcohol abuse that had led to repeated hospitalizations for alcohol poisoning. However, she indicated that she had had nothing to drink for the past two weeks.

You provide a form of emotion-focused treatment rooted in the traditions of client-centered therapy, existential therapy, and Gestalt therapy as well as the research on emotions in cognitive science and neuroscience (Greenberg & Goldman, 2007; Perls, Hefferline, & Goodman, 1951; Rogers, 1951). You believe that people have an innate, emotion-based system that helps them derive meaning from their experiences and motivates them to grow and develop. Ellen comes to you in a state of distress and doesn't want you pointing her in the wrong direction. She doesn't need to worry about that. You would never tell her that her lesbianism is a problem or is not a problem. She is the expert on her experiences, and only she will be able to decide if something is adaptive or maladaptive for her. She also has a natural capacity to grow and change in an adaptive way, if she can trust herself to fully process her experiences. Your role will be to facilitate this process (Greenberg & Goldman, 2007;

Rogers, 1951). The following more detailed analysis of emotion-focused treatment is drawn from Elliott and Greenberg (1995).

Ellen is constantly creating meaning from her experiences so that she can understand herself, others, and her situation. Healthy functioning results when she processes her internal and external experiences thoroughly so that the meaning derived from them can guide her flexibly and adaptively. As she does this processing, she needs to keep her emotional arousal at a level that is optimal for her. There are times when she will need to access her emotions, heighten them, and tolerate them so that she can recognize the importance of the situation (the meaning of it) and take appropriate action. At other times, the meaning-creation process will be blocked unless she can reduce her state of arousal by containing or distancing herself from these emotions so she'll be able to think adaptively about the situation and act appropriately. Emotional regulation is critical to Ellen's adaptive functioning and consists of knowing when to be more in touch with her emotions so that they can guide her and when she needs to keep her emotions under control so that she can process her experiences using reason. If Ellen's present functioning is maladaptive, it is the result of blocked emotional processing.

Ellen has recently begun trusting her internal experiences. This has led her to redefine herself as a lesbian rather than a heterosexual. She is now struggling with the meaning this shift in sexual orientation has for other aspects of her life. Ellen did not change her view of herself in the world overnight. Rather, this view has always been in a state of construction as she has integrated new and old experiences. Old experiences, in the form of emotion schemes, serve as a filter for new experiences. Emotion schemes develop during childhood and then operate automatically and unconsciously to guide behavior in an anticipatory and pattern-determined fashion. This innate, emotion-based system provides a holistic sense of how things are going for Ellen on a moment-to-moment basis.

An emotion scheme could be developed around a primary or secondary emotion. Primary emotions occur in direct reaction to something that has happened. If Ellen is angry at her father, this anger is a primary emotion. However, if immediately upon experiencing the anger Ellen experiences fear that her father will hit her if she expresses anger, then fear becomes a secondary emotion that serves to cover up the primary emotion of anger. To gain constructive meaning from these experiences, Ellen will need to work through the fear until the primary emotion surfaces and then fully process her anger. Negative emotions always serve as cues to areas of experience that need further processing for meaning.

Emotion schemes are not simple feelings. Although feelings play a key role in their development, emotion schemes represent high-level organizing structures in which feelings, bodily sensations, cognitions (beliefs, perceptions, expectations), and motivational tendencies or action tendencies are brought together to help Ellen understand who she is, how she relates to others, and what is important to her. While these emotion schemes automatically influence her behavior, Ellen's processing of new experiences, or further processing of older experiences, can serve to modify or transform her already created emotion schemes as well as to create new ones.

Ellen's strengths come from healthy emotion schemes and adaptive emotions, while her difficulties are the result of either maladaptive emotion schemes or adaptive emotions in the face of problematic experiences. Healthy schemes will help guide Ellen to get her needs met in a life-enhancing manner. They will each contain feelings, bodily sensations, cognitions, and motivations or action tendencies. Incomplete, unhealthy, or contradictory schemes will not guide Ellen adaptively but will still be an attempt to get her legitimate needs met.

What might a healthy emotion scheme be? Ellen always did well in school. This may be due to a healthy scheme that guides her in learning academic material effectively. This scheme might contain feelings of confidence, expectations that she can learn new things, and perceptions that she has been successful in learning in the past. This might be coupled with motivational tendencies that lead her to pay attention in class and study. This scheme would be adaptive in helping Ellen learn within an academic environment and would bode well for her being able to learn new things within the treatment environment.

What is an adaptive emotion? It is an emotion that guides Ellen adaptively in her present circumstances. If someone insults Ellen at work, she might feel angry. If in response to this anger, she responds with assertive behavior to defend herself, then the anger is functioning as an adaptive emotion that leads her to take adaptive action. Similarly, if she is in a situation with a romantic partner and being treated with kindness and love, Ellen might feel love in return. If she responds by expressing love and affection to her partner, then this love is acting as an adaptive emotion.

Ellen has some emotional-processing problems, so all of her experiences are not organized into healthy and complete emotion schemes. What goes wrong if Ellen has an incomplete scheme? For example, Ellen could have a desire or motivational tendency to form an emotionally intimate relationship with another adult. However, this scheme could exist solely as inchoate longings for emotional connection (an unclear felt sense). This scheme is incomplete and therefore not helpful in guiding Ellen in how she should act to get this need met. In treatment, you would help Ellen become more aware of her longing for emotional connection. She could discuss it and put into words what the longing means to her (symbolize it). Through focusing her attention on her bodily sensations, she may come to label these sensations as reflecting a feeling of sadness that she doesn't know how to develop emotional intimacy even though she's very motivated to experience it. By processing this longing more deeply, Ellen may recognize that she doesn't know how to share her feelings with another person. From this further emotional processing, her unclear felt sense has been transformed into a complete and adaptive scheme in which she has feelings of hope, cognitions that she has learned effectively in the past and can continue to do so, and a motivation to try hard and practice new social skills so that she can develop emotional intimacy with another person.

What about a complete but maladaptive emotion scheme? Due to her father's abusive behavior, Ellen may have developed a scheme for interacting with men that includes cognitions that all women need to be submissive in order to be safe. Her motivational tendencies may lead her to engage in submissive behavior, including the bodily responses of looking down, speaking quietly, and always agreeing with men. She may feel unfulfilled but safe. While this scheme might have been functional in decreasing her father's abusive behavior, it is rigidly guiding her behavior with both violent and nonviolent men. Thus, it couldn't guide her to have an emotionally satisfying relationship with Frank.

How might two conflicting schemes influence Ellen? She might have two emotion schemes that guide her in incongruent ways; this may cause a self-evaluative split in which Ellen is torn between two competing aspects of her experience. For example, she might have an emotion scheme guiding her sexual behavior. This developed through her childhood as she watched her parents, and other visible sexual partners, interact. Ellen also heard a lot of homophobic comments as she was growing up, so the scheme guiding her sexual behavior might include cognitions that appropriate sexual behavior occurs only between a man and a woman and that lesbian and gay sexual behavior is always unacceptable. In contrast to this scheme that developed in childhood, as an adult Ellen has a newly developed scheme that supports her in a lesbian personal identity. At this time, this scheme might consist of feelings of hope and contentment; sensations of excitement; and cognitions that she understands herself better, that she wasn't a loser as a marital partner, and that being a lesbian is part of the solution to her problems. This scheme might contain motivational tendencies that lead her to reach out to date other lesbians. However, her "sexual behavior" scheme that tells her how to behave in sexual relationships is incongruent with her "personal identity" scheme that motivates her to date lesbians. This leaves Ellen in a state of confusion and internal conflict, unable to date unless she is drunk so that alcohol can dampen her contradictory cognitions and action tendencies.

Finally, Ellen might experience problems due to an adaptive emotion that developed in response to problematic experiences during childhood, as her father was very physically abusive to her and she witnessed his sexual abuse of her mother. She may have learned that when someone (her father) experienced anger, someone else (herself, her mother) would become seriously injured, leading Ellen to fear the emotional expression of anger. Fear may have become an adaptive emotion because it led her to engage in behavior that would protect her. Whenever her dad raised his voice, her fear may have motivated her to be submissive, and this may have moderated her father's rage—thus, it was adaptive. Now, this formerly adaptive emotion may be limiting her ability to express anger herself or work through problems with others who are angry. Treatment could help her fully explore this emotion and decrease its potency so that she can understand its role in her relationships. Ellen could then decide if her submissive actions are functional for her in dealing with angry people and if it is safe for her to be angry with other people.

Ellen may have predominantly healthy emotion schemes and adaptive emotions guiding her in processing meaning from her experiences and have only minimal or circumscribed emotional-processing problems. On the other hand, she may have developed a problematic global processing style that interferes with appropriate emotional regulation much of the time. This problematic processing style could reflect emotional overregulation (the person is cut off from emotions), emotional underregulation (the person is a sea of emotions), too heavy a reliance on experiential processing (the person overuses emotional or bodily awareness), or too heavy a reliance on conceptual processing (the person overuses reasoning strategies).

If Ellen has a problematic processing style, it is associated with intensely painful emotions (core pains) or overwhelming thoughts (core issues). These emanate from one of four causes: difficulty in putting her experiences into words so that she can conceptually process them; intrapersonal dynamics such as struggles with self-esteem or self-definition; interpersonal dynamics such as struggles in forming attachments that balance her need for intimacy with her need for autonomy; and existential dynamics where she struggles with the meaning of death, loss, life, and so forth. Ellen could have more than one core pain or issue. Each of these is a component of a dysfunctional or underarticulated emotion scheme or an adaptive emotion in the face of a problematic experience.

As long as Ellen is not fully processing her experiences, her freedom of choice and action are limited. Treatment will focus on helping her (a) become more fully aware of her experiences, (b) process those experiences more fully for meaning, and (c) decide if any aspect of an emotion scheme is not functional for her. If she decides this, then she will modify it, transform it, or create something new that was missing. As a result of this functional processing of her emotions, Ellen will have a new view of herself in the world, a new view of others, and a greater understanding and acceptance of herself.

THE ROLE OF THE CLINICIAN

How will you help Ellen? Overall, you will follow two overarching principles. The first is to foster a collaborative, prizing, and genuine treatment relationship. To do so, you will focus on developing empathetic attunement to Ellen's frame of reference, you will develop a prizing relationship with her, and you will involve her in a process of mutual goal setting and participation in treatment tasks. The second principle is that, while you will be nondirective as to the content of the treatment session, as Ellen is an expert on what she needs to discuss, you will facilitate her self-exploration through providing opportunities for her to engage in specific treatment tasks. The tasks will facilitate her full processing of painful emotional states and thematic material and incorporation of these new experiences into her constructions of herself and her situation. Your challenge is to create a balance between therapeutic attunement to Ellen's self-exploration, which is critical to helping her learn to trust her internal experience, and the introduction of specific tasks that will aid Ellen in constructing meaning from her experiences.

How will you decide what tasks will help Ellen in the moment? You will listen attentively and track her emotions in the moment. You will look for markers that indicate an emotional-processing problem (unresolved cognitive-affective problems) and then suggest a task that could help with this in-the-moment block to her fully experiencing her internal and external world. You can also examine the quality of Ellen's voice as she relates her experiences, as this can provide clues to what she needs from you. Four different vocal qualities have been identified. If she speaks with a focused voice, she is ready to put into words some new aspect of her experience. An emotional voice indicates that she is tuned in to her feelings. If she is speaking with a limited voice, she is concerned about what would happen if she got in touch with her emotions. In this situation, Ellen needs to develop trust and a greater sense of safety within the treatment relationship before she can explore her experiences more fully. Finally, if Ellen has an external voice, she is describing her experiences in a rehearsed or rote manner with her attention on the reaction that this description will evoke in you rather than on developing an internal understanding of their meaning. In this case, you will help her turn inward and reenact each experience in a vivid way so that it can be processed within the immediacy of the moment.

Will Ellen proceed with a task you suggest? Her autonomy and self-directed exploration are critical, and thus she will take on a task only if she feels ready to do so. Ellen is always in the process of incorporating new experiences into her sense of self and her world; as she does this, she is recreating herself and what she needs in the moment. As a result, no plan of action carries directly over from one session to another. She will determine the pace and direction of each session. However, you expect that if she has a core pain or core issue, it will recur across sessions. Each time you see Ellen, you will wait to see what emerges from her and follow her lead as you build a collaborative, egalitarian treatment relationship. You will never impose meanings on her experiences, as this could impede the treatment process and prevent her from reorganizing her experience in the manner that is most helpful to her.

Markers of experiences that should be explored could come from Ellen's global processing style of overregulating her emotions. Thus, at the first sign, or marker, that she is minimizing her experience of emotions, you could suggest a task that would facilitate her more fully experiencing them instead. A marker could also be something small that occurs within the immediacy of the moment, such as an aspect of nonverbal behavior. For example, Ellen might look down when discussing something (nonverbal expression). You would draw her attention to her bodily sensations around this behavior and help her first symbolize it (put it into words) and then consider what it might mean.

Six different types of emotional-processing problems (process diagnoses) will be discussed. For each type, there is a related treatment task that could help Ellen explore and/or transform it for adaptive meaning. The first type is called a problematic reaction, in which Ellen recognizes that there is a discrepancy between her expected reaction and her actual reaction; she finds the experience puzzling or troubling in some way. The task that is helpful in this case is systematic evocative unfolding. Ellen will be helped to vividly reexperience and explore this problematic reaction while you respond empathically. You will slow down the processing of the puzzling experience so you can help Ellen more deeply examine every small piece of it. She will come to recognize the perceptual trigger (what happened immediately before the reaction), the immediate thoughts she has around it (further symbolization of the experience), her feelings in response to it (how the experience feels), and her motivations (what she wants to feel and think about it). As a result, Ellen will be able to draw more adaptive meaning from the problematic experience.

People have a multiplicity of selves, not a single executive self. Ellen is in a constant state of constructing a unified sense of herself. If she has a second type of processing problem, a self-evaluative split, two aspects of herself are working against each other rather than being fully integrated within her sense of herself. For example, one aspect of her identity could be critical of or coercive to another. One may criticize her as incapable of a relationship, since her marriage failed. The other may insist that it was sexual confusion, not an inability to relate, that led to the failure. These two aspects need to be integrated adaptively into Ellen's self-concept. The treatment technique of a two-chair dialogue is helpful in this situation. Ellen will personify each aspect of herself (the critic of her role as a wife vs. her newly developed identity as a lesbian). You will coach her in having one aspect talk to the other until the messages of both voices are fully processed. This will aid her in integrating both voices. She may have previously denied some aspect of her experience because it was traumatic or unacceptable to her. Ellen will be helped to show compassion and self-acceptance, as this aspect of her experience is a valid part of herself.

In a related vein, a third type of problem is a self-interruptive split. It's possible that Ellen went for years with one aspect of herself (the part trying to be the good wife) interrupting or minimizing her ability to express or fully experience her emotion of dissatisfaction in the marriage. In this case, a two-chair enactment task might be helpful. Ellen will slowly process this split by bringing the interrupting good wife (who is overregulating her emotion of dissatisfaction) under her deliberate control. Ellen will then be able to fully express her dissatisfaction and process it for constructive meaning.

A fourth type of problem is called a sense of vulnerability. This represents painful emotions relevant to some aspect of her experience that Ellen may have kept secret from everyone in the past. Perhaps Ellen always believed that she deserved the abusive treatment she got from her father as she wondered if she was inherently bad or worthless. Whenever this sense of vulnerability begins to surface, she may shy away from experiencing it, fearing that to take in this experience will mean she is bad and worthless. In this case, the task of empathic affirmation is needed. You will demonstrate to Ellen that you understand and value her for who she is—a divorced, lesbian mother of two who was abused as a child and so forth; you value her whole self. This acceptance will help Ellen develop a greater sense of hope and strength so that she can accept all aspects of herself.

A fifth processing problem is an absent or unclear felt sense. This is relevant to Ellen if she has a confusing or an absent physiological reaction around some aspect of her experience. Experiential focusing is a task that is particularly helpful in this situation. Assume Ellen always feels numb when she turns off the lights prior to going to bed, but she has no idea why. You help Ellen turn inward and pay close attention to this numbness while giving herself permission to process it more. She is helped to intensify her feeling of numbness so that she can give it a label that helps her visualize this sensation. She says the numbness is like being an ice cube, frozen and suspended until it melts and she is lost. Keeping this ice cube metaphor in mind, Ellen can now symbolize (put into words or further symbols) that as an ice cube, she didn't have to feel pain as her father beat her. Afterward she melted away because her mother treated her as if the experience didn't occur. Ellen can construct new meaning from this intense focusing on this unclear felt sense. While her past cannot be changed, the meaning of the beatings can. She can stop believing she is just water melting away. She can now believe that her father was abusive and that her mother was in denial of this. Her sense of self now contains recognition that as an adult she can protect herself from abuse. She may now turn off the lights at night, remaining fully aware, as the adult Ellen is safe in bed.

The last type of processing marker is called unfinished business. Perhaps Ellen's mother died when she was 5, and Ellen has unresolved feelings of abandonment or anger over this event. A dialogue using an empty chair (where her mother is imagined to be sitting) can be a valuable task in this situation. First Ellen talks from her own perspective while looking at the empty chair. Then, Ellen moves to sit in the "mother's chair" and continues the dialogue from her mother's perspective. Ellen keeps changing chairs, and points of view, until she has fully fleshed out all aspects of the unfinished business. She can now come to an adaptive conclusion where she has resolved her feelings toward her mother's death.

All process diagnoses (recognition of markers) are tentative and may or may not be confirmed by further emotional processing. All six treatment tasks serve to bring unconscious and automatic emotion schemes into Ellen's awareness, where they can be explored in depth. If Ellen finds a scheme that can guide her constructively but that she has minimized in the past, she can pay more attention to it to increase its potency in guiding her. If she discovers that one of her guiding schemes is destructive, she can reorganize it, transform it, or create a different scheme that is more helpful to her.

What will Ellen have gained at the end of treatment? She will have full access to her emotions and be able to use them to guide her actions. If she is feeling overwhelmed with her emotions, she will have learned skills to reduce her arousal using strategies such as self-soothing, seeking support from others, and distracting. In contrast, if she is cut off from her emotions, she will have learned skills such as how to attend to her bodily sensations and take an inner focus so that she can become aware of her emotional states. Overall, she will be able to trust her own experience, make use of a greater range of emotional information, and develop an ability to reflect on her own way of thinking and feeling about her experiences. She will learn that she can be herself in a relationship with someone else because she is a worthwhile person and can guide her own destiny.

CASE APPLICATION: INTEGRATING THE DOMAIN OF SEXUAL ORIENTATION

Ellen's case will now be examined in detail. There are many domains of complexity that might be relevant to her case. The domain of sexual orientation has been chosen to be examined within an emotion-focused case conceptualization and treatment plan.

Interview With Ellen (E) From an Emotion-Focused Perspective

C: Welcome. (pause) Where would you like to start?

E: (sad, looking down) I recently divorced my husband, Frank. I met him in high school. He was my first and only serious relationship and he always took charge of our money, where we lived, and how we lived. He was my one and only friend. (looking up)

C: How hard to divorce your only friend.

E: (dejected) Yes, it was very hard. I have casual friends, but (pause; desolate) I need a new partner, someone to love—I am so lonely at night after my sons go to sleep.

C: You're seeking a way out of the loneliness. (pause) What might you do?

E: (embarrassed) I know I need to meet (long pause) other lesbians. But how do I approach other women? I have always found it hard to meet new people. Frank was the one who approached me—I wouldn't have been able to approach him. (defensively) I went to a gay bar last weekend. I was just planning to drink just enough to help me be (pause) social. But (pause; looking down) it took me a long time and a lot of alcohol, but I managed to start talking to someone. We went to some hotel, and (long pause) I don't remember the woman's name or what I did. (looking up, disgustedly) I woke up the next morning alone at the hotel. I looked at myself in the bathroom mirror and suddenly began to throw up all over myself. (angry) I had to go back home and face my kids. (long pause) They saw me come in wearing the same clothes as the day before (pause) all stained from vomit; they just stared at me. I lied. I said I had the flu and went to the hospital. (pause; sadly) It felt bad, really bad to lie to them. (confused) But what else was I to do?

C: It didn't feel right. You couldn't remember what happened. (pause; *E* looks down) You lied. (pause) Waking up to vomit and lying to your kids isn't the life you are looking for. (*E* looks up)

E: (firmly) No, it's not. This wasn't the first time I had a blackout. Before I got my life together, I spent a lot of time drunk. My kids often saw me passed out on the coach. (pause; firmly) I am not going to get drunk again! I am through with that trap.

C: You sound determined not to get drunk. (*E* nods) How hard is this going to be?

E: (firmly, looking down) I don't drink. (pause; looking up) I mean, I hadn't had any alcohol since I realized I was gay. (confused) But when I went to that bar I just fell back into the bottle.

C: You look confused.

E: (softly) Yes, I am. I spent most of my life hiding from myself. (long pause; firmly) Now that I know who I am, my hiding is over. So, why did I get drunk?

C: It felt as if the new you, who understood yourself, would not make this kind of mistake.

E: (long pause; looking up at *C*) Am I strong or not?

C: Do strong people ever struggle to understand themselves? Do they always know what to do?

E: (sadly) I guess that is unrealistic. (long pause) I said it's okay to have sex with a woman—even when Frank yelled at me that it isn't. That made me feel so strong I assumed nothing could go wrong again.

C: That would have been so great. (pause) After all you had to go through in the past, to finally be free of insecurity and pain.

E: (long pause; agitated) I was so scared about talking to another lesbian, I had to get drunk. (strong) That is why I am here. I am facing my fears from now on, not using alcohol to cover them up.

C: You are turning to treatment, not alcohol, for help. (long pause) Is there anything else helping you avoid the alcohol trap?

E: (thoughtfully) My boys deserve an attentive mother. They have never done well in school. (pause; painfully) I have been so caught up with my own struggles that I neglected them like my parents did me. My mother was always drunk. I didn't want to be like her, but I was. I never helped them with their homework—even when teachers wrote me notes. They were held back last year, and (pause; choked up) it made them so unhappy. (long pause; determinedly) I let myself be drunk and uncaring—that's over.

C: Your concern for your boys increases your determination not to drink. (*E* nods) You are willing to struggle to understand yourself and be a good parent.

E: (firmly) Yes, I am determined to help myself and my kids. (anxiously) There is so much I don't know about being a good mother. I feed and clothe them, but that's about it. I notice sometimes they look unhappy, but I don't know what to do. Chances are, something happens and I end up just screaming at them—I sound just like my dad and I hate that! I know, (choked up) deep down, they need a better mom. (sobbing)

C: (long pause) There is so much pain in this room; it comes from deep within you.

E: (tearfully) My boys need more than a drunk for a mother. They have had to wake me up, when I was in a drunken sleep, so I could get them something to eat. I've already been such a bad mother. (fearfully, sinking in the chair) How will they react if they know I'm a lesbian? Frank has said such terrible things. Will they think he's right? He just wants me back, but he is doing a terrible thing to talk that way about me.

C: So much pain. (pause) So much worry. (pause) Your body looks like it is trying to hide in the chair. (long pause)

E: (shakily) No, I can't. (sits up) I can't hide. That would be the old me; the one who neglected her kids and stayed with Frank even though it felt wrong. The new me is going to learn to be a good mom. (pause) But my stomach churns every time I try to be strong and tell the boys I'm gay. (looking down) They have to know. (anxiously) I want them to accept me and love me for who I am.

C: It would be frightening to think they will react like Frank. (long pause) You worry they won't love you anymore. (long pause) They loved you when you were drunk in bed. They came to you for food; they knew you would get it for them. Could they have this same confidence in you as a sober, lesbian mom? (long pause)

E: (looking up; strong and clear) Yes, they could. (pause) The home Frank and I built together has been a miserable place. Frank and I should have divorced years ago. If I give the boys a predictable, happy home, there should be more love, not less. But I don't always feel strong enough to do it. I can get so lonely; it is just so hard for me to meet new people. Frank calls and says he knows I am alone and feeling bad. (long pause) He wants the sad, submissive me—even though she was a drunk. (confused) I need more, but I don't know how I will get it.

C: Married to Frank, you knew things weren't right. (pause) You tried to find your way out through alcohol, but you know that was just a trap. You have a growing awareness of what you need, but not how to get it. Frank doesn't understand that things have to change.

E: (soft) The change just started on its own. I was in the hospital yet again for alcohol poisoning. After pumping me up with IV fluids, the doctors and nurses started asking me the same questions they always did about my drinking. (long pause; amazed) There was one doctor who was a young, attractive woman; I was very aware of her. That was it. I understood myself. (pause) I was a lesbian. It felt so good all day long to know myself—even though I was in the hospital. (pause) But the nights are so hard for me: The boys are asleep, I am alone. (softly) I ache with it. Frank calls; he is lonely too. (pause) He says he will always want me.

C: You and Frank help each other not feel lonely. You tried that way; it wasn't enough. Inside (pause) it always felt wrong. (long pause) Now you know why it didn't work with Frank.

E: (long pause, shaking herself energetically) Knowing I'm a lesbian didn't solve all my problems, but it did make it easy to quit drinking. Sober, I know I don't want to keep using Frank.

C: Your body had blended into the chair and your voice sounded so demoralized when you were talking about Frank. Now you seem taller as you talk of how self-knowledge has helped you. In your face, I can see the freedom you feel after accepting something so intrinsic to yourself—your sexuality. It has energized and freed you to explore your life.

E: (ambivalent) Yes, I do feel free sometimes, but I also feel so scared and confused. Frank keeps saying that being a lesbian is my problem. My dad was so homophobic. He was so insulting to anyone he thought might be gay. Once he beat a guy up just because he thought he was gay. (tensely, loudly) Frank said you would cure me of this lesbian thing and then I would come back home!

C: You felt so free until Frank denied your sexuality. He thinks you need to be cured of it. Your dad might beat you up if he knew. Are you wondering if I agree with your dad and Frank?

E: (long pause, softly) Do you?

C: No, I don't. (pause) As I look at you, your body seems to be saying something. Can you allow yourself to focus on what your body is saying right now?

E: (long pause) I feel so tense and so angry. (pause) I have to let go of it or people will move away from me, and I am lonely enough.

C: I won't move away if you want to experience your anger more.

E: (long pause; speaking furiously) I am just boiling inside a lot of the time. Frank likes me as a drunk. I was a punching bag for my dad. My mom ignored me most of the time because she was a drunk—I wanted her to help me and she never did. (body rigid) I have no one who will accept me for myself.

C: Your body looks so tight and controlled.

E: (strongly, body rigid) It feels terrible. I have to stop.

C: You can stop anytime, (pause) but your feelings are part of you. Maybe it needs to feel terrible for a while. Your dad abused you, your mom neglected you, Frank is saying you have to go back to being a drunk. You feel *boiling hot*. (long pause) That sounds so hot, so intense, yet you look contained, as if no steam is rising from your boiling insides.

E: (panicky) I can't let the steam out; I might explode.

C: Your dad did explode; he treated you like a punching bag, not a child who needed a father to care about her. (Ellen nods and sobs) There is so much anger inside you. Will it destroy you to experience it more?

E: (tensely) I can control it, push it down.

C: You can control your anger. It is yours to control. Yet it may have something important to tell you.

E: (tensely) I don't want to hurt anyone.

C: Does anger have to lead to you punching someone? (*E* looks intently at *C*) Anger doesn't have to be dangerous.

E: (puzzled) What if you're wrong?

C: I could be wrong. Only you know for sure. Do you have thoughts of harming others?

E: (intent) No. I might yell, but I have never hit my kids or anyone else. (long pause, looking furious) When I let myself think about it, I am angry at all of them—Frank included. I was getting drunk all the time. Obviously, I was in trouble and needed help, yet no one seemed to notice or care!

C: You look angry now. (pause) You sounded angry. (long pause) Yet, you aren't boiling over into violence. (long pause) What might this mean?

E: (pause) I am a lonely person, but I have never hit anyone. I don't want to explode and yell at my kids or yell at Frank. (long pause) I want acceptance. I want them to love me, care about me, (pause) even lesbian me.

C: You deserve acceptance.

E: (softly) I need it to be okay with everyone that I'm a lesbian. If I could feel safe about retaining custody of my boys . . . (long pause; looking off in space)

C: Why are you looking away? (long pause) Are you afraid you will lose custody?

E: (softly) I don't know. Frank has never threatened me directly with it. But he wants me back. He has made some teasing comments to the kids that are homophobic. When he finally realizes I'm not coming back, (whispering) he might become spiteful—he can be that way.

C: Your voice has gotten softer and softer.

E: (painfully) I heard nothing but insults about lesbians as I grew up. I guess this is part of why I hid from myself for so long. If it came to a court fight, my father would definitely work against me. My mom, (pause) I always wish she would be on my side, but she would be too afraid to contradict my dad. He would beat and rape her — I could hear her screams. (pause) What would the judge do if Frank said he had to get the kids because I was a bad influence? (questioningly) What if I just denied the truth in court, (pause) just said I made it up to punish Frank?

C: You sound ambivalent.

E: (firmly) I don't want to lie. I've done that for too long. I want my kids to know who I am and understand it's all right. One of them might be gay. I wouldn't want either of my sons to suffer like I have. I want them to like themselves.

C: Self-acceptance is important.

E: (painfully, sinking down into the chair) I'll be in chaos if I lie again. I might drink again. (long pause; sitting up, shaking herself, confidently) No. I won't do that. Things are going to be different. I have a plan to stay strong. I am coming here. And, I'm starting with changing my name.

C: I felt despair turn to something else when you mentioned a new name.

E: (smiling) I have created a new name for myself. I hated my dad. He was an alcoholic and abusive I don't want his name. My marriage to Frank was really a lie, so his name isn't mine either. I am going to create my own name to mark my new beginnings.

C: I can really feel your power as you talk about this.

E: (smiling) I do feel more important somehow when I consider what name to pick.

C: You're smiling. You look relaxed.

E: (sincerely) I know what I want even though I'm not sure how to start, (pause) but I'm not going into a coma this time to avoid feeling lonely.

C: Lonely feels bad, but being in a coma is worse—you lose yourself. There is so much excitement ahead as you come out of the coma and truly experience life.

E: (long pause; anxiously) I'm going to need help.

C: I'm here. (pause; *E* smiles) You smiled and sank lower in that chair.

E: It's such a relief that Frank was wrong. You aren't going to make me change.

C: You were afraid that I wouldn't accept you or accept your goals for yourself. (*E* nods) You feel good about yourself as a lesbian. You feel more personal control, and you're symbolizing it by picking a new name. (*E* nods) What's confusing is how to integrate this new understanding of yourself into finding a romantic partner, becoming an attentive mother, and finding out how to relate to Frank and your parents.

E: (smiling) Yes. (pause) Thank you for listening!

Emotion-Focused Case Conceptualization of Ellen: Assumption-Based Style

Ellen grew up in an abusive and neglectful environment that led her to develop a global style of inhibiting her experience of emotions and being inattentive to her bodily felt senses. This made it difficult for her to develop healthy, fully articulated emotion schemes for guiding her behavior. Instead, many are incomplete or maladaptive. For example, Ellen developed an overly articulated emotion scheme around a desire for physical safety. In this scheme, she experiences fear when a man becomes angry, has cognitions that she must behave submissively or will be in danger, speaks quietly and agrees with whatever the man says, looks down so as not to challenge his power, and provides sexual services if required. In addition, for developing emotional intimacy, Ellen had only an incomplete scheme consisting of feelings of loneliness and a longing for emotional connection. It had no cognitions for interpreting what was dysfunctional about her parents' relationship or how to reach out to others without being drunk. Her emotion scheme around her sexuality revolved around an unclear felt sense she couldn't label and cognitions that were homophobic. Recently, Ellen has become more in touch with her emotions and bodily sensations that are relevant to her sexuality. She has been able to label her previously unclear felt sense as sexual arousal. This processing has led to a more complete scheme that now includes the motivation to develop a sexual relationship with another woman. Unfortunately, Ellen still doesn't have any adaptive behavior to use in approaching another woman, so she abused alcohol again to do so. Despite her brief relapse into dysfunctional behavior, Ellen's greater awareness of her sexuality feels very good to her. Ellen is ready to further retreat from her global processing style of over-controlling her emotions. She has contacted a clinician to gain help in developing positive new self-identities as a lesbian woman, partner, and mother. She wants to raise her sons free of homophobia. Her greater openness to emotional processing bodes well for her being able to process even more of her experiences for constructive meanings so that she can transform more of her maladaptive emotion schemes into functional ones.

Ellen developed a global processing style of suppressing her emotions as a result of her abusive and neglectful upbringing. This style was most heavily reinforced by her overly articulated safety scheme. She developed this scheme in response to intense fear of her father, and it contained cognitions that she must be submissive if a man is angry, speak quietly and agree with whatever a man says to her, look down to not challenge his power, and provide sexual services if required. While Ellen was never involved in sexual activities with her father, she witnessed many acts of sexual violence perpetrated by her father on her mother; thus, she came to expect that men might both beat her and sexually assault her. Ellen describes her father as physically abusive and someone who treated her like a punching bag. She describes her mother as someone who ignored her most of the time—someone who was more interested in alcohol than in parenting. To escape the fear, pain, and anger that these relationships caused her, Ellen learned to withdraw into herself and not feel her emotions of pain (be numb) rather than allowing herself to be aware of a litany of negative emotions. Whenever the emotions threatened to spill over into her awareness, Ellen used alcohol to keep them under control. To Ellen, awareness of emotions meant being overwhelmed by them and perhaps harming someone else. To let go of her global processing style of "nonexperiencing," Ellen needs support in learning how to regulate her emotions of anger, loneliness, and love so that they can guide her effectively rather than overwhelm her. While she is frightened of her emotions, the positive impact that she has experienced, after being aware of her sexual attraction to a female doctor, motivates her to take the risk of being more emotionally attuned.

To develop emotional intimacy, Ellen has only an incomplete emotion scheme consisting of feelings of loneliness and a longing for connection. She has only inchoate thoughts of wanting closeness. She never saw any signs of emotional closeness in her parents' behavior toward her or toward each other. Her father's social behavior around the house was either physical or verbal abuse. Her mother was either being victimized or getting drunk. Ellen could not learn any healthy emotional connection skills from them. Ellen describes herself as having always wanted more relationships with people but being too shy to initiate these relationships. She met Frank early in her life. Frank recognized the loneliness in Ellen and approached her. Ellen quickly fell into the pattern of letting him be the initiator of all their social interactions in order to avoid her paralyzing anxiety. Frank didn't seem to care that she became an alcoholic and submissive wife. He still wants her this way. In the past, she was too grateful not to be alone to question why. Ellen allowed herself to believe, on and off for 10 years, that she had a friend and partner in Frank and would not be lonely again. Episodically, she could not avoid the recognition that her marriage was not satisfying to her. At these times, she would leave Frank. However, she only had to be lonely for a short time before he would lure her back into their relationship. While he has never done anything to actively harm her, he has insisted that if she is a lesbian, she must change. He has begun to make teasing comments in front of the children that are homophobic. While this frightens her, on the other hand it has also brought out her confidence that she will not return to a life of numbness. She also doesn't want her children hearing homophobic comments in case her boys might one day find out they are gay. This might be the beginning of an emotion scheme for a more self-confident Ellen who is a champion for her children's welfare.

While motivated to be a good parent, Ellen's emotion scheme for intimacy does not contain any behaviors for acting as an effective parent. It contains only guidance for how not to act; she knows she must not ignore her children and she knows she must not beat them. However, she learned nothing growing up about how to be a responsive parent who could effectively guide her children's behavior. While adult Ellen has been successful at not physically abusing her children, she does lose control of her anger and yell at them a great deal—like her father yelled at her. When she knows they have done badly at school or is aware that she has let them down, she numbs herself with a bottle like her mother did. She criticizes herself for yelling at her children, being drunk in front of them, and not helping them with their schoolwork. However, she doesn't praise herself for feeding, clothing, and bathing them. Somehow she has managed to teach them that, even drunk, she will feed them if they let her know they are hungry. Thus, some of her parenting behaviors are likely to be better than she currently perceives them to be. At the least, she is aware that it is important for children to learn in school, that parents should help their children with schoolwork, and that her children's suffering at school is a problem. This knowledge may form the basis for a healthy emotion scheme around her mothering. Ellen fears that Frank will try to take custody of her children from her if she refuses to go back to him. While Frank never threatened to do this when she was a drunken mother, she has observed him being vindictive with others. She fears he will become vindictive toward her if she denies him a sexual relationship, and he has made teasing homophobic comments to suggest that he has begun to think about it. While she considers hiding her sexuality from the court if it comes to a custody fight, her greater awareness of the impact of lying on her sense of herself may prevent her from doing so. Ellen has come out of a state of emotional confusion, and it bodes well for her future that she does not want to return to this state.

Until recently, the only emotion scheme guiding Ellen's sexuality directly involved an unclear felt sense she couldn't label and cognitions that were homophobic. In addition to harming her physically, her father was verbally abusive, and among his hateful comments were many slurs against sexual minorities. These comments, coming from someone who terrified her, further numbed Ellen's ability to recognize any of the cues within her body regarding her lesbianism. It was only recently that Ellen suddenly became in tune with her bodily sensations of sexual arousal. She has now been able to put her sexual attraction for a female doctor into words and realize she is a lesbian. Prior to this insight, Ellen had worked hard to suppress all her emotions. She had assumed that if she experienced emotions, she would lose control of them, like her father always did. However, when she was attracted to the female doctor, she was able to regulate her emotions of attraction, she kept them to herself, and she did not harm anyone.

Ellen was involved in an unsatisfying heterosexual marriage for 10 years. The only emotion that Ellen had allowed herself to be aware of was loneliness. Her response to these physical signs was to engage in sexual relations with Frank, the one and only close friend she has ever had. While this removed her immediate sensations of loneliness, her intimate relationship with Frank was never fully satisfying to her. She had an unclear felt sense that it was not right for her. However, whenever she attempted to move away from this relationship and explore this unclear felt sense, her fear of loneliness drove her back to Frank. Self-knowledge may have been gradually building over the years, but she felt as if it came at her in a rush when she was in the emergency room. Her unclear sense of "wrongness" seemed to disappear as she became aware of how good she felt as she contemplated her new understanding of herself as a lesbian. Suddenly, her failures in feeling satisfied with her relationship with Frank made sense as being due to sexual orientation rather than to a lack of competence as a sexual partner. The greater sense of competence and completeness that this self-awareness has brought her has increased her motivation to understand herself further and to help her boys develop the skills they will need to understand themselves fully as sexual beings.

Ellen was raised in an abusive and neglectful environment where, for her own safety, she developed a global processing style of repressing her emotions. She used a limited voice and, when interacting with others, always kept her emotions under tight control. She believed that expressions of emotion always led to danger to others, and Ellen didn't want to ever harm her children. Despite her long history of alcoholism, a window of opportunity has opened up that may end Ellen's need for alcohol once and for all. This window opened because of an empowering experience that caught Ellen completely by surprise. While getting treatment in the hospital, Ellen felt a rush of sexual arousal toward another woman.

As a result of this positive experience with her emotions, Ellen has begun accepting parts of herself that she forced out of her conscious awareness as a developing child. The pleasure she has gained from this awareness of her sexuality has motivated her to choose therapy, over alcohol, as her new strategy for gaining a coherent sense of herself. However, she is still new to allowing herself to experience her emotions and becomes quickly overwhelmed. The clinician will need to be attentive to signs that Ellen has had enough experiencing for the moment so that Ellen doesn't relapse back into abusing alcohol. In her evolving sense of herself, Ellen has begun taking a series of constructive actions to make being a lesbian a part of the solution to her problems. To further symbolize this transformation, Ellen has created a new last name for herself to highlight the beginning of her new self-awareness. This is a positive sign that this may be Ellen's time to truly learn to accept herself.

Emotion-Focused Treatment Plan: Assumption-Based Style

Treatment Plan Overview. Ellen needs help in further processing her experiences so that she develops a flexible processing style where she can experience her emotions at levels appropriate to the situations that she is in. Long-Term Goal 1 is designed to help her become aware of her gut reaction to withdraw from any person or situation that evokes an emotional response from her. It is likely that she will need to proceed at least partially through this goal before proceeding to the other goals in her plan. However, she will be allowed to process any aspect of her experience that is most present for her at any time rather than following these goals in any predefined order. Long-Term Goals 1 through 3 will each focus on one of the three emotion schemes that is guiding most of her behavior at this time. She has an overly articulated emotion scheme around safety as a result of her abusive upbringing, an incomplete scheme for supporting emotional intimacy, and an incomplete scheme for guiding her behavior as a lesbian woman. (This treatment plan follows the *problem format*.)

PROBLEM: Ellen prefers to escape from her emotions rather than experience them.

LONG-TERM GOAL 1: Ellen will become fully aware of her global processing style of distancing herself from her emotions.

Short-Term Goals

1. Ellen will become aware of the last incident in which her father frightened her and describe it in as much detail as possible.

2. Ellen will articulate what she is feeling in her body as she describes this incident.

3. Ellen will become aware of her gut reaction to this incident in terms of where she wants to look, what she hopes to hear, and what she would prefer to do.

4. Ellen will become aware of the last incident in which she felt tremendously lonely and describe it as much detail as possible.

5. Ellen will articulate what she is feeling in her body as she describes this incident.

6. Ellen will become aware of her gut reaction to this incident in terms of where she wants to look, what she hopes to hear, and what she would prefer to do.

7. Ellen will become aware of the last incident in which she felt she had to have sexual relations with Frank.

8. Ellen will articulate what she is feeling in her body as she describes this incident.

9. Ellen will become aware of her gut reaction to this incident in terms of where she wants to look, what she hopes to hear, and what she would prefer to do.

10. Ellen will consider any patterns in how she responded to these incidents.

11. Ellen will consider if this pattern of behavior is helping her achieve her goals of being a good woman, a good mother, and a good sexual partner.

12. Other goals will be added if needed to support Ellen in recognizing that she responds to all emotions with the gut reaction of withdrawal.

LONG-TERM GOAL 2: Ellen will become fully aware of her safety emotion scheme so that she can decide if it needs to be modified to adaptively guide her as a lesbian adult who interacts with both violent and nonviolent individuals.

Short-Term Goals

1. Ellen will become aware of the last time she remembers being terrified of her father.

2. Ellen will become aware of the sensations she is having in her body as she gets in touch with her fears of her father.

3. Ellen will stay with the sensations she is experiencing in the moment and put her fear into words.

4. Ellen will articulate the sensations she has in her body as she gets fully in touch with her fear.

5. Ellen will articulate any further meaning that she associates with these experiences.

6. Ellen will consider whether her safety scheme is guiding her effectively in any current encounters with her father.

7. Ellen will consider whether her safety scheme is guiding her effectively in her relationship with Frank.

8. Ellen will consider whether her safety scheme is guiding her effectively in her relationship with men who are not violent.

9. Ellen will consider whether her safety scheme will guide her effectively as her sons enter adolescence and become man sized.

10. Ellen will process these experiences for further meaning and modify or change her safety scheme as appropriate to the person she's interacting with.

11. Other goals will be added as needed to support Ellen in developing a flexible safety scheme that guides her effectively in both violence and nonviolent relationships.

LONG-TERM GOAL 3: Ellen will fully articulate her emotional intimacy scheme so that it can guide her effectively as a lesbian mother.

Short-Term Goals

1. Ellen will become aware of the last incident she can remember in which she longed for an emotional connection with her mother.

2. Ellen will become aware of the sensations she feels in her body as she thinks about her relationship with her mother.

3. Ellen will symbolize these sensations in words.

4. Ellen will articulate any motivations that she has to begin, leave alone, or end her relationship with her mother.

5. Ellen will derive more meaning from her prior experiences with her mother and decide whether, as a lesbian adult, she wants to continue seeking emotional intimacy from her mother or seek this out from another older, adult woman who might be more able to respond to her overtures in an adaptive manner.

6. Ellen will become aware of the last incident she can remember in which she longed for a better emotional connection with one of her sons.

7. Ellen will fully explore the sensations she feels in her body as she remembers this incident.

8. Ellen will symbolize these feelings in words.

9. Ellen will fully explore the feeling of numbness that she had the last time she was drunk while parenting her sons.

10. Ellen will fully explore the sensations in her body as she remembers this incident.

11. Ellen will symbolize these sensations in words.

12. Ellen will describe any motivations that she has as a result of this emotional processing.

13. Ellen will focus her attention on her desire to be an active and helpful parent.

14. Ellen will fully explore the sensations in her body as she thinks about being an active and helpful parent.

15. Ellen will put into words her desire to be an active parent and what she would like to say to her children about her past parenting as well as what she would like to say to them about the new type of relationship she seeks to build with them.

16. Other goals will be developed as needed to support Ellen in developing healthy, age-appropriate emotional intimacy with others.

LONG-TERM GOAL 4: Ellen will fully articulate her sexuality scheme so that it can guide her effectively as a lesbian woman.

Short-Term Goals

1. Ellen will vividly recall her visit to the emergency room, particularly the moment she became aware of the sexually attractive doctor.

2. Ellen will explore the bodily sensations that she experiences as she vividly recalls this experience.

3. Ellen will symbolize these bodily sensations in words.

4. Ellen will articulate any fears that she has that the clinician will reject her or try to change her into a heterosexual.

5. Ellen will explore the sensations that she has in her body as she considers whether the clinician is homophobic.

6. Ellen will symbolize these sensations in words.

7. Ellen will consider the meaning it might have for her if the clinician, like Frank, did not consider her to be a lesbian.

8. Ellen will vividly recall the incident when she got drunk in order to be able to approach another lesbian.

9. Ellen will explore the sensations that she has in her body as she remembers her revulsion the next day.

10. Ellen will symbolize these sensations in words.

11. Ellen will articulate any action tendencies that she has as a result of vividly remembering this incident.

12. Ellen will fully process her same-sex experience for adaptive meaning and develop a plan for how to be fully ready to engage in a respectful and enjoyable same-sex experience.

13. Other goals will be added as needed to help Ellen develop a healthy sexual relationship with another lesbian adult.

Emotion-Focused Case Conceptualization of Ellen: Interpersonally Based Style

In the past, Ellen's views of how to relate to a romantic partner, how to be a good mother, and how to relate to herself were based on the assumption that she was heterosexual. In this regard, Ellen saw herself as a loser who had been a failure as a wife and a mother. In processing these experiences, she used a global style of avoiding her emotions; her alcohol abuse served to support this style. However, it left her with deep-seated fears of loneliness and unresolved anger. Recently, these negative perceptions and feelings about herself have undergone a substantial change. Her awareness of her internal experiences has deepened, and this has led her to the recognition that she is a lesbian. Through this greater self-knowledge, she has reevaluated the meaning of her past "failures." She has realized that a denial of internal experience around her sexuality was a root cause of her difficulties. Although her self-awareness has grown, she continues to overregulate her emotions. She needs help fully processing the meaning her lesbianism has for her within her relationships with an intimate partner, her children, and her extended family. Ellen's strengths lie in her increased awareness of the value of attending to her internal experiences, her recognition and acceptance of her sexual feelings for other women, and her trust in her internal felt sense of "wrongness" when she was drunk that led her to stop drinking.

Ellen learned recently that she wants to relate to another woman in an intimate relationship. She had entered a hospital for treatment of alcohol abuse. Surprisingly, she found herself sexually attracted to her female, attending doctor. This triggered a deeper understanding of a previously unclear felt sense around her sexuality. This increased understanding helped her construct an understanding of why she had "failed" to establish a satisfying intimate relationship with her husband. She has tried to reach out to form new relationships based on her greater sexual awareness. She found, however, that she could reach out only when abusing alcohol because she was afraid and conflicted about how to behave. In reflecting on her experience after an alcohol-precipitated date, she recognizes that it "felt wrong." Processing this problematic reaction point on her own, Ellen recognizes that her behavior was not congruent with her motivation to respect herself within her relationships with others. She recognizes that she is unsure of how to guide herself to develop a healthy intimate relationship.

Ellen has reflected on her past romantic relationship with Frank and recognizes that he did not provide her with the type of support she wants from a romantic partner. She wants support for being a more aware person, and he was satisfied with her being numb and drunk. After constant avoidance, she has finally allowed herself to become aware of how her fear of loneliness led her to be involved in a 10-year marriage in an unhappy home. Having sex with Frank kept her from feeling lonely in the moment but wasn't enough to ward off her deep, aching vulnerability. Frank was underaware of her desire to be a good mother and didn't show concern over her self-destructive use of alcohol. She did try to separate from him many times, but her fear of loneliness would always send her back. Similarly, Ellen has remained in contact with her parents despite their inability, or lack of interest, in meeting her physical and emotional needs. Currently, Ellen recognizes that Frank and her father are both homophobic and might fight her in court for custody of her sons if she maintains a lesbian identity. Frank has never directly threatened her with this, but she fears he may turn on her and "be spiteful" if she clearly rebuffs his desire for reconciliation and openly maintains a lesbian identity. Ellen's concern about a custody fight represents a realistic fear, as some judges have made homophobic custody decisions. Despite her fear of losing custody, Ellen is aware that she cannot return to a time when she denies her own needs as a human being. Her strengths lie in her desire for self-acceptance and her recognition that her boys need to learn how to accept their own sexual selves as well; she doesn't want to be a bad role model for them. She doesn't know what to do, but she does know that numbing her feelings with alcohol is not the answer and that running back to Frank to momentarily escape loneliness isn't either. While still feeling confused about what actions to take, a strength Ellen brings to this challenge is her increased awareness that, in the past, she entered into relationships out of a sense of loneliness and vulnerability and gave in to the wishes of others to gain their acceptance. Her deep craving to remain true to herself and relate authentically to others, when more completely processed, will help her discover the behaviors she needs to actualize this motivation.

Ellen has come to recognize that she was an uninvolved and passive mother. She came to these conclusions after focusing her awareness more intensely on her parenting behavior and her children's welfare. She recognized that, while her boys have been experiencing problems in school for a long time, she never helped them with their schoolwork and did not request any meetings with their teachers to try to assess what help her children needed. Ellen also has some awareness that she was neglected as a child by her mother and only screamed at or beaten by her father. She hasn't processed these experiences beyond a vague sense that she doesn't want to parent like they did, but she has not constructed meaning that would help her parent her own children in a positive way. Ellen may have a self-evaluative split in which "a critical voice" demeans her past mothering behavior while a "passive voice" plaintively expresses confusion over how to do things differently. Ellen needs to fully integrate and accept both aspects of herself as a mother. This will facilitate her search for parenting behaviors that will enhance her boys' welfare. She is also unsure if, or how, her lesbianism should influence her parenting, and when and how she should explain her sexuality to her boys. Her strengths, as she seeks to develop a positive mothering role, lie in her recognition that for her boys to develop a positive sense of themselves as males, they need to respect their own internal experiences; she does not want them to undergo the same struggles in understanding their sexuality that she has undergone in understanding hers. In addition, she may have begun to develop an emotion scheme around effective parenting as signified by her inchoate hopes that she has the potential to develop into a good mother. Her concern for her boys has also increased her resolve to avoid alcohol, as it previously served as a barrier to her taking constructive actions.

Ellen has recently developed a stronger relationship with herself as a result of trusting her internal experience and discovering the truth about her sexuality. Prior to this, Ellen used alcohol to keep herself unaware, or only partially aware, of many of her internal experiences; this prevented her from developing a positive identity and engaging in constructive relationships with others. Her fears of rejection and loneliness were the motivations behind her using alcohol as a barrier to fully processing her experiences. Her mental numbness has now ended. Despite continuing to be fearful, her increased sense of agency and her desire for self-determination are propelling her toward adaptive growth. She has been empowered by exploring her feelings and trusting her intuitions about herself. She is symbolizing this change by selecting a new last name to identify herself with. Thinking about this name fills her with feelings of confidence and excitement. Fully articulating this fledgling emotion scheme may help further power positive self-growth. A barrier to her continued growth at this time is her realistic fears about losing custody of her sons as an "out" lesbian mother. However, she is open to personal collaboration with someone who is willing to listen and treat her self-knowledge with respect. She is highly motivated to continue on her path of self-discovery through processing her experiences for constructive and life-enhancing meaning.

Emotion-Focused Treatment Plan: Interpersonally Based Style

Treatment Plan Overview. Ellen's long-term goals are interpersonal in nature. They may be refined or refocused as treatment progresses and she comes to a deeper understanding of her feelings and needs. Ellen will determine which interpersonal relationship is a focus of the treatment session at any given time. The clinician will need to monitor Ellen's alcohol usage due to her past history of abuse. (This treatment plan follows the *basic format.*)

LONG-TERM GOAL 1: Ellen will fully explore how to relate to other adults in a same-sex, intimate relationship.

Short-Term Goals

1. Ellen will fully process the problematic reaction she had when she was drunk and on her first lesbian date.
   a. She will intensify the feeling of "wrongness" and put into words how this experience served to increase her motivation to respect herself when relating to a lesbian partner.
   b. Ellen will intensify her feeling of fear in initiating same-sex relationships and put into words the relationships between this fear, her abuse of alcohol on her date, and her feeling of "wrongness."

2. Ellen will become aware of her feelings of loneliness and experience how quickly they intensify in terms of their accompanying bodily sensations.
   a. Ellen will articulate the cognitions accompanying these sensations.
   b. Ellen will consider how the intensity of these emotions may have stopped her from trying to form new relationships.

3. Ellen will fully process her feelings of "wrongness," fear, and loneliness to develop constructive meaning that will guide her to take actions that might bring a feeling of "rightness" when on a date.

LONG-TERM GOAL 2: Ellen will explore how to relate to her children as a lesbian parent.

Short-Tem Goals

1. Ellen will fully explore her conflicting cognitions of self-criticism and passivity through personifying them and taking turns speaking with the voice of each one until they are fully understood.
   a. Ellen will become aware of her body as she takes on the role of each voice and identify the emotion, motivation, and action tendencies that go along with these physical sensations.
   b. Ellen will draw new meaning from this processing that allows her to accept the constructive aspects of both voices into her parenting.

2. Ellen will fully explore her inchoate hopes and feelings of determination around parenting.
   a. Ellen will put these feelings into words that describe her beliefs about being an effective parent.
   b. Ellen will focus attention on her desire to be an active parent and consider what types of actions might bring this desire to fruition.

3. Ellen will explore the confusing thoughts she has about coming out to her sons, including her fear that her boys will hate her for being a lesbian.
   a. Ellen will put into words her concern that her boys may internalize homophobic ideas and hate themselves if they are gay if she remains closeted until they are adults.
   b. Ellen will fully explore the outcomes that might result from coming out and the meaning these outcomes would have for her and decide on a course of action.

LONG-TERM GOAL 3: Ellen will explore the contradictory feelings guiding her in relating to her ex-husband and extended family members as a lesbian family member.

Short-Term Goals

1. Ellen will explore the boiling-over-with-anger feeling that she experiences in her relationships with her ex-husband and extended family through focusing on her bodily sensations as her anger builds.
   a. Ellen will put into words the motivation that comes from this experience and whether it is tied to others wanting her to be submissive and not true to herself.
   b. Ellen will fully process her more deeply understood anger and determine if directly communicating her needs to family members would serve her well at this time.

2. Ellen will explore the vulnerable feelings of pain and isolation that she has when relating to her ex-husband and extended family through experiencing these feelings vividly.
   a. Ellen will put into words the motivation that comes from this experience.

    b. Ellen will construct meaning from this vividly re-created experience and decide whether it would be adaptive to try to change her role in relating to her ex-husband and extended family at this time.

3. Ellen will become aware of how her feelings of pain and isolation are motivating her to behave very differently than are her feelings of anger in trying to relate to her ex-husband and parents.

    a. Ellen will focus her attention first on her motivation to approach them (to avoid the pain of isolation) and then on her motivation to avoid them (to increase her sense of personal control and self-affirmation).

    b. Ellen will further process these discrepant tendencies until she can develop meaning that will guide her adaptively at this time of self-discovery when she has realistic concerns about losing custody of her sons.

LONG-TERM GOAL 4: Ellen will explore her feelings of confidence and excitement evoked by her new name and how this influences her relationship to herself as a lesbian.

Short-Term Goals

1. Ellen will reexperience her feelings of confidence and excitement associated with her new name.

    a. Ellen will use words to describe what this new name means to her, including her motivations and behaviors in regard to it.

    b. Ellen will consider whether alcohol will be a part of this newly named person's life.

    c. Ellen will consider whether heterosexual behavior will ever be a part of this newly named person's life.

2. Ellen will reexperience the feelings of freedom and self-acceptance that occurred when she recognized her new sexual motivation, allowing herself the psychological space to stay fully aware of these emotions.

    a. Ellen will use words to describe the meaning these feelings have for her.

    b. Ellen will consider what behaviors will be most valuable to her in maintaining these positive emotions.

    c. Ellen will discuss her new narrative of herself, how she wants to interact with others, and how she will maintain a healthy lifestyle.

PRACTICE CASE FOR STUDENT CONCEPTUALIZATION: INTEGRATING THE DOMAIN OF VIOLENCE

It is time to do an emotion-focused analysis of Nicole. There are many domains of complexity that might provide insights into her behavior. For this case, you are asked to integrate the domain of violence into your case conceptualization and treatment plan.

Information Received From Brief Intake

Nicole is an 18-year-old White female living in a rural town. She is presently a senior in high school. She has an excellent academic record and will be attending college next year. She comes from a nuclear family in which she has three older brothers who are still living at home. Her father is the proprietor of a car mechanic's shop, and his sons work for him. Nicole says that her father and brothers have made a lifestyle out of beating women, including herself and her mother. She now has the opportunity to leave home and move in with her boyfriend, Tim; however, she is afraid to go. She wants help making the decision about whether she should leave or stay.

Nicole referred herself for treatment after completing a high school psychology course. Her parents are not aware that she has sought treatment, and Nicole wants this information kept private. During a brief mental status exam, there were no clinical signs of homicidal or suicidal ideation or severe psychopathology. However, Nicole showed some anxiety when the limits of confidentiality were raised. This anxiety subsided when she was reassured that, at 18, she is no longer under the purview of child protective services. She preferred to receive help from the first clinician who had an opening.

Interview With Nicole (N) From an Emotion-Focused Perspective

C: Hello, Nicole. How can I help?

N: (earnestly) My boyfriend is pressuring me to move in with him when we graduate this spring. (confused) I don't know what to tell him. (pause) We've been hanging out together since our freshman year. He's really my best and only friend, but . . . (pause)

C: (pause) But . . . (pause)

N: (uncertainly) I do care, but he wants more, and I don't know if I can give it.

C: He wants more than friendship, and you aren't sure if you do.

N: (certain) I do want him physically. This edgy feeling just overwhelms me whenever I think of having sex with him. Just kissing is hard enough.

C: Do you know what this edginess means?

N: (anxiously) I don't know, and whenever I have tried to talk to Tim about it, he gets angry and avoids me for a while. (pause) Then we just forget about it.

C: It's confusing. You don't really understand it and haven't been able to work it through. Would you like to try to experience it more now?

N: (long pause, then panicky) It's like my skin is crawling. I feel doomed. (whispering) I am not going to keep doing this.

C: (pause) When you experienced it more, it went beyond edgy into something threatening that you had to get away from.

N: (anxiously) This is just great. I come here to get help for this, and I can't stand talking about it. (pause) I am such a loser.

C: The feeling is overwhelming now, but does this mean it always will be?

N: (sadly) Do you think this is a waste of time?

C: You want to work it out, but at this particular moment it feels too hard.

N: (tentatively) Maybe if we talk about something else first, I can handle it later.

C: What feels right to discuss?

N: (long pause; anxiously) I want you to tell me everything is going to work out.

C: It would feel reassuring if I could promise that.

N: (sadly) You won't promise anything, huh?

C: I will promise to listen, to attend to what you say, and to put all my energy into understanding you.

N: (pause; hopefully) Would you really do that for me?

C: You are important. (N smiles) You smiled. It would feel good to experience someone as finding you important.

N: (cautiously) I can't really take it in somehow. I know I'm important to Tim. I know how much he loves me—he tells me so all the time. He is always gentle, but I feel scared when he touches me. (pause; anxiously) I don't know why; he has never forced anything on me. (pause) I don't want to lose him.

C: He is important to you. You don't want to lose feeling valued.

N: (tense) No, (pause) I don't, (pause; anxious) but moving in . . . (long pause)

C: You don't want to lose Tim, but your body gets tense and you feel uneasy about moving in with him.

N: (confused) Yeah, and it's so weird because I have always hated living at home, and here is my chance to get away.

C: (long pause) You're wondering what's stopping you from escaping from it.

N: I'm a punching bag at home, and so is my mom. I can't remember a time when one of us didn't have bruises healing up somewhere.

C: I'm worried that you're in danger.

N: (emphatically) No. I am okay. I have been living with this all my life. I know how to escape from the house when I need to.

C: This dangerous situation is commonplace to you. (pause) How bad is it?

N: (matter-of-factly) I used to be hurt really bad when I was younger. I didn't know how to recognize the signs of impending disaster. A few times I ended up with a broken arm or leg. Since I've been a teenager, I haven't gotten more than a few bruises. I can tell when things are heating up and can back out the door and get to Tim's house fast. I've done it many times.

C: How do you back out the door?

N: (matter-of-factly) After the first blow, I can always escape. I may pretend to back down and act like I'm going to do what they want, or I get them fighting with each other; that's *easy* to do. Then I take off out the bathroom window or through the front door, whichever is closer.

C: Once you're out of the house, how do you get to Tim's?

N: He's just a few blocks away. His parents have him living in their basement. I can go in the basement door, and they don't even know I'm there.

C: What if Tim's gone?

N: I have a key. (sincerely) Really, this is commonplace for me. I have never needed it, but I know where the battered women's shelter is if I ever do.

C: You have thought about this a lot. You have an escape plan, (pause) but (*N* interrupts)

N: Honestly, I know I have to get out at some point. I want to, (pause) but what will happen when I do?

C: There is danger at home, (pause) but you know how to escape. In a new situation, there is the unknown.

N: Exactly. (long pause; anxiously) Maybe it will be worse somewhere else.

C: A frightening thought.

N: (hurriedly) I'm scared. I want to feel safe.

C: You sound anxious. You want to feel safe. Have you ever been safe?

N: (calmly) At school I am. There isn't any hitting at school.

C: School has been a safe place. Anyplace else?

N: (softly, looking down) Tim has never hit me. He gets *mad*, but . . . (pause)

C: But?

N: (hurriedly) I haven't *lived* with him.

C: Tim has gotten mad, and nothing scary has happened so far. You wonder if this would change if you lived in the same house.

N: (anxiously) When people live together, things get very intense.

C: Living together increases intensity, and maybe scary things happen.

N: (pause) It's risky. I don't think I can stand this. (pause) Let's talk of something else.

C: Your fear is filling the room.

N: (desperately) Help me, (pause) please.

C: You're trembling. All the fear inside is pouring out.

N: (yelling) *I am going to explode!*

C: (whispering) So much fear. Fear you have had all your life. If it all comes out . . . (long pause)

N: (anxiously) I don't like this. It feels *terrible.*

C: Even though the fear is washing over you, it is safe here to be aware of it.

N: (with forced calm) I need to escape from this before I do something bad. (pause; panicky) I need to stop this *now!*

C: Escape if you need to.

N: (desperately) *School.* It will be *okay* if we talk about school more.

C: (long pause) School. (long pause)

N: (taking deep breaths) School is calm. If you do your work, the teachers smile at you. The worst thing that happens is the teachers jerk you around a little.

C: Calm, smiles, maybe some jerking around.

N: (relaxed) The jerking stuff is nothing. The teachers make the decisions. They can be bossy. I can go with it. They tell you what to do, but they don't hurt you. A lot of them have encouraged me; that has felt good.

C: Teachers have more power than you, but some have believed in you.

N: (amazed) They like me. I don't know if I would've ever realized I was smart enough for college if so many of them hadn't told me so.

C: They helped you see yourself as an intelligent person. How does it feel?

N: (reflectively) Nice, I guess. It's the only place I feel at ease with myself.

C: How do you feel here? (long pause; *N* looks thoughtful) I can see that you're thinking deeply about something. Can you tell me about it?

N: (calmly) I do feel safe here too. It's strange in a way, because I just met you and I don't believe in jumping to conclusions.

C: What do you mean?

N: (tense) There's a lot of uncontrolled anger in the world. I have to be very careful to protect myself.

C: Anger is out there in the world, and it feels dangerous to you.

N: (anxious) I don't want more hurt. I might escape from it by moving in with Tim. Tim says he wants to share a safe place with me.

C: He needs a safe place; you need a safe place.

N: (seriously) No one is threatening Tim. He's just ignored by his family—kind of an outcast. I'm really his family. I like it, but . . . (*N* is looking overwhelmed)

C: You look lost. (*N* nods) You need physical safety; he needs emotional safety. You each get some of that with each other. (pause) But you fear that if Tim gets too close, he might stop being a safe person for you.

N: (anxiously) He would go ballistic if he heard me say that. He has been my best friend through a lot of scary stuff at home.

C: He has been your best friend. But this fear of anger is always with you.

N: (nodding her head) Yeah . . . (pause) I can't . . . (long pause) I don't . . . (long pause)

C: You are really struggling to put your feelings into words.

N: (longingly) I need to understand this more. I don't want to fear my best friend. Sometimes I think it is so weird that I could ever be scared of Tim. He knows how much pain I have been in sometimes over my family, and I know he cares for me.

C: But the fear is still there. It's real. It surrounds you.

N: (sadly) It's never completely gone. (pause) I always hold back.

C: How does it feel in your body when you hold back?

N: (puzzled) I don't know. Tim gets engrossed in me all the time. I see the love in his eyes. I do love him. (looking away) There is always a part of me looking on from afar, kind of examining what is going on at a safe distance.

C: He doesn't fear you, so he can let himself go fully into the relationship. You hold back a part of yourself so you can feel safe.

N: (nodding) Sometimes I have to rush off to the bathroom for a breather. In the mirror I see this look on my own face. (pause) I don't know what it means, but I have seen this look on my mother's face.

C: You don't understand it, but you recognize it. Would your mother understand?

N: (dismissively) I don't know. We don't talk much. What's the point? (pause) She has never helped me. She never will.

C: You share a look with your mother, but you don't share your thoughts. (long pause) Why doesn't she help you?

N: (angrily) I used to cry out for her help when I was little until I figured out she was a total puppet for my dad. The only thing she ever did was keep my hiding place in the kitchen a secret when my dad was hunting for me.

C: She never actively helped you, but did she show she cared by letting you escape?

N: (unconvinced) I don't know if she was showing that she cared. I think she was just showing how passive she was—never doing anything unless she was told to do it. (long pause; angrily) I used to ask myself why my teachers cared more about me than my own mother. (pause; with resignation) I'm used to it now.

C: The attention from your teachers felt good, but it also made you angry because you weren't getting this attention from your mother. What do you think was going on?

N: (long pause; thoughtfully) My dad could never tolerate my mom paying the smallest amount of attention to me; he demands constant attention on himself. When my brothers and I were little, we were all getting slammed by him constantly. Now that they can hold their own against him, he treats them as buddies. He laughs if one of them punches my mom for not doing something fast enough for them. They try to treat me as their slave, but I escape a lot.

C: First your dad and then your brothers use force to keep your mother their slave. You are trying to escape from this.

N: (slumping down in the chair) I feel exhausted. I have really had it for the day.

C: You have experienced a lot of difficult things today. You are ready for a rest. Still, I'm worried about you being safe at home.

N: (tiredly) It's kind of you to care but unnecessary. My dad and brothers work late during the week; I only cross their paths on the weekend. If things look ugly, I can take off. If I get caught by surprise, after the first blow, I can always escape.

C: Even one bruise is too much. You deserve safety. If you were seventeen, I would be calling child protective services in to protect you from this abuse.

N: (skeptically) Child protective services was called in a few times when I was younger. My dad always outsmarted them. Don't worry; I'm going to be OK.

C: I respect your right to decide. I just strongly believe in your right to be safe.

N: (reflectively) I can tell that you mean it. (pause) I'll think about it.

Exercises for Developing a Case Conceptualization of Nicole

Exercise 1 (four-page maximum)

GOAL: To verify that you have a clear understanding of emotion-focused theory.

STYLE: An integrative essay comprising Parts A through C.

NEED HELP?   Review this chapter (pages 237–244).

A. Develop a concise overview of all the assumptions of emotion-focused theory (the theory's hypotheses about key dimensions in understanding how clients change; think broadly, abstractly) as an introduction to the rest of this exercise.

B. Develop a thorough description of how each of these assumptions is used to understand a client's progression through the change process in paragraphs that provide specific examples to fully explain each assumption.

C. Conclude your essay by describing the role of the clinician in helping the client change (consultant, doctor, educator, helper), the major approach taken to treatment, and common treatment techniques. Provide enough specific examples to clarify what is distinctive about this approach.

Exercise 2 (four-page maximum)

GOAL: To aid application of emotion-focused treatment to Nicole.

STYLE: A separate sentence outline for each section, A through G.

NEED HELP?   Review this chapter (pages 327–244).

A. What does Nicole view as her weaknesses (concerns, issues, problems, symptoms, skill deficits, treatment barriers, areas in which her growth is blocked) at this time? For each of these, consider the following:

1. What marker of an emotional-processing problem, adaptive emotion vis-à-vis a problematic experience, or aspect of a maladaptive emotion scheme might each weakness represent?

2. Looking across all the information above, what maladaptive emotion schemes might be operating in Nicole's life?

a. Several weaknesses could be part of the same emotion scheme.

b. Maladaptive schemes can be incomplete, they can be complete but guide the client in maladaptive ways, or they can provide conflicting guidance in relation to other schemes.

B. Looking across the markers of emotional processing problems and their underlying emotion schemes, does Nicole have a global processing style (emotionally overregulated, emotionally underregulated, engaged in mostly conceptual processing, engaged in mostly experiential processing)?

1. Based on your responses to Part A, what core pain or core issue is associated with this global processing style? (There may be more than one core pain or issue.)

2. Does the core pain or issue relate to an inability to symbolize internal experience, intrapersonal problems, interpersonal problems, or existential concerns?

C. Discuss the type of voice (focused, emotional, limited, external) Nicole uses over the course of the interview, giving specific examples to support your choice. Then, discuss the implications of this for her ability to profit from emotion-focused treatment in general, as well as the types of techniques she may profit from most at this time.

D. For each marker you indicated in Part A, discuss the type of emotional-processing task it suggests Nicole might profit from at this time. Does the voice you indicated she has in Part C have any influence in facilitating or inhibiting how much Nicole would profit from each task at this time?

E. What does Nicole view as her strengths (strong points, positive features, successes, skills, factors facilitating change, areas in which her growth is not blocked) at this time? For each of these, consider the following:

1. What component of healthy emotional processing, aspect of an adaptive emotion scheme, or adaptive emotion might each strength reflect or have developed from?

2. Looking at all the information above, what healthy or incomplete but partially healthy emotion schemes seem to be operating in Nicole's life? (Several strengths could be part of the same scheme.)

3. How might Nicole's strengths reflect a positive tendency toward self-growth, and how could these strengths be given more attention so that they can help Nicole with her current difficulties?

F. Considering the information from Parts A through E, what types of meaning is Nicole currently creating from her experiences about herself, others, and her situation, and how does this relate to her overall level of functioning?

G. What barriers or windows of opportunity currently exist in regard to Nicole's fully processing her experiences and drawing adaptive meaning from them at this time?

Exercise 3 (three-page maximum)

GOAL: To develop an understanding of the potential role of violence in Nicole's life.

STYLE: A separate sentence outline for each section, A through J.

NEED HELP?   Review Chapter 2 (pages 92–102).

A. Assess the risk factors for violence and the protective factors discouraging violence that are currently in place for Nicole, considering the following questions:

1. What adverse childhood events has Nicole been exposed to in the past? Consider events such as living with a drug addict; having divorced parents; severe family disruption, such as repeated moves or homelessness; having a parent who was depressed or mentally ill; living with someone who committed suicide or attempted to commit suicide; living with someone who committed a serious crime or went to prison; being physically, sexually, or emotionally abused or neglected; and witnessing violence.

2. What adverse adult events has Nicole been exposed to? Consider events such as living with a drug addict; severe family disruption; living with someone who is depressed or mentally ill; living with someone who committed or attempted to commit suicide; living with someone who committed a serious crime or went to prison; being physically, sexually, or emotionally abused; or witnessing violence or living in fear of violence.

3. What *internal* factors are within Nicole that might be protective against violence? Consider whether she has the ability to control impulses, set limits on her own behavior, regulate emotions, engage in reflective problem-solving, or understand the emotions and behaviors of others.

4. Did the *long-term* social network and environment during Nicole's childhood support or constrain violence? Consider whether there were traumatic, ambivalent, or nonexistent emotional bonds versus positive emotional bonds; the level of family violence; the level of family toleration for violence as a problem-solving strategy; positive or negative school or neighborhood experiences; and religious background.

5. Are there *currently* environmental supports or constraints on violence from Nicole's family relationships, peer relationships, educational attainment, vocation, current neighborhood, or current religious beliefs?

6. Are there any *immediate* eliciting or triggering factors that might serve to justify a violent or prosocial response or make it more likely? Consider such things as the presence or absence of a weapon, the level of alcohol or drug use, the level of frustration or anger, and the encouragement or discouragement of violence from others in Nicole's life.

B. Assess Nicole's exposure to violence across her life span.

1. Types of exposure (direct, indirect)

2. Frequency of exposure

3. Severity of incidents

4. Nicole's role in the exposure (witness, victim, perpetrator, victim-perpetrator)

5. The current impact of the violence exposure in terms of emotional, cognitive, physical, and social functioning

C. Assess Nicole's worldview, whether violence plays a generalized or circumscribed role in it, and whether it is currently generating or promoting violence or generating or promoting prosocial behavior.

D. Assess Nicole's danger and that of others within her environment at this time. Consider whether—and if so, how—safety could be enhanced in both the immediate and the longer term; include careful consideration of the *characteristics* of the perpetrator of the violence in Nicole's life. On a scale of 1 to 10, how dangerous is her environment at this time? On a scale of 1 to 10, how much control of this danger does Nicole have?

E. Assess Nicole's safety and that of others within her personal, social, and cultural worlds.

F. Assess the overall psychological and physical impact of violence on Nicole and others in her life, evaluating whether there are more forces supporting violence or supporting nonviolence and determining Nicole's prognosis in terms of her being able to live a life free of violence at this time.

G. What is your current knowledge of the impact of violence and neglect on individuals and their families?

1. How many courses have you taken that give you background on the impact of neglect, violence, and trauma on the physical and emotional welfare of clients?

2. How many workshops have you taken that give you background on the impact of neglect, violence, and trauma on the physical and emotional welfare of clients?

3. What professional experiences have you had that give you background on the impact of neglect, violence, and trauma on the physical and emotional welfare of clients?

4. What personal experiences have you had that give you background on the impact of neglect, violence, and trauma on the physical and emotional welfare of clients?

5. What cohort effects might influence the worldview of individuals with a background of neglect, violence, and trauma in terms of what is important in the world, how people communicate, and what is rewarded and punished in this world?

H. What is your current level of awareness of issues relevant to clients who come from violent or neglectful backgrounds?

1. Discuss your stereotypes of neglectful and violent lifestyles and whether this might influence your view of Nicole at this time.

2. Discuss your past experiences or exposure to violence and how this might influence your view of Nicole at this time.

3. Discuss your stereotypes of good romantic relationships and stereotypes of good parent-child relationships and whether these might influence your view of Nicole at this time.

4. Discuss how your past exposure to violence and neglect might influence your reactions to Nicole.

5. Discuss your stereotypes of clients from violent and neglectful backgrounds and how these might influence your work with Nicole.

6. Discuss the experiences you have had that could support your effective work with Nicole as well as experiences you have had that might lead to negative bias or marginalization of Nicole's point of view or current situation.

I. What are your current skills in working with clients from violent or neglectful backgrounds?

1. What skills do you currently have that are of value in working with individuals who have a background of neglect, violence, or trauma?

2. What skills do you feel it would be important to develop to work effectively with individuals who have a violent or neglectful background?

3. What can you do to increase the likelihood of a positive outcome with Nicole, considering that she has a violent and neglectful background?

J. What action steps can you take?

1. What can you do to prepare yourself to be more skilled in working with Nicole, considering that she comes from a violent and neglectful background?

2. Discuss any biases related to your treatment approach in terms of neglect of or inappropriate interventions for individuals who were victims of violence.

3. How might you structure the treatment environment to increase the likelihood of a positive outcome with Nicole, considering that she comes from a violent and neglectful background?

4. What processes of treatment might you change to make them more welcoming to Nicole, considering that she comes from a violent and neglectful background?

5. Discuss any experiences you have had that might be of value as you seek to develop an effective therapeutic relationship with Nicole, a victim of violence. Consider whether any of these experiences might lead to negative bias or marginalization of Nicole's point of view, or whether they might increase your understanding of Nicole. Discuss what you might try to do to increase the likelihood of a positive outcome for Nicole and why you think this might help.

6. Assess whether your past experiences with violence, your stereotypes of violent lifestyles, or biases embedded in your treatment approach might lead to negative bias, marginalization of Nicole's point of view, or an increase in danger for Nicole and others in her life, and consider what you might do to modify your approach to increase the likelihood of a positive outcome.

Exercise 4 (six-page maximum)

GOAL: To help you integrate your knowledge of emotion-focused treatment and violence issues into an in-depth conceptualization of Nicole (who she is and why she does what she does).

STYLE: An integrated essay consisting of a premise, supportive details, and conclusions following a carefully planned organizational style.

NEED HELP?   Review Chapter 1 (pages 1–7) and Chapter 2 (pages 92–102).

STEP 1: Consider what style you should use in organizing your emotion-focused understanding of Nicole. This style should (a) support you in providing a comprehensive and clear understanding of how she processes emotion and (b) support language she might find persuasive in her current state of confusion.

STEP 2: Develop a concise premise (overview, preliminary or explanatory statements, proposition, thesis statement, theory-driven introduction, hypotheses, summary, concluding causal statements) that explains Nicole's difficulty in deciding where to live. If you have trouble with Step 2, remember it should be an integration of the key ideas of Exercises 2 and 3 and that it should (a) provide a basis for her long-term goals, (b) be grounded in emotion-focused treatment and be sensitive to issues of violence, and (c) highlight the strengths Nicole brings to emotion-focused treatment.

STEP 3: Develop your supporting material (a detailed case analysis of strengths and weaknesses, supplying data to support an introductory premise) from an emotion-focused perspective, incorporating within each paragraph a deep understanding of Nicole as a victim of violence. If you need help with Step 3, consider the information you'll need to include in order to (a) support the development of short-term goals, (b) be grounded in emotion-focused treatment that is sensitive to violence issues, and (c) integrate an understanding of how Nicole's strengths could be used in processing her emotions for further meaning.

STEP 4: Develop your conclusions and broad treatment recommendations, including (a) Nicole's overall level of functioning, (b) anything facilitating or serving as a barrier to her fully processing her experiences at this time, and (c) her basic emotional-processing needs at this time in terms of enhancing her natural tendency for positive growth, being careful to consider what you said in Part H and J of Exercise 3 (be concise and general).

Exercise 5 (three-page maximum)

GOAL: To develop an individualized, theory-driven action plan for Nicole that considers her strengths and is sensitive to violence issues.

STYLE: A sentence outline consisting of long- and short-term goals.

NEED HELP? Review Chapter 1 (pages 7–27).

STEP 1: Develop your treatment plan overview, being careful to consider what you said in Parts H and J of Exercise 3 to try to prevent any negative bias in your treatment plan and individualize treatment to Nicole's unique needs as an individual.

STEP 2: Develop long-term (major, large, ambitious, comprehensive, broad) goals that *ideally* Nicole will reach by the termination of treatment and that will lead her to be free to grow adaptively from her new experiences and live in a nonviolent environment. If you have trouble with Step 2, reread your premise and support topic sentences, looking for ideas to transform into goals that will support emotional processing of internal and external experiences (use the *style* of Exercise 4).

STEP 3: Develop short-term (small, brief, encapsulated, specific, measurable) goals that Nicole and you can expect to see accomplished within a few weeks and that will help you chart her progress in processing her experiences, instill hope for change, and plan time-effective treatment sessions. If you have trouble with Step 3, reread your support paragraphs, looking for ideas to transform into goals that (a) might help her fully process her experiences of violence and nonviolence, (b) might enhance factors facilitating the development of new meaning from her experiences or decrease barriers to such development, (c) utilize her strengths in processing her experiences whenever possible, and (d) are individualized to her needs as a victim of abuse rather than generic.

Exercise 6

GOAL: To critique emotion-focused treatment in the case of Nicole.

STYLE: Answer Questions A through E in essay form or discuss them in a group format.

A. What are the strengths and weaknesses of this model for helping Nicole (a teen with a history of violence)?

B. Discuss the pros and cons of taking a feminist approach with Nicole instead of an emotion-focused approach (include consideration of its compatibility with Nicole's view of her difficulties, her potential motivation to work on a treatment plan within its framework, and its responsiveness to issues of violence).

C. Using the domain of age, describe how Nicole's childhood exposure to violence influenced her physical, cognitive, and psychosocial functioning. Include an analysis of how it influenced her strengths and her weaknesses as an emerging adult.

D. What ethical issues are raised by using a treatment approach with Nicole that gives her the power to decide if she does or does not discuss her physical safety during the course of a session? Can you try to ensure Nicole's safety while continuing to treat her as an expert on her own experience and an equal partner in the treatment relationship?

E. The clinician in emotion-focused treatment uses a process-directive but content-nondirective approach. Discuss your own personal style as a clinician and consider how compatible it is with this type of treatment approach. Does your style fit best overall with the more directive forms of treatment, such as behavioral and cognitive therapy, or with more nondirective forms, such as emotion-focused and constructivist therapy?

RECOMMENDED RESOURCES

Books

Elliott, R., Greenberg, L. S., & Lietaer, G. (2004). Research on experiential psychotherapies. In M. J. Lambert (Ed.), *Handbook of psychotherapy and behavior change* (5th ed., pp. 493–539). New York, NY: John Wiley & Sons.

Geller, S. M., & Greenberg, L. S. (2012). *Therapeutic presence: A mindful approach to effective therapy.* Washington, DC: American Psychological Association.

Greenberg, L., & Goldman, R. (2007). Case-formulation in emotion-focused therapy. In T. D. Eells (Ed.), *Handbook of psychotherapy case formulation* (2nd ed., pp. 379–411). New York, NY: Guilford Press.

Greenberg, L. S. (2011). *Emotion-focused therapy: Coaching clients to work through their feelings.* Washington, DC: American Psychological Association.

Greenberg, L. S., McWilliams, N., & Wenzel, A. (2013). *Exploring three approaches to psychotherapy.* Washington, DC: American Psychological Association.

Videos

American Psychological Association (Producer), & Greenberg, L. S. (Trainer). (n.d.). *Process-experiential therapy* (Systems of Psychotherapy Video Series, Motion Picture #4310290). (Available from the American Psychological Association, 750 First Street, NE, Washington, DC 20002–4242)

Ellis, D. J. (Featured). (2014). Rational emotive behavior therapy [Video series episode]. In *APA psychotherapy video series: I. Systems of psychotherapy.* Washington, DC: American Psychological Association.

Goldman, R. N. (Featured). (2014). Case formulation in emotion-focused therapy: Addressing unfinished business [Video series episode]. In *APA psychotherapy video series: II. Specific treatments for specific populations.* Washington, DC: American Psychological Association.

Johnson, S. (2014, Feb. 19). Emotionally focused therapy [Video file]. Retrieved from https://www.youtube.com/watch?v=xQCg-jC25fo

Paivio, S. C. (Featured). (2014). Emotion-focused therapy for trauma [Video series episode]. In *APA psychotherapy video series: II. Specific treatments for specific populations.* Washington, DC: American Psychological Association.

PsychotherapyNet. (2012, May 21). Sue Johnson emotionally focused couples therapy (EFT) in action video [Video file]. Retrieved from https://www.youtube.com/watch?v=xaHms5z-yuM

Websites

Emotion-Focused Therapy Clinic. http://www.emotionfocusedtherapy.org

International Centre for Excellence in Emotion Focused Therapy. http://www.iceeft.com

International Society for Emotion Focused Therapy. http://www.iseft.org

EIGHT

Dynamic Case Conceptualizations and Treatment Plans

INTRODUCTION TO DYNAMIC THEORY

You have just received a referral from the juvenile probation department due to your expertise in working with adolescents. Sergio, a 17-year-old Latino male, was recently arrested for selling marijuana to his high school classmates. He was sentenced to one year of probation and mandated into treatment. Sergio's parents, along with a large extended family, live in a rural farming community where there has been significant racial tension between the Mexican and non-Mexican populations. Sergio's siblings include Raoul (age 12), Ana (age 10), and José (age 8). Sergio's parents and extended family are migrant workers who originally came to the United States for the spring and summer months and then returned to Mexico for the rest of the year. Now they have settled permanently in the United States. Their income is below the poverty level. Within his family, Sergio is described as a respectful son and responsible family member. At school, Sergio's academic performance has always been in the average range, and he has never been in trouble before now.

In a brief mental status screen, there were no signs of cognitive confusion, suicidal or homicidal ideation, or substance abuse, although Sergio admits to both drinking alcohol and smoking marijuana.

You practice a form of time-limited dynamic treatment that considers interpersonal relationships as primary to both adaptive and maladaptive functioning. The goals of treatment will be to improve Sergio's manner of relating to himself and others. Time-limited dynamic treatment has roots in object relations theory, interpersonal theory, and self-psychology as well as other psychological theories (Levenson & Strupp, 2007). Sergio, like all people, has biologically programmed needs for human connections in which he will feel safe and loved (Bowlby, 1973; Levenson & Strupp, 2007). Sergio may come to treatment complaining about symptoms of anxiety, depression, or anger. However, it will be his interpersonal style, not these symptoms, that will be the focus of treatment. The following detailed description of time-limited dynamic treatment is taken predominately from the work of Levenson and Strupp (2007) and Strupp and Binder (1984).

How do dysfunctional interpersonal styles develop? They arise from faulty interpersonal relationships, particularly those of early childhood. Sergio will not be pathologized if he has developed a dysfunctional style of relating to others; it will have developed in his realistic attempts to get his basic needs for human connection met. These faulty patterns of relating may be modified or completely transformed based on new life experiences. An adult will maintain rigid patterns learned in childhood only if they are supported by current relationships.

How can Sergio's interpersonal problems be modified or resolved in treatment? The curative factors will develop within an effective treatment relationship. Sergio will inevitably re-create any cyclic maladaptive pattern(s) (CMP[s]) of relating he has developed as he tries to relate to you. However, in the treatment relationship, he will (a) experience a new outcome when relating to you, as opposed to what he received from others, and (b) develop a new understanding of how he has been relating to others, including himself, in his current and possibly his past relationships.

While all clients in time-limited dynamic treatment will experience a new outcome and gain a more flexible pattern of relating to others, not all clients will be guided to experience insights into the development of their CMP(s). Sergio may benefit from insight because he is very intelligent and has shown the ability to reflect on both his motivations and the motivations of others. Some clients may not be capable of this, but they can still profit from time-limited dynamic treatment. For these clients, the clinician will help them develop a healthy interaction style within the treatment setting, and then they will be guided to generalize this to relationships outside of treatment.

Why might Sergio need treatment at this time? Although the focus of treatment will be on Sergio's current life functioning, his need for treatment will be embedded in his early development. In healthy development, Sergio's basic needs for intimacy (ability to relate to others, to form and maintain attachments, to give and gain affection, and to have emotional access) and autonomy (a sense of independence and self-regulation acquired through exploration of one's abilities) will have been met effectively and consistently in his relationships with caregivers (Bowlby, 1973; Strupp & Binder, 1984). Through these healthy interpersonal relationships, Sergio will have learned to accept limitations on his caregivers' ability to respond to him, and he will have learned to tolerate reasonable delays in getting his needs met. Through these age-appropriate and minimal frustrations, the young Sergio will have learned to soothe himself when necessary. As a result of these experiences, he will have a positive sense of self (trust in himself), realistic and adaptive expectations of himself and others, and a flexible way of relating to people. These healthy attitudes and patterns of relating will have been internalized into a model of how the interpersonal world works.

In contrast, if Sergio's needs were not met consistently in his early interpersonal relationships, he will have developed one or more CMPs (Bowlby, 1973; Strupp & Binder, 1984). Sergio will have developed these faulty and rigid patterns of relating in an indirect attempt to get his needs met and avoid anxiety or depression. Sergio will have developed an internalized model of the interpersonal world that contains self-defeating expectations of himself and others. He will have poor self-esteem and low self-efficacy.

Sergio's internal model of the interpersonal world represents his personal interpretation of reality and consists of the roles he casts for himself, including his thoughts, feelings, and wishes in relationship to others; the roles he casts for others, including his expectations and perceptions within interpersonal interactions; and his introjects about himself. These introjects contain his thoughts, feelings, and wishes in relation to himself. Sergio's internalized model of the interpersonal world should contain many different interpersonal patterns of relating so that Sergio can respond flexibly to the situation he is in and the person he's relating to. However, if Sergio has a maladaptive model of the interpersonal world, he will have at least one CMP and possibly more. In this case, time-limited dynamic treatment will focus Sergio's attention on his most pervasive or problematic style of relating.

Will Sergio's early life experiences inevitably influence his present behavior? Environmental circumstances may change with age; however, Sergio's interpersonal behavior could still be guided by fantasies, fears, and misconceptions developed early in life. If this is so, Sergio's dysfunctional interpersonal patterns could be replicated in all of his current interpersonal relationships, including sibling or peer relationships, work or academic relationships, parental relationships, and the treatment relationship. However, his model of the interpersonal world is always open to change and will respond to changes within his ongoing relationships as a teenager. When he leaves home and engages in a fully adult life, Sergio's internal model of the interpersonal world will continue to be open to change based on interactions with new people in his life and any changes in their behavior. Thus, if Sergio developed a dysfunctional style of relating in early life, it will only be continued, unchanged, if the maladaptive patterns continue to be fostered in his current relationships.

How might current relationships foster dysfunctional styles of relating? One way would be for Sergio to enter into complementary maladaptive relationships with other individuals who also have dysfunctional interpersonal patterns. Assume that in Sergio's childhood, he was able to receive nurturance from his authoritarian parents only if he engaged in submissive behavior. Although he may have desired greater independence, he may have preferred to subvert this need to maintain a sense of emotional connection to his parents. As an adult, Sergio may now unintentionally seek out relationships with autocratic individuals because he understands how to get his needs for nurturance met through such individuals.

Another way Sergio's dysfunctional patterns could be reinforced is by his unintentionally soliciting from others exactly those reactions that he most fears or wants. For example, by his submissive behavior, Sergio might elicit authoritarian behavior from others. Finally, Sergio may interpret social interactions in a manner consistent with maladaptive expectations. For example, if a teacher asks him what project he would like to work on for class, Sergio might interpret this as a setup in which the teacher is looking for ways to criticize his behavior if he does not choose the "right" project. Thus, the behavior of others in Sergio's current relationships could inadvertently reinforce Sergio's maladaptive pattern of relating. A dysfunctional interpersonal episode that occurred once in response to an unusual circumstance in Sergio's life would not be a CMP. For example, if there was a tyrannical teacher at his high school around whom all of the students behaved submissively, Sergio's submission in reaction to this teacher would say more about the teacher than about Sergio. In addition, it will be important to examine whether some of his interpersonal patterns are typical for his cultural group and/or represent adaptations to cultural demands rather than being idiosyncratic interpersonal patterns of Sergio. Although Sergio is consciously aware of some aspects of his internal model of the interpersonal world, much of it is preconscious or unconscious (Strupp & Binder, 1984).

THE ROLE OF THE CLINICIAN

In time-limited dynamic treatment, you are a participant/observer of interpersonal behavior who provides Sergio with a new model to identify with and who collaborates with Sergio, as a trustable and reliable ally, in the process of examining his interpersonal behavior. Broadly, there will be two treatment goals: (a) to create a new interpersonal experience within the therapeutic relationship and (b) to create a new understanding for Sergio of how he relates to himself and other people. You will need to be very aware of your thoughts and feelings as you relate to Sergio. These will provide key data for you to use in both figuring out the nature of his interpersonal problems and determining what to do differently to provide the new experience that Sergio needs to have within the treatment relationship.

Your first task is to determine if Sergio has one or more CMPs that, though they may be historically significant, can be clearly related to his present life struggles. In addition, if appropriate, this pattern will be explained to Sergio using terms that he can understand. If you determine that insight into the pattern is not in Sergio's best interests, you will discuss his relationship problems only in terms that are directly relevant to his specific presenting problems.

To evaluate Sergio's interpersonal relationships and determine if there is a rigid and dysfunctional pattern of relating, you seek to answer four questions:

1. What is Sergio's role for himself in interacting with others? This includes how he behaves toward other people as well as his feelings, thoughts, and intentions toward other people. Sergio may act in ways to evoke certain feared or wished-for reactions from others.

2. How does Sergio expect other people to respond to his interpersonal behavior? This includes all the thoughts Sergio has that anticipate how other people will respond to his interpersonal behavior.

3. What are the acts of others toward Sergio (how do others relate to him), and how does he perceive this interpersonal behavior? This includes how other people respond to Sergio's interpersonal behavior and how he interprets the meaning of their responses. Sergio may also misconstrue the behavior of others as meeting his prior expectations.

4. What is Sergio's role in relating to himself (his introjects)? This includes how he behaves toward himself (self-punishing, self-nurturing, and so forth) as well as his thoughts, feelings, and intentions toward himself. He is likely to treat himself in the same way he perceives significant others as treating him.

Trying to understand Sergio's interpersonal model by organizing his interpersonal behavior into these four categories is valuable because it helps reduce a large amount of information about his experiences into a concise format; it may also help you clarify Sergio's reactions to you and your reactions toward him. At times it may be confusing to you to determine exactly which of Sergio's thoughts, feelings, and behaviors are directed at others or at himself. It may not be critical to make this discrimination if it won't interfere with your understanding of his overall interpersonal style. The identified CMP represents your hypothesis for explaining Sergio's current interpersonal difficulties. It may need to be modified as more information about his relationships becomes available. You may also become aware that some of Sergio's interpersonal behavior represents flexible and adaptive patterns; these reflect his interpersonal strengths.

As Sergio is intelligent enough and reflective enough to benefit from it, once you have developed an understanding of Sergio's focused CMP, your second task will be to help Sergio develop insight into it as he relates to you within the treatment session. Once this is accomplished, your next task will be to help him explore the ramifications of it for his current life. Over the course of treatment, once Sergio begins to show signs of improved relating within the session and outside of it, it is important for you to comment on this and help Sergio value his interpersonal strengths (Levenson & Strupp, 2007).

How are these tasks accomplished? You must create a good working relationship with Sergio through communicating interest in him, listening empathetically to him, and developing an understanding of his inner world. You will also provide a new model for Sergio to identify with that is more adaptive than the models available to him in childhood. At first, Sergio may not be able to benefit fully from this good relationship. If conflicted, he will attempt to re-create his CMP with you. As a participant-observer of this interpersonal process, you will routinely step out of the process to observe and then comment to Sergio about what is happening within the treatment relationship in terms of transference and countertransference phenomena. Transference is Sergio's inevitable attempt to repeat his internalized interpersonal patterns (ideas and beliefs about self, others, and the interaction of self and others) with you. You need to be vigilant to, and comment on, Sergio's attempts to elicit a type of interpersonal response such as domination, control, manipulation, exploitation, criticism, and so forth in order to re-create his CMP.

You will also experience countertransference reactions to Sergio's behavior. Countertransference provides important clues to you as to what Sergio needs as a corrective experience. First, you will determine the pattern you have been pulled into, and then you will determine how you should start behaving, within your role as a clinician, to disrupt this rigid interpersonal pattern. By choosing, from the many relationship-enhancing manners of responding to Sergio, what would be most valuable to him, you are individualizing treatment to his interpersonal needs. Perhaps he needs you to be matter-of-fact, not angry, when he engages in teasing behavior. Perhaps Sergio needs you to show respect for his desire to be treated as an adult male. If the countertransference you show is not parallel to how other significant others are relating to Sergio, then you need to examine whether the countertransference really relates to your own unique history rather than to Sergio.

Your interpretation of the interpersonal process provides Sergio with cognitive and experiential learning about his cyclic maladaptive patterns of relating to others. Whether the interpretations are concrete and very much tied to the presenting problem or reflect more insight-inducing comments about the interpersonal pattern depends on Sergio's ability to think and reflect about himself and others. Interpretations in the here and now are emphasized more than those of early childhood relationships. Narrative truth is considered more important than historical validity. Inferences should be kept to a minimum, and interpretations should be tied to a reality that he understands. The interpretation process can be damaging if you communicate too complexly or are rejecting. As Sergio lives through affectively painful and ingrained interpersonal scenarios yet receives a different reaction from you (i.e., different from what he expected based on past relationships), he will gain a greater ability to question his prior assumptions about his self-image and about the attitudes and intentions of others. As Sergio gains confidence in examining his own CMP, he will develop an increased ability to confront his previously repressed emotions and fantasies associated with them. You are a reliable and trustworthy ally in this process. Through the context of a good relationship with a supportive and empathetic listener, Sergio can develop new patterns of thinking, feeling, and acting within relationships. Time limits must be set at the beginning of treatment and discussed on a continuing basis with Sergio. A planned termination is considered essential to solidifying treatment gains within short-term, dynamic treatment.

CASE APPLICATION: INTEGRATING THE DOMAIN OF RACE AND ETHNICITY

Sergio's case will now be examined in detail. There are many domains of complexity that might be appropriate to apply to him. The domain of race and ethnicity has been selected to consider within a dynamic case conceptualization and treatment plan. As racism is an important issue in this case, assume the clinician has no Mexican heritage.

Interview With Sergio (S) From a Dynamic Perspective

C: Good afternoon, Sergio. As you know, your probation officer called me yesterday to set up this appointment. He selected me because I work a lot with teenagers. He told me that your family is from Mexico. I have never been there, but I have seen pictures and it's a very beautiful country. (long pause) Would you mind telling me why you're here from your point of view? (long pause) I was told that your family speaks Spanish at home. Spanish is a powerful language for expressing yourself. (pause) I'm sorry that I don't speak it. Perhaps you would prefer to talk to someone who can speak Spanish?

S: (sullenly, looking down) I am here because I have to be here.

C: It has been forced on you. (pause) You have a lot of self-control to come here when you feel forced.

S: (starts calmly but gets sullen) Yes, I have control. Is that so surprising to you?

C: I was meaning to show respect for your point of view, but the meaning of it became garbled somehow and you feel insulted.

S: (angrily) I want to be treated with respect and not jerked around by you and everyone else.

C: Jerking people around is wrong. I don't ever intentionally do that. However, if you ever feel jerked around, I would appreciate you letting me know.

S: (pause; sincerely) If you mean it, (looks briefly up at C) that is good.

C: I do mean it. (pause) I read the court records on your case, and I saw that your entire family came to court with you.

S: (defiantly) My family is everything to me.

C: I wonder if you think I can't ever understand how much you love your family. (S nods and looks down; long pause) Would you tell me about them?

S: I live with my mother and father in a house next to my mother's parents. All over the neighborhood there are other Mexican families, many of whom are related to us or who lived near us in Mexico. My uncle José came here first. When his boss at the farm, Mr. Zuckerman, needed more help, we all began to come. We work very hard for this man on his farm during the summer. He is a good man. He isn't like the other Whites in this town.

C: You love your family, and you respect this man. You are dedicated to them.

S: I respect my parents and grandparents. (pause; emphatically) Everyone should respect them. They have always worked hard. (pause; lovingly) They do everything for me, my brothers, and my sister.

C: Their role is to care for you, and they do it with love. (S nods) What do you do?

S: (sincerely) I try to help. We all help bring in crops over the summer, and my mother also sews in a factory during the other months when the farm doesn't need us. When she is working, I watch my younger brothers and sister a lot. I try to help them with their schoolwork and their duties at home.

C: How do your brothers and sister react to this?

S: (smiling down at his lap) They look up to me. I watch out for them.

C: You describe a very close-knit and caring family. Are there any problems?

S: (sullenly) We have no problems. We have a tight community—we stay together. We try to avoid the Whites, except at work, but they still cause us trouble.

C: What do you mean?

S: (disgustedly) Some of our neighbors are White, and they are always spying on us.

C: What are they doing?

S: (sarcastically) They come out on their porches to watch us doing yard work or playing ball, to listen to us talk.

C: How good are they at spying?

S: (with a chuckle) They don't understand Spanish. So they don't know what we're saying. They just pretend to be busy, but they aren't doing much of anything.

C: Do you always speak Spanish at home?

S: (defensively) It's our language.

C: I wasn't trying to insult you. I just wondered if you were speaking Spanish so your neighbors couldn't listen in on your conversation or because you speak Spanish at home. (long pause) Could your neighbors be making mistakes, like I am, out of ignorance, but not doing it to be disrespectful?

S: (calmly) No, their faces and actions give it away. (pause; angrily) They reported my parents last year to the police because I was out late at night.

C: You have so much respect for your parents that it must have made you very angry that anyone considered they were bad parents. (*S* nods) What happened?

S: (angrily) Some child protective services worker investigated us. (pause) They were so disrespectful to my parents, but my father, (pause) he insisted we just answer their questions and then be quiet. They told him I had to be in the house by eleven; that is the curfew for teenagers. He said OK to them, but (pause) my parents know what is right for me—not those ignorant people.

C: What do your parents expect from you?

S: (reflectively) On a weekday, I need to come home right after school ends to take care of my brothers Raoul and José and my sister Ana. On the weekend, my parents let me run around as much as I want with my *primos.* (*C* looks confused) Sorry, I mean my cousins. They don't expect me home until I get there.

C: So you might come home really late at night.

S: (calmly) Sometimes not until morning. I can handle myself. We have a good time.

C: Your parents trust you and respect your decision about when you are ready to come home.

S: (calmly) They know I am a man now. They respect my judgment.

C: You expect this respect from them. They understand you can be trusted.

S: (smiling) Yes. (pause) Of course, when I was little, they guided me, babied me. I don't need that now.

C: What are you doing when you are out with your cousins?

S: (smiling) We are just hanging out in someone's house or yard eating, listening to music, joking around, maybe cruising in a car. (pause) It's nobody else's business.

C: How are you feeling when you're with your cousins?

S: (smiling) Great. I always feel accepted by them. They know who I am. (*S* is silent)

C: What are you thinking about?

S: (tensely) Are you going to tell my probation officer that I'm out late sometimes past the stupid curfew he set for me?

C: No. I wouldn't do that. But I know the probation department is serious about its rules. If your probation officer finds out, he will come down hard on you.

S: (reflectively) My parents worry about this too.

C: They do? (*S* nods) What would it mean to you to come home earlier while you are on probation?

S: (emphatically) I don't want to be told what to do by that officer who doesn't know who I am and doesn't respect me.

C: When you feel respected, like by your parents, are you willing to listen?

S: (calmly) Of course. Elders are there to guide us, (angrily) but my probation officer knows nothing about me at all. He has no respect for me!

C: What does he do that is disrespectful?

S: (tensely) I am not treated as a man and allowed to speak. He just tells me to sit, listen, and do what he says. It is only out of respect for my parents' wishes that I go to see him (pause) and come here—not because of him!

C: Even though this officer does things you find disrespectful, you are still showing up for your appointment with him out of your deep respect for your parents.

S: (sincerely) I don't want to bring more trouble to my parents. I was trying to help them when I got into all this trouble to begin with.

C: With the marijuana?

S: (resignedly) The laws here on marijuana are just stupid. Many people smoke in Mexico just to relax. It is nothing. I know guys who bring it with them when they come across the border each summer. Money was tight at home, so I asked these guys if I could have some to sell to make money for my parents; some of those White kids at school have lots of money to spend.

C: Did your parents know what you were doing?

S: (sadly) No, and they were angry when they found out. They say it's against the law here and that I should respect the law.

C: Do your parents smoke?

S: (angrily) No, of course not!

C: I'm sorry, but you said "it was nothing" and that "many people smoke."

S: (sheepishly) My father thinks it is a waste of a life to smoke, and he has forbidden me to smoke. Still, it is true that a lot of people I know do smoke. No one cares when a White person does it.

C: How do you know that?

S: (frustrated) I have eyes. I had seen a lot of drugs around the high school before. Some people have gotten caught, but I have seen only *me* getting sent to the police.

C: You were the only one sent to the police?

S: (angrily) Yes, I'm Mexican, and they blame everything bad on us.

C: It was obvious to you that racism was the real problem at school, not selling marijuana.

S: (angrily) They are punishing me for being Mexican and going to their school. The people want us in the summer to work on their farms, but they don't want us staying in town afterward. We are supposed to go back to Mexico until the next summer. They don't care how hard it is to live without a permanent home.

C: (softly) They don't get how hard it is. What do they do to show this attitude?

S: (angrily) No one wanted to rent a house to my parents except in the crummy part of town. All the Mexican families live in these broken-down houses, while on the other side of town most Whites live in beautiful places. When we go shopping, they look at us funny, and they won't let their kids hang out with us at school.

C: You sound angry.

S: (reflectively) I don't know. I guess I'm used to it, but Ana was in tears the other day because four other girls in her class were going to some birthday party she hadn't been invited to. I told her to forget those girls—they are bad. We don't need any of them. Our community has parties all the time, and those girls aren't invited. We have lots of good times. We don't need any of them.

C: You feel close to family members, and you enjoy your time with them. But why do you say those girls are bad? What do you know about them?

S: (emphatically) I asked Ana; they are all White. With a few exceptions, like Mr. Zuckerman and some of my teachers, the Whites here don't trust us.

C: It feels clearly racist to you. You are a strong brother and don't want your sister hurt. (pause) Is it possible that any of the girls are like Mr. Zuckerman and really like Ana?

S: (pause; reflectively) I guess so. I didn't think about that. I know that some of them are probably all right like Mr. Zuckerman, but most are racist, and it's safer for Ana to realize that.

C: You want to protect Ana from the pain racist behavior has caused you. (S nods) What else has happened?

S: My parents don't speak English well and can't read the signs at stores or the labels on things. I shop for them because English came easily to me. At all the stores, I'm followed around like I'm a thief. At first, I didn't know what to do. Now I play some games with the employees. Sometimes I say, "I'm too busy to shoplift today. Maybe I'll come back tomorrow." Then I just leave the store without buying anything.

C: It hurts to feel distrusted. (S nods) You sometimes respond by teasing people. How do they react?

S: (ironically) They get scared; they take it seriously. They are just stupid. My family works hard for the money I spend in their stupid stores. Everyone in our community works hard. We are honest people, and we deserve respect.

C: Hard work does deserve respect. When people follow you, you have a right to feel angry about it. You tease them; they get scared. (pause) Do you always do this?

S: (reflectively) Sometimes I just take a long time to find the money at the cash register.

C: Do they know you are teasing them?

S: (tensely) They just think I'm stupid and slow, (pause) like all Mexicans.

C: Mexicans aren't stupid or slow.

S: (angrily) I have heard them saying this when they think I can't hear them.

C: Their comments hurt you. (pause) Does part of you believe what they say?

S: (reflectively) Only when I am with them. Once I'm home, I know I am not stupid. I do well in school. My math teacher is trying to get me to work harder. He is one of the good teachers at school. He doesn't care about skin color; he just tries to help everyone. He has noticed I can follow everything he says in class—even when many others are lost. I could do better if I had more time to do my homework, but my brother José—he is eight—he has lots of trouble learning, and I have to spend a lot of time helping him; that must come first.

C: You are dedicated to all of them, but José—he particularly needs you. What do your parents think about your behavior at the stores?

S: (calmly) They don't want me to play these games, so I'm trying to break the habit. (pause) My father says it's childish. He's right. I am a man and shouldn't do it.

C: You are very focused on doing the right thing as a man. What are your plans right now?

S: (emphatically) I need to decide how to help my parents. When I first heard about their money trouble, I told them I would drop out of school and work full time, but they were against it. They are proud to think I could graduate from high school—I would be the first in the family. But my family needs more money.

C: Could anyone help you find a part-time job?

S: (earnestly) I asked Mr. Zuckerman if he could give me work. He says he doesn't need extra help in the winter and doesn't know anyone who does. He did say he would give me a good reference if I need one.

C: Can anyone in the Mexican community help you?

S: (calmly) No, we are all hungry in the winter.

C: It's painful to know your community doesn't get enough of basic things like food.

S: (sadly) It's the reality we live with. If the Whites were all like Zuckerman, we would be all right.

C: Mr. Zuckerman knows who you really are. How would he describe you as an employee?

S: (calmly) He would say I am always on time, I never take days off, and I work hard.

C: That sounds like the type of man anyone would want to hire. (*S* nods) You have confidence in this. Could your probation officer help you find work?

S: (uncertainly) Why would he help me? To him, I'm dirt. That's why he orders me around.

C: No one likes to be ordered around. He should treat you with respect. I'm not saying he isn't racist. I am just saying, he might do this even to Whites on probation. He may think people won't shape up if he doesn't act tough.

S: (reflectively) He's White, so I just assumed he hates Mexicans.

C: (firmly) He may. Or he may think he is doing what probation officers are supposed to do.

S: (long pause) I play stupid around him, and maybe that's not the right thing to do.

C: If you showed him who you really are, could something better happen? (*S* is silent) Could a racist probation officer learn that you are a man who deserves respect and maybe help get you a job?

S: (uncertainly) I don't know.

C: There is a lot of racism in this town. However, whether someone is racist or not, how you treat them can have an influence, in the long run, on how many of them will treat you. Not all; some are so racist nothing you do makes a difference. I appreciate the respectful way you have treated me and my questions. Would you be willing to come back next week? (*S* nods yes) Thank you for coming.

Dynamic Case Conceptualization of Sergio: Assumption-Based Style

Sergio comes from a close-knit Mexican family in which his basic needs for nurturance, closeness, and emotional connection as well as his needs for autonomy and independence have been well met. He has identified strongly with his parents, whom he perceives as loving and self-sacrificing. As a result, he has developed a generally adaptive internal model for understanding himself, other people, and interpersonal relationships. This adaptive model is reflected in his predominantly healthy narratives about himself and his family, as reflected in his positive acts toward others, his realistic expectations of others, his accurate perceptions of the reactions of others to himself, and his constructive personal introjects. Sergio's parents have faced an intense, ongoing struggle to support their children financially within what appears to be a highly racist White community. They have only other extended family (Mexicans) to turn to for help. This may have fostered an "us" versus "them" (Mexicans versus Whites) mentality. By his strong identification with his parents, Sergio may have internalized this tendency in the form of negative perceptions and expectations of Whites. This is not a true split of good versus bad, as Sergio has been able to perceive differences among Whites and possibly non-Mexicans who aren't White (neighbors and store owners versus teachers and the clinician). However, these negative expectations and perceptions are important factors in Sergio's recent conflicts with some White community members and the legal system.

How does Sergio act toward others? He is an active and socially outgoing individual who engages in positive interpersonal relationships with his parents, siblings, and extended family. His acts of self toward the Mexican community consist of socially outgoing and responsible behavior in which he values others, defers to the wishes of his elders, and is responsive to the needs of his younger siblings. His acts of self toward Whites range from flexible to rigid. Toward Whites and non-Mexicans whom he perceives as being condescending toward him, not respecting him, or reviling of him (neighbors, school peers, store owners), he responds with withdrawal, passive-aggressive behavior, or minor acts of verbal aggression. Toward Whites and non-Mexicans he perceives as relatively accepting (some teachers, Mr. Zuckerman, the clinician), he can be open, clear thinking, and assertive.

What are Sergio's expectations of others? He has positive expectations for how other Mexicans will react to him. He has a solid faith in his parents' love and respect for him as a growing man. He views them as trusting his ability to be independent and to make decisions about his own life. He is confident that his siblings love him and appreciate the time he takes to care for them and encourage their growth. His baseline expectations for the White community are negative. He expects the behavior of Whites in the neighborhood, schools, and stores to be disrespectful and demeaning; it is likely these oppressive behaviors are occurring. However, he is behaving in ways that can elicit the very negative behavior and stereotyping he most hates and fears from Whites and non-Mexicans who might not mistreat him without this evocative behavior. Sergio has shown the ability to test out his baseline expectations and take in clearly positive interpersonal feedback from Whites and non-Mexicans (some teachers, Mr. Zuckerman, the clinician) despite his overall negative perceptual set. Sergio's negative expectations have a foundation in reality, as there have been racial incidents within his community.

How do other people respond to Sergio, and how does he perceive this interpersonal behavior? His Mexican family and friends enjoy his company and respect his judgment, and he perceives this positively. On the other hand, he has negative perceptions of most White people's behavior. He views many of them as distrusting and reviling him. While there have been racial incidents within the community, he may have misperceived or not perceived some ambiguous or nondiscriminatory community behavior. For example, the curiosity that all new neighbors tend to arouse in a neighborhood may have appeared to Sergio as antagonism. Similarly, the aloofness that a new student can arouse in a close-knit school group may have been misperceived by Sergio as racial antagonism. The report of neglect made against his family, while inappropriate within a culturally aware context, is not out of keeping with the reporting laws for abuse and neglect within the United States. However, the fact that White students were not arrested for bringing drugs to school whereas he was clearly suggests he was targeted because he is Mexican. Thus, while some of his perceptions of oppression are accurate, it is important for Sergio to recognize the role he sometimes plays in furthering or possibly initiating negative views of Mexicans by his intentionally irritating, provocative, or intimidating responses to White community members. Sergio has shown openness to considering when his perceptions are and are not accurate.

What are Sergio's introjects? He views himself as a competent, loving, and responsible family member and believes that, if given the chance, he can be a successful worker. He is proud of his ability to care for his siblings. He primarily treats himself in a positive manner and appreciates and respects his capabilities. He experiences pride and self-respect when he considers the recommendation Mr. Zuckerman is willing to give him for his work on the farm. He experiences strong feelings of shame when he does things that are counter to his parents' values, such as selling marijuana in the schools and teasing store owners. There are some signs, in the comments he makes about his White peers and neighbors, that he may have taken in some negative Mexican stereotypes.

Sergio has learned how to get his intimacy and autonomy needs met effectively within his relationships with Mexicans. His fully adaptive functioning is presently inhibited by his rigid, but not inflexible, negative perceptions and expectations for Whites. These, added to what may be cultural confusion over the ethics of marijuana usage, have resulted in his current status as a drug offender. His drug dealing is not believed to reflect antisocial tendencies, and his conviction, which resulted in probation, may serve as a window of opportunity for challenging Sergio to reexamine his negative perceptions and beliefs about Whites within the treatment setting. Within a treatment relationship, Sergio can experience a reaction to any of his interpersonally distancing behavior, such as teasing and acting stupid or showing hostility, that is different from what he has experienced from the non-Mexicans in his town. Sergio can explore his unconscious struggle for acceptance from the White community and his tendency to use the defense of splitting (good/bad). He will recognize that his style of interacting with Whites is less effective than the one he uses with Mexican Americans. This insight will help ensure his probation ends satisfactorily and that his conviction does not have a continuing negative impact on his ability to succeed in the dominant culture of the United States. Sergio is highly motivated to gain employment, and an active approach in helping him do so will heighten his motivation for change, serve to further reinforce his interpersonal competencies within the White community, and support his positive identity as an adult male who provides emotionally and financially for his family.

Dynamic Treatment Plan: Assumption-Based Style

Treatment Plan Overview. The clinician needs to be sensitive to the likelihood that Sergio will experience further acts of overt or subtle racism during the course of treatment; otherwise, these will create a barrier to treatment success. Long-Term Goal 1 will focus on the treatment relationship and then expand as appropriate to include other relationships (probation officer, teachers, neighbors, peers, parents). Long-Term Goal 2 will be completed as part of the termination process. While helping Sergio find paid employment is not a typical goal from a dynamic perspective, it is considered a critical component of culturally sensitive treatment in Sergio's case, as this is the goal he is most motivated to achieve in order to help his family. The competencies Sergio has shown in reflecting about his conflict-ridden interpersonal transactions with Whites suggest that short-term treatment will be effective. (This treatment plan follows the *basic format*.)

LONG-TERM GOAL 1: Sergio will use his experience within the treatment relationship to increase the flexibility of his internal model of the interpersonal world with Whites and non-Mexicans.

Short-Term Goals

1. Sergio will become aware of the role he has taken on within most White and non-Mexican relationships he is currently involved in; he will make a list of these individuals to facilitate this.

    a. Sergio will become aware of how he has acted within his relationship with Mr. Zuckerman and how this has increased the likelihood of Mr. Zuckerman's maintaining or developing positive stereotypes of Mexicans.

    b. Sergio will become aware of how he has used eliciting maneuvers, such as teasing store owners, that have increased the likelihood that some of these Whites and non-Mexicans will reject him and how his behaviors have supported their maintaining negative stereotypes of Mexicans.

    c. Sergio will become aware of his emotions, fantasies, and wishes involving each of these people and become aware of how his negatively cast ones may have led to his good/bad (Mexican vs. White/non-Mexican) categorization.

2. Sergio will become aware of how he expects to be treated by specific Whites and the emotions that accompany these expectations.

    a. Sergio will become aware of his negative expectations for how each White person will treat him and how these influence his emotions during interactions with this person during the week.

    b. Sergio will become aware of his positive expectations for treatment by Mexicans and how these influence his emotions during interactions with specific Mexican people during the week.

3. Sergio will discuss his perceptions of the treatment he has received during the week from others and the evidence he has to support the accuracy of his perceptions about specific Mexicans, Whites, and non-Mexicans.

    a. Sergio will discuss his positive perceptions of Mexicans, Whites, or non-Mexicans during the past week and the evidence he has to support them.

    b. Sergio will discuss his negative perceptions of Mexicans, Whites, or non-Mexicans during the past week and the evidence he has to support them.

4. Sergio will become more aware of his introjects as he takes on the role of a Mexican, son, brother, young adult, person on probation, and person in treatment.

    a. Sergio will more fully experience his feelings of anger and shame engendered by episodes of racism during the week within any of his roles and consider whether negative community stereotypes are influencing his introjects.

b. Sergio will more fully experience his feelings of pride, love, and respect that are engendered by positive interactions within any of his roles and consider how these interactions are influencing his introjects.

c. Sergio will more fully experience his needs as a young adult for emotional intimacy and independence and consider how well these needs are met within the roles he takes on and how these influence his introjects.

LONG-TERM GOAL 2: Sergio will increase his ability to meet his need for autonomy (being perceived by himself, his family, and others as an adult) through gaining paid employment to support his family's financial health.

Short-Term Goals

1. Sergio will become aware of the role he took on within his work for Mr. Zuckerman as well as his emotions, fantasies, and wishes for himself as an employee for someone else who is likely to be White or non-Mexican.

2. Sergio will explore, with the clinician, teachers, and the probation officer, the expectations of employers within the United States for their employees' behavior, particularly as they relate to on-the-job behavior and drug use.

3. Sergio will become aware of his own perceptions of his treatment by Mr. Zuckerman as well as his emotions, fantasies, and wishes regarding how White and non-Mexican employers may treat him when he first comes to work for them and what actions he could take to encourage a positive stereotype of Mexicans.

4. Sergio will become aware of his introjects about himself as a good employee and further explore any positive or negative emotions he has about his identity as a young adult seeking to help his family financially.

Dynamic Case Conceptualization of Sergio: Interpersonally Based Style

Sergio's interpersonal relationships with his parents, siblings, White boss, and White community members paint contrasting views of his areas of strength and weakness. Sergio is trying to acculturate to the new expectations of others now that he is living in the United States after living much of his earlier childhood in Mexico. He was referred for treatment by his probation officer because he was using marijuana and selling it at school. Sergio perceives it to be racism that he was arrested and put on probation in the first place. He expects that the White teachers and White police officers will treat him and his family disrespectfully because they are Latinos. While Sergio's parents may share his view of marijuana and the racism in their community, they have adamantly requested that he stop using, as it is against the law in the United States. His probation officer expects him to stop being out late at night, although his parents are not concerned about this because it is typical for young men in Mexico. While Sergio's interpersonal relationships with many White individuals involve his acting oppositional toward all he perceives to be racist, Sergio's manner of interacting with his family is quite different. He has a deep commitment to helping his younger siblings with their homework and trying to provide money to help his family purchase basic necessities. His perceptions of himself are that he is a hard worker and that his White employer, Mr. Zuckerman, would give him a good recommendation. His ability to relate differently with others, depending on the situation, bodes well for his being able to develop a new model of relating to White people who may have no experience with the Mexican culture.

Sergio's role with his parents is to be a respectful son. He recognizes that coming to live in the United States has been more difficult for his parents than for him, as he has become fluent in English and they have not. Despite being followed at stores and overhearing racist comments from other people in the stores, Sergio continues to do the family shopping. He perceives his parents to be wiser than he and expects that they will always advise him of his best interests. He is very aware of all the hard work they have done to support him and his siblings. Sergio is willing to leave high school and work to earn more money so his family and extended family won't be hungry in the winter. However, his parents want him to succeed in school and are proud that he will be the first family member to graduate from high school. Sergio's introjects about his elders are that they deserve his admiration, that his extended family help each other, that they are all hardworking and fine people, and that he is proud to be one of them.

Sergio's role with his siblings is to be the helpful older brother. He comes home directly from school to help his brother José with his homework. Even when he needs more time for his own work, he puts helping José first. Sergio perceives José as having more trouble learning than he does himself and acts to be a responsible and dependable helper. He perceives it to be his responsibility to help José learn. He also considers his siblings' happiness to be his concern. He is deeply pained when he perceives his sister Ana to have been victimized by racism. Young girls she perceived to be her friends did not include her in a recent birthday party. Sergio is quick to label this as racism, and, given his experiences in town, it is not an unlikely reason for her exclusion. However, he is able to consider that his expectations and perceptions of racism may not always be accurate. Sergio's introjects about himself as an older brother include that he cares deeply for them, that they care deeply for him, and that he is being a responsible older brother to always put their needs ahead of his own.

Sergio's role as a Mexican in a White community ranges from flexible to rigid. Toward Whites or non-Mexicans he perceives as relatively accepting (some teachers, Mr. Zuckerman, the clinician), he can be open, clear thinking, and assertive. His acts of self toward White Mr. Zuckerman are to take on the role of a hardworking and dependable employee. He works all summer on Mr. Zuckerman's farm and is valued for his efforts by Mr. Zuckerman, who has offered to be a reference for any winter work Sergio applies for. Mr. Zuckerman is White, and Sergio has been able to perceive that his behavior is not racist and that he recognizes that Sergio and his family members are deserving of respect. Sergio expects that he can be successful in the world of work and perceives that good bosses will appreciate this hard work, even if they are White. Sergio's introjects about himself as a worker are that he is always on time, works hard, and never takes time off.

Sergio's role as a Mexican, toward Whites and non-Mexicans whom he perceives as being condescending toward him, not respecting him, or reviling him (neighbors, school peers, storeowners) is to respond with withdrawal, passive-aggressive behavior, or minor acts of verbal aggression. He has come to expect the behavior of Whites in the neighborhood, schools, and stores to be disrespectful and demeaning. These expectations may well have been built up on real oppressive behavior; Sergio lives in a community where there have been many acts of racism. However, he is behaving in ways that can elicit the very negative behavior and stereotyping he most hates and fears. There may be more Whites or non-Mexicans who would not mistreat him if he didn't engage in provocative behavior, such as pretending to have trouble finding his money when he is at the cash register of a store. Sergio has shown himself to have the ability to test out his baseline expectations and take in clearly positive interpersonal feedback from Whites and non-Mexicans (some teachers, Mr. Zuckerman, the clinician) despite his overall negative perceptual set. While there have been racial incidents within the community, Sergio may have misperceived or not perceived some ambiguous or nondiscriminatory community behavior. For example, the curiosity that all new neighbors tend to arouse in a neighborhood may have appeared to Sergio as antagonism. Similarly, the aloofness that a new student can arouse in a close-knit school group may have been misperceived by Sergio as racial antagonism. His introjects contains strong feelings of shame when he does things that are counter to his parents' values, such as selling marijuana in the schools and teasing store owners.

Sergio has a flexible pattern of responding in interpersonal relationships. He can be a hardworking, dependable, and kind son and older brother. He can be a conscientious, respectful, and grateful employee to Mr. Zuckerman. He can be an irritating, slow, and provocative adolescent on probation. At this time, Sergio is hiding his positive identity, as a hardworking and dependable family member, from his probation officer. His perceptions, expectations, and introjects all reinforce his belief that he is only on probation because he is Mexican. It is possible that Sergio's beliefs are accurate. It is also possible that his probation officer is a racist. These would serve as powerful barriers to Sergio getting off probation and developing more effective skills for living within a non-Mexican community. However, Sergio's strong motivation to help his parents financially is also a window of opportunity for change. It is possible that his probation officer, his teachers, or other members of the community might be able to help him find paid employment even if they hold some racists beliefs. Receiving effective help from White members of the community is more important to the health of Sergio's family then the brief feelings of satisfaction Sergio gets from successfully provoking individuals he considers to be racist. This knowledge may help Sergio more fully explore how he can relate to White community members, teachers, and his probation officer without breaking their rules so that he can be proud of his Mexican American heritage and still remain on the pathway to employment success.

Dynamic Treatment Plan: Interpersonally Based Style

Treatment Plan Overview. The clinician needs to be sensitive to the likelihood that Sergio will experience further acts of overt or subtle racism during the course of treatment; otherwise, these will create a barrier to treatment success. In addition, if the clinician is White, he or she needs to recognize that Sergio will test the relationship to see if his expectation that the clinician is a racist is accurate. As a result, Long Term Goal 1 and then

Long Term Goal 2 will be initiated first so that there will be many opportunities for the clinician to show respectful behavior toward Sergio's family. Helping Sergio find paid employment (Long Term Goal 1) is not a typical goal from a dynamic perspective; however, it is considered a critical component of culturally sensitive treatment in Sergio's case, as this is the goal he is most motivated to achieve in order to help his family. The competencies Sergio has shown in reflecting about his conflict-ridden interpersonal transactions with Whites suggest that short-term treatment will be effective. (This treatment plan follows the *basic format*.)

LONG-TERM GOAL 1: Sergio will fully explore how he relates to his Mexican American parents to develop a plan for helping them financially without coming into contact with the law.

1. Sergio will become aware of the role he takes on as a respectful young male with his Mexican American parents.

2. Sergio will explore the expectations he has for his Mexican American parents' behavior toward him and how they view his use of marijuana.

3. Sergio will become aware of his own perceptions of his treatment by his parents both before and after his arrest for using and selling marijuana.

4. Sergio will become more aware of his introjects about himself as a Mexican American son who wants his parents to be proud of him as a man, and how this has been affected by his being arrested for using and selling marijuana.

LONG-TERM GOAL 2: Sergio will fully explore how he relates to his Mexican-American siblings and how he can be a role model for them as they acculturate to White society in the United States.

1. Sergio will become more aware of the role he takes on as an older sibling along with all that means to his younger siblings as they learn to be Mexican Americans.

2. Sergio will explore the expectations he has for his siblings and how they are impacted by his use and selling of marijuana.

3. Sergio will become aware of his own perceptions of his treatment by his siblings both before and after his arrest for using and selling marijuana.

4. Sergio will become more aware of his introjects of himself as a Mexican American older brother who is his siblings' role model of a young man and how this has been affected by his being arrested for using and selling marijuana.

LONG-TERM GOAL 3: Sergio will fully explore how he relates to his White employer Mr. Zuckerman and how he can be proud of his Mexican American heritage without engaging in oppositional behavior with Whites who may hold racist expectations and perceptions of Mexican Americans.

Short-Term Goals

1. Sergio will become aware of the role he took on within his work for Mr. Zuckerman as well as his emotions, fantasies, and wishes for himself as an employee for someone else who is likely to be White or non-Mexican.

2. Sergio will explore, with the clinician, teachers, and the probation officer, the expectations of employers within the United States for their employees' behavior, particularly as they relate to on-the-job behavior and drug use.

3. Sergio will become aware of his own perceptions of his treatment by Mr. Zuckerman as well as his emotions, fantasies, and wishes regarding how White or non-Mexican employers may treat him when he first comes to work for them and what actions he could take to encourage a positive stereotype of Mexicans.

4. Sergio will become aware of his introjects of himself as a good employee and how these have been affected by his being arrested for using and selling marijuana.

LONG-TERM GOAL 4: Sergio will fully explore how he can relate to White community members, teachers, and his probation officer without breaking their rules so that he can be proud of his Mexican American heritage and still remain on the pathway to employment success.

Short-Term Goals

1. Sergio will become aware of the role he has taken on with most White community members, such as teachers, store employers, and his probation officer.

   a. Sergio will become aware of how he has acted within his relationship with Mr. Zuckerman and how this has increased the likelihood of Mr. Zuckerman's maintaining or developing positive stereotypes of Mexicans.

   b. Sergio will become aware of how he has used eliciting maneuvers, such as teasing store owners, that have increased the likelihood that some of these Whites or non-Mexicans will reject him, and of how his behaviors have supported their maintaining negative stereotypes of Mexicans.

   c. Sergio will become aware of his emotions, fantasies, and wishes involving each of these people and become aware of how his negatively cast ones may have led to his good/bad (Mexican vs. White/non-Mexican) categorization.

2. Sergio will become aware of how he expects to be treated by specific Whites and the emotions that accompany these expectations.

   a. Sergio will become aware of his negative expectations for how each White person will treat him and how these influence his emotions during interactions with this person during the week.

   b. Sergio will become aware of his positive expectations for treatment by Mexicans and how this influences his emotions during interactions with specific Mexican people during the week.

3. Sergio will discuss his perceptions of the treatment he has received from others during the week and the evidence he has to support the accuracy of his perceptions of specific Mexicans, Whites, and non-Mexicans.

   a. Sergio will discuss his positive perceptions of Mexicans, Whites, or non-Mexicans during the past week and the evidence he has to support them.

   b. Sergio will discuss his negative perceptions of Mexicans, Whites, or non-Mexicans during the past week and the evidence he has to support them.

4. Sergio will discuss the introjects he could have about himself if he behaved respectfully toward all individuals, whether they were racists or not.

   a. Sergio will discuss the roles this might open up for him as he searches for paid employment.

   b. Sergio will discuss the emotional frustration or pain he might suffer if he is respectful to those who are not respectful to him.

   c. Sergio will discuss how his behavior might bring positive benefits to himself and his family.

   d. Sergio will discuss the sacrifices adult males have to make in order to take good care of their families.

PRACTICE CASE FOR STUDENT CONCEPTUALIZATION: INTEGRATING THE DOMAIN OF GENDER

It is time to do a dynamic analysis of Steve. There are many domains of complexity that may be appropriate to him. You are asked to integrate the domain of gender into your dynamic case conceptualization and treatment plan.

Information Received From Brief Intake

Steve is a senior in college. He has majored in art. He describes himself as a talented artist and as being in excellent health. He lives in an apartment off campus with several friends and periodically visits his parents, who live in a city about two hours away. He comes from an upper-middle-class family, which has provided the financial support for his college attendance. He has referred himself because, as he approaches graduation, now just one month away, he is becoming increasingly concerned about his ability to be financially independent after leaving college.

During a brief mental status exam, he demonstrated a moderate level of anxiety about his future; however, he showed no signs of suicidal or homicidal ideation or severe psychopathology. He expressed a preference for a male clinician but was willing to take a female if that would give him an earlier appointment.

Interview With Steve (S) From a Dynamic Perspective

C: I understand from the phone intake that you have been feeling stressed for about a month.

S: (angrily) I feel really stupid being here. I should be able to handle this on my own.

C: You are angry about needing help from someone.

S: (confusedly) I don't really know why I came. I have always solved my problems on my own. (emphatically) All my friends solve their own problems. I'm sorry that I've wasted your time.

C: Are you sure that asking for help is a waste of my time?

S: (with determination) Of course. If you can't take care of yourself, you are a loser. (pause) Why would anyone want to help a loser?

C: Might I have any other perceptions of you?

S: (dismissively) No. If any of my friends knew that I had come here, they would be laughing it up.

C: I will see you as a loser, and your friends will laugh.

S: (intently) You bet. They know how independent I am. (thoughtfully) At first, they would think I was kidding about coming here. Then they would make fun of me and maybe call me "Mr. Psycho."

C: Your friends don't help you when you have a problem?

S: (derisively) Only losers have problems. All of my friends are artists; they are very self-sufficient. They talk of art, art theory, the stupidity of some of the art profs around here, or the moronic taste of most of the students here.

C: You belong to a group of young artists who keep separate from most of the other students here.

S: (calmly) Yes, we keep pretty much to ourselves; our goals are just on a different plane. We each have our own talent and work hard to develop it within ourselves.

C: It sounds like you are alone a lot.

S: (emphatically) Of course, you must be alone to create. (fervently) It's unbelievable to be on your own, creating something really important that maybe only a few people will ever truly appreciate.

C: You are alone with your art, your problems . . . even with your friends. (pause) You keep changing your position. How are you feeling right now?

S: (with increasing stress) My back has been hurting a lot lately; it's been keeping me from doing my work.

C: The pain in your body has slowed you down and given you more time to think.

S: (intently) Yes, I have been thinking a lot, but these aren't the types of thoughts I share with my friends. (softly) They would just laugh and then find a reason to walk out.

C: *What will happen if you tell me?*

S: (reflectively) I guess it's your job to listen. (pause) I hear seniors talking all the time about their plans for after graduation. Some are getting married; some have jobs. All of them seem to be having parties or something to celebrate. I haven't been invited to any parties, and my parents haven't suggested I have one. (confused) Not that I need that kind of thing—it's really irrelevant.

C: But it feels strange not to be connected to friends the way most of the other students seem to be.

S: (nodding) Yeah, I never have been even as a child. I have always been self-sufficient, even from my folks. I only need my art.

C: Your art. (pause) What does it mean to you?

S: (sounding happy for the first time) I feel really free and expressive.

C: Has something changed? (pause) You don't look like you feel free.

S: (softly) It used to feel great, but now it doesn't. In the studio, I look over at my friends painting, and I wonder who they are.

C: Have you asked them?

S: (sarcastically) They would just laugh if I asked them something like that. We are always laughing at the boring lives most people lead, constantly fighting with each other and being jealous of each other. (anxiously) I'm not laughing now. I don't have anyone to be jealous of and yet, I don't know.

C: You feel alone even when you're with your friends because you don't feel you can safely share your thoughts. Is there anyone you can turn to when you feel alone?

S: (firmly) No. My folks are very busy and very independent. They wouldn't understand at all. My father is still bent out of shape that I chose to major in art. He thinks I've wasted his money. He would really blow his top if he knew that I wasn't even sure about art anymore.

C: *Why have you wasted his money?*

S: (sarcastically) Well, he's the director of a bank. (pause) Since I was a kid, all that he's had time for is money. He can't understand why I chose art. He says since I am not Picasso, I am going to be dependent on him forever.

C: But (pause) you are so self-sufficient.

S: (anxiously) I don't need people. (pause) But, if I don't make money, I'll be under my father's control forever.

C: His control?

S: (intently) If I need his money to start an art studio, he'll make me grovel for it.

C: Grovel?

S: (impatiently) Spend time at the bank, go to his parties, try to suck up to his friends. (head in his hands, fearfully) I can't paint; I feel so pressured!

C: You can't express yourself with your parents, your friends, now even your art . . . (pause)

S: (desperately) I have to get out of this chair; my back is killing me.

C: This is the second time that, when discussing loneliness, you have shifted the conversation to your back. I wonder what role the pain is playing in your life.

S: (angrily) It's been building these past few months, ever since my last talk with my folks about money.

C: What happened?

S: (intently) I have to make money. I have always known that in the back of my mind. (pause) But art isn't about money and competition. It's about what's inside you. I have had this fight repeatedly with my dad. (angrily) He's a brick wall. He keeps saying, "You'll be like a kept woman."

C: He puts your manhood on the line.

S: (sarcastically) Ever since I was about two.

C: Tell me more about this.

S: (furiously) I can still hear my dad's voice in my head saying "Be a man" every time I asked for help.

C: Help with what?

S: (sarcastically) My shoes, my homework . . . (pause) I was a real pain to them as a kid, but I learned as fast as I could and tried not to ask for help with the same thing twice.

C: You wanted your parents' approval, and they didn't approve of your needing help.

S: (calmly) In our house, to ask for help is to be a loser. I heard it a thousand times: "Do it yourself, try harder, be a man, or you'll always be a loser!"

C: Who said that?

S: (angrily) They both did, but my dad was the loudest.

C: In your family, independence was important; needing help was stupid. How did you experience that?

S: (with determination) I thought my parents were right. I was a loser.

C: You say demeaning things to yourself. Did you learn to treat yourself this way from your parents?

S: (matter-of-factly) Sure, but my friends call dependent people losers too. People need to take care of themselves. Don't you agree?

C: Your parents, your friends, and your inner voice all criticize you for needing help, and you assume I will. What else could it mean for children or adults to need help besides that they are losers?

S: (long pause; calmly) Maybe it's OK for children to need help; you aren't born knowing everything. But this is different—I'm an adult man.

C: You have said that men have to be competitive, make money, and not need anything. Is this really true?

S: (confusedly) Why am I still sitting here? What's the point?

C: Part of you is ready to go. Part of you wonders if it's okay for a man to get help.

S: (jumping up; angrily) I'm tired of your stupid comments. (shaking a fist toward *C*) Maybe you are the loser!

C: (loudly) I don't like being called a loser, and I don't like people shaking their fists at me!

S: (sitting down; defensively) I didn't mean . . . (long pause) I just feel so edgy, and I can't create anything, and . . . (hanging his head down)

C: (long pause; calmly) I apologize for yelling. I don't like being called a loser. You don't either. (*S* looks up; long pause) Have you ever noticed that when someone yells at you, something inside wants to make you yell back?

S: (reflectively) That's what always seems to happen with my dad, even when I tell myself ahead of time to stay cool.

C: It's a normal reaction. (pause) Just in case you're wondering, I don't think you're a loser.

S: (soft) Thanks. (pause; tense) I want to paint.

C: You need to paint. (pause) Being an artist is a critical part of who you are. (*S* nods) We won't forget that as we do our work together.

Exercises for Developing a Case Conceptualization of Steve

Exercise 1 *(four-page maximum)*

GOAL: To verify that you have a clear understanding of time-limited dynamic theory.

STYLE: Integrative essay incorporating Parts A through C.

NEED HELP?   Review this chapter (pages 277–282).

A. Develop a concise overview of all the assumptions of time-limited dynamic theory (the theory's hypotheses about key dimensions in understanding how clients change; think broadly, abstractly) as an introduction to the rest of this exercise.

B. Develop a thorough description of how each of these assumptions is used to understand a client's progression through the change process in paragraphs that provide specific examples to fully explain each assumption.

C. Conclude your essay by describing the role of the clinician in helping the client change (consultant, doctor, educator, helper), the major approach taken to treatment, and common treatment techniques. Provide enough specific examples to clarify what is distinctive about this approach.

Exercise 2 (four-page maximum)

GOAL: To aid application of dynamic theory to Steve.

STYLE: A separate sentence outline for each section, A through C.

NEED HELP?   Review this chapter (pages 277–282).

A. Assess how adaptively or maladaptively Steve is relating to his parents, his peers, and his teachers, and analyze his interaction style within each type of relationship using either a CMP, an adaptive pattern of relating, or a mixed pattern with both adaptive and maladaptive features. Be sure to include in each interpersonal pattern his role for himself in relating to others, his expectations of others' attitudes and intentions toward him, his perceptions of the behavior of others toward him, and his role toward himself (introjects).

B. Overall, how well is Steve relating to the clinician at this time, considering (a) any signs of transference from Steve, (b) any signs of countertransference from the clinician, and (c) any signs of openness to interpretations of his interpersonal patterns?

C. Over all his relationships, what strengths (strong points, positive features, successes, skills, factors facilitating change) and weaknesses (concerns, issues, problems, symptoms, skills deficits, treatment barriers) does Steve bring to the interpersonal process, and how well is he getting his needs for intimacy and autonomy met across all these relationships?

D. Does Steve bring any strengths or weaknesses to treatment that are separate from his manner of relating to others? If so, how might the weaknesses affect the treatment process, and how might the strengths be used to support treatment success?

Exercise 3 (four-page maximum)

GOAL: To develop an understanding of the potential role of gender in Steve's life.

STYLE: A separate sentence outline for each section, A through I.

NEED HELP?   Review Chapter 2 (pages 41–51).

A. Assess the personal costs or benefits of the gender role currently guiding Steve in terms of his self-image, emotional life, expectations, perceptions, behavior, and access to personal resources.

B. Assess the interpersonal costs or benefits of the gender role currently guiding Steve in terms of his relationships with romantic partners, family, and friends.

C. Assess the social costs or benefits of the gender role current guiding Steve in terms of his educational or work relationships and access to social resources.

D. How much are traditional gender roles positively or negatively influencing Steve's mental or physical health, and how aware is Steve of these influences?

E. Overall, how much power and choice does Steve have to live life as a nongendered individual with unique needs and goals, and how strong are counterpressures on Steve to be a gendered individual?

F. What is your current knowledge of gender issues?

   1. How many courses have you taken that give you background on issues relevant to gender?

   2. How many workshops have you taken that give you background on gender issues?

   3. What professional experiences have you had that were informed by a gender analysis?

   4. What personal experiences have you had in which you have considered the impact of gender on individuals?

   5. What cohort effects might influence your worldview of gender, the roles of men and women in society, how men and women communicate, and what is rewarded and punished for males and females?

G. What is your current level of awareness of how gender has played a role in your life?

   1. What gender role is currently guiding you in your life?

   2. How similar or different is this gender role to that of Steve?

   3. What stereotypes of gender within U.S. culture might influence your views of the client?

   4. Discuss any stereotypes of the male gender that you know.

   5. Discuss experiences you have had that could support your effective work with Steve as well as experiences you have had that might lead to negative bias or marginalization of Steve's point of view or current situation.

H. What are your current skills in working with Steve?

   1. What skills do you currently have that are of value in working with Steve?

   2. What skills might it be important to develop to carry out an effective gender analysis of Steve?

3. What could you do to develop a positive working relationship with Steve?

4. What aspects of your treatment approach might be gender biased, and how will you deal with this?

I. What action steps can you take?

1. What can you do to prepare yourself to be more skilled in working with Steve?

2. How might you structure the treatment environment to increase the likelihood of a positive outcome for Steve?

3. What processes of treatment might you change to make them more welcoming to Steve?

Exercise 4 (six-page maximum)

GOAL: To help you integrate your knowledge of dynamic theory and gender issues into an in-depth conceptualization of Steve (who he is and why he does what he does).

STYLE: An integrated essay consisting of a premise, supportive details, and conclusions following a carefully planned organizational style (see Chapter 2).

NEED HELP?   Review Chapter 1 (pages 1–7) and Chapter 2 (pages 41–51).

STEP 1: Consider what style you should use for organizing your dynamic understanding of Steve. This style should (a) support you in providing a comprehensive and clear understanding of his dynamics and (b) support language that Steve might find persuasive, considering his fear that needing treatment means he's a loser.

STEP 2: Develop a concise premise (overview, preliminary or explanatory statements, proposition, thesis statement, theory-driven introduction, hypotheses, summary, concluding causal statements) that explains Steve's overall functioning as a young man fearful of his ability to succeed as an artist. If you have trouble with Step 2, remember that this should be an integration of the key ideas of Exercises 2 and 3 and that it should (a) provide a basis for Steve's long-term goals, (b) be grounded in dynamic theory and sensitive to gender issues, and (c) highlight the strengths Steve brings to dynamic treatment.

STEP 3: Develop your supporting material (a detailed case analysis of strengths and weaknesses, supplying data to support an introductory premise) from a dynamic perspective, incorporating within each paragraph a deep understanding of Steve and his struggles with society's definition of masculinity. If you need help with Step 3, consider the information you need to include in order to support the development of short-term goals that (a) are grounded in dynamic theory and sensitive to gender issues and (b) integrate an understanding of Steve's strengths in interpersonal relating whenever possible.

STEP 4: Develop your conclusions and broad treatment recommendations, including (a) Steve's overall level of functioning, (b) anything facilitating or serving as a barrier to his changing his interpersonal patterns at this time, and (c) his basic needs in the interpersonal process at this time, being careful to consider what you said in Part G and I of Exercise 3 (be concise and general).

Exercise 5 (three-page maximum)

GOAL: To develop an individualized, theory-driven action plan for Steve that considers his strengths and is sensitive to gender issues.

STYLE: A sentence outline consisting of long- and short-term goals.

NEED HELP?   Review Chapter 1 (pages 7–24).

STEP 1: Develop your treatment plan overview, being careful to consider what you said in Parts G and I of Exercise 3 to try to prevent any negative bias in your treatment plan and to ensure that you adapt your treatment approach to Steve's unique needs as an individual.

STEP 2: Develop long-term (major, large, ambitious, comprehensive, broad) goals that will help Steve develop a flexible pattern of relating to others as an adult male and that *ideally* he will reach by the termination of treatment. If you have trouble with Step 2, reread your premise and support topic sentences, looking for ideas to transform into goals that will help give Steve insight into his interpersonal style and the ability to relate in a flexible manner to others (use the *style* of Exercise 4).

STEP 3: Develop short-term (small, brief, encapsulated, specific, measurable) goals that Steve and you can expect to see accomplished within a few weeks and that will help you chart Steve's progress in developing interpersonal insights and skills, instill hope for change, and plan time-effective treatment sessions. If you have trouble with Step 3, reread your support paragraphs, looking for ideas to transform into goals that (a) might help Steve gain a new experience within the interpersonal process with the clinician; (b) might help him gain a new understanding of how he relates to others as a man; (c) might enhance factors facilitating development of a flexible style of relating or getting his needs for autonomy and nurturance met, or decrease barriers to such development; (d) utilize his strengths to build a flexible style of relating as an adult male whenever possible; and (e) are individualized to his interpersonal needs rather than generic.

Exercise 6

GOAL: To critique short-term dynamic treatment in the case of Steve.

STYLE: Answer Questions A through E in essay form or discuss them in a group format.

A. What are the strengths and weaknesses of this model for helping Steve, a college student struggling with rigid gender role stereotypes?

B. Discuss the strengths and weaknesses of using emotion-focused treatment with Steve in comparison to dynamic treatment. Be sure to consider his goals for treatment (greater emotional intimacy, career direction) as well as his ability to be motivated to work within this approach.

C. Discuss Steve considering the domain of socioeconomic status. How might having been raised in a wealthy family have influenced his interpersonal style and contributed to his fears about the future? Compare the importance of class versus gender issues in guiding Steve's treatment. Overall, how big a difference would it make in your treatment plan?

D. Steve is socially isolated, involved in serious family discord, and feeling hopeless about his future. Discuss whether supporting Steve in departing from the gender role stereotypes of his family would increase or decrease his risk for suicide. What more do you need to know from Steve in the next session to feel confident in your assessment of his risk?

E. Dynamic treatment requires a great deal of self-awareness on your part along with strategic use of your own internal reactions to the client. Consider your internal reactions to Steve as you peruse the interview again, this time taking note of which comments from him evoked which reactions from you. Discuss these countertransference issues and how much you consider them to be a reaction to Steve's pattern of relating and how much they are a result of your own personal history.

RECOMMENDED RESOURCES

Books

Binder, J. L. (2004). *Key competencies in brief dynamic psychotherapy: Clinical practice beyond the manual.* New York, NY: Guilford Press.

Greenberg, L. S., McWilliams, N., & Wenzel, A. (2013). *Exploring three approaches to psychotherapy.* Washington, DC: American Psychological Association.

Levenson, H. (2010). *Brief dynamic therapy.* Washington, DC: American Psychological Association.

Levenson, H., & Strupp, H. H. (2007). Cyclic maladaptive patterns: Case formulation in time-limited dynamic psychotherapy. In T. D. Eells (Ed.), *Handbook of psychotherapy case formulation* (2nd ed., pp. 164–197). New York, NY: Guilford Press.

Videos

American Psychological Association (Producer), & Freedheim, D. K. (Trainer). (n.d.). *Short-term dynamic therapy* (Systems of Psychotherapy Video Series, Motion Picture #4310833). (Available from the American Psychological Association, 750 First Street, NE, Washington, DC 20002–4242)

Frederickson, J. (2011, October 5). Intensive short term dynamic psychotherapy part 1 [Video file]. Retrieved from https://www.youtube.com/watch?v=cKzmk2-xnzY

PsychotherapyNet. (2009, May 6). Time-limited dynamic psychotherapy (TLDP) with Hannah Levenson video [Video file]. Retrieved from https://www.youtube.com/watch?v=yTHM2o3dvao

Websites

California Society for Intensive Short-Term Dynamic Psychotherapy. http://www.istdp.com/

Hanna Levenson, PhD. http://www.hannalevenson.com/institute.html

Society for Psychotherapy Research. http://www.psychotherapyresearch.org/?104

N I N E

Family Systems Case Conceptualizations and Treatment Plans

INTRODUCTION TO FAMILY SYSTEMS THEORY

You have just received a referral from Mrs. Walters, a third-grade teacher. She says a 9-year-old White girl named Alice has been a constant behavior problem; Alice is disrespectful and will not follow instructions in class. In addition, Alice is described as bossy and immature in relating to her peers. Alice is a new student in the school. She moved into the district when her mother (Katherine, age 30) and her father (Dave, age 32) were divorced this past summer. While Katherine has primary custody, Alice spends almost every weekend with her father and her paternal grandmother. Dave is using Alice as a confidant. He wants Katherine to return to the marriage, and his mother supports him in this. He has asked Alice to spy on Katherine so that he can find a way to get their family back together. Dave was respectful of Katherine's role as mother prior to the divorce, but now, everything seems to be forgotten as he single-mindedly pursues reconciliation with Katherine; the thought that his behavior might have the opposite effect hasn't seemed to cross his mind. Katherine revealed all this information to Mrs. Walters during a parent-teacher conference last week; Mrs. Walters told Katherine she would make the referral to you but that Katherine would have to directly contact you to get an appointment.

A short intake was scheduled, and during a mental status screen, both Alice and Katherine appeared to be of at least average intelligence. There were no signs of any cognitive confusion or learning disabilities in Alice that could be playing a role in her academic difficulties. Katherine showed no signs of cognitive confusion, homicidal or suicidal behavior, or impulse control difficulties.

Your approach to Alice's situation will be based on the structural family approach of Salvador Minuchin. Alice might have an individually focused problem, such as a learning disability, that is leading her to misbehave in school. However, the power of your approach comes through its recognition that Alice's problems might be a reflection of family conflict. Much of the conflict that Alice experiences in her life will involve her interactions with others. Considering her family as a unit, determined by its interactional patterns, provides many new and nonblaming explanations for Alice's situation; she is an individual, doing her best to get her needs met within the context of her relationships—most particularly her family relationships.

Every family is a social group that has a structure. The purpose of this structure is to ensure accomplishment of family tasks, such as paying the bills, cleaning the house, helping children with homework, and caring for sick family members. The structure also determines how each family member's needs for independence and emotional closeness get met. For a family's structure to be functional, the tasks need to be coordinated, and personal needs must be met in a dependable fashion.

The structure of a family can be analyzed in terms of its basic features. One important feature is its subsystems or the smaller units that make up the family system. Subsystems may develop around specific functions that need to be achieved in the family, such as parenting children. Family subsystems may also develop around gender, generation, or both. Another important structural feature is the boundaries that develop between subsystems and between the family system as a whole and nonfamily members. Boundaries determine how much subsystems communicate with each other and how much family members are encouraged to individuate versus how much emotional closeness is encouraged. Family structure also carries within it a hierarchy that determines who is in charge of coordinating tasks and making decisions. This hierarchy of power and authority often has a spousal subsystem at the top.

If Alice's family is functioning well, it will be encouraging developmentally appropriate autonomy (individuation) and developmentally appropriate relatedness (a sense of belonging) for all family members. If Alice's family system is malfunctioning, treatment will intervene to help family members alter their interactional patterns and develop a structure that is more effective in meeting their needs as a unit and as individuals. The following more detailed paragraphs are based on the work of Salvador Minuchin and his colleagues (Minuchin, 1974; Minuchin & Fishman, 1981; Minuchin, Nichols, & Lee, 2007; Nichols, 2008).

When Katherine and Dave married and moved in together, they created a new family system. Their family had only two members (Katherine and Dave), but it had three smaller family groupings or subsystems: the Katherine subsystem, the Dave subsystem, and the spousal subsystem. Each subsystem had tasks to accomplish, and members within each subsystem were likely to develop roles complementary to each other. At first, Dave and Katherine needed to adjust to, and negotiate with each other, who would do what tasks in the family. They also needed to develop rules related to how to communicate with each other and how to resolve conflicts. While Katherine and Dave needed to have loyalty to their couple as a unit (spousal subsystem), they still needed to maintain loyalty to themselves as individuals (Dave subsystem, Katherine subsystem). This personal loyalty helped ensure that while Katherine and Dave made some accommodation to each other, they continued to support their own autonomy needs.

As enduring patterns were developed between Dave and Katherine, they each began to use only a limited number of the behaviors they were capable of; this is because each had been delegated to engage in only certain family tasks. For example, at the beginning of the marriage, Dave may have initiated early social contacts between the family and extended family because his relations lived close by. However, as this continued to occur over time, he and Katherine may have developed the expectation that he would always be in charge of this, establishing an enduring pattern within their family; the longer this pattern endured, the more it seemed necessary rather than optional. Thus, a family rule may have developed that only Dave could set up social engagements. The family rules that develop over time may be explicit or implicit and govern the range of behaviors that are considered appropriate for each family member.

As more members enter a family, more subsystems develop. When Alice was born, two new subsystems formed. The parental subsystem was formed to be responsive to Alice's developing needs, and Alice formed her own subsystem. Alice and her mother could also have formed a subsystem of females. The parents interacted with each other and with Alice to carry out socialization functions. Alice, in interacting with her parents, learned what to expect from people who had more strength and greater resources. She learned what brought rewards and what brought punishments.

If other children had entered the family system, then a sibling subsystem would have formed. Within a sibling subsystem, children learn important interpersonal skills, such as how to accommodate and negotiate with peers and what to expect from individuals with power equal to theirs. If at first an older child stands up for a younger one in a fight with another child, this begins to develop an expectation, and then a family rule, that the older one will take care of the younger one; this rule may continue even after it is not functional because the "younger one" is now old enough to take care of himself or herself. If the older one remains the protector, the younger one may not learn to stand up for himself or herself. Thus, expectations between family members, if they continue to be met, establish family rules for how each member "should" behave.

What boundaries developed among the subsystems of Alice's family? Boundaries are invisible barriers that determine how frequently and in what manner subsystems interact with each other. A boundary also exists around the family system as a whole in its interactions with the outside world. Minuchin describes boundaries as being clear, diffuse, or rigid. Clear subsystem boundaries exist when family members are supported, nurtured, and allowed to individuate. In this case, although the parental subsystem has the most power, the parents will modify the family rules to accommodate, for example, the growing need of teenagers to make decisions and have control over aspects of their day-to-day lives. There is frequent communication among subsystems. Thus, subsystems can communicate and negotiate with one another, and family rules accommodate to situational and developmental challenges.

Diffuse boundaries exist when family members are supported and nurtured but not allowed to individuate. There is no clear hierarchy of authority, and family members negotiate with and accommodate to each other too much. This may lead family members to become enmeshed (extremely dependent on one another emotionally). Enmeshed children are immature and rely too much on their parents and not enough on their own abilities. The growing children may need more personal control but fear either that individuation will be a rejection of family members or that they cannot successfully be independent. Parents may fear disastrous consequences if children have more autonomy. On the other hand, a child who is enmeshed with a parent may believe he or she has the right to interrupt this parent and demand attention even when the parent is engaged in a vital task or in an important communication with another person; the parent's authority in the family is not respected. In interacting with individuals outside the family, enmeshed family members continue to expect to be cared for and will make unrealistic demands on others.

Rigid boundaries exist when family members are encouraged to individuate and master personal interests but needs for nurturance go unmet. Rigid boundaries restrict interpersonal contact between family members, leading to emotional disengagement (emotional isolation). Family members have little room to negotiate and accommodate to each other. There is only restricted access between subsystems. As a result, each family member may be an island, facing successes and failures alone.

It may be that some members of a family are disengaged from each other while others are enmeshed. For example, Katherine and Alice may have become emotionally overinvolved (enmeshed) with each other to make up for their feelings of loss following the divorce. On the other hand, Dave may have become emotionally distanced (disengaged) from Alice because his time with her was reduced following the divorce. Dave may have sought to get his needs met by his parents again, as he did as a child, becoming enmeshed with them. Boundaries between the entire family and the outside world can also be clear, diffuse, or rigid.

How have authority and power been distributed in Alice's family? A family's hierarchy refers to who in the family has the most power and authority to make rules and decisions. In a healthy family, parents have more power and authority than children, and older children may have more power and authority than younger children. For a well-functioning parental subsystem, Katherine and Dave should have a strong, positive coalition with each other so that they work as a team to raise Alice. This coalition reflects mutual respect and concern so that they do not undermine each other's authority as parents. In addition, members of the extended family, such as grandparents, should support the authority of parents. When a child is born, the child's needs for autonomy and nurturance are respected, but the child is not allowed to disrupt the parental coalition or make important family decisions. In a healthy family, it is the adults who have the ultimate authority, and all the children in the household have their dependency needs as children respected.

In a malfunctioning family, cross-generational alliances may have formed that disrupt the family hierarchy. For example, an alliance may have developed in which the paternal grandmother and the father exclude or demean the participation of the mother in the parenting subsystem. Another type of cross-generational alliance can occur when a child is brought into a coalition with one of the parents. Although the child may gain the benefit of additional authority within the family, the child's own developmental needs go unmet. The child may be expected to make decisions or to handle situations that he or she doesn't have the skills or experience for; this puts the child under stress.

There are times when a family's structure remains stable (periods of homeostasis); however, all families go through periods of stress and growth resulting from internal or external demands for change (periods of disequilibrium). Internal demands for change can come from the birth or death of family members or through the changing needs of family members that come with age. If family members stay together, Minuchin considers them to progress through four stages: couple formation, families with young children, families with older or adolescent children, and families with grown children. External demands include employment changes, educational changes, and deaths of extended family members. Change requires the family to accommodate and negotiate (modify the family rules) so that the needs of family members are still met.

All families have problems, but healthy families have functional strategies for dealing with these problems. While a healthy family may struggle at first in times of change, it will be able to accommodate to these changed circumstances. Unhealthy periods of homeostasis occur when there are legitimate pressures for change but the family is attempting to maintain its past structure and not adapt. Unhealthy periods of disequilibrium represent a disintegration of the family structure when it is under pressure to change.

As a result of divorce, Alice is no longer part of a nuclear family system. Family systems come in many other configurations, including extended families, single-parent households, divorced couples, and stepfamilies. It is not the configuration of a family per se that determines its health but the ability of the system to balance the needs of its members for nurturance and autonomy in times of homeostasis and disequilibrium. You will assume that Alice's family is basically healthy but is in need of reorganizing itself so that it can solve its own problems; the goal of treatment is to alter the family structure.

To help Alice's family, you will progress through a four-step intervention model (Minuchin et al., 2007). The first step will be to discuss the family's point of view on the presenting complaint and then open up alternative explanations for it for their consideration. The second step will be to highlight how current family interactions are maintaining the presenting complaint. The third step will be to explore the past, from a structural perspective, to give adult family members some cognitive insight into how their childhood experiences are related to the current problem within their family. The final step will be to help the family members explore alternative ways of relating to each other and determine how they will use their strengths and resources to overcome their problems and develop a more functional family structure.

During this treatment process, you and Alice's family members will not discover the "truth" about what caused their current problems and the "right way" for the family to be structured. Rather, each family member will participate in a construction of the family's current reality or story and will be involved in any reconstructions that may help the family function within a created family story that they find more satisfying and adaptive.

THE ROLE OF THE CLINICIAN

How will you help Alice? You are an expert, a coach, a collaborator, and a helper. Your first task will be to understand the family. You will join with it in a collaborative stance to help understand how each person experiences the family, and you will experience this reality with each of them; this is called joining the family. You will convey an understanding of, and respect for, every family member. The family usually locates the problem within one individual. You have an alternative view, or a reframing of the problem, by which you perceive that there are complementary roles played by family members and that the problems are located within the family structure rather than within an individual.

The family is the context for understanding its members. Thus, to help them develop an understanding of their structural problems, all of them will need to attend at least the initial sessions. Later on, it may be valuable to have meetings with just subsystems or even individuals. Within sessions, you will encourage family members to communicate directly with one another and thus bring their patterns and processes of interacting into the treatment session; when family members interact in their normal manner, it is called an enactment. You will alternate between observing these interactions and participating in them.

Once you develop an understanding of the dysfunctional family structure, you'll develop a new formulation of the identified problem that explains how it encompasses the interactions of all family members rather than residing in one person. There are many techniques you could use to widen the family's view of the presenting complaint. One is to have each family member articulate a strength he or she sees in the symptom bearer (the person who is supposed to be the problem). The strengths and weaknesses of all family members may also be highlighted. This helps take the identified patient off the hot seat of being the "trouble" in the family. The role each family member plays in maintaining the problem will be underscored in a nonblaming and nonjudgmental manner, and alternative conceptualizations, or reframes of the problem, will be discussed that may open up alternative interaction patterns within the family. There is no one "true" reframing of the problem. If a reframe helps the family reorganize in a constructive manner, then it is a successful one for the family.

The third step in treatment will be to help adult family members develop cognitive insight into the unproductive family assumptions that are limiting their views of themselves and others. In the early history of structural theory, insight was not considered important—the goal was just to change family interactions until a functional structure developed. However, recent work suggests that helping adult family members develop cognitive insight into how their past childhood experiences are related to their current family interactional struggles serves to increase their willingness to see themselves and their family members in more flexible ways and maintain changed interaction patterns in the long run (Minuchin et al., 2007).

These discussions of the past will always be tied clearly to the presenting concerns of the family members so that they can understand why the family is "stuck" in dysfunctional patterns. This will lead into the fourth step of treatment, where you will help the family members consider ways of getting "unstuck" that involve trying out a variety of different ways of relating to each other; the goal is to expand their choices in developing a new family structure. Each family member who would need to do something different will be asked to consider what he or she would and would not do to get his or her family moving into a new pattern of interactions; you ask for such willingness because you cannot force a family member to interact differently. You want to build collaboration between family members for trying new things; if any family members change their interaction style, it will have an influence on the entire family system. Within each session, you will help family members actively experience a new way of relating to each other. This new way of functioning as a family is based on the reframes you developed together; this represents a constructed truth about the family. If this new construction opens up interactions that are more satisfying than the old ones, the family may choose to keep using it.

How will you provide Alice's family members with new experiences in relating to each other? Your overall plan will be to disrupt the old structure. This may involve adjusting boundaries and realigning subsystems in a manner that will be more functional for the family at its current stage of development. How will you begin? You will actively disrupt the old subgroups as they are interacting within the immediacy of the session; you will respond to what you see and experience within the session while still treating with respect family members' own descriptions of what is happening within their family at home.

You may increase the experienced intensity of the family members' conflicts so that they will need to question their manner of interaction and search for alternatives to the behaviors, cognitions, and affective responses they have been using. Structural treatment offers many techniques for raising intensity. For example, Katherine and Dave could be asked to discuss their conflicts with each other while seated facing each other with their knees touching; this is a method of raising intensity through manipulating physical proximity. As another example, if Katherine said, "I feel sad about my marriage failing," you could say, "You feel tortured by your marriage failing"; this method raises intensity through manipulating language.

Treatment is individualized to each family, and a variety of techniques exist for helping family members interact more productively with each other. A few common ones will be discussed, including strengthening appropriate coalitions and developing clear boundaries. While you will be sensitive to the needs of individual families, you believe that a healthy family with children needs to have a cohesive parental subsystem. Thus, you will work to create a strong parental coalition between Dave and Katherine and support the authority of the parental subsystem over the child subsystem of Alice despite the divorce. Second, if there are enmeshed subsystems, you will strengthen boundaries and encourage individuation of family members when needed. Third, if there are disengaged subsystems, you will increase direct communication among family members to strengthen their emotional connections with each other. For example, Dave may have limited his contact with Alice (become disengaged) because he sees the divorce from Katherine as requiring his being "divorced" from Alice. You could provide Dave with a renaming or reinterpretation of this divorce context, such as "Now that you don't have to fight daily with Katherine, you can have the freedom to really enjoy your time with Alice." This reframing of Dave's divorced family reality will be successful if it frees Dave to reestablish his emotional connection to Alice. You could build on Dave's strengths by pointing out relationships where he has maintained emotional connection and show faith in Dave's ability to reconnect with Alice. Shaping competence (building on strengths) will encourage Dave to use constructive behaviors in his interactions with Alice and Katherine that are alternatives to those he is currently using.

Another important technique is called boundary making. If a child is interrupting a parent, you will encourage the parent to tell the child to stop; this helps the parent take on a higher level of parental authority and strengthens the boundary between the parent and child subsystems. The child may have previously been a "parentified child." This is a child who has been allowed to take on some of the power of a parent. While this gives the child added freedom and power, it also puts him or her in a position where he or she is making decisions that he or she isn't developmentally ready to make. If a parent keeps interfering when two siblings fight, he or she will be told to stay out of it so that the siblings can learn how to solve their own problems.

In the technique of "unbalancing," you change the relationship between members of a subsystem. For example, a family can be stalemated in problem-solving when two people who holding opposing views are not able to reach a compromise; fear of change is often behind this. You could take the side of one member of the power struggle, shifting power to this person. The intent is to shake both of them out of the stalemate so that they can work toward a solution of balance and fairness. During the course of treatment, you will align with every family member in turn, as needed, to aid problem-solving.

How much do you need to do? Each family has within it the ability to move itself toward an adaptive structure. You will keep trying different techniques until you facilitate family members' moving beyond their presenting concerns to develop a functional structure that supports the welfare of all of them. It is not the techniques themselves that are critical to change; it is your being able to help the family develop a new and more satisfying way of carrying out family tasks that supports the needs of each member for age-appropriate autonomy and nurturance.

CASE APPLICATION: INTEGRATING THE DOMAIN OF AGE

Alice's case will now be examined in detail. There are many domains of complexity that might be relevant to her case. The domain of age has been chosen to examine within a family systems case conceptualization and treatment plan.

Interview With Alice (A) and Katherine (K) From a Family Systems Perspective

C: Hello, Katherine, Alice. Can you tell me why you're here?

K: (calmly) Alice is having trouble adjusting to a new (Alice interrupts)

A: (accusatorily) Everyone at school is mean to me.

C: What were you going to say, Katherine?

K: (calmly looking at *C*) The teacher thinks that Alice doesn't know how to cooperate and share with the other children.

C: Look at Alice and tell her what you think.

A: (venomously) I hate that Mrs. Walters. She is always telling me what to do, and she will never help me!

C: Alice, your mother has something important to tell you.

K: (turning to Alice, calmly) I want you to have friends.

A: (angrily) I don't want to be friends with any of them. They are selfish. We do all these projects in class. They never give me the stuff I want to use. They always say, "Wait. It's not your turn." (*K* tries to stroke *A*'s hand, but *A* jerks it away) Then, if I grab it from their grubby hands, Mrs. Walters takes *me* away from the group!

C: You feel angry and treated unfairly. Ask your mom what you could do about it.

A: (dismissively) She can't help me. People always push her around.

K: (looking at C, calmly) Dave has always bossed me around. I don't like to boss people. The teacher says Alice is very bossy at school; she learned this from Dave.

C: You seemed to cringe, Alice.

A: (angrily) She is saying bad things about Dad again. They both do it. (Stomping her feet) *I hate it!* Why do they have to say mean things?

C: Tell your mom what you want her to do.

A: (glaring at K, yelling) Mom, stop talking to me about Dad and stop fighting with Dad in front of me. (turning to C) They are so loud; they just scream at each other in front of me all the time.

C: Keep looking at your mom. She needs to know how you feel.

A: (shaking her fist at her mom and yelling) *I hate this!* If you would just move back home, these fights could end!

K: (calmly but squirming) Alice, your dad and I are divorced. I am never going to move back. Our home is here now.

A: (condescendingly) Dad says you will come home when you come to your senses.

K: Don't talk to me like that, Alice. (Alice interrupts)

A: (condescendingly) He says you have forgotten your promises to him. You went out and got a job instead of staying home to care for me like you should. Grandma and Dad *both* say so!

C: Katherine, Alice interrupts you a lot. Is this OK with you?

K: (concernedly) Well, this divorce hurt her a lot. It took an interminable three years because Dave had to fight over every possible little detail. She has always been close to her dad. I don't want to disrupt that. I tried for a long time to work things out with her dad. I'm not surprised his mother is still blaming me. She always did that.

C: You're a good mom. You are aware of her feelings about the divorce and you realize her dad is important to her. But, is it okay that she interrupts you all the time? Remember, you are the mother.

K: (reflectively) I think Alice wants to be the boss. She doesn't listen to me, and the teacher says Alice doesn't listen at school.

C: What do you think Alice needs?

K: (firmly) She needs to be able to listen to her teacher and learn from her, and she needs to have friends her own age.

C: You have a good grasp of her academic and social needs. What about her adjustment to the divorce?

K: (calmly) I don't mean to complain to her about Dave. He is still so angry at me that he picks a fight with *me* whenever he comes to get her. I used to let Dave and his mother push me around. Now, I stand up for myself; the fights do get loud.

C: The fight is between you and Dave. So, Alice shouldn't be drawn into it. Look at her and tell her what she needs to hear from you.

K: (Looking at *A*) I'm sorry that I let you get in the middle of my fights with your dad. We are going to keep fighting for a while until we work some problems out. I will try not to do it in front of you.

C: (*A* is looking down) Alice, can you look at your mom? (*A* looks at *K*)

K: (sincerely) I am going to try, Alice, but I need *you* to try too.

A: (dismissively) I'm not going to follow those stupid rules! I've told Dad, and he says I don't have to follow them.

K: (angrily) He has no (*C* interrupts)

C: Katherine, you are forgetting not to complain about Dave. Tell Alice what you think about the rules and say it in a voice that tells her you mean it.

K: (firmly) The teacher told me you are more impatient, share less, and are less helpful than the other kids at school. You are really smart and sweet, Alice. You could be the teacher's favorite student. It's my fault. Before the divorce, I did all the housework and organized your homework. I didn't see that you were growing up.

A: (looking at *K*, whiningly) I hate cleaning up. I don't want to do it.

C: You are setting a good example for your mother, Alice. You looked right at her and told her what was on your mind without blaming anyone.

A: (looking at *K*, whiningly) Mom, I like it when you do everything.

C: OK, that was simple and clear—but only babies have their moms do everything. You are nine. Find out what nine-year-old goodies you might get if you take on the responsibilities of a nine-year-old.

A: (aggressively) Mom, if I do the stupid cleanup, are you going to give me something fun?

K: Alice, your teacher says (*C* interrupts by whispering in *K*'s ear, "Tell her what *you* think") Alice, if you are responsible and do your chores and homework, I could let you invite a friend to stay overnight.

A: (excitedly and loudly) *Tonight?*

K: I don't know. (looks at *C*) Alice, I'm not ready to have a friend come over tonight. We need to work out the chores first. Let's think about who you could have over next week if you act responsibly.

A: (sadly) All the kids at school hate me.

K: (sadly) I don't really know how to start with that problem.

C: Alice can do a lot of things for herself that she isn't aware of yet—like making friends at school. Alice, who were your friends before you moved here?

A: (calmly) My dad's farm is way out in the country. I mostly played with my older cousins. They were neat to play with. They always let me choose what to do. They weren't pushy like the kids here.

C: Do you see your cousins now?

A: (angrily) Only if I'm with my dad. They are all from his side of the family, and none of them are speaking to my mom.

C: Why not?

A: (angrily) They say my mom is bad for leaving my dad.

C: They put you in the middle of the fight again. What would happen if you told them that it made you feel bad to be in the middle of the fight?

A: (anxiously) Maybe they would hate me like they hate Mom.

C: That would hurt, and no one wants that to happen.

A: (whiningly and demandingly) So, how am I going to make friends?

C: Let's see if your mother could be a good example for you to learn from. Katherine, are there any grown-ups helping you with your own hurt?

K: (sadly) My parents died before Alice was born. I was an only child.

C: Friends?

K: (reflectively) The farm was isolated. We socialized with Dave's family. I have met some new people, but I don't know them well.

C: Katherine, what is going on with Alice as we talk?

K: (calmly) She looks very sad.

C: Can you help her?

K: (calmly) It's hard for me to make friends too, Alice, but I'm going to find a way to help you. I know you need friends.

C: You are a perceptive mother, Katherine. Is there something you can do right now to help Alice? (*K* goes over and hugs *A*)

A: (crawls into *K*'s lap and cuddles; *K* cuddles back, and they both smile)

C: You are both smiling now and look happy. Families can't be happy all the time, but we need to make your family happy for as much of the time as we can. We know that Alice needs friends. She also needs to be responsible for kids' stuff like home-work, and *not* grown-up stuff like the divorce.

K: (still cuddling *A* but twisting to look her in the face) Alice, we will keep coming back here until we have worked these problems out. I really love you.

A: (sweetly) I love you too, Mommy.

C: Katherine, it would be best if Dave came in also so that you could both help Alice understand her new families and how to behave at school.

K: (sighing, looking quickly at *A* and then back to *C*) That would be all right with me, but I don't know if Dave would come in.

C: Alice, do you know your dad's phone number by heart? (*A* nods) Great; you can give it to me. I will call your dad and invite him to come. Whether he says yes or not, we three will all meet next week.

Family Systems Case Conceptualization of Alice: Assumption-Based Style

Alice's family entered a period of chaotic disequilibrium when a parental divorce took three years to finalize and split her family in two. Even though Alice was only 6 at the start of it, Katherine and Dave were both so angry that the parental coalition was allowed to completely shatter. No clear hierarchy of authority was established within the Katherine-Alice family or the Dave-Alice-Grandma family, as all the adults lost touch with the fact that Alice still needed to be nurtured and given age-appropriate guidance. In Katherine's family, Alice was given too little autonomy. Katherine did every little thing for Alice to make her feel loved, so that Alice continues to behave like a spoiled 6-year-old even though she is now 9. In Dave's house, she was brought into a pseudo-adult role with her father and grandmother. In this role, they all gossip about Katherine, blaming her for the divorce. Dave and his mother have either directly or indirectly given Alice the idea that it is her job to convince her mother to return to Dave. Given that Alice has too much authority in one home and none in the other, it isn't surprising that she gets into conflicts over authority with her teacher. Alice has become the symptom bearer for the family and has been referred for treatment by her schoolteacher because she is by turns bossy, immature, and sad. She needs to be taken out of the middle of her parents' conflicts and returned to the world of 9-year-olds so she can learn how to relate effectively with her peers. While all the family rules and responsibilities seem to have flown out the win-dow, Dave and Katherine did work effectively as a parenting subsystem before the divorce. In addition, Alice is a very bright young girl. This bodes well for her being able to learn effectively from her parents and her teacher and resume age-appropriate behavior once a new family equilibrium has been established.

Karen and Dave do not have an effective parental coalition that allows them to share important information about Alice and guide her effectively as their child. Prior to the divorce, Dave worked the family farm and Katherine was a stay-at-home mom. They were both very attentive to Alice. Unfortunately, the divorce was a three-year endurance contest during which well-adjusted 6-year-old Alice grew into irritable and bossy 9-year-old Alice.

It is likely that, due to her age, Alice considered herself responsible for the divorce. Her father and grandmother unintentionally feed into this belief by putting her in charge of convincing her mom to return to the farm. The conflicting information Alice gets from her mother is that the divorce is final. This information only serves to make Alice angry with her mother. Katherine responds to this with overindulgence, thus further giving Alice the message that she is in charge of what happens in the family. Despite there being three adults intimately involved in her care, no one is giving Alice enough guidance at home. The divorce has also substantially decreased Alice's time with her father, and his anger over the divorce has interfered with his ability to recognize and respond to Alice's developmental needs. Katherine and Dave unintentionally have placed Alice in the middle of their conflicts by fighting in front of her and by complaining about each other to her. Dave's mother has supported this. Alice feels torn between her parents and responsible for helping them reconcile, but unsure of what her role should be; no 9-year-old would have these skills or should be put in this position.

Neither Katherine nor Dave has established an appropriate hierarchy with Alice at home where the parent was clearly in charge and Alice followed her or his rules for her behavior. Nine-year-old Alice would have found it confusing just having two different sets of rules in her mom's versus her dad's house. However, the lack of rules has really made it difficult for her to even accept adults as authority figures. The family hierarchy was clear before the divorce. Dave was a dominating husband and father. He always had to have the final say and served as a role model of authority. While something of a bully, he did treat Katherine's role as mother with respect and would never have allowed Alice to speak disrespectfully to her mother in front of him. Post-divorce, Katherine has tried not to allow Dave to boss her around. However, this has led to many loud confrontations in front of Alice, which is very distressing for her. Being a bright little girl, Alice soon discovered that she got more of what she wanted at her dad's house by siding with him and her grandma against her mom. The three of them trade gossip about Katherine. Alice also found she could gain more power at home with Katherine by crying about the divorce whenever her mom tried to set limits on her behavior. Katherine was easily manipulated by Alice's tears to remove any limits she had tried to set. While Alice has gained power since the divorce, she hasn't been developing age-appropriate emotional control or learning important social skills like how to share and compromise. In addition, Alice frequently feels irritable and angry, as she is constantly in the middle between her parents. Alice needs to return to the child subsystem at home and only take on responsibilities that are age-appropriate.

Neither Katherine nor Dave established with Alice what the appropriate hierarchy should be at school, with the teacher making the rules and Alice cooperating and sharing with the other children. Alice's parents did not set age-appropriate expectations for Alice's behavior at home, and so she went to school expecting that the teacher wouldn't set limits on her behavior or would back down from any limits that were set. At the present time, Alice is struggling to retain her pseudo-adult role at school. However, unlike her parents, Mrs. Walters is not backing down and has even taken steps to help Katherine and Dave not back down either by referring them to treatment. Alice is at a time of life when making friends is becoming important, and it will only grow more important as the years go by.

Katherine recognizes that Alice needs to learn to share, compromise, and make friends her own age. Unfortunately, living out on the farm, Alice played primarily with adults and much older cousins, who always altered games to suit Alice. Her peers at school will not do this for Alice, and she doesn't have the social skills to deal with this situation effectively. Instead, she responds by escalating her bossy, controlling behavior, trying to force the other students to live life her way. While becoming socially isolated, Alice sees the conflicts with other children at school to be their fault.

The family of Alice and Katherine and the family of Alice, Dave, and Grandma are both in a period of chaotic disequilibrium in which prior family roles have been disrupted and a new homeostasis has not yet emerged. Within each family, the parents need to be in charge and Alice needs to be supported in learning age-appropriate academic and social skills. However, at this time, the parents appear to be most motivated to fight and blame each other. It is painful for Alice to be the family scapegoat. However, her taking on this role may provide a window of opportunity for the clinician to encourage family change. The only thing that Dave and Katherine can agree on is that they love Alice. Her significant problems in school, in dealing with both the teacher and her peers, may motivate them to look beyond their own pain and see Alice's. Unfortunately, one barrier to change is that the all-important decision of "who is in the family" has not been answered in a unified manner by everyone. It is understandable that 9-year-old Alice wants her family to reunite. Dave also wants this. However, Katherine does not; for her, the divorce is final. The clinician will have to find a way to help them beyond this stalemate so that homeostasis can develop in each family.

Family Systems Treatment Plan: Assumption-Based Style

Treatment Plan Overview. The optimal plan would be for some of the treatment sessions to revolve around the Katherine-Alice family, some to revolve around the Dave-Alice family, and some to include Katherine, Dave, and Alice in support of effective coparenting. However, due to the current acrimony between Katherine and Dave, this may not be possible. The treatment plan has been developed with optimal family participation in mind, but goals involving Dave will be deleted or modified it Katherine is correct and he will not participate. (This treatment plan follows the *problem format.*)

PROBLEM: Alice has gotten caught in a divorce war between her parents, and it has negatively affected her development.

LONG-TERM GOAL 1: Karen and Dave will reestablish an effective parental coalition even though they are divorced so that they can share important information about Alice and take good care of her as their child.

Short-Term Goals

1. Katherine will tell Dave about Alice's problems at school based on the teacher's report, showing him her report card.

2. Katherine and Dave will discuss concretely how Alice is currently in emotional turmoil as a direct consequence of their public disagreements with each other.

3. Katherine and Dave will develop a plan together for how to handle exchanges of Alice between their respective homes to minimize acrimony between them.

4. Katherine and Dave will be shown the "potential goals" for the coparenting appointments that include them and Alice and discuss in what ways they agree and disagree with these goals.

5. Katherine and Dave will discuss together whether they will agree to attend these coparenting appointments with Alice, and if they don't, what will happen instead to ensure clear communication about Alice.

LONG-TERM GOAL 2: The parents will establish the appropriate hierarchy at home with the parents in charge and Alice following the rules.

Short-Term Goals

Mom's House Rules

1. Katherine will develop age-appropriate rules for Alice's behavior at home and consequences if these rules are not followed.

2. Katherine will discuss with Alice her responsibility for her homework and for caring for her room at home. She will tell her that, when she completes these responsibilities, she is acting like a 9-year-old and will be able to stay up 15 minutes longer at night, but that if she is not being responsible, she will go to sleep 15 minutes earlier.

3. Katherine and Alice will watch appropriate movies and TV shows together where Katherine can point out good friendship behaviors between kids Alice's age.

4. Katherine will coach Alice to play a board game with the clinician where Alice cooperates, shares, and is a good sport.

5. Katherine will help Alice pick out a person from her class to invite over for a play date along with this person's mother or father.

6. Katherine will help Alice make this a fun play date by providing fun snacks and supervise a game.

Dad's House Rules

7. Dave will develop age-appropriate rules for Alice's behavior (at the farm, grandmother's house, cousin's house) and consequences if these rules are not followed.

8. Dave will discuss with Alice her responsibility for her room on the farm. He will tell her that, when she is acting like a 9-year-old and doing an appropriate chore on the farm that he will pick, she will be able to stay up 15 minutes longer at night, but that if she is not being responsible, she will go to sleep 15 minutes earlier.

9. Dave, his mother, and Alice will watch appropriate movies and TV shows together, and Dave and his mother will point out good friendship behaviors between kids Alice's age.

10. Dave, his mother, and Alice will play a board game where Alice is expected to show the type of good sportsmanship a 9-year-old should show so that Alice can learn how to play effectively with other kids her own age.

11. Dave and his mother will invite an older cousin over to play with Alice, and both will be instructed to follow appropriate rules for the game so that Alice can learn how to play effectively with other kids her own age.

LONG-TERM GOAL 3: The parents will establish the appropriate hierarchy at school, with the teacher and the parents making the rules for Alice to follow and Alice cooperating and sharing with the other children.

Short-Term Goals:

1. Katherine and Dave will discuss with Alice what she thinks the role of the teacher at school is and what her own role as a student is.

2. Katherine and Dave will discuss with each other what the consequences should be if Alice's teacher calls with a complaint that Alice was not following her instructions. Alice can listen but not interrupt.

3. Katherine and Dave will discuss with Alice what the consequences will be if she comes home from school and she has listened and followed instructions at school, and what the consequences will be if the teacher was not satisfied.

4. Alice will tell her parents about a specific problem she had with one particular child at school and ask them for advice about what to do if it happens again.

5. Katherine and Dave will discuss with each other what might be good strategies for Alice to try. Alice can listen but not interrupt.

6. Katherine and Dave will discuss their best ideas with Alice, and she will tell them which she would like to try first.

7. Alice will tell her parents about a child she would like to make friends with and ask them for advice on how to start making friends without doing something to make her teacher mad.

8. Katherine and Dave will discuss with each other what might be good strategies for Alice to try. Alice can listen but not interrupt.

9. Katherine and Dave will discuss their best ideas with Alice, and she will tell them what she would like to try first.

10. Katherine and Dave will discuss with Alice what to do if the other child does not want to be friends.

11. Other goals will be developed as appropriate to help Alice take on an age-appropriate role at school with her teacher and her peers.

LONG-TERM GOAL 4: Katherine and Dave will establish clear communication with Alice about their divorce in order to take her out of the middle of their conflicts, putting her back in the child subsystem with themselves in the parental coalition.

1. Katherine and Dave will each give an example of one behavior in their daughter Alice that they are very proud of.

2. Katherine will give an example of something Dave did with Alice that she respects.

3. Dave will give an example of something Katherine did with Alice that he respects.

4. Katherine and Dave will discuss the problems that Alice is having at school that are a result of her being torn between her parents.

5. Katherine and Dave will discuss whether they will make a commitment to not complaining about each other in front of Alice because it distresses her.

6. Katherine and Dave will discuss whether they will make a commitment to a family session in which they will discuss the divorce together with Alice.

7. Alice will talk about fun memories of their family when it was together and look at family albums with her parents in session.

8. Alice will sit on her mother's lap while Katherine tells her things she likes about Dave and expresses regret that their old family system had to change (giving Alice hugs for emotional support when needed).

9. Alice will sit on her father's lap while Dave tells her things he likes about Katherine and expresses regret that their old family system had to change (giving Alice hugs for emotional support when needed).

10. Katherine will clearly tell Alice that the divorce is final despite what she hears at her dad's house, but that she wants Alice to continue loving her dad with all her heart.

11. Dave will clearly tell Alice that the divorce is final despite what she has heard in the past and that he wants Alice to continue loving her mom with all her heart.

12. Other goals will be developed as appropriate to help Alice feel she is no longer caught in a divorce war between her parents.

Family Systems Case Conceptualization of Alice: Symptom-Based Style

Alice has been referred for treatment by the school system because she is bossy, immature, and sad. Although she appears to be a bright and verbal 9-year-old, she behaves immaturely for her age and engages in disruptive behavior with adults and peers. At her age, she should be developing significant peer friendships. Instead, she is struggling with the earlier developmental tasks of learning to cooperate and share. While still being connected strongly to her parents, a 9-year-old should be turning to teachers and other adults as additional role models. Instead, Alice does not seek to acquire her teacher's approval or recognize the teacher's authority. Alice is also feeling sad and stressed by her parents' post-divorce conflicts. These symptoms can be viewed as reflections of a malfunctioning family system. Structural dysfunctions within Alice's nuclear family resulted in her not acquiring a realistic view of her own power vis-à-vis adults and not developing the ability to accommodate and negotiate with peers. These skill deficits became more problematic for Alice as her nuclear family dissolved and her divorced family began the struggle of creating new subsystems and boundaries. Family strengths that are emerging during this period of disequilibrium include Katherine's commitment to her role as a parent, her ability to recognize and respond to Alice's needs for emotional support, and both Katherine's and Alice's willingness to explore new patterns of relating.

Why is Alice bossy with adults? Within her nuclear family, Katherine and Dave did not have a strong parental coalition. Dave had the final authority for making decisions in the family. However, he did require Alice to treat Katherine with respect as her mother. Since the divorce, he has encouraged both his own mother and his daughter to devalue Katherine's role as a mother out of revenge. Katherine, having developed a complementary pattern to her husband during their marriage of submitting to his will to avoid conflict, is now doing the same thing with Alice, thereby unintentionally delegating her authority as a parent to her daughter. Katherine's submissive behavior also made it unnecessary for Alice to develop the negotiation and accommodation skills she needed to develop constructive relationships with adults. Brought into a pseudo-parental role by her father, Alice developed a false sense of her power within child–adult relationships. Alice has tried to bring this increased power into the school setting. While seeing that other children in school follow the teacher's rules, she does not think that the rules apply to her. At the present time, Alice is struggling to retain her infantilized role with Katherine, as she doesn't want to have to help out at home; Katherine recognizes it is healthier for Alice to act her age and follow rules both at home and at school. Dave's views aren't known at this time.

Why is Alice immature in her peer relationships? As an only child, Alice socialized primarily with adults and older cousins. These older individuals accommodated to her wishes. Because they always yielded to Alice, the egocentric play style that would be expected of a preschool-age Alice has in many ways been maintained, unintentionally, within Alice's family and extended family system. Thus, when she interacts in school with peers and needs to alter her style to fit relationships of equal power, she doesn't know how. She responds by escalating her bossy, controlling behavior to try to force these other individuals into her familiar pattern of relating where others have always submitted to her demands. Alice sees her conflicts with other children at school as their fault. Katherine recognizes that Alice needs to learn to share, compromise, and make friends her own age.

Why is Alice sad? Katherine and Dave were both highly committed to their role as parents. They were loving and attentive to Alice. Although this led to emotional connections, these connections are now disrupted. The divorce has substantially decreased Alice's time with her father, and his anger over the divorce has interfered with his ability to recognize and respond to Alice's developmental needs. Katherine and Dave have unintentionally placed Alice in the middle of their conflicts by fighting in front of her and by complaining about each other to her. Dave's family has supported this. Alice feels torn between her parents and responsible for helping them reconcile, but unsure of what her role should be; no 9-year-old would have these skills or should be put in this position. With the clinician's support, Alice was able to ask her mother to stop putting her in this role; she is willing to try to do the same thing with her father and grandmother. Katherine has taken responsibility for blurring the parent–child boundary in the past; she is open to support from the clinician in taking on a fully adult role in her new family with Alice.

Alice, Katherine, and Dave are in a period of disequilibrium in which prior family roles have been disrupted and a new homeostasis has not yet emerged. Dave may be trying to reinstate the old family structure and boundaries. Katherine, with Alice, is trying to establish a new family system. Within this new system, Katherine needs to increase her authority as a parent, and Alice needs to take on age-appropriate responsibilities and learn how to accommodate and negotiate with people of greater authority (parents, teachers) as well as with people of equal authority (peers). Alice is at a stage in development in which she has the cognitive ability to understand cause-and-effect relationships and can understand the needs of others if they are presented in concrete terms. These competencies will serve her well as she seeks to expand her repertoire of interpersonal behavior to fit the multiple systems in which she is a member (her mom's family, her dad's family, the school system). Katherine is highly motivated to be an effective parent for Alice. However, Dave and his family may be more focused on post-divorce conflicts than Alice's need to grow and develop at this time; if so, their behavior may serve as a barrier to treatment success.

Family Systems Treatment Plan: Symptom-Based Style

Treatment Plan Overview. Alice's difficulties in school have developed within the context of disturbed family relationships. The most helpful plan for Alice would be if all the adults who are parenting her would attend treatment. However, while Dave and his mother will be asked to participate, few goals have been developed for them because it is not clear if they will come. The clinician will invite them in, emphasizing Alice's problems as a hook for them to consider establishing coparenting strategies despite their anger over the divorce. Goals 1, 2, and 3 will be introduced at the same time. (This treatment plan follows the *basic format*.)

LONG-TERM GOAL 1: Alice will decrease her sadness concerning her parents' divorce.

Short-Term Goals

Katherine and Alice Family System Appointments

1. Katherine will ensure that Alice is out of the room and not listening when she has discussions with Dave about parenting before and after visitation.

2. Katherine will learn not to talk to Alice about her problems with Dave.

3. Katherine and Alice will talk about fun memories of their family when it was together and look at family albums in session.

4. Alice will sit on her mother's lap while Katherine tells her things she likes about Dave and expresses regret that their old family system had to change (giving Alice hugs for emotional support when needed).

5. Katherine will clearly tell Alice that the divorce is final despite what she hears at her dad's house but that she wants Alice to continue loving her dad with all her heart and hopes that someday Dave won't be mad about the divorce anymore.

6. Katherine will talk to Alice about fun memories they have together as a new family, and the clinician will take fun photos of them together during the session for them to put in a new family album.

7. Other goals will be developed as appropriate to help Alice feel loved by Katherine and clearly allowed to continue loving Dave as her father.

Dave, Grandma, and Alice Family System Appointments if Possible (otherwise, Alice will be given homework assignments to do the following on visitation)

8. Alice will ask her dad not to talk about his problems with her mom in front of her and explain that it makes her sad.

9. Alice will ask her dad to help her tell her grandma that it makes her sad to hear her criticize her mom.

10. Dave and his mom will discuss how to parent Alice without criticizing Katherine while Alice listens but isn't allowed to interrupt.

Katherine and Dave Divorced Family System Appointments

11. Katherine and Dave will discuss how they can continue parenting Alice, for her benefit, and keep their own disagreements with each other out of it.

All Family Systems

12. Other goals will be developed as appropriate for strengthening these new family systems in their ability to parent a happy Alice who can love her parents and grandmother.

LONG-TERM GOAL 2: Alice will decrease her immature behavior so that she can establish friendships with peers.

Short-Term Goals

Katherine and Alice Family System Appointments

1. Katherine will discuss with Alice her responsibility for her schoolwork and her room at home. She will tell her that, when she is acting like a 9-year-old, she will be able to stay up 15 minutes longer at night, but if she is not being responsible, she will go to sleep 15 minutes earlier.

2. Katherine will discuss with the clinician adults she could try to be friends with and how she might start a friendship. Alice will be allowed to listen but not interrupt this adult conversation so that her mom can role-model friend-seeking behavior for her.

3. Katherine will invite one of these potential friends out to lunch, bringing Alice along so that Katherine can model the good friend behavior of cooperating, listening, and sharing. If Alice acts like a 9-year-old, she will get dessert at lunch. If she doesn't act like a 9-year-old, she will not get dessert at lunch, and she won't get it at dinner either.

4. Katherine and Alice will watch appropriate movies and TV shows together where Katherine can point out good friendship behaviors between kids Alice's age.

5. Katherine will coach Alice to play a board game with the clinician where Alice cooperates, shares, and is a good sport.

6. Katherine will help Alice pick out a person from her class to invite over for a play date along with this person's mother or father. Katherine will call the mother or father and pick the day and time first, and then coach Alice to very nicely ask this person over on the phone.

7. While maintaining an appropriate adult–child boundary, Katherine will help Alice make this a fun play date so that this person will want to come back over.

8. Other goals will be developed as appropriate to help Alice socialize appropriately with peers.

LONG-TERM GOAL 3: Alice will decrease her bossy behavior with adults.

Short-Term Goals

1. Katherine will discuss with the clinician the rules that she wants Alice to follow at home, and Alice will be allowed to stay up 15 minutes later that night if she doesn't interrupt the conversation and have to go to bed five minutes earlier for each time she interrupts the conversation.

2. Katherine will make a behavior chart containing the rules that Alice needs to follow at home, and Alice will earn five points for every rule she follows each day.

3. Alice will discuss with her mother how many points she will need to earn each week to be considered a good enough listener to go out to dinner.

4. Alice will discuss with her mother how many points she will need to earn to be a good enough listener to have a new friend spend the night over at their house.

5. Other goals will be developed as appropriate to help Alice behave respectfully toward her mother and other appropriate adults.

PRACTICE CASE FOR STUDENT CONCEPTUALIZATION: INTEGRATING THE DOMAIN OF RACE AND ETHNICITY

It is time to do a family systems conceptualization and treatment plan for Tanisha and Marcus, an African American couple. Although many domains of complexity may have relevance for them, you are asked to try to integrate the domain of race and ethnicity into your case conceptualization and treatment plan. As a conflict between the clinician and the clients over race and ethnicity is critical to the interview, assume that the clinician is not African American.

Information Received From Brief Intake

Tanisha, a 30-year-old African American, and Marcus, a 32-year-old African American, have been married for seven years. They moved to western Pennsylvania about two years ago from a suburb of Detroit, Michigan. Tanisha indicates that her marriage is generally happy but that she and Marcus need help dealing with the death of their infant daughter, Latisha. Tanisha was referred to treatment by a close friend who was very happy with the outcome of her own marital treatment with this clinician. Marcus doesn't know that Tanisha is making this appointment, but she is confident he will come.

During a brief mental status exam, Tanisha showed signs of clinical depression but had no signs of suicidal or homicidal ideation or other serious psychopathology. Tanisha's description of Marcus suggested he was not depressed or showing signs of significant psychopathology.

Interview With Tanisha (T) and Marcus (M) From a Family Systems Perspective

C: Tanisha, Marcus. Thank you for coming in. I had a chance to talk with Tanisha earlier and explain how I generally conduct treatment sessions and the ethical and legal rules of privacy that I follow. Marcus, are there any questions you have about any of this before we start?

M: (tensely) No. Tanisha filled me in and showed me those pamphlets you gave her.

C: Great. If you have any questions about what I'm doing or the treatment process itself, please don't hesitate to ask. (pause) Could we start with one of you telling me about your family?

T: (tensely) Marcus and I are the only members of our family living here. (*T* looks at *M*, who is looking down) A while back, (pause) we decided we needed a fresh start, and Marcus accepted a promotion that led us to move here. We both have a lot of family back in Detroit. We try to get back there to see them four to five times a year. We still talk regularly by phone and e-mail. It was hard to move far away, but Marcus and I have always emphasized our careers.

C: So, the family back in Detroit is very important to you. (pause) Is anyone else living with you, or around you, right now? (long pause)

T: (looking briefly at *M*, regretfully) No. Marcus's younger sister did live with us last summer to take some courses at the university near us—we were the only ones really encouraging her to get a college degree and would have liked her to stay with us. But she's at Wright State now, and it has the advantage of being around the corner from where her mom and our other relatives live.

C: Both getting an education and being around family were important to her.

T: (tentatively) Yes (*M* breaks in)

M: (angrily) What is the point of this? The family in Detroit is fine, so talking about them is a waste of time.

C: Marcus, I don't mean to waste your time. Knowing who is in your family is part of the process of my understanding what you need from me. (*M* and *T* are glaring at each other; *T*'s fists are clenched)

C: Look at your fists, Tanisha. (*T* relaxes her hands) You need to say something. Why don't you turn your chair toward Marcus, rather than me, so that the two of you can discuss together how you want to tell me what your family needs right now. (*T* turns her chair toward *M* and then looks up at *C*, who nods)

T: (hesitantly, looking at *C*) I guess (pause) I'll start by telling you (*C* interrupts)

C: I apologize for interrupting. I need you to discuss it with Marcus. I'll listen.

T: (hesitantly, looking at *M*) I know we came here to get a new start, but I still can't stop thinking about our little girl dying five years ago. (pause) I just can't stop crying over her. You've been able to get on with things. (pause) I feel I have gone on at work but not at home. (pause) You want another child, and I love children but I don't think I (long pause; *T* leans forward with her face in her hands; *M* leans toward her and pats her knee softly)

C: It's devastating to lose a child. (long pause) What happened?

M: (speaking calmly but emphatically) I think it's better if we don't go into all those details. It's just going to make Tanisha cry, and it's not going to change anything.

C: It's a very painful topic.

M: (with an edge to his voice) And, the topic is closed.

T: (tearfully) Marcus, this is what we're here for. This is what I came here for. Our baby, Latisha, was born with some kind of birth defect; they don't know why. My pregnancy was healthy. There were no problems in delivery, but as soon as she was born, (pause) it was clear something was wrong. She had heart and lung defects. They transferred her to the Cleveland Clinic because they had a specialty unit there for babies like her. She never left that hospital. I went to visit her every weekend for a year. My poor little darling had tubes up her nose. Never got to play, rarely got to see her family outside of me because the hospital was so far away. My dad is in really bad health, and my mom was always afraid to leave him and drive out with me. My mother-in-law came with me a few times. (starts to cry softly)

M: (angrily) I told you this was a bad idea. (glaring at *C*) Let's just go home, sweetheart; this isn't going to help us. (*M* stands up and gently pulls on *T*'s hand)

T: (fiercely) No, I'm staying. I know you don't like talking about it, Marcus. But what we've been doing isn't working, and I need help. We need help. (*M* sits back down)

M: (glowering at *C*) Talking about Latisha is not going to help.

C: I can see that I've made you angry. I didn't mean to do that. Of course, you know Tanisha a lot better than me, but my eyes tell me that she needs to work this through.

M: (accusingly) Excuse my bluntness, but you aren't African American, so you can't know what she needs.

C: Even if I was African American, my goal would be to help you two figure it out together; I wouldn't try to push my agenda on you. (pause) I can see what a strong couple you are. Could you give me a chance to try to help you deal with the traumatic death of your Latisha?

M: (sinking into his chair; tiredly) Look, I have nothing against you, but Tanisha has to let go of this. I'd like to have another child, but if she doesn't want to try again—I'll live with that. We have a good life as it is. (begins to move forward in the chair as if to stand up again)

C: I can see you don't want to talk about your daughter, but would you be willing to talk more with Tanisha about the good life you have together?

M: (looking away from *C* and back at *T*, who sits back against her chair, tiredly) Okay, I'll talk about that. (looking at *C*) I'm a postmaster in a town about twenty minutes from here. I make a good living. So does Tanisha. She's the regional manager for Rite Aid. Together, we have made enough money to buy a really nice home and fill it with beautiful things. We take a great vacation every year. Last year, we went to Mexico, and the year before that we went on an Alaskan cruise. (looking at *T*, emphatically) Tanisha, you've got to admit we're living the good life.

T: (sadly) I never said we weren't. I'm grateful for the good things we have. But I wanted our little girl to grow up. I had a plan. I was going to stop working and have a big family like my mother did. I loved growing up in a house full of kids. (wistfully) I didn't care that we would be giving up a lot of money if I stayed home.

M: (softly) I wanted that too. We could still do that.

T: (shaking her head, sadly) You just don't get it. Our Latisha is dead. I don't want another child. I want *her*. (long pause as she holds her face in her hands)

C: Try to look at Marcus, Tanisha. He wants to remind you what a beautiful life you have together despite the terrible loss of your daughter. He wants to remind you how much strength and love you have together, even without her. (*T* looks up at *M* and gives him a little smile) The two of you love each other but are in a different phase of family life. He has finished grieving over the tremendous loss of his Latisha, and what he has left is his love for you and a desire to try to be a father to another child. Tanisha, you are still deeply in grief. The pain and suffering have been so heavy that you feel mired in the horror of her death. You can't consider, right now, even the idea of another child. (pause) Can you take Marcus's hands and just experience his strength to help you pull back from some of this pain?

M: (pushes his chair backward as *T* begins to take his hands; glaring at *C* and yelling) *I won't stand any more of this! We are not puppets. Stop ordering us around!*

C: You're both strong people and nothing like puppets. (long pause) Is it the techniques I'm using to try to help the two of you talk that are the problem, or am I the problem?

M: (firm but polite) You aren't African American. You don't understand our families. You just aren't going to understand what we're going through, so I want you to stay out of it.

T: (angrily) Marcus, I think about our girl every day, but you don't want to hear that. This is what you always do. I need to talk about it, but you just get mad and walk away. Well, you're not the only one who gets mad. I've kept more than my pain about our little girl in my heart for so long. I have to tell you how mad I am that you never went with me to visit our girl.

M: (defensively) There was no point going there. She couldn't see us, and she couldn't hear us—the doctors said so.

T: (loudly) I held her hand. She might have been able to feel that. She was ours. She needed us.

C: The two of you understood what the doctor said in different ways. Tanisha heard that she couldn't help Latisha by talking. So, she tried touching. You, Marcus, heard that there was no hope, and you began to grieve for her even before she actually died.

M: (angrily) Don't try to manipulate me. I told you I wasn't going to discuss Latisha. Tanisha, we need each other, but we don't need this. Look at yourself; you're more depressed now than you were when we began driving here.

T: (tiredly) I'm just letting out what I've had inside. I want to be here. If you don't want to be here, (long pause) you can leave. (long pause)

C: Marcus, I know that being here is not what you want, but could you consider staying, because it feels like the right place for Tanisha to be right now?

M: (shakes his head no; long pause) I don't feel comfortable with you or with this situation.

C: It's strange to be talking about such private things with someone who not only isn't African American, but also is someone you just met. (pause) Marcus, you feel manipulated. I'm sorry you feel that way. My way of helping couples talk through problems is very directive. I'm honestly trying to help you two talk about Latisha in a way that's different from what you two have done before. I heard Tanisha say she needs help working through the reality of Latisha's death. I was trying to help set up a conversation that might help Tanisha with this—not because I want to force something on you. If this doesn't help, my plan would be to suggest we try something else. I'm willing to keep trying until we find something that works for both you and Tanisha that feels right. (pause) What do you think?

M: (intently) You might try, but you can't understand us because you aren't the right race. I know that's blunt, but I can't pretend.

C: You're right. Whatever I have gone through in my life, it isn't due to being African American, so I will never understand your experiences like you do.

M: (jumping on this) Then, we agree this was a mistake.

C: I agree that I am not African American, and this difference between us might represent a barrier to our working together successfully. But, on the other hand, something I noticed that we do share is we are hardworking and ambitious without forgetting the importance of loving connections to family. I don't want to make you live "my way." I want to help you find a way to relate to Latisha as parents that allows you to continue this wonderful and strong couple of Marcus and Tanisha.

T: (demandingly) Marcus, you are not helping me with this. I want to drop this racial thing and talk about our girl.

M: (angrily) No. We can't just drop it. (long pause)

C: My not being African American is clearly very important. Why don't I go into the next room and give you two time alone to discuss what it means to each of you to work with me? You can come and get me once you decide if we should work further together or if I should give you the names of other clinicians and tell you about their cultural affiliations and strengths.

T: (emphatically) No. I don't want to talk about that. Marcus, focusing on race is just another way to not talk about Latisha. I want to talk about her.

M: (compellingly) Tanisha, someone who isn't African American can't understand and will make things worse even with the best intentions.

C: That would be terrible if instead of helping I made things worse. I can understand why you would want to prevent that. (long pause) My goal in being here is to support the strength within you two, not to try to transform your marriage into my image of what a marriage should be. There are lots of things I won't understand about what you need unless you help me understand. (*T* starts to cry again)

M: (emphatically) Can't you see how you are hurting her with this? I can't allow that.

C: You love her. You want to protect her from pain. But, is it possible to protect her from the pain of your daughter's birth defects and death?

T: (leans over and takes *M*'s hand; calmly) He's a good man, and he does a lot to take care of me. But, you're right. He doesn't understand that I can't just go on and forget about our Latisha. We bought our house outside Detroit so she would have a back-yard to play in. (painfully) That's one of the reasons we moved away from Detroit. What was the point of that house, especially after Marcus gave away Latisha's things—leaving me with nothing but memories? He couldn't take those away.

M: (frustratedly) I didn't just give the stuff away. Your sister needed it for her son. She didn't have the money to buy her own. It wasn't doing any good, locked away in that room. It was better for you to get it out of the house.

T: (calmly) I guess we spent our first three years of marriage with him being the big boss, as you can see now. But you can't boss me out of this. (moving her chair farther away from *M*) I want to be here. I need to be here. I can't be silent about it anymore. I've tried that. It doesn't work for me.

M: Why here? If we have to do this, let's find someone else.

T: Someone I trust got help here. Marcus, please give this a chance.

M: (torn) I'll give in to this for one more week. But I still don't buy it that this will help.

C: Your wife's been crying for five years; one week isn't enough time. How about three weeks? Then, if you two talk and decide I'm the problem, I'll try to help you find someone else. But if you think maybe it could be working, you keep coming.

M: (firmly) OK, you've got three weeks. (sardonically) You've got a fast mouth; I'll give you that.

C: I can't argue with that.

Exercises for Developing a Case Conceptualization of Tanisha and Marcus

Exercise 1 (four-page maximum)

GOAL: To verify that you have a clear understanding of family systems theory.

STYLE: An integrative essay incorporating Parts A through C.

NEED HELP?   Review this chapter (pages 309–316).

A. Develop a concise overview of all the assumptions of family systems theory (the theory's hypotheses about key dimensions in understanding how clients change; think broadly, abstractly) as an introduction to the rest of this exercise.

B. Develop a thorough description of how each of these assumptions is used to understand a client's progression through the change process in paragraphs that provide specific examples to fully explain each assumption.

C. Conclude your essay by describing the role of the clinician in helping the client change (consultant, doctor, educator, helper), the major approach taken to treatment, and common treatment techniques. Provide enough specific examples to clarify what is distinctive about this approach.

Exercise 2 (four-page maximum)

GOAL: To aid application of family systems theory to Tanisha and Marcus.

STYLE: A separate sentence outline for each section, A through E.

NEED HELP?   Review this chapter (pages 309–316).

A. What are the strengths (strong points, positive features, resources) that you see in Tanisha and Marcus, both as individuals and as a couple, at this time?

B. What are the weaknesses (concerns, issues, symptoms, problems, treatment barriers) that you see in Tanisha and Marcus, both as individuals and as a couple, at this time?

C. Provide a detailed analysis of how these strengths and weaknesses could be understood within a family context by describing the following:

1. Whom do Marcus and Tanisha consider to be members of their family, and do they agree or disagree about this?

2. What are the family subsystems, and what is the composition and function of each?

3. What type of boundaries exist between subsystems, between the family and extended family, and between the family and other social systems?

4. Who has the power in the family to do what, what are the family rules, and is this a change from the past? (That is, what are the issues of hierarchy and alignments?)

5. How well are the needs of each family member, and of the system as a whole, being met in terms of emotional intimacy and independence?

6. What role does Latisha play in the family system at this time?

7. Do Tanisha and Marcus have the same perceptions of the impact of Latisha's birth defects on their family system, and how has this influenced their expectations and behaviors within their current family system?

D. What stage of development is the family in now? Is the family in a period of homeostasis or disequilibrium? How well is the family functioning overall?

E. What changes in family structure might be beneficial at this time? What strengths does the family bring to the process of treatment? Are there any factors facilitating or inhibiting structural change at this time?

Exercise 3 *(four-page maximum)*

GOAL: To develop an understanding of the potential role of African American heritage in Tanisha and Marcus's marriage and current situation.

STYLE: A separate sentence outline for each section, A through J.

NEED HELP?   Review Chapter 2 (pages 53–57).

A. Assess the role of Tanisha and Marcus's African American heritage in their lives in terms of the strengths, resources, and power it may be bringing to them within personal, family, social, vocational, and political spheres.

B. Consider what entrenched dominant cultural worldviews, institutions, policies, and practices might be leading to discrimination, prejudice, and racism and setting up barriers to Tanisha and Marcus's healthy development at this time.

C. Consider what current events might be leading to increased discrimination, prejudice, and racism and thus setting up barriers to Tanisha and Marcus's healthy development at this time.

D. Consider what historical events have influenced the couple's African American heritage and assess whether any of their current problems could be a result of direct or indirect oppression or trauma, their responses to this oppression, assimilation stress, discrimination, prejudice or racism, or a mismatch in values with the dominant society and its institutions.

E. Assess how well the couple is functioning overall in terms of their values, beliefs, and behaviors, both through the worldview of African American heritage and through the worldview of the dominant cultural group; discuss if any of their behavior within the dominant society might represent a healthy adaptation to injustice that would be supported by their African American heritage.

F. Consider if successful treatment will involve more internal awareness or actions on the part of the couple or if it will involve more actions to change policies, procedures, and values of an environment that is oppressing the couple; consider if there are any culturally specific resources, treatment strategies, or helpers Tanisha and Marcus would value at this time that might be effectively used within your treatment plan.

G. What is your current knowledge of African American heritage?

   1. How many courses have you taken that give you background on African American heritage?

   2. How many workshops have you taken that give you background on African American heritage?

   3. What professional experiences have you had with clients who are African American?

4. What personal experiences have you had with African Americans?

5. Describe the worldview(s) of the African American cultural group.

H. What is your current level of awareness of issues relevant to this cultural heritage?

1. Describe the stereotypes you have heard about African Americans.

2. Describe how the dominant culture's White cultural biases may have operated in your life.

3. Describe the role your racial and ethnic cultural groups have played in your life.

4. In comparing your racial and cultural affiliations to those of Tanisha and Marcus, what differences could lead to communication problems, values conflicts, or difficulty understanding the couple's lifestyle or experiences, or an invalidation of their strengths?

I. What are your current skills in working with Tanisha and Marcus?

1. What skills do you currently have that are of value in working with Tanisha and Marcus?

2. What skills do you feel it will be important to develop to work effectively with African Americans?

J. What action steps can you take?

1. What might you change in how you interact within the rapport-building phase to develop a more effective working alliance with African American clients?

2. How might you structure the treatment environment to increase the likelihood of a positive outcome with African American clients?

3. What aspects of the theoretical orientation you are planning to use with Tanisha and Marcus might contain implicit cultural or racial biases, and what will you change to promote effective treatment?

4. What might you change in the treatment-planning phase to increase the likelihood of a positive outcome with Tanisha and Marcus?

Exercise 4 (six-page maximum)

GOAL: To help you integrate your knowledge of family systems theory and racial and ethnic issues into an in-depth conceptualization of Tanisha and Marcus (who they are and why they do what they do).

STYLE: An integrated essay consisting of a premise, supportive details, and conclusions following a carefully planned organizational style.

NEED HELP? Review Chapter 1 (pages 1–7) and Chapter 2 (pages 53–57).

STEP 1: Consider what style you should use for organizing your family systems understanding of this couple. This style should (a) support you in providing a comprehensive and clear understanding of the family's structure and how it is functioning and (b) support language that Tanisha and Marcus might find persuasive, considering their disagreement over the need to get help outside of their family and the African American community.

STEP 2: Develop a concise premise (overview, preliminary or explanatory statements, proposition, thesis statement, theory-driven introduction, hypotheses, summary, concluding causal statements) that explains Tanisha and Marcus's issues as a couple whose child died and who disagree about whether they need to process this loss further than they already have. If you have trouble with Step 2, remember that it should be an integration of the key ideas of Exercises 2 and 3 and that it should (a) provide a basis for the family's long-term goals, (b) be grounded in family systems theory and be sensitive to Tanisha and Marcus's African American heritage, and (c) highlight the strengths the family brings to family systems treatment.

STEP 3: Develop your supporting material (a detailed case analysis of strengths and weaknesses supplying data to support an introductory premise) from a family systems perspective, incorporating within each paragraph a deep understanding of Tanisha and Marcus as an African American couple. If you have trouble with Step 3, consider the information you'll need to include in order to (a) support the development of short-term goals, (b) be grounded in family systems theory and sensitive to racial and ethnic issues, and (c) incorporate an understanding of the structural strengths within Tanisha and Marcus's family whenever possible.

STEP 4: Develop your conclusions and broad treatment recommendations, including (a) the couple's overall level of functioning, (b) anything facilitating or serving as a barrier to the couple's developing a new family structure at this time, and (c) the couple's basic needs as a family system at this time, being careful to consider what you said in Part H and J of Exercise 3 (be concise and to the point).

Exercise 5 (three-page maximum)

GOAL: To develop an individualized, theory-driven action plan for Tanisha and Marcus that considers their strengths and is sensitive to their African American heritage.

STYLE: A sentence outline consisting of long- and short-term goals.

NEED HELP?   Review Chapter 1 (pages 7–24).

STEP 1: Develop your treatment plan overview, being careful to consider what you said in Parts H and J of Exercise 3 to try to prevent any negative bias in your treatment plan and individualize it to Tanisha and Marcus's unique needs.

STEP 2: Develop long-term (major, large, ambitious, comprehensive, broad) goals that *ideally* Tanisha and Marcus will reach by the termination of treatment and that will lead them to reach an adaptive homeostasis in their marriage that acknowledges the role of Latisha in their lives. If you have trouble with Step 2, reread your premise and support topic sentences for ideas, paying careful attention to how they could be transformed into structural goals (use the *style* of Exercise 4).

STEP 3: Develop short-term (small, brief, encapsulated, specific, measurable) goals for the family's structure that Tanisha, Marcus, and you can expect to see accomplished within a few weeks and that will help you chart progress, instill hope for change, and plan time-effective treatment sessions. If you have trouble with Step 3, reread your support paragraphs looking for ideas to transform into goals that (a) might enhance cognitive insight into the different family expectations Tanisha and Marcus brought into their marriage based on their childhood families; (b) might support structural change; (c) might enhance factors facilitating or decrease barriers to their effectively dealing with the death of their daughter; (d) might utilize their individual, relationship, and extended family strengths whenever possible; and (e) are individualized to their needs as an African American couple rather than generic.

Exercise 6

GOAL:　　　　To critique family treatment in the case of Tanisha and Marcus.

STYLE:　　　　Answer Questions A through E in essay form or discuss them in a group format.

A. What are the strengths and weaknesses of family systems theory for helping Tanisha and Marcus (an African American couple in grief, separated by a large distance from extended family, who have experienced cultural oppression)?

B. Discuss the pros and cons of feminist treatment for Marcus as a member of a minority group and an *individual* for whom issues of oppression may be very salient. Discuss how important it is to integrate gender issues into this couple's treatment.

C. Discuss the validity of Marcus's concerns that a White clinician will not be able to understand him, Tanisha, and their situation. What might or might not change if the clinician was a person of color but not African American? What might or might not change if the couple was White but the clinician was African American?

D. What ethical issues are raised once Marcus expresses concerns about the clinician being culturally different from his own family and therefore unable to provide competent treatment? What needs to be assessed further before the clinician can decide whether to try to treat this family himself or herself or refer Tanisha and Marcus elsewhere?

E. How did you react personally to Marcus's challenging comments to the clinician, and how might you handle the situation if it happened to you? (If you are African American, assume the couple is White and that the husband raised the same concerns.) If you are culturally different from a family in one or more ways, what could you do to try to foster a strong treatment relationship and a positive outcome? Consider how you would prepare yourself prior to treatment, how you might handle the structure of the sessions differently, and what differences might need to occur in the process of the sessions.

RECOMMENDED RESOURCES

Books

Alexander, J. F., Waldron, H. B., Robbins, M. S., & Need, A. A. (2013). *Functional family therapy for adolescent behavior problems*. Washington, DC: American Psychological Association.

Minuchin, S., Nichols, M. P., & Lee., W.-Y. (2007). *Assessing couples and families: From symptom to system*. Boston, MA: Allyn & Bacon.

Nichols, M. P. (2008). *Family therapy concepts and methods* (8th ed.). Boston, MA: Pearson Education.

Videos

Alexander, J. F. (Featured). (2014). Functional family therapy for high-risk adolescents [Video series episode]. In *APA psychotherapy video series II: Specific treatments for specific populations*. Washington, DC: American Psychological Association.

Family Institute of Kansas City, Missouri (Producer), & Corales, R. (Trainer). (1986). *The major theories of family therapy teaching tapes: VT 112 structural* [Motion picture]. (DVD #7AQ3717 available from Insight Media, 2162 Broadway, New York, NY 10024, 1–800–233–9910)

Jamestermcb. (2009, August 2). Structural family therapy [Video file]. Retrieved from https://www.youtube.com/watch?v=91wTCgPa_xw

PsychotherapyNet. (2009, June 30). Kenneth Hardy family systems therapy video [Video file]. Retrieved from https://www.youtube.com/watch?v=WBfaIN0rKWM

PsychotherapyNet. (2009, August 4). Tools and techniques for family therapy video [Video file]. Retrieved from https://www.youtube.com/watch?v=62HTYRM14rs

RockinChikk. (2012, February 24). Structural family therapy example [Video file]. Retrieved from https://www.youtube.com/watch?v=bOrnOcHWXgA

ToniHerbineBlank's channel. (2012, January 23). About internal family systems [Video file]. Retrieved from https://www.youtube.com/watch?v=_Yz4JNKIK_Q

Websites

American Association for Marriage and Family Therapy. http://www.aamft.org/

Bowen Center for the Study of the Family: Georgetown Family Center. http://www.thebowencenter.org

Family Systems Institute. http://www.thefsi.com.au

Cultural Case Conceptualizations and Treatment Plans

INTRODUCTION TO CULTURAL THERAPY

Amber (age 45) is the CEO of a computer software company in California. She has never been married but did live with Martin (age 46) in a committed relationship for five years in her mid-20s. He ended their relationship when he decided he was ready to have children and she was not. Amber is the oldest of three adult children, who while they were growing up lived with their wealthy parents in an exclusive neighborhood in San Francisco. Amber returned to California after graduating with a bachelor's degree from Harvard and a doctorate from Yale in computer engineering. Amber sees her parents once a week; she sees her siblings on an erratic basis, as they live out of state.

Amber's father is White and her mother is African American. While he was a successful banker and she was a successful artist, they were actively excluded by some friends and relatives as a result of their marriage. Amber indicates her parents were very happy together and have a very egalitarian relationship. While Amber indicates that she is very satisfied with her professional life, considering herself to be a self-made success, she also indicates experiencing a profound loneliness that began about six months ago.

An in-depth mental status exam was conducted that included intellectual and personality assessment. On the Wechsler Adult Intelligence Scale, Fourth Edition (WAIS-IV), Amber functioned in the superior range of intelligence. She showed no signs of cognitive confusion or difficulties with memory. On the Minnesota Multiphasic Personality Inventory–2 (MMPI-2), Amber appeared to be responding in an open and honest manner. There were no signs of significant pathology, although her scores on anxiety and depression were somewhat elevated.

You practice multicultural therapy (MCT) as developed by Hays (2008, 2013). Multicultural therapy (MCT) considers every encounter between people to be a multicultural experience, as everyone's identity is influenced by his or her membership in many different social groups. To understand her loneliness, Amber will need to understand how her complex cultural influences are interacting to give her a sense of herself, others, and how to operate in the world. The number of social groups, or cultural influences, in Amber's life may grow or contract at different points in her life. Because it is a natural, human process, all social groups form stereotypes of themselves and others. Over time, they may come to perceive their own values and experiences as more normal or valid than those of other groups. Unfortunately, this leads to in and out groups and the accompanying unequal distribution of power in society. MCT perceives the oppression that Amber may experience as a member of one or more out groups to be the major source of her psychological distress. The dominant groups in society have shaped institutions and social norms to reflect their "truth." If Amber is departing from the social norms that society deems appropriate, she may be the target of aggression or microaggressions from others. Developing a multicultural understanding will help Amber recognize that there are many possible ways for her to live her life that are all valuable, and they are all embedded in a cultural context that is more or less visible to dominant and minority groups. Amber's loneliness may be a result of factors that are particular to her, or they may be the result of oppressive behavior from others. Determining this causality will have a major impact on treatment. In areas where her pain comes from social injustice, she may need to become an activist in her personal or social life for her personal distress to be truly alleviated.

Amber was born into a complex cultural context that consisted of many intersecting social groups. Each social group had its own worldview that guided members' beliefs, expectations, values, behaviors, and rules for living (Sue & Sue, 2013). Being the child of a mixed-race couple may have meant that, from the moment of conception, Amber's development was impacted by differing cultural expectations for her White father and her African-American mother about how to handle a pregnancy. The fact that some of her parents' relatives and friends stopped interacting with them after their marriage may have meant Amber's birth was not met with the universal approbation that many children receive. Both parents were very successful in their careers despite not having full family support; however, perhaps due a lack of family support, Amber played a major caretaking role in the family. Throughout her development, how Amber viewed the world, how she came to value computer engineering, and how she made decisions about how to act as a woman were influenced on both unconscious and conscious levels by the "truths" about the right way to live emanating from the social groups that are always influencing her identity. Amber's truths about living were first shaped by her parents' values and beliefs and then, to an ever-increasing degree, by the many social groups she became a part of or was excluded from (Sue & Sue, 2013). To understand Amber from a cultural perspective, you must go far beyond the fact that she is a woman with dark brown skin who has a slim physique and carries a doctorate in computer engineering. You will need to understand what her cultural heritage means to her, what it has meant to her parents and her ancestors, and how it influences her current worldview. It may be that Amber has developed her own special life path through blending all of her cultural influences together. On the other hand, there may be one source of cultural influence that has had an overarching influence on her beliefs, values, and attitudes (Comas-Diaz, 2012).

In MCT, you will start by pulling apart and analyzing each of Amber's cultural influences. At any point in time, some of these cultural influences play a greater role in her identity than others. MCT will use the ADDRESSING framework to help Amber understand the full impact of cultural influences on her attitudes, emotions, behaviors, and relationships with others. These cultural influences include: (a) <u>A</u>ge and generational influences,

(b) Developmental or other Disabilities, (c) Religion and spiritual orientation, (d) Ethnic and racial identity, (e) Socioeconomic status, (f) Sexual orientation, (g) Indigenous heritage, (h) National origin and primary language, and (i) Gender-related information, including roles, expectations, and relationships. While there are other sources of cultural influence on Amber, the ones highlighted in the ADDRESSING framework represent areas in which there has been systematic oppression from the institutions of the United States (Hays, 2013). It is external oppression that is likely to be playing a significant role in her feelings of loneliness.

In evaluating these nine cultural influences on Amber, you will be determining when she is a member of the dominant or minority group. Dominant group membership does not necessarily reflect numerical superiority. Dominance reflects the group's ability to control the environment. It is dominant social groups that are in control of the institutions of society at large and thus set most of the rules for day-to-day living. Members of dominant groups find their values reflected in institutions such as schools and criminal justice systems. Members of dominant groups find it easy to celebrate their religious holidays, as they are reflected in national holidays or traditional days off from school or work (Hays, 2008). Dominant groups are free to consider their experiences and values as normal and their values as representing "truth." They have the opportunity to live their day-to-day lives without awareness of the physical and emotional realities of members of minority groups. Members of the dominant group may have limited contact with those in the minority position. For example, families with children may live close to schools and seniors may live in adult-only communities. Wealthy people may live in gated communities in the suburbs while the poor live in the inner city. This physical separateness can fuel the respective groups' misunderstandings of each other's beliefs and values.

Minority status represents having one's access to power limited by the dominant group. It means having the reality of one's lifestyle misrepresented by mainstream institutions, such as media, that seek to maintain the current power structure. Only by keeping the minority members marginalized and excluded from positions of influence can the dominant group maintain its power and control of society. Members of minority communities must be very aware of the values, beliefs, and expectations of the dominant culture(s) that have power and influence; they are dependent on the dominant group for employment, housing, education, and social services. The environment people live in is very powerful in influencing their psychological adjustment. Social justice fosters mental health, and experiences of injustice are the major source of psychological distress and dysfunction (Sue & Sue, 2013). While being part of a minority culture leads to greater exposure to oppression, it also brings with it culturally specific strengths, such as a sense of group cohesion and pride, positive traits and qualities promoted by the culture, and natural helpers and practices. Having to deal with racism and discrimination may have taught Amber how to tie her self-esteem to her own judgments of her achievements rather than to rely on the judgments of others around her.

Within age and generational influences, children (23.5%) and elders (13.7%) are minority groups in the United States (Vespa, Lewis, & Kreider, 2013). Amber is a 45-year-old adult, and within the United States, she is part of the privileged group that is given more respect. Amber recognizes that on entering menopause, she has begun the long tumble down from the dominant group of adults with the most social respect, into the group of supposedly inferior, older adults with cognitive and health problems. If Amber were 65 rather than 45, ageism might be an important component in her loneliness. Palmore (2001) found that ageism is frequent and extends from microaggressions, such as people assuming that someone is too old to drive safely, to more serious discrimination where someone is denied a promotion or a loan based on the assumption that he or she is losing competence or may develop a debilitating disease that will prevent him or her from repaying the loan.

In addition to her age per se, Amber has generational influences that have affected her view of herself and others. Amber was born in 1969. There was a great deal of social activism in her youth around racial prejudice and discrimination; Martin Luther King Jr. had been assassinated a year before her birth. Thus, the meaning of being biracial might be substantially different for her cohort than for biracial individuals born in 2000, who would see the election of Barack Obama as the first biracial—African American and White— president of the United States.

Within the social influences of developmental disabilities and those acquired later in life, people with disabilities are in the minority group, representing 19% of the total population of the United States in 2010 (Brault, 2012). There are currently five federal laws that seek to protect individuals with disabilities from being discriminated against, including the Americans With Disabilities Act, the Rehabilitation Act, the Workforce Investment Act, the Vietnam Era Veterans' Readjustment Assistance Act, and the Civil Service Reform Act. However, these laws don't force restaurants or employment buildings that were in existence before these laws were enacted to make their buildings accessible. If Amber is physically able, she has many invisible privileges, such as the ability to enter any building and climb the stairs if an elevator doesn't exist or is out of service. She can attend weddings or go to parties at new locations without researching in advance if the location allows reasonable access for someone with mobility problems. If Amber were in a wheelchair, she might be lonely because, when she traversed the halls at work, no one would say hello to her because they were looking at their own eye level, not closer to the ground where Amber was. At this time, you have no information suggesting that Amber has any disabilities. However, as she ages, the likelihood that she will experience at least temporary disabilities increases. As the CEO, she may be responsible for policies that save money for the company but that makes the work environment less friendly or inaccessible to less able-bodied individuals.

Within the cultural influences of religious and spiritual orientations, people who are not Christians are in the minority group within the United States. Based on 2008 census data (U.S. Census Bureau, 2012c), Christians made up 57% of the population. Of these, 31% who identified themselves as Christians indicated they were Protestant, and 19% identified themselves as Catholic. The next largest category included individuals who indicated they considered themselves to be not religious/secular. These individuals represented 11% of the population. Of the many minority religions that were represented on the census, the next largest groups were Jewish (0.9% of the population), Muslim (0.4%), Buddhist (0.4%), and Hindi (0.2%). While Amber is likely to be a Protestant Christian, and thus from the dominant religious group, there has been a long-standing separation between the White Christian churches and the African American Christian churches as a result of long-standing discrimination and prejudice (Boyd-Franklin & Lockwood, 2009). Where does Amber belong? If Amber lives close to her parents, she may continue to belong to the church they raised her in. However, if it is populated by White, wealthy individuals, then she may be part of the tolerated minority within her own home church.

In terms of ethnic and racial influences, people who are not White are in the minority group. Amber's father is White (like 77.9% of the population) and her mother is African American (like 13.1% of the population). Where does she fit? Biracial individuals currently represent 2.4% of the population based on census data (U.S. Census Bureau, 2012d). Can Amber hate the Whites who discriminate against her when they look like family? What about when they don't accept her as family? As a biracial individual, Amber may experience daily microaggressions perpetrated by members of the dominant White social group against members of the African American community—to which her mother belongs. She may also be very aware of the negative stereotypes of White people—her father's group—held by many members of the African American community. Biracial people may be put under pressure to choose a "side." For example, in attending religious services, she may have to choose between a church attended primarily by White group members and one attended primarily by African Americans. These are choices she and her sisters "have to make" because they are both White and African American. Each of Amber's racial groups may think there is only one path to a healthy and adaptive life, leaving Amber in conflict over which path to take (Comas-Diaz, 2012). On the other hand, her rich biracial cultural identity may have helped her develop significant resilience in the face of life stress. She may have learned the best problem-solving strategies and best coping strategies from both cultural groups. She may have learned how to function successfully within both the White and the African American community, providing her with many social resources. She may have learned to exert power, where she has it, in a compassionate and respectful way toward those of less power (Comas-Diaz, 2012).

In terms of sexual orientation, all who are not exclusively heterosexual are in the minority group. Amber lived with a male for five years and appears interested in pursuing further male partners. This suggests she is part of the heterosexual dominant group. However, if Amber were to be aware of herself as a bisexual person, a lesbian, or a member of another sexual minority, she would be part of a group that was quantitatively smaller than the dominant group and actively discriminated against (American Psychological Association, 2008). While professional groups such as the American Psychological Association (2005a, 2012), the American Psychiatric Association (American Psychiatric Association, Commission on Psychotherapy by Psychiatrists, 2000), and the Association for Lesbian, Gay, Bisexual, and Transgender Issues in Counseling (2012) all stress that sexual minority individuals are following different but adaptive patterns of development, considerable discrimination and prejudice continues to exist against these individuals. They may develop more psychological difficulties as a result of living within a hostile environment (American Psychological Association, 2008; Herek & Garnets, 2007).

Within the culture of socioeconomic status, people with less money, less education, or lower status occupations or who live in rural areas are in the minority group. Having lived in San Francisco with a banker for a father and a successful artist for a mother, Amber was raised as a member of the elite. She is likely to have lived within an upper-class neighborhood and to have mingled with the children of the wealthy and powerful in society. She was provided with a first-class education and an accelerated entrée into the world of success.

She thinks of herself as a self-made success. She is currently unaware of the privilege she was raised with and how big an impact that may have played in her current position as CEO. Amber was raised to be a member of the capitalist group who represent 2% of the labor force. This group has the power to dominate in the workplace and in the political arena (Zweig, 2008). In shocking comparison, the poor are a numerically superior group representing 15% of the population; most of these individuals live below the poverty line (Macartney, Bishaw, & Fontenot, 2013). Despite their numerical superiority, they have little power to control any employment they might get, where they live, what they eat, and where their children go to school. It is not uncommon for individuals living within different ranges of socioeconomic status to have very little knowledge of each other's circumstances. This is because they live in different neighborhoods, they have different places of employment, and their children go to different schools (Books, 2007; Lott, 2002). Thus, Amber may be unaware of how much privilege she has in her life and how it helped elevate her to her current position as CEO of a software company.

In terms of indigenous heritage, American Indians and Alaska Natives represent the original inhabitants of North America. There are currently 5.1 million people who identify as indigenous (U.S. Census Bureau, 2012a). Amber lives in San Francisco, where there is a yearly protest held by the indigenous to abolish Columbus Day (Pan Tribal Secession Against the Empire, 2012). The soul wound created in indigenous peoples as a result of White colonial efforts to eradicate their cultures and their physical existence (Duran, 2006) may resonant personally with Amber. While she is a member of the dominant, nonindigenous group, she has heard family stories, and seen art created by her mother, detailing slavery and racism in the United States. This may have may have sensitized her to the genocide perpetrated against the indigenous peoples of the United States, and she may be more sensitive to not committing aggressions or microaggressions against an indigenous person.

In terms of national origin, refugees, recent immigrants, and international students are in the minority group. There are many unauthorized immigrations in the United States, with an estimated 11.7 million coming from Latin America (Passel & Cohn, 2009). Whether immigration is lawful or unlawful has major implications. Under President Obama, prosecutions for unlawful entry more than doubled between 1992 and 2012, and most individuals sentenced for unlawful entry go to prison (Passel & Cohn, 2009). Even when they are aware that they need social services, illegal immigrants may not seek physical or mental health services due to fear of deportation, language barriers, a lack of interpreters, and cultural differences (Bemak & Chung, 2008).

In terms of national origin, Amber is in the dominant group as she, her parents, and her grandparents were born in the United States. However, acts of racial prejudice and discrimination are still common in the United States. Amber's own experience with prejudice may make her more sensitive to the needs of immigrant groups, or she may feel more threatened by them as potentially taking opportunities away from members of her own social groups.

Finally, in terms of gender, women and transgender people are minority groups (American Psychological Association, 2012; American Psychological Association, Join Task Force, 2006; U.S. Census Bureau, 2010a). In 2010, women represented 51% of the population of the United States, and this majority increases as men and women age

(U.S. Census Bureau, 2010a). Despite the fact that women constitute the numerical majority, men continue to hold more positions of power and authority than women. Amber may have experienced a great deal of prejudice and discrimination as she pursued her education at Harvard and Yale, as there would have been few women in her computer-engineering classes. Amber admits that many of her new clients assume she is a secretary when they come for meetings and ask her for coffee. While these acts would be considered microaggressions, Amber is likely to have experienced this type of behavior over and over, and it may have created significant stress for her (Sue & Sue, 2013). Transgender individuals represent less than 1% of the population and are a minority group. This group is highly discriminated against (American Psychological Association, Task Force on Gender Identity, Gender Variance, and Intersex Conditions, 2006) and currently has no power or social influence.

Amber is a member of both dominant and minority groups. Her identity in the moment, as she relates to some specific person within some specific social situation, will be influenced by differences in social power between her and the other person. From individuals from whom she expects, perceives, or receives oppression, Amber will experience stress due to her relative lack of power to control important aspects of her life. Conversely, in interactions where she expects, perceives, or receives power, she will experience an increase in resources and strength. Thus, just as Amber may have been victimized by dominant group members in some situations, she may also have been acting as an oppressor in other situations. Understanding when Amber may be the oppressor and when she may be the oppressed will help determine how much Amber needs to be making personal changes to reduce her loneliness and how much she needs to be engaging in social activism to change an oppressive environment. Seeking social justice is a key component of treatment using MCT, as oppression is the major cause of psychological stress and dysfunction. Treatment will help Amber discover that there are many ways to live a valuable life, each pathway embedded in a multicultural context.

THE ROLE OF THE CLINICIAN

Your major role will be to help Amber identify the impact of her cultural influences on her sense of herself, others, and her worldview. Through an analysis of the sources of power and oppression in Amber's life, you will help her become aware of when her isolation is influenced by external forces of oppression and when it is coming from her own personal expectations, perceptions, and behavior. MCT is a technically eclectic model. As Amber's cultural identity is very complex, many different types of interventions may be needed, including interventions that are not typically considered part of mainstream psychotherapy (Hays, 2008). You need to remain flexible in your thinking and respectful of Amber's values and beliefs as you consider techniques that might build on her personal strengths and resources in culturally congruent ways. For example, you might include culturally specific healing rituals in Amber's treatment plan. Historically, the church has played a major role in the welfare of the African American community. If church services are a source of cultural strength for Amber, they will be integrated into her treatment plan. Cultural influences could impact the treatment plan in many ways. For example, African

American culture values respect within relationships. Amber has indicated that, within her role as CEO, she believes her instructions to staff are treated with less respect than she deserves. Amber could reflect more on her African American culture and how respect is shown in relationships. She could then decide whether a meeting with her staff as a whole, meetings with individual staff members, a memo to staff, or something else would be the best framework for educating her staff as to how she wants her instructions handled. It could be that staff members are behaving in ways she finds disrespectful due to cultural disconnects rather than intentional disrespect. However, Amber may need to make practical changes in her work environment. If employee racism is at the base of this disrespect, Amber needs to consider whether she wants to be patient and work toward building more constructive relationships with her employees or if it is time to use her power within the company to fire the problematic employees and hire new ones, thus taking action to change a hostile environment.

Before Amber walks in the door, you need to prepare yourself to be an effective clinician for her as an individual. Every interaction between two people, including the treatment relationship, is a multicultural experience (Comas-Diaz, 2012). Cultural differences between you and Amber will influence treatment. As a result, you will need to be very aware of how your belief systems and worldview influence your work with her. Listening to Amber about her experiences will be important. However, you must first find ways to expand your contact with individuals who will help you recognize the limits of your worldview (Hays, 2008, 2013). You will need to reflect on what you consider to be appropriate interventions for therapy and how these might be influenced by your own worldview rather than the "truth" about what might be the best interventions for Amber at this time (Sue & Sue, 2013). However prepared you think you are to be an effective helper, you need to approach treatment from a position of humility. There may be sources of knowledge that you don't consider "traditional" that will help you gain a greater understanding of Amber. For example, are there experiences you could gain from music, food, movies, literature, religious observations, and so forth that would help you understand sources of cultural influence on Amber? You need to go beyond traditional sources of knowledge, as they are limited by your own cultural stereotypes (Hays, 2013).

How will you know where to expand your knowledge base? You will start by using the ADRESSING model to compare your own areas of privilege and oppression to Amber's. For example, Amber talks of beginning to experience menopause. Have you had any personal experience with menopause? How much value do you place on fertility as an aspect of a woman's identity? How much are you educated about the impact of this developmental milestone on women? Are you aware of negative or positive stereotypes about older women? Becoming self-aware of what you know and don't know about older women's issues is your first step in preparing yourself for Amber's treatment. Your second step is to educate yourself about menopause so you can more fully understand how Amber may be thinking, feeling, and experiencing becoming an older woman (Hays, 2013). Amber comes into treatment identifying as biracial. Are you monoracial, biracial, or multiracial? How will you feel at the gut level if she asks you how many biracial individuals you interact with on a daily basis? It is hard not to feel defensive and close your mind when you feel that in some way you are being criticized or having your competence questioned. However, to help Amber, you must demonstrate compassion for her viewpoint and for her experiences (Hays, 2008, 2013). If your experience with biracial individuals is limited, admit it. Validate her right to be concerned about whether you have enough experience with biracial individuals to be helpful to her. It is an assumption of privilege to assume that treatment will progress satisfactorily without your having this experience when she is concerned that it will not. Forming categories and stereotypes is a typical human coping strategy; helpers are not immune to this. The fact that you enter the relationship with the desire to help Amber does not automatically give you the skills to do it (Hays, 2013).

In your first treatment session with Amber, you will ask her to describe herself from her own perspective and also how the people within her social network might describe her. Using the ADDRESSING system, you will help her become aware of the complex cultural influences within her life. She is likely to be most aware of identities in which she is currently feeling oppressed and least likely to be aware of areas in which she is privileged. This is because individuals in dominant groups are not encouraged to be aware of the privileges and power their identity gives them. It just surrounds them like an invisible cloud and influences less powerful people to act in a differential, and preferential, manner. Members of minority groups are raised to be sensitive of differentials in power, while members of dominant groups may take their privilege for granted. When listening to Amber, you will need to be alert for signs of sociocultural bias that are leading her to be oppressed or leading her to oppress others.

After you and Amber collaborate in this culturally responsive assessment of her loneliness, you will be aware of what changes Amber needs to make in how she interacts in the world. For example, Amber may be unconsciously committing microaggressions that keep others at a distance. On the other hand, external sources of oppression may need to change. Perhaps employees close to her in power resent her being their boss. If they cannot learn to respond respectfully to her valid requests, Amber may need to find new employees who will. It may be that it is a combination of both internal and external attitudes or behaviors that are leaving Amber lonely. You have no preconceived plan for how Amber will become more socially connected. You believe that there are many different routes out of loneliness that are equally valid roads to a life worth living (Comas-Diaz, 2012). Thus, you will build Amber's view of what she wants to achieve, and what she would consider treatment success, into your treatment plan to help her find satisfaction in her life. There may be times when your own worldview and values comes into conflict with Amber's. While you will not impose your cultural values on her, it is possible that you will seek to expand her options in order to help her balance the needs she may have across her many social identities.

Whatever interventions you choose to help Amber, using the ADDRESSING framework will create an environment where the need for social justice becomes explicit. Amber will recognize in which aspects of her identity she is currently experiencing oppression and how specifically this has affected her. In addition, she will recognize in which aspects of her identity she has been behaving oppressively toward others. Amber will have more power to make changes in environments in which she has been the source of oppression than in those in which she is the recipient (Hays, 2013).

CASE APPLICATION: INTEGRATING THE DOMAIN OF AGE

Amber's case will now be examined in detail. There are many domains of complexity that might be relevant to her case. The domain of age has been chosen to examine within a cultural conceptualization and treatment plan.

Interview With Amber (A) From a Cultural Perspective

C: I understand you're here because you're feeling deeply lonely. Can you start by telling me about yourself?

A: (analytically) I just turned forty-five . . . (pause) It's stupid, but suddenly my age is bothering me.

C: It feels stupid to you in this moment, but it might be valuable to understand how your age might be defining you.

A: (irritated) It's stupid to care about my age. It's not like I'm on death's door. I just have a few wrinkles.

C: Young women are glamorized in advertisements and movies, while old women are stereotyped as irritating or obsolete.

A: (irritated) I don't like to think of myself as believing that crap. I know who I am . . . (long pause)

C: Most of us take in the stereotypes around us even when we aren't aware of it. (long pause) Stereotypes can help us understand things we aren't familiar with, but they can also constrain or harm us if we don't consciously examine their validity for guiding us.

A: (looks speculatively at C) Turning forty-five last month has made me feel more lonely than usual. I had a big blowout party. I kept finding myself standing in a dark corner, watching all my guests eating and laughing. Everyone seemed to be having fun but me. (long pause) It's stupid, because I never wanted children.

C: But now?

A: (angry) I have begun to have an erratic menstrual cycle and hot flashes. My gynecologist says I have begun menopause. The symptoms don't make me feel that bad, (pause) but I keep remembering things I don't want to think about.

C: Menopause reminds you that you won't be giving birth. Before it was your choice, but now biology is choosing for you.

A: (angry) I like to be the one who makes the choices. I have worked hard to have the power and control to be the chooser.

C: Biology doesn't care that you are a powerful CEO. (long pause) Do you regret not having children?

A: (softly) Both my parents pressured me to have children. It was exhausting always having to affirm my right to not have children. I had enough of having to take care of children when I was growing up. (long pause)

C: You had to care for children?

A: (analytically) I didn't have to exactly. My parents were always rushing around accomplishing things. I really admired my parents and wanted to have the same type of drive. On the other hand, I was the eldest, and my two younger sisters clung to me like glue when my parents were gone; they were always crying that they were lonely. I didn't mind at first, being the one to tuck them in and help with homework. But I did get tired out being the one they always turned to. I would have to work late into the night to get my own homework done. When I left to go to college, I went far from home—all the way to Boston; I wanted to finally just look after myself.

C: Just you, (pause) and . . . (pause)

A: (happy) I feel selfish to say so, but I loved it. The years sped by. I met a great guy in graduate school; we moved in together and had five great years. (excited) My career began to really take off as I approached thirty, and I was really enjoying the ride. (pause; irritated) Then, he gave me the "It's time to settle down" speech. (pause) What kind of crap was that? I had been clear from the start that I wanted a career. Both of us were working hard and doing great. In what way hadn't "we" settled down?

C: You felt you had been honest in indicating that your career was a priority. However, somehow he felt it was a young woman's spree rather than a long-term choice.

A: (angry) Exactly. He admitted that he had assumed that when we were older I would stop working and be a full-time mother. I don't know where he got this. I never expressed an interest in this. (getting loud) What infuriated me the most was that he was so sure his plan was right and something was wrong with me if I didn't see it that way. (long pause; softer) I brought this up, and he said I had to decide right then or he was walking out . . . (long pause) and he did.

C: What a shock. (long pause)

A: (angry) I feel angry just thinking about it. We had always talked about being equal partners. He always seemed to listen to me talk about work like I listened to him. (frustrated) I could understand that he might have changed his mind about kids— he hadn't wanted them either when we first met. (long pause) But it seemed as if he had always just assumed I didn't mean it when I said I didn't want kids. (long pause; angry) When I said he was taking control and changing all the rules in our relationship, he said he could tell what my decision was, packed his bags, and off he went. He dated other women for about four months, got married, and now has three kids. (sigh)

C: (tentative) What does the sigh represent?

A: (calm) I don't regret that the relationship ended. I don't think I regret not having children. I think I regret not screaming my lungs out at him that he was acting like a sexist from the Stone Age. I was supposed to change, but he didn't need to. We were together for five years. Then, after a few months, he got married to someone else. I was to give up my position of authority—that I had worked so hard to get—but he was to keep his and get the relationship.

C: He didn't have to choose; he could have both power and the relationship. Could your loneliness represent you buying into this to some extent?

A: (angry, loud) I refuse to let that be true. My parents were partners. I think I always expected we would be partners and was shocked to see what a jerk I had been living with all those years.

C: You wanted him to know you had been genuine about what you wanted and that it was he who was changing the rules, not you. You regret not saying more to him before he walked out.

A: (calmly) Yes, it felt too much like he was leaving me rather than that we were deciding not to stay together. It was also so abrupt. I thought it over many times and I didn't see it coming from him—though I wondered about his parents. (*C* looks questioningly at *A*) We always had Friday night dinner with my parents and Sunday morning brunch, after church, with his. They never seemed comfortable with me, even though we shared a meal every weekend for five years!

C: (surprised) It doesn't make sense.

A: (earnestly) I had asked him once if it was because my dad was White; both his parents are African American. He denied it, but while I had my parents invite them to Friday night dinner every once in a while, they never had my parents over. They seemed as uncomfortable with my parents as they were with me.

C: (matter-of-factly) You noticed the same pattern.

A: (matter-of-factly) While I didn't have the kind of parents who played games with me or tucked me in at night, they did talk to all of us about not being naive about the racial divide. They said they both came under a lot of social pressure to end their engagement. They refused to be divided, but it came at a price; they both had family and friends who found excuses to not be around much after they got married.

C: (pause) Found excuses?

A: (angry) They weren't going to admit they were bigots. Both my parents made a lot of money before they even met each other. So it couldn't have been anything but race.

C: Both of your parents had the power and privilege that money can bring. Yet, in relation to some of your relatives, they were still oppressed because when it came to race, being a mixed-race couple put them in a minority group and they faced oppression at a really personal level.

A: My mother was proud to be African American. Her art was a powerful combination of both her African heritage and the black slave experience. She knows all about her family for generations back. They told stories until they had the freedom to be able to write them down. My mother was the first to paint rather than write. She was proud of her race and her family.

C: She was aware of the pain your family had suffered in slavery, as well as the strengths that came to the family from sharing the story down through the generations. I wonder if she anticipated the pain she might feel if her biracial children were rejected by either African Americans, European Americans, or both?

A: Her way of dealing with it was just to paint a very angry painting and then tell us to blow it off.

C: Do you think being biracial has anything to do with your current loneliness?

A: (irritated but thoughtful) That would make sense, wouldn't it. New clients are very disrespectful to me. In fact, they often assume I'm a secretary and ask me to get them coffee. (long pause) It could be my skin color, but I think the disrespect comes more from my being a woman. It infuriates me that women get treated this way. As adults, we are the majority of the general population—a small majority, but still . . . (pause)

C: Domination comes from having the most power and control in society, not having the greatest numbers.

A: (sighs) Well, I hate thinking of the world this way. (sincerely) I have to admit that I do like the power and control I have at work. Getting the job done well carries so much satisfaction with it. (long pause; happily) I truly love what I do, and my hard work has given me both intellectual challenges and financial security. (long pause; angrily) I shouldn't be lonely! It is just infuriating. I should be able to handle this. I handle things well. I do.

C: At work, when problems come up, you can handle it, but later you feel so lonely. What might be behind it?

A: (long pause; softly) Men go out with women who make less money than they do all the time. But when I meet someone, he always asks what I do, and when I tell the truth, the light goes out of his eyes.

C: If you tell the truth?

A: (calm) I have tried hedging—just saying I'm in computer software. But then they want to pick me up at home or drop me off, rather than meeting at a restaurant; they want to be invited up. But if they see my apartment, they act like they found out I had an STD.

C: It's frustrating that you need to hide from people an area of your life that you actually have a right to be very proud of—your achievements at work.

A: (emphatically) Yes! Men get to be proud. When I think about it, my mother's paintings hung all over the house, but at the dinner table, when we were together as a family, we were always listening to what my father was doing.

C: Your father may have had no idea that by monopolizing the family conversations, he was subtly telling the family that your mother's accomplishments weren't as important as his.

A: (vehemently) He was proud of her work. He is proud of me. I am sure of it, because I have overheard him telling his friends about my having a bachelor's degree from Harvard and a doctorate from Yale. (pause) I don't remember him actually listening to me talk about what I studied at either place or what I'm doing at work right now.

C: Bias can operate on the unconscious level. He may absolutely have been proud of both of you, yet still not really listened. While you have the power at work to set the agenda of what gets discussed, at home, it has been your father who has the power to decide this. Whenever you interact with anyone, issues of power and control come up. Whoever is on top may consciously or unconsciously oppress the other person by treating his or her opinions or experiences with less respect.

A: (irritably) Not feeling listened to makes me feel angry. Why do you think it relates to my feeling lonely?

C: It might not relate to your loneliness. But could the men you go out with unconsciously expect to set the agenda? Then, when you walk in full of personal power, it makes them uncomfortable and they put you at a distance?

A: I don't care about the money, so why must they?

C: It might be because men expect to make more money. It might just be that your confident tone and your assurance in stating your opinions are all subtle ways of showing that you have experienced a lot of power and privilege in your life. It may be this package that makes men assume you won't be interested in them.

A: (frustrated) I know so many men who make more than the women they're with.

C: That fits the stereotype that women like successful men. Where are the cultural images showing men with successful women? (pause)

A: They are the underlings that follow in her shadow, not her equals. (pause) If she falls for him, in the movies, it's because the guy somehow knows more about living life or understanding people. Somehow they make the guy superior to the woman in some way even though she makes more money.

C: Social stereotypes are very powerful, even when we try to fight against accepting them. (long pause) You look angry, not lonely, right now.

A: (angry) I'm mad at myself; I can't hide from it. I want to say the problem is my being dark skinned; I want to say it's the money.

C: You want to, but . . . (long pause)

A: (still angry) Even last year, I can remember enjoying it that some men jumped back five feet from me when they found out I was a CEO.

C: But . . . (pause)

A: (angry) It's my age. I am so furious with myself. A few wrinkles and hot flashes and I'm expecting to be alone for the rest of my life.

C: It's harder for women to have these signs of age, because you see middle-aged men still being romantic leads in movies, but they are with twenty-something women, (pause) not women their own age. Men often divorce their wives, and when they remarry, it's to a much younger woman.

A: (angry) I swear I still don't want to have children. But I think I do want to settle down and stop all the dating.

C: We've spent a lot of time talking about what cultural influences might be behind your loneliness. Do you think we've missed anything that might be relevant right now?

A: (tired) I think we've got it. It's just old wrinkly me.

C: Next week, we would be doing something that parallels this. We would be going through and examining how all your cultural influences bring you strengths or give you options for how to work through this loneliness. (*A* is looking down) Do you want to come back and do this?

A: (pause; looks up) Absolutely.

Cultural Case Conceptualization of Amber: Assumption-Based Style

Amber belongs to many social and cultural groups whose norms influence her interactions with others and her view of how the world works. Could her loneliness be the result of racial oppression? Amber is biracial, with an African American mother and a European American father. In both communities, she doesn't "fit" or feel comfortable. Could her membership in the upper class set her apart? As CEO of a new company, she earns a salary and enjoys a sense of power and control over her day-to-day work environment experienced by only 2% of the population. What about her gender? The world of software engineering is dominated by men. Amber feels her male colleagues are treated with more respect than she is. What about her recent awareness of herself as middle-aged? Amber has begun menopause, and her negative stereotypes of older women may be causing her distress. Issues of power and control pervade every social encounter Amber has. In some interactions, her loneliness may be a function of oppression coming from others—such as racial discrimination. In other interactions, it may stem from instances in which she has taken on the oppressor role and set herself apart from someone else— for example, by treating a restaurant server as invisible. Through developing a deeper respect for cultural differences, Amber can define her own unique path to happiness and not be constrained by any one group's definition of the "true" path. Amber's prior success in forging her own way to educational and employment success bodes well for her ability to find ways to use her personal power constructively and learn how to seek social justice when external forces of oppression stand in her way.

Amber's racial influences come from both the African American and White cultural groups. As a biracial person, Amber makes up part of a very small minority of the population that faces active discrimination. Where does she belong? The worldview of African Americans is often described as collectivist, valuing communal welfare, strong interdependent emotional connections with family and extended family members, and a present-day orientation. The White culture is often described as individualistic, valuing autonomy, personal responsibility, and a future orientation. Where does Amber fit in this? She may be experiencing significant oppression as she is torn between two worldviews and never quite belonging to either group. On the other hand, she may have had the opportunity to draw strengths from both cultural influences as a bicultural person. Amber's parents tried to prepare her for the oppressive experiences she might have. She heard stories from her mother and father about how they lost friends and relatives when they married. Amber's mother told her family stories of racism and oppression. These stories helped Amber draw strength from her African American cultural heritage. In addition, from her father, she gained the belief that with hard work and perseverance, she could be another member of the family to succeed at prestigious universities like Harvard and Yale. Amber respects the achievements of both her parents, and thus has personal knowledge that both cultural groups can experience success. Thus, when biracial Amber experienced microaggressions for five years from her African American boyfriend's family, it made her feel uncomfortable. However, it did not influence her assessment of her own worth as a person.

In terms of the cultural influence of socioeconomic status, Amber has a great deal of social power. She is a highly educated, wealthy woman from a wealthy family. She is the CEO of a computer software company. Her worldview, as a wealthy individual, is that she deserves the power and privileges she has earned through what she sees as her own hard work and personal abilities. As Amber grew up, she developed the expectation and perception that when you work hard and have great ideas, you can achieve success. Therefore, she is very aware of how hard she worked in college and graduate school, as well as in the world of work, to achieve the position she now has as a CEO. Amber has no awareness of how her parents' wealth supported her in becoming a computer engineer with a doctoral degree. Few families living in San Francisco could have afforded to send a child to a private school in Boston. In addition, if Amber hadn't gone to a highly competitive high school, she would have had a much harder time developing the academic skills needed to gain entrance to Harvard. These privileged experiences cut Amber off physically and emotionally from the experiences of individuals who were not wealthy and powerful. Thus, Amber has the freedom to consider her current experiences with success "normal" and herself a self-made success. When people do not listen to what she says or treat her opinion with respect, she is taken aback. Because of her wealthy background, leading a good life means Amber will pursue success, power, influence, and money. It is possible that her current loneliness is due to her behaving in a directly oppressive way toward others with less power than her. She may also be committing microaggressions that put people at a distance. Amber has some growing awareness of how her wealth may be playing a role in her loneliness, as she has begun to try to keep the fact that she is a CEO out of the equation when she first meets a potential romantic partner. Amber recognizes on some level that it takes only one look at her apartment for a date to end abruptly. While Amber can see that her wealth itself is setting people at a distance, she currently remains unaware of how her attitudes and behavior might also play a role.

In terms of the cultural influence of gender, Amber is frustrated by the fact that although she is part of the numerically superior group, as a woman she is treated with less respect than her male colleagues. She is likely to have been the recipient of many forms of active discrimination as well as the microaggressions she talks about, such as being taken for a secretary at meetings. Despite her dedication and hard work, Amber is aware that her male colleagues had a smoother upward career path. Even now, as the CEO of the company, there are times she has to insist before a male executive follows her instructions. This has less to do with Amber and more to do with the fact that the society in the United States is still heavily embedded in patriarchy. As such, men hold most of the positions of power and authority, and woman leaders are considered less competent or anomalous. Amber behaves as an androgynous person in many regards. She has taken on the female worldview that it is important to have an enduring relationship with a man. However, she has rejected the view that as a woman, her major life satisfaction should come from giving birth and raising children. She took care of her two younger sisters as they were growing up, and she feels this was her stint with nurturing young lives. She has taken on the male worldview in valuing competition, success, and making money as exciting and satisfying. When she began a relationship with her ex-boyfriend, Martin, they both indicated they didn't want children and were excited at the prospect of working together as equal partners in a relationship. Five years later, in a shocking change of face, Martin told her he was leaving her if they didn't marry and have children. When she reiterated she did not want to have children, he walked out, and within a few months was marrying another woman, who quickly became a stay-at-home mother. Martin was a member of the dominant group of powerful males. He was socialized to not recognize the barriers that were in Amber's path to success that he did not have to face. Privileged people don't have to know the differences between themselves and the less advantaged or the rules of society. He "just expected" that Amber would come around to his point of view. He may have had no conscious awareness that he held this expectation. However, as the years rolled by and she didn't change, he asserted his power to control the future of their relationship—which wasn't as egalitarian as Amber thought. Traditional gender role stereotypes include that women should marry good providers and that male providers will be wealthier than they are. The reverse stereotype is not true. The unflattering male stereotype is that if a man marries a woman who makes more money than he does, he is a kept man. This may be why, on seeing her luxury apartment, men seem to flee. Amber, with no steady romantic partner and entering menopause, is violating the stereotype of what makes a woman a success. Amber may be lonely knowing the barriers she is facing to developing a satisfying, intimate relationship.

In terms of the cultural influence of age and generation, Amber is middle-aged and thus a member of the privileged group that holds the stable positions in society. There are stereotypes for how people will behave and what their life will be like at different ages. Childhood is supposed to be carefree. It wasn't for Amber, as the fast pace her parents led in their careers left Amber and her two younger sisters alone a great deal. Amber took over the mothering role, making lunches for her sisters to take to school and making sure their homework got done. The stereotype of the college years is that they are carefree. Amber made sure she could put herself first by intentionally going to a college that was literally across the continent from her home. She loved it, and after achieving her bachelor's degree at Harvard, went on to receive a PhD at Yale. It was at Yale graduate school that she met the man she thought she would be spending her life with. They were both completely committed to a fast-paced life in computer software. She was loving it and taken completely by surprise when, just as she was closing in on 30 and being very successful in her career, her partner said it was time to get married and for her to stay home and take care of their children. Amber was blindsided by this. She had thought they had an equal partnership and that neither of them wanted children. While she could accept his changing his mind, the manner in which he left made her feel oppressed and disrespected, as he quickly married someone else. Amber is now 45. The stereotype of middle age indicates that she is at a time when she can expect the most employment stability and economic success. Earlier in her career, she was struggling for recognition of her ideas. Now, she is the CEO of a company. While generally successful, she is still treated disrespectfully by some of her employees. Generational influences may have led this cohort of workers to still see all CEOs as male and feel uncomfortable with her management style.

Stereotypes of aging include mental deterioration and incompetence. These may be influencing Amber at a conscious or unconscious level. Amber has just begun to experience hot flashes, and she is recognizing that she is now headed down the slippery slope to being an older woman—the type of woman who is described in population literature as a bitter old woman, an old maid, a crone. Amber identifies age and generational influence as having the greatest impact on her loneliness at this time. She isn't concerned about the wrinkles per se, but they represent the slippery slope into old age. Male CEOs are often found bringing young women to business events. Female CEOs may bring their husbands, or a son perhaps. Who is Amber going to bring? She has loved the fast past of the technology field. Whereas earlier in her life she wanted to put her career first, now, as the option for having children seems to be biologically fading away, she doubts her decisions. As the years have melted away, she is beginning to wonder how many of the choices were hers and how many were forced on her by societal pressures that don't force the same choices on ambitious men.

Amber is experiencing significant loneliness that has lasted for six months. It is unclear at this time if her loneliness is more a result of external factors, such as discrimination and prejudice, or of internal factors, such as the fact that Amber works too many hours to meet enough people. It would be a microaggression to blame Amber for emotional pain that had more to do with the environment than her own attitudes or actions. Currently, she has identified four areas of cultural influence that are most salient in her life at this time, including her racial heritage, her socioeconomic status, her gender, and her age and generational influences. Whenever one of these cultural influences puts Amber in the minority group, she is in a position where she may have been marginalized and oppressed by the dominant group. At this time, she is feeling very aware of being oppressed as a middle-aged woman, someone who is left over, not chosen by a man and not able to give birth to children. In areas where she is in the dominant group, such as socioeconomic status, Amber may need to increase her awareness of how her attitudes and behaviors that exert power and privilege may be serving to oppress others and set her apart from them. Windows of opportunity for change include the fact that Amber's position as a CEO gives her a great deal of power that she could exert in a positive way to help herself and her employees have less stressful lives.

Cultural Treatment Plan: Assumption-Based Style

Treatment Plan Overview. Amber comes in for help dealing with her intense loneliness. The cultural influences that she is most aware of at this time include her age and generational influences, her gender, her racial and ethnic influences, and her socioeconomic status. For each of Long-Term Goals 1 through 4, Amber will evaluate the differences in power and privilege she experiences within each of these cultural influences and how they might relate to her loneliness. They build in order to Long-Term Goal 5, which will represent the culmination of her treatment. (This treatment plan follows the *basic format.*)

LONG-TERM GOAL 1: Amber will examine the impact that her age and generational influences may have on her current experience of loneliness.

Short-Term Goals

1. Amber will articulate her stereotypes of young adults, middle-aged adults, and seniors in terms of their strengths and weaknesses.

2. Amber will articulate the strengths and weaknesses she perceives herself to have had as a young adult, those she perceives herself to have as a middle-aged adult, and those she perceives she will have as a senior.

3. Amber will research her generation in terms of their expectations for themselves as individuals and for society and then consider if any of these generational influences have led her to have certain expectations of herself or affected how she sees the world.

4. Amber will read a book on development to compare and contrast her current views on aging with medical and psychological data.

5. Amber will examine a relationship she currently has with a young adult and consider the impact of her middle age on this relationship, considering generational influences on her behavior as well as the influences she thinks come from age differences in particular.

6. Amber will examine a relationship she currently has with a senior and consider the impact of her middle age on this relationship, considering generational influences on her behavior as well as the influences she thinks come from age differences in particular.

7. Amber will articulate any age or generational influences that may play a role in her current loneliness, including the impact of environmental stressors outside her control as well as personal influences within her control as an aging person.

8. Amber will develop action steps to reduce any emotional distance she may be experiencing with people due to age and generational factors in her personal, social, and work environments.

9. Amber will consider the power she has in terms of financial, educational, and social resources and create two agendas for herself, one for her personal life and one for her work life, containing action steps for using her power to reduce the oppression of older people within her personal, social, and work environments.

LONG-TERM GOAL 2: Amber will examine the impact that her wealthy background and employment as a CEO have on her current experience of loneliness.

Short-Term Goals

1. Amber will articulate her stereotypes of poor, middle-class, and wealthy individuals in terms of their strengths and weaknesses.

2. Amber will articulate the strengths and weaknesses she perceives herself to have had as an individual fresh out of school in her first job, the strengths and weaknesses she perceives she has in her life as a CEO, and what she expects her income and lifestyle to be when she retires.

3. Amber will read a book on the current economic situation and its impact on the poor, middle class, and wealthy and discuss in what ways this new knowledge did or did not change her social stereotypes of people at different ranges of socioeconomic status.

4. Amber will examine a recent interaction she had with a secretary or someone from the cleaning staff of her company and consider the impact of their differential incomes and power on what they talked about, the language they used, the way they noticed or didn't notice other people during this interaction, and who had the power to initiate social contact and who had the power to end the social contact.

5. Amber will examine a recent interaction she had with another software CEO and consider the impact of their greater income and power on what they talked about, the language they used, the way they noticed or didn't notice other people during this interaction, and who had the power to initiate social contact and who had the power to end the social contact.

6. Amber will articulate any socioeconomic influences that may play a role in her current loneliness, including the impact of environmental stressors outside her control as well as personal influences within her control as an aging, wealthy CEO.

7. Amber will consider the power she has in terms of financial, educational, and social resources and create two agendas for herself, one for her personal life and one for her work life, containing action steps for using her power to reduce oppression of lower-income groups within her personal, social, and work environments.

LONG-TERM GOAL 3: Amber will examine the impact that her female gender has on her current experience of loneliness.

Short-Term Goals

1. Amber will articulate her stereotypes of men and women in terms of their strengths and weaknesses.

2. Amber will articulate the strengths and weaknesses she perceives herself to have as a woman and how similar or different she believes her experiences have been to those of other women.

3. Amber will read a book on the role of gender in personal and social environments and consider in what ways a gender analysis does and does not provide insights in her current situation.

4. Amber will consider the relationship she had with Martin when they were in their 20s and articulate in what ways male and female stereotypes may have played a role in the initiation and termination of this relationship.

5. Amber will examine a relationship that she currently has with a male who is not her employee and consider the impact of her female gender on this relationship, considering signs such as who interrupts whom, who sets the topic of conversation, who changes the subject, who has the power to the end this social contact, who has the power to initiate another social contact, and who has the most power in the relationship.

6. Amber will examine a relationship she currently has with another woman who is not her employee and consider the impact of her female gender on this relationship, considering signs such as who interrupts whom, who sets the topic of conversation, who changes the subject, who has the power to the end this social contact, who has the power to initiate another social contact, and who has the most power in the relationship.

7. Amber will join a businesswomen's association and consider the dynamics of the organization and what she thinks the strengths and weaknesses of this organization are compared to those of a male-dominated organization, such as one she belongs to as a software engineer.

8. Amber will articulate any gender influences that may play a role in her current loneliness, including the impact of environmental stressors outside her control as well as personal influences within her control as an aging, wealthy, female CEO.

9. Amber will create an agenda of action steps to take in which she will use her androgynous strengths of caring about the development of long-term relationships, ability to develop an agenda, ability to set reachable goals, and ability to solve problems using a future orientation to reduce gender discrimination in her personal, social, and work environments.

LONG-TERM GOAL 4: Amber will examine the impact of her biracial heritage on her current experience of loneliness.

1. Amber will articulate her stereotypes of Whites, African Americans, and biracial individuals in terms of their strengths and weaknesses.

2. Amber will articulate the strengths and weaknesses she perceives her mother, her father, and herself to have and how similar or different she believes her family experiences with race are to what happens in the general population.

3. Amber will read a book about biracial experiences in the United States and consider in what ways it does and does not provide her with insights about her current situation.

4. Amber will examine a relationship that she currently has with a White person who is not her employee and consider the impact of her biracial identity on this relationship, considering signs such as who interrupts whom, who sets the topic of conversation, who changes the subject, who has the power to end this social contact, who has the power to initiate another social contact, and who has the most power in the relationship.

5. Amber will examine a relationship she currently has with an African American person who is not her employee and consider the impact of her biracial identity on this relationship, considering signs such as who interrupts whom, who sets the topic of conversation, who changes the subject, who has the power to the end this social contact, who has the power to initiate another social contact, and who has the most power in the relationship.

6. Amber will examine a relationship she currently has with someone who is biracial or multiracial and not a member of her family and consider the impact of her biracial identity on this relationship, considering signs such as who interrupts whom, who sets the topic of conversation, who changes the subject, who has the power to the end this social contact, who has the power to initiate another social contact, and who has the most power in the relationship.

7. Amber will articulate any racial and ethnic influences that may play a role in her current loneliness, including the impact of environmental stressors outside her control as well as personal influences within her control as an aging, wealthy, female, and biracial person.

8. Amber will consider whether the strengths she has in planning and controlling her schedule, stemming from her White heritage, could be used to give her more time to socialize with others.

9. Amber will consider whether a greater integration of the collectivist worldview of her African American heritage into her personal attitudes and behaviors toward others would reduce her loneliness.

10. Amber will articulate what she would like to do personally to reduce racial and ethnic discrimination in her personal, social, and work environments.

LONG-TERM GOAL 5: Amber will examine the impact of having differing worldviews, originating from cultural influences surrounding her age and generation, socioeconomic status, gender, and race, on her loneliness and create her own unique truth for pursuing a happy and successful life.

1. Amber will articulate any conflicts she experiences between her age and generational influences and her CEO identity.

2. Amber will articulate any conflicts she experiences between her age and generational influences and her identity as an attractive woman.

3. Amber will articulate any conflicts she experiences between her African American and White cultural stereotypes of middle-aged and senior people.

4. Amber will articulate any conflicts she experiences between her African American and White cultural stereotypes of women.

5. Amber will articulate any conflicts she experiences between her African American and White cultural stereotypes of wealthy people.

6. Amber will articulate any conflicts she experiences between how she is to behave as a person who happens to be a woman and how she is to behave as a CEO.

7. Amber will articulate her worldview of how best to operate in the world based on her analysis of cultural influences on herself.

8. Amber will consider what she would like to do, in terms of both personal actions and social justice, that might alleviate her loneliness.

9. Amber will consider whether taking on a multicultural worldview would add to her sense of satisfaction in her personal, social, and work environments and how treating cultural groups with more respect in these environments could decrease her social isolation from others.

Cultural Case Conceptualization of Amber: Diagnosis-Based Style

Amber is a multicultural person, and every interaction she has with someone else is a result of the interaction of their cultural influences with hers. She has a flexible mindset and can take strengths from both her African American and White cultural heritage. She has learned that persistence and hard work pay off, as she gained entry into first Harvard for a bachelor's degree and then Yale for a doctorate in computer engineering. Amber is a very independent person within her work environment and currently has earned a great deal of power and privilege as the CEO of a computer software company. Despite her many successes, Amber has been very lonely for the past six months. This problem with social connection will be examined within her cultural influences of age, gender, race, and socio-economic status to determine whether it is a result of external sources of oppression, of internal sources such as her beliefs and actions, or of both. Although Amber is lonely, she has also continued to achieve at a very high level at work, socialize regularly with her parents, and continuing to socialize with others. On psychometric testing, she showed no signs of cognitive confusion, suicidal or homicidal ideation, or impulse control problems. Her superior level of intelligence and long history of hard work and persistent reflect an individual who has the personal resources to make progress in attaining her goals of developing a more satisfying personal life. Her working DSM-5 diagnosis at this time is V60.3 Problem Related to Living Alone (American Psychiatric Association, 2013). She is currently functioning at a very high level occupationally, is financial secure, has a family support system, and has the resources she needs to attend treatment.

Amber is a multicultural person, and while she may not consciously identify herself as such, she has developed the flexible mindset of a multicultural person. She is able to recognize that there are many pathways to happiness and many adaptive ways to live a life. Amber may have developed this flexible perspective because she was raised within a home that combined the African American and White cultural traditions. Amber's mother comes from a long line of African Americans who tracked their heritage across the generations, even into the slave years. They used first oral and then written stories to keep their family history alive. Amber grew up hearing these stories and seeing how her mother visualized them in her paintings. Both hearing the stories and seeing her mother transform the written words into images may have encouraged Amber to think about the past and how it influenced the present. Using words and using images are two different ways to capture experiences and maintain their impact; whether it was at the conscious or unconscious level, Amber learned there was more than one way to express powerful ideas.

Amber's father introduced Amber to the White cultural tradition. He was very successful in the banking world. From him, she learned how to take on a future orientation and pursue long-term goals in a persistent and effective manner. Her father introduced her to a fast-paced career, and she found it exhilarating. However, while her White heritage encouraged her independence and a high level of achievement, her African American heritage encouraged strong family connections. Perhaps as an attempt to balance her two cultural traditions, Amber moved back to San Francisco so that she could see her family regularly while living the life of a CEO. Amber recognizes that while her parents took different paths, both of them ended up very successful and are not socially isolated. However, Amber has experienced significant oppression as a woman and a biracial person, and now she is facing more as an older person; these may all be factors that have led to her current loneliness.

Amber multicultural mindset has also allowed her to take on a flexible view of what it means to be a man or a woman. Both of her parents were highly ambitious and career oriented. However, her mother painted pictures and her father was a banker. Whether consciously or unconsciously, Amber learned there were multiple pathways to leading a successful life and that she didn't have to take on exclusively the female or male gender role stereotype to have such a life. As a result, Amber took on an androgynous role. From the male gender role, she incorporated a single-minded focus on pursuing control, power, and prestige within the business world. From the female gender, she incorporated a value for spending time with family and having a lifelong partner. Amber shares a meal with her parents once a week. When she and her ex-boyfriend Martin were living together, they shared a meal with his parents once a week. She was significantly distressed when their five-year relationship failed, as she thought she'd found a lifelong partner who valued an egalitarian relationship. However, when she realized he wanted to be the authority in the home, she recognized that this was not the kind of relationship she wanted. Amber values having a stable family life and would like to marry. The pool of wealthy, male, single CEOs is quite limited, and this may play a role in her current loneliness. Amber's flexible mindset allows her to think of men who earn less money than she does as romantic partners. But, at this time, she has found the reverse not to be true. Men seem to find her financial success a barrier to remaining in a romantic relationship with her. While Amber currently doesn't know how to find her lifelong partner, she is clear that she wants an egalitarian relationship, and she is fearful that her middle age will serve as an impediment to developing one.

Amber's hard work and persistence first began to show their power as she achieved at a high level and was accepted into Harvard as an undergraduate. She did not burn out there. She continued her excellence in performance and gained entry into a premier doctoral program at Yale. She had selected computer engineering as her field, which was dominated by men. However, despite gender bias slowing down her upward mobility, she continued to work hard and produce excellent work and is now CEO of a software company. While she is frustrated that her male executives don't always follow her instructions, when she insists, they do. She has the power, and at 45, Amber can expect to hold it for a long time to come. However, while 45 is a "good thing" as far as years left to work, 45 is a "bad thing" in the world of biology. Although Amber actively rejected parenthood in her 20s, her signs of menopause have made her feel as if she has lost control of her choice to have or not have children. Amber's awareness of herself as an older woman is what she identifies as the main force behind her feelings of loneliness. She wonders if the pool of men her age who are not married contains her partner for life. Will she still be attractive to him? Amber has seen male CEOs walking around with younger women, but she can't see her crowd accepting her coming to a function with a younger man. Her stereotypes of older woman are all negative. Concerns about living the rest of her life alone may be playing a leading role in her current social isolation.

Amber values independence and the ability to set her own agenda. Therefore, although she was deeply committed to Martin, when he told her that her choice was to give up her career and have children or give up her relationship with him, she picked maintaining her career. Amber doesn't dwell on the loss of Martin as a partner per se; however, entry into menopause has caused her to be more aware that her pool of prospective partners is dwindling. Amber identifies her increasing age as the most likely cause of her current loneliness despite continuing to date and throw parties. Amber doesn't value having sexual encounters with many partners. Perhaps due to a collectivist orientation from her mother or female gender role stereotypes, Amber seeks a stable relationship with a man who will value his own independence as well as hers. While she has been feeling lonely for six months, Amber has been functioning at a high level at work and has maintained her weekly connections with her parents and an active social calendar. She has a multiplicity of strengths, including a flexible mindset, a history of hard work and persistence, the ability to think on her feet in a fast-paced work environment, and the ability to function independently as well as within interconnections with others. A window of opportunity for change at this time is that Amber is ready to take active steps to reduce her social isolation. She is aware of the many cultural issues that may be impacting her at this time, and she has a history of success in solving complex problems. Her parents have been role models for an egalitarian partnership in which both parties get to excel at their individual talents. Finally, her flexible mindset makes her open to the new ideas that come up in treatment sessions. If Amber becomes more aware of her myriad of cultural influences, she may be able to create a worldview that fits her unique identity. Finding a partner who will treat her as an equal may be a smoother process once she has clarified her own values and beliefs for herself.

Cultural Treatment Plan: Diagnosis-Based Style

Treatment Plan Overview. Amber is a very bright woman with many strengths. Her treatment goals build on each other sequentially, and she may be able to progress swiftly through the plan. Her issues with loneliness will first be described from her point of view. Then, information garnered from other sources will be summarized. Finally, a detailed plan that builds on her unique strengths will be presented. (This treatment plan follows the *adapted SOAP format.*)

Subjective Data

Amber's presenting complaint is that she is very lonely and has been lonely for quite some time. While her social disconnection is causing her distress on the personal level, particularly as signs of aging remind her that her child-bearing years are over, across many domains of cultural influence Amber experiences a lot of privilege and power.

Objective Data

Standardized testing revealed that Amber was performing in the superior range of intellectual functioning on the Wechsler Adult Intelligence Scale, Fourth Edition (WAIS-IV). Her performance on the Minnesota Multiphasic Personality Disorder–2 (MMPI-2) revealed that she was responding in an open and honest manner and showed no signs of significant pathology; however, there were signs of some depression and anxiety. She has very good verbal communication skills. She maintains regular contact with her parents and siblings. She frequently dates and is very successful in the work environment. Thus, her feelings of loneliness are most compatible with a DSM-5 diagnosis of V60.3 Problem Related to Living Alone. However, Amber is living in a society that is still highly racist. Thus, her biracial heritage may be found to play a significant role in her current difficulties. If this turns out to be true, other potential diagnoses, such as V62.4 Acculturation Difficulties or V62.4 Target of Adverse Discrimination or Persecution, may be found to be more appropriate explanations for her current loneliness.

Assessment

Amber expected to feel satisfied and empowered by her current lifestyle as a CEO. While having money and power, she has found these achievements to be satisfying professionally, but they have left her feeling deeply lonely within her personal life. She finds some of this dissatisfaction to be coming from external sources, such as possibly being a target of racism by her ex-boyfriend's parents and society's general treatment of individuals as "African American" to the exclusion of their other cultural identities. She also has felt herself to be the target of a gender double standard by her ex-boyfriend and some men within the work environment. However, she doesn't believe these are the predominant sources of her current loneliness. There are some indications that the approach of menopause is having a significant impact on how she views herself as a woman, and this may play a significant role in her loneliness, as she may fear that she will be less appealing to men and therefore less likely to find a life partner. Although she is not showing significant symptomatology at this time, her deep feelings of loneliness are important to address. Her superior level of intelligence and long history of hard work and persistence reflect an individual who has the personal resources to make progress in attaining her goal of developing a more satisfying personal life.

Amber's working diagnosis at this time is V60.3 Problem Related to Living Alone, single, mild. She is currently functioning at a very high level occupationally, is financially secure, and has a family support system and the resources she needs to attend therapy.

Plan

Treatment plan overview: Long-Term Goals 1 through 4 can be addressed in any order. Long-Term Goal 5 should be addressed after the first three are complete.

LONG-TERM GOAL 1: Amber will examine how her flexible mindset has provided her with strengths to use as she examines cultural influences on her loneliness.

Short-Term Goals

1. Amber will articulate her stereotypes of young adults, middle-aged adults, and seniors in terms of their strengths and weaknesses.

2. Amber will articulate the strengths and weaknesses she perceives herself to have had as a young adult, those she perceives herself to have as a middle-aged adult, and those she perceives she will have as a senior.

3. Amber will research her generation in terms of their expectations for themselves as individuals and for society and then consider if any of these generational influences have led her to have certain expectations of herself or have affected how she sees the world.

4. Amber will read a book on development to compare and contrast her current views on aging with medical and psychological data.

5. Amber will articulate her stereotypes of poor, middle-class, and wealthy individuals in terms of their strengths and weaknesses.

6. Amber will articulate the strengths and weaknesses she perceives herself to have had as an individual fresh out of school in her first job, the strengths and weaknesses she perceives she has in her life as a CEO, and what she expects her income and lifestyle to be when she retires.

7. Amber will read a book on the current economic situation and its impact on the poor, middle class, and wealthy and discuss in what ways this new knowledge did or did not change her social stereotypes of people at different ranges of SES.

8. Amber will articulate her stereotypes of men and women in terms of their strengths and weaknesses.

9. Amber will articulate the strengths and weaknesses she perceives herself to have as a woman and how similar or different she believes her experiences have been to those of other women.

10. Amber will read a book on the role of gender in personal and social environments and consider in what ways a gender analysis does and does not provide insights in her current situation.

11. Amber will articulate her stereotypes of Whites, African Americans, and biracial individuals in terms of their strengths and weaknesses.

12. Amber will articulate the strengths and weaknesses she perceives in her mother, her father, and herself, and how similar or different she believes her family experiences with race have been to what happens in the general population.

13. Amber will read a book about biracial experiences in the United States and consider in what ways it does and does not provide her with insights about her current situation of being lonely.

14. Amber will spend a week keeping a diary of her thoughts as she moves through the day and sees people of different ages, genders, generations, socioeconomic statuses, racial heritages, and so forth, and consider what she has learned that she can use to create her own unique worldview in terms of how to live a successful and happy life.

15. Further goals will be developed as needed.

LONG-TERM GOAL 2: Amber will examine how she could use her strengths of hard work and persistence to decrease her sense of loneliness.

Short-Term Goals

1. Amber will attend church services and intentionally sit next to people older than her, initiate small talk before and after the services, and be aware of her feelings of social connection or disconnection while she is doing it.

2. Amber will take two action steps at work that could reduce any emotional distance she may be experiencing with people due to age and generational factors and be aware of her feelings of social connection of disconnection while she is doing them.

3. Amber will take two action steps in her personal life that could reduce any emotional distance she may be experiencing with people due to age and

generational factors and be aware of her feelings of social connection of disconnection while she is doing them.

4. Amber will consider the power she has in terms of financial, educational, and social resources and create two agendas for herself, one for her personal life and one for her work life, that will support healthy views of aging, and be aware of her feelings of social connection or disconnection as she implements them.

5. Amber will attend a businesswomen's association meeting and consider how she feels at this meeting compared to how she feels in a male-dominated meeting and if this influences her feelings of social connection or disconnection.

6. Amber will create an agenda of action steps to take in which she will use her androgynous strengths of caring about the development of long-term relationships, ability to develop an agenda, ability to set reachable goals, and ability to solve problems using a future orientation to reduce gender discrimination in her personal, social, and work environments.

7. Amber will take turns working out in the gym of the YMCA and the gym in a wealthy private club and compare her feelings of social connection and disconnection at each place.

8. Amber will consider the power she has in terms of financial, educational, and social resources and create two agendas for herself, one for her personal life and one for her work life, containing action steps for using her power to reduce oppression of lower-income groups within her personal, social, and work environments.

9. Amber will attend an NAACP meeting and a Republican club meeting and consider whether these environments enhance her feelings of social connection or disconnection.

10. Amber will consider whether the collectivist worldview of her African American heritage or the individualistic worldview of her White heritage is having more impact on her manner of interacting with others, how much time she gives herself to interact socially, and the places she goes to interact with others.

11. Amber will develop one strategy for planning ahead (from her White heritage) and one strategy for interacting with people using a present orientation (from her African American heritage) to try to increase her sense of social connection.

12. Amber will articulate what she would like to do personally to reduce racial and ethnic discrimination in her personal, social, and work environments.

13. Further goals will be developed as needed.

LONG-TERM GOAL 3: Amber will use her valuing of and ability for independent action to set her own agenda and build her own multicultural worldview that will maximize her feelings of social connection.

Short-Term Goals

1. Amber will articulate any conflicts she experiences between her age and generational influences and her CEO identity.

2. Amber will articulate any conflicts she experiences between her age and generational influences and her identity as an attractive woman.

3. Amber will articulate any conflicts she experiences between her African American and White cultural stereotypes of middle-aged and senior people.

4. Amber will articulate any conflicts she experiences between her African American and White cultural stereotypes of women.

5. Amber will articulate any conflicts she experiences between her African American and White cultural stereotypes of wealthy people.

6. Amber will articulate any conflicts she experiences between how she is to behave as a person who happens to be a woman and how she is to behave as a CEO.

7. Amber will articulate her worldview of how best to operate in the world based on her analysis of cultural influences on herself

8. Amber will consider what she would like to do, in terms of both personal actions and social justice, that might alleviate her loneliness.

9. Further goals will be developed as needed.

PRACTICE CASE FOR STUDENT CONCEPTUALIZATION: INTEGRATING THE DOMAIN OF VIOLENCE

It is time to do a multicultural analysis of Dan. There are many domains of complexity that might provide insights into his behavior. Within this analysis, you are asked to try to integrate the domain of violence into your case conceptualization.

Information Received From Phone Intake

Dan is a 75-year-old male widower of five years. When his wife Connie died, their daughter Helen moved back into the family home to care for Dan. Dan and Connie had been married 52 years and had lived in the same house their entire life together. Dan was an architect who inherited the family architectural firm from his father Meyer. Dan and Connie had two children. Their oldest son, Gerry (age 50), moved to France after completing his college degree and rarely returns to the United States for visits. Their daughter Helen (age 48) had moved back to her hometown after she graduated from college and lived in a small condominium near her parents' home. Helen got married, at the age of 36, to a Mexican citizen, Rodrigo, who emigrated to the United States and became a citizen. He worked as a chef in a Mexican restaurant, and Helen worked as a dental assistant. They had one son, Juan, who is currently 12 years old. Helen and Rodrigo divorced when Juan was 10 years old.

Dan looked painfully thin and gaunt when he attended his interview. His doctor had filed a mandated report to adult protective services when Dan came in to get his pneumonia shot and the nurse noticed that his arms were covered in bruises. Dan denied that there were any problems at home but agreed to come in for this interview in order to get the doctor to promise not to contact Helen or ask her any questions. When Dan came in for this brief intake, he was angry and responded to questions very briefly. During a mental status exam, Dan showed signs of functioning in the superior range of intelligence. He made a lot of sarcastic comments about himself, using labels such as *demented*, *senile*, *an idiot*, and *retarded*. He showed no signs of cognitive confusion, memory loss, depression, or suicidal ideation. There were some signs that Dan drank regularly by himself every day, but he refused to provide enough information to screen in or screen out the possibility of substance abuse. While his referral for treatment had been a result of indications of elder abuse, he denied all the allegations.

Interview With Dan (D) From a Cultural Perspective

C: I read the report from your internist. (long pause) It said your arms were bruised.

D: (angrily) I don't want to talk about that, and I want you to know that I am not a man who is used to being pushed around. You can't make me talk about those stupid bruises if I don't want to talk about them.

C: You are very right about that. (long pause) You describe yourself as a man who doesn't want to be pushed around. (*D* glares directly at *C*) Would it be all right for us to talk more about who you are as a strong man?

D: (cautiously) What do you want to know?

C: Honestly, I want to know all about who you are. Could we start with what it does or doesn't mean that you are seventy-five years old?

D: (caustically) I am not demented, if that's what you are insinuating. I did not get bruised because I'm clumsy. I have always been athletic, and I am still playing tennis and golf.

C: Tennis is a great sport. (long pause) Most people today seem blind about how important exercise is for their bodies and mind. (pause) So, where did your bruises come from, since you are not clumsy?

D: (with pride) Don't think you can trap me into talking about something I don't want to talk about. My memory is just as sharp now as it has been all my life. Just like my weight is exactly the same as it was when I graduated from college. I have never been one to overindulge in food. Now my daughter Helen, that's a different story. How she let herself get so fat has always been beyond me.

C: You started out by being proud of your own athleticism. How did you end up criticizing Helen?

D: (caustically) Why shouldn't I criticize her? She's my daughter. She got fat when she hit her teens—just when she should have been paying more attention to her looks. My wife tried to help her with diets. Connie was like me. We met on our college tennis team and both stayed fit all our lives. My oldest child, Gerry, he can also swing a racket and has also stayed fit; at least he looks fit in the pictures he sends home. Helen was always the outsider in our family, sneaking food out of the kitchen; she eats all day now.

C: You are feeling physically fit and feel that you always have been. Is anything about your age important for me to know in understanding your life now?

D: (angrily) Well, I lost my Connie five years back, and now Helen is living with me. What a terrible exchange! Helen never learned to cook decently—she loves food so much, you'd think she would put more effort into cooking. She is such a nag, always trying to make me do things I don't want to do. My Connie wasn't like that. But there is no point crying over it anymore; she's dead. That's what I try to tell Helen, but she's still crying.

C: (questioningly) You don't like to hear her cry? (pause; D nods yes) Do you ever try to comfort her?

D: (snapping) I didn't believe in that emotional spoiling when she was a small child, and I certainly don't believe in it now that, to put it mildly, she is full grown.

C: So you never had that type of relationship some dads have with their daughters, where when she was little, she crawled into your lap crying and you comforted her?

D: (proud) In my family, we learn early to keep a stiff upper lip. There is no point in everyone knowing how you're feeling. You are the only one who cares anyway. It's babyish and immature to cry.

C: It sounds like you value stoicism?

D: (tense) Any sane man would.

C: Not all cultural traditions consider men unemotional. For example, Latino and Italian cultures encourage men to be emotionally expressive.

D: (emphatic) My family is from Vermont. There is not an emotional bone in our bodies— and thank the good Lord for that.

C: I get it. You are glad to be stoic. So, why did Helen move in after Connie died?

D: (frustrated) I didn't ask her to. (pause; irritated) I sprained my ankle last year and needed help getting back and forth to the doctor. Helen used this as an excuse to stop working and move in with me. I didn't want her to. All I wanted was a little help getting to the doctor. She said my appointments were getting her into trouble at work. She never could stand up for herself. She just quit her job. Typical of her, she never had any strength of character.

C: You sprained your ankle and needed some help getting to appointments. Has your full mobility returned?

D: (explosively) Do you see crutches? A wheelchair? Are you blind!

C: (firmly) I apologize for touching a raw nerve. I was not suggesting that you had any difficulties. I am just trying to understand who you are right now. I can hear how angry you are. (long pause) Sometimes people go from being able-bodied to being disabled, and this is quite a blow to their freedom—it makes them angry.

D: (hostile) I am completely self-sufficient. (with emphasis) It is Helen who has all the self-sufficiency of an eight-year-old.

C: You have said a lot of demeaning things about Helen today. Why is that?

D: (pause; ignoring the question) My problems with Helen are not a big deal. I told my doctor that. (pause) But he had to make the bruises I had on my arms a big deal by calling those protective services—as if I need to be protected from anybody. I'll tell you what happened, but don't you go making a big deal about it. (pause) Helen had gotten on my nerves nagging at me, so I went into my den and knocked back a few scotches while I watched TV. I guess I had a few too many because I don't remember getting any bruises. But I can't deny it—I am not blind or deaf. I did have quite a few that day at the doctor's office.

C: It seems very important to you that I know you aren't impaired in any way.

D: (squirming and angry) Well, wouldn't you?

C: Yes, I would want people to know that too. (long pause) If I was having problems hearing or seeing, this impairment would weigh heavily on me. I spend my days listening to people and looking at them carefully to try to understand them. This would be really hard for me to do if I developed a sensory impairment.

D: (with hostility) You admit it; your identity is tied up in being a good spy.

C: (calmly) What are all these put-downs about? (long pause while *C* looks into *D*'s eyes) I wonder if you feel it is necessary to let me know you are a powerful person by insulting me.

D: (matter-of-factly) Well, I am a powerful man. I was the head of a successful company, like my father before me. I was the head of my household and everyone in the family knew it.

C: Did you and your wife share any of this power?

D: (explosively) Don't you read your Bible? The husband is the head of the house.

C: You sound angry again. I wasn't trying to be disrespectful of your religious beliefs. What should I understand about them so I don't misunderstand your family?

D: (long pause, glaring intently at *C*) Okay, you got me there. I am not a religious man. I was just trying to yank you out of this irritatingly calm attitude you have.

C: (looking directly in *D*'s eyes) I haven't stayed calm to play a power game with you. (pause) Being such a powerful man all your life has made seeking help from me an alien experience. (long pause) Usually, my being calm helps others feel more comfortable in talking about why they're here. It doesn't seem to work that way with you.

D: (surprised) You talk as if you mean what you say.

C: I do. Let me assure you of one thing. I have heard all your insults today. But it's up to me if I say anything about it or not. (pause) I'm stoic.

D: (laughing) Well, if you recognize I can get your goat, I guess I can stop trying so hard to do it.

C: Great; let's see what else we can agree on. You have always been a strong man with decided opinions. You are a very successful man at work who also likes to be in charge at home. You have grown older with the years, but these things have not changed who you are. But you have some concerns that others might consider you senile or decrepit just because you're older. You are a wealthy man from a wealthy family, and everything was going according to plan until your wife died. Religion didn't help you then, and it's not relevant now because you aren't religious.

D: (disgruntled) Connie was in great health; she wasn't supposed to die. It made no sense. We were about to go to Europe to visit our son, Gerry; we hadn't seen him in years. (long pause) Well, let's change the subject. Dwelling on her death won't bring her back. I've told Helen over and over that crying won't help. I offered her some scotch once, but she flung it away—it made a mess on the carpet! It makes more sense to have a few drinks than cry. At least the scotch tastes good (*D* is looking down and nodding to himself). No point crying over it, as I've told Helen over and over.

C: Different people need to grieve in different ways. You've made it clear that you and Helen were cut from different cloth. You love sports; she doesn't. Why would you grieve in the same way?

D: (matter-of-factly) Because there is a smart way and a stupid way, and Helen always manages to take the stupid way. She has always been a disappointment to me—but I can't kick her out of my house. The fool quit her job. She's middle-aged; she's fat. Who would want to hire her? And she's got that boy. She needs to stay home and take good care of him—if she's capable of it.

C: Why are you calling your grandson "that boy"?

D: (angry) I can call him anything I want. She is the one who named him Juan, which is a name I hate. No one in our family has been named Juan. Now, John is a good name, but Helen won't hear of it, even though the dumb Mexican never even stayed with her.

C: Do you talk like that about Juan and his dad at home?

D: (sharply) No, of course not. I told you I'm not an idiot. I don't want to hurt the kid; it's not his fault. It's all Helen's fault. She went on a trip to Mexico with some of her friends, and she comes back married to someone who just wanted to be an American citizen.

C: How long were they together?

D: (sharply) Ten years too long if you ask me.

C: Ten years sounds like a long time to stay together if you only want citizenship. Maybe, just like fifty percent of the marriages in the United States, they got a divorce because they weren't getting along.

D: (angry) That's just what Connie said, but she was always making excuses for Helen, and it didn't help Helen any. (long pause) Connie thought it was sweet how Rodrigo—that was his name—would make tacos for dinner or some other Mexican something or other. What's he, a woman? Why is he cooking?

C: Lots of men like to cook.

D: (yelling) In my day, men were men, and they certainly didn't cook for their wives. If he is working hard, he doesn't have time to cook.

C: You feel very strongly about what men should and shouldn't do. By the way, (long pause) you don't have to yell at me. I will listen to what you say, even if you speak quietly.

D: (firm) If you don't try to push that feminist nonsense on me that men can cook, I won't need to yell. No one is going to make me believe something I don't want to believe.

C: I am not trying to force anything on you. No two people share all the same beliefs. But I think taking on a more open perspective, that there are a lot of good ways to live a life, is more respectful of others, and you aren't the only one who wants to be treated with respect.

D: (irritated) I am proud to be an outspoken person. I tell people what I think.

C: Can you be both outspoken and respectful of others? (long pause) From my perspective, many of your comments would be offensive to people with Mexican heritage, women, people with disabilities, and most particularly Helen.

D: (beginning to stand up) If you think I will tolerate you calling me a racist, I will just leave. I told the same to Helen; if she objected to how I referred to her husband, she could just leave.

C: It would be very lonely for you if everyone left. (*D* looks down; long pause) My role is not to insult you. But I have to be honest and say that what you consider being outspoken, I often find offensive, even when the comments are not directed at me. You have lost your beloved wife; do you want to lose Helen and Juan?

D: (sarcastic) Calling me a racist will help me not hurt Helen and Juan?

C: You used the word *racist*, not me. (long pause) While you didn't choose it, part of your identity now is being the father of a woman who married into a Mexican family. (long pause) You now have a Mexican American grandchild. You are proud of coming from Vermont. (long pause) Should Helen want Juan to be proud of coming from Vermont and Mexico?

D: (irritated) Okay, no need to get all sensitive on me. Yes, I do call Helen names; she's my daughter, for God's sake, and Juan is my grandson. I am the head of the house; I can say what I want and I always have. So don't describe me as a racist again.

C: Did I hurt your feelings? (*D* nods) Sorry, (pause) I'm not buying it. Remember, you told me you were stoic. (*D* laughs; long pause) However, you have made it clear that Helen isn't stoic. I'm worried that you got those bruises because you mouthed off about somebody Helen loved, like Juan, and she beat you for it.

D: (quiet for a few minutes, looking down) No, I've been in the business world; I know how to keep my mouth shut. You can stop worrying. It was an accident, but it didn't happen the way I told my doctor it did. I've told you before that it irritates me how much Helen eats. It was late at night; I was tired. I had told her a million times I didn't want my money spent on junk food. However, once again she'd gone to the store and bought a lot of crap to eat. I told her I'm trying to help Juan learn how to play tennis, and that requires a healthy diet. (looking down)

C: (long pause) So, she went to the store and bought more junk food. What happened next?

D: (sharply) I have to say I am proud that she's showing some spunk. The only thing she stands up to me about is that damn food. (looking down, rubbing his arms)

C: Could you describe exactly what happened?

D: (sharply) Of course I could, but (long pause)

C: I know it's hard to talk about, but I assure you, I can take it. Tell me.

D: You don't have to sound so dramatic. It wasn't anything. She came home Sunday with a cake, cookies, you name it. I yelled at her that it was my money and I didn't want that crap in the house. She cut herself a big piece of cake and swung it back and forth in front of my face. I reached out and pushed the cake off her plate. She put her plate down and came toward me. I should've stood my ground, but I took a step back and fell down over a rip in the carpet.

C: (long pause) Sorry, I don't buy it again. (pause, looking directly at *D*) A rich man like you doesn't have ripped carpet.

D: (long pause) Would you believe it if I said that boy (sees look on *C*'s face), I mean Juan, gave me a shove? (*C* shakes head no) Okay, so it was Helen. She pulled me toward her, and then when I started to yell, she pushed and pulled me back and forth a few times and then let go suddenly, and I lost my balance and fell backward. She knows I work out. She figured I could take it. She didn't know she was going to bruise my arms and make me fall. My doctor should have minded his own business.

C: The doctor had to do something. There is a law against elder abuse, and his code of ethics requires him to try to protect you, just like mine does, even though a powerful man like you doesn't feel in need of any protection from others.

D: (very red in the face and loud) That's right. I don't need help.

C: I can hear that you are angry again. Does Helen have your temperament?

D: (mumbling) No, Helen isn't anything like me. She's not like Connie either. She's more like my mother-in-law. She was fat too.

C: Physical appearance is very important to you. I don't know if you realize it, but you haven't told me anything about Helen besides that she is fat, stupid, and married a man who used her.

D: (hostile) I can see what you're doing, and I don't like you saying insulting things about my family.

C: You can say it, and it's not insulting, but if I say it, it is? (*D* nods) If Helen was under eighteen and I had heard you insulting her like that, over and over, I would be mandated to report you to child protective services for verbal abuse.

D: (sarcastic) You have got to be kidding!

C: (looking steadily at *D*) No. Trying to teach Juan to eat lots of fruits and vegetables rather than cake and cookies, that's a parent's choice respected under the law. However, if you called him "the boy" to his face over and over, never using his name, and called his father a dumb Mexican in front of him, you would be verbally abusing him under the child protective services law.

D: (matter-of-factly) Laws keep changing. I can't imagine what my father would have thought of that child abuse law. Verbal abuse to call a kid names? Geez, my father used to take his belt off and beat my back black and blue at the drop of a hat. Did I get a B plus on a paper, not an A; off came the belt. What would he think of your child abuse law? (looking down and shaking his head)

C: Yes, society has really changed its views on parenting over the years. If your father took his belt to your back today, I would be making a report and you would probably be sent to foster care for a while.

D: (intent) Is that what you are going to do to me? Have me sent off somewhere out of my own house because Helen got a little rough?

C: No. The difference is that you are an adult. You are smart and in complete charge of your faculties. If you don't want to press charges against Helen, nothing is going to happen.

D: (emphatic, but squirming) Good, that's what I want. No interference.

C: Is seeing me interference?

D: (sarcastic) Why should I come back here?

C: I know you like scotch, but that isn't the best way to prevent things from getting bad again at home.

D: (looking down, tense) You think Helen might do it again?

C: (looking directly at *D*) Yes. (pause) I think you and I should work on this together.

D: (looking at *C*, tense) Maybe I will come back. This wasn't as awful as I thought it would be. But I'll have to think about it.

Exercises for Developing a Case Conceptualization of Dan

Exercise 1 (four-page maximum)

GOAL: To verify that you have a clear understanding of cultural theory.

STYLE: An integrative essay incorporating Parts A through C.

NEED HELP?   Review this chapter (pages 343–351).

A. Develop a concise overview of all the assumptions of cultural theory (the theory's hypotheses about key dimensions in understanding how clients change; think broadly, abstractly) as an introduction to the rest of this exercise.

B. Develop a thorough description of how each of these assumptions is used to understand a client's progression through the change process in paragraphs that provide specific examples to fully explain each assumption.

C. Conclude your essay by describing the role of the clinician in helping the client change (consultant, doctor, educator, helper), the major approach taken to treatment, and common treatment techniques. Provide enough specific examples to clarify what is distinctive about this approach.

Exercise 2 (four-page maximum)

GOAL: To aid application of multicultural theory to Dan.

STYLE: A separate sentence outline for each section, A through F.

NEED HELP?   Review this chapter (pages 343–351).

A. Create a list of Dan's weaknesses (concerns, issues, problems, symptoms, skill deficits, treatment barriers) and indicate which of them Dan wants help with.

B. Create a list of Dan's strengths (strong points, positive features, successes, skills, factors facilitating change) and indicate which of them Dan is aware of having.

C. For each of the nine cultural domains of influence in the ADDRESSING model, discuss (a) how much power and privilege Dan experiences, (b) whether Dan experiences oppression or oppresses others in this domain, (c) what power and prestige Dan draws from this domain, (d) what sources of oppression Dan draws from this domain, and (e) how salient this domain is in Dan's overall view of himself at this time.

D. What are Dan's most salient domains of cultural influence at this time and why?

E. Considering what you said in Part D, how would you describe Dan's overall worldview and values?

F. Considering what you said in Part D, in what ways are Dan's current difficulties a result. of internal influences and in what ways are they a result of external influences?

Exercise 3 (six-page maximum)

GOAL: To develop an understanding of the potential role of violence in Dan's life.

STYLE: A separate sentence outline for each section, A through J.

NEED HELP?   Review Chapter 2 (pages 92–102).

A. Assess the risk factors for engaging in violence and the protective factors discouraging violence that are currently in place for Dan, considering the following questions:

   1. What adverse childhood events has Dan been exposed to in the past? Possible events include living with a drug addict; having divorced parents; severe family disruption, such as repeated moves or homelessness; having a parent who was depressed or mentally ill; living with someone who committed suicide or attempted to commit suicide; living with someone who committed a serious crime or went to prison; being physically, sexually, or emotionally abused or neglected; and witnessing violence.

   2. What adverse adult events has Dan been exposed to? Possible events include living with a drug addict; severe family disruption; living with someone who is depressed or mentally ill; living with someone who committed or attempted to commit suicide; living with someone who committed a serious crime or went to prison; being physically, sexually, or emotionally abused; or witnessing violence or living in fear of violence.

3. What *internal* factors are within Dan that might be protective against violence? Consider whether he has the ability to control impulses, set limits on his own behavior, regulate emotions, engage in reflective problem-solving, or understand the emotions and behaviors of others.

4. Did the *long-term* social network and environment during Dan's childhood support or constrain violence? Consider whether there were traumatic, ambivalent, or nonexistent emotional bonds versus positive emotional bonds; the level of family violence; the level of family toleration for violence as a problem-solving strategy; positive or negative school or neighborhood experiences; and religious background.

5. Are there *currently* environmental supports or constraints on violence from Dan's relationships, peer relationships, educational attainment, vocation, current neighborhood, and current religious beliefs?

6. Are there any *immediate* eliciting or triggering factors that might serve to justify a violent or prosocial response or make it more likely? Consider such things as the presence or absence of a weapon, the level of alcohol or drug use, the level of frustration or anger, and the encouragement or discouragement of violence from others.

B. Assess Dan's exposure to violence across his life span. Consider the following:

1. Types of exposure (direct, indirect)

2. Frequency of exposure

3. Severity of incidents

4. Dan's role in the exposure (witness, victim, perpetrator, victim-perpetrator)

5. Current impact of the violence exposure in terms of Dan's emotional, cognitive, physical, and social functioning

C. Assess Dan's' worldview and whether violence plays a generalized or circumscribed role in it and whether it is currently generating or promoting violence or generating or promoting prosocial behavior.

D. Assess Dan's danger and that of others within his environment at this time, and if, and how, safety could be enhanced in both the immediate and the longer term. Include careful consideration of the *characteristics* of the perpetrator of the violence in his life. On a scale of 1 to 10, how dangerous is Dan's environment at this time? How much control of this danger does Dan have?

E. Assess Dan's safety and that of others within his environment at this time, including in his personal, social, and cultural worlds.

F. Assess the overall psychological and physical impact of violence on Dan and others, whether there are more forces supporting violence or supporting nonviolence, and Dan's prognosis for living a life free of violence at this time.

G. What is your current knowledge of the impact of violence and neglect on individuals and their families?

1. How many courses have you taken that give you background on the impact of neglect, violence, and trauma on the physical and emotional welfare of clients?

2. How many workshops have you taken that give you background on the impact of neglect, violence, and trauma on the physical and emotional welfare of clients?

3. What professional experiences have you had that give you background on the impact of neglect, violence, and trauma on the physical and emotional welfare of clients?

4. What personal experiences have you had that give you background on the impact of neglect, violence, and trauma on the physical and emotional welfare of clients?

5. What cohort effects might influence the worldview of individuals with a background of neglect, violence, and trauma as to what is important in the world, how people communicate, and what is rewarded and punished in this world?

H. What is your current level of awareness of issues relevant to Dan as an individual who comes from a violent or neglectful background?

1. Discuss your stereotypes of neglectful and violent lifestyles and whether this might influence your view of Dan at this time.

2. Discuss your past experiences or exposure to violence and how this might influence your view of Dan at this time.

3. Discuss your stereotypes of good romantic relationships and stereotypes of good parent–child relationships and whether these might influence your view of Dan at this time.

4. Discuss how your past exposure to violence and neglect influence your reactions to Dan.

5. Discuss experiences you have had that could support your effective work with Dan as well as experiences you have had that might lead to negative bias or marginalization of Dan's point of view or Dan's current situation.

I. What are your current skills in working with clients from violent or neglectful backgrounds?

1. What skills do you currently have that are of value in working with Dan?

2. What skills do you feel it would be important to develop to work effectively with Dan?

3. What can you do to increase the likelihood of a positive outcome with Dan?

J. What action steps can you take?

1. What can you do to prepare yourself to be more skilled in working with Dan?

2. Discuss any biases related to your treatment approach in terms of its neglect of appropriate interventions or inclusion of inappropriate interventions for Dan, who is both a victim and perpetrator of violence.

3. How might you structure the treatment environment to increase the likelihood of a positive outcome with Dan?

4. What processes of treatment might you change to make them more welcoming to Dan or another client from a violent or neglectful background?

Exercise 4 (seven-page maximum)

GOAL: To help you integrate your knowledge of multicultural theory and issues relevant to socioeconomic status into an in-depth conceptualization of Dan (who he is and why he does what he does).

STYLE: An integrated essay consisting of a premise, supportive details, and conclusions following a carefully planned organizational style.

NEED HELP? Review Chapter 1 (pages 1–7) and Chapter 2 (pages 92–102).

STEP 1: Consider what style you should use for organizing your multicultural understanding of Dan. This style should (a) support you in providing a comprehensive and clear understanding of his social and cultural groups and (b) support language that he might find persuasive in protecting himself from further elder abuse.

STEP 2: Develop a concise premise (overview, preliminary or explanatory statements, proposition, thesis statement, theory-driven introduction, hypotheses, summary, concluding causal statements) that explains Dan's overall level of functioning as an individual who is struggling to understand his changes in power as a result of changes in his life circumstances and able-bodiedness due to advanced age. If you have trouble with Step 2, remember that it should be an integration of the key ideas of Exercises 2 and 3 and that it should (a) provide a basis for Dan's long-term goals of being free of both victimizing his daughter and being victimized by her, (b) be grounded in multicultural theory and sensitive to issues of violence, and (c) highlight the strengths he brings to multicultural treatment whenever possible.

STEP 3: Develop your supporting material (a detailed case analysis of strengths and weaknesses, supplying data to support an introductory premise) from a multicultural perspective that integrates an in-depth understanding of Dan, an older adult who has acquired disabilities and was recently abused by his adult daughter. If you have trouble with Step 3, consider the information you'll need to include in order to (a) support the development of short-term goals, (b) be grounded in multicultural theory and sensitive to issues of violence and neglect, and (c) integrate an understanding of Dan's strengths in analyzing his worldview and values.

STEP 4: Develop your conclusions and broad treatment recommendations, including (a) Dan's overall level of functioning, (b) anything facilitating or serving as a barrier to his developing his cultural strengths at this time, and (c) his basic needs as he evaluates his worldview and values, being careful to consider what you said in Parts H and J of Exercise 3 (be concise and general).

Exercise 5 (four-page maximum)

GOAL: To develop a theory-driven action plan for Dan that considers his cultural strengths and is sensitive to issues of violence and neglect.

STYLE: A sentence outline consisting of long- and short-term goals.

NEED HELP?   Review Chapter 1 (pages 7–24).

STEP 1: Develop your treatment plan overview, being careful to consider what you said in Parts H and J of Exercise 3 to try to prevent any negative bias in your treatment and to ensure that you adapt your plan to fit Dan's unique needs as an individual.

STEP 2: Develop long-term (major, large, ambitious, comprehensive, broad) goals that *ideally* Dan will reach by the termination of treatment and that will lead to an adaptive worldview and a recognition of the role of violence in his family relationships. If you have trouble with Step 2, reread your premise and support topic sentences for ideas, paying careful attention to how they could be transformed into goals that are realistic for Dan's needs and situation (use the *style* of Exercise 4).

STEP 3: Develop short-term (small, brief, encapsulated, specific, measurable, subsidiary) goals that Dan and you can expect to see accomplished within a few weeks and that you can use to chart Dan's progress in becoming aware of his worldviews and values, particularly around violence and power; instill hope for change; and plan time-effective treatment sessions. If you have trouble with Step 3, reread your support paragraphs, looking for ideas to transform into goals that (a) might help Dan engage in hypothesis testing in regard to his specific values around power and how changes in his life circumstances and his able-bodiedness have required him to reassess his manner of relating to people, (b) might enhance factors facilitating or decrease factors inhibiting his ability to pursue a safety plan, (c) might utilize his strengths in analyzing his life whenever possible, and (d) are individualized to him as an older adult who is both a victim and perpetrator of violence.

Exercise 6

GOAL: To critique multicultural treatment in the case of Dan.

STYLE: Answer Questions A through E in essay format or discuss them in a group format.

A. What are the strengths and weaknesses of this model for helping Dan (an adult who has been a victim of elder abuse)?

B. Consider how taking a dynamic perspective, where you would help Dan integrate an understanding of the role of his cyclic maladaptive pattern of emotionally abusing and dominating women, would change the treatment plan. What role has Dan taken on with woman? What perceptions and expectations does he have of women? What might Dan's introjects of himself as a man be? Which approach do you consider more valuable to Dan at this time, dynamic or multicultural, and why?

C. Assume that Dan's domination of his daughter, Helen, is reflective of how he treated everyone at work who was a subordinate of him, while he treated with deference anyone in a position of authority over him. Considering what you know from the domain of race and ethnicity, how effective might it be to educate Dan on how being raised within the White cultural group has influenced his interpersonal relationships with Helen and his subordinates? How motivated might Dan be to consider racial and ethnic issues, given that you have already introduced him to cultural treatment? How hard do you think it might be to discuss issues of Whiteness with him, considering your own cultural background?

D. Considering Dan's family situation and the research on violence, discuss Dan's current risk for suicide. Are there particular issues you need to assess in more depth to develop an accurate assessment of this? What could happen if Helen becomes aware of what he is talking about in treatment? Might this increase or decrease his risk for suicide?

E. How did learning about Dan's abuse of Helen influence your own attitudes toward him in particular and victims of elder abuse in general?

RECOMMENDED RESOURCES

Books

Comas-Dias, L. (2012). *Multicultural care: A clinician's guide to cultural competence.* Washington, DC: American Psychological Association.

Hays, P. (2013). *Connecting across Cultures: The helper's toolkit.* Thousand Oaks, CA: SAGE.

Sue, D. W., & Sue, D. (2013). *Counseling the culturally diverse: Theory and practice* (6th ed.). Hoboken, NJ: John Wiley & Sons.

Videos

Hays, P. (2012). *Culturally responsive cognitive-behavioral therapy in practice* [DVD]. Washington, DC: American Psychological Association. Available at www.apa.org/pubs/videos/4310900.aspx

Lindner, E. (2011, October 31). Linda Hartling: Relational-cultural theory [Video file.] Retrieved from https://www.youtube.com/watch?v=Ew4zBnz_GVc

McGill Transcultural Psychiatry. (2013). Community mental health and cultural therapy in Jamaica [Video file]. Retrieved from http://vimeo.com/52488730

Wellesley Centers for Women. (2014). Forming healthy, thriving connections [Video file]. Retrieved from http://www.wcwonline.org/Videos-by-WCW-Scholars-and-Trainers/forming-healthy-thriving-connections

Websites

Dr. Pamela Hays. http://www.drpamelahays.com

Jean Baker Miller Training Institute. http://www.jbmti.org

Constructivist Case Conceptualizations and Treatment Plans

INTRODUCTION TO CONSTRUCTIVIST THEORY

Zechariah arrives at an appointment made for him by the disciplinary board of a midsized, rural university. He is a 19-year-old African American freshman. He has a 17-year-old sister and two younger brothers aged 15 and 13. They have been raised by his mother and his grandmother in a large northeastern city about four hours away from the university. The Christian religion plays an important role in Zechariah's family's life, and he was named after the Prophet Zechariah, whose teachings were repeatedly quoted to him during his childhood. Zechariah has been referred for anger management. He disagrees with the referral, believing it reflects a racist university system. However, he plans to cooperate. He is determined to succeed academically and become the first member of his family to graduate from a university. In a brief mental status screen, there were no signs of cognitive confusion, homicidal or suicidal ideation, or impulse control problems.

The postmodern tradition encompasses many different viewpoints rather than providing a unified theory for clinicians to follow. This tradition was influenced by a confluence of approaches, including feminist, humanistic, and systemic (Neimeyer, 2009). What these diverse, constructivist approaches have in common is the belief that individuals are always making meaning from their experiences to understand themselves and the world. To do this, individuals need to impose order on the phenomena they experience. The order they impose helps them understand their experiences and derive meaning from them. In fact, this order, and the emphasis individuals places on certain aspects of their experience, shapes their view of their lives and contributes to both their strengths and their difficulties. This is because the meanings they derive from their experiences represent socially constructed realities rather than an objective reality that holds true for themselves across time, across different individuals, within a culture, or across cultures. While there is an objective world of external stimuli, Zechariah's meaning making is much more a function of his socially constructed world. While there is no absolute "truth," social constructions that stem from dominant social groups and institutions may impose their view of reality on less powerful individuals and groups (Neimeyer, 2009).

You are a relational constructivist. Thus, you believe that it is the conversational exchanges Zechariah has with himself and others that serve as the medium for imposing order on his experiences so that meaning construction can take place. Zechariah is the protagonist within the story of his life, and in order to understand it, Zechariah must talk about it with you. This dyadic dialogue is the process that allows him to construct knowledge for understanding himself, you, and his situation; this meaning creation is mediated by the language used in the dialogue. As he tells you what he is going through at the university, he is engaging in a social performance that is, by its nature, a relational act. You will take a very ideographic approach to helping him. Until Zechariah comes to his appointment, you'll have no plan about how you will proceed beyond encouraging him to tell his story and intending to fully participate with him in cocreating a healing experience. It is a cocreated experience because who (Zechariah) tells what (his problems with his roommate) to whom (you) when (after a disciplinary board hearing) is highly influential in what story unfolds and the meaning that Zechariah draws from it (Neimeyer, 1995, 2000).

Relational constructivism "emphasizes the primacy of interpersonal relationships and conversational exchanges in human life" (Neimeyer, 2000, p. 216) and seeks to explain that all-important concept, "the self." You believe that Zechariah maintains a coherent sense of himself through the stories he tells about his past. These "storied selves" are always open to revision as he explores and elaborates on his experiences within conversational exchanges; Zechariah does not have a true self that is knowable or that is real as an entity. His stories are first-person narrations used to (a) integrate his disparate experiences together into a coherent whole, (b) position him in relation to others, and (c) temporarily provide him with fictional coherence for understanding himself. Who in fact is Zechariah? A university student? An African American male? An eldest son? An angry young man? The answer will depend on who he is relating to in any given moment and what type of relational exchange he is engaged in with this other person; even his immediate sense of himself is a process under construction within every interpersonal exchange (Neimeyer, 2000). Thus, whether he experiences himself as a university student, an eldest son, or an angry man depends more on what is functional for him, in the moment, than what is objectively "true" or reality based.

Zechariah is continuously in the process of trying to make meaning from his experiences through exploring and elaborating on them. The past experiences Zechariah is attempting to incorporate within his self-understanding are in fact heterogeneous, complex, and at times contradictory. Thus, many different stories are possible, and no one is more objectively true than another. How will a dialogue proceed? As Zechariah relates his life to you, he will organize his experiences into units that seem meaningful to him in the moment. He may perceive patterns or themes within these experiences as he does so. For example, he may remember many instances in which he helped his younger siblings. The meaning he creates or draws from these stories about himself could include that he is a loving older brother (who he is) who actively seeks to help his siblings (what he does). This understanding of himself, or self-theory, can be considered functional for him if it is plausible within the constraints of his current day-to-day life, if it offers opportunities for expansion or revision so that it can integrate new experiences, and if it leads to positive mood states.

Does Zechariah need treatment? It depends on whether he has a coherent and life-enhancing narrative guiding him in the moment. To determine if this is the case, consider the following questions: Is he experiencing a lot of positive emotions? Does his current narrative give him an adaptive and coherent view of himself? Is he relating effectively to others? Is he taking actions that support adaptive goals within his family, school, and work environments? Is he able to adaptively accommodate new experiences into his ongoing narrative? If so, then his narrative is life enhancing, and he doesn't need treatment. On the other hand, if he is experiencing a lot of negative emotions; if he is experiencing a disorganized, negative, incoherent, or overly rigid view of himself; if he is struggling within dysfunctional relationships; if he is unable to take adaptive actions; or if he is unable to be responsive to new experiences, then treatment is indicated.

At this moment in time, Zechariah is defining his identity using a problem-saturated narrative; the problems he has faced as a new student, his roommate's accusation that he is violent, the behavior of the disciplinary board, and his feelings of oppression and invisibility within society are dominating his view of himself and his world. Other aspects of his experiences, such as his success in his coursework, his happiness at finding African American friends, and the love and respect he receives from his family members, are thin (not well-elaborated) stories that are not experienced as potently at this time as the thick (well-elaborated) story of oppression. If he chooses to participate in treatment, his awareness of these positive experiences and the emotions they evoke could be enhanced through further exploration and elaboration so that they could form powerful counternarratives to the painful one that is currently dominating his constructions. Zechariah would be in charge of any meaning he draws from these treatment experiences, but through attending to his emotional responses (verbal and nonverbal), you would guide him to develop a more life-enhancing narrative (Neimeyer, 1995, 2000), one that gives him more choices for constructive action (Neimeyer, 2009).

THE ROLE OF THE CLINICIAN

Your therapeutic sessions would involve interventions regarding the meaning that Zechariah draws from his experiences (Neimeyer, 2009). It starts with a conversation between Zechariah and you. While his words and actions are going to define how treatment starts, you are not a passive participant in his reality. You need to be fully present as you listen to him and free of any agendas or distractions. You need a "from–to" presence in which you are aware of yourself as an individual as you are relating to him as an individual (Neimeyer, 2009, p. 60). You will be part of his narrative process by asking questions, reflecting on what he's said, and encouraging him to experience his emotions and bodily sensations more deeply. By doing this, you and Zechariah will be temporarily creating segments of his experience (subplots). These have an assumed beginning and end that punctuate a seemingly linear event, even though no objective linear cause–effect relationships are actually possible (Kelly, 1955).

For example, Zechariah may have found an experience in his morning psychology class confusing. You will encourage him to explore this experience more deeply by helping him recall further details of the class to enable him to consider his actions, thoughts, feelings, and interactions with others from multiple perspectives. Through this process, he will gain deeper meaning from what he experienced. In the moment, he says that a particular statement made by the professor was subtly insulting and "caused" him to feel rejected. Zechariah has worked hard in this class and doesn't understand why the professor would mistreat him. Fully processing negative emotions plays an integral part in the meaning-making experience of treatment, so Zechariah's emotion of rejection will be explored fully. You will help him find the meaning he has constructed from the words of the professor. This will not be a passive relating of what occurred in class—you will help him affectively experience what he is relating to you, and you will be aware of your own experiential reaction to what he is relating. You will also help Zechariah look for deeper themes behind this particular story and other stories that he tells you that may play key roles in his overall constructions of his life (Neimeyer, 2009).

Zechariah defines the beginning of this experience as the professor's comment and the end of it as his feeling of rejection. However, if a different segment of time had been chosen, a different interpretation of cause and effect might have enfolded. For example, based on your questions, you might determine that, due to a faulty alarm clock, Zechariah rushed into class late. This entry disrupted the class discussion. The professor responded by criticizing Zechariah for coming in late. In this way, "the lateness" is now the cause of the rejection, not the professor's comments. Thus, there is no true linearity that can be used to determine cause and effect, only a perceived linearity.

As Zechariah tells his story, you will try to achieve narrative empathy—where you are attuned to his feelings and thoughts and are engaged in reflecting on and validating his identity as it unfolds. You will be curious and encourage exploration rather than being directive or didactic. His emotions always carry important meaning, and they will be actively explored whenever signs of them, either verbal or nonverbal, emerge in the session. To process his experiences and support meaning construction, you will engage him in three basic processes: articulating his story as fully as possible; elaborating any aspects of it that might be confusing, incomplete, or problematical; and negotiating interpersonal meanings from his experiences that support understanding of his world and his place in it, with a sense of coherence and optimism, and that support an adaptive lifestyle (Neimeyer, 2009).

Both of you are bound in some ways by the language you use while conversing. Treatment can turn its attention to this language, within which the assumptions of the dominant culture are embedded, along with the family or cultural assumptions behind Zechariah's self-theories; some of these may be guiding him in adaptive ways, but others may be problematic and need to be challenged. For example, a son involved in an incestuous relationship with his father could be labeled an "incest victim," an "incest survivor," or a "thriver despite incest." Subtle and not-so-subtle changes in language can have a potent impact on the son's view of himself in relation to others. Thus, Zechariah's created understanding of his situation may limit him more in exploring options for himself than the external contingencies of the university; therapy seeks to expand his options. If social constructions of the university are oppressive to Zechariah, the therapist may act as an agent for social change. The therapist may help Zechariah modify, reinterpret, or resist cultural stories that are oppressive to him or others (Neimeyer, 2009).

How will you encourage adaptive meaning construction? The overall process will start with you and Zechariah deconstructing his story (taking it from one whole into many parts, such as the setting, characters, and plot) and then elaborating further aspects of it that he may not have fully attended to. This will allow him to draw more meaning from it. There are many techniques you could use in this process. While you listen actively, you will suggest techniques that might resonate with his needs in the moment. As the treatment process is highly collaborative, a technique will never be imposed on Zechariah; he will be asked about whether he wants to try something or not. Techniques developed from many different schools of treatment may prove useful within the spontaneous interactions that unfold during the session. However, the storied-self metaphor can be used to provide practical guidance for encouraging Zechariah in the meaning construction process. This metaphor can be explored and elaborated along three dimensions, including its (a) narrative form and features, (b) points of view and voice, and (c) issues of authorship and audience. Each dimension offers ideas for how your conversation with Zechariah could intervene in the meaning construction process to make more narrative possibilities available. Narratives that don't open up opportunities for new meaning construction are considered thin and in need of further exploration and expansion; this is called thickening the narrative. The following descriptions of how to use these dimensions in opening up new narrative possibilities for Zechariah, the "author-protagonist," come from Neimeyer (2000).

Narrative form and features is a structure for understanding Zechariah's autobiographical account that includes articulating details of the setting (where), the characterization (who), the plot (what), the themes (why), and the goals (purpose) of the narrative. The setting emerges from a step-by-step account of what is going on during a particular aspect of his history and indicates the where and when of a segment of experience. You will help Zechariah recall as many details of the setting as possible, and you will accent the meaning he is attaching to them so that he can explore his constructions more thoroughly.

Characterization refers to defining who the actors are within the story as well as the hypothetical intentions of these individuals as told by the narrator. While Zechariah may be sure he understands his roommate's motivation, you may help him explore alternative possibilities. Individuals often have complex intentions. By considering these possibilities, Zechariah will add greater psychological depth to his story. This process may leave Zechariah with a deeper insight into other people. Zechariah's own intentions can also be examined in this way, and you may offer metaphors or other methods for helping him understand his own complex internal experiences. Finally, this work will help Zechariah see how his "self" and "other" constructions are interrelated within his story.

Helping Zechariah articulate the plot of his story, or what happened in a certain episode (or subplot) of his story, will be used to increase his awareness of all the actions that occurred and the order in which they occurred. Inadequate understanding of events will interfere with Zechariah's having a coherent sense of his identity. If he is having trouble recalling details of a subplot, you will help him vividly reexperience it. Through this, he will be guided to fill in gaps in the story. For example, Zechariah may have aspects of himself that he has kept secret from others in an attempt to separate himself from trauma, negative experiences, or some disliked or disowned behavior on his part. You will help him clarify the *meaning* of these parts of himself in a more self-affirming and accepting way. Similarly, he may be confused because aspects of his experience are directing him to behave in contradictory ways. You will help him clarify these confusing experiences, negotiate meaning that takes all of them into account, and develop a plan of action that directs him in a life-affirming way. You will then help him consider how each part of the experience helps him understand what has happened.

The wherefore of the narrative is the well-defined, if fictional, goals that you will help Zechariah set for himself. These goals are future oriented and will reflect positive actions that he could take to sustain himself in living within a coherent self-understanding while he relates adaptively to others. While in fact no particular goal represents the reality of how he "should" be, these goals represent possibilities that are open to him. They may also include attempts to seek social validation for his new positive self-constructions. While these goals may be satisfying to him or designed to satisfy the university's disciplinary board, success in treatment is never based on goal attainment per se, as his life is an ongoing process of construction without a knowable endpoint. Goals are successful if they set Zechariah on a forward-moving narrative into the future.

As Zechariah relates his narrative to you, there is both an intrapersonal and an interpersonal focus. The intrapersonal focus is highlighted by the point of view and voice of the narrative. Zechariah can choose from five different points of view in telling his story. In the first, he can be engaged in an interior monologue, where he is providing an uncensored, free-flowing description of his experiences as they spontaneously occur to him. Second, he may be engaged in a dramatic monologue, where he is attempting to explicitly persuade the listener of his point of view. Third, he may be engaged in a letter narrative, which, like the internal monologue, is a form of self-exploration. However, in writing the letter, it is more organized and less free floating. The writer assumes that the reader of the letter will form a response to it; therefore, the narrative needs to be made clear to this potential other. Fourth, Zechariah could relate his narrative in the style of a detached autobiography, where he tries to show objectivity in examining his life. Finally, in anonymous narration, Zechariah could articulate the viewpoints of more than one character within the story. In this way, the story wouldn't have an "I" focus.

In telling the story, the voice Zechariah chooses to use may provide clues to the meaning he has been drawing from it. For example, does he use a pleading voice, as if telling himself that he has done the best he could? Does he use a condemning tone of voice where he blames himself for what has happened? Zechariah has many voices within himself. If only one can be heard, he risks ignoring important aspects of himself in constructing his identity.

Why is Zechariah choosing to mention some details of his story but not others? How is this intended to influence you? Storytelling is an interactive process with reciprocal influence between the teller (author) and the listener (audience). From this perspective, it has an interpersonal focus. Zechariah is implicitly or explicitly bringing you in as a listener and participant in how he decides to tell you his story and in how he decides which of his heterogeneous experiences to share with you. In addition, the very language he uses in talking about himself is influenced by his social context. The culture Zechariah lives in provides the language that he can use to try to understand his experiences and that he can use to reshape his experiences. You will help Zechariah understand how languaging (the using of words to describe experience) is a process that occurs in the context of one person communicating to another. The language an individual uses implicitly or explicitly punctuates experience and thus can bias the individual's construction of meaning from a story. Zechariah may need new words to use in developing a more functional meaning from aspects of his story or to use in plotting an alternative narrative.

In summary, many techniques, performed orally or in writing, can help Zechariah deconstruct a problem-saturated narrative and begin creating a more life-enhancing one. The process of deconstruction will provide Zechariah with new possibilities for how he can think, feel, or behave as he reconstructs a new life story. At the end of treatment, Zechariah will be telling his story in a more life-enhancing manner. What will that reflect? His stories about himself will include self-acceptance, validation, and continuity. He will have positioned himself in a positive way in relation to others. He will have active, positive ways of connecting to the social world that receive positive validation from others. His new story will be able to guide him toward achieving his goals as a student and loving family member. You will have validated any constructive changes Zechariah made in how he sees himself, how he sees his place in the world, and how he interacts with others. However, strong, health-seeking identities are best validated by significant others in his life beyond the treatment setting. Thus, you will have helped him determine if, how, and when he will document any new aspects of himself in his interactions with other people. You will have supported Zechariah in developing his own idiosyncratic meanings from the patterns he has punctuated in his life, as recognition of his uniqueness is primary in your view of him. The healthy meanings he has constructed will lead him to goal-directed and health-discovering behavior, thoughts, and emotions. You will have helped relieve him of personal and social constructions that have constrained or oppressed him (Neimeyer, 2009). How long will treatment be? Each session will end with a consideration of its value and whether the client feels another consultation would be of value (Neimeyer, 1995, 2000).

CASE APPLICATION: INTEGRATING THE DOMAIN OF SOCIOECONOMIC STATUS

Zechariah's case will now be examined in more detail. While there are many domains of human complexity that could provide insights into his constructions of himself, others, and his situation, the domain of socioeconomic status has been selected to integrate within a constructivist case conceptualization and treatment plan.

Interview With Zechariah (Z) From a Constructivist Perspective

C: (handing Z a copy of the report) Here is the disciplinary board report. I thought you would want to see it. (long pause while Z reads through the document) I found it very confusing. You've got an outstanding academic record for your first semester here—a 4.0. To me, this means you must be a disciplined, high-achieving young man. Yet, the board describes you as impulsive and angry.

Z: (tightly gripping the report, calmly but with intensity) This is all racist bullshit. What's wrong with everybody here? (loudly and firmly) I got angry a few times at the hearing because my roommate was lying about me. That doesn't make me an angry person. (pause) I could tell the moment I walked in that the board had pre-judged me and found me guilty.

C: What told you that?

Z: (matter-of-factly) There were ten of them all sitting across from me and just staring at me throughout the hearing—all wearing fancy suits. I was wearing my church clothes, but they were from Kmart; I doubt those people ever needed to shop at Kmart.

C: You felt their clothes set them apart from you. It was hard to imagine that people who were so much wealthier than you would treat you fairly. Was there anything else?

Z: (angrily) I was separated by a stupid screen from my roommate. My lawyer warned me about this in advance (pause) but, I . . . (choked up)

C: The screen hit you hard. What did it mean to you?

Z: (angrily) It was saying I was set apart—invisible. He was free to accuse me of anything, and . . . (pause) Henry—my roommate—told the board that he was so scared of me, he couldn't testify if he saw me, (pause, hands on chair, knuckles white) and they let him get away with it.

C: It was an ordeal, painful, and it felt rigged against you.

Z: (intently) I had to sit there and listen to all this testimony where he insisted I'd been threatening him from day one. I could see his hands on the table because the screen wasn't very large. He was clutching a Bible like he was some pious man. The panel questioned him gently as if he was on the brink of a breakdown. When it was my turn, I asked him if it wasn't true that I tried over and over to befriend him; he just kept muttering I was just trying to intimidate him. (voice getting louder) I asked him if it wasn't true that I was hardly ever in the room except to sleep. He said that was because I was always off drinking. (fists pounding the side of the chair) I wasn't out drinking. I was in the library studying, but he assumes everything bad he can about me.

C: Why does he do that?

Z: (intently, looking down) He's a racist, pure and simple. (looking up, sarcastically) Are you one of those people who believes racism is a thing of the past?

C: The world, including this campus, is still filled with stories of oppression, pain, and suffering. (pause) I'm sorry these stories are still being created. Every student has a right to feel welcomed and respected here.

Z: (quietly) I dreamed of a university being like that, ever since I was little. I can still remember my mother taking me downtown to walk around the public library every

Saturday—it was huge. She would say that universities were full of buildings like this and, one day, I could go if I worked hard enough. I was so excited. I did work hard, and I got here. That first day started out joyfully. But, now . . . (pause)

C: Thinking of a university was exhilarating, (pause) but something went seriously wrong.

Z: (intently) I knew I was headed for a challenge coming here.

C: (pause) What do you mean by "challenge"?

Z: (ironically) I've grown up around African Americans. Looking at the brochures this school sent me, I saw nothing but White faces. I knew I would be an outsider here. I wanted to go to Hampton University in Virginia. It's a private school for African Americans (pause), but this is a public school, and the tuition is much lower. I could see the look in my mom's eyes as we sat at the kitchen table looking at my acceptance to both schools. She didn't have to say anything; there was pride, but there was . . . (pause; tearing up)

C: (softly) You needed . . . (pause) your family needed to put the cost first?

Z: Yeah, (pause) this place gave me the most money, and I really needed to go where the money was. (long pause where he is looking at his hands thoughtfully) I knew it wouldn't be easy, but I was not prepared for that fool Henry. When I first saw this skinny White kid moving into my room, I honestly just couldn't believe it. I assumed I'd be rooming with a brother. Henry couldn't even look at me when I greeted him. He had these two heavy suitcases. They looked too heavy for him; he's such a small guy. I came over and took one and swung it up on his bed. I wasted my breath all weekend being friendly.

C: You tried to help him and reach out, but he didn't understand the meaning of what you were trying to do even though you did obvious things like helping with his suitcase.

Z: (softly) He barely answered me when I asked him questions, but I was cool with it. I told myself he was shy and kept trying. On Sunday morning, I saw he was reading the Bible. Being a regular churchgoer myself, I tried to talk with him about Jesus, but (pause) he was so rigid. I'm a Baptist Christian, and he doesn't think I'm going to heaven. He thinks only people from his church hear the true word of God and the rest of us are damned. (pause; intently) Jesus saved us all, (pause) but I was respectful and just waved as I left. I prayed hard on it in church, but I just couldn't feel any spiritual connection to him. (sounding sad and looking up at *C*)

C: You still sound sad about it. You kept reaching out to him. You tried hard to build the foundation for a friendship, but there was nothing to build. Even talking about God left the room feeling empty of understanding.

Z: (sadly) Yeah, it was an empty room, and I felt lonely, so I wrote letters to my sister and brothers to help myself. It all slammed down fast the next day. I came back in the room, just out of the shower, and saw him hiding his money underneath his mattress. This really hurt. The day before I was talking about God with him and telling him how much Jesus was in my life, yet he thought I'd steal. I was so mad I walked out as soon as I could grab my clothes.

C: You tried to share your soul with him, but he rejected the chance to know you, holding on fast to his false image of you.

Z: I didn't come back until five p.m. By then I was chilled out and tried another time to get through to him. (pause) The Prophet Zechariah had a tough job trying to get the tribe of Israelites back to the word of God after they lost their way, so I thought surely I had the strength to move this one White boy. I decided not to tell him what I saw. I just invited him to go to dinner. He said no, not even looking up from the computer screen. At that moment, I wanted to just move out to an apartment, but I had no money for it. (shaking his head) That would have settled the whole thing. But I had to stay.

C: Lack of money kept you feeling trapped.

Z: (sadly) Yeah, you got it. No matter what I said, he couldn't hear me. I was raised to speak the truth to my neighbor—that's from Zechariah 8:16. It's a tough standard to always speak the truth, but I work at it every day. I told the truth to the disciplinary board, but they were deaf to me. Henry is the problem. (emphatically) Not me. Henry. I have never been, and never will be, violent. I am following the path of Jesus Christ.

C: Violence has no place in your story. It's crafted around a deep and sincere faith in God. I can hear your strength of purpose.

Z: (intently) Thank you for understanding that violence thing is a lie. (pause) I decided I would forgive my roommate for his ignorance but stay away from him. I set out to find some brothers. It's a big place; they had to be somewhere.

C: You were looking for friends, so you persisted, like you persist with your schoolwork. You recognized Henry wasn't going to be a friend, and you moved on.

Z: (smiling) I was lucky and found a group of brothers hanging out in the cafeteria. They've been on campus since last year—they got it right away what was happening.

C: I can see that it was a relief to find people who understood what was happening.

Z: (emphatically) They understood how bad I felt inside and reached out to help. It started with a party to welcome me. Then, we went to the mall, and they helped me buy some posters to hang in my room. I didn't bring anything but my clothes. Henry had signs of himself everywhere. The posters would rid my side of its emptiness. They would make *me* visible.

C: That's a really important theme in your life, wanting to be visible, to leave your mark.

Z: (intently) I was tired of feeling ignored, like the space only belonged to him and he could decide if I was in the room or not. To be fair, he never told me to get out.

C: The way he talked to you and the way he didn't talk to you seemed to say, "Stay out."

Z: (softly) You got it. (smiling) Well, we hung the posters when I knew Henry would be in class. (seriously) I'll give him that, (pause) he does go to class.

C: He's really hurt you, but you still try to be fair to him. (pause) In the report, Henry accused you of hanging up posters to scare him out of the room.

Z: (seriously) They were pictures of my heroes—Reverend Martin Luther King, W. E. B. Du Bois, and Malcolm X. I figured that seeing those posters every day would remind me to be strong and fight injustice in my own way. I did wonder how Henry would react to my being visible—I pretended to read when he walked in. He just flipped out and ran. I started laughing, (pause) it was just so crazy, but I'm not laughing now.

C: I'm puzzled by why you were watching for his reaction. (pause) Did you expect something to go wrong?

Z: (sheepishly) I knew that Henry was ignorant and wouldn't understand the words on the posters. (long pause)

C: What did they say?

Z: (intently) Dr. King was saying, "A man can't ride your back unless it's bent."

C: What did that mean to you?

Z: (seriously) That my roommate, or other people, could insult me and try to degrade me but they couldn't succeed if I didn't let them.

C: That's a powerful message. It's self-affirming that others can't take away who you are. (long pause) What about the others?

Z: (forcefully) W. E. B. Du Bois was saying, "Now is the accepted time, not tomorrow, not some more convenient season . . ."

C: What does that mean to you?

Z: (calmly) I needed to study and listen hard and learn as much as I could as this was my time. (pause) It was the Malcolm X poster I was watching his face about. I knew, in my heart, that I should have bought a different one. (looking up, sheepishly) Malcolm X has his fist raised high. (pause) I guess my anger took over and left the forgiveness behind when I picked that poster.

C: He rejected you in a lot of painful ways. You had a right to feel angry. But, the quote?

Z: (intently) "Be peaceful, be courteous, obey the law, respect everyone; but if someone puts his hand on you, send him to the cemetery."

C: Maybe it was the cemetery part that bothered him. (both *Z* and *C* are chuckling)

Z: (serious again) Malcolm has inspired me my whole life. I regret using him that way to scare my roommate. It was just supposed to shock him for a second. It made me feel sick inside when I saw, at the hearing, that the fool's hand was actually shaking. He really is scared of me, and it hurts. I am *not* dangerous.

C: You have many parts of yourself, (pause) but they all seem to contain religious convictions and following the path of peace, not violence. Your interactions with Henry have contained anger because his constructions of you involve preconceived, negative beliefs. Henry knows very little of the Zechariah you have striven to be all your life. That particular poster carried with it potent negative meaning for Henry because his constructions of African Americans appeared full of fear.

Z: (angrily) He thinks we're all violent. To me, the poster meant I should continue living my life as my family taught me to live it and, if someone tried to keep me down, I should fight for my right to live as I choose; I was strong, not invisible.

C: The report said something about you threatening to kill him.

Z: (sadly) That night, the brothers and I were going out for dinner, but I realized I left my wallet, so I rushed back upstairs and found Henry looking through my chest of drawers. I told him off the same way I've told off my younger brothers and sister anytime they got into my stuff. (angrily) Sure, I used a strong voice and strong words, but he had no business going through my drawers. My lawyer pointed that out at the hearing.

C: Did he say what he was up to?

Z: (snorting) He was looking for guns and drugs. He decided my friends and I were some kind of gang, and he was looking for evidence to bring to the police.

C: Did he admit this at the hearing?

Z: (angrily) Yes, but he justified it by saying he didn't know where else I could get the money to be here. I got a presidential scholarship, and I got it from my hard work all through school. I earned my way here, and it wasn't easy. I'm buying all my books used so I can send part of my scholarship money home to help my sick grandmother. (looking down tearfully)

C: Even though you worked hard to get here and need the money, you send some of it to those you love.

Z: (firmly) My family would do anything for me, and I would do anything for them.

C: When you began talking of your family, love was shining in your face, but then the light went out.

Z: (sadly) His accusation that I didn't earn my way really hurt. My family didn't have much. But what we have, we earned through hard work. My mother works two jobs, one cleaning an apartment building during the day and one cleaning a department store at night. She comes home exhausted, but she always found time to ask me about my schoolwork. My grandmother should have retired, but we just can't afford for her to stop working. It hurts me to know she's working when her arthritis is so bad.

C: Your family story is full of self-sacrifice and love. (pause) When you talked about your grandmother's arthritis, I could see the pain in your face.

Z: (looking down) My grandmother should be seeing a doctor now. My mom says she's so worried about me that she can't sleep. She can't go to the doctor because we owe him too much money. My sister told me the emergency room was really rude to my mom last weekend, saying my grandmother wasn't an emergency case and shouldn't be there. Nobody wants to help us. Most folks just don't have the time for us or care what happens to us. We don't count to them. (firmly) I say we do count.

C: Your grandmother, such a wonderful and self-sacrificing individual, needs health care, and she's not getting it. That's an ugly theme that keeps resurfacing, that the world is treating your family like they are invisible even though they are good, hard-working people who deserve everyone's respect.

Z: (firmly) I wasn't going to be invisible at that board hearing. My lawyer told me not to say much, but I just couldn't sit there and say nothing—maybe I did yell. I have rights like everyone else. (softly) That's what the student handbook says anyway.

C: I understand why you didn't want to be invisible. How would the board be able to tell you had the righteous anger of a wrongly accused person rather than the anger of a young man who was out of control?

Z: (strongly) Shouldn't my record in my classes count for anything? This report has only one line about my good grades. Everything else is how they're judging me based on one night. Yes, I lost my cool that night and yelled my lungs out at him. Still, I never touched Henry and had no intention of ever touching him. (sadly) He claims to be a man of God, yet he lied about me. (reading from the report) "He threatened to kill me." Maybe I said those words, but he took it all wrong. How could he not get that?

C: You were both there and heard the same words, yet you each took very different meaning from them.

Z: (frustratedly) I've said those same words to my friends, my brothers, and my sister all the time. Man, why did he make such a big deal about it? I was staying out of his face. Why couldn't he stay out of mine? All they need to do is give me a new room-mate. I don't need anything else. I don't need to be here.

C: I hear you, and I have to say that I agree. I have to write a report to the board about whether I think you're a danger to others or not. (Z frowns) I will be saying that you're a credit to the university and we're very lucky to have you here.

Z: (long pause) Thank you, I appreciate that.

C: I don't know what they will do in response. They might just drop their demand that you come here. They might not. Would an appointment next week be useful to you?

Z: (firmly) I don't think so. But, I need this degree, so I'll come back if they insist. (pause) It has been a relief in a way to talk to you. I don't want to worry my family about this.

C: You talked a number of times of having rights like everyone else. I just want you to know that you have the same right as every other student on this campus to come here and talk about racism on this campus, the stress of worrying about your grandmother, or wanting to figure out a career for yourself after graduation. The Counseling Center is free to all students here.

Z: (calmly) I'll definitely be back if the disciplinary board tells me it's required. If they don't, (pause) I'll think about what you said and let you know. I like the idea of taking advantage of a service that's free to me, especially when at home every service comes at such a high price.

C: I'll be here if you decide to talk some more.

Constructivist Case Conceptualization of Zechariah: Assumption-Based Style

Zechariah understands his referral to the Counseling Center through the lens of four major life stories, one involving his mother and feelings of love and hope, one involving his African American friends at the university and feelings of understanding and acceptance, one involving his roommate Henry and feelings of rejection and spiritual pain, and one involving the university's disciplinary board and feelings of anger and impotence. Within each of these stories, Zechariah is creating a storied self that is influenced by who is listening to the story, the details that Zechariah uses to punctuate the story, and the meaning that Zechariah derives from telling the story; he has no real self, just a constantly emerging sense of someone who wants to be visible to other people. At this time, the meaning that Zechariah is drawing from his stories is that he is a hardworking student, a loyal friend, a loving brother and son, and a deeply religious man. In sharp contrast, in the story told by Henry to the disciplinary board, Zechariah is a thief, drug dealer, drunk, and dangerous young man who should be thrown off campus. These stories are vastly discrepant. Neither represents an objective reality. Both were cocreated between the teller (Zechariah, Henry) and the listener (clinician, disciplinary board). Zechariah can achieve his goals of gaining a college degree and helping his family out of poverty only if he cocreates a functional reality for himself that can guide him in adaptive ways to achieve these goals.

When Zechariah arrived at the university, he was living his dream of being the first member of his family to attend college. This story started in the public library when he was a little boy, when his mother showed him all the books and began to tell him what a college was all about. As Zechariah punctuated this story during the interview, it included details such as his love of books and the escape reading could bring from life in an impoverished neighborhood. Another character in this story was his hardworking mother, who worked two jobs to care for her children but who always found the time to ask Zechariah about school and check in on his homework. Another was his grandmother, who had bad arthritis and should retire, but instead kept working to help the family stay housed and fed. The last main characters were his three younger siblings, who looked up to him as he smiled down at them, their proud older brother. The plot of this story concerns a loving family struggling to make ends meets as the adults struggle with minimum-wage jobs, a lack of higher education, and no medical care. Zechariah wants the plot to end with details that include his graduation from college, his being hired for a good job after graduation, his being able to move his family out of the slums, and his being able to help his younger siblings go to college. The emotions he feels during this story are love and hope for a better life. The meaning that Zechariah is currently drawing from this story, as he awaits the final decision of the disciplinary board, is that the university is full of racists who will do whatever it takes to try to smash his dreams and hold his family down. He is willing to attend the Counseling Center to try to prevent his expulsion from this university even though he denies all charges against him.

The story of the university as a haven from poverty and pain began to go wrong almost immediately. In Zechariah's original story, he would attend a private, African American college where he would be surrounded by brothers and sisters who would understand his life context. Unfortunately, the cost of a private education was impossible. A public university offered him a presidential scholarship based on his excellent high school record. While wary, Zechariah understood that for the sake of his family, he needed to rewrite the plot of his education and attend this predominantly White school. While knowing in advance that the school had few African Americans, Zechariah was shocked to discover that the new character in his life, his roommate, was to be a White, skinny, fundamentalist Christian—not a fellow African American, a brother. Trying to embrace this new person within his storyline of a four-year dream ride, Zechariah took one of Henry's suitcases and swung it up on the bed for him. Zechariah punctuated the story at this point as one where, despite his first sense of shock, he reached out to be friendly and include Henry in his dream ride. Henry's version of that same first moment in the plot of move-in day is likely to begin at a very different point. After trudging to his room, carrying suitcases that were too heavy for him, Henry was suddenly confronted by a large, African American male, the last person Henry imagined he would be rooming with at a predominantly White school. As if this weren't frightening enough, this intimidating young man grabbed one of his suitcases without saying a word first. Sure, Zechariah put the suitcase on Henry's bed, but his intent had been to show Henry just how much bigger and stronger he was, and Henry felt fear of Zechariah for the first time. Neither young man was writing the story he originally planned about his first day with a new roommate, but just how differently they were punctuating the events that followed would set the stage for further, more serious cultural miscommunications.

Sunday morning, their second day at the university, Zechariah and Henry had the opportunity to begin the second chapter of their mutual story. As always, this was to be a coconstruction between the two of them; again they would punctuate different aspects of it and draw very different meanings from it. For Zechariah, the story started with a feeling of happiness to see that Henry was reading a Bible in bed. Zechariah's family was deeply religious, and he himself had been named after the Prophet Zechariah. In trying to begin this story with Henry, Zechariah joyfully told him that he was a Baptist and that perhaps the two of them could talk about the words of Jesus Christ together. Zechariah wanted to find a mutual connection with Henry, something they both cared about that could serve as the basis for a real friendship. Whether intending to be insulting or not, Henry indicated to Zechariah that they weren't going to be talking about Jesus Christ together because only members of his church truly understood those words; only members of his church would be going to heaven. Zechariah didn't know what to make of Henry and his beliefs. As a member of a minority group, he had often been treated as if he was invisible to White people. Now, despite Zechariah's deep faith, Henry was telling him that he was invisible to God. Rather than expressing the pain he felt at these comments, he waved good-bye and went to church. He prayed hard but couldn't find any way to make a spiritual connection with Henry. For Henry, the fact that Zechariah could wave good-bye, after hearing that he was going to hell, may have further reinforced his belief that Zechariah was not the deeply spiritual man he professed to be. Perhaps, through years of being told that no one else was going to heaven, Henry had become inured to the reactions of the alleged damned. At this point in their mutual story, neither young man could understand the other.

The third chapter of the story involving Zechariah and Henry continued its downward path of misunderstanding. Zechariah accidentally came upon Henry hiding his money under his bed mattress. How Henry justified this behavior is unknown, as Zechariah never asked him about it. Within Zechariah's narrative, Henry was calling him a thief and once again showing a complete disregard for the Christian heritage that was so much a part of Zechariah's upbringing. Filled with anger but controlling himself, Zechariah left the dorm without Henry ever being aware he had been caught in this behavior. Zechariah went across campus in search of brothers, other African American men, who could create stories with him that were less perplexing than the ones that kept occurring between Henry and him. He found them in the cafeteria, and with relief, shared his story involving Henry and his intense feeling of invisibility. Zechariah and his brothers shared stories. They all had been part of plots where their character was victimized by racism. Sharing these stories recharged Zechariah's feelings of hope that he could success at the university despite racism and oppressive experiences.

Zechariah and his brothers set to work creating a story where he would not be invisible in his own dorm room. They helped him purchase, and hang in his dorm room, posters with inspirational messages from W. E. B. Du Bois, Malcolm X, and the Reverend Martin Luther King. The meaning Zechariah drew from this experience was of loyalty from his friends and strength and persistence from strong African American heroes who had faced their own oppression head on. Each poster punctuated part of the African American experience. From differing perspectives, each underscored that through determination, hard work, and defending their rights as human beings, African Americans would overcome racism. Zechariah intended to see these posters each day as a reminder of his cultural strengths and a reminder that he was not invisible. However, a voice of anger continued to exert some influence on Zechariah, and he chose a poster of Malcolm X that was intended to disturb Henry: "Be peaceful, be courteous, obey the law, respect everyone; but if someone puts his hand on you, send him to the cemetery." While Zechariah was a deeply spiritual young man, part of him knew Henry would find this poster intimidating, and part of him could not resist. Henry was shocked by Malcolm's words, just as Zechariah had hoped he would be. However, Zechariah had only wanted to shock Henry in the moment; he never intended that Henry should fear him.

The final chapter of Zechariah and Henry's mutual story occurred within the context of a disciplinary board hearing. Zechariah was filled with righteous indignation and anger that he had been accused of violent behavior by Henry. Watching the members of the disciplinary board, Zechariah noted that all of the characters looked alike; they were White, dressed in expensive clothes, and looking hostile and disbelieving as he told his story. They didn't seem to consider his excellent attendance and GPA of 4.0 as a sign that Henry was casting him as the wrong character in the story. Zechariah understood himself to be the character making continuously friendly gestures toward Henry that were being continuously rejected. The story Henry told the disciplinary board was shocking to Zechariah. Henry was casting him as a dark character. He alleged that Zechariah was on campus to sell drugs, not get an education; his brothers were gang members, not real college students. Even more shocking to Zechariah was how Henry's hands were clutching a Bible so tightly that his knuckles were white. The meaning Zechariah drew from Henry's posture was that Henry actually believed he was dangerous; all Zechariah's acts of friendliness and religiosity had been invisible to Henry.

What was the crux of Henry's story plot of violence? The night Zechariah came back to the room to find Henry searching through his possessions, Zechariah yelled his lungs out at Henry. Both men include the yelling in their stories of that night; however, the meanings they draw from it are highly divergent. Zechariah was merely angry and vented this anger in threats he never intended to carry out. This mirrored his behavior back home when he had caught his siblings invading his privacy. Zechariah was both infuriated and perplexed that Henry could actually take these threats seriously; he had never laid hands on Henry or any of Henry's things. While having a lawyer with him who punctuated Henry's culpability in searching through Zechariah's possessions, the board made a decision that Zechariah considered only a racist reality could explain. Zechariah was mandated into anger management treatment at the Counseling Center as a condition for staying at the university. Zechariah felt angry and impotent. It should have been Henry mandated into treatment for his racism and paranoid intrusiveness. However, the board members made their judgments based on Henry's point of view.

Zechariah is determined to graduate from college, so he attended an appointment at the Counseling Center despite feeling that racism, not justice, had triumphed at the disciplinary hearing. He has met a new character in his college story, a clinician who has no difficulty seeing his strengths of hard work, persistence, friendliness, spirituality, and deep connection to family. The clinician has some power to influence the disciplinary board and intends to tell them that Zechariah is not a danger to others and that the university is lucky to have him in attendance. Zechariah is not violent and has many strengths. Should he attend appointments with the clinician? He is under a lot of pressure to succeed, as his family is counting on him to be the one to draw them all out of poverty. He also has many family concerns weighing on him due to his grandmother's ill health and his family's inability to afford health insurance. Attending sessions at the Counseling Center could serve as a window of opportunity for Zechariah to step out of invisibility on campus, receive social support in the face of the racism on campus, and gain allies in activism to reduce racism on campus—without incurring any financial burdens on himself or his family. Zechariah is the protagonist of his own life story. It is his decision whether he will use his referral to the Counseling Center as an opportunity to gain deserved social support or if he will rely on his own, myriad strengths to bring the plot of his education to an exciting conclusion at his graduation ceremony.

Constructivist Treatment Plan: Assumption-Based Style

Treatment Plan Overview. Zechariah may not return to treatment if the disciplinary board does not mandate it. He has many strengths and can successfully graduate from college using only his brothers on campus and his family at home as social support. The following plan was developed in case he decides to take advantage of the opportunity to receive further support from the Counseling Center. (This treatment plan follows the *problem format*.)

PROBLEM: Zechariah has been accused of violent behavior and faces disciplinary charges at the university.

LONG-TERM GOAL 1: Zechariah will re-story what happened between him and Henry to develop further meaning from it that will reduce his feelings of rejection and spiritual pain.

Short-Term Goals

1. Zechariah will recall his thoughts about sharing a room with a stranger rather than his siblings when he first came to college.

2. Zechariah will retell his story of attending a White college, sharing a room, and meeting Henry and more fully explore the details that relate to his family's poverty.

3. Zechariah will retell his story of his first impressions of Henry, including additional details that might indicate Henry's socioeconomic status.

4. Zechariah will pray about what happened between him and Henry, searching for additional details that can help him draw meaning from how two young men, both deeply spiritual, could have been involved in such a destructive narrative.

5. Zechariah will involve his brothers on campus in developing a story for using their determination and persistence to be positive role models for academic success on campus.

6. Zechariah will decide whether including the clinician in the retelling and expanding of his story with Henry would support his spiritual healing and help him move forward on his academic goals.

LONG-TERM GOAL 2: Zechariah will re-story his experiences of being invisible to reduce his feelings of impotence and anger.

Short-Term Goals

1. Zechariah will explore developing a story where he reduces his feelings of invisibility on campus by becoming active in student groups.

2. Zechariah will attend an NAACP meeting and consider what meaning he might draw from becoming part of a national group in support of African American rights.

3. Zechariah will meet with one professor a week to discuss his future goals and increase his visibility as a successful student so that he can get effective mentoring on campus.

4. Zechariah will meet one new student from a minority group that is not African American to explore issues of invisibility on campus.

5. Zechariah will consider his personal story of being invisible due to coming from a poor family and consider whether he can draw any new meaning from this story based on the details he punctuated in earlier goals.

6. Zechariah will decide whether cocreating a story with the clinician about how to end his invisibility would support his positive growth.

LONG-TERM GOAL 3: Zechariah will re-story what is happening between him and his family members to deepen the meaning he draws from it and enhance his feelings of hope and love.

Short-Term Goals

1. Zechariah will call his mother and share about his experiences with Henry at the disciplinary board hearing and hear her perspective on Henry, how he himself should process it, and what meaning they can draw from it together.

2. Zechariah will talk to each of his siblings in turn about his experiences with Henry at levels they can understand to put racism into a context that won't negatively affect their self-constructions.

3. Zechariah will talk to his grandmother and share about his experiences with Henry at the disciplinary board hearing and hear her perspective on Henry, how he himself should process it, and what meaning they can draw from it together.

4. Zechariah will talk to his brothers on campus and share about his experiences with Henry at the disciplinary board hearing and hear their perspective on Henry, how he himself should process it, and what meaning they can draw from it together.

5. Zechariah will talk to his minister at school and share about his experiences with Henry at the disciplinary board hearing and hear his perspective on Henry, how he himself should process it, and what meaning they can draw from it together.

6. Zechariah will talk to the clinician and share all the additional story elements that have developed through his reaching out for social support and decide whether attending sessions to discuss this further would be of value to him.

7. Other goals will be developed if needed to move Zechariah forward in developing constructive meaning from his experiences with Henry and the disciplinary board.

Constructivist Case Conceptualization of Zechariah: Symptom-Based Style

Zechariah is feeling depressed, confused, angry, and alienated as a result of negative experiences he has had at the university—particularly the discrimination and oppression he's experienced in interacting with his roommate and the university disciplinary board. He came to the university filled with excitement and hope that, in this setting, he could achieve academic success and begin his family's journey out of poverty. His self-constructions were filled with the love of his family, strong spiritual beliefs, and pride in his African American heritage. Now, he is prey to strongly contrasting emotions that flicker back and forth in his self-constructions as he attempts to adjust his dreams of university life with his perceived reality of the recent past. Zechariah is currently relating a problem-saturated narrative in a voice of rejection. Dominating his story are constructions of himself as an "other" functioning on the margins of dominant society. While his negative emotions are running painfully deep at this time, he has a contemplative voice that allows him to easily attune to alternative aspects of his experience; this voice can serve as a powerful ally within a treatment relationship. In addition, Zechariah has found positive and adaptive meaning from his religion, his family, and his academic achievements in the past. This bodes well for his being able to coconstruct a new and more life-enhancing narrative to propel him toward an adaptive future free of poverty.

Zechariah feels depressed; however, this reflects a profound change in his emotional state. His narrative of life at the university began with exhilaration at his being the first member of his family to study at the university level. As a young child, his mother had started him on a future-oriented narrative in which, through educational achievement, he could enter a world filled with large buildings and books; it was to be a way out of poverty for him and his younger siblings. Zechariah began working hard then, and continues to work hard now, on his goal of becoming well educated so that he will be prepared to succeed financially. While poverty and racism have served as anchors dragging his family down in the past, the voice that predominated after he gained the prestigious presidential scholarship was confident and hopeful that he was finally on the road out of poverty and invisibility and that he would be able to bring his family along with him.

Zechariah became increasingly confused and disappointed as interactions with his roommate indicated that they would not be "brothers" interacting within an evolving, joint subplot of academic success. Rather, Henry seemed determined to coconstruct a stable narrative that was replete with negative racial stereotypes and that actively ignored counternarratives presented by Zechariah's open and friendly behavior and deeply expressed religious beliefs. None of his efforts, such as his reaching out for Henry's suitcase, inviting him to meals, or engaging him in discussions of scriptures, showed any sign of influencing Henry's constructions of their relationship; in telling about this, Zechariah's narrative voice begins to lack confidence. Throughout his life, Zechariah had been forced to interact within oppressive relationships, and these had always left him with feelings of invisibility and marginalization. He had hoped to escape into a more uplifting reality when he went off to school. Given a free choice, he would have gone to Hampton University, a private school for African Americans; in this context, he would have had the freedom to be surrounded by people of his own race and not have "race" made an issue throughout his day-to-day life. However, poverty served to deny him this context of acceptance. He needed to put his personal desires aside and take the larger scholarship offered by a primarily White, public university. Here, he expected to continue facing invisibility as an African American. However, in a voice of dejection, he relates that he hadn't expected to face it in his new home—his dormitory room; in past constructions, home had always been a context of acceptance and love.

Zechariah struggled with deep feelings of anger and disappointment as Henry continued to reject his overtures of friendship. He had assumed his interactions as a roommate would fit the pattern of his interactions as a loving son, grandson, and older brother. Thus, what he was experiencing was doubly upsetting to him. However, Zechariah tried to find meaning from these experiences that could hold angry constructions at bay. He explained Henry's behavior to himself through a lens of forgiveness and kindness; he assumed that Henry's behavior was the result of shyness or poor social skills. Zechariah had wanted to be like his namesake, the Prophet Zechariah, and lead Henry out of ignorance and into friendship. Such a self-construction became untenable once Henry's behavior deteriorated from subtly rejecting to overtly insulting. The day Henry hid money underneath his mattress and seemed, from Zechariah's perspective, to be degrading his spiritual beliefs was the day that a plot of oppression and racism seemed fully formed between them; Zechariah's constructions of their relationship now came through only with voices of anger and disappointment.

However, Zechariah did not want to passively accept a stable story dominated by these negative emotions. He sought out other African American students, hoping that in finding support for his past constructions of pride in his African American heritage, acts of racism would stop dominating his university constructions. When Zechariah was able to share his feelings of anger and disappointment with these students, they reciprocated with their own stories of racism on campus; Zechariah's sense of invisibility as an individual was lessened. They actively sought to help Zechariah regain his feelings of hope and optimism. They helped him purchase, and hang in his dorm room, posters with inspirational messages from W. E. B. Du Bois, Malcolm X, and the Reverend Martin Luther King. The meaning Zechariah drew from this experience was of loyalty from his friends and strength and persistence from strong African American heroes who had faced their own oppression head on. In addition, the posters served to make him feel visible in his room and to have a sense of ownership of it; his experienced value as a human being increased. However, a voice of anger continued to exert some influence on Zechariah, and he chose a poster of Malcolm X that was intended to disturb Henry.

Zechariah was satisfied with the changes his posters brought to the dorm room, but this mood quickly shifted back to anger once he experienced the poisonous construction Henry drew from all of them. Ignorant of African American culture, and perhaps with a determination to maintain a stable sense of reality for himself, Henry appeared to draw meaning from these posters that reinforced and deepened his negative stereotypes of African Americans. Within this reality, the posters represented threats to his safety, and he became highly fearful of Zechariah. Henry then took actions that seemed justified to him—he searched through Zechariah's belongings in search of illegal drugs and weapons. Zechariah caught Henry in the act. Responding in the justifiable anger of the moment, Zechariah threatened Henry using the same strong language and nonverbal behavior that he had often used before in dealing with his own friends and siblings. However, having grown up in an extremely restricted religious community and seeming to have no positive constructions of African

Americans, Henry took this outburst of anger as representing a serious intent to harm him; he reported Zechariah to the disciplinary board. Poverty continued to exert a powerful influence on the plot of this story. With more money, Zechariah could have moved out of the dorm room. However, he was trapped by his straitened circumstances in a stable and hostile reality with Henry. The themes of poverty and racism once again dominated Zechariah's narratives of himself, his family, and the world; the voice of discouragement predominated within his storytelling.

Zechariah's constructions of reality were dominated by feelings of fear as he faced the disciplinary board. He feared that his grandmother's health was in serious jeopardy, as money she needed for medicine was being spent on his defense. He was also fearful that his dream of a future free of poverty would end if he was expelled from the university. While his family emphasized spirituality and loving relationships as more important than worldly goods, Zechariah was deeply conscious of the benefits affluence could bring in terms of access to higher-quality medical care, housing, and educational resources for his family. This made the personal sacrifice of having to suppress his anger and accommodate to the disciplinary board's view of reality one he was willing to try to make. However, the harshness of the setting and the behavior of his roommate and the board members served to make the plot seem stacked against him. Based on Zechariah's story, it appears as if his roommate's White privilege did carry weight at the university, as most roommate disputes are settled at the residence hall level. This same privilege may have been in Henry's favor at the hearing. Despite his fears, Zechariah made some attempts to defend his view of reality, and this may have made some positive impact as, while the board seemed supportive of Henry, Zechariah was mandated into treatment rather than expelled.

Zechariah attended his appointment at the Counseling Center feeling very alienated by his referral for anger management. Despite this, Zechariah has within him a voice of rationality that allows him to easily become aware of possibilities for more positive meaning construction. At this time, Zechariah's life narrative as an African American, freshman male is heterogeneous and full of conflicting positive and negative emotions. He has segmented his university experiences in a manner that highlights themes of invisibility and racism; past experiences, since childhood, have supported the strength of these themes in his meaning construction. However, he has shown significant resilience in building narratives that are future oriented, hope enhancing, and filled with themes of family love and religious conviction, despite the often desperate financial circumstances in which he and his family find themselves. Zechariah doesn't need anger management. However, he might profit from support in navigating the prejudices and stereotypes of others who might serve as barriers to his educational success. His willingness to consider appointments at the Counseling Center as a resource open to all students, rather than as a place he is mandated to go, may provide a window of opportunity for him to profit from treatment at this time. While a coconstructed treatment narrative may still contain racist or oppressive segments within it, the meanings that he draws from them would hopefully no longer be destructive to his continued pursuit of achieving a bachelor's degree, supporting his siblings in attending a university, and using the money he makes as a university graduate to help his family out of poverty. The disciplinary board holds a lot of power over Zechariah. The treatment relationship might be a powerful tool for removing this barrier to Zechariah's achievement of his life-enhancing goals.

Constructivist Treatment Plan: Symptom-Based Style

Treatment Plan Overview. Zechariah was sent to the Counseling Center for help with anger management. He does not need help in this regard, as he has a deep well of positive emotions, adaptive thoughts, and behaviors that he has drawn on in continuing to construct his life story as a successful student. However, the Counseling Center and the treatment relationship might be a resource that he can use, without negative impact to his family, for support in being successful within an environment where he has experienced oppression for his lack of financial resources and his African American heritage. These goals will be offered to Zechariah within a collaborative framework, and if they represent what is meaningful to him, they will be worked on simultaneously. (This plan follows the *problem format.*)

PROBLEM: Zechariah has developed a problem-saturated narrative based on negative interactions he had with his roommate and the university disciplinary board.

LONG-TERM GOAL 1: Zechariah will reduce his feelings of depression by coconstructing a new reality with the clinician about how life at the university differed from his prior expectations.

Short-Term Goals

1. Zechariah will discuss with the clinician the reactions that each of his family members had when he told them he had been admitted to the university.

2. Zechariah will discuss with the clinician the reactions that his neighbors and fellow church members had when they talked with him about his acceptance to a university.

3. Zechariah will discuss with the clinician in detail the joyful story he had coconstructed with his family about what life was going to be like the first day he arrived on campus.

4. Zechariah will take notes during the day about anything positive that he sees or that happens that fits within the joyful story he coconstructed prior to his arrival on campus.

5. Zechariah will discuss these positive story details with the clinician and consider the meaning they have for him as he works to build a new narrative about achieving his goal of a joy-filled university education.

6. Zechariah will meet with his brothers at the university and discuss these positive story details with them and ask them to tell him about anything positive they have seen or experienced on campus.

7. Zechariah will consider the meaning that these positive experiences have for him as he considers whether his initial joyful story has some validity for guiding his life at this time.

8. Other goals will be developed if Zechariah still feels depressed when he thinks about his educational goals.

LONG-TERM GOAL 2: Zechariah will reduce his feelings of confusion by coconstructing a new reality with the clinician regarding how to interact within the faith community and the academic community.

Short-Term Goals

1. Zechariah will make an appointment with a minister of his own faith and discuss with the minister his confusion over Henry's story that only members of his particular sect of Christianity will go to Heaven.

2. Zechariah will discuss with the minister how he could become a familiar and accepted member of the minister's congregation.

3. Zechariah will discuss with the clinician his experiences in working with the minister to coconstruct a religious community for himself at the university.

4. Zechariah will make an appointment with one of his college professors and work with this professor to construct a clear narrative about the expectations that faculty on campus have of students.

5. Zechariah will discuss with the clinician his experiences in working with the faculty member to coconstruct a clear role for himself within the university community.

6. Other goals will be developed as needed to help Zechariah feel clear about the expectations that faculty have for students on campus.

LONG-TERM GOAL 3: Zechariah will reduce his feelings of anger by coconstructing a new reality with the clinician about how to interact with individuals who may have negative stereotypes of African Americans.

1. Zechariah will observe students he sees each day who are not African American and take notes on the signs he sees that one of them might share with him a friendly and caring attitude toward others.

2. Zechariah will discuss with the clinician how he might begin a story of potential friendship with this other caring student.

3. Zechariah will approach this student and try to initiate a narrative of being a new student at the university who is trying to develop a social network with others.

4. Zechariah will discuss with the clinician the success or lack of success he had with this potential friend and what details he has that support his belief that this encounter was a beginning of a friendship narrative or a blind corner that requires a new effort.

5. Zechariah will discuss his efforts to engage with a non–African American student with his brothers at the university and listen to details about the experiences they may have had in doing similar things.

6. Zechariah will discuss with his brothers the clubs they might consider joining together on campus so that none of them will be the only African American in the club and so that they can demonstrate, just by participating together, that not all African Americans are alike.

7. Zechariah will discuss with the clinician his experiences of trying to develop positive narratives of his interactions with students who are not African American and expand the details within his narratives to include the individual characteristics of these students.

8. Other goals will be developed if needed so that Zechariah feels satisfied, rather than angry, about his experiences with students on campus who are not African American.

LONG-TERM GOAL 4: Zechariah will reduce his feelings of fear by coconstructing a new reality with the clinician about how to be successful at the university following his experience with the disciplinary board.

1. Zechariah will discuss with the clinician his fear of losing his opportunity to get a university education if the disciplinary board continues to perceive him as violent and how he might restory their views of him.

2. Zechariah will consider whether a further meeting with his attorney might be needed to ensure that his right to an education at the university is upheld.

3. Zechariah will contact his family and discuss his grandmother's condition and whether her health is improving or deteriorating.

4. Zechariah will further develop a story of how he can emotionally support his grandmother and his family while maintaining academic success at college.

5. Zechariah will develop a detailed emergency plan for how he will leave the university to visit his grandmother, if needed, while following appropriate university policies for unplanned absences.

6. Other goals will be developed if needed to make certain that Zechariah feels confident he has taken the best precautions he can to ensure his educational success while maintaining his family connections.

LONG-TERM GOAL 5: Zechariah will reduce his feelings of alienation by coconstructing a new reality with the clinician about himself as a visible member of the university community.

1. Zechariah will come to each of his classes with a thoughtful question to ask about the material to be covered that day, and he will ask the question before, during, or after class to begin establishing his visibility with each of his professors.

2. Zechariah will take notes of these exchanges in terms of how he perceived the professor to react to his questions and what details he has that support his perceptions.

3. Zechariah will discuss his notes with the clinician and construct a narrative of how the experience was for him and whether continuing this pattern of intentional interactions with faculty members will increase his feelings of visibility on campus.

4. Zechariah will ask a question himself, or respond to a question from the professor, in each of his classes to begin establishing with the other students in his classes the reality that he is a well-prepared and articulate student who is visible and deserving of their respect.

5. Zechariah will discuss these experiences with the clinician and develop other goals for increasing his feelings of visibility on campus if needed.

PRACTICE CASE FOR STUDENT CONCEPTUALIZATION: INTEGRATING THE DOMAIN OF VIOLENCE

It is time to do a constructivist analysis of Josephina. There are many domains of complexity that might provide insights into her behavior. You're asked to integrate the domain of violence into your constructivist conceptualization and treatment plan.

Information Received From Brief Intake

Josephina is a 17-year-old Mexican American mother; she was born in the United States. She has been married to Roberto, a 25-year-old Mexican male, for 13 months; they met three months before their marriage. He is a distant relative who had just emigrated, illegally, from Mexico. They have a son, Carlos, who is 16 months old. The family has been living in a small home in a rural area for the past year. They moved to this area from New Mexico, where Josephina's father owns a small store, due to the promise of agricultural work. Both Josephina and Roberto worked picking a variety of crops on a local farm until Carlos was born. At that point, Josephina stayed home to care for him. Josephina was referred for treatment by child protective services (CPS) following her physical abuse of Carlos. Roberto suddenly left the family and has not been heard from since CPS began its investigation two weeks ago. At this time, Carlos is in foster care.

During a brief mental status exam, Josephina showed signs of significant depression and anxiety, although there were no indications of suicidal or homicidal ideation or severe psychopathology. Josephina became completely overcome as the clinician reviewed the limits of confidentiality and said that CPS would be expecting regular reports on her progress in treatment to determine when and if it was safe to return Carlos to her care. CPS has selected you as Josephina's clinician; she had no say in the matter.

Interview With Josephina (J) From a Constructivist Perspective

C: Welcome to my office. (pause) As you know, your CPS caseworker thinks that you need help with your parenting skills. (long pause) I would appreciate it if you would tell me about yourself and what you consider it important for us to talk about. (*J* is looking down and clutching something hanging from her neck) I see that something important is hanging from your neck.

J: (looking up and down quickly; softly) Yes, it is important.

C: (long pause) Can you tell me what meaning it holds for you?

J: (whispering) It helps to protect me. (tearing up) You will think I'm bad like those other people do.

C: What people?

J: (hopelessly) Those people at CPS who say how dangerous I am to my son. But this rosary brings me close to the Virgin, Guadalupe—I need to be a mother like her. I pray to her every day asking for help.

C: Your Catholic faith is very important to you. (*J* nods) Can you tell me how the Virgin is helping you?

J: (tears flowing down her face, whispering) I am praying to her, but since I've been condemned as a child abuser, I haven't felt her presence.

C: "Child abuser." (pause) Those are harsh words.

J: (anxiously) It's my duty to be a good mother. I do try, but Carlos cries and cries no matter how tired I am. (pause) He doesn't want to stop. Carlos was a small baby, and the doctor explained that this is why he cries so much. I don't really understand it exactly, because my little cousins didn't cry so much. (very anxiously) The doctors and nurses were very cold and rude to me, so I was afraid to ask them any more questions.

C: You want to understand why Carlos seems so difficult to take care of, but you feel alone in figuring it out.

J: (deadpan) His crying makes Roberto very angry because he needs his sleep after working hard all day. Roberto told me only a terrible mother could make her son so unhappy.

C: Your face looks very pale and sad as you say this. (long pause)

J: (painfully) I was just remembering . . . (pause; deadpan) Never mind; it isn't important.

C: I can see in your face that it is important. (long pause) Could you tell me?

J: (whispering) Roberto hits me for being a bad mother and making his son cry.

C: You make him cry?

J: Roberto thinks a good mother keeps her son happy, so it's my fault that Carlos cries. (desperately) I always tried hard to get Carlos to sleep before Roberto came home, but (sadly) Roberto drinks after work and then makes so much noise he always wakes Carlos up. I tried so many things that didn't work. (whispering) A few weeks ago, my hairbrush was close by. I thought it couldn't hurt Carlos if I just took my hairbrush and struck him lightly on his feet—just as a sign of my disapproval, not to hurt him. His eyes went very wide, and he quieted down quickly. I thought it was a safe way to handle him.

C: How often did you strike him?

J: (whispering) At first, I just struck him lightly, just once and he stopped crying. (long pause; looking down) The second night, I don't know why, but the first strike didn't work and I hit him a second time—just to keep him quiet because Roberto was drunk, and . . . (long pause)

C: You were afraid Roberto would beat you.

J: (anxious) Not beat, no. Just hit me with his belt a few times. (looking down)

C: It hurts your body and your mind when he strikes you with his belt.

J: (sad) Yes, and now, I have done this same thing to Carlos, but (pause; in a rush) last week Carlos was crying so much I just couldn't stand it and then I noticed a look on his face—he looked like Roberto. (deadpan) I knew I would have to be strict, or he would grow to be a bad man like his father.

C: Since Carlos looked like Roberto, you feared he might hurt others, like his father hurt you, if you didn't raise him properly. (pause) Is a mother supposed to be strict?

J: (emphatically) No, my mother was loving—and the Virgin was too. (whispering) I am so ashamed. (pause) But I was desperate. I thought maybe if I was just consistent, and struck him on the feet every time he started to cry, but . . . (long pause) then I noticed how bad his feet looked, (pause) and I did stop. I did, (pause) but it was too late; there had already been a report.

C: Is there anyone who can help you?

J: I did try to ask the doctor once what to do, but he was in a big hurry, and he said Carlos was just teething. (pause) He had no time to help me; others were waiting.

C: You realized you needed help. You asked the doctor, but he didn't give you the help you needed. (J is crying) Did you try reaching out to your parents for advice?

J: (sadly) I did try once to call my mother when I first came back from the hospital. I was so tired, and Carlos seemed to do nothing but cry. My father answered the phone and asked so coldly what I wanted. (pause) I tried to explain that I didn't know what to do. He hung up, saying, "Go ask your husband." But I can't ask him. He would just get mad.

C: What about another relative?

J: (listlessly) I know my godmother would help, but she doesn't have a phone. I wrote her a letter, but it was so hard to write down what was happening. She misunderstood me. She just wrote back saying my parents really miss me and if I can just act like a good woman they will forgive me. (sadly) They won't forgive. They will hear about me being a child abuser, and that will be the end.

C: The end? What does that mean?

J: (sadly) They will be done with me. I've really hurt Carlos. My father would be so angry. What kind of a mother hurts her child? (stares blindly ahead)

C: You look lost. (J nods) Has there been a time when you were not lost and people weren't calling you a child abuser?

J: (whispering) It's been a long, long time. The day of my *quinceañera*, last year—that was my last day as a good person. (long pause) I was so excited. All my teachers noticed me smiling. I worked hard in school but was always quiet. I tried so hard to be a humble and sweet girl like my mother. But, on that day, I couldn't keep my mind on my schoolwork. I kept thinking about all the food I helped my mother prepare and all the relatives who were coming to see me.

C: You were feeling excited. What did you think of yourself?

J: (calmly) I was a good girl. I know that. I always helped my mother and any relatives who needed me. I helped a lot of my cousins with their schoolwork. I wanted to be just like my mother, but . . . (long pause)

C: But . . . (pause)

J: (softly) I wanted to be as warm and kind as her. I learned all of her special recipes. But, ever since I was very little, I was interested in healing. We had a female healer, a *curandera*, in our town who everyone used instead of the doctors at the hospital, who were very cold and disrespectful to us. (smiling) Whenever anyone in the family was sick, she would come with candles and a special cross she would put over the head of the sick person. She would use herbs to brew special medicine and pray to God with special invocations. (earnestly) I wanted to be like her. I felt like God had chosen me to be a healer, but I also wanted to go on to medical school to learn everything else I could. I wouldn't have been like the doctors at the hospital. (her voice like a thread) I would have treated my people with respect like the *curandera*. I would have known her healing, and . . . (sobs into her hands while still clutching her rosary)

C: (long pause) That rosary must have tremendous meaning for you. Your knuckles are white from your painful grip on it.

J: (softly) It is the special rosary I got at my *quinceañera*. I use it to pray to God and call out to Guadalupe to help me.

C: Before your *quinceañera* you had images of yourself as a good woman like your mother—kind, caring—and you were going to take this caring even further to become a *curandera* and help your people when they were sick. (pause) How did God choose you?

J: (confidently) I could feel it. When I was with the *curandera*, she would look me in the eyes, and I felt a strong pulse coming into me. I would dream of being a healer that night. This was God's message to me. I worked so hard in school to try to make it come true. But instead, I . . . (looks desperately at *C*)

C: Pain is overwhelming you. (*J* nods) You feel you had a destiny that you and your family would have been proud of, one in which you would help your people. The self you see now you define as a bad woman. That self doesn't make sense to me because I have heard your deep commitment to helping others.

J: (painfully, choking) Quick, so quick, everything changed. (pause) While the priest was blessing me, I knelt on a pillow with my name on it. My godmother knew of my dream to be a healer, and she had embroidered my name and special symbols she had created herself to give more power to my dreams. As I knelt there, with this rosary on for the first time, I was surrounded by God and the love of my family. (softly) My father changed my shoes to show the family I was now a woman. He had tears in his eyes, tears of pride. (pause) He looked like a thundercloud as he said good-bye after I married Roberto. All pride was gone.

C: Quickly, so quickly, things changed. (long pause) How did it happen?

J: (in a tight, high-pitched voice) I think the party went to my head. I had nothing to drink, but I felt giddy with all the attention I got. I was wearing a tiara in my hair, a fancy necklace, and earrings to go with the beautiful gown my mother had sewn for me. (pause; sadly) I sound so selfish.

C: It was a very important day full of meaning. It made sense to be excited.

J: (intently) My father was supposed to lead me in a dance, but some children spilled punch all over him. He was laughing and saying he must change when Roberto strode over, took my hand, and said he would dance with me. I was so surprised he wanted to dance with me. He was a cousin from Mexico who had just arrived in the USA. My father had a letter from his father that he was coming, and so of course he was invited to my party. He was so tall and so attractive. (long pause) My hand tingled in his. At the end of the dance, he whispered in my ear to meet him outside the house. (long pause; painfully) I said no, but he just laughed.

C: Why did he laugh?

J: (sadly) He could tell what kind of a woman I was. (pause; intently) I really just thought about a romantic walk outside and (pause) maybe a kiss good-night. I have some friends at school who date. I knew dating wasn't for me, but their stories excited me.

C: You knew you shouldn't go on a date, but he danced with you at your *quinceañera*. He was family, so you believed he was a good man.

J: (intently) I did think that. My father let him take my hand. I just assumed he was good.

C: What would your father have said if he heard Roberto whispering to you?

J: (emphatically) He would have sent him out of the house. He would've been angry. I knew it was a little bit wrong, but I never expected . . . (long pause; whispering) It is all my fault. I shouldn't have let it happen.

C: What was your fault?

J: (long pause; tearfully) I had sex with Roberto like a bad woman.

C: You look confused. (*J* nods and looks blank; long pause) What happened?

J: (fearfully) I got scared right away. Roberto smelled of alcohol. I knew he was older than me and would be offered a drink, but I had never seen a man drunk before. I tried to pull away from him, but he was much stronger. I can't . . . (wracked with sobs)

C: It is very traumatic for you to remember this.

J: I was supposed to be pure until I married. On that first night of being a woman, I lost my chastity. (pause) I have no excuse for my immoral behavior.

C: Roberto was so much older than you. He had been a man for years. He should have known better. He should have treated you with respect.

J: (long pause) Now that you say that, (pause) yes, he should have listened to me. I told him I wanted to go back in the house as soon as I smelled the alcohol, but he ignored this and my trying to push him away. He pulled my clothes up. (long pause; woefully) It is still my fault.

C: The meaning that comes through for me is different. This was your special night and your first night as a woman. You didn't have experience making adult decisions. You made a mistake by trusting your honor to a relative you didn't know well.

J: (sincerely) He looked so handsome I assumed he was good.

C: A young woman mistake. (long pause) Did you tell your family what happened?

J: (desperately) How could I? I would have taken away all their pride in me. It happened anyway, but at least they had three more months to love me.

C: What happened when they found out?

J: (whispering) They were deeply ashamed. My father is a gentle man, but he struck me. He had never done it before. Then he left the house for a few days. When he came back, he would not talk to me. My mother prayed with me every day. Then the letter came from Roberto's father in Mexico; my father had written him about me. They both agreed that we must marry. Roberto did not want to, but it was that or return to Mexico. He only had a counterfeit work visa, and my father knew that. (weeping)

C: Your pain is so intense—the meaning of the events so destructive—that you stopped viewing yourself as a good person, even though you have done so many good things.

J: (softly) I don't seem like such a wicked person when I hear my story from your lips. But nothing can change the evil of what I have done to my son.

C: The good is still in you, despite the mistakes you have made. You did hurt Carlos; the injuries were serious.

J: (sadly) I know. I am ashamed that I let things go that way.

C: Under the law, you did abuse him. Yet, you are a young mother whose husband beats her, whose family lives far away, whose young son needs a lot of care. This is a reality where many things can go wrong.

J: (sadly) I will keep praying.

C: Your deep faith and your prayers to the Virgin are all important starting points. But, an important part of your story is your deep attachment to family. You need other people to help you with being a good mother. If your father knew that you did not consent to have sex with Roberto, if he knew that Roberto beats you, might he change his view of how you fit in his family? (long pause) Might he at least forgive you enough to take you back home where your family can help you with Carlos?

J: (anxiously) I don't know. I would be afraid to ask. What if he says no? (long pause) I don't know how to start, but I want my son back home. I want to be his mother.

C: Would you like to come back tomorrow and talk more about this?

J: (softly) I will keep praying, (pause) and yes, I will come back tomorrow.

Exercises for Developing a Case Conceptualization of Josephina

Exercise 1 (four-page maximum)

GOAL: To verify that you have a clear understanding of constructivist theory.

STYLE: An integrative essay addressing Parts A through C.

NEED HELP?   Review this chapter (pages 389–395).

A. Develop a concise overview of all the assumptions of constructivist theory (the theory's hypotheses about key dimensions in understanding how clients change; think broadly, abstractly) as an introduction to the rest of this exercise.

B. Develop a thorough description of how each of these assumptions is used to understand a client's progression through the change process in paragraphs that provide specific examples to fully explain each assumption.

C. Conclude your essay by describing the role of the clinician in helping the client change (consultant, doctor, educator, helper), the major approach taken to treatment, and common treatment techniques. Provide enough specific examples to clarify what is distinctive about this approach.

Exercise 2 (five-page maximum)

GOAL: To aid the application of constructivist theory to Josephina.

STYLE: A separate sentence outline for each section, A through E.

NEED HELP?   Review this chapter (pages 389–395).

A. Create a list of Josephina's weaknesses (concerns, issues, problems, symptoms, skill deficits, treatment barriers).

B. Create a list of Josephina's strengths (strong points, positive features, successes, skills, factors facilitating change).

C. Write a brief synopsis of each of Josephina's main life stories.

　　1. For each synopsis, illustrate each component of the narrative, including the setting (where), the characterization (who), the plot (what), the themes (why), the goals (purpose) of the narrative, and the voice in which the story is told.

　　2. For each synopsis, highlight areas of the story that are confusing, incomplete, problematic, and/or tied to negative emotion.

　　　　a. Discuss how these might be related to one or more of Josephina's weaknesses.

　　　　b. What types of deconstruction of the story might be valuable in aiding Josephina in developing more adaptive meaning from these troubling experiences?

　　3. For each synopsis, highlight areas of the story that are complete, tied to positive emotions, and/or related to positive meaning construction.

　　　　a. Discuss how these might be related to one or more of Josephina's strengths.

　　　　b. What type of further attention to, or elaboration of, these positive aspects of her story might open up possibilities for new interpersonal meanings within the development of a life-enhancing narrative?

D. Discuss how problem saturated Josephina's life narrative is at this time, considering her storied self, her relationships to others, her view of her situation and past trauma, any negative emotions, any maladaptive goals, and her level of rigidity or difficulty in accommodating new experiences and integrating them into her ongoing narrative.

E. Discuss how resilient Josephina's life narrative is at this time, considering her storied self, her relationships to others, her view of her situation and positive experiences, any positive emotions, any adaptive goals, and her level of flexibility or ease in accommodating new experiences and integrating them into her ongoing narrative.

Exercise 3 (six-page maximum)

GOAL: To develop an understanding of Josephina, her family, and her situation using the domain of violence.

STYLE: A separate sentence outline for each section, A through J.

NEED HELP? Refer to Chapter 2 (pages 92–102).

A. Assess the risk factors for engaging in violence and the protective factors discouraging violence that are currently in place for Josephina, considering the following questions:

1. What adverse childhood events has Josephina been exposed to in the past? Consider events such as living with a drug addict; having divorced parents; severe family disruption, such as repeated moves or homelessness; having a parent who was depressed or mentally ill; living with someone who committed suicide or attempted to commit suicide; living with someone who committed a serious crime or went to prison; being physically, sexually, or emotionally abused or neglected; and witnessing violence.

2. What adverse adult events has Josephina been exposed to? Consider events such as living with a drug addict; severe family disruption; living with someone who is depressed or mentally ill; living with someone who committed or attempted to commit suicide; living with someone who committed a serious crime or went to prison; being physically, sexually, or emotionally abused; or witnessing violence or living in fear of violence.

3. What *internal* factors are within Josephina that might be protective against violence? Consider whether she has the ability to control impulses, set limits on her own behavior, regulate emotions, engage in reflective problem-solving, or understand the emotions and behaviors of others.

4. Did the *long-term* social network and environment during Josephina's childhood support or constrain violence? Consider whether there were traumatic, ambivalent, or nonexistent emotional bonds versus positive emotional bonds; the level of family violence; the level of family toleration for violence as a problem-solving strategy; positive or negative school or neighborhood experiences; and religious background.

5. Are there *currently* environmental supports or constraints on violence from Josephina's family relationships, peer relationships, educational attainment, vocation, current neighborhood, or current religious beliefs?

6. Are there any *immediate* eliciting or triggering factors that might serve to justify a violent or prosocial response or make it more likely? Consider such things as the presence or absence of a weapon, the level of alcohol or drug use, the level of frustration or anger, and the encouragement or discouragement of violence from others in Josephina's life.

B. Assess Josephina's exposure to violence across her life span. Consider the following:

1. Types of exposure (direct, indirect)

2. Frequency of exposure

3. Severity of incidents

4. Josephina's role in the exposure (witness, victim, perpetrator, victim-perpetrator)

5. Current impact of the violence exposure in terms of emotional, cognitive, physical, and social functioning

C. Assess Josephina's worldview, whether violence plays a generalized or circumscribed role in it, and whether it is currently generating or promoting violence or generating or promoting prosocial behavior.

D. Assess Josephina's danger and that of others within her environment at this time. Consider whether—and if so, how—safety could be enhanced in both the immediate and the longer term; include careful consideration of the *characteristics* of the perpetrator of the violence in Josephina's life. On a scale of 1 to 10, how dangerous is Josephina's environment at this time? On a scale of 1 to 10, how much control of this danger does she have?

E. Assess Josephina's safety and that of others within her personal, social, and cultural worlds.

F. Assess the overall psychological and physical impact of violence on Josephina and others in her life, evaluating whether or not there are more forces supporting violence or supporting nonviolence and determining Josephina's prognosis in terms of her being able to live a life free of violence at this time.

G. What is your current knowledge of the impact of violence and neglect on individuals and their families?

1. How many courses have you taken that give you background on the impact of neglect, violence, and trauma on the physical and emotional welfare of clients?

2. How many workshops have you taken that give you background on the impact of neglect, violence, and trauma on the physical and emotional welfare of clients?

3. What professional experiences have you had that give you background on the impact of neglect, violence, and trauma on the physical and emotional welfare of clients?

4. What personal experiences have you had that give you background on the impact of neglect, violence, and trauma on the physical and emotional welfare of clients?

5. What cohort effects might influence the worldview of individuals with a background of neglect, violence, and trauma as to what is important in the world, how people communicate, and what is rewarded and punished in this world?

H. What is your current level of awareness of issues relevant to Josephina as an individual who comes from a violent or neglectful background?

1. Discuss your stereotypes of neglectful and violent lifestyles and whether these might influence your view of Josephina at this time.

2. Discuss your past experiences or exposure to violence and neglect and how these might influence your view of Josephina at this time.

3. Discuss your stereotypes of good romantic relationships and stereotypes of good parent–child relationships and whether these might influence your view of Josephina at this time.

4. Discuss experiences you have had that could support your effective work with Josephina as well as experiences you have had that might lead to negative bias or marginalization of Josephina's point of view or current situation.

I. What skills do you have or can you develop in working with clients from violent or neglectful backgrounds?

1. What skills do you currently have that will be of value in working with Josephina?

2. What skills do you feel it would be important to develop to work effectively with Josephina?

3. What can you do to increase the likelihood of a positive outcome with Josephina?

J. What action steps can you take?

1. What can you do to prepare yourself to be more skilled in working with Josephina?

2. Discuss any biases in the treatment approach you have chosen for Josephina in terms of its neglect of appropriate interventions or inclusion of inappropriate interventions for individuals who were victims or perpetrators of violence.

3. How might you structure the treatment environment to increase the likelihood of a positive outcome with Josephina?

4. What processes of treatment might you change to make them more welcoming to Josephina or another client from a violent or neglectful background?

Exercise 4 (seven-page maximum)

GOAL: To help you integrate your knowledge of constructivist theory and violence issues into an in-depth conceptualization of Josephina (who she is and why she does what she does).

STYLE: An integrated essay consisting of a premise, supportive details, and conclusions following a carefully planned organizational style.

NEED HELP?   Review Chapter 1 (pages 1–7) and Chapter 2 (pages 92–102).

STEP 1: Consider what style you should use to organize your constructivist understanding of Josephina. This style should (a) support you in providing a comprehensive and clear understanding of her story and how life enhancing it is and (b) support language she might find persuasive as a mandated referral for child abuse.

STEP 2: Develop your concise premise (overview, preliminary or explanatory statements, proposition, thesis statement, theory-driven introduction, hypotheses, summary, concluding causal statements) that explains Josephina's story as a wife and new mother who has lost a sense of who she is outside of a violent and abusive story. If you have trouble with Step 2, remember that it should be an integration of the key ideas of Exercises 2 and 3 and that it should (a) provide a basis for Josephina's long-term goals, (b) be grounded in constructivist theory and sensitive to issues of violence, and (c) highlight the strengths Josephina brings to constructivist treatment.

STEP 3: Develop your supporting material (a detailed case analysis of strengths and weaknesses, supplying data to support an introductory premise) from a constructivist perspective, incorporating within each paragraph a deep understanding of Josephina, a young woman whose storied self includes being both a victim and a perpetrator of violence. If you have trouble with Step 3, consider the information you'll need to include in order to (a) support the development of short-term goals, (b) be grounded in a constructivist perspective and sensitive to violence issues, and (c) integrate an understanding of the strengths Josephina brings to the coconstruction of a new and coherent storied self.

STEP 4: Develop your conclusions and broad treatment recommendations, including (a) Josephina's overall level of functioning, (b) anything facilitating or serving as a barrier to her constructing a more life-enhancing narrative at this time, and (c) her basic needs in the construction of a life-enhancing narrative, being careful to consider what you said in Parts H and J of Exercise 3 (be concise and general).

Exercise 5 (four-page maximum)

GOAL: To develop an individualized, theory-driven action plan for Josephina that considers her strengths and is sensitive to issues of violence.

STYLE: A sentence outline consisting of long- and short-term goals.

NEED HELP? Review Chapter 1 (pages 7–24).

STEP 1: Develop your treatment plan overview, being careful to consider what you said in Parts H and J of Exercise 3 to try to prevent any negative bias in your treatment plan and to ensure that you adapt your treatment approach to Josephina's unique needs as an individual.

STEP 2: Develop long-term (major, large, ambitious, comprehensive, broad) goals that *ideally* Josephina will reach by the termination of treatment and that will create an adaptive, violence-free narrative for her and Carlos. If you have trouble with Step 2, reread your premise and support topic sentences for ideas, paying careful attention to how they could be transformed into goals for deconstructing or reconstructing Josephina's stories (use the *style* of Exercise 4).

STEP 3: Develop short-term (small, brief, encapsulated, specific, measurable) goals that Josephina and you can expect to see accomplished within a few weeks and that you can use to chart Josephina's progress in integrating new experiences into her prior stories of herself, instill hope for change, and plan time-effective treatment sessions. If you have trouble with Step 3, reread your support paragraphs, looking for ideas to transform into goals that (a) might help Josephina in the deconstruction and then reconstruction of her storied self and are sensitive to violence issues, (b) would enhance factors facilitating or decrease barriers to her parenting effectively at this time, (c) would utilize her strengths in developing new adaptive meaning from her life stories whenever possible, and (d) are individualized to Josephina as both a victim and a perpetrator of violence rather than generic.

Exercise 6

GOAL: To critique constructivist treatment in the case of Josephina.

STYLE: Answer Questions A through E in essay form or discuss them in a group format.

A. What are the strengths and weaknesses of constructivist treatment for Josephina (a young mother cut off from extended family who is both a victim and a perpetrator of violence)?

B. Discuss the pros and cons of using family systems treatment with Josephina and her family of origin. Comparing this approach to your constructivist one, which do you believe has the most utility for helping Josephina at this moment, considering the facts of this case? How would it alter your decision if you entered Josephina's story when she first recognized she was pregnant?

C. What role does Josephina's Mexican American heritage play in her current situation? Discuss in detail how it might be adding risk factors for violence and/or protective factors that would support a nonviolent outcome.

D. You have an ethical responsibility as a mandated reporter to do your utmost to ensure Carlos's safety, and you do not have a parallel responsibility to Josephina. Considering this, discuss how safe Carlos would be, in the short run, if you used constructivist treatment with his mother. Do the risks increase or decrease in the long run, and why or why not? How might you tailor your treatment plan to assess safety issues, session by session, within a constructivist framework?

E. What would be your personal challenges in providing effective treatment to someone who has abused an infant? Do the facts of Josephina's case change these challenges in any way? Is there anything about this case that might make it difficult for you to provide treatment, considering her gender, Mexican American heritage, and religious background?

RECOMMENDED RESOURCES

Books and Articles

Neimeyer, R. A. (2000). Frameworks for psychotherapy. In R. A. Neimeyer & J. D. Raskin (Eds.), *Constructions of disorder: Meaning-making* (pp. 207–242). Washington, DC: American Psychological Association.

Neimeyer, R. A. (2004, February 15). *Constructivist psychotherapies.* Retrieved from the Internet Encyclopaedia of Personal Construct Psychology website at http://www.pcp-net.org/encyclopaedia/const-psther.html?new_sess=1

Neimeyer, R. A. (2009). *Constructivist psychotherapy.* New York, NY: Routledge.

Videos

American Psychological Association (Producer), & Neimeyer, R. (Trainer). (n.d.). *Constructivist therapy* (Systems of Psychotherapy Video Series, Motion Picture #4310704). (Available from the American Psychological Association, 750 First Street, NE, Washington, DC 20002–4242)

Construtivismo Clínico SPPC. (2011, July 13). Part I: Constructivist psychotherapies distinctive features and evolution [Video file]. Retrieved from https://www.youtube.com/watch?v=GgiqgyrjxBs

Websites

Constructivist Psychology Network. http://www.constructivistpsych.org

Society for Constructivism in the Human Sciences. https://sites.google.com/site/constructingworlds/

Transtheoretical Case Conceptualizations and Treatment Plans

INTRODUCTION TO TRANSTHEORETICAL THEORY

Jake is a 25-year-old White male. He is married to Jennifer, who is a 24-year-old White female. They have a son, Jamie, age 6. The family lives in a small midwestern city in a blue-collar neighborhood. Jake earns his living driving a truck for a large food distribution company. Because he gets paid a bonus for "getting there fast," he frequently drives for several days at a time without sleeping. His wife is a homemaker. They have no contact with extended family members and no friendship network. Jamie has been removed from the home for the last week because of a report of child physical abuse. Jake's participation in treatment has been required by the court system as a prerequisite to child protective services (CPS) returning Jamie to his home. CPS will be making weekly home visits to monitor the home environment.

In a brief mental status screen, Jake showed no signs of cognitive confusion and appeared to be of at least average intelligence. He showed no signs of suicidal or homicidal ideation; however, he became angry very quickly and showed significant signs of impulsivity. He refused to answer any questions about alcohol or drug use.

You are a proponent of the transtheoretical model, a systematically eclectic approach developed through research on the change process (Prochaska & DiClemente, 1984, 1986). Will Jake change to get his son back home? The answer is not a simple yes or no, as you view change as an ongoing process rather than a static state. In addition, you believe that Jake will be most motivated to change something that he himself views as a problem. Although Jake may not be ready to modify his violent behavior immediately—a change from the court's viewpoint—he may be ready to think about his behavior and what it means in his life (an early stage in the process of changing). The following summary of the transtheoretical model is drawn from the work of Pro-change Behavior Systems (2008), Prochaska (2005), Prochaska and DiClemente (1984, 1986), and Prochaska and Norcross (2009).

How could you define what Jake needs to change? The transtheoretical model posits that there are five equally valid *levels of change* at which Jake could define, perceive, or understand each of his problems: symptom/situational (Level 1), maladaptive cognitions (Level 2), current interpersonal conflicts (Level 3), family/systems conflicts (Level 4), and intrapersonal conflicts (Level 5). All behavioral models of treatment intervene at Level 1. All cognitive models intervene at Level 2. All interpersonal models intervene at Level 3. All family systems models intervene at Level 4. Constructivist, dynamic, emotion-focused, and feminist treatment are examples of intrapsychic/intrapersonal Level 5 interventions. Although defining his problems at any of these levels is legitimate, as the problem definition moves from symptom/situational toward intrapersonal conflicts, Jake will be less and less aware of the causes of his problems, the antecedents of these problems will be deeper and deeper in his past history, and the length of treatment needed to resolve these problems will be longer and longer. The transtheoretical model both respects the value of the diverse set of theoretical perspectives available for guiding treatment and provides a set of guidelines for choosing among these perspectives to maximize the likelihood that Jake will both attend (versus drop out of) treatment and change (versus just showing up).

Jake may define his problems at only one level of change; however, the levels of change are distinct only on theoretical grounds. Jake is always thinking, feeling, and being influenced by his past history and present relationships, and thus his symptoms and life problems occur in an interrelated, multilevel context. For example, Jake has been referred to treatment because of his abusive behavior toward his son. On the symptom/situational level, he may be likely to lose control in situations in which he feels angry or threatened, and this tendency to lose control may be increased if he is drinking or unable to perceive negative consequences to his acting out. At the maladaptive cognitions level, Jake may think, in hearing a request, "I can never be safe if someone has power over me." At the current interpersonal conflicts level, Jake may be struggling with issues of control in his relationship with his wife that are accentuated by any attempts at "control" from others.

When Jake was growing up, he witnessed his father beating his mother, and he was abused by both his parents. Thus, at the family systems level, Jake considers violence a natural part of family life. At the intrapersonal level, Jake now feels helpless, out of control, and fearful unless he is in a position of domination over others. His experiences of pleasure and self-esteem are all tied to his ability to exert his will over others. Only in these situations does he feel he is acting like a man. When a spouse or another adult tries to develop a give-and-take relationship with Jake, he may react with violence because of unconscious and profound fears of dependence. From a transtheoretical perspective, it is legitimate to view Jake's problem with anger at any of these five levels, and interventions on any of these levels could help him continue in the process of constructive change. If he has more than one problem, you will analyze each one at each level of change. Then, you will need to select a level or levels to use in defining each problem during treatment; Jake will be most motivated to change a problem if you define it at a level that makes sense to him.

Jake's motivation to change can be viewed as being represented by one of five possible *stages of change.* These stages reflect a sequence of increasing motivation to make a change, including Jake's attitude toward the problem behavior as well as any actions he may have taken in regard to it. If Jake is in the first stage of change for his abusive behavior, *precontemplation*, he is unaware or underaware that it is a problem, and he has no intention of changing his behavior in the foreseeable future. He sees more benefits to continuing his violence than disadvantages that come from it. If Jake is in the second stage of change, *contemplation*, he is aware that a problem exists and is considering what to do about it. He is considering the pros and cons of making a change; however, he has no commitment to take action and is highly ambivalent about doing so. If he is in the third stage of change, *preparation*, Jake plans to take action to change in the next month, and he may have taken small steps to change or have unsuccessfully tried to take action to change in the past year; he might tell others of his plan to change.

If he is in the fourth stage of change, *action*, Jake is actively modifying his behavior and trying to overcome his violent tendencies. Action involves the most overt behavioral signs of change; however, Jake needs to go through the thoughtfulness of the earlier stages to be prepared to take effective action. To be in this stage, Jake must have successfully altered his violent behavior for at least one day. His changes may last for six months; Jake's challenge is to not slip back into violence. If Jake has reached the fifth stage of change, *maintenance*, he is working hard to prevent relapses into violent behavior and working to consolidate the effective changes that he has made. This stage lasts from six months to an indeterminate period of time past the initial action to change. If Jake goes beyond maintenance into *termination*, he has absolute confidence (100% self-efficacy) that he has overcome his violent tendencies, and he is experiencing no temptation to relapse. It is unusual for anyone to reach termination; most people continue to experience temptation to relapse (Prochaska, 1999).

When Jake comes into treatment, what stage of change will he likely be in for his violent behavior? The vast majority of clients (80%) come to treatment in the early stages of change and will resist a treatment plan that requires immediate action. Treatment will need to provide Jake with experiences that change his "decisional balance" so that the pros of moving to the next stage of change outweigh the cons of not doing so (Pro-change Behavior Systems, 2008). Thus, for treatment to be effective, you must correctly identify which stage of change Jake is in for a problem and then design treatment goals to move him forward to the next stage of change for this problem. Jake could be at a different stage of change for each of his problems.

While you prefer Jake to progress in a linear manner through the stages of change, his progression is more likely to follow a spiral. Individuals often start a pattern of change, relapse, and then progress forward again. Each time Jake moves toward action and maintenance, he will grow stronger and more effectively committed to the change process. Jake will develop increased confidence (self-efficacy) that he can maintain change despite temptations to relapse.

What will facilitate Jake's progression in the change process? There are 10 *processes of change* that Jake uses or can potentially learn to use to be able to change. A process of change is a type of activity that Jake can use to modify thinking, behavior, or affect related to a particular problem. Research with populations both in and out of treatment suggests that successful changers have used similar processes of change. Transtheoretical theory labels these change processes as helping relationships, consciousness raising, self-liberation, self-reevaluation, counterconditioning, stimulus control, reinforcement management, dramatic relief, environmental reevaluation, and social liberation.

If Jake makes use of a helping relationship, he is being open and trusting about his problems with someone who cares. If he is involved in consciousness raising, Jake is increasing his information about himself and his problems. Jake's self-liberation would involve his increasing his commitment to change and believing in his own ability to do so. Self-reevaluation would involve Jake's assessing how he feels and thinks about himself with respect to his problems and recognizing that adaptive replacements for violence are what he wants for himself. Counterconditioning would involve Jake in substituting alternative behaviors and cognitions for his problematic ones. Stimulus control would consist of Jake's avoiding or countering stimuli that elicit his problem behaviors and increasing his exposure to cues and reinforcements that support his adaptive behavior. In reinforcement management, Jake would reward himself or be rewarded by others for making changes; in addition, the negative consequences that result from his violence would be increased. Dramatic relief would involve Jake's deeply experiencing and expressing his feelings about his problems as well as the feelings that could come from potential solutions to them. In environmental reevaluation, Jake would assess how both his problems and his adaptive behaviors could affect his relationships with others and his environment. Finally, in social liberation, Jake would recognize that society is much more supportive of nonviolent than violent behavior; thus, if he changed, he would have more alternatives for how to live his life that wouldn't include social control agencies such as child protective services.

Research indicates that individuals within the precontemplative, contemplative, and preparation stages of change are helped the most by insight-provoking treatment interventions, although the preparation stage can also involve small action steps. In contrast, individuals in the action and maintenance stages are most helped by action-oriented treatment interventions. Thus, you will help Jake use the processes of change that are most appropriate to help him progress forward from his current position in the change process. It may not be a smooth progression. Jake might reach an impasse through the overuse, misuse, or neglect of an important process of change. Your role will be to determine what has impeded change and then provide Jake with a strategy to resume the change process.

THE ROLE OF THE CLINICIAN

Treatment is a collaborative, interpersonal endeavor. You will serve as a consultant or coach facilitating Jake's ability to initiate constructive change. The first step in treatment will be for you to teach Jake about the stages of change, processes of change, and levels of change. This educational effort will serve to empower Jake because it will allow him to see himself as involved with the change process, whether he is presently in precontemplation or action.

The second step in treatment will be to assess each of Jake's problems at all five levels of change. Which level will be selected? While interventions at any level of change have value for Jake, whenever possible you should help Jake change at the level at which he could change most quickly; this is often the symptom/situational level, because clients' level of awareness of their problems is usually greatest at this level. If Jake can succeed in reaching maintenance at the symptom/situational level, then no further treatment will be needed. If he is most motivated to change at a different level, you will attempt to "meet Jake" at his definition of the problem unless you have a very compelling reason for not doing so. For your definition to help him change, you will need to persuade Jake that your reason is valid; you can't impose change—he must be an active participant in the process.

The third step in treatment will be to assess Jake's stage of change for each problem he is currently experiencing. A basic strategy for selecting the level of change at which to plan treatment is to be guided by the level where Jake is already furthest along in the change process. For example, if Jake is precontemplative at Levels 4 and 5, contemplative at Levels 1 and 2, and in preparation at Level 3, you will select Level 3 for intervention unless for some reason Jake is against it.

Finally, you will help Jake implement the processes of change that will help him move through the stages of change, at the level of change that has been selected for intervention for each problem. This matching is critical for a positive treatment outcome. A precontemplative Jake is in need of insight-oriented processes. If, instead, you try to engage Jake in action-oriented processes when he is precontemplative, it will disrupt the treatment alliance, and he may drop out. Before implementing new processes of change focused on his violent behavior, you will assess what, if anything, Jake currently is doing to control his violent behavior himself and what, if any, processes he has tried in the past. You will attempt to maximize Jake's self-change efforts by facilitating neglected processes, deemphasizing overused processes, correcting inappropriately used processes, and teaching new processes that may be more appropriate to Jake's stage and level of change. Jake's insights will be treated with respect, and you will actively seek out Jake's strengths to use in the treatment process. An example of how you would assess Jake's violence using the levels, stages, and processes of change is provided in Table 12.1.

There are three treatment strategies to consider using to support Jake in the change process for his violent behavior. The first is called the *shifting-levels strategy*. First, you bring Jake through as many stages of change as you can at the symptom/situational level. If Jake can reach maintenance at this level, then treatment ends. If he gets stuck in the change process before reaching maintenance, you shift to the cognitive level of change and again work to bring Jake to the maintenance stage at this level. If you are successful, then treatment will end. If Jake once again becomes stuck in the change process, treatment will shift down to the interpersonal level, and so on, until Jake successfully reaches the maintenance stage for his violence.

A second approach is the *key-level strategy*. Treatment can begin at the level of change identified by Jake and/or you as particularly relevant to the problem that is the focus of change. If Jake indicates he wants to work on his relationship with his son at the current interpersonal level, you can follow his lead and use techniques (processes of change) specialized to his stage of change at that level. However, you might disagree with Jake. Based on your assessment, you might consider interventions at the intrapersonal level to be most critical to his being successful at changing. You cannot impose work at a particular level of change on Jake. Change will not be possible at this "key" level unless you can motivate Jake to define his difficulty at this level.

A final treatment strategy is the *maximum impact strategy*. This strategy involves intervening at up to all five levels simultaneously. This approach may be appropriate in complex clinical cases in which it is evident that multiple levels are actively involved in the etiology or maintenance of a client's problem. Intervening at multiple levels will be challenging for you and is most appropriate when a client, like Jake, has complex problems that will require lengthy treatment.

Table 12.1   How Jake's Violence Might Be Assessed Using Levels, Stages, and Processes of Change

Levels of Change	Stages of Change	Processes of Change That Are Appropriate*
1. Symptom/situational		
Jake is violent.	Precontemplative	Insight oriented
2. Maladaptive cognitions		
Jake has violent thoughts.	Precontemplative	Insight oriented
3. Current interpersonal		
Jake is in conflict with his wife and son.	Preparation	Insight and action oriented
4. Family/systems		
Jake was raised in a violent family.	Precontemplative	Insight oriented
5. Intrapersonal		
Jake has a profound, unconscious fear of dependence.	Precontemplative	Insight oriented

* Processes of change that promote insight include consciousness raising, dramatic relief, social liberation, and environmental reevaluation. Processes of change that promote action include reinforcement management, helping relationships, counterconditioning, and stimulus control.

CASE APPLICATION: INTEGRATING THE DOMAIN OF VIOLENCE

Jake's case will now be examined in detail. There are many domains of complexity that may be relevant to his case. The domain of violence has been chosen to examine within a transtheoretical case conceptualization and treatment plan.

Interview With Jake (J) From a Transtheoretical Perspective

C: I understand that Ms. Newton from child protective services recommended that you come here.

J: (angrily) It wasn't a recommendation. It was blackmail. I come here or they won't consider bringing Jamie home from foster care.

C: Why did they take Jamie away?

J: (angrily) They say I'm a dangerous man.

C: You sound very angry.

J: (rigidly) This is nothing; this is calm.

C: This is what you sound like when you're calm?

J: (ironically) Sure, am I scaring you? My caseworker says I'm scary.

C: I'm sure you could scare me. But I'm not scared now. I'm curious about how you're feeling now. You sound angry to me; your face looks angry, your body looks tense, but you say you're calm.

J: (tensely) Let's talk about my son; that's why I'm here. He's scared of me. I don't want that. I was scared of my old man, and I don't want that for my kid!

C: He's important to you.

J: (furiously) *Of course he's important to me! He is myyyy kid!*

C: Are you angry with me?

J: (tensely) Not exactly, but . . . Jamie freaked out last week and ran to the neighbors'. They called child protective services. That's why I have to talk to you.

C: He freaked out?

J: (confusedly) I was yelling at him that he had to clean up the mess he made in the kitchen. He started gibbering, so I hit him a few times to calm him down, but instead of calming down, he ran right through the glass door in the kitchen to get away from me.

C: He must have been terrified. What happened?

J: (matter-of-factly) I chased him to the neighbors' house, put him on my motorcycle, and took him to the hospital. The glass from the door had cut him up. Riding my bike calmed me down. It always does. But he was still trembling. I had to drag him off my bike to get him into the emergency room. While we were waiting for the doctor, the child protective services jerks showed up. I told them to leave Jamie alone. (pause) Then the weird thing happened.

C: What was that?

J: (confusedly) He went with them right away. I told him to stay with me. He went with *them*. He had this funny, kind of familiar look on his face. Riding home on my bike, I remembered that it was the look on my face when I saw my old man.

C: You don't want him to look at you that way.

J: (angrily) No. I am not like my old man. I hated him. I am not him.

C: What was he like?

J: (deadpan) He wasn't even human. He hated anything that lived—people, animals, plants. He was a destroyer. He tried to destroy me, but I outsmarted him.

C: How did you do that?

J: (proudly) I lived. Trying to snuff me out was a habit with him. He couldn't do it. I was too strong for him.

C: Were you always too strong for him?

J: (tensely) When I was real little, he had the upper hand. He did me in plenty of times, and I was really scared of him. But then it all changed when I was eight. I will never forget the day it happened. I had a bad cold. I woke up screaming from some dream. I had wet the bed. I tried to clean it up before he could find out. He caught me, shoved my face into the sheets, and beat me black and blue. Then he made me sit with the wet sheets around my head. Even a dog shouldn't be treated like that. I stopped being scared and started to plan.

C: Plan?

J: (with satisfaction) Plan how I would get even. I started that very night. He got drunk and crashed on the living room sofa. I went out in the yard, let in the dog, and put dog shit all over my dad's back.

C: What happened?

J: (half laughing) When he woke up, he shot that poor stupid dog to bits. He was wrong. That dumb dog didn't do it. *I did it*. He never even suspected.

C: How did your mom fit into this?

J: (dismissively) She was the invisible woman.

C: Invisible?

J: (dismissively) She was there but not there. She was terrified of him.

C: Why?

J: (calmly) For every beating I got, she got *two*. Periodically, after beating her up, my dad would dump her at some hospital. Later, he would get her out, and she would be real quiet for a while. He knew how to control her.

C: Control?

J: (matter-of-factly) Keep her from interfering, make her jump to it.

C: Was there anyone who tried to help you or your mom?

J: (tensely) In this world, you have to save yourself. I learned that early in life. I was fourteen when I saved myself and my mom. I had finally grown to be as big as my dad. I picked my moment. He was drunk. But he still fought back. I threw him out the back door a bleeding wreck. In the morning, he was gone. He never came back.

C: You were finally safe. He was gone.

J: (thoughtfully) Not exactly gone. He's in my head a lot.

C: What do you mean?

J: (angrily) If anything goes wrong, his voice screams abuse inside my head. Only a bike ride helps. If I gun the engine, if I really go fast, his stupid voice shuts off.

C: How long have you been hearing his voice?

J: (angrily) It seems like my whole life.

C: How do you know it's his?

J: (furiously) It's his words, not him. I heard them day and night for fourteen years. They're *imprinted* on my brain!

C: The words are his, but the voice comes from you.

J: (furiously) *Of course!*

C: You sound really angry with me again.

J: (glaring, loudly) How many times do I have to say that I'm not angry?

C: I'm sorry that you feel contradicted. I just want you to know that if I make you angry, I want you to tell me about it.

J: (glaringly) Fine. Let's just get on with this.

C: What's important is to build a relationship with Jamie, where you're confident he's not scared of you. You also don't want to be like your old man.

J: (emphatically) I'm not anything like him! (pause) Jamie should like me.

C: Tell me about what you like to do with Jamie.

J: (thoughtfully) I've taken him on bike rides. I figure it's something we could do together. When he's older, I would get him a bike, and we could rev off together.

C: Does Jamie like to go with you?

J: (frustratedly) He cries. My wife says he's terrified of the bike because I go so fast. That's stupid. You need to go fast. The kid will have to get used to it.

C: You want him to enjoy it, but he gets scared of you instead.

J: (emphatically) He's scared of the bike!

C: How often do you take him out?

J: (tensely) Maybe once a week. I can't take him more because his mother interferes.

C: Your wife stops you?

J: (uncertainly) Yeah, she thinks he's too young to ride on a bike; she says he should be home learning to read.

C: Does that make sense to you?

J: (tensely) Well, she's a good mother. She pays attention to the kid. I want Jamie to survive. It's a tough world. (thoughtfully) It's good she pays attention to him. (pause) She pays attention to me, too.

C: Your wife cares for you.

J: (long pause) We're having problems, but I think it will work out.

C: What problems?

J: (angrily) It's this child abuse crap. Protective services said if I didn't come to see you, I would have to leave the house, or Jamie would stay for at least six months in foster care. My wife begged me to come here or get out because she wants Jamie back as soon as possible.

C: So you chose to come here?

J: (furiously) I had no choice! I want to keep my wife and kid. I can live with coming here. (pause) I am not going to disappear like my dad.

C: Are there any other problems in your marriage?

J: (pause; calmly) She pretty much does just what I tell her to do. She is always waiting for me to come home. She talks a lot. Like you, she always asks a lot of questions. I'm usually OK with it.

C: Your wife and son are really important to you, and you want to keep things going the way they were before the abuse report.

J: (firmly) Yeah.

C: Have you ever beaten anyone else besides your dad and Jamie?

J: (angrily) I didn't beat Jamie. I hit him a few times.

C: Have you ever hit anyone else?

J: (angrily) Sometimes people need to meet force before they back off. It's no big deal.

C: There are times when you feel you have to hit people?

J: (tensely) Nothing serious. Maybe one time a few years ago, things got out of hand at a football game, and I had to spend the weekend in jail. I have lost a few jobs because I had to get physical with some people on the job.

C: You had to?

J: (furiously) You bet I had to. Since my dad, I vowed to never let another guy slam me down ever again. No boss, no one on this earth.

C: It sounds like you have gotten into a lot of physical fights.

J: (dismissively) It's a tough world. People are always looking to see you screw up. There are a lot of people like my old man out there. But I get the drop on them fast so I don't get slammed.

C: Does your wife get a drop on you?

J: (dismissively) No, she's OK.

C: Do you ever hit her?

J: (tensely) No, I told you I am not like my dad!

C: Is there anyone out there now you need to get a drop on?

J: (angrily) CPS is full of jerks, but I can't touch them.

C: Why not?

J: (furiously) Don't act stupid. I'd lose my wife and kid.

C: You can keep yourself from slamming them to save your family?

J: (tensely) Yeah, I'm in control.

C: Am I out to get a drop on you?

J: (ironically) You seem more of a talker than a fighter.

C: You're right. (pause) It seems like the most important thing for us to talk about is what you could do besides bike riding to help Jamie like you.

J: (tensely) That's what I want.

Transtheoretical Case Conceptualization of Jake: Assumption-Based Style

Jake's violence can be understood at five different levels of change, including that (a) there are certain situations where Jake behaves violently; (b) there are certain interactions that trigger Jake to have violent thoughts; (c) Jake is more likely to engage in violent behavior in interactions with individuals he feels are trying to dominate him; (d) Jake comes from a family where his father was extremely violent toward him, his mother, and the family dog; and (e) Jake, having been raised in fear and neglect, developed an insecure attachment to both his parents and developed introjects that the only way to protect himself from terrifying situations was to be in control of everyone else. These five different ways of understanding Jake's violence are all equally valid, but he is most likely to consider changing to a nonviolent lifestyle if the problem is defined in the manner that makes the most sense to him. Currently, he is most aware of his violence at the interpersonal level of change. At this level, he recognizes that his relationship with his son Jamie is in serious jeopardy. He doesn't understand his role in creating this problem; however, he seeks to remain an active parent in Jamie's life. At all the other ways of understanding his violence, Jake is unaware or underaware of any need to change. He sees far more benefits to continuing to dominate individuals he relates to than disadvantages. Jake's current strengths are that he is able to reflect on the situations where he is most and least likely to be violent, he can recognize the behavioral signs of fear in others, and he recognizes the things his father did that made him a bad husband and father. These skills can be used in helping Jake progress from preparation into action on becoming a less violent individual in his relationship with his son.

At the symptom/situational level, Jake is violent in response to any cues of possible physical aggression from others and from any comments he considers to being attempts to control him. For example, when he attends a football game, if he is pushed by anyone, he assumes it is intentional aggression and he reacts with rage. His immediate response to any problem is anger. This led him to reflexively yell at Jamie when the child made a mess in the kitchen, and this yelling was an immediate antecedent that led to the consequence of CPS becoming involved with Jake's family. Jake is in the precontemplative stage of change in regard to the concept that he is ever violent. Jake doesn't typically reflect on his own emotions and thoughts before acting. Instead, something happens, and he immediately becomes angry and behaves aggressively. He was unaware that by his first yelling at and then hitting Jamie, his son became terrified and ran through the glass in the kitchen door to escape from him. However, Jake is able to think back about the event. Thus, when reflecting later on the puzzling look he saw on his son's face in the hospital, Jake is able to recognize it as a look of fear. He does not want Jamie to fear him as he feared his own father. Jake is motivated to be close to his son and have a positive father–son relationship. Thus, he may be willing to learn to use processes of change that can help him build a positive relationship with Jamie. Jake can also stop and think when he is not on an adrenaline rush. For example, he recognizes that if he is violent in any way toward the child protective service worker, he will lose custody of his son. Similarly, he recognizes that if he wants to get Jamie back home with his wife, he can't say provocative things to the clinician. Thus, Jake's desire to be in control of a situation can be moderated by the outcome that he desires to attain. Processes that may be helpful to Jake at the symptom/situational level include increasing his awareness of the immediate triggers of his anger and strategies he can use to calm himself in the moment so that he doesn't lose control of his behavior.

At the maladaptive cognitions level, Jake has many violent thoughts. In addition to the violent thoughts he has about others, his self-talk is full of abusive messages he says to himself whenever he makes a mistake. Jake says he has internalized his father's voice and hears his emotionally abusive comments over and over again. Jake is precontemplative that any of his thoughts are different than anyone else's. Having grown up in a very dangerous family environment, he assumes that everyone has violent thoughts. Having heard his father scream abuse at him throughout his childhood, Jake assumes everyone's father was like this—except him; he doesn't think he is anything like his father. In considering the world as a whole, Jake views it as a dangerous place full of people who will take advantage of you if you don't get the drop on them first. Not all of Jake's beliefs revolve around violence. He also believes that his wife is a good mother, and he can articulate specific things she does to take good care of him. He also believes that it is important for a husband and father to support his family. As a result, even though he has sometimes lost control at work and lost his job, he always seeks out and gets another one. While losing temporary custody of Jamie shocked Jake, he is still precontemplative that he needs to change his basic approach to the world. Processes of change that may help Jake recognize this include raising his awareness of Jamie's behavior on the day of the accident and on other occasions where he took Jamie for rides on his motorcycle. If Jake becomes aware of how his current belief systems are interfering in his developing a close relationship with his son, he may be more likely to evaluate the validity of his current beliefs.

At the current interpersonal level, Jake denies that he has ever been violent at home. However, it isn't clear what Jake's definition of violence is, as he does admit to hitting Jamie the night that CPS became involved with his family. Jamie was afraid enough of his father that night to run through a glass door and to the neighbor's house. Jamie's behavior at the hospital in turning to the CPS worker, instead of him, has moved Jake from precontemplation, through contemplation, and into preparation in regard to his relationship with his son. Jake's awareness comes from three sources. First, he recognized on his son's face signs of fear that was directed at himself rather than the CPS worker. Rather than feeling like a powerful man, Jake was shocked to see this look of fear on his son's face. Second, he respects Jennifer's ability to mother their son, and she begged him to come to treatment appointments so they wouldn't risk losing custody of Jamie. Finally, CPS sent Jamie to foster care and has the power to keep Jamie away from even Jennifer's custody if Jake doesn't follows through with treatment. Jake is intrinsically motivated to have a good father–son relationship. Now that he recognizes that any relationship at all with Jamie is in jeopardy, he wants to change something and is prepared to listen to Jennifer, and even the clinician if necessary. As he is prepared to act but doesn't know what to do, some insight-focused processes to help him find good parenting strategies are needed. He will need to first learn some new parenting strategies, practice these strategies, and then work on using them to build a good relationship with Jamie. One of Jake's strengths is that he recognizes that his wife pays careful attention to his son and acknowledges that this makes her a good mother. Some violent men are jealous of the attention their wives give their children, and it evokes more violence. This is not true of Jake. He wants his son to get this attention. Jake is also very aware that he needs to keep his new relationships with the clinician and the CPS worker violence free if Jamie is to be returned to his custody. Jake has been able to keep his aggressive behavior under control even though he is extremely angry about the current situation.

At the family systems level, Jake was raised in a violent home where both he and his mother were abused by his father. He talks about his father as the embodiment of evil. Throughout his early childhood years, he was in a constant state of fear and had no control over the violence within his home. However, he recognized that his father was the one person safe in the home. Jake became motivated to be the member of the family who was not afraid. He set out to become physically strong so he could defend himself. He talks about a key moment in childhood when he recognized he could outsmart his father. Jake planned his moment carefully; then, once his father had passed out on the couch, Jake covered him in dog filth. When his father killed the family dog and didn't come after him, Jake knew he had put one over on his father; it was the beginning of the end for Jake's terror of his dad. Jake rid himself of his father for good when, as a teenager, he interfered when his father was beating his mother. His dad became the victim as Jake gave him a severe beating. His father left the home the following day and never returned, Unfortunately, Jake had already internalized his emotionally abusive style of talking with family members. Currently, Jake is completely unaware that when he took on a new family role to protect himself and his mother, he became the family victimizer. He now terrifies his own son Jamie just as his own father used to terrify him. Processes of change that might help him understand his childhood role in the family, his role in the family as a teenager, and his current role as an adult child of a violent parent might increase Jake's awareness of how he wants his current wife and son to feel in relation to him.

At the intrapersonal level, Jake has a profound and unconscious fear of being dependent on other people. His father let him down by directly abusing him physically and emotionally and by indirectly abusing him through allowing Jake to see his violent assaults on his mother. Jake's mother could not protect him in any way from violence. Whether intentionally or unintentionally, she allowed Jake to be terrorized by his father and did not provide him with any context for understanding that the violence was not a normal part of family life. As a result, Jake developed introjects that the world is a violent place, parents can't be relied on, and the only protection from violence comes from being the strongest and most powerful person in every relationship. Jake was also not given any help in learning to regulate his own emotions or in learning nonviolent problem-solving skills. As a result, Jake became increasingly more aggressive as he aged. However, Jake did get married and does say he respects his wife's behavior as a mother. Adult Jake values his wife's opinions and wants his son to enjoy spending time with him. This suggests that Jake still desires emotional intimacy with family members despite not having the skills to maintain secure attachments himself or to help Jamie to do so.

Jake behaves violently when frustrated, has cognitions that the world is full of violence, has repeatedly terrified his son, was terrified of his own father, and has deeply ingrained thoughts and feelings about the lack of safety in the world. At most of these levels of understanding violence, Jake has no awareness that there is a need for him to change. At the current interpersonal level of change, however, Jake recognizes that he has done things that have directly led to his losing custody of his son, and he very much wants his son back home. Thus, while not agreeing that he is violent per se, Jake has shown openness to learning strategies that can help him build a positive parent–child relationship with Jamie. A window of opportunity in support of this change is that CPS has the power to keep Jamie in foster care if Jake doesn't follow through with their recommendations for treatment.

Transtheoretical Treatment Plan: Assumption-Based Style

Treatment Plan Overview. Jake denies that he has any problems with anger or violence. On the other hand, he does recognize that he can't regain custody of his son if he doesn't change something. Jake was always motivated to have a good relationship with Jamie, but until the accident had been completely unaware that he didn't in fact have such a relationship with him. Now, the shock of seeing fear on Jamie's face has put Jake into the preparation stage of change for improving his relationship with his son. Thus, his ability to inhibit his violent behavior and engage in constructive relationship behavior will be worked on at a key level of change—the current interpersonal level. First, Jake will be moved from preparation to action and then from action to maintenance at the interpersonal level of change. Risks of violence will need to be assessed throughout treatment, and additional goals will be added as needed. (This treatment plan follows the *problem format*.)

PROBLEM: Jake wants to have a loving relationship with his son Jamie, but Jamie shows signs of being fearful of spending time with Jake.

LONG-TERM GOAL 1: Jake will become more aware of the reasons his son Jamie might have shown fear of him the day he lost custody.

Short-Term Goals (Preparation to Action at the Interpersonal Level of Change)

1. Jake will watch a children's movie with Jennifer and come back to treatment and discuss what the children in the movie were afraid of and why he thinks they were afraid.

2. Jake will read a book about children's fears and come back to treatment to discuss what surprised and didn't surprise him about what he read.

3. Jake will discuss with the clinician a book about children's games and also discuss which games he thinks Jamie might be ready to play and why.

4. Jake will watch a TV program with the clinician and note how children react to being yelled at by adults.

5. Jake will talk, step by step, about what happened before, during, and after he yelled at Jamie to clean up his mess and consider whether he has learned anything about child development that might help explain why Jamie began to jibber in response to Jake's yelling.

6. Jake will discuss with the clinician how he showed concern for Jamie after the accident with the glass and consider whether he has learned anything about child development that might help explain why Jamie ran through the glass after Jake struck him a few times.

7. Jake will discuss with the clinician how he showed his concern for Jamie when he took him from the neighbors' house, onto his motorcycle, and to the hospital, and consider whether he has learned anything about child development that might help explain Jamie's behavior when they arrived at the hospital.

8. Jake will discuss with the clinician whether he has learned anything about child development that might help explain why Jamie ran to the CPS worker instead of him at the hospital.

9. Jake will read a popular book about parenting young children and decide what skills within this book might be useful for building a fear-free relationship with Jamie.

10. Jake will watch two hours of television shows that involve parents and children and discuss in session what behaviors of the parents led to positive reactions from the children.

11. Jake will discuss with the clinician specific behaviors he thinks he needs to practice so that he can guide Jamie's behavior without provoking any fear.

12. Other goals will be developed as needed to increase Jake's knowledge of child development and support him in practicing the skills he needs to be a parent who can guide his son without causing fear.

LONG-TERM GOAL 2: Jake will begin taking steps to increase his positive interactions with Jamie.

Short-Term Goals (Action to Maintenance at the Interpersonal Level of Change)

1. Jake will read a book on anger management and discuss whether there is anything in this book that might be of value to Jake as he works toward developing a stronger relationship with Jamie.

2. Jake will read a book on relaxation training and stress management and discuss whether there is anything in this book that might be of value to Jake as he works toward developing a stronger relationship with Jamie.

3. Jake will discuss whether there are any types of relaxation, stress management, or anger management strategies that he would like to practice with the clinician so that he can keep his voice low while playing with Jamie.

4. Jake will practice one of the skills he chose in each of the next three treatment sessions.

5. Jake will practice one of the skills he chose in each of the next three consecutive days outside the session.

6. Jake will practice one of the skills he chose in each of the next three treatment sessions after the clinician intentionally says something to be provoking.

7. Jake will discuss whether there are other skills he would like to practice to ensure that he keeps his voice low while playing with Jamie.

8. Jake will practice playing a board game in session while the clinician brings to his attention what young children sometimes do that irritates parents during these games.

9. Jake will practice reading a children's book in the session while the clinician brings his attention to what young children sometimes do that irritates parents while they read them stories.

10. Jake will bring Jennifer in to practice playing a board game and practice reading a story together to get ready to try one of these activities with Jamie in session.

11. Jake will practice taking a personal time-out so that he has a strategy to use if he begins to feel frustrated while playing with Jamie.

12. Jake, Jennifer, and the clinician will plan the emergency word that Jennifer will use if she feels Jamie is getting scared and needs a personal time-out.

13. Jake and Jennifer will each practice taking a personal time-out in case something begins to frustrate either of them during the game with Jamie.

14. Jamie will come in to hear a story read by Jake while he sits with Jennifer's arm around him and while the clinician observes everyone and suggests personal time-outs if anyone looks as if he or she needs one.

15. Jamie will come in to play a game with Jake and Jennifer while the clinician observes everyone and suggests personal time-outs if anyone looks as if he or she needs one.

16. Other goals will be developed as needed to get Jake to maintenance on controlling his anger, understanding child development, and using effective parenting skills so that Jamie enjoys spending time with his dad in a violence-free environment.

Transtheoretical Case Conceptualization of Jake: Theme-Based Style

"To be safe, I must be violent." This is Jake's code. He sees violence as his only protection against a hostile world. At the symptom/situational level, Jake has been precontemplative about whether he could be safe without violence or if he should care about the negative consequences his violent behavior brings to others; his violence has been an integral part of himself. Despite losing several jobs and spending time in jail, he has never before been motivated to reexamine his code. Recently, he has developed some openness to change at the current interpersonal level. His son is terrified of him, and he does not like this. The environmental demands from his wife Jennifer and CPS that he change his violent behavior, coupled with the failure of his only strategy for having fun with Jamie, have put him in the preparation stage of change about his father–son relationship. Jake's strengths lie in his current greater openness to improving his relationship with Jamie, his willingness to talk about how to build a positive relationship with him, his desire to maintain his marriage, and his ability to reflect on his life despite being mandated into treatment.

Can Jake feel safe for more than a moment at a time? At the symptom/situational level, whether at home, on the job, or at recreational activities, there are cues that trigger a rage response in Jake. He is aware of the immediate precipitants of his anger and violence. For example, he can state that "being pushed" at a football game can trigger an aggressive response. He is unaware, however, of how his violent behavior has terrorized Jamie. Although it may seem as if his only response to perceived threat is violence, he can at times stop and think. For example, although terrified of his own father, he was able to plan how to defend himself. In addition, within the present mandated treatment situation, he has been able to think about the impact of his losing control with a CPS worker. He has also been able to perceive that the clinician, though making him angry, is not a threat to his security. The research literature on violence suggests a priming effect of violent TV, alcohol use, and other environmental forces. Thus, it will be important to assess these and other variables to determine what helps versus hinders Jake's ability to control his aggression.

Jake will need to become aware of the immediate and long-term impact of his violent discipline on his son's thoughts and behavior if he wants to improve their relationship; this might motivate him to consider change at this level.

Can Jake be safe if he listens to himself? At the maladaptive cognitions level, Jake indicates that he has a mental stream of self-talk that "screams abuse" at him whenever he makes a mistake. Like many violent individuals, he views the world as a hostile place, interpreting neutral events as aggressive. In relating to others, their behavior is interpreted through a negative lens. In his words, people are always trying to get him to "screw up" or "get the drop on him." An exception to this is his wife. He perceives her as being a good person and caring about him. He denies any hostile thoughts toward her and doesn't appear to have thoughts of interfering with or degrading her parenting as is common within battering relationships. Overall, his hostile thoughts toward coworkers and strangers serve as predisposing factors for further violent behavior.

Can Jake be safe if he interacts with people? At the interpersonal level, Jake has no close friendships with his peers. His code requires him to take an aggressive posture with others to prevent their "getting the drop" on him. This has led to physical confrontations at work and has cost him several jobs. He is presently unaware of how his violence scares others off or brings out their own hostile and/or aggressive behavior. However, there are signs that Jake can improve his interpersonal functioning. He may have ignored his code in interactions with his wife; he firmly denies ever responding violently to her. Within the home, he can recognize that she takes good care of him and his son and doesn't want his marriage to end. This wish may not be reciprocal. Jennifer is at least a witness to his child-abusive behavior, and he may be verbally abusive to her. Violent men who are controlling their physical aggression often continue to express their aggression verbally. There are indications that this may be occurring in Jake's home. For example, he states that Jennifer always does what he asks her to do, carefully attends to him, and begged him, rather than asked him, to follow through with the CPS recommendations so that Jamie would return home from foster care. Other forms of violence, such as spouse abuse or verbal abuse, are common correlates of child physical abuse and will need to be assessed further as rapport builds within the treatment relationship. Jake has been abusing Jamie, but he perceives himself to be working toward a good father–son relationship. He is in the preparation stage of change for his own parenting behavior. He knows what he won't do—he won't disappear as his father did—but he is currently stymied as to what he needs to do to develop a better relationship with his son. He tried to share with Jamie the bike riding that he finds so relaxing and enjoyable; however, this backfired. Through self-reevaluation following the incident in the emergency room, Jake has realized that he has a poor relationship with his son, and he is committed to changing this so that his son will not hate him as he hated his own father. At this time, he is willing to "talk" about it with the clinician. Other strengths are that he has shown an ability to observe his wife, recognize that her parenting strategies differ from his, and periodically follow her lead without resorting to violence.

Could Jake, the child, be safe at home? At the family/systems level, as Jake was maturing, the power to survive was centered on whoever could most effectively use physical force. For a long time, Jake's father threatened both Jake's and his mother's physical survival. An 8-year-old Jake moved temporarily from precontemplation into preparation and tested whether he could fight back against his father's violence. He had a small success and recognized that, if he planned carefully, he could free himself from his dad's violence. His mother, the invisible person, was never involved in the major decision of who was in the family and what the family rules would be. Thus, Jake's experience taught him that to be safe in a family, you needed to be successful at using violence. The survival struggle at home shifted when Jake was 14 and big enough to seize the power firmly from his father. Jake is unaware how the violent code he learned within his family to protect himself is now serving to alienate him from the very person he most desires to connect with—his son. He is aware of his son's fear but unaware that he is reenacting the role of his own father within his new family. Although he literally kicked his father out of his life, his father's violence continues to victimize him through shaping his relationships with other people and preventing him from ever feeling "safe" in the world. Although Jake can talk about his family relationships and evaluate how he felt about them, he is precontemplative about the role of his father's victimizing behavior in his own current behavior.

How can Jake survive? At the intrapersonal level, Jake feels that he must constantly fight to survive. Unable to protect his integrity without violence, he has intimidated most of the people he relates to. Presently, he is struggling with the issue of how to be close to people while still being physically safe. Jake is precontemplative about how his fears for his own security have led him to behavior that blocks him from forming positive emotional attachments. This combination has led him to become in many ways just like the figure he most hates and dreads, his own father. He is precontemplative about the similarity between his current lifestyle and personality and that of his father's. His strengths lie in his clear recognition that his father's lifestyle was unacceptable and his desire to not be like him.

Must Jake remain violent? As a child, Jake had to use violence to survive. As an adult, he continues to use violence as a mechanism for feeling safe in the world. Violence has become deeply embedded in every aspect of his life, and he is unaware of how this violence is blocking his ability to relate positively to others, particularly his son. Although he is precontemplative about his need to end his violent behavior at most levels of change, he is in the preparation stage about making changes in "something" so that he can develop a more positive relationship with his son; this greater openness to change may serve as a window of opportunity for modifying Jake's code. A potential barrier to Jake's progression in the change process is that his level of dangerousness to others is not static; it fluctuates due to both situational and interpersonal factors. While Jake is precontemplative about change at the symptom/situational level, if he loses control of his anger, he could lose both his marriage and custody of his son. Thus, increasing his immediate ability to control his anger, in addition to working on his father–son relationship, is critical at this time. There are several environmental pressures supporting this type of change at this time. Jake recognizes the power CPS has to keep his child from him. Jake recognizes the look of terror he brought to his son's face and doesn't want to see this look again. Jake respects his wife's mothering skills and doesn't dismiss her input out of hand. The clinician may be able to use these pressures and strengths to help Jake contemplate the benefits of a life free from violence.

Transtheoretical Treatment Plan: Theme-Based Style

Treatment Plan Overview. It will be difficult to assess accurately how dangerous Jake is until genuine therapeutic rapport has been developed, so close collaboration with CPS and the court system will be needed, and a maximum impact strategy will be used to try to decrease the risk of violence as much as possible. Goals will target the symptom/situational and current interpersonal relationships levels of change. The long-term goals will be initiated in numerical order. The short-term goals are labeled to indicate which stage of change they target and the level of change that is the focus of the intervention; this is done as a teaching tool for the reader. When two levels are worked on for the same stage of change, the short-term goals may be accomplished in an intermixed fashion. (This treatment plan follows the *problem format.*)

PROBLEM: Jake's code is interfering in his developing the relationship he wants with his son.

LONG-TERM GOAL 1: Jake will consider whether he can relate safely with others without resorting to his code and if this could help him develop a closer relationship with his son.

Short-Term Goals (Precontemplation to Contemplation at the Symptom/Situational Level of Change)

1. Jake will increase his awareness of the immediate cues/behaviors on the part of others that make him feel unsafe, and strategies for avoiding the cues that trigger him to feel unsafe will be discussed.

2. Jake will increase his awareness of what he does to inhibit his aggressive behavior, for example, with CPS workers, even when the cues/behaviors for eliciting anger are present.

3. Jake will increase his awareness of the specific behaviors CPS needs to see to consider it safe to return Jamie home.

4. Jake will increase his awareness of the negative consequences of further aggressive behavior by discussing foster care with the CPS worker and how foster care would decrease his time with Jamie.

5. Other insight-focused goals will be added if needed to move Jake to the contemplation stage of change at this level.

LONG-TERM GOAL 2: Jake will consider whether another code exists for resolving interpersonal conflicts that would keep him feeling safe and in control, yet help improve his relationship with Jamie.

Short-Term Goals (Contemplation to Preparation at the Symptom/Situational Level of Change)

1. Jake will observe role models (the clinician, his wife, coworkers) and increase his awareness of how they display or respond to anger, and he will discuss the pros and cons of using these strategies himself.

2. Jake will read about nonviolent strategies for responding to provocation such as passive, aggressive, assertive, and humorous strategies and consider if any of these strategies might help him stay safe yet not decrease Jamie's or other people's safety.

3 Jake will consider the situations he finds provocative within the treatment relationship and discuss which of the strategies he read about earlier might be effective in responding to these provocative situations without jeopardizing his safety or that of the clinician.

4. Jake will observe the behavior of his wife, his coworkers, and CPS staff and, during the treatment session, discuss his perceptions of their behavior as positive, neutral, and/or negative and consider how accurate his perceptions are in distinguishing truly provocative from nonprovocative behaviors.

5. Jake will read about relaxation strategies and consider whether any of these might be valuable to him to use when he is beginning to become angry yet recognizes that his safety is not jeopardized.

6. Jake will keep a record of his level of anger before and after he engages in his typical media experiences, including television, video games, and music, and determine when these media calm his anger or intensify it.

7. Jake will consider using the media that decrease his anger to calm himself down at times he recognizes that he is getting angry. If he finds that some of his media experiences intensify his anger, he will consider avoiding them and finding instead media that help him feel calm and relaxed.

8. Other insight-focused goals will be developed if needed to move Jake into the preparation stage of change.

LONG-TERM GOAL 3: Jake will consider whether he can feel safe and more emotionally connected to his son and other people when interacting with them using a different code of conduct.

Short-Term Goals (Preparation to Action at the Symptom/Situational Level of Change)

1. Jake will be given opportunities within sessions to practice responding nonaggressively whenever he experiences the clinician's behavior as provocative and discuss whether he felt safe.

2. Jake will ask the clinician to verbalize the motivation behind the "provocative" behavior to explore whether it was truly provocative or whether it was "neutral" or "positive," and Jake will consider how he feels during this discussion.

3. Jake will develop a list of behaviors that he sees during the week in his current interpersonal relationships and that he finds provocative and then explore with the clinician whether these behaviors might or might not have been intended to be provocative.

4. Jake will select a strategy that he would like to use for relaxing when he recognizes that he is getting angry yet also recognizes that the behavior of the other person is not intended to be provocative.

5. Jake will be given opportunities to use these strategies within sessions with the clinician, after being warned that intentional provocation will occur, and consider afterward whether he felt safe and in control.

6. Jake will become aware of what cues/behaviors his wife uses that make him feel good in his interactions with her and consider using them himself.

7. Jake will become aware of the cues/behaviors his wife uses when interacting with Jamie that appear to make Jamie feel comfortable and happy and consider using them with Jamie himself.

8. Jake will become aware of what cues/behaviors occur within the treatment setting that make him feel good and consider using them himself in his interactions with Jamie and others.

9. Jake will read about effective communication strategies and consider which of these he might be able to use while still maintaining his own safety and that of others.

10. Other insight-focused goals or small action steps will be developed if needed to move Jake into the action stage at the symptom/situational level of change.

Short-Term Goals (Preparation to Action at the Current Interpersonal Level of Change)

1. Jake will practice, within role plays with the clinician and then with his wife in conjoint sessions, how to use positive cues/behaviors to make others feel good.

2. Jake will discuss how he would like his father–son relationship to change, first in role plays with the clinician and then in conjoint sessions with his wife where he assertively asks for her advice.

3. Jake will first practice with the clinician and then implement with his wife asking what behaviors of his she perceives as having pushed Jamie away from him, using relaxation strategies if he feels provoked by her opinions.

4. Jake will practice effective communication skills to use with Jamie and his wife, first within role plays with the clinician, then with his wife in conjoint sessions, and finally with his son and Jennifer in family sessions, with the clinician pointing out any positive or negative consequences of these new behaviors within the session.

5. Other insight-focused goals and small action steps will be developed if needed to move Jake into the action stage of change at the current interpersonal level.

LONG-TERM GOAL 4: Jake will help his son, and others, feel safe and emotionally secure through responding to them using his new code of nonviolence even when he is angry.

Short-Term Goals (Action to Maintenance at the Symptom/Situational Level of Change)

1. Jake will learn to identify when his aggressive urges become strong and ride his motorcycle to calm down if possible.

2. Jake will use other relaxation strategies to calm down whenever the situation does not allow for riding his bike yet he feels his anger rising.

3. Jake will avoid his son when he knows that his anger level is high in order to keep his son from feeling unsafe.

4. Jake will avoid his wife and other people when he knows that his anger level is high in order to keep them from feeling unsafe.

5. Jake will read a book on parenting and decide if anything in the book might be valuable to try within his interactions with his son so that he can teach his son how to grow and develop while maintaining a safe home.

6. Jake will read a book on successful marriages and decide if anything in the book might be valuable to try within his interactions with his wife to keep the home a safe place.

7. Other goals will be developed if needed to move Jake into maintenance at the symptom-situational stage of change.

Short-Term Goals (Action to Maintenance at the Current Interpersonal Level of Change)

1. Jake will assertively ask Jamie what he likes to play and explain to his son how riding a motorcycle is play to him.

2. Jake will practice how to play with Jamie within role plays with the clinician using a game or activity Jamie has said he likes to play.

3. Jake will generate a list, during the treatment session, of things Jamie might do during a play session that could frustrate him or make him angry and consider how he could calm himself down in this situation.

4. Jake will invite his son to play, will notice if his son looks afraid, and if he does, will assertively remove himself from the play session if he becomes angry about this.

5. Jake and his wife will talk about the parenting strategies they want to use with their son, and the clinician will help them compromise when needed. Jake will calm himself down if he finds that the need to compromise makes him angry.

6. Jake will practice assertive strategies for disagreeing with his wife over parenting decisions, first within role plays with the clinician and then at home with his wife, using his relaxation strategies or avoidance strategies whenever necessary to keep his anger under control.

7. Jake will use his new communication and anger management strategies outside his family life, reminding himself that these strategies can keep CPS and the

police from becoming involved in his life again and to ensure the success of his new code of nonviolence.

8. Other action-focused goals will be added if Jake has not progressed securely to the maintenance stage of change at the current interpersonal level.

PRACTICE CASE FOR STUDENT CONCEPTUALIZATION: INTEGRATING THE DOMAIN OF RACE AND ETHNICITY

It is time to do a transtheoretical analysis of Kayla. There are many domains of complexity that might provide insights into her behavior. You are asked to integrate the domain of race and ethnicity into your case conceptualization and treatment plan.

Information Received From Brief Intake

Kayla is a 24-year-old single Lakota Sioux. She is a journalist working for Greenpeace. She travels worldwide in helping this organization publicize environmental concerns. She is presently on a leave of absence because of ill health. While on leave, she is living in an apartment in Watertown, Massachusetts (a suburban area of Boston). Kayla has referred herself for treatment, within a private practice setting, because of an overall feeling of malaise and perceived lack of direction to her life. Kayla initiated contact at this time because of situational constraints. Although she has been feeling the need for help for the last year, only in the past week did she return to the United States and find herself in a position to seek help.

During a brief mental status exam, Kayla showed signs of depression and anxiety, but not at clinical levels. There were also no signs of suicidal or homicidal ideation or severe psychopathology. Kayla was open to help from whichever clinician at your practice had the first opening. Greenpeace will be sending her abroad in six months.

Interview With Kayla (K) From a Transtheoretical Perspective

C: Kayla, I understand that you are coming in because you are dissatisfied with the general direction your life is taking. Can you tell me more?

K: (forlornly) Well, I have been working for Greenpeace since I graduated from college. It's a great organization, and they are doing work that is full of personal meaning for me. Yet, I feel an emptiness, (pause) a disconnectedness from everyone. I can't really put my finger on it. I have always felt this way. I thought that this malaise would go away once I had my degree and some important work to do.

C: You've had this feeling your whole life?

K: (forlornly) My family was poor. I never had the same clothes as everyone else. The community was small. Everyone seemed to belong to the Protestant church but us. I was a Sioux; they were all White. I was always bullied or rejected by the other kids.

C: It sounds like a traumatic experience.

K: (thoughtfully) It was. No one, not even my family, seemed to understand what I was going through until my high school guidance counselor came along. He realized I needed help and sent me to treatment for the first time.

C: First?

K: (calmly) I have been in treatment three times now. Each time it really helped me through a life crisis. However, they never really made me feel like I was part of this world. I always continued to feel that I was disconnected.

C: What parts of the treatment helped you?

K: (reminiscently) In my first round, I learned about relaxation. I had never really known what it was like to relax before. I was always tense, on edge, ready to fight for little or no reason at all. The sessions taught me a lot of relaxation exercises and anger control strategies. This clinician was great, one of the few people I have ever felt connected to. I still use many of those relaxation exercises. If anyone at work or at home gets me going, I just give myself a personal time-out. I haven't had any real fight with anyone since I was about fifteen years old.

C: No fights?

K: (satisfied) None that really count. I might get a little irritated with someone, but if it goes beyond that, I immediately withdraw and pull myself back together.

C: Does anyone think he or she fights with you?

K: (confusedly) No, and that's the ironic thing. This lack of fighting is actually what my old boyfriend said blew up our relationship.

C: The relationship is over?

K: (sadly) Yes. We both worked for Greenpeace and had been living together for two years. He said that I was too emotionally cold—a ghost, there but not there.

C: Do you know what he meant by that?

K: (pause; hesitantly) He complained that I was only there for the good times. There were a lot of times when he felt that I wasn't around when he needed me.

C: Were you around?

K: (adamantly) I was physically there. But when he was in trouble, I felt overwhelmed with anger at whoever or whatever was causing the problem and I needed to cool off before I exploded. He saw my coping as pulling back from him and not allowing myself to care deeply about anything. (long pause) He left Greenpeace.

C: Is there anybody new in your life?

K: (dejectedly) No, I don't think I can handle a relationship right now. I have never been really good at closeness. In college, I only had what my last clinician called superficial friends. We would joke around a lot together, but we made it a point to always keep our emotions under control.

C: What did you feel was beneficial about that treatment experience?

K: (calmly) It really helped me understand interpersonal relationships better. I realized that I had been purposefully distancing myself from others because I was afraid of rejection. I had never experienced any close attachments—I hadn't thought I needed them. But I came to see how very lonely and isolated I was. I learned how to reach out to people and developed my first real friendships.

C: What changed so that your friendships became real rather than superficial?

K: (reflectively) I had been living a kind of hermitlike existence. I was always holed away in my room, writing for hours on end. I loved to write, and I was doing something I thought was meaningful. Yet I was getting a lot of feedback from my English professors that my work seemed to be lacking a sense of purpose. At first, I thought that my professors were rejecting my work because I was a Sioux. But treatment helped me realize that I was rejecting criticism because I was afraid I didn't have enough talent to write. I forced myself to express these fears to my professors and the students in class and began to feel closer to them. They seemed to show a greater interest in me too; I made real friends.

C: By being vulnerable, you established more connections.

K: (calmly) Yes, and I know I still need more connections, but it can be so hard. You guys always seem to know what I'm thinking and what I need to learn next; it's easier to relate to you than anyone else.

C: What about your family?

K: (calmly, sighing) I am a reject to them. (pause) I am not exaggerating. I had to give up completely on them. I did try. In fact, that was a major focus of my second treatment experience. I was really struggling with trying to understand my identity. My high school teachers had helped me get to college on a full scholarship. I wanted so much to be there, but my family was against it. They saw it as my rejecting my Sioux background and completely cut me off for a while.

C: How did that feel?

K: (sadly) I felt traumatized at first that I had lost my family. But, in treatment, I realized that nothing had changed that much. I have really always been an outcast in my family. I had always tried to develop a balance between what they wanted for me and what I wanted so that they would accept me. My clinician encouraged me to learn about the Lakota Sioux and draw on my heritage for strength. I read up on everything I could. I began to realize that my confusion over family rituals was because my parents themselves were confused.

C: What do you mean?

K: (seriously) Many Indians in my grandparents' generation were forced away from traditional Indian life, sent to boarding schools, punished for speaking their native language. How could they have taught my parents how to be Sioux? I think my parents are trying to recapture their traditional ways, but they don't know exactly how to do it except to hate outsiders. I approached my mother about this. (pause) I told her I was trying to understand, (pause) but she just walked away from me.

C: You felt rejected. You were trying to understand, and she walked away.

K: (confusedly) I always seem to repel them. (pause) I have become more of a White than an Indian in some ways, but I did learn things maybe they don't even know by reading about the Sioux. After graduation, I picked Greenpeace because it values the land; it was the right amount of connectedness for me.

C: Connectedness is important to you.

K: (emphatically) My family and our people value nature and the environment. My family always talked of how much the land means, although they left our Sioux reservation after my grandmother died and bought our tree farm in Maine. I always worked so hard on the farm, to show I cared too; my dad never seemed to notice.

C: What do you mean?

K: The only attention I got was from the teachers at school. When I applied to go to college, my family accused me of betraying our people and continuing to prefer the company of outsiders. I tried to explain my love for writing to them, but they just said I was turning my back on them. I tried to show them that the land was important to me, using my writing. (pause) I thought they would see my work with Greenpeace as important since its aim is to protect the earth.

C: How do they see it?

K: (dully) It's just following a White path, not a Sioux one. Coming to school was my dream, but I should have put my family's welfare first. I did try to do this during my childhood, but I couldn't fit in. (anxiously) I had to find a place to fit in. After my first semester at the university, my uncle came after me. He said to come home now and listen or to never come home again.

C: Does your uncle speak for everyone?

K: (resignedly) Yes, he always has. My parents, my older sisters, and my uncle and aunt had a meeting to discuss my final insult to the family and decided I was out.

C: Everyone but you was there.

K: (resignedly) Even when I was at home, I was never included.

C: (long pause) Unconnected. (pause) Were you always that way?

K: (resignedly) Spiritually, yes. Physically, we were together every day after school, and every weekend we would go into the woods together and plant or harvest trees. We also have to cut wood to use in heating our house. If our wood supply gets low, we get cold. Self-sufficiency is very important to my family. We hunt in the woods, although my mother does go to the supermarket for some things. We use as little of the White community services as we can.

C: You and your family have life skills that few people have these days.

K: (sadly) Yes. I was also the best wood chopper in the family, but no one ever said anything. I know it's not the Sioux way to expect thanks for your work, but I just wanted some sign I counted for something; I only got disapproval.

C: Disapproval hurts.

K: (sadly) It did hurt. Whatever I did, starting as far back as I can remember, they accused me of preferring outsiders—particularly Whites. Calling me a White is the biggest insult they can come up with.

C: Why?

K: (intently) My parents hate all of our White neighbors. I think there was some trouble about my parents getting the tree farm, but I don't know what. My parents just always told me that we can't trust Whites and I should stay away from them.

C: Do your mother and father always agree?

K: (intently) Yes. My father makes all the decisions. My mother goes along. Sometimes, I feel she doesn't really agree, and I beg her to take my side. She won't. Later, she will say, "Learn silence, or you will always be in conflict."

C: What does learning silence mean?

K: She meant if I stuck up for myself I would always be in conflict. If I was quiet, there would be no conflict.

C: Does your mother always follow the rule to be silent?

K: She does now, but I think there was a time when she wasn't so silent. I have vague memories of my parents fighting when I was really young. After one big fight, I was sent to live with my aunt and uncle for three years. My sisters stayed at home. No one would tell me why I'd been sent away. The first night I was with them, I overheard talk about my mother being in a hospital. I got really scared and ran into the room. They were very angry about this and wouldn't discuss it with me. I wondered if my mom was sent to the hospital for not being silent.

C: How did it feel to be sent away and cut off from your parents and sisters?

K: (anxiously) I was scared and confused, but I knew that if I wanted to get home, I had to be silent. I was sent home when it was time for kindergarten. When I got there, they acted as if I had never left. I had so many questions. Why was I sent away and not my sisters; why had my mother gone to the hospital; why had I been sent back; why was it so important to always be silent?

C: Some people are very curious, and some people are not.

K: (emphatically) I'm the curious kind. I loved kindergarten from the very first day because the teachers always encouraged and answered my questions. My parents have always believed I respected my teachers more than them.

C: Did you?

K: (resignedly) I just fit in there better. I wasn't alone like I was at home. I tried to understand what it meant to be a Sioux, but family holidays never made sense. It's weird; my parents say particular days are special to the Sioux, but they don't seem to do anything on these days but smoke and drink. They always get mad if I ask any questions. I'm not sure they know what they're celebrating.

C: They didn't respond to direct questions, but did they ever try to teach you about the holidays through stories or some other teaching ritual?

K: (disgustedly) They seemed to just sit in a circle and get drunk.

C: Who are they?

K: (disgruntledly) My parents, my older sisters, my uncle, and his wife. They just sit in silence. That is what they always said they wanted from me.

C: How much do they drink?

K: (calmly) Until they pass out. But they aren't alcoholics if that's what you think.

C: There are a lot of families where alcohol is a big problem.

K: (insistently) I don't drink, and I don't think my family drinks too much except maybe on the holidays.

C: I can feel your loyalty to your family. Do you think I assume they are drunks because they are Sioux? Or do you feel they don't have a drinking problem?

K: (sadly) I don't drink at all. (pause) Maybe alcohol is part of their problems.

C: Do you think turning to school is what separated you from the family?

K: (emphatically) It made it worse, but my father has always treated me differently than my sisters. He is a quiet man, but he does talk to them. To me, he has always been cold. I can still remember as a small child following him around trying to help him on the farm. He never acknowledged that I was there. I loved school because it's not wrong to talk there.

C: At home you felt different and alone; at school you felt connected, but it took you even further from your parents.

K: (intently) I was always speaking up despite my mother's injunctions to be silent and my father's obvious disapproval. I wanted to fit in like my sisters, but I couldn't be quiet like them. I always had this independent spirit. I fit in with my coworkers at Greenpeace. I am Sioux. I am not trying to make money to collect things; I'm trying to help keep the earth healthy for everyone. I have caused a lot of conflict in my family; a good Sioux should not do that, but it's not against our culture to try and find your own path. (pause) It's not. (long pause; dejectedly) Sometimes I think that if my work at Greenpeace was really of value, my father would talk to me. Why would I feel so empty if my work had meaning?

C: Since you feel empty, you think your work can't be important?

K: (determinedly) I wrote a particularly good article for Greenpeace—I received a literary award for it; I sent it to my parents. Shouldn't they respect how I'm trying to protect the earth? Maybe they thought I sent the article to impress them; that is not our way. (bright red, embarrassed) I think about this a lot. I have this voice in my head that seems to drone on, "Do something important and your parents will want you back." There are times when I feel like I must be going nuts because I have arguments with this voice; I say, "I am doing something important; they just don't want me." Just talking about it aloud makes me feel tired and worn out.

C: The voice demands a level of perfection and importance that no one can reach.

K: (adamantly) Yes, and it never stops.

C: And your response to the voice is to feel tired?

K: (resignedly) It's so hard to keep trying, but I know that I must.

C: Why?

K: (forcefully) I guess I have always been a fighter—even as a kid. It's one of those things about me that made me so visible to my parents when they wanted me to be invisible; I can't give up. You guys sometimes play this game suggesting I can stop trying, but really you always demand that I be strong.

C: Are we perfectionistic too?

K: (calmly, smiling) Yes, you won't let me be weak and fall apart. That's one thing that keeps me coming back to treatment; you like it when I'm strong.

C: You have told me a lot about yourself, and you seem to have a lot of insight into your own difficulties. Why do you need to be here?

K: (thoughtfully) I'm feeling stuck and lost. I can't seem to move on with my life. This has happened before, and treatment has really helped me regain direction.

C: What do you think is behind this stuckness and lost feeling?

K: (nervously) I can't say right now. (pause) It's hard to admit everything that's happened. It's easy to not share something unless someone asks specifically. I've kept some secrets from my previous clinicians because they didn't ask. (pause; looks down) I answered any questions they asked, but if they didn't ask . . . (long pause)

C: What secrets?

K: (nervously) I didn't mention to any of them that I had been in treatment before. I thought they would think I was a real loser needing treatment repeatedly.

C: You're a loser if you need treatment more than once?

K: (emphatically) Even coming once was a sign of weakness—I'm supposed to be self-sufficient.

C: So, you feel that coming to treatment is turning your back on your traditions?

K: (emphatically) Absolutely! I'm supposed to be self-sufficient and silent and do what I'm told. Instead, I'm living with outsiders, needing help, asking questions, and ignoring my family's wishes!

C: Is everyone who isn't a Sioux an outsider?

K: (resignedly) The clinicians, the teachers, my friends, and my coworkers.

C: What would other American Indians outside your family think about you?

K: (confusedly) I don't know. There are other Indians involved politically, like those in the American Indian movement. I could contact them, (pause) but I have found a place I fit—it's Greenpeace. It's where I want to be connected. But . . . (long pause)

C: But even from these most connected people, you have kept secrets. (*K* nods) What important secret is left to tell me today?

K: (nervously) I must handle it alone.

C: What will happen if I know this secret?

K: (panicky) I will lose the little connection that I have. You will kick me out.

C: Kicking you out is not an option.

K: (panicky) You would! You would realize what an outcast I am.

C: I know a lot about you now, and I respect you. It's hard for me to imagine that I could learn something now that would lead me to cast you out.

K: (confusedly) What opinion can you have of me? This is our first session!

C: There is a lot I don't know about you. But what I do know is that you are a tremendously creative and hardworking person, a courageous person, a lonely person. Your family has rejected you, and in a way you have rejected yourself. Could you forgive yourself—for whatever the secret is—and let yourself be connected to me, your colleagues, and other people?

K: (determinedly) I want to, but I don't know if I can.

C: Maybe we could work it out together, or maybe you could work it out for yourself.

K: (panicky) Am I such a loser you won't accept me for treatment?

C: You are such a winner I'm not sure I have anything to offer you that you don't already know you need to do for yourself.

K: (panicky) I can't be alone anymore.

C: You need to be connected to others. But do you need me to help you?

K: (pleadingly) Yes; I told you I can't handle things anymore on my own.

C: You are not alone. I'm here. Let's each do something important for next week. I will think about what you've shared with me so far and have some ideas to suggest to you. You think about your secret and think about your strengths. Come up with some ideas to suggest to me about your plan of action to end this empty feeling.

K: (calmly) I can do that.

Exercises for Developing a Case Conceptualization of Kayla

Exercise 1 (four-page maximum)

GOAL: To verify that you have a clear understanding of transtheoretical theory.

STYLE: An integrative essay incorporating Parts A through C.

NEED HELP?   Review this chapter (pages 429–434).

  A. Develop a concise overview of all the assumptions of transtheoretical theory (the theory's hypotheses about key dimensions in understanding how clients change; think broadly, abstractly) as an introduction to the rest of this exercise.

  B. Develop a thorough description of how each of these assumptions is used to understand a client's progression through the change process in paragraphs that provide specific examples to fully explain each assumption.

  C. Conclude your essay by describing the role of the clinician in helping the client change (consultant, doctor, educator, helper), the major approach taken to treatment, and common treatment techniques. Provide enough specific examples to clarify what is distinctive about this approach.

Exercise 2 (five-page maximum)

GOAL: To aid application of the transtheoretical theory to Kayla.

STYLE: A separate sentence outline for each section, A through C.

NEED HELP?   Review this chapter (pages 429–434).

  A. Create a list of Kayla's problems (concerns, weaknesses, problems, symptoms, skill deficits, treatment barriers), and for each discuss the following:

    1. At what level of change is Kayla defining the problem?

2. Which stage of change is Kayla in regarding the problem?

3. Are there any processes of change Kayla has used to try to overcome the problem, and has this produced effective, ineffective, or mixed results? Have the processes of change she has used been appropriate, considering 1 and 2 above?

B. Create a list of Kayla's strengths (strong points, positive features, successes, skills, factors facilitating change), and for each discuss the following:

1. How aware is Kayla of this strength, and in what ways is it benefiting her?

2. Is Kayla using this strength in an attempt to overcome any of her problems (be specific)?

a. A strength could help her understand her problem at one or more levels of change.

b. A strength could be used as a *process of change* to move her through a stage of change.

c. A strength could enable her to *make effective use* of a process of change.

C. Based on Part A, what is Kayla most motivated to change at this time? For each of these problems, discuss the following:

1. The treatment strategy you would select for each problem that will be a focus of treatment and why you chose it.

2. The specific change processes that are needed to support change for each problem, within each treatment strategy, and why you chose them.

3. Considering Part B, how might Kayla's strengths be used within your treatment strategy for each problem?

Exercise 3 (four-page maximum)

GOAL: To develop an understanding of the potential role of Kayla's Sioux heritage in her life.

STYLE: A separate sentence outline for each section, A through J.

NEED HELP?   Review Chapter 2 (pages 58–65).

A. Assess the role of Kayla's self-identified Sioux heritage in terms of the strengths, resources, and power it may be bringing to her within her personal, family, social, vocational, and political spheres.

B. Consider what entrenched dominant cultural worldviews, institutions, policies, and practices might be leading to discrimination, prejudice, and racism and setting up barriers to Kayla's healthy development at this time.

C. Consider what current events might be leading to increased discrimination, prejudice, and racism and thus setting up barriers to Kayla's healthy development at this time.

D. Consider what historical events have influenced Kayla's identification with the Sioux(s) and assess if any of her current problem(s) could be a result of direct or indirect oppression or trauma, her responses to this oppression, assimilation stress, discrimination, prejudice and racism, or a mismatch in values between the Sioux and the dominant society and its institutions.

E. Assess how well Kayla is functioning overall in terms of her values, beliefs, and behaviors, both through the worldview of the Sioux and through the worldview of the dominant cultural group; discuss if any of her behavior within the dominant society might represent a healthy adaptation to injustice that would be supported by the Sioux.

F. Consider if successful treatment will involve more internal awareness or actions on Kayla's part or if it will involve more actions to change policies, procedures, and values of an environment that is oppressing her and the Sioux Nation; consider if there are any culturally specific resources, treatment strategies, or helpers Kayla would value at this time that might be effectively used within your treatment plan.

G. What is your current knowledge of the Sioux people?

   a. How many courses have you taken that give you background on the Sioux or other Native people?

   b. How many workshops have you attended that give you background on the Sioux or other Native people?

   c. What professional experiences have you had with the Sioux or other Native people?

   d. What personal experiences have you had with the Sioux or other Native people?

   e. Describe the worldview(s) of the Sioux or other Native people.

H. What is your current level of awareness of issues relevant to the Sioux or other Native people?

   a. Describe the stereotypes you have heard about the Sioux or other Native people.

   b. Describe how the dominant culture's White cultural biases may have operated in your life.

   c. Describe the role your racial and ethnic cultural groups have played in your life.

   d. In comparing your racial and cultural affiliations to Kayla's, what differences could lead to communication problems, values conflicts, difficulty understanding Kayla's lifestyle or experiences, or an invalidation of Kayla's strengths?

I. What skills do you have or can you develop in working with members of the Sioux Nation or other Native people?

    a. What skills do you currently have that are of value in working with the Sioux or other Native people?

    b. What skills do you feel it would be important to develop to work effectively with the Sioux or other Native people?

J. What action steps can you take?

    a. What might you change in how you interact within the rapport-building phase to develop a more effective working alliance with Kayla or other members of the Sioux Nation?

    b. How might you structure the treatment environment to increase the likelihood of a positive outcome with Kayla or other members of the Sioux Nation?

    c. What aspects of the theoretical orientation you are planning to use with Kayla might contain some implicit cultural or racial biases, and what will you change to promote effective treatment?

    d. What might you change in the treatment-planning phase to increase the likelihood of a positive outcome with Kayla or other members of the Sioux Nation?

Exercise 4 *(seven-page maximum)*

GOAL: To help you integrate a transtheoretical orientation and racial and ethnic issues into an in-depth conceptualization of Kayla (who she is and why she does what she does).

STYLE: An integrated essay consisting of a premise, supportive details, and conclusions following a carefully planned organizational style.

NEED HELP?   Review Chapter 1 (pages 1–7) and Chapter 2 (pages 58–65).

STEP 1: Consider what style you should use in organizing a transtheoretical understanding of Kayla. This style should (a) support you in providing a comprehensive and clear understanding of where she is in the change process and what she needs in order to move forward toward maintenance and (b) support language Kayla might find persuasive as she struggles with whether revealing her secret will make her more or less of an outcast.

STEP 2: Develop a concise premise (overview, preliminary or explanatory statements, proposition, thesis statement, theory-driven introduction, hypotheses, summary, concluding causal statements) that explains Kayla's overall level of functioning as an individual struggling to feel connected to others and find meaning in her life. If you need help with Step 2, remember that this should be an integration of the key ideas of Exercises 2 and 3 and that it should (a) provide a basis for Kayla's long-term goals, (b) be grounded in a transtheoretical perspective and be sensitive to racial and ethnic issues, and (c) highlight the strengths she brings to transtheoretical treatment.

STEP 3: Develop your supporting material (a detailed case analysis of strengths and weaknesses, supplying data to support an introductory premise) from a transtheoretical perspective, incorporating within each paragraph a deep understanding of Kayla, a woman who has struggled her whole life to fit in. If you need help with Step 3, consider the information you'll need to include in order to (a) support the development of short-term goals, (b) be grounded in transtheoretical theory and sensitive to racial and ethnic issues, and (c) integrate an understanding of Kayla's strengths into the change process whenever possible.

STEP 4: Develop your conclusions and broad treatment recommendations, including (a) Kayla's overall level of functioning, (b) anything facilitating or serving as a barrier to her reaching the maintenance stage for each of her problems at this time, and (c) her basic needs in the change process, being careful to consider what you said in Part H and J of Exercise 3.

Exercise 5 (four-page maximum)

GOAL: To develop an individualized, theory-driven action plan for Kayla that considers her strengths and is sensitive to her Sioux heritage.

STYLE: A sentence outline consisting of long- and short-term goals.

NEED HELP? Review Chapter 1 (pages 7–24).

STEP 1: Develop your treatment plan overview, being careful to review what you said in Parts H and J of Exercise 3 to try to prevent any negative bias in your treatment plan and ensure that it is individualized to Kayla's unique needs as a Sioux woman.

STEP 2: Develop long-term (major, large, ambitious, comprehensive, broad) goals that *ideally* Kayla will reach by the termination of treatment for each of the problems identified, so that at the end of treatment she will be interpersonally connected and find meaning in her life. If you have trouble with Step 2, reread your premise and support topic sentences for ideas to transform into goals that will move Kayla through the change process on each of her identified problems (use the *style* of Exercise 4).

STEP 3: Develop short-term (small, brief, encapsulated, specific, measurable) goals that Kayla and you can expect to see accomplished within a few weeks and that you can use to chart her progress in the change process for each of her problems, instill confidence that she is progressing, and plan time-effective treatment sessions. If you have trouble with Step 3, reread your support paragraphs, looking for ideas to transform into goals that (a) will support Kayla in moving through the stages of change on one of her problems, using insight- or action-oriented processes of change, as appropriate, at the level of change at which the problem is identified; (b) will enhance factors facilitating and decrease factors inhibiting her ability to change and find meaning in her life at this time, (c) utilize strengths she has developed both in and out of treatment whenever possible, and (d) are individualized to her personal journey for meaning as a Sioux woman rather than generic.

Exercise 6

GOAL: To critique the transtheoretical model in the case of Kayla.

STYLE: Answer Questions A through E in essay form or discuss them in a group format.

A. What are the strengths and weaknesses of this model for helping Kayla (a successful professional with acculturation conflicts), and how will you encourage the change process without further encouraging Kayla's dependence on treatment to begin the change process?

B. Discuss the strengths and weaknesses of using a relational constructivist approach with Kayla, considering her interpersonal problems, her quest for meaning in her life, and her contradictory narratives of being an outcast and being a successful writer.

C. Assume Kayla's secret is that she is a lesbian. Discuss in detail how knowing this might deepen and/or change your understanding of her personal and family dynamics. Discuss how this might influence or change your treatment plan.

D. What ethical dilemmas would be raised if Kayla told you that she felt closer to you than she'd ever felt to anyone else and admitted to having sexual fantasies involving you? Explore how this makes you feel, particularly as it relates to how attractive you find Kayla as an individual. How will you handle it if she asks you out on a date? (If you are female, assume Kayla is a lesbian; if you are male, assume she is heterosexual.)

E. To use the transtheoretical model, you need to be capable of using treatment frameworks and processes of change from many different theoretical orientations, and you must be comfortable with working with Kayla at the stage of change she is in. Discuss the strengths and weaknesses of you personally using this approach and provide specific examples to back up your points.

RECOMMENDED RESOURCES

Books and Articles

Brooks, G. R. (2010). *Beyond the crisis of masculinity: A transtheoretical model for male-friendly therapy.* Washington, DC: American Psychological Association.

Duncan, B. L. (2014). *On becoming a better therapist: Evidence based-practice one client at a time* (2nd ed.). Washington, DC: American Psychological Association.

Lambert, M. J. (2010). *Prevention of treatment failure: The use of measuring, monitoring, and feedback in clinical practice.* Washington, DC: American Psychological Association.

Prochaska, J. O., & Norcross, J. C. (2009). *Systems of psychotherapy: A transtheoretical analysis.* Pacific Grove, CA: Brooks/Cole.

University of Rhode Island Cancer Prevention Research Center. (2008). *Trans-theoretical model: Detailed overview of the transtheoretical model.* Retrieved from http://www.uri.edu/research/cprc/TTM/detailedoverview.htm

Videos

Allyn & Bacon Professional (Producer). (n.d.). *Stages of change for addictions with John Norcross* (Part of the brief therapy for addictions hosted by Judy Lewis & Jon Carlson) [Motion picture, ISBN 0–205–31544–5, http://abacon.com/videos]. (Available from Pearson Education Company, 160 Gould Street, Needham Heights, MA)

Websites

Motivational Interviewing. http://www.motivationalinterview.org

Pro-change Behavior Systems. http://www.prochange.com/staff/james_prochaska

Psychotherapy Integration. http://www.psychotherapy-integration.com

T H I R T E E N

Discussion and Extension
of the Model

Research indicates that 80% of individuals who receive treatment for their emotional or behavioral difficulties, are better off than those who do not seek help (Lambert, 2013; Miller, Hubble, Duncan, & Wampold, 2010). However, it also suggests that nearly 50% of people who initiate treatment will prematurely drop out and, for those who remain in treatment, up to 30% to 50% do not continue to benefit after their initial visits (Duncan, Miller, & Hubble, 2007).

You have just been assigned a new client, Juliet, age 15. You wholeheartedly want to help her. You certainly do not want her to drop out of treatment or have her parents pull her out after calling you an incompetent cretin. How will you decide which of the 10 different theoretical perspectives you now have practiced is best suited to helping her?

Juliet has come to you for help with an eating disorder. Should you help her control the antecedents and consequences of her eating behavior (Chapter 3)? Should you find out what thoughts are going through her head immediately before she begins to put her fingers down her throat (Chapter 4)? Do you want her to learn how to be mindful and present oriented so that she can recognize that she is the one in control of her thoughts and behaviors rather than their being in control of her (Chapter 5)? What about helping Juliet understand how unrealistic images of women have led even the most beautiful to be dissatisfied with their bodies (Chapter 6)? Could she be cut off from her feelings and need help further processing them (Chapter 7)? Perhaps she has a dysfunctional interpersonal style in which she always pulls away from others whenever they try to get close to her (Chapter 8). Are her parents very controlling, and so she needed to learn how to do something as a teen that was solely under her control (Chapter 9)? Perhaps she is having cultural conflicts with her parents, as she is the first generation of her family to be born in the United States (Chapter 10). Perhaps she has always planned to be a star on Broadway and, although hungry, has included her dance teacher's construction of a healthy body rather than that of her parents in her storied self (Chapter 11). Any of these approaches might help Juliet eat in a healthier manner. It may be best to select the approach that defines her eating in the way that makes the most sense to Juliet (Chapter 12).

Is it valid to let Juliet, who has no experience with treatment, have so much power in the treatment selection process? Absolutely; after all, none of these approaches has been found to be generally superior to the other. Rosenzweig (1936) dubbed this clinical finding the "Dodo bird verdict." In addition, the research literature has indicated that there are certain common factors, independent of theoretical orientation or technique, that are important for you to try to maximize as you work with Juliet according to whichever model of treatment guides you. These common factors include extratherapeutic factors (what Juliet brings into treatment), the therapeutic relationship (whether or not a warm and trusting working relationship is developing between you and Juliet), models and techniques, expectancy and hope, and your responding to Juliet's feedback as treatment progresses (Wampold, 2010). It is also important for you to track whether Juliet is showing any signs of changing. Research indicates that an important sign of positive outcome is whether Juliet begins experiencing signs of positive change within her first six visits. What are the signs you should look for? Actually, clinicians have often been found to overestimate how much their clients are gaining from treatment. Thus, what predicts positive outcome for Juliet is her own perspective on whether treatment is working or not (Duncan et al., 2007).

A last critical predictor of client outcome is you. We all want to be great clinicians. The average effectiveness of a clinician is 50%, while excellent clinicians have a 70% effectiveness rating (Walfish, McAllister, & Lambert, 2012).There is a short list of strategies found to discriminate the work of excellent clinicians from the work of less effective ones (Duncan, Miller, & Sparks, 2004). First, highly effective clinicians pay careful attention to whether clients view their treatment sessions as helpful. These practitioners actively solicit feedback on how treatment is progressing for their clients, starting at the end of visit one. Excellent clinicians don't hedge. They directly ask their clients how comfortable they are with the therapeutic alliance and how well they consider treatment to be going. When they receive negative feedback, these clinicians address them actively and immediately (Miller, Hubble, & Duncan, 2007). Effective clinicians fight the tendency to go on automatic pilot in treatment. They are measuring, strategizing, reviewing, and changing things in the moment as needed based on client feedback. Finally, they have deep knowledge of interpersonal strategies and can make effective use of negative client feedback (Fleming & Asplund, 2007). While it is intimidating, you must ask Juliet every session if she is dissatisfied in any way with how things are going. If you don't ask, or don't take effective steps to address the problematic issues right away, she will end up dropping out or not benefiting from treatment with you.

INDIVIDUALIZING TREATMENT TO ENSURE QUALITY CARE

The clients in this text have had complex stories. For each client, you were given one domain of human complexity to use in individualizing treatment to the unique characteristics and needs of each client. Should you have considered two domains? Three? Deeper and more complex conceptualizations are interesting, but they take more time to develop. Thus, although many domains of human complexity might have value for a particular client, assessing all of them would be an overwhelming, if not impossible, task.

For which clients might it be useful to increase the complexity of your clinical tools? Bohart and Tallman (2010) suggest that you make the choice based on the complexity and severity of the client's presenting problems. If the presenting problems are relatively straight-forward and symptomatic, then short-term treatment may be called for; research indicates that 50% of clients improve in the first 5 to 10 sessions. In contrast, if the presenting problems are severe and complex, then complex case conceptualizations and treatment plans may be needed to guide longer-term treatment; at least 20% to 30% of clients with severe problems need more than 25 sessions and are prone to relapse (Asay & Lambert, 1999).

What if you are unsure of how complex and severe a case is? Consider it severe if the client shows signs of having issues with (a) danger (violence, sexual abuse, suicide, homi-cide), (b) reality contact, and/or (c) substance abuse. Your client may not trust you enough at the beginning to provide you with the information you need to effectively assess these issues. When in doubt, assess further after you have had a chance to build more rapport. Early change is an indication that you are on the right path. It doesn't have to be a big change, but it needs to be a step in the right direction. If this isn't happening, you need to do something differently (Asay & Lambert, 1999; Hubble, Duncan, & Miller, 1999).

Whether the case is complex or not, how do you decide what area of human complex-ity to integrate into your treatment plan? Consider your clients as partners in the concep-tualization process and ask them. If clients say that spirituality is a guiding principle of their lives, then make spirituality a cornerstone of your treatment plan. A strong therapeutic alliance is an important common factor of effective treatment; it is the client's view of the alliance, by the third to fifth session, that is predictive of outcome. Thus, you need to respect the client's point of view on how well the process of treatment is going as well as on what is critical to include in the treatment plan. While it does take more time to write a treatment plan that's individualized to the client, this has been found to enhance the therapeutic alliance (Wampold, 2010).

CASE CONCEPTUALIZATION AND TREATMENT PLANNING OVER TIME

Effective clinical practice does not require a clinician to develop a flawlessly accurate con-ceptualization and treatment plan at the beginning of treatment that is carried out unvary-ingly until termination. Instead, effective treatment may involve shifting, modifying, or refining the treatment plan over time as new information about clients serves to enhance or reframe their current difficulties. Early in treatment, you must make a judgment about what domain or domains of complexity are most critical to your client at the present time. You then develop a theoretical model for understanding the client that incorporates these domains. If the client can change constructively, this may be the only time that you develop a conceptualization and treatment plan.

If barriers to progress arise in treatment, case conceptualizations and treatment plans may need to be revised. The case of Kayla, introduced in Chapter 12, will be further exam-ined to illustrate how a case conceptualization and treatment plan can evolve over the course of treatment. Kayla has returned for treatment two years after she was seen in Chapter 12.

The Case of Kayla

Kayla, a 26-year-old Sioux woman, has just referred herself to a clinician with an expertise in family systems treatment. This is the fifth time Kayla has initiated treatment with a clinician. Kayla was sexually abused by her uncle throughout her childhood and adolescent years. The abuse ended only when she left her home to attend college. Kayla has been in treatment before but never revealed the abuse. She feels she is ready now to face why she has always felt like an outcast.

The Beginning Stage of Treatment

In the first stage of treatment, you and Kayla will work together to form an effective working alliance and develop a clear view of her presenting concerns. A model for understanding Kayla (case conceptualization) will be developed so that a treatment plan can be designed and initiated.

Kayla is intelligent, verbal, and very responsive to your validating comments, and the treatment alliance seems to solidify quickly. Kayla is very articulate in describing her past dysfunctional patterns of relating to others. With support from you, she identifies two areas that she would like to address within treatment. First, she wants to resolve her feelings about her prior sexual abuse so that it no longer influences her relationships with men. Second, in pursuing her own professional goals, she has become alienated from her Sioux parents, and she would like to reconnect with them. At this time, the domains of sexual abuse and race and ethnicity seem most relevant to integrate into a family systems perspective on Kayla.

Kayla, similar to other victims of sexual abuse, has trouble trusting other people. Thus, she intentionally keeps some important information from you. This is not unusual. Conceptualizations and treatment plans developed at the beginning of treatment may well lack some relevant information for understanding the client. This may or may not inhibit Kayla's treatment, as not everything needs to be known about her to develop an effective treatment plan.

The Middle Stage of Treatment

In the middle stage of treatment, the major goals of the treatment plan have been broken down into small steps (accomplishments, tasks, etc.), and you are helping Kayla make active progress in goal attainment. You have developed what you consider to be an effective working relationship with Kayla. She has acquired insight into the role of her prior sexual abuse in her distrust of others, particularly men, and she is reaching out more constructively in interpersonal relationships. No progress has been made, however, on her goal of developing an emotional connection to her parents. In reviewing your case conceptualization, you wonder if, by not being a Sioux, you have been a poor liaison for a family with strong acculturation conflicts. You discuss with Kayla your idea of trying to locate a Sioux healer who might help her in the process of reconnecting with her parents instead of you. She accepts this idea, and you find a healer living in Maine, and he contacts Kayla's parents. They adamantly reject his help and indicate that Kayla is no longer their daughter. The healer then meets with Kayla on several occasions and offers further support to her if she wants it. In his opinion, something besides culture is behind the family's rejection of Kayla. She chooses to continue working on these issues with you rather than the healer. Together, you discuss the need to explore further the structure of her family in terms of its hierarchy, boundaries, and subsystems. Kayla trusts you more than she did in the beginning stage of treatment. This time, as you obtain a more detailed assessment of her family and her role in it, she reveals that she and her mother were physically abused by her father.

You develop a deeper conceptualization integrating cultural, sexual abuse, and violence issues. Using this, you redesign your plan with the potential of danger to Kayla and her mother in mind. The first step of the plan is for Kayla to explore what her goals are for this "family reconnection." Kayla comes to recognize that the emotional connection she wants is with her mother. Kayla contacts her mother again when she knows that her father will be absent. Hesitantly, her mother agrees to one meeting.

In the family session, Kayla's mother clarifies the family struggles that ultimately led to Kayla's being sexually abused when she was 4 years old. Kayla's parents married young and lived below the poverty line on a reservation. Their family structure revolved around the maternal grandmother, who was a highly respected member of the tribe and at the top of the family hierarchy. When Kayla was 1 year old, this grandmother died suddenly from cancer. The grandmother's presence had kept the family living on the reservation. Her death was instrumental in the family (mother, father, older sisters, Kayla, uncle) resettling in Maine. Their life on the reservation had been difficult. There had been no employment for Kayla's father or uncle on the reservation. Her father and uncle, now the heads of the family, quarreled with the tribal elders over the wisdom of leaving the reservation in search of work. They moved to Maine in response to advertisements for work within the tree industry. When they arrived, however, they faced active discrimination from their White neighbors, but they worked and saved; they felt trapped in Maine by economic necessity. The adults' suspicion of Whites turned into an implacable hatred when they bought a tree farm from a retiring couple amid community action to stop the sale from being finalized; once their purchase was confirmed, they built strong boundaries between themselves and the community. They had rejected their tribe and thus had no one to turn to for support in their struggles but one another. Kayla's father and uncle turned to alcohol to dampen their feelings of frustration and anger.

As the family grew more and more isolated, the domestic violence and child abuse began. When Kayla was 4, her battered condition was noticed by community members, who reported the family to child protective services (CPS). CPS insisted that Kayla be sent temporarily either to her uncle's home or to an outside foster placement. Although having her move in with her uncle seemed at first to be a good solution to the intrusion of the Whites in their lives, Kayla's mother began to suspect the sexual abuse about two years later. It still took her another year to get her husband to agree to bring Kayla back home. CPS did not intervene. Her mother remained silent about both the past physical abuse and the current sexual abuse because she believed that no good would come of discussing them. Kayla's mother had developed a code of silence. When she was silent, she was not beaten; if she was silent, problems could be forgotten. To survive, she felt Kayla must also develop this code.

Kayla and her mother developed a deeper connection with each other during this one session. The emotional neglect Kayla had experienced throughout her childhood was now reframed as her mother's best attempts to teach her to survive in a dangerous world. Kayla wanted further sessions with her mother and expressed fear for her mother's safety. Her mother was not afraid. She said that the domestic violence had ended when Kayla had moved away. Her mother's code of silence had been transformed into a code of loyalty. Her mother believed in the spiritual benefit of enduring hardship and living in balance. She and her husband had survived poverty, discrimination, and loneliness together. She could not come back for further sessions because she believed this would be a betrayal of her husband's trust. She felt strongly that Kayla would never be safe at home and should not return. Discussing the abuse issues had freed Kayla's mother from her torment of silence. She was able to express her love for Kayla directly and to encourage her to find a balance for herself in her new life as a writer.

As a result of this family intervention, Kayla understood her role as "outcast" or "scapegoat" in her family. She symbolized for them their rejection from White society, their poverty, and their pain. Through casting her out, they were distancing themselves from some of the trauma that had engulfed their lives. She recognized her role now and was able to reject its validity for herself as a person. It was true that White society had rejected her parents, but she had had no part in the decision to leave the reservation. CPS had crossed the family's boundaries, but this had been due to her father's physical abuse of her. Her uncle's sexual abuse of her had led to a disruption of the family hierarchy because her mother had challenged her father's authority for the first time by bringing Kayla home, but again, the disruption had been a result of her uncle's actions, not Kayla's. She had developed loyalties to White teachers and White clinicians; however, this came as a response to her rejection by her own family.

When Kayla was a child, a feedback loop had developed, with family rejection leading Kayla to identify more strongly with White community members, leading to greater family rejection. In trying to meet her needs for nurturance, Kayla had unintentionally alienated herself from her cultural heritage. As an adult, Kayla's chronic emptiness was relieved when the family code of silence was broken and Kayla could be fully aware of her past traumas. Kayla was able to free herself from her emptiness and fill it with pride in Greenpeace's efforts to take care of the land and with new efforts to establish emotional connections with others.

The End Stage of Treatment

At the end of treatment, the clinician is helping Kayla consolidate the gains she has made and empowering her with a sense of self-efficacy for addressing any further concerns. Would it be useful at this point to proceed with a deeper case conceptualization? This could be useful in two circumstances. One circumstance would be if Kayla might be returning to treatment. A revised conceptualization could be a resource for guiding her next treatment. Is this likely? Kayla has participated in treatment on many occasions, starting when a school counselor noticed her isolation when she was 14 years old. Each time, she made effective use of treatment and continued in the process of constructive change. Once she developed the necessary skills or insights to move forward, she terminated treatment and continued the process on her own. When her self-change efforts became stymied, she reinitiated treatment. Thus, although Kayla has shown herself to be a bright and resilient individual who can learn effectively both within and outside treatment, her history suggests that she might resume treatment at some point.

A second circumstance that would justify an end-stage conceptualization would be if Kayla's treatment was being reviewed for ethical, insurance, or other professional purposes. An end-stage conceptualization could be used to support your judgments concerning the type and length of treatment that she received. The following is an end-stage premise to support Kayla's long-term treatment.

Premise

Kayla came from a Sioux family consisting of her, her mother, her father, her two sisters, and her paternal aunt and uncle. The family was socially isolated from other tribe members as a result of geographic and economic constraints. The family members intentionally isolated themselves from their White neighbors in reaction to racism and discrimination. The family structure was chaotic. There were few boundaries between adults and children, and family subsystems were emotionally disengaged from one another. The boundaries between the family and the outside world were rigid and inflexible. Within the family, Kayla's developmental needs for nurturance and guidance were either ignored or responded to with physical, sexual, and emotional abuse. She often considered suicide. In reaching out for help to White teachers and clinicians, Kayla received support. These contacts, however, intensified her acculturation conflicts. Despite her traumatic history, Kayla developed many strengths based on her family's cultural emphasis on self-sufficiency and attunement with nature. As an adult, she is an intelligent, self-directed individual with a well-developed social conscience. This is epitomized by her success as a writer for Greenpeace. Kayla attended a total of 44 individual treatment sessions and one family session with her mother. This long-term treatment is justified based on her severe and complex history of victimization, social isolation, and cultural alienation. These factors, coupled with her family history of alcohol abuse, all placed Kayla at risk for suicide or other self-destructive behavior.

CONCLUSION

Human beings are complex, and our conceptualizations will of necessity consist of only part of the whole picture that is a human being. This book is only an introduction to case conceptualization and treatment planning. There are many other psychological theories, many more domains of complexity, and many more thought-provoking research articles to be mastered as you work toward developing your own personal style as an effective and competent clinician. It is a bias of this book that to become one of those highly effective clinicians, you must be open to new research developments and continue to strengthen your skills throughout a lifetime of clinical practice.

RED-FLAG GUIDELINES FOR DEVELOPING A CASE CONCEPTUALIZATION AND TREATMENT PLAN

1. Distill the theory down to its major assumptions to ensure that you grasp it.

2. Apply these assumptions to the specifics of your client.

3. Review the domain or domains of human complexity that are most relevant and distill them down to guidelines that can be applied to your client.

4. Integrate the information from Steps 2 and 3 into a case conceptualization.

5. Develop a treatment plan that is suited to the uniqueness of the client and that actively takes advantage of the client's strengths.

6. Actively monitor and review treatment in collaboration with the client.

7. If the client provides negative feedback about treatment or about the treatment relationship, actively initiate change.

References

Acierno, R., Hernandez, M. A., Amstadter, A. B., Resnick, H., Steve, K., Muzzy, W., & Kilpatrick, D. G. (2010). Prevalence and correlates of emotional, physical, sexual, and financial abuse and potential neglect in the United States: The national elder mistreatment study. *American Journal of Public Health, 100*(2), 292–297.

Addis, M. E., & Mahalik, J. R. (2003). Men, masculinity, and the contexts of help seeking. *American Psychologist, 58,* 5–14.

Albee, G. (1977, February). The Protestant ethic, sex, and psychotherapy. *American Psychologist,* 150–161.

American Civil Liberties Union. (1998, July). *ACLU factsheet: Chronology of bottoms vs bottoms: A lesbian mother's fight for her son.* New York, NY: Author. Retrieved June 19, 2008, from https://www.aclu.org/lgbt-rights_hiv-aids/overview-lesbian-and-gay-parenting-adoption-and-foster-care

American Psychiatric Association. (2002). *Documentation of psychotherapy by psychiatrists: Resource document* [Ref. #200202]. Washington, DC: Author.

American Psychological Association. (2002a). Criteria for practice guideline development and evaluation. *American Psychologist, 57*(12), 1048–1051.

American Psychological Association. (2002b). *A reference for professionals: Developing adolescents.* Retrieved from http://www.apa.org/pi/families/resources/develop.pdf

American Psychological Association. (2004). Guidelines for psychological practice with older adults. *American Psychologist, 59,* 236–260.

American Psychological Association. (2005a). *Lesbian and gay parenting.* Retrieved from http://www.apa.org/pi/lgbt/resources/parenting.aspx

American Psychological Association. (2005b). *Resolution on male violence against women.* Washington, DC: American Psychological Association.

American Psychological Association. (2007a). Guidelines for psychological practice with girls and women. *American Psychologist, 62,* 949–979.

American Psychological Association. (2007b). *Parenting: Communication tips for parents.* Retrieved May 29, 2009, from http://www.apahelpcenter.org/articles/article.php?id=48

American Psychological Association. (2007c). Record keeping guidelines. *American Psychologist, 62*(9), 993–1004.

American Psychological Association. (2008). *Answers to your questions: For a better understanding of sexual orientation and homosexuality.* Washington, DC: Author. Retrieved from http://www.apa.org/topics/sorientation.pdf

American Psychological Association. (2012). Guidelines for psychological practice with lesbian, gay, and bisexual Clients. *American Psychologist, 67,* 10–42.

American Psychiatric Association (2013). *Diagnostic and statistical manual of mental disorders* (5th ed.; DSM-5). Washington, DC: American Psychiatric Publishing.

American Psychological Association. (2013). *Guidelines for psychological practice with older adults.* Retrieved from http://www.apa.org/practice/guidelines/older-adults.aspx?item=9

American Psychological Association. (2014). *Just the facts about sexual orientation & youth: A primer for principals, educators, & school personnel.* Retrieved April 26, 2014, from http://www.apa.org/pi/lgbt/resources/just-the-facts.aspx

475

American Psychiatric Association, Commission on Psychotherapy by Psychiatrists. (2000). Position statement on therapies focused on attempts to change sexual orientation (reparative or conversion therapies). *American Journal of Psychiatry, 157,* 1719–1721.

American Psychological Association, Committee on Lesbian and Gay Concerns. (1991). *American Psychological Association policy statements on lesbian and gay issues.* Washington, DC: American Psychological Association.

American Psychological Association, Committee on Lesbian, Gay, Bisexual, and Transgender Concerns. (2006). *Answers to your questions about transgender people, gender identity, and gender expression.* Retrieved August 22, 2013, from http://www.apa.org/topics/transgender.html

American Psychological Association, Joint Task Force. (2006, July). *Summary of guidelines for psychological practice with girls and women.* Washington, DC: American Psychological Association.

American Psychological Association, Task Force on Gender Identity, Gender Variance, and Intersex Conditions. (2006). *Answers to your questions about transgender people, gender identity, and gender expression.* Retrieved April 23, 2014, from http:/www.apa.org/topics/sexuality/transgender.pdf

Anderson, R. (2011). Dynamics of economic well-being: Poverty, 2004–2006. *Current Population Reports* (pp. 70–123). Washington, DC: U.S. Census Bureau.

Archer, J. (2002). Sex differences in aggression between heterosexual partners: A meta-analytic review. *Psychological Bulletin, 126,* 651–681.

Asay, T. P., & Lambert, M. J. (1999). The empirical case for the common factors in therapy: Quantitative findings. In M. A. Hubble, B. L. Duncan, & S. D. Miller (Eds.), *The heart & soul of change: What works in therapy* (pp. 23–55). Washington, DC: American Psychological Association.

Asendorpf, J. B. (1990). Beyond social withdrawal: Shyness, unsociability, and peer avoidance. *Human Development, 33,* 250–259.

Asendorpf, J. (1993). Abnormal shyness in children. *Journal of Child Psychology and Psychiatry and Allied Disciplines, 34,* 1069–1081.

Association for Lesbian, Gay, Bisexual, and Transgender Issues in Counseling. (2012). *ALGBTIC competencies for counseling lesbian, gay, bisexual, transgender, queer, questioning, intersex, and ally individuals.* Retrieved from http://www.counseling.org/docs/ethics/algbtic-2012-07.pdf?sfvrsn = 2

Atkinson, D. R., Morten, G., & Sue, D. W. (1979). *Counseling American minorities: A cross-cultural perspective.* Boston, MA: McGraw-Hill.

Aud, S., Fox, M.A., & KewalRamani, A. (2010). *Status and trends in the education of racial and ethnic groups* (NCES 2010-015). Washington, DC: National Center for Education Statistics.

Bacigalupe, G. (2008). *SOAP notes handout.* Retrieved May 23, 2008, from http://www.umb.edu/forum/1/family_therapy_internship/res/SOAP_Notes_Handout.doc

Bancroft, L., & Silverman, J. (2002). *The batterer as parent: Addressing the impact of domestic violence on family dynamics.* Thousand Oaks, CA: SAGE.

Bancroft, L., & Silverman, J. (2004/2005, Fall). The parenting practices of men who batter. *APSAC Advisor, 11–14.*

Bandura, A. (1986). *Social foundations of thought and action: A social-cognitive theory.* Englewood Cliffs, NJ: Prentice Hall.

Barnett, R. C., & Hyde, J. S. (2001). Women, men, work, and family: An expansionist theory. *American Psychologist, 56,* 781–796.

Bartoli, E., & Gillem, A. R. (2008). Continuing to depolarize the debate on sexual orientation and religion: Identity and the therapeutic process. *Professional Psychology: Research and Practice, 39*(2), 202–209.

Bates, J. E., & Pettit, G. S. (2007). Temperament, parenting, and socialization. In J. E. Grusec & P. D. Lastings (Eds.), *Handbook of socialization: Theory and research* (pp. 153–190). New York, NY: Guilford Press.

Bauermeister, J. A., Johns, M. M., Sandfort, T. G. M., Eisenberg, A., Grossman, A. H., & D'Augelli, A. R. (2010). Relationship trajectories and psychological well-being among sexual minority youth. *Journal of Youth and Adolescence, 39*(10), 1148–1163. doi: 10.1007/s10964-010-9557-y

Baumrind, D. (1967). Child care practices anteceding three patterns of preschool behavior. *Genetic Psychology Monographs, 75,* 43–88.

Beck, A. T. (1991). Cognitive therapy: A 30-year retrospective. *American Psychologist, 46,* 368–375.

Beck, A. T., & Weishaar, M. (2000). Cognitive therapy. In R. Corsini & D. Wedding (Eds.), *Current psychotherapies* (6th ed., pp. 241–272). Itasca, IL: F. E. Peacock.

Beck Institute for Cognitive Therapy and Research. (2008). Retrieved April 8, 2009, from http://www.beckinstitute.org/Library/InfoManage/Guide.asp?FolderID=200&SessionID={1C10428F-9375-4F78-89AF-E9B106C7DD19}

Beck, J. S. (2011). *Cognitive behavior therapy: Basics and beyond* (2nd ed.). New York, NY: Guilford Press.

Beckstead, L., & Israel, T. (2007). Affirmative counseling and psychotherapy focused on issues related to sexual orientation conflicts. In K. J. Bieschke, R. M. Perez, & K. A. DuBord (Eds.), *Handbook of counseling and psychotherapy with lesbian, gay, and transgendered clients* (2nd ed., pp. 221–240). Washington, DC: American Psychological Association.

Belgrave, F. Z., Chase-Vaughn, G., Gray, F., Addison, J. D., & Cherry, V. R. (2000). The effectiveness of a culture- and gender-specific intervention for increasing resiliency among African American preadolescent females. *Journal of Black Psychology, 26,* 133–147.

Bemak, F., & Chung, R. C.-Y. (2008). Counseling refuges and migrants. In P. B. Pedersen, J. G. Draguns, W. J. Lonner, & J. E. Trimble (Eds.), *Counseling across cultures* (6th ed., pp. 307–324). Thousand Oaks, CA: SAGE.

Bergen, G., Chen, L. H., Warner, M., & Fingerhut, L. A. (2008). *Injury in the United States: 2007, Chartbook.* Hyattsville, MD: National Center for Health Statistics.

Bernal, G., & Enchautegui-de-Jesus, N. (1994). Latinos and Latinas in community psychology: A review of the literature. *American Journal of Community Psychology, 22*(4), 531–557.

Billie, J. E. (2013). Like the old Florida flag: "Let us alone!" *Seminal Tribune: Voice of the Unconquered.* Retrieved May 1, 2014, from http://www.semtribe.com/SeminoleTribune/Archive/2013/SeminoleTribune_October%2025_2013v2.pdf

Black, M. C., Basile, K. C., Breiding, M. J., Smith, S. G., Walters, M. L., Merrick, M. T., . . . Stevens, M. R. (2011). *The National Intimate Partner and Sexual Violence Survey (NISVS): 2010 summary report.* Atlanta, GA: Centers for Disease Control and Prevention, National Center for Injury Prevention and Control.

Bohart, A. C., & Tallman, K. (2010). Clients: The neglected common factor in psychotherapy. In B. L. Duncan, S. D. Miller, B. E. Wampold, & M. A. Hubble (Ed.), *The heart and soul of change: Delivering what works in therapy* (2nd ed., pp. 83–111). Washington, DC: American Psychological Association.

Books, S. (2007). Devastation and disregard: Reflections on Katrina, child poverty, and educational opportunity. In S. Books (Ed.), *Invisible children in the society and its schools* (3rd ed., pp. 1–22). Mahwah, NJ: Lawrence Erlbaum.

Bowlby, J. (1973). *Attachment and loss: Vol. 2. Separation, anxiety, and anger.* New York, NY: Basic Books.

Boyd-Franklin, N., & Lockwood, T. W. (2009). Spirituality and religion: Implications for psychotherapy with African American families. In F. Walsh (Ed.), *Spiritual resources in family therapy* (2nd ed., pp. 141–155). New York, NY: Guilford Press.

Bramlett, B. H., Gimpel, J. G., & Lee, F. E. (2011). The political ecology of opinion in big-donor neighborhoods. *Political Behavior, 33,* 565–600.

Brannon, L. (2002). *Gender: Psychological perspectives.* Boston, MA: Allyn & Bacon.

Brault, M. W. (2012). *Americans with disabilities: 2010.* Washington, DC: U.S. Census Bureau. Retrieved June 9, 2014, from http://www.census.gov/prod/2012pubs/p70-131.pdf

Brems, C. (2008). *A comprehensive guide to child psychotherapy and counseling* (3rd ed.). Long Grove, IL: Waveland Press.

Brodkin, K. (2001). How Jews became White. In P. S. Rothenberg (Ed.), *Race, class, and gender in the United States: An integrated study* (5th ed.). New York, NY: Worth.

Broidy, L. M., Nagin, D. S., Tremblay, R. E., Bates, J. E., Brame, B., Dodge, K. A., . . . Vitaro, F. (2003). Developmental trajectories of childhood disruptive behaviors and adolescent delinquency: A six-site, cross-national study. *Developmental Psychology, 39*(2), 222–245.

Brown, D. W., Anda, R. F., Tiemeier, H., Felitti, V. J., Edwards, V. J., Croft, J. B., & Giles, W. H. (2009). Adverse childhood experiences and the risk of premature mortality. *American Journal of Preventive Medicine, 37*(5), 389–396. doi: 10.1016/j.amepre.2009.06.021

Capps, R., & Fix, M. E. (2005, November). *Undocumented immigrants: Myths and reality.* Retrieved from http://www.urban.org

Carpenter, S. (2001, October). Sleep deprivation may be undermining teen health. *Monitor on Psychology,* 42–45.

Carreon, G., Drake, C., & Barton, A. C. (2005). The importance of presence: Immigrant parents' school engagement experiences. *American Educational Research Journal, 42,* 465–498.

Carson, E. A., & Golinelli, D. (2013, December). *Prisoners in 2012. Trends in admissions and releases, 1991–2012.* U.S. Department of Justice, Office of Justice Programs, Bureau of Justice Statistics. Retrieved May 1, 2014, from http://www.ojp.usdoj.gov

Carson, E. A., & Sabol, W. J. (2012, December). *Prisoners in 2011* (NCJ 239808). U.S. Department of Justice, Office of Justice Programs, Bureau of Justice Statistics. Retrieved May 1, 2014, from http://www.bjs.gov/content/pub/pdf/p11.pdf

Case, K. A. (2012). Discovering the privilege of Whiteness: White women's reflections on anti-racist identity and ally behavior. *Journal of Social Issues, 68,* 78–96.

Caughy, M. O., O'Campo, P. J., & Muntaner, C. (2004). Experiences of racism among African American parents and the mental health of their preschool-aged children. *American Journal of Public Health, 94,* 2118–2124.

Centers for Disease Control and Prevention. (1998). Lifetime annual incidence of intimate partner violence and resulting injuries. *Morbidity and Mortality Weekly Report, 47,* 846–853.

Centers for Disease Control and Prevention. (2002). Abuse of the elderly. *World Report on Violence and Health.* Retrieved May 1, 2014, from http://www.who.int/violence_injury_prevention/violence/global_campaign/en/chap5.pdf

Centers for Disease Control and Prevention. (2006). *Intimate partner violence during pregnancy: A guide for clinicians.* Retrieved October 25, 2008, from http://www.cdc.gov/Reproductivehealth/violence/IntimatePartnerViolence/sld001.html

Centers for Disease Control and Prevention. (2013a, May 16). Mental health surveillance among children—United States 2005–2011. *Morbidity and Mortality Weekly Report, 62,* 1–35. Retrieved March 11, 2014, from http://www.cdc.gov/mmwr/preview/mmwrhtml/su6202a1.htm?s_cid=su6202a1_w

Centers for Disease Control and Prevention. (2013b). *Saving lives in protecting people: Preventing violence against children and youth.* Retrieved March 11, 2014, from http://www.cdc.gov/injury/about/focus-cm.html

Centers for Disease Control and Prevention. (2014). *Suicide prevention: Youth suicide.* Retrieved March 11, 2014, from http://www.cdc.gov/violenceprevention/pub/youth_suicide.html

Centers for Disease Control and Prevention, National Vital Statistics System, National Center for Health Statistics. (2010). *10 leading causes of death by age group, United States—2010.* Retrieved February 2, 2014, from http://www.cdc.gov/injury/wisqars/LeadingCauses.html

Central Intelligence Agency. (2013). *World factbook*. Retrieved January 23, 2013, from https://www.cia .gov/library/publications/the-world-factbook/geos/print/country/countrypdf_mx.pdf

Children's Defense Fund. (2008). *The state of America's children 2008*. Washington, DC: Author.

Christian, M. D., & Barbarin, O. A. (2001). Cultural resources and psychological adjustment of African American children: Effects of spirituality and racial attribution. *Journal of Black Psychology, 27*(1), 43–63.

Chung, R. C.-Y., Bemak, F., & Kudo-Grabosky, T. (2011). Multicultural-social justice leadership strategies: Counseling and advocacy with immigrants. *Journal for Social Action in Counseling and Psychology, 3*, 86–102.

Cochran, S. (2001). Emerging issues in research on lesbian and gay men's mental health: Does sexual orientation really matter? *American Psychologist, 56*, 931–947.

Comas-Diaz, L. (2008). The Black Madonna: The psychospiritual feminism of Guadalupe, Kali, and Monserrat. In L. B. Silverstein & T. J. Goodrich (Eds.), *Feminist family therapy: Empowerment in social context* (pp. 147–160). Washington, DC: American Psychological Association.

Comas-Diaz, L. (2012). *Multicultural care: A clinician's guide to cultural competence*. Washington, DC: American Psychological Association.

Comer, J. P., & Hill, H. (1985). Social policy and the mental health of Black children. *Journal of the Academy of Child Psychiatry, 24*(2), 175–181.

Consortium for Longitudinal Studies of Child Abuse and Neglect. (2006). *LONGSCAN research briefs* (Vol. 2). Retrieved August 22, 2008, from http://www.iprc.unc.edu/longscan/pages/researchbriefs/ LONGSCAN%20Research%20Briefs%20(Volume%202).pdf

Cooper, L., & Cates, P. (2006). *Too high a price: The case against restricting gay parenting*. New York, NY: American Civil Liberties Union Foundation.

Copen, C. E., Daniels, K., Vespa, J., & Mosher, W. D. (2012). First marriages in the United States: Data from the 2006–2010 National Survey of Family Growth. Centers for Disease Control and Prevention, Division of Vital Statistics. *National Health Statistic Reports, 49*, 1–22.

Coplan, R., Prakash, K., O'Neil, K., & Armer, M. (2004). Do you "want" to play? Distinguishing between conflicted shyness and social disinterest in early childhood. *Developmental Psychology, 2*, 244–258.

Crawford, M. (2006). *Transformations: Women, gender & psychology* (2nd ed.). New York: NY: McGraw-Hill.

Currie, C., Zanotti, C., Morgan, A., Currie, D., de Looze M., Roberts, C., . . . Barnekow, V. (2012). Health behavior in school-aged children: International report from the 2009/2010 survey. *Health Policy for Children and Adolescents,* No. 6. Geneva, Switzerland: World Health Organization.

Curtis, J. (2013). Middle class identity in the modern world: How politics and economics matter. *Canadian Sociological Association, 50*(2), 204–226.

DeAngelis, T. (2002). A new generation of issues for LGBT clients. *Monitor on Psychology, 33*(2), 42–44.

Delgado, G. (2006). Mexican American religion and spirituality. In E. Dowling & W. Scarlett (Eds.), *Encyclopedia of religious and spiritual development* (pp. 289–291). Thousand Oaks, CA: SAGE. doi: 10.4135/9781412952477.n155

Delphin, M., & Rowe, M. (2008). Continuing education in cultural competence for community mental health practitioners. *Professional Psychology: Research and Practice, 39*(2), 182–191.

DeNavas-Walt, C., Proctor, B. D., & Smith, J. C. (2013). Income, poverty, and health insurance coverage in the United States: 2012. *Current Population Reports,* P60-245. Washington, DC: U.S. Census Bureau. Retrieved May 1, 2014, from https://www.census.gov/prod/2013pubs/p60-245.pdf

Denham, S. A., Basset, H. H., & Wyatt, T. (2007). The socialization of emotional competence. In J. E. Grusec & P. D. Hastings (Eds.), *Handbook of socialization: Theory and research* (pp. 614–637). New York, NY: Guilford Press.

Dixon, L., & Stern, R. K. (2004). *Compensation for losses from the 9/11 attacks* (Monograph MG-264-IC, p. xviii). Santa Monica, CA: RAND Corporation.

Dixon, S. V., Graber, J. A., & Brooks-Gunn, J. (2008). The roles of respect for parental authority and parenting practices in parent–child conflict among African American, Latino, and European American families. *Journal of Family Psychology, 22*(1), 1–10.

Dodge, K. A., Pettit, G. S., Bates, J. E., & Valente, E. (1995). Social information-processing patterns partially mediate the effect of early physical abuse on later conduct problems. *Journal of Abnormal Psychology, 104*, 632–643.

Dong, X. Q., Simon, M. A., Beck, T. T., Farran, C., McCann, J. J., Mendes de Leon, C. F., . . . Evans, D. A. (2011). Elder abuse and mortality: The role of psychological and social wellbeing. *Gerontology, 57*, 549–558.

Du Bois, W. E. B. (1997). *The souls of Black folk.* Boston, MA: Bedford Books. (Original work published 1903)

Duncan, B., Miller, S., & Hubble, M. (2007, November/December). How being bad can make you better. *Psychotherapy Networker*, pp. 36–45, 57.

Duncan, B. L., Miller, S. D., & Sparks, J. A. (2004). *The heroic client: A revolutionary way to improve effectiveness through client-directed, outcome-informed therapy* (Rev. ed.). San Francisco, CA: Jossey-Bass.

Duran, E. (2006). *Healing the soul wound: Counseling with American Indians and other Native peoples.* New York, NY: Teachers College Press.

Dye, M. L., & Davis, K. E. (2003). Stalking and psychological abuse: Common factors and relationship-specific characteristics. *Violence and Victims, 18*, 163–180.

Eagleton Institute of Politics. (2014). *Current numbers of women officeholders.* Rutgers, the State University of New Jersey, Center for American Women and Politics. Retrieved March 2, 2014, from http://www.cawp.rutgers.edu

Editors of Consumer Reports. (2004, October). Drugs versus talk therapy. *Consumer Reports,* pp. 22–29.

Egan, G. (2007). *The skilled helper* (8th ed.). Belmont, CA: Brooks/Cole.

Elliott, R., & Greenberg, L. S. (1995). Experiential therapy in practice: The process-experiential approach. In B. Bongar & L. E. Beutler (Eds.), *Comprehensive textbook of psychotherapy: Theory and practice* (pp. 123–139). New York, NY: Oxford University Press.

Englund, M. M., Kuo, S. I.-C., Puig, J., & Collins, W. A. (2011). Early roots of adult competence: The significance of close relationships from infancy to early adulthood. *International Journal of Behavior Development, 35*(6): 490–496. doi: 10.1177/0165025411422994.

Ennis, S. R., Ríos-Vargas, M., & Albert, N. G. (2011, May). *The Hispanic population: 2010* (2010 Census Briefs). Retrieved from http://www.census.gov/prod/cen2010/briefs/c2010br-04.pdf

Erikson, E. H. (1963). *Childhood and society* (2nd ed.). New York, NY: Norton.

ESPN.com News Services. (2005, August 12). NCAA American Indian mascot band will begin Feb. 1. *ESPN College Sports.* Retrieved May 1, 2014, from http://sports.espn.go.com/ncaa/news/story?id=2125735

Evans, G. W. (2004). The environment of childhood poverty. *American Psychologist, 59*(2), 77–92.

Evans, G. W., Li, D., & Whipple, S. S. (2013). Cumulative risk in child development. *Psychological Bulletin, 139*(6), 1342–1396. doi: 10.1037/a0031808

Fantuzzo, J., & Mohr, W. (1999). Prevalence and effects of child exposure to domestic violence. *Future of Children, 9*(2), 21–32.

Feather, N. T., & Sherman, R. (2002). Envy, resentment, Schadenfreude, and sympathy: Reactions to deserved and undeserved achievement and subsequent failure. *Personality and Social Psychology Bulletin, 28*, 953–961.

Feder, J., Levant, R. F., & Dean, J. (2007). Boys and violence: A gender-informed analysis. *Professional Psychology: Research and Practice, 38*, 385–391.

Feeney, J. A. (2008). Adult romantic attachment: Developments in the study of couple relationships. In J. Cassidy & P. R. Shaver (Eds.), *Handbook of attachment: Theory, research, and clinical applications* (2nd ed., pp. 456–481). New York, NY: Guilford Press.

Felitti, V. J. (2002). The relation between adverse childhood experiences and adult health: Turning gold into lead. *Permanente Journal, 6*(1), 44–47.

Finkelhor, D., Turner, H., Ormrod, R., & Hamby, S. (2005). The victimization of children and youth: A comprehensive national survey. *Child Maltreatment, 10*(1), 5–25.

Finkelhor, D., Turner, H., Ormrod, R., & Hamby, S. (2009). Violence, abuse, and crime exposure in a national sample of children and youth. *Pediatrics, 124,* 1411–1423.

Fleming, J., & Asplund, J. (2007). *Human sigma.* New York, NY: Gallup Press.

Ford, D. Y. (1997). Counseling middle-class African Americans. In C. C. Lee (Ed.), *Multicultural issues in counseling* (2nd ed., pp. 81–108). Alexandria, VA: American Counseling Association.

Frankenberg, R. (2008). Whiteness as an "unmarked" cultural category. In K. E. Rosenblum & T. C. Travis (Eds.), *The meaning of difference: American constructions of race, sex and gender, social class, sexual orientation, and disability* (5th ed., pp. 81–87). Boston, MA: McGraw-Hill.

Freedom to Marry. (2013). *Winning the freedom to marry: Progress in the states.* Retrieved August 16, 2014, from http://www.freedomtomarry.org/states/.

French, L. A. (1997). *Counseling American Indians.* Lanham, MD: University Press of America.

Frieze, I. H. (2005). Female violence against intimate partners: An introduction. *Psychology of Women Quarterly, 29,* 229–237.

Fuligni, A. (1998). Authority, autonomy, and parent–adolescent conflict and cohesion: Study of adolescents from Mexican, Chinese, Filipino, and European backgrounds. *Developmental Psychology, 34,* 782–792.

Garbarino, J. (1999). *Lost boys: Why our sons turn violent and how we can save them.* New York, NY: Free Press.

Gates, G. (2010). *Sexual minorities in the 2008: General Social Survey: Coming out and demographic characteristics.* Retrieved May 1, 2014, from http://williamsinstitute.law.ucla.edu/wp-content/uploads/Gates-Sexual-Minorities-2008-GSS-Oct-2010.pdf

Ge, X., Conger, R. D., & Elder, G. H., Jr. (2001). Pubertal transition, stressful life events, and the emergence of gender differences in adolescent depressive symptoms. *Developmental Psychology, 37,* 404–417.

Glaze, L. E., & Herberman, E. (2013, December). *Correctional populations in the United States, 2012* (NCJ 24393). U.S. Department of Justice, Office of Justice Programs, Bureau of Justice Statistics. Retrieved February 9, 2014, from http://www.bjs.gov/content/pub/pdf/cpus12.pdf

Goodrich, T. J. (2008). A feminist family therapist's work is never done. In L. B. Silverstein & T. J. Goodrich (Eds.), *Feminist family therapy: Empowerment in social context* (pp. 3–15). Washington, DC: American Psychological Association.

Graber, J. A, Lewinsohn, P. M., Seeley, J. R., & Brooks-Gunn, J. (1997). Is psychopathology associated with the timing of puberty development? *Journal of the American Academy of Child and Adolescent Psychiatry, 36,* 1768–1776.

Graham-Kevan, N., & Archer, J. (2005). Investigating three explanations of women's relationship aggression. *Psychology of Women Quarterly, 29*(3), 270–277.

Greenberg, L., & Goldman, R. (2007). Case-formulation in emotion-focused therapy. In T. D. Eells (Ed.), *Handbook of psychotherapy case formulation* (2nd ed., pp. 379–411). New York, NY: Guilford Press.

Greene, B. (1997). Psychotherapy with African American women: Integrating feminist and psychodynamic models. *Journal of Smith College Studies in Social Work: Theoretical, Research, Practice and Educational Perspectives for Understanding and Working With African American Clients, 67,* 299–322.

Grusec, J. E., & Goodnow, J. J. (1994). Impact of parental discipline methods on the child's internalization of values: A reconceptualization of current points of view. *Developmental Psychology, 30,* 4–19.

Haas, E., Hill, R., Lambert, M. M., & Morrell, B. (2002). Do early responders to psychotherapy maintain treatment gains? *Journal of Clinical Psychology, 58,* 1157–1172.

Hagan, J. (2013, June 27). The 10 dumbest things ever said about same-sex marriage: The worst logical fails, nastiest hate speech and most deeply confused metaphors from the anti-gay movement. *Rolling Stones.* Retrieved April 18, 2014, from http://www.rollingstone.com/politics/news/the-10-dumbest-things-ever-said-about-same-sex-marriage-20130627#ixzz2xJU8QlEU

Halberstadt, A. G., & Eaton, K. L. (2003). A meta-analysis of family expressiveness and children's emotion expressiveness and understanding. *Marriage and Family Review, 34,* 35–62.

Haldeman, D. (2000). Therapeutic responses to sexual orientation: Psychology's evolution. In B. Greene & G. L. Croom (Eds.), *Education, research, and practice in lesbian, gay, bisexual, and transgendered psychology: A resource manual* (pp. 244–262). Thousand Oaks, CA: SAGE.

Hall, R. L., & Greene, B. (2008). Contemporary African American families. In L. B. Silverstein & T. J. Goodrich (Eds.), *Feminist family therapy: Empowerment in social context* (pp. 107–120). Washington, DC: American Psychological Association.

Hamby, S., & Grych, J. (2013). *The web of violence: Exploring connections among different forms of interpersonal violence and abuse.* New York, NY: Springer.

Hanson, R. F., Self-Brown, S., Fricker-Elhai, A. E., Kilpatrick, D. G., Saunders, B. E., & Resnick, H. S. (2006). The relations between family environment and violence exposure among youth: Findings from the National Survey of Adolescents. *Child Maltreatment, 11,* 3–15.

Hays, P. (2008). *Addressing cultural complexities in practice: Assessment, diagnosis, and therapy* (2nd ed.). Washington, DC: American Psychological Association.

Hays, P. (2013). *Connecting across cultures: The helper's toolkit.* Thousand Oaks, CA: SAGE.

Herek, G. M., & Garnets, L. D. (2007). Sexual orientation and mental health. *Annual Review of Clinical Psychology, 3,* 353–375.

Hershberger, S. L., & D'Augelli, A. R. (2000). Issues in counseling lesbian, gay, and bisexual adolescents. In R. Perez, K. DeBord, & K. Bieschke (Eds.), *Handbook of counseling and psychotherapy with lesbian, gay, and bisexual clients* (pp. 225–247). Washington, DC: American Psychological Association.

History Learning Site. (2008). *Family life.* Retrieved August 13, 2008, from http://www.historylearning site.co.uk/familylife.htm

Hofmann, A. D., & Greydanus, D. E. (1997). *Adolescent medicine.* Stamford, CT: Appleton & Lange.

Holmes, S. A., & Morin, R. (2006, June). Being a Black man: The poll. *Washington Post.* Retrieved June 5, 2009, from http://www.washingtonpost.com/wp-dyn/content/discussion/2006/06/02/DI2006060201012.html

Holt, M. K., Finkelhor, D., & Kantor, G. K. (2007). Multiple victimization experiences of urban elementary school students: Associations with psychosocial functioning and academic performance. *Child Abuse and Neglect, 31,* 503–515.

Hubble, M. A., Duncan, B. L., & Miller, S. D. (1999). Directing attention to what works. In M. A. Hubble, B. L. Duncan, & S. D. Miller (Eds.), *The heart and soul of change: What works in therapy* (pp. 407–447). Washington, DC: American Psychological Association.

Human Rights Campaign. (2000). *Finally free* [Research report]. Washington, DC: Author.

Ignatieff, M. (2005, September 25). The broken contract. *New York Times.* Retrieved June 13, 2009, from http://www.nytimes.com/2005/09/25/magazine/25wwln.html?_r=1&scp=1&sq=Ignatieff%20 broken%20contract&st=cse

Ignatiev, N. (1995). *How the Irish became White.* New York, NY: Routledge.

Indians.org. (2014). *Native American healing.* Retrieved May 1, 2014, from http://www.indians.org/articles/native-american-healing.html

Ingram, B. L. (2012). *Clinical case formulations* (2nd ed.). Hoboken, NJ: John Wiley & Sons.

Jaffe, P., & Geffner, R. (1998). Child custody disputes and domestic violence: Critical issues for mental health, social service, and legal professionals. In G. Holden, R. Geffner, & E. Jouriles (Eds.),

Children exposed to marital violence: Theory, research, and applied issues (pp. 371–408). Washington, DC: American Psychological Association.

Jefferson National Expansion Memorial. (2013). Lakota Sioux. Retrieved May 1, 2013, from http://www.nps.gov/jeff/historyculture/the-lakota-sioux.htm

Jensen Racz, S., McMahon, R. J., & Luthar, S. S. (2011). Risky behavior in affluent youth: Examining the co-occurrence and consequences of multiple problem behaviors. *Journal of Child and Family Studies, 20,* 120–128. doi: 10.1007/s10826-010-9285-4

Johnson, M. P. (1995). Patriarchal terrorism and common couple violence: Two forms of violence against women. *Journal of Marriage and the Family, 75,* 283–294.

Johnson, M. P., & Leone, J. M. (2005). The differential effects of intimate terrorism and situational couple violence: Findings from the National Violence Against Women Survey. *Journal of Family Issues, 26,* 322–349.

Just the Facts Coalition. (2008). *Just the facts about sexual orientation and youth: A primer for principals, educators, and school personnel.* Washington, DC: American Psychological Association. Retrieved April 23, 2014, from http://www.apa.org/pi/lgbc/publications/justthefacts.html

Kagan, J. (1997). *Galen's prophecy: Temperament in human nature.* Boulder, CO: Westview Press.

Kantor, G. K., & Little, L. (2003). Refining the boundaries of child neglect: When does domestic violence equate with parental failure to protect? *Journal of Interpersonal Violence, 18*(4), 338–355.

Kaufman, M. (1994). Men, feminism, and men's contradictory experiences of power. In H. Brod & M. Kaufman (Eds.), *Theorizing masculinities* (pp. 142–163). Thousand Oaks, CA: SAGE.

Keenan, J. M. (2008). *Review of SOAP note charting.* Retrieved May 23, 2008, from http://www.meded.umn.edu/students/residency/documents/06_Keenan_Review_SOAP_Note_Charting.pdf

Kelly, G. A. (1955). *The psychology of personal constructs.* New York, NY: Norton.

Kessler, R. C., Chiu, C., Demier, W., & Walters, E. (2005). Prevalence and comorbidity of 12-month DSM-IV disorder in the National Comorbidity Survey Replication. *Archives of General Psychiatry, 62,* 617–627.

Kimmel, M. S. (2008). The gendered society. In K. E. Rosenblum & T. C. Travis (Eds.), *The meaning of difference: American constructions of race, sex and gender, social class, sexual orientation, and disability* (5th ed., pp. 81–87). Boston: McGraw-Hill.

Kochhar, R., Fry, R., & Taylor, P. (2011). Wealth gaps rise to record highs between Whites, Blacks, Hispanics. *Pew Research: Social and Demographic Trends.* Retrieved May 1, 2014, from http://www.pewsocialtrends.org/2011/07/26/wealth-gaps-rise-to-record-highs-between-whites-blacks-hispanics/

Kosciw, J., Greytak, E., Diaz, E., & Bartkiewicz, M. J. (2010). *The 2009 National School Climate Survey: The experiences of lesbian, gay, bisexual, and transgender youth in our nation's schools.* New York, NY: Gay, Lesbian and Straight Education Network.

Kosciw, J. G., Palmer, N. A., Kull, R. M., & Greytak, E. A. (2013). The effect of negative school climate on academic outcomes for LGBT youth and the role of in-school supports. *Journal of School Violence, 12*(1), 45–63. doi: 10.1080/15388220.2012.732546

Koss, M. P., Bailey, J. A., Yuan, N. P., Herrera, V. M., & Lichter, E. L. (2003). Depression and PTSD in survivors of male violence: Research and training initiatives to facilitate recovery. *Psychology of Women Quarterly, 27,* 130–142.

Krieder, R. M., & Elliot, D. B. (2009, September). America's families and living arrangements: 2007. *Current Population Reports.* U.S. Department of Commerce, Economics and Statistics Division, U.S. Census Bureau. Retrieved February 8, 2012, from http://www.census.gov/prod/2009pubs/p20-561.pdf

Krogstad, J. M. (2014). *Near Civil Rights Act anniversary, only a quarter of Blacks report recent improvement in Black people's lives.* Pew Research Center. Retrieved from http://www.pewresearch.org/fact-tank/2014/04/10/near-civil-rights-act-anniversary-only-a-quarter-of-blacks-report-recent-improvement-in-black-peoples-lives/

Krogstad, J. M., & Fry, R. (2014). *More Hispanics, Blacks enrolling in college, but lag in bachelor's degrees.* Pew Research Center. Retrieved from http://www.pewresearch.org/fact-tank/2014/04/24/more-hispanics-blacks-enrolling-in-college-but-lag-in-bachelors-degrees/

Krugman, P. (2005, September 19). Tragedy in black and white. *New York Times,* p. A25.

Laible, D. J., & Thompson, R. A. (2007). Early socialization: A relational perspective. In J. Grusec & P. Hastings (Eds.), *Handbook of socialization* (Rev. ed., pp. 181–207). New York, NY: Guilford Press.

Lambert, M. J. (2013). The efficacy and effectiveness of psychotherapy. In M. J. Lambert (Eds.), *Bergin and Garfield's handbook of psychotherapy and behaviour change* (6th ed., pp. 169–218). Hoboken, NJ: John Wiley & Sons.

Lambert, M. J., Garfield, S. L., & Bergin, A. E. (2004). Overview, trends, and future issues. In M. J. Lambert (Ed.), *Bergin and Garfield's handbook of psychotherapy and behavior change* (5th ed., pp. 805–821). New York, NY: John Wiley & Sons.

Lansford, J. E., Miller-Johnson, S., Berlin, L. J., Dodge, K. A., Bates, J. E., & Pettit, G. S. (2007). Early physical abuse and later violent delinquency: A prospective longitudinal study. *Child Maltreatment, 12,* 233–245.

LaRue, A., & Majidi-Ahi, S. (1998). African-American children. In J. T. Gibbs & L. N. Huang (Eds.), *Children of color: Psychological interventions with culturally diverse youth* (pp. 143–170). San Francisco, CA: Jossey-Bass.

Lee, R. M., & Dean, B. L. (2004). Middle-class mythology in an age of immigration and segmented assimilation: Implication for counselling psychology. *Journal of Counseling Psychology, 51*(1), 19–24.

Levenson, H., & Strupp, H. H. (2007). Cyclic maladaptive patterns: Case formulation in time-limited dynamic psychotherapy. In T. D. Eells (Ed.), *Handbook of psychotherapy case formulation* (2nd ed., pp. 164–197). New York, NY: Guilford Press.

Light, M. T., Lopez, M. H., & Gonzalez-Barrera, A. (2014). *The rise of federal immigration crimes: Unlawful reentry drives growth.* Pew Research Center. Retrieved from http://www.pewhispanic.org/2014/03/18/the-rise-of-federal-immigration-crimes/

Lipton, E., & Nixon, R. (2005, September 26). Many contracts for storm work raise questions. *New York Times,* p. A1.

Liu, W. M. (2005). The study of men and masculinity as an important multicultural competency consideration. *Journal of Clinical Psychology, 61*(6), 685–697.

Lofquist, D. (2011). Same-sex couple households. *American Community Survey Brief, ACSBR/10–03.* Retrieved May 1, 2014, from http://www.census.gov/prod/2011pubs/acsbr10-03.pdf

Lopez, M. H., Gonzalez-Barrera, & Motel, S. (2011). *As deportations rise to record levels, most Latinos oppose Obama's Policy.* Washington, DC: Pew Hispanic Center. Retrieved May 1, 2013, from http://www.pewhispanic.org/2011/12/28/as-deportations-rise-to-record-levels-most-latinos-oppose-obamas-policy/

Lott, B. (2002). Cognitive and behavioral distancing from the poor. *American Psychologist, 57*(2), 100–110.

Luthar, S. S., & Latendresse, S. J. (2005). Children of the affluent challenges to well-being. *American Psychological Society, 14*(1), 49–53.

Macartney, S., Bishaw, A., & Fontenot, K. (2013, February). Poverty rates for selected detailed race and Hispanic groups by state and place: 2007–2011. *American Community Survey Briefs, 11–17.* Retrieved May 1, 2014, from http://www.census.gov/prod/2013pubs/acsbr11-17.pdf

Macartney, S., & Mykyta, L. (2012). Poverty and shared households by state: 2011. *American Community Survey Briefs, 11–05.* Retrieved May 1, 2014, from http://www.census.gov/prod/2012pubs/acsbr11-05.pdf

Mahalik, J. R., Locke, B. D., Ludlow, L. H., Diemer, M., Scott, R. P. J., Gottfried, M., & Freitas, G. (2003). Development of the Conformity to Masculine Norms Inventory. *Psychology of Men and Masculinity, 4,* 3–25.

Mahalik, J. R., Morray, E. B., Coonerty-Femiano, A., Ludlow, L. H., Slatter, S. M., & Smiler, A. (2005). Development of the Conformity to Feminine Norms Inventory. *Sex Roles, 52*, 417–435.

Mallinckrodt, B., & Wei, M. (2005). Attachment, social competencies, social support, and psychological distress, *Journal of Counseling Psychology, 52*(3), 358–367.

Mann, C. C. (2005). *1491 new revelations of the Americas before Columbus.* New York, NY: A. A. Knopf.

Markus, H. R., & Conner, A. (2013). *Clash! 8 cultural conflicts that make us who we are.* New York, NY: Hudson Street Press.

Marshall, J. M. (2001). *The Lakota way: Stories and lessons for living.* New York, NY: Penguin Compass.

Masten, A. S. (2001). Ordinary magic: Resilience processes in development. *American Psychologist, 56*, 227–238.

Masten, A. S. (2014). Global perspective on resilience in children and youth. *Child Development, 85*(1), 6–20.

Masten, A. S., & Narayan, A. J. (2012). Child development in the context of disaster, war and terrorism: Pathways of risk and resilience. *Annual Review of Psychology, 63*, 227–257. doi: 1146/annurev-psych-120710–100356

Mazure, C. M., Keita, G. P., & Blehar, M. C. (2002). *Summit on women and depression: Proceedings and recommendations.* Washington, DC: American Psychological Association.

McCormick, C. M., Kuo, S. I., & Masten, A. S. (2011). Developmental tasks across the lifespan. In K. L. Fingerman, C. Berg, T. C. Antonucci, & J. Smith (Eds.), *Handbook of life-span development.* New York, NY: Springer.

McIntosh, P. (2008). White privilege: Unpacking the invisible knapsack. In K. E. Rosenblum & T. C. Travis (Eds.), *The meaning of difference: American constructions of race, sex and gender, social class, sexual orientation, and disability* (5th ed., pp. 368–372). Boston, MA: McGraw-Hill.

Mellander, C., Florida, R., & Rentfrow, J. (2011). The creative class, post-industrialism and the happiness of nations. *Cambridge Journal of Regions, Economy, and Society*, pp. 1–13.

Mellinger, T. N., & Liu, W. M. (2006). Men's issues in doctoral training: A survey of counseling psychology programs. *Professional Psychology: Research and Practice, 37*(2), 196–204.

Meltzoff, A. N. (2005). Imitation and other minds: The "like me" hypothesis. In S. Hurley and N. Chater (Eds.), *Perspectives on imitation: From neuroscience to social science* (Vol. 2, pp. 55–77). Cambridge, MA: MIT Press.

Messner, M. A. (1997). *Politics of masculinities: Men in movements.* Thousand Oaks, CA: SAGE.

Miller, S. D., Hubble, M. A., & Duncan, B. L. (2007). Supershrinks. *Psychotherapy Networker, 31*(6), 26–35, 56.

Miller, S. D., Hubble, M. A., Duncan, B. L., & Wampold, B. E. (2010). Delivering what works. In B. L. Duncan, S. D. Miller, B. E. Wampold, & M. A. Hubble (Eds.) *The heart and soul of change: Delivering what works in therapy* (2nd ed., pp. 421–429). Washington, DC: American Psychological Association.

Minami, T., Wampold, B., Serlin, R., Hamilton, E., Brown G., & Kircher, J. (2008). Benchmarking for psychotherapy efficacy. *Journal of Consulting and Clinical Psychology, 76*, 116–124.

Minuchin, S. (1974). *Families and family therapy.* Cambridge, MA: Harvard University Press.

Minuchin, S., & Fishman, H. (1981). *Family therapy techniques.* Cambridge, MA: Harvard University Press.

Minuchin, S., Nichols, M. P., & Lee, W.-Y. (2007). *Assessing couples and families: From symptom to system.* Boston, MA: Allyn & Bacon.

Moffitt, T. E. (1993). Adolescent-limited in life-course-persistent antisocial behavior: A developmental taxonomy. *Psychological Review, 100*(4), 674–701.

Monro, F., & Huon, G. (2005). Media-portrayed idealized images, body shame, and appearance anxiety. *International Journal of Eating Disorders, 38*, 85–90.

Monroe, C. R. (2005). Why are "bad boys" always Black? Causes of disproportionality in school discipline and recommendations for change. *Clearing House, 79,* 45–50.

Montemurro, B. (2003). Not a laughing matter: Sexual harassment as "material" on workplace-based situation comedies. *Sex Roles, 48,* 433–445.

National Center for Health Statistics. (2002, April 24). Deaths: Injuries, 2002. *National Vital Statistics Reports, 54*(10). Retrieved February 3, 2009, from http://www.cdc.gov/nchs/data/nvsr/nvsr54/nvsr54_10.pdf

National Scientific Council on the Developing Child. (2004). *Children's emotional development is built into the architecture of their brains* (Working Paper #2). Retrieved from http://www.developingchild.net

National Scientific Council on the Developing Child. (2005). *Excessive stress disrupts the architecture of the developing brain* (Working Paper #3). Retrieved April 10, 2014, from http://www.developingchild.net

National Scientific Council on the Developing Child. (2007). *The science of early childhood development.* Retrieved from http://www.developingchild.net

Neal-Barnett, A. M., & Crowther, J. H. (2000). To be female, middle class, anxious, and Black. *Psychology of Women Quarterly, 24,* 129–136.

Neimeyer, R. A. (1995). An invitation to constructivist psychotherapies. In R. A. Neimeyer & M. J. Mahoney (Eds.), *Constructivism in psychotherapy* (pp. 1–8). Washington, DC: American Psychological Association.

Neimeyer, R. A. (2000). Narrative disruptions in the construction of the self. In R. A. Neimeyer & J. D. Raskin (Eds.), *Constructions of disorder: Meaning-making frameworks for psychotherapy* (pp. 207–242). Washington, DC: American Psychological Association.

Neimeyer, R. A. (2009). *Constructivist psychotherapy.* New York, NY: Routledge.

Nelson, S. (2008). *Welcome message to iask.inc.* Retrieved July 24, 2008, from www.iaskinc.org

New York Life. (2008). *African American wealth: Powerful trends and new opportunities.* Retrieved June 14, 2008, from http://www.newyorklife.com/nyl/v/index.jsp?vgnextoid=921e3c5ac59d2210a2b3019d221024301cacRCRD

Ng, F. F., Pomerantz, E. M., & Lam, S. (2007). European American and Chinese parents' response to children's success and failure: Implications for children's responses. *Developmental Psychology, 43*(5), 1239–1255.

Nichols, M. P. (2008). *Family therapy: Concepts and methods* (8th ed.). Boston, MA: Pearson Education.

Nolen-Hoeksema, S. (2000). The role of rumination in depressive disorders and mixed anxiety/depressive symptoms. *Journal of Abnormal Psychology, 109,* 504–511.

Nzinga-Johnson, S., Baker, J. A., & Aupperlee, J. (2009). Teacher–parent relationships and school involvement among racially and educationally diverse parents of kindergartners. *Elementary School Journal, 110,* 81–91.

Official Site of the Rosebud Sioux Tribe. (2013). *Rosebud Sioux Tribe.* Retrieved from http://www.rosebudsiouxtribe-nsn.gov/

Ogbu, J. (2003). *Black American students in an affluent suburb: A study of academic disengagement.* Mahwah, NJ: Lawrence Erlbaum.

Palmore, E. (2001). The ageism survey: First findings. *Gerontologist, 41*(5), 572–575.

Pan Tribal Secession Against the Empire. (2012, October). *American Indian/Alaska Native—Attack the system: Abolish Columbus Day protest and occupied Cascadia screening—Seattle 2012.* Retrieved from http://aianattackthesystem.com/2012/10/01/columbus-day-protest-seattle-2013/

Papp, P. (2008). *Gender, marriage, and depression.* In L. B. Silverstein & T. J. Goodrich (Eds.), *Feminist family therapy: Empowerment in social context* (pp. 211–223). Washington, DC: American Psychological Association.

Passel, J. S., & Cohn, D. (2009, April 14). *A portrait of unauthorized immigrants in the United States.* Washington, DC: Pew Hispanic Center.

Passel, J. S., & Cohn, D., & Gonzalez-Barrera, A. (2012, April 23). *Net migration from Mexico falls to zero—and perhaps less.* Washington, DC: Pew Hispanic Center. Retrieved August 26, 2014, from http://www.pewhispanic.org/2012/04/23/net-migration-from-mexico-falls-to-zero-and-perhaps-less/

Pavlov, I. (1927). *Conditioned reflexes.* London, UK: Oxford University Press.

Pedrotti, J. T., Edwards, L. M., & Lopez, S. J. (2008). Working with multiracial clients in therapy: Bridging theory, research, and practice. *Professional Psychology: Research and Practice, 39*, 192–201.

Peplau, L. A., & Fingerhut, A. (2007). The close relationships of lesbian and gay men. *Annual Review of Psychology, 58,* 405–424.

Perls, F., Hefferline, R., & Goodman, P. (1951). *Gestalt therapy.* New York, NY: Dell.

Piaget, J. (1952). *The origins of intelligence in children* (M. Cook, Trans.). Oxford, UK: International Universities Press. (Original work published 1936)

Pincus, F. L. (2001/2002, Winter). The social construction of reverse discrimination: The impact of affirmative action on Whites. *Journal of Intergroup Relations, 38*(4), 33–44.

Pinderhughes, E. E., Dodge, K. A., Bates, J. E., Pettit, G. S., & Zelli, A. (2000). Discipline responses: Influences of parents' socioeconomic status, ethnicity, beliefs about parenting, stress, and cognitive-emotional processes. *Journal of Family Psychology, 14*, 380–400.

Pritchard, J. (2002). Male victims of elder abuse: Their experiences and needs. *Violence and Abuse Series.* London, UK: Jessica Kingsley.

Pro-change Behavior Systems. (2008, March). *About us.* Retrieved April 8, 2009, from http://www.prochange.com/staff/james_prochaska

Prochaska, J. (1999). How do people change, and how can we change to help many more people? In M. A. Hubble, B. L. Duncan, & S. D. Miller (Eds.), *The heart and soul of change: What works in therapy* (pp. 227–255). Washington, DC: American Psychological Association.

Prochaska, J. (2005). Reply to Callaghan: Stages of change and termination from psychotherapy. *Psychotherapy: Theory, Research, Practice, Training, 42*(2), 247–248.

Prochaska, J., & DiClemente, C. (1984). *The transtheoretical approach: Crossing traditional boundaries of change.* Homewood, IL: Dorsey.

Prochaska, J., & DiClemente, C. (1986). The transtheoretical approach. In J. Norcross (Ed.), *Handbook of eclectic psychotherapy* (pp. 163–200). New York, NY: Brunner/Mazel.

Prochaska, J. O., & Norcross, J. C. (1999). Comparative conclusions: Toward a transtheoretical therapy. In J. O. Prochaska & J. C. Norcross (Eds.), *Systems of psychotherapy: A transtheoretical analysis* (4th ed., pp. 487–532). Pacific Grove, CA: Brooks/Cole.

Prochaska, J. O., & Norcross, J. C. (2009). *Systems of psychotherapy: A transtheoretical analysis.* Pacific Grove, CA: Brooks/Cole.

Quinn, D. M., & Crocker, J. (1999). When ideology hurts: Effects of belief in the Protestant affect and feeling overweight on the psychological well-being of women. *Journal of Personality and Social Psychology, 77*(2), 402–414.

Rabinowitz, F. E., & Cochran, S.V. (2002). *Deepening psychotherapy with men.* Washington, DC: American Psychological Association.

Ramirez, O. (1998). Mexican American children and adolescents. In J. T. Gibbs, L. N. Huang, & Associates (Eds.), *Children of color: Psychological interventions with culturally diverse youth* (2nd ed., pp. 215–239). San Francisco, CA: Jossey-Bass.

Raeff, C. (2014). Demystifying internalization and socialization: Linking conceptions of how development happens to organismic-developmental theory. In J. B. Benson (Ed.), *Advances in child development and behavior* (Vol. 46, pp. 1–32). Burlington, VT: Academic Press.

Rhule, D. M. (2005). Take care to do no harm: Harmful interventions for youth problem behavior. *Professional Psychology: Research and Practice, 36*(6), 618–625.

Riggle, E. D. B., Whitman, J. S., Olson, A., Rostosky, S. S., & Strong, S. (2008). The positive aspects of being a lesbian or gay man. *Professional Psychology: Research and Practice, 39*(2), 210–217.

Rios, R., Aiken, L. S., & Zautra, A. J. (2012). Neighborhood contexts and the mediating role of neighborhood social cohesion on health and psychological distress among Hispanic and non-Hispanic residents. *Annuals of Behavioral Medicine, 43,* 50–61.

Rodriguez, C. E. (2008). Latinos and the U.S. race structure. In K. E. Rosenblum & T. C. Travis (Eds.), *The meaning of difference: American constructions of race, sex and gender, social class, sexual orientation, and disability* (5th ed., pp. 81–87). Boston, MA: McGraw-Hill.

Rogers, C. (1951). *Client-centered therapy.* Boston, MA: Houghton Mifflin.

Rosenzweig, S. (1936). Some implicit common factors in diverse methods of psychotherapy. *American Journal of Orthopsychiatry, 6,* 412–415.

Russo, N. F., & Tartaro, J. (2008). Women and mental health. In F. L. Denmark & M. A. Paludi (Eds.), *Psychology of women: A handbook of issues and theories* (2nd ed., pp. 440–481). Westport, CT: Greenwood Press.

Ryder, J. A. (2014). *Girls & violence: Tracing the roots of criminal behavior.* Boulder, CO: Lynne Rienner.

Samuelson, S. L., & Campbell, C. D. (2005). Screening for domestic violence: Recommendations based on a practice survey. *Professional Psychology: Research and Practice, 36*(3), 276–282.

Sanchez, K. S., Bledsoe, L. M., Sumabat, C., & Ye, R. (2004). Hispanic students' reading situations and problems. *Journal of Hispanic Higher Education, 3,* 50–63. doi: 10.1177/1538192703259531

Santana, S., & Santana, F. (2001). *An introduction to Mexican culture: For rehabilitation service providers.* Retrieved August 5, 2008, from http://cirrie.buffalo.edu/monographs/mexico.pdf

Savin-Williams, R. C. (2001). *Mom, Dad, I'm gay: How families negotiate coming out.* Washington, DC: American Psychological Association.

Schneider, M. S., Brown, L. S., & Glassgold, J. (2002). Implementing the resolution on appropriate therapeutic responses to sexual orientation: A guide for the perplexed. *Professional Psychology: Research and Practice, 33*(3), 265–276.

Schooler, D., & Ward, L. M. (2006). Average Joes: Men's relationships with media, real bodies, and sexuality. *Psychology of Men and Masculinity, 7,* 27–41.

Schwartz, C. E., Kunwar, P. S., Greve, D. N., Moran, L. R., Viner, J. C., Covino, J. M., . . . Wallace, S. R. (2010). Structural differences in adult orbital and ventromedial prefrontal cortex predicted by infant temperament at 4 months of age. *Archives of General Psychiatry, 67*(1), 78–84. doi: 10.1001/archgenpsychiatry.2009.171

Schwartz, D., & Proctor, L. J. (2000). Community violence exposure and children's social adjustment in the school peer group: The mediating roles of emotional regulation and social cognition. *Journal of Consulting and Clinical Psychology, 68,* 670–683.

Schwartz, D., Toblin, R., Abou-ezzeddine, Shelley, T., & Stevens, K. (2005). Difficult home environments in the development of aggressive victims of bullying. In K. Kendall-Tackett & S. M. Giacomoni (Eds.), *Child victimization: Maltreatment, bullying and dating violence, prevention and intervention* (pp. 11–19). Kingston, NJ: Civic Research Institute.

Segal, Z. V., Williams, J. M. G., & Teasdale, J. D. (2013). *Mindfulness-based cognitive therapy for depression* (2nd ed.). New York, NY: Guilford Press.

Shapiro, I., Greenstein, R., & Primus, W. (2001, May 31). *Pathbreaking CBO study shows dramatic increases in income disparities in 1980s and 1990s: An analysis of CBO data.* Retrieved June 12, 2008, from http://www.cbpp.org/5-31-01tax.html

Shidlo, A., & Schroeder, M. (2002). Changing sexual orientation: A consumers' report. *Professional psychology: Research and practice, 33*(3), 249–259.

Singh, G. K., & Ghandour, R. M. (2012). Impact of neighborhood social conditions and household socioeconomic status on behavioral problems among US children. *Maternal Child Health Journal, 16,* 158–169.

Skinner, B. F. (1938). *The behavior of organisms: An experimental analysis.* New York: Appleton.

Smith, L., Constantine, M. G., Graham, S. V., & Diz, B. (2008). The territory ahead for multicultural competence: The "spinning" of racism. *Professional Psychology: Research and Practice, 39*(3), 337–345.

Smith, T. (2011). Public attitudes toward homosexuality. *General Social Survey 2010*. Retrieved April 16, 2014, from http://www.norc.org/PDFs/2011%20GSS%20Reports/GSS_Public%20Attitudes%20Toward%20Homosexuality_Sept2011.pdf

Snow Owl. (2004, September). *Native American people/tribes: The great Sioux nation*. Retrieved August 13, 2008, from http://www.snowwowl.com/peoplesioux.html

Solorzano, D., Ceja, M., & Yosso, T. (2000, Winter). Critical race theory, racial microaggressions, and campus racial climate: The experiences of African American college students. *Journal of Negro Education, 69*, 60–73.

South Dakota Department of Tribal Relations. (2011). *Lower Brule Sioux Tribe*. Retrieved April 28, 2014, from http://www.sdtribalrelations.com/lowerbrule.aspx

Sroufe, A. (2005). Attachment and development: A prospective, longitudinal study from birth to adulthood. *Attachment and Human Development, 7*(4), 349–367.

Steinberg, L. (2007). Risk-taking and adolescence: New perspectives from brain and behavioral science. *Current Directions in Psychological Science, 16*, 55–59.

Steinberg, L. (2008). A social neuroscience perspective and adolescent risk-taking. *Developmental Review, 28*, 78–106.

Steinberg, L., Albert, D., Cauffman, E., Banich, M., Graham, S., & Woolard, J. (2008). Age differences in sensation seeking and impulsivity as indexed by behavior and self-report: Evidence for dual systems model. *Developmental Psychology, 44*, 1764–1778.

Steinberg, L., Cauffman, E., Woolard, J., Graham, S., & Banich, M. (2009). Are adolescents less mature than adults? Minors access to abortion, the juvenile death penalty, and the alleged APA "flip-flop" in parentheses. *American Psychologist, 64*, 583–594.

Steinberg, L., Graham, S., O'Brien, L., Woolard, J., Cauffman, E., & Banich, M. (2009). Age differences in future orientation and delay discounting. *Child Development, 8*, 28–44.

Steinberg, L., & Monahan, K. (2007). Age differences in resistance to peer influence. *Developmental Psychology, 43*, 1531–1543.

Steinberg, L., & Scott, E. (2003). Less guilty by reason of adolescence: Developmental immaturity, diminished responsibility, and the juvenile death penalty. *American Psychologist, 58*, 1009–1018.

Strupp, H., & Binder, J. (1984). *Psychotherapy in a new key: A guide to time-limited dynamic treatment*. New York, NY: Basic Books.

Stuart, R. B. (2005). Treatment for partner abuse: Time for a paradigm shift. *Professional Psychology: Research and Practice, 36*(3), 254–263.

Sudak, D. M. (2006). *Psychotherapy in clinical practice: Cognitive behavioral therapy for clinicians*. Philadelphia, PA: Lippincott Williams & Wilkins.

Sue, D. W., Arredondo, P., & McDavis, R. J. (1992). Multicultural counseling competencies and standards: A call to the profession. *Journal of Counseling and Development, 70*, 477–486.

Sue, D. W., & Sue, D. (2013). *Counseling the culturally diverse: Theory and practice* (6th ed.). Hoboken, NJ: John Wiley & Sons.

Surgeon General. (2001). *Youth violence: Report from the surgeon general*. Retrieved August 1, 2007, from http://www.ncbi.nlm.nih.gov/books/NBK44294/

Terhune, C., & Perez, E. (2005, October). Roundup of immigrants in shelter reveals rising tensions. *Wall Street Journal*, p. B1.

Timmons Fritz, P. A., & O'Leary, K. D. (2007). The course of physical and psychological aggression across time. In K. A. Kendall-Tackett & S. M. Giacomoni (Eds.), *Intimate partner violence* (pp. 1–19). Kingston, NJ: Civic Research Institute.

Tutwiler, S. W. (2007). How schools fail African-American boys. In S. Books (Ed.), *Invisible children in the society and its schools* (3rd ed., pp. 1–22). Mahwah, NJ: Lawrence Erlbaum.

United States v. Windsor, 133 S. Ct. 2675 (2013). Retrieved April 19, 2014, from http://www.supreme court.gov/opinions/12pdf/12–307_6j37.pdf

U.S. Bureau of Labor Statistics. (2013, October). Highlights of women's earnings In 2012. *BLS Reports.* Retrieved April 28, 2014, from http://www.bls.gov/cps/cpswom2012.pdf

U.S. Census Bureau. (2003). *Married-couple and unmarried-partner households.* Retrieved June 3, 2008, from http://www.census.gov/prod/2004pubs/censr-5.pdf

U.S. Census Bureau. (2004). *U.S. interim projections by age, sex, race, and Hispanic origin.* Retrieved May 30, 2008, from http://www.census.gov/ipc/www/usinterimproj/

U.S. Census Bureau. (2006). *State and county quick facts.* Retrieved May 21, 2008, from http://www .census.gov

U.S. Census Bureau. (2010a). *Census briefs.* Retrieved November 29, 2013, from http://www.census .gov/2010census/data/2010-census-briefs.php

U.S. Census Bureau. (2010b). *Indian entities recognized and eligible to receive services from the United States Bureau of Indian Affairs.* Retrieved from http://www.bia.gov/idc/groups/xraca/documents/ text/idc011463.pdf

U.S. Census Bureau. (2010c). *Profile of general population and housing characteristics: 2010.* Retrieved from http://factfinder2.census.gov/faces/nav/jsf/pages/community_facts.xhtml

U.S. Census Bureau. (2011a). *2006–2010 American Community Survey / Fact finder: Selected social characteristics in the United States.* Retrieved November, 30, 2013, from http://www.census.gov/acs/www/

U.S. Census Bureau. (2011b). *Profile America: Facts for features.* Retrieved from http://www.census.gov/ newsroom/releases/archives/facts_for_features_special_editions/cb11-ff09.html

U.S. Census Bureau. (2012a). *American Indian and Alaska Native Heritage Month: November 2012.* Retrieved from http://www.census.gov/newsroom/releases/pdf/cb12ff-22_aian.pdf

U.S. Census Bureau. (2012b). *Current population survey: Annual social and economic supplement.* Retrieved from http://www.census.gov/cps/

U.S. Census Bureau. (2012c). *Statistical abstract of the United States / Table 75. Self-described religious identification of adult population: 1990, 2001, and 2008.* Retrieved June 9, 2014, from http://www .census.gov/compendia/statab/2012/tables/12s0075.pdf

U.S. Census Bureau. (2012d). *Total ancestry reported* (B04003). Retrieved from http://www.census.gov/ fsrscripts/tracker.html?siteid=0&name=census.gov&domain=census.gov

U.S. Census Bureau. (2012e). U.S. Census Bureau projections show a slower growing, older, more diverse nation a half century from now. *Newsroom.* Retrieved March 2, 2014, from http://www .census.gov/newsroom/releases/archives/population/cb12-243.html

U.S. Department of Health and Human Services. (1999). *Report of the Surgeon General's Conference on Children's Mental Health: A national action agenda.* Retrieved February, 6, 2001, from http://www .surgeongeneral.gov/cmh/default.htm

U.S. Department of Health and Human Services, Administration for Children and Families. (2006). *Summary: Child maltreatment 2006.* Retrieved August 22, 2008, from http://www.acf.hhs.gov/ programs/cb/pubs/cm06/summary.html

U.S. Department of Health and Human Services, Federal Interagency Forum on Child and Family Statistics 2000. (2008). *America's children in brief: Key national indicators of well-being.* Retrieved June 19, 2009, from http://www.childstats.gov/americaschildren

U.S. Department of Health and Human Services, Health Resources and Services Administration, Maternal and Child Health Bureau. (2009). *The National Survey of Children's Health 2007.* Rockville, MD: U.S. Department of Health and Human Services.

U.S. Department of Health and Human Services, Office of Minority Health. (2006). *American Indian/ Alaska Native profile.* Retrieved June 2, 2008, from http://www.omhrc.gov/templates/browse .aspx?lvl=3&Ivlid=26

U.S. Department of Health and Human Services, Office of Minority Health. (2009). Infant mortality and American Indians/Alaska Natives. Retrieved from http://minorityhealth.hhs.gov/templates/ content.aspx?ID=3038

U.S. Department of Justice. (2002). *American Indians and crime: A BJS statistical profile, 1992–2002.* Retrieved August 23, 2014, from http://www.ojp.usdoj.gov/bjs/abstract/aic02.htm

U.S. Department of Justice. (2006). *Lifetime likelihood of going to state or federal prison.* Retrieved June 3, 2008, from http://www.ojp.usdoj.gov/bjs/abstract/llgsfp.htm

U.S. Department of Justice, Office of Violent Crimes. (2010). *In their own words: Domestic abuse in later life.* Madison, WI: National Clearinghouse on Abuse in Later Life.

Vespa, J., Lewis, J. M., & Kreider, R. M. (2013). America's families and living arrangements: 2012. *Current Population Reports,* P20–570. Washington, DC: U.S. Census Bureau. Retrieved May 1, 2014, from https://www.census.gov/prod/2013pubs/p20–570.pdf

Vieth, V. & I., & Johnson, M. (2013). The key to Indian Country: Lessons learned from front line professionals. *APSAC Advisor, 3,* 18–20.

Vygotsky, L. S. (1978). *Mind in society: The development of higher psychological processes* (M. Cole, V. John-Steiner, S. Scribner, & E. Souberman, Eds.). Cambridge, MA: Harvard University Press. (Original work published 1935)

Vygotsky, L. (1986–1987). *Thought and language.* Cambridge, MA: MIT Press.

Walfish, S., McAllister, B., & Lambert, M. J. (2012). An investigation of self-assessment bias in mental health providers. *Psychological Reports, 110,* 639–644.

Wampold, B. E., (2010). The research evidence for the common factors models: A historically situated perspective. In B. L. Duncan, S. D. Miller, B. E. Wampold, & M. A. Hubble (Eds.), *The heart and soul of change: Delivering what works in therapy* (2nd ed., pp. 49–81). Washington, DC: American Psychological Association.

Washington, A. T. (2005). Katrina riles, rallies Black America. *Bellingham Herald,* p. A3.

Watkins, N. L., Labarrie, T. L., & Appio, L. M. (2010). Black undergraduates' experiences with perceived racial microaggressions in predominately White colleges and universities. In D. W. Sue (Ed.), *Microaggressions and marginality* (pp. 25–51). Hoboken, NJ: John Wiley & Sons.

Watson, D. L., Andreas, J., Fischer, K., & Smith, K. (2005). Patterns of risk factors leading to victimization and aggression in children and adolescents. In K. Kendall-Tackett & S. Giacomoni (Eds.), *Child victimization* (pp. 1–23). Kingston, NJ: Civic Research Institute.

Weber, M. (1958). *The Protestant ethic and the spirit of capitalism* (T. Parsons, Trans.). New York, NY: Scribner's. (Original work published 1904–1905)

Werner, C. A. (2011). *2010 census briefs: the older population* (C 20110BR-09). U.S. Census Bureau. Retrieved November 29, 2013, from http://www.census.gov/2010census/data/2010-census-briefs.php

Werner, H. (1957). The concept of development from a comparative and organismic point of view. In D. B. Harris (Ed.), *The concept of development: An issue in the study of human behavior* (pp. 125–148). Minneapolis, MN: University of Minnesota Press.

White, J. W., & Smith, P. H. (2004). Sexual assault perpetration and re-perpetration: From adolescence to young adulthood. *Criminal Justice and Behavior, 31*(2), 182–202. doi: 10.1177/0093854803261342

Wolak, J., & Finkelhor, D. (1998). Children exposed to partner violence. In J. Jasinski & L. Williams (Eds.), *Partner violence: A comprehensive review of 20 years of research* (pp. 73–111). Thousand Oaks, CA: SAGE.

Worell, J., & Remer, P. (2003). *Feminist perspectives in therapy: Empowering diverse women.* New York, NY: John Wiley & Sons.

World Health Organization. (2000, June 21). *World Health Organization assesses the world's health systems* (World Health Organization Press Release WHO/44). Retrieved June 12, 2008, from http://www.who.int/whr/2000/media_centre/press_release/en/

World Health Organization. (2002). *World report on violence and health: Summary* (NLM classification HV6625). Geneva, Switzerland: Author.

World Health Organization. (2014). *Health for the world's adolescents: A second chance in the second decade.* Retrieved March 14, 2014, from http://www.who.int/adolescent/second-decade

Wright, M. O., Masten, A., & Narayan, A. J. (2013). Resilience processes in development: Four waves of research on positive adaptation in the context of diversity. In S. Goldstein & R. B. Brooks (Eds.), *Handbook of resilience in children* (p. 15). New York, NY: Springer Science & Business Media. doi: 10.1007/978-1-4614-3661-4_2

Zea, M. C., & Nakamura, N. (2014). Sexual orientation. In F. T. L. Leong (Ed.), *APA handbook of multicultural psychology* (Vol. 1, pp. 395–411). doi: 10. 1037/14189-022

Zurbriggen, E. L., Collins, R. L., Lamb, S., Roberts, T. A., Tolman, D. L., Ward, L. M., & Blake, J. (2007). *Report of the APA Task Force on the Sexualization of Girls.* Washington, DC: American Psychological Association.

Zweig, M. (2008). What's class got to do with it? In K. E. Rosenblum & T. C. Travis (Eds.), *The meaning of difference: American constructions of race, sex and gender, social class, sexual orientation, and disability* (5th ed., pp. 81–87). Boston, MA: McGraw-Hill.

About the Author

Pearl S. Berman, PhD, joined the psychology department of Indiana University of Pennsylvania in 1986, where she is now a full professor and the assistant chair of the department. She is also a licensed clinical psychologist. Her long-standing interest in violence prevention has led her to integrate information and skill building relevant to interpersonal violence into all of her teaching at both the undergraduate and doctoral level. Her undergraduate coursework has included General Psychology, Child Psychology, and Personality Theories. Her doctoral coursework has included Methods of Intervention I, Methods of Intervention II, Therapist Techniques lab, Child Clinical Psychology, Advanced Psychotherapy With Children, Family and Child Clinic, Child Assessment Clinic, Advanced Psychological Practicum, Family Therapy, and Children and Youth Practicum. She is an active member of the National Partnership to End Interpersonal Violence and the National Committee to Prevent Elder Abuse, and is collaborating with the National Child Protection Training Center to expand their Child Advocacy Studies courses across the country and offer an expansion of the project called Child and Adult Advocacy Studies. Her areas of clinical and research expertise include child physical and sexual abuse, neglect, spousal violence, violence prevention, and professional training. She is the author of three doctoral-level books. Her first book is titled *Therapeutic Exercises for Victimized and Neglected Girls: Applications for Individual, Family, and Group Psychotherapy* (Professional Resource Press, 1994). Her second book was the first edition of *Case Conceptualization and Treatment Planning: Exercises in Integrating Theory With Clinical Practice* (SAGE Publications, 1997); this book was translated into Korean by Hak Ji Sa in 2007. The second edition of this book was published by SAGE in 2010. Her third book is *Interviewing and Diagnostic Exercises for Clinical and Counseling Skills Building* with her colleague Susan Shopland, PsyD (Lawrence Erlbaum & Associates, 2005). She has also published 8 book chapters and 11 professional articles. She has presented 55 professional papers and 13 professional workshops in her areas of expertise. Finally, she is a member of many professional groups working toward the cessation of victimization, including the American Psychological Association, the American Professional Society on the Abuse of Children, the Association of Women in Psychology, the National Partnership to End Interpersonal Violence, the National Committee to Prevent Elder Abuse, the Southern Poverty Law Center, and the National Organization for Women.

⑨SAGE research**methods**

The essential online tool for researchers from the world's leading methods publisher

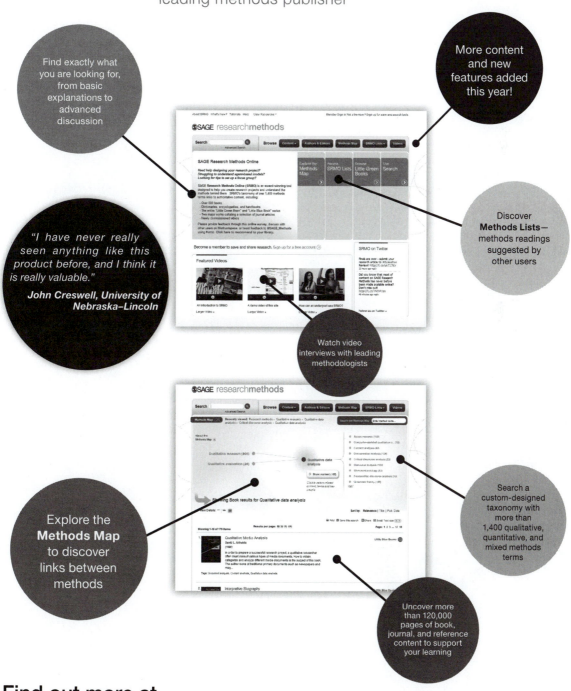

Find exactly what you are looking for, from basic explanations to advanced discussion

More content and new features added this year!

"I have never really seen anything like this product before, and I think it is really valuable."

John Creswell, University of Nebraska–Lincoln

Discover Methods Lists— methods readings suggested by other users

Watch video interviews with leading methodologists

Explore the Methods Map to discover links between methods

Search a custom-designed taxonomy with more than 1,400 qualitative, quantitative, and mixed methods terms

Uncover more than 120,000 pages of book, journal, and reference content to support your learning

Find out more at
www.sageresearchmethods.com